NEW VIEW
A L M A N A C

Computer Graphics by
David C. Bell, Signature Graphics

Text by
Jenny Tesar

Bruce S. Glassman, *Editor*

B L A C K B I R C H   P R E S S ,   I N C .
W O O D B R I D G E ,   C O N N E C T I C U T

Published by Blackbirch Press, Inc.
260 Amity Road
P.O. Box 3575
Woodbridge, CT 06525
web site: www.blackbirch.com
email: staff@blackbirch.com

Printed in the U.S.A.
10 9 8 7 6 5 4 3 2 1

The New View Almanac™ Staff

Executive Editor: Bruce S. Glassman
Assistant Editor: Jenifer Corr Morse
Production Manager: Calico Harington
Production and additional graphics: Mindi Englart and Jane Vaughn

The New View Almanac™ is a trademark of Blackbirch Marketing, Inc.

Library of Congress Cataloging-in-Publication Data

Tesar, Jenny.
　　The new view almanac / computer graphics by David C. Bell; Bruce S. Glassman, editor; text by Jenny Tesar. — 2nd ed.
　　　　p.　　cm.
　　Includes index.
　　Summary: Provides facts and figures on a wide variety of topics, including health and nutrition, science and technology, and sports and records, accompanied by easily understood graphics.
　　　　ISBN 1-56711-150-5 (library binding: alk. paper)
　　　　1. Almanacs, Children's. 2. United States—Statistics—Juvenile literature.
　　[1. Almanacs.] I. Bell, David C., ill. II. Glassman, Bruce, ed. III. Title.
AY81.J8T47　　2000
031.02—dc20
　　　　　　　　　　　　　　　　　　　　　　　　　　　　　　　　　　　　95-40618
　　　　　　　　　　　　　　　　　　　　　　　　　　　　　　　　　　　　CIP
　　　　　　　　　　　　　　　　　　　　　　　　　　　　　　　　　　　　AC

TABLE OF CONTENTS

1

HEALTH
AND
NUTRITION

THE AMERICAN DIET

A well-balanced diet consists of a wide variety of important nutrients, including carbohydrates, proteins, fats, vitamins, and minerals. The lack of any one of these—or too much of any one—can cause malnutrition and possibly disease.

No single food can supply all the important nutrients in the amounts you need. To have a nutritious diet, you must eat a variety of foods. In 1992, the U.S. government introduced what it calls a "food pyramid" (see page 18). This diagram shows what proportions of foods are recommended for good health. It helps people make healthy dietary choices. Today, nutrient information can be found on almost every kind of food package in the U.S. Many packages display the food pyramid.

What people eat has changed drastically over the last 30 years. Americans have improved their diets by eating more fruits and vegetables and by avoiding fats. For example, Americans reduced the amount of fat in their diets from 42% in the mid-1960s to 34% in 1994. Health experts recommend that daily sodium intake be no more than 3,000 milligrams. They also recommend that sugars be eaten only in moderation. A diet with lots of sugar has too many calories and too few nutrients for most people.

Food alone does not make a person healthy or unhealthy. One's state of health also depends on other factors, such as heredity, environment, medical care, and lifestyle. In that food supplies fuel for the body, though, food choices are certainly a critical element of our health that is well within our control.

FINGERTIP FACTS

☞ Americans are eating less fat and cholesterol. In 1994, the American adult's average fat consumption had dropped to 34% of calories. This trend has helped to reduce the risk of heart disease.

☞ Despite the drop in fat consumption, the American diet has seen an increase in calorie consumption. In 1994, Americans were eating an average of 231 more calories per day than they did in 1984.

☞ In 1994, more than 12.4 million Americans—7% of the population—said they were vegetarians. That's almost 10 times as many as in 1978.

☞ Vegetarians are 28% less likely than meat-eaters to die of heart disease and 39% less likely to die of cancer.

☞ Yogurt consumption was 4 times greater in 1994 than in 1971.

☞ In 1997, Procter & Gamble introduced WOW Potato Chips with Olestra, a nonfat substance that has the taste and texture of real fat but cannot be absorbed by the body.

☞ Soft drinks are Americans' favorite beverage. Water ranks #2, and milk is #3.

☞ The average American drinks about 52 gallons of soft drinks per year.

☞ Vegetable consumption has risen sharply in the last 6 years. In 1990, the average American ate 386 pounds of vegetables. In 1996, the average yearly consumption climbed to 412 pounds.

AVERAGE U.S. PER CAPITA CONSUMPTION OF PRINCIPAL FOODS
(Annual consumption, in pounds)

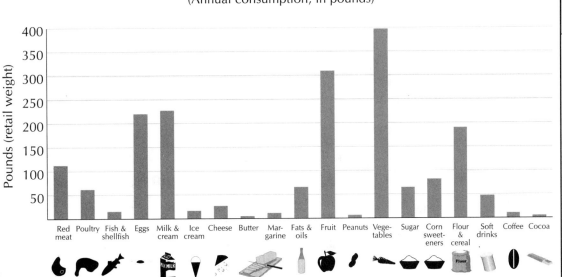

Source: U.S. Department of Agriculture

YEARLY U.S. YOGURT CONSUMPTION, PER CAPITA

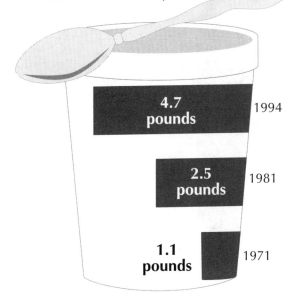

4.7 pounds — 1994
2.5 pounds — 1981
1.1 pounds — 1971

Source: U.S. Department of Agriculture

CONSUMPTION OF SELECTED BEVERAGES, 1970 vs. 1996
(Annual per capita consumption, in gallons)

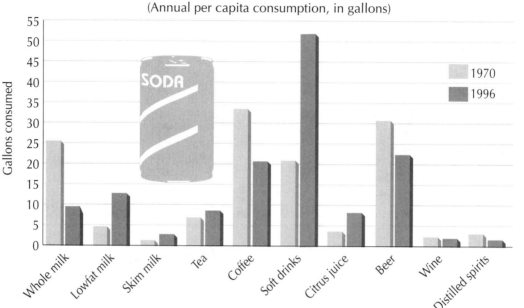

ALCOHOLIC VS. NON-ALCOHOLIC BEVERAGES, 1970 vs. 1996
(Annual per capita consumption, in gallons)

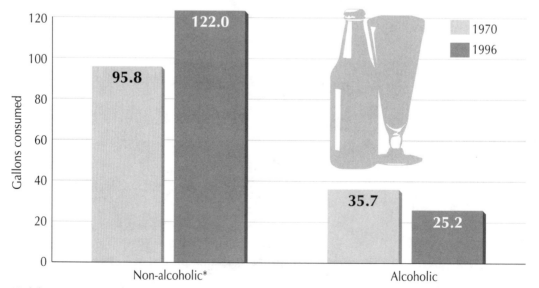

* Excludes water.

Source: U.S. Department of Agriculture, Economic Research Service, *Food Consumption, Prices, and Expenditures,* annual

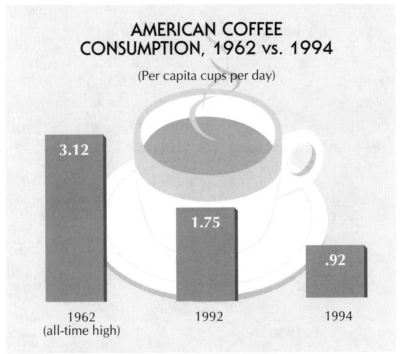

AMERICAN COFFEE CONSUMPTION, 1962 vs. 1994

(Per capita cups per day)

3.12 — 1962 (all-time high)

1.75 — 1992

.92 — 1994

Source: U.S. Department of Agriculture

AMERICA'S MOST POPULAR BEVERAGES

Americans drink an average of 183 gallons of beverages per year.
The most-consumed drinks per person are:

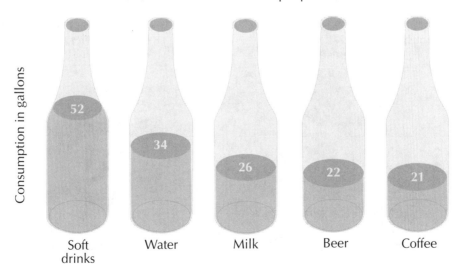

Consumption in gallons

Soft drinks	Water	Milk	Beer	Coffee
52	34	26	22	21

Source: U.S. Department of Agriculture

SKIM MILK CONSUMPTION vs. WHOLE MILK, 1986 vs. 1993

(Percentage of milk drinkers)

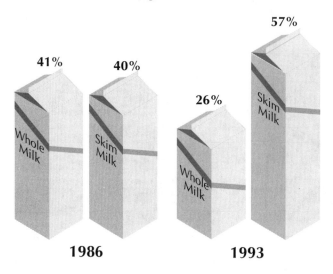

Source: U.S. Department of Agriculture

AMERICA'S SWEET TOOTH

Americans consume huge quantities of sugar, despite rising rates of obesity and diabetes. Soda is one of the top sources.

Per Capita U.S. Sugar Consumption, 1972 vs. 1997
(In pounds)

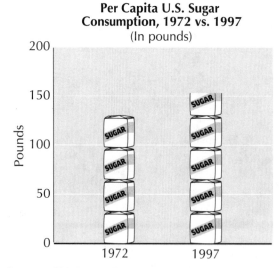

Per Capita Soft Drink Consumption Regular vs. Diet, 1997
(In gallons)

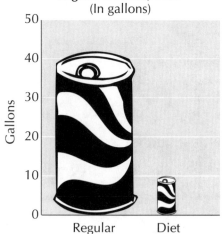

Sources: USDA, *Beverage Digest*

TOP U.S. BEVERAGE COMPANIES, 1997

(In net revenues)

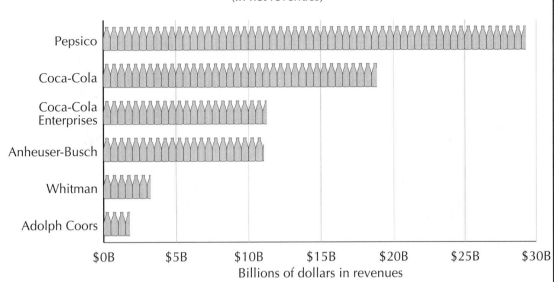

Billions of dollars in revenues

Source: Fortune Magazine

TOP BEVERAGE BRANDS, 1997
(As percentage of all top beverages sold)

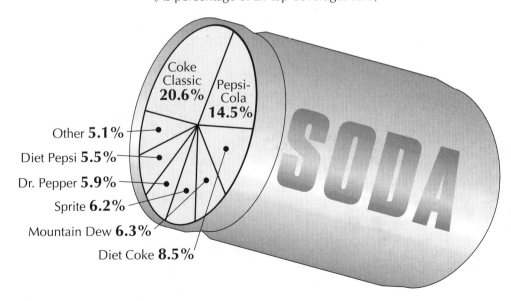

Coke Classic **20.6%**
Pepsi-Cola **14.5%**
Other **5.1%**
Diet Pepsi **5.5%**
Dr. Pepper **5.9%**
Sprite **6.2%**
Mountain Dew **6.3%**
Diet Coke **8.5%**

Source: *Beverage Journal*

FAST FOOD BREAKDOWN
(Calories and fat content of some favorite fast foods)

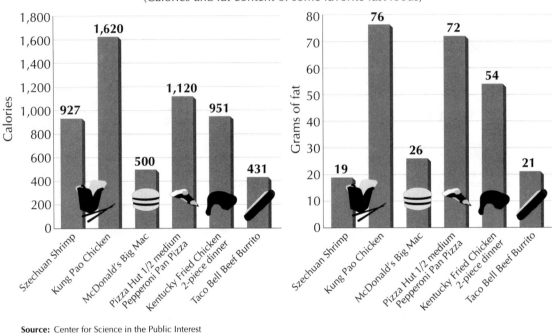

Source: Center for Science in the Public Interest

TOP 5 U.S. MAC CITIES

The Big Mac is the most popular fast-food hamburger in America.
Here are the top 5 cities in annual per capita Big Mac consumption:

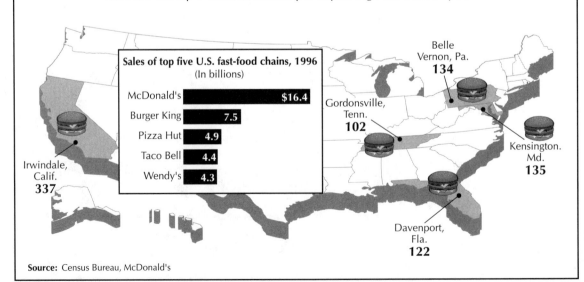

Sales of top five U.S. fast-food chains, 1996
(In billions)

McDonald's	$16.4
Burger King	7.5
Pizza Hut	4.9
Taco Bell	4.4
Wendy's	4.3

Belle
Vernon, Pa.
134

Gordonsville,
Tenn.
102

Kensington.
Md.
135

Irwindale,
Calif.
337

Davenport,
Fla.
122

Source: Census Bureau, McDonald's

THE U.S. ICE CREAM MARKET

(The most popular kinds of ice cream, based on percentage of market share)

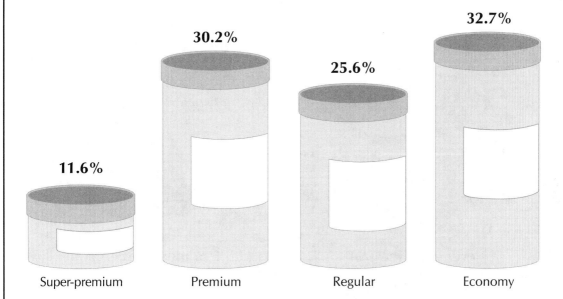

11.6%   30.2%   25.6%   32.7%

Super-premium   Premium   Regular   Economy

AMERICA'S MOST POPULAR ICE CREAM FLAVORS

(As percentage of all ice cream sold)

4.5%   5.1%   6.1%   8.8%   25.2%

Peach   Strawberry   Neapolitan   Chocolate   Vanilla

Source: Information Resources, Inc.

PERSONAL HEALTH PRACTICES OF THE AVERAGE AMERICAN ADULT, BY SELECTED CHARACTERISTIC

(Percentage of population, ages 18 and older)

Sleeps 6 hours or less

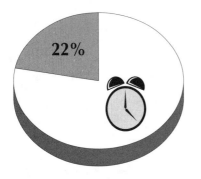

Doesn't exercise regularly

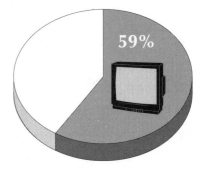

Never eats breakfast

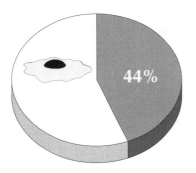

Has 5 or more drinks on any day

Current smoker

Snacks every day

20% or more overweight

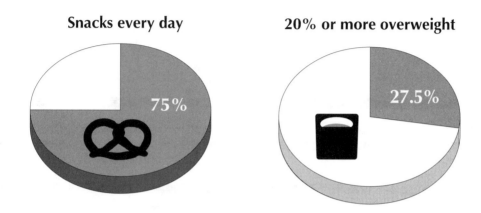

75%

27.5%

Source: Based on statistics from U.S. National Center for Health Statistics

DIETARY HABITS IN THE U.S.

(What Americans say about their eating habits, by sex)

Do all they can to maintain a healthy diet

Select foods carefully to maintain a healthy diet

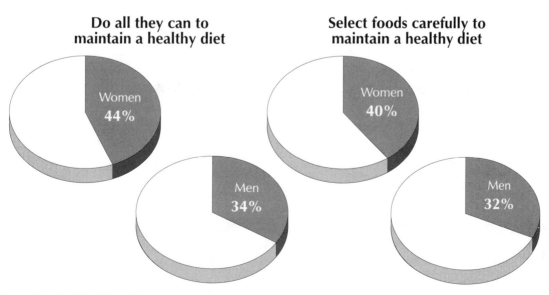

Women
44%

Men
34%

Women
40%

Men
32%

Source: American Dietetic Association

SELECTED CHARACTERISTICS OF COMMON FOODS, PER PORTION

Food	Measure	Grams (weight)	Calories	Fat (grams)
DAIRY PRODUCTS				
Cheese, cheddar	1 oz.	28	115	9
Cheese, cottage, small curd	1 cup	210	220	9
Half-and-half	1 tbsp.	15	20	2
Cream, sour	1 tbsp.	15	25	3
Milk, whole	1 cup	244	150	8
Milk, nonfat (skim)	1 cup	244	85	T
Milkshake, chocolate	10.6 oz.	300	355	8
Ice cream, hardened	1 cup	133	270	14
Sherbet	1 cup	193	270	4
Yogurt, fruit-flavored	8 oz.	227	230	3
EGGS				
Fried in butter	1	46	85	6
Hard-boiled	1	50	80	6
Scrambled in butter (milk added)	1	64	95	7
FATS & OILS				
Butter	1 tbsp.	14	100	12
Margarine	1 tbsp.	14	100	12
Mayonnaise	1 tbsp.	14	100	11
MEAT, POULTRY, & FISH				
Bluefish, baked with butter or margarine	3 oz.	85	135	4
Clams, raw, meat only	3 oz.	85	65	1
Crabmeat, white or king, canned	1 cup	135	135	3
Fish sticks, breaded, cooked, frozen	1 oz.	28	50	3
Salmon, pink, canned	3 oz.	85	120	5
Shrimp, French-fried	3 oz.	85	190	9
Tuna, canned in oil	3 oz.	85	170	7
Bacon, broiled or fried crisp	2 slices	15	85	8
Ground beef, broiled, 10% fat	3 oz.	85	185	10
Roast beef, relatively lean	3 oz.	85	165	7
Beef steak, lean and fat	3 oz.	85	330	27
Lamb, chop, lean and fat	3.1 oz.	89	360	32
Liver, beef	3 oz.	85	195	9
Ham, light cure, lean and fat	3 oz.	85	245	19
Pork, chop, lean and fat	2.7 oz.	78	305	25
Bologna	1 slice	28	85	8
Frankfurter, cooked	1	56	170	15
Sausage, pork link, cooked	1 link	13	60	6
Veal, cutlet, braised or broiled	3 oz.	85	185	
Chicken, drumstick, fried, bones removed	1.3 oz.	38	90	4
Chicken, half broiler, broiled, bones removed	6.2 oz.	176	240	7
FRUITS				
Apple, raw, 2 3/4 in. diam.	1	138	80	1
Apricots, raw	3	107	55	T
Banana, raw	1	119	100	T
Cherries, sweet, raw	10	68	45	T
Grapefruit, raw, medium, white	1/2	241	45	T
Grapes, Thompson seedless	10	50	35	T
Cantaloupe, 5 in. diam.	1/2	477	80	T
Orange, 2 5/8 in. diam.	1	131	65	T
Peach, raw, 2 1/2 in. diam.	1	100	40	T
Raisins, seedless	1 cup	145	420	T
Strawberries, whole	1 cup	149	55	T
Watermelon, 4 by 8 in. wedge	1	926	110	T
GRAIN PRODUCTS				
Bagel, egg	1	55	165	2
Bread, white, enriched, soft-crumb	1 slice	25	70	1
Bread, whole wheat, soft-crumb	1 slice	28	65	1
Oatmeal or rolled oats	1 cup	240	130	2
Bran flakes (40% bran), added sugar, salt, iron, vitamins	1 cup	35	105	1
Corn flakes, added sugar, salt, iron, vitamins	1 cup	25	95	T

Food	Measure	Grams (weight)	Calories	Fat (grams)
Rice, puffed, added iron, thiamin, niacin	1 cup	15	60	T
Wheat, shredded, 1 biscuit or 1/2 cup	1	25	90	1
Cake, angel food, 1/12 of cake	1	53	135	T
Cupcake, 2 1/2 in. diam. with chocolate icing	1	36	130	5
Boston cream pie with custard filling, 1/12 of cake	1	69	210	6
Brownie, with nuts, from commercial recipe	1	20	85	4
Cookies, chocolate chip, from home recipe	4	40	205	12
Crackers, graham	2	14	55	1
Crackers, saltine	4	11	50	1
Doughnut, cake type	1	25	100	5
Muffin, corn	1	40	125	4
Noodles, enriched, cooked	1 cup	160	200	2
Pizza, cheese, 1/8 of 12 in. diam. pie	1	60	145	4
Popcorn, popped, plain	1 cup	6	25	T
Pretzels, stick	10	3	10	T
Rolls, enriched, brown & serve	1	26	85	2
Rolls, frankfurter & hamburger	1	40	120	2
Spaghetti with meatballs & tomato sauce	1 cup	248	330	12
LEGUMES, NUTS, & SEEDS				
Beans, Great Northern, cooked	1 cup	180	210	1
Peanuts, roasted in oil, salted	1 cup	144	840	72
Peanut butter	1 tbsp.	16	95	8
Sunflower seeds	1 cup	145	810	69
SUGARS & SWEETS				
Candy, caramels	1 oz.	28	115	3
Candy, milk chocolate	1 oz.	28	145	9
Fudge, chocolate	1 oz.	28	115	3
Candy, hard	1 oz.	28	110	T
Honey	1 tbsp.	21	65	0
Jams & preserves	1 tbsp.	20	55	T
Sugar, white, granulated	1 tbsp.	12	45	0
VEGETABLES				
Asparagus, canned, spears	4 spears	80	15	T
Beans, green, from frozen cuts	1 cup	135	35	T
Broccoli, cooked	1 stalk	180	45	1
Cabbage, raw, coarsely shredded or sliced	1 cup	70	15	T
Carrots, raw, 71/2 by 11/8 in.	1	72	30	T
Celery, raw	1 stalk	40	5	T
Collards, cooked	1 cup	190	65	1
Corn, sweet, cooked	1 ear	140	70	1
Lettuce, iceberg, chopped	1 cup	55	5	T
Mushrooms, raw	1 cup	70	20	T
Onions, raw, chopped	1 cup	170	110	T
Peas, frozen, cooked	1 cup	160	110	T
Potatoes, baked, peeled	1	156	145	T
Potatoes, frozen, French fried	10	50	110	4
Potatoes, mashed, milk added	1 cup	210	135	2
Potato chips	10	20	115	8
Potato salad	1 cup	250	250	7
Spinach, chopped, from frozen	1 cup	205	45	1
Sweet potatoes, baked in skin, peeled	1	114	160	1
Tomatoes, raw	1	135	25	T
MISCELLANEOUS				
Cola-type beverage	12 fl. oz.	369	145	0
Ginger ale	12 fl. oz.	366	115	0
Gelatin dessert	1 cup	240	140	0
Olives, pickled, green	4 medium	16	15	2
Pickles, dill, whole	1	65	5	T
Popsicle, 3 fl. oz.	1	95	70	0
Soup, tomato, prepared with water	1 cup	245	90	3

T = Trace
Source: *Home & Garden* Bulletin No. 72, U.S. Government Printing Office

NUTRITION PROFILE: U.S. ADULTS, 1991 vs. 1993

(By percentage of population

Adults who consider nutrition:

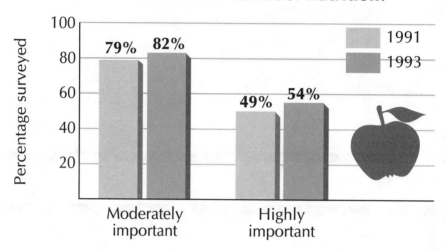

Percentage of surveyed adults who improved diet by:

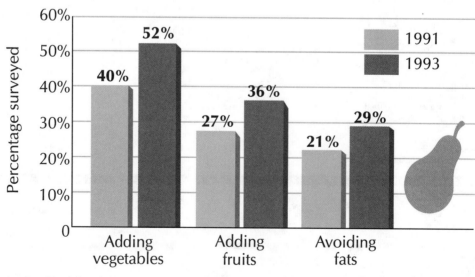

Source: American Dietetic Association

Most Americans were concerned about diet and nutrition because they . . .

wished to maintain health:	**69%**
wished to maintain or lose weight:	**31%**

Considered physical activity as important as diet for good health   **88%**

Most Americans failed to maintain a healthy diet because they...

feared having to give up favorite foods:	**39%**
believed it would take up too much time:	**22%**

Source: American Dietetic Association

THE FOOD PYRAMID

The U.S. Department of Agriculture (USDA) has created this recommended balance of food groups for good nutrition.

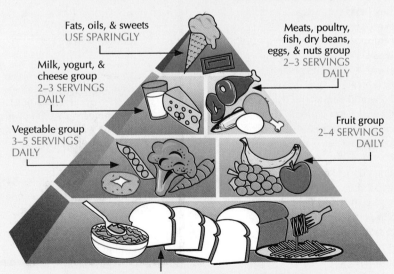

Fats, oils, & sweets
USE SPARINGLY

Meats, poultry, fish, dry beans, eggs, & nuts group
2–3 SERVINGS DAILY

Milk, yogurt, & cheese group
2–3 SERVINGS DAILY

Fruit group
2–4 SERVINGS DAILY

Vegetable group
3–5 SERVINGS DAILY

Bread, cereal, rice, & pasta group 6–11 SERVINGS DAILY

Source: U.S. Department of Agriculture

P E R S O N A L   H E A L T H

Americans are getting heavier. In 1998, approximately 36% of adults in the U.S. were estimated to be overweight. This was a 33% increase since 1980. Equally problematic is the fact that 21% of U.S. teenagers are overweight. Excess weight has been linked to a number of serious health problems, including cancer, cardiovascular disease, diabetes, and gallbladder disease.

There are two main reasons why people gain weight: they eat too much food and get too little exercise. On average, Americans are consuming more calories than their bodies can burn. They are sitting in front of television sets for hours on end, and jumping into automobiles for short trips instead of walking. A 1993 survey reported that only 33% of Americans engaged in strenuous exercise at least 3 days a week. Many do not exercise at all.

Many people need to change their lifestyles if they want to maintain good health. They need to engage in regular physical exercise, with at least 20 minutes of continuous aerobic activity 3 to 5 days a week. Any kind of regular physical exercise can improve health. Some people prefer vigorous exercise, such as skiing and running. Others prefer less strenuous activities, such as walking and biking. Of course, more strenuous activities burn calories more quickly.

The benefits of keeping fit are many. A good diet and regular exercise help to build bones and fight disease. They also improve one's mental outlook—another important factor in one's overall health.

FINGERTIP FACTS

- Obesity is defined as being 20% or more above your desirable weight.

- In 1993, about 34 million Americans were overweight. By 1999, the number had jumped to 97 million.

- About 70% of children who are overweight at ages 10 to 13 will become overweight adults.

- The U.S. diet industry (diet foods, books, programs, etc.) has total estimated annual revenues of $40 billion to $50 billion.

- Only 37% of high school students say they exercise regularly.

- Boys are more physically active than girls. Statistically, white high school students exercise more regularly than African-American students.

- Americans spend more than $2 billion per year on exercise equipment alone.

- The more money people make, the more likely they are to exercise regularly. More than half of all people who earn $50,000 or more exercise; only 35% of people who earn $15,000 or less exercise.

- Aerobics is a heavily female-dominated form of exercise; 84% of all aerobic sessions are done by women.

IDEAL WEIGHTS FOR ADULTS

Height	Weight, in pounds	
	19–34 years	35 years and over
5'0"	97–128	108–138
5'1"	101–132	111–143
5'2"	104–137	115–148
5'3"	107–141	119–152
5'4"	111–146	122–157
5'5"	114–150	126–162
5'6"	118–155	130–167
5'7"	121–160	134–172
5'8"	125–164	138–178
5'9"	129–169	142–183
5'10"	132–174	146–188
5'11"	136–179	151–194
6'0"	140–184	155–199
6'1"	144–189	159–205
6'2"	148–195	164–210
6'3"	152–200	168–216
6'4"	156–205	173–222
6'5"	160–211	177–228
6'6"	164–216	182–234

Source: National Research

CALORIES USED PER MINUTE, ACCORDING TO BODY WEIGHT

Activity	Weight, in pounds					
	100	120	150	170	200	220
Volleyball (moderate)	2.3	2.7	3.4	3.9	4.6	5.0
Walking (3 mph)	2.7	3.2	4.0	4.6	5.4	5.9
Table tennis	2.7	3.2	4.0	4.6	5.4	5.9
Bicycling (5.5 mph)	3.1	3.8	4.7	5.3	6.3	6.9
Calisthenics	3.3	3.9	4.9	5.6	6.6	7.2
Skating (moderate)	3.6	4.3	5.4	6.1	7.2	7.9
Golf	3.6	4.3	5.4	6.1	7.2	7.9
Walking (4 mph)	3.9	4.6	5.8	6.6	7.8	8.5
Tennis	4.5	5.4	6.8	7.7	9.1	10.0
Canoeing (4 mph)	4.6	5.6	7.0	7.9	9.3	10.2
Swimming (breaststroke)	4.8	5.7	7.2	8.1	9.6	10.5
Bicycling (10 mph)	5.4	6.5	8.1	9.2	10.8	11.9
Swimming (crawl)	5.8	6.9	8.7	9.8	11.6	12.7
Jogging (11-min. mile)	6.1	7.3	9.1	10.4	12.2	13.4
Handball	6.3	7.6	9.5	10.7	12.7	13.9
Racquetball	6.3	7.6	9.5	10.7	12.7	13.9
Skiing (downhill)	6.3	7.6	9.5	10.7	12.7	13.9
Mountain climbing	6.6	8.0	10.0	11.3	13.3	14.6
Squash	6.8	8.1	10.2	11.5	13.6	14.9
Skiing (cross-country)	7.2	8.7	10.8	12.3	14.5	15.9
Running (8-min. mile)	9.4	11.3	14.1	16.0	18.8	20.7

Source: *Home & Garden* Bulletin No. 72, U.S. Government Printing Office

U.S. AEROBIC EXERCISERS, BY SEX

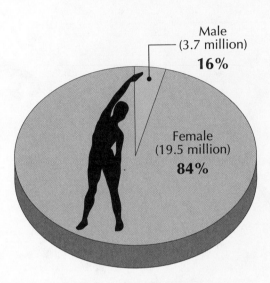

Male
(3.7 million)
16%

Female
(19.5 million)
84%

U.S. RUNNERS AND JOGGERS, BY SEX

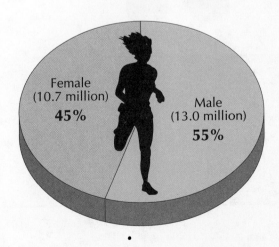

Female
(10.7 million)
45%

Male
(13.0 million)
55%

Source: U.S. Census Bureau

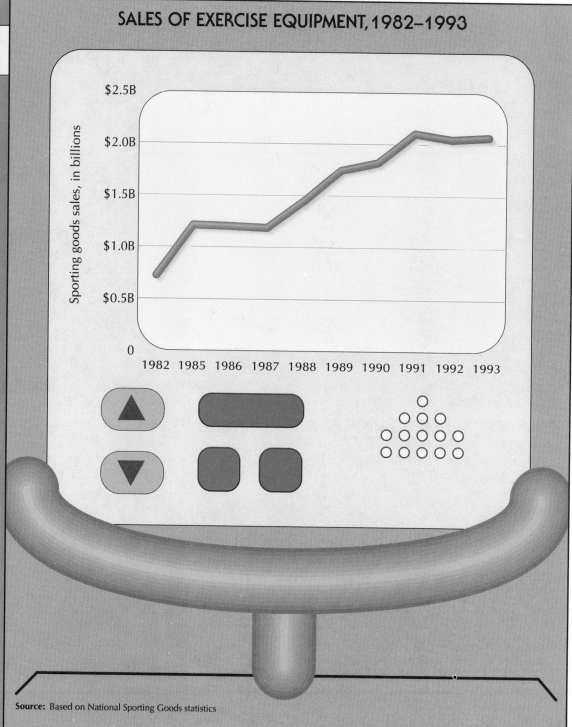

SALES OF EXERCISE EQUIPMENT, 1982–1993

Sporting goods sales, in billions

Source: Based on National Sporting Goods statistics

WHO WORKS OUT?

(Percentage of people, by level of income, who do and don't exercise often or at all)

 Do exercise 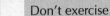 Don't exercise

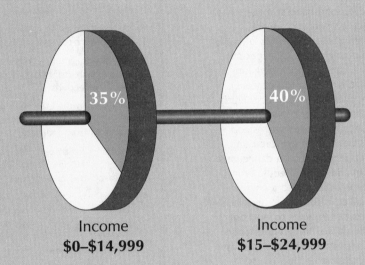

Income
$0–$14,999

Income
$15–$24,999

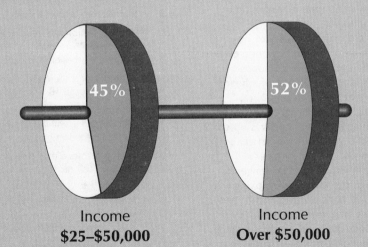

Income
$25–$50,000

Income
Over $50,000

Source: U.S. Centers for Disease Control and Prevention

S M O K I N G

Each year, more than 400,000 people in the U.S. die as a result of smoking. Most of these people were smokers. But almost 50,000 people die because they inhaled second-hand smoke—that is, other people's tobacco smoke.

Smoking increases the risk of many serious and deadly diseases, especially heart disease, cancers (including lung, mouth, throat, breast, colon cancers), emphysema, pneumonia, and bronchitis. Smoking robs the body of vitamins, weakens bones, interferes with sleep, and doubles the risk of eye cataracts.

Smoking is more than a dangerous habit. It is an addiction. People who smoke become addicted to a chemical in tobacco called nicotine. Many smokers report that they want to quit but are unable to do so. They experience physical withdrawal symptoms as they try to break their addiction to this powerful drug. The majority of studies show that women have a harder time quitting than men.

There are major benefits to be gained from quitting smoking, regardless of a person's age. Within 24 hours of quitting smoking, the chance of a heart attack decreases. Within 48 hours, nerve endings begin to regrow. Within 3 months, lung function improves up to 30%. Within 5 years, the risk of cancer declines sharply.

In general, smoking is no longer fashionable in the U.S. Anti-smoking campaigns and bans on smoking in many public places have encouraged many people to "kick the habit." In many other parts of the world, however, smoking is commonplace and still growing in popularity. Experts predict that if current trends continue, smoking will cause 10 million deaths worldwide each year by the year 2020.

FINGERTIP FACTS

- Smoking is the most preventable cause of death in the U.S.

- Smokers are twice as likely as nonsmokers to have strokes.

- Worldwide, smoking kills 3 million people each year. That's 1 person every 10 seconds.

- Each year in the U.S, there are twice as many deaths from second-hand smoke as from murder.

- Women who smoke during pregnancy are 10 times more likely to miscarry than nonsmokers.

- In 1964, when the government released its first report warning that smoking was unhealthy, 40% of Americans smoked. In 1997, some 29% smoked.

- About 75% of U.S. adults who smoke regularly had their first cigarette before they were 18 years old.

- Over 3 million U.S. teenagers smoke cigarettes. More than 1 million teen males use smokeless tobacco.

- One out of 4 teenagers uses tobacco by age 18.

- About 32% of young people who start smoking will die of smoking related disorders.

- Each year, more than 4 million U.S. smokers use nicotine patches in efforts to stop smoking.

- In the U.S., 5.17 trillion cigars were sold in 1997. That's enough to give every person on Earth about 8 cigars.

- It is estimated that smoking costs the nation more than $100 billion per year in lost productivity, medical bills, insurance, and other health-related expenses.

PROFILE OF ADULT U.S. CIGARETTE SMOKERS
(Percentage, by selected characteristics)

By sex

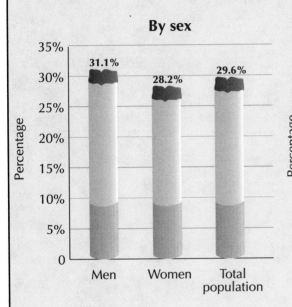

By race

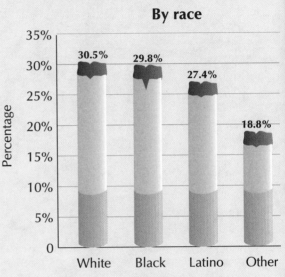

By age group

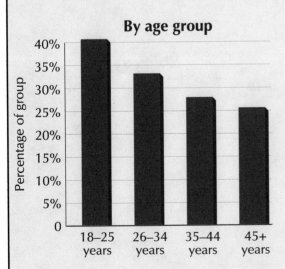

By education

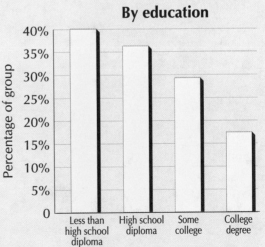

Source: U.S. Department of Health and Human Services, U.S. Centers for Disease Control

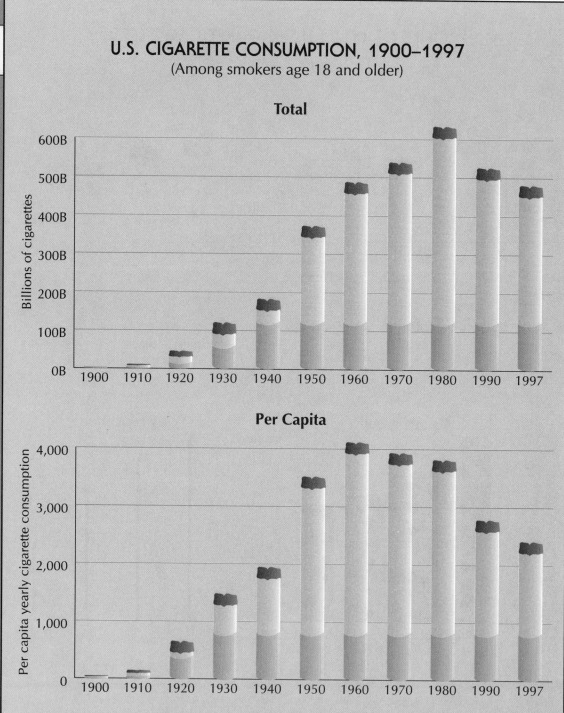

U.S. CIGARETTE CONSUMPTION, 1900–1997
(Among smokers age 18 and older)

Total

Per Capita

Source: U.S. Dept. of Health and Human Services

CHILDREN WHO SMOKE

(Percentage of U.S. kids in
each age group who smoke)

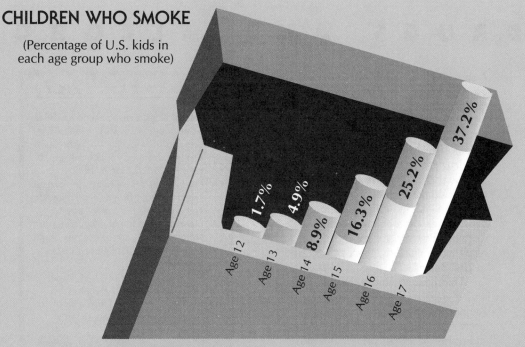

Age 12 — 1.7%
Age 13 — 4.9%
Age 14 — 8.9%
Age 15 — 16.3%
Age 16 — 25.2%
Age 17 — 37.2%

Source: Statistics based on National Household Survey on Drug Abuse

IQ AND SMOKING

(The average 4-year-old's IQ, compared to that of a 4-year-old whose mother
smokes 10 or more cigarettes during pregnancy)

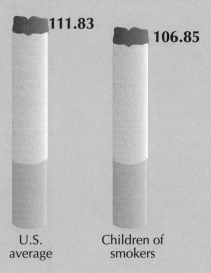

111.83

106.85

U.S.
average

Children of
smokers

Source: Cornell University/University of Rochester

D R U G S   A N D   A L C O H O L

A shockingly large number of Americans use illegal drugs. A 1997 survey estimated that 24.1 million people ages 12 and older used illegal drugs in the past year. The good news is that this represents a significant decline from peak U.S. drug use in the mid 1980s. The bad news is that drug abuse causes tremendous health and social problems. Addiction—a physical or psychological dependency—is a common result. Cocaine addiction, for example, can result in convulsions, heart attacks, and sudden death.

The most commonly abused illegal drug is marijuana, followed by cocaine. People also abuse legal drugs, such as alcohol, cold medicines, amphetamines, and tranquilizers. Alcohol is the most commonly abused legal drug in America. A 1997 survey concluded that approximately 109 million Americans ages 12 and older had used alcohol in the previous month. Alcohol is the "drug of choice" among adolescents, with more than 53% of high school seniors reporting current use.

Alcohol is a factor in more than 100,000 deaths annually. Some of these deaths are from diseases, such as of the heart and liver. Even moderate drinking can be dangerous. For example, some studies suggest that a woman who has only a few drinks a week has a significantly greater risk of developing breast cancer than do non-drinkers.

The consumption of alcohol is also associated with accidents—in homes, workplaces, and on the road. More than one-third of all traffic fatalities in the U.S. are alcohol related. These statistics mean that one alcohol-related traffic death occurs in the U.S. every 26 minutes. More than one-third of these deaths occur among people ages 25 or younger.

FINGERTIP FACTS

- Use of illegal drugs peaked in 1985, when there were 34.1 million drug users in the U.S. By 1995, the number had dropped to 22.6 million. It rose to 24.1 million in 1997.
- People ages 18 to 25 are the biggest users of illegal drugs. People age 35 and older are the lowest users.
- Most users of illegal drugs are white, but the rate of use per capita is somewhat higher among blacks than whites.
- Males are heavier users of illegal drugs than females. People who have not completed high school are heavier users than people with more education.
- Marijuana is the most commonly used illegal drug, taken by about 77% of drug users.
- People who start to drink before age 15 are more likely to use marijuana or cocaine.
- Among graduating high school seniors in 1998, 54.1% had used an illegal drug at least once before senior year.
- A government study estimated that alcohol abuse costs the U.S. about $85 billion a year; drug abuse costs another $58 billion.
- Deaths caused by drunk driving are declining. In 1982, more than 42.7% of motor vehicle deaths were alcohol related. By 1997, the number had dropped to 38.6%.
- Men ages 21 to 35 are responsible for more than 50% of all alcohol-related car fatalities in the U.S.
- About 40% of all people in the U.S. will be involved in an alcohol-related traffic crash during their lifetimes.
- By mid-1994, some 44 states mandated prison time for drivers with 2 convictions for drunken driving.

LIFETIME DRUG USAGE RATES FOR 8TH, 10TH, AND 12TH GRADERS BY PERCENTAGE, 1997

(Percentage by grade of students with a minimum one-time use)

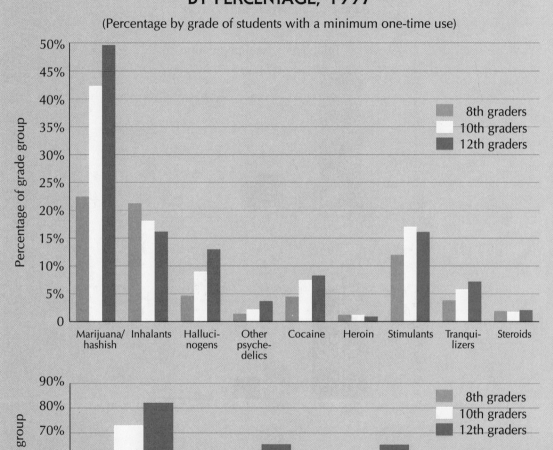

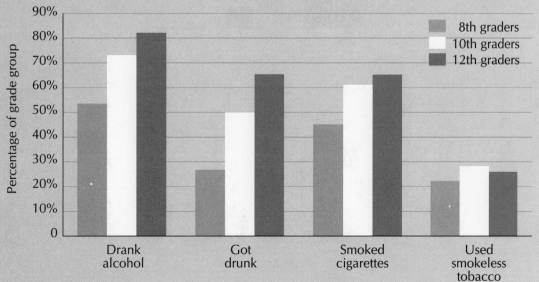

Source: National Institute on Drug Abuse, National Institutes of Health; University of Michigan

PROFILE: DRUG USE BY U.S. HIGH SCHOOL STUDENTS

(Percentage of student population who used drugs
during the 30 days before survey)

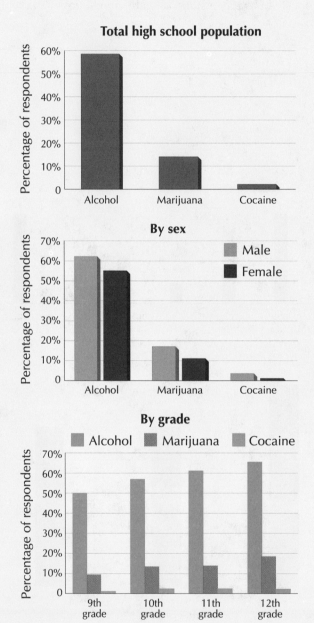

Source: U.S. Department of Health and Human Services, U.S. Centers for Disease Control

DRUG USAGE IN HIGH SCHOOL, 1975, 1980, 1998

(Percentage of students reporting use in prior year)

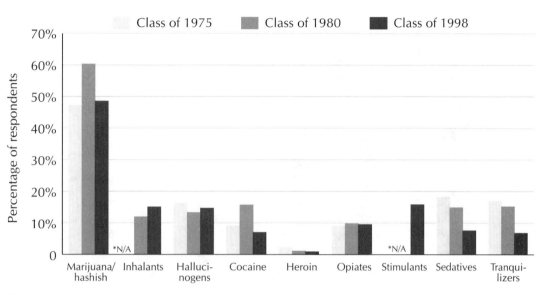

* N/A = Not available

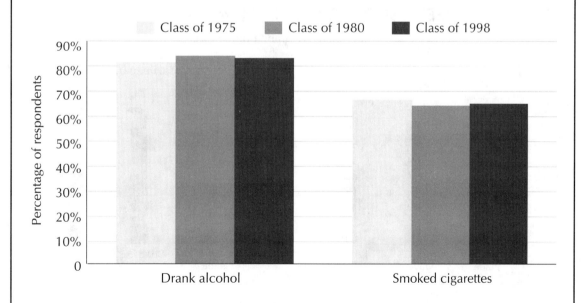

Source: National Institute on Drug Abuse; National Institutes of Health; University of Michigan

DRUG USE BY U.S. HIGH SCHOOL SENIORS, 1975–1997

(As percentage of total senior population)

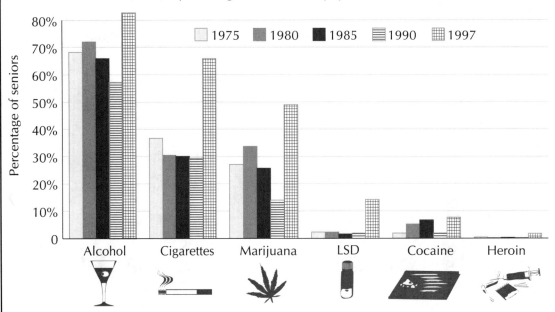

Legend: 1975   1980   1985   1990   1997

Y-axis: Percentage of seniors (0 to 80%)

Categories: Alcohol, Cigarettes, Marijuana, LSD, Cocaine, Heroin

TEENAGE DRUG USE, 1991 vs. 1998

(As percentage of grade population)

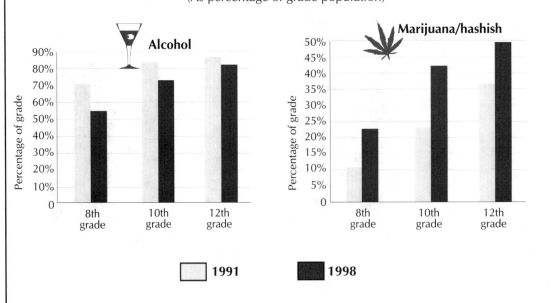

Alcohol — Percentage of grade (0 to 90%): 8th grade, 10th grade, 12th grade

Marijuana/hashish — Percentage of grade (0 to 50%): 8th grade, 10th grade, 12th grade

Legend: 1991   1998

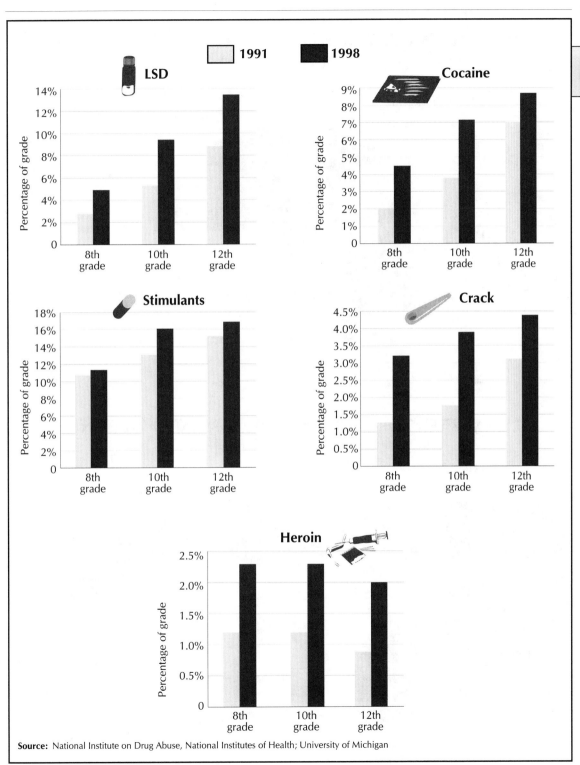

Source: National Institute on Drug Abuse, National Institutes of Health; University of Michigan

DRUG-ABUSE-RELATED EMERGENCY ROOM EPISODES, 1997

(Percentage by type of drug involved)

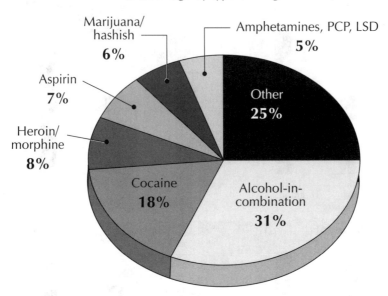

Marijuana/
hashish
6%

Amphetamines, PCP, LSD
5%

Aspirin
7%

Other
25%

Heroin/
morphine
8%

Cocaine
18%

Alcohol-in-
combination
31%

Source: U.S. National Center for Health Statistics, *Monthly Vital Statistics Report;* and unpublished data.

U.S. EMERGENCY ROOM DRUG-ABUSE-RELATED INCIDENTS

(January to June 1997)

Number of incidents

Total episodes	**466,897**
Alcohol-in-combination	**145,394**
Cocaine	**80,000**
Heroin/morphine	**38,000**
Aspirin	**34,980**
Marijuana/hashish	**33,000**
Methamphetamine	**8,000**
PCP/PCP combinations	**3,500**
LSD	**3,700**

Source: U.S. Department of Health and Human Services, National Institute on Drug Abuse; Drug Abuse Warning Network

PERCENTAGE OF PEOPLE WHO SAY THEY HAVE USED MARIJUANA

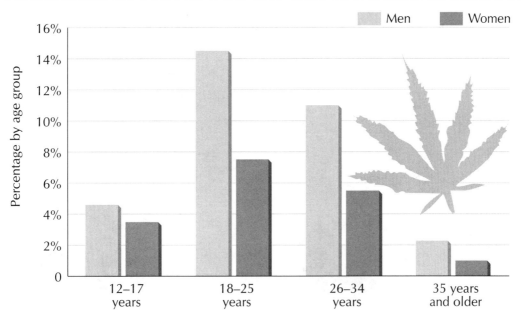

PERCENTAGE OF PEOPLE WHO SAY THEY HAVE USED CRACK AT LEAST ONCE

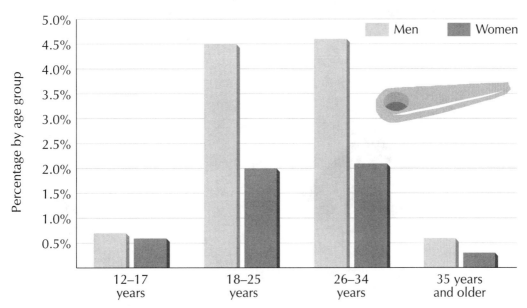

Source: U.S. Substance Abuse and Mental Health Services Administration

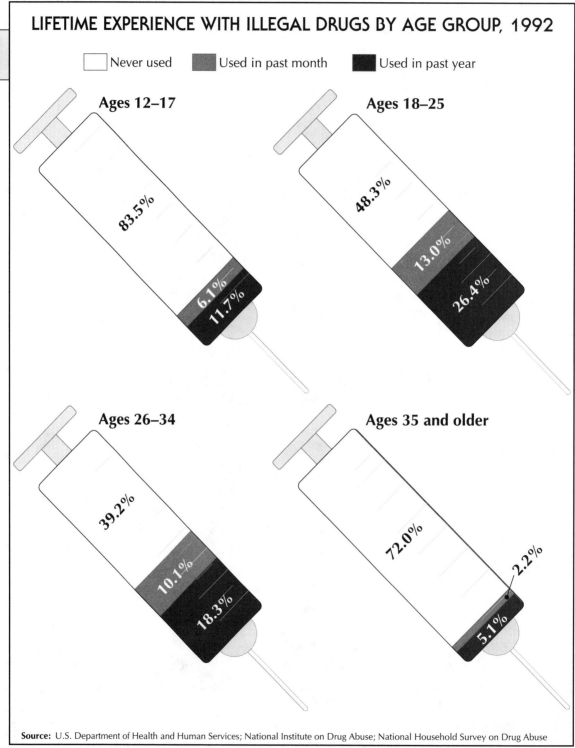

LIFETIME EXPERIENCE WITH ILLEGAL DRUGS BY AGE GROUP, 1992

Never used   Used in past month   Used in past year

Ages 12–17

83.5%

6.1%

11.7%

Ages 18–25

48.3%

13.0%

26.4%

Ages 26–34

39.2%

10.1%

18.3%

Ages 35 and older

72.0%

2.2%

5.1%

Source: U.S. Department of Health and Human Services; National Institute on Drug Abuse; National Household Survey on Drug Abuse

AGE AND PERCENTAGE OF PERSONS
REPORTING ILLEGAL DRUG USE, 1979–1995

Ever used　　Used in past year　　Used in past 30 days

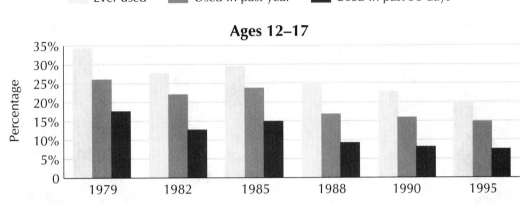

Ages 12–17

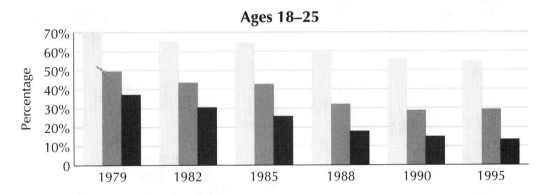

Ages 18–25

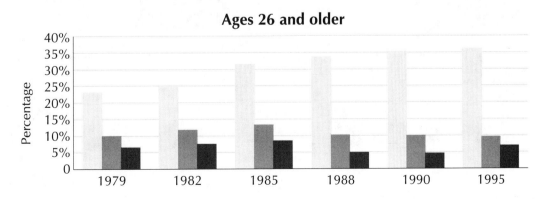

Ages 26 and older

Source: National Household Survey on Drug Abuse

PROFILE: HEAVY ALCOHOL CONSUMPTION, BY AGE, RACE, AND SEX

Heavy users are defined as those drinking 5 or more drinks per day for
5 or more days within past month:

By age

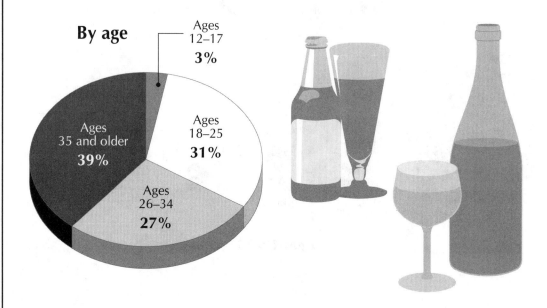

Ages
12–17
3%

Ages
18–25
31%

Ages
26–34
27%

Ages
35 and older
39%

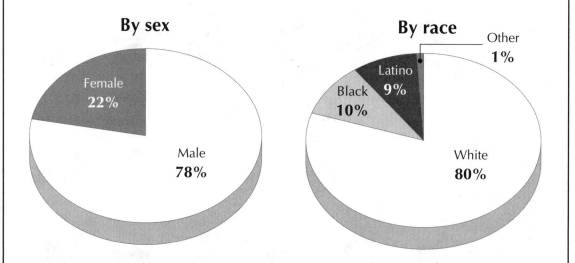

By sex

Female
22%

Male
78%

By race

Other
1%

Latino
9%

Black
10%

White
80%

Source: U.S. Department of Health and Human Services

ALCOHOL DEPENDENCE AND ABUSE IN THE U.S., BY AGE AND SEX

By age

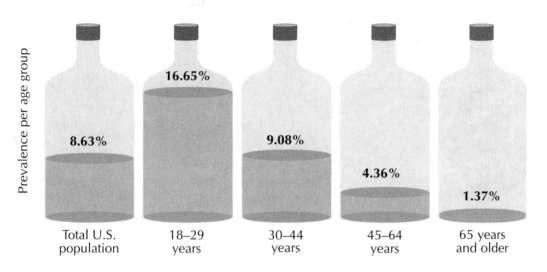

Prevalence per age group

8.63%	16.65%	9.08%	4.36%	1.37%
Total U.S. population	18–29 years	30–44 years	45–64 years	65 years and older

By sex and age

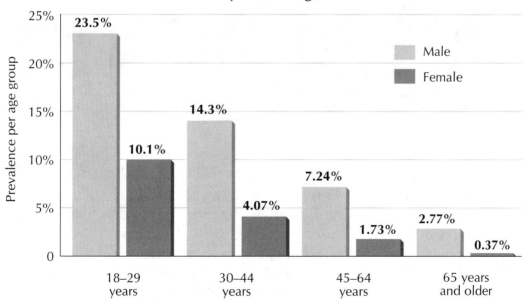

Prevalence per age group

Male
Female

	18–29 years	30–44 years	45–64 years	65 years and older
Male	23.5%	14.3%	7.24%	2.77%
Female	10.1%	4.07%	1.73%	0.37%

Source: U.S. Department of Health and Human Services, National Institute on Alcohol Abuse & Alcoholism

ALCOHOLISM IN THE U.S.

**Americans affected by
alcoholism in their family**

**Americans who lived with an
alcoholic while growing up**

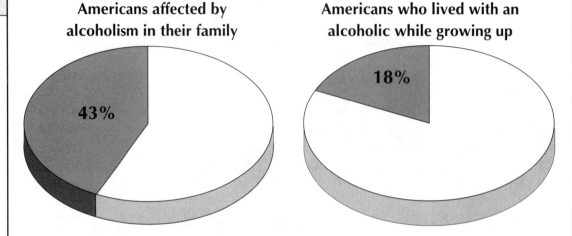

43%

18%

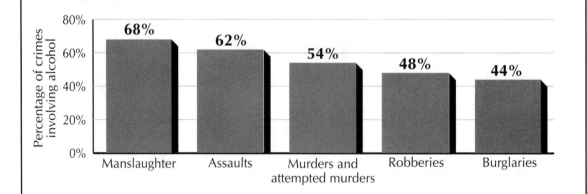

Percentage of crimes
involving alcohol

80%

68%

62%

60%

54%

48%

44%

40%

20%

0%

Manslaughter   Assaults   Murders and
attempted murders   Robberies   Burglaries

- There are an estimated 26.8 million children of alcoholics in the
  United States; over 11 million are under age 18.
- Children of alcoholics are four times more likely to develop
  alcoholism.
- Roughly 1 in 8 U.S. adult drinkers is an alcoholic.
- The total health care costs of children of alcoholics is 32% higher
  than children from non-alcoholic families.

Source: National Clearinghouse for Alcohol and Drug Information

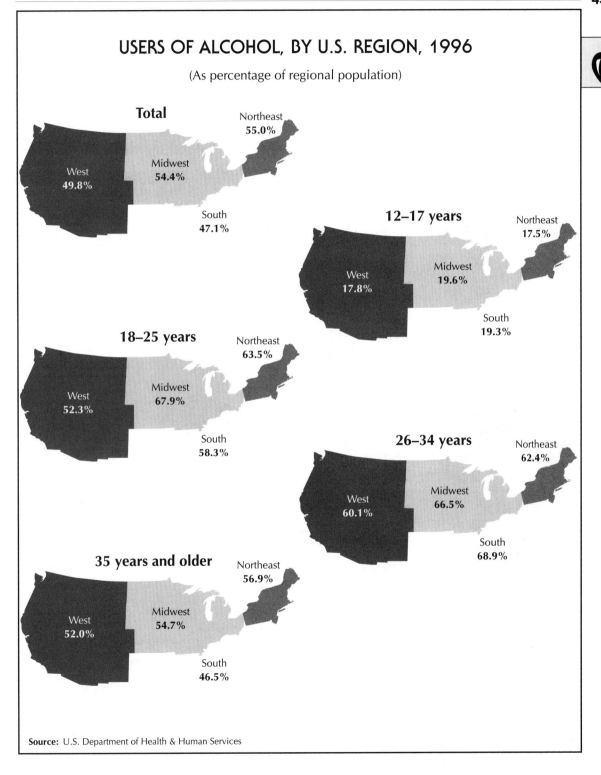

USERS OF ALCOHOL, BY U.S. REGION, 1996

(As percentage of regional population)

Total

Northeast
55.0%

West
49.8%

Midwest
54.4%

South
47.1%

12–17 years

Northeast
17.5%

West
17.8%

Midwest
19.6%

South
19.3%

18–25 years

Northeast
63.5%

West
52.3%

Midwest
67.9%

South
58.3%

26–34 years

Northeast
62.4%

West
60.1%

Midwest
66.5%

South
68.9%

35 years and older

Northeast
56.9%

West
52.0%

Midwest
54.7%

South
46.5%

Source: U.S. Department of Health & Human Services

INITIATION OF DRUG USE, AGES 12–17, 1991 vs. 1996

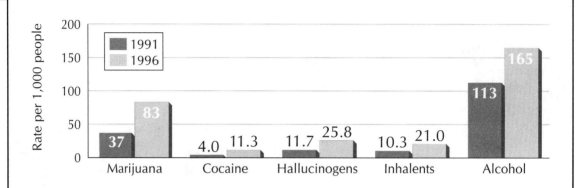

Rate per 1,000 people

- 1991
- 1996

	Marijuana	Cocaine	Hallucinogens	Inhalents	Alcohol
1991	37	4.0	11.7	10.3	113
1996	83	11.3	25.8	21.0	165

ILLICIT DRUG USE, 1997

60% use marijuana only

20% use only illicit drugs other than marijuana

20% use marijuana and other illicit drugs

13.9 million Americans (6.4%) were current drug users. 80% of them used marijuana, while 40% used drugs other than marijuana.

ILLICIT DRUG USE BY RACE, 1997

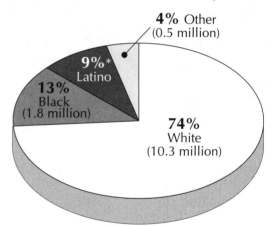

4% Other (0.5 million)

9%* Latino

13% Black (1.8 million)

74% White (10.3 million)

*(1.3 million)

The drug use rate for blacks (7.5/100) remained higher than for whites (6.4/100) and Latinos (5.9/100).

Source: National Center for Disease Control

DRUG USE IN THE U.S., 1997

(As percentage of total population)

By Region

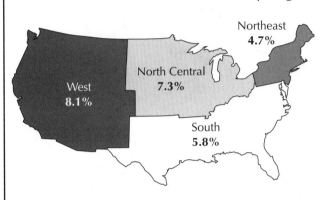

Northeast
4.7%

North Central
7.3%

West
8.1%

South
5.8%

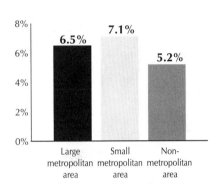

By Gender

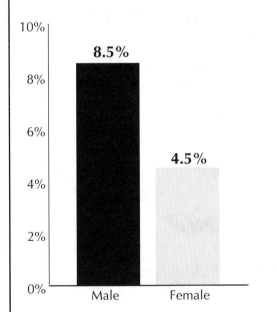

By Education

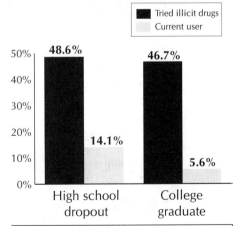

Although a very similar number of high school dropouts and college graduates have tried illicit drugs, 29% of dropouts continued using while only 12% of college graduates did.

Source: National Center for Disease Control

PROFILE: TOP 10 STATES* IN PER CAPITA SPENDING FOR MENTAL HEALTH PROGRAMS

(With rankings)

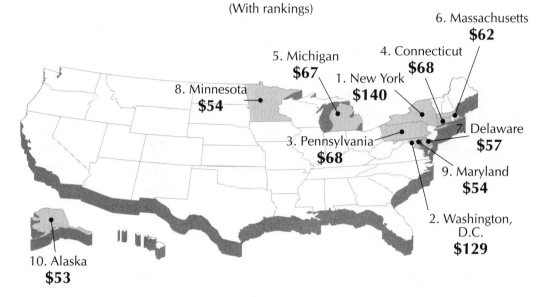

6. Massachusetts
$62

4. Connecticut
$68

5. Michigan
$67

1. New York
$140

8. Minnesota
$54

7. Delaware
$57

3. Pennsylvania
$68

9. Maryland
$54

2. Washington, D.C.
$129

10. Alaska
$53

PROFILE: BOTTOM 10 STATES* IN PER CAPITA SPENDING

(With rankings)

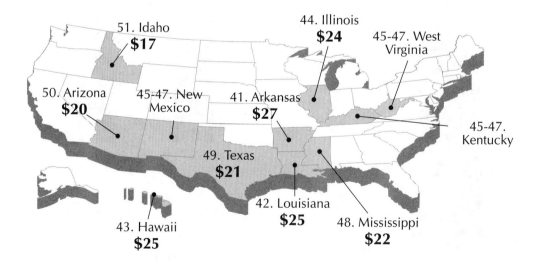

51. Idaho
$17

44. Illinois
$24

45-47. West Virginia

50. Arizona
$20

45-47. New Mexico

41. Arkansas
$27

45-47. Kentucky

49. Texas
$21

42. Louisiana
$25

48. Mississippi
$22

43. Hawaii
$25

* Includes Washington, D.C.
Source: U.S. Department of Health and Human Services

MENTAL ILLNESS IN AMERICA, BY DISORDER, 1998

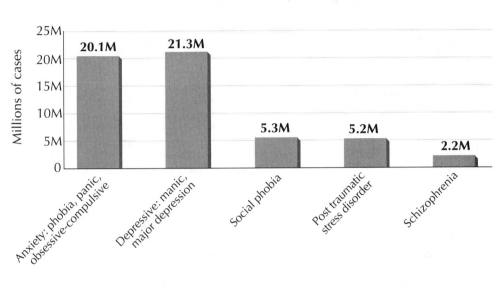

Source: National Institute of Mental Health

PROFILE: TREATMENT FOR DRUG DEPENDENCY

Most drug-dependent people are not in treatment. Only about 15% of people with a chemical dependency are actively involved in treatment programs. People in treatment, by race:

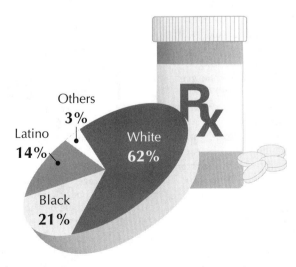

Source: National Drug and Alcoholism Treatment Survey

LIFE EXPECTANCY AND BIRTH RATE

People are living longer. An American born in 1900 could expect to live 47.3 years. An American born in 1996 could expect to live 76.1 years. Life expectancy has increased because death rates have fallen. Better health care, sanitation, and nutrition account for much of the drop in death rates.

Infants are at risk of dying from pregnancy complications, premature birth, low birthweight, respiratory ailments, and other causes. But infants' chances of surviving have steadily improved.

The infant mortality rate—the number of infant deaths per 1,000 live births—has fallen dramatically. But it has fallen much faster, and much further, for whites than for African-Americans. From 1980 to 1996, the rate of white infant deaths in the U.S. fell 44%, from 10.9 to 6.1 per 1,000 births. The rate for blacks fell 34%, from 22.2 to 14.7 per 1,000 births.

The U.S. birth rate has also fallen. The birth rate is the number of births per 1,000 people. In 1910, the U.S. birth rate was 30.1. It fell to 14.6 in 1975, then rose gradually to 16.3 in 1991. In 1997, it fell back to 14.5.

Because people are living longer, there are more older people than ever before. Between 1980 and 1997, the number of people ages 85 or older increased by 40%, to 3.7 million.

Many factors affect life expectancy and birth rates, including age, sex, race, occupation, and nutrition. Life expectancy and birth rates also vary from one country to another. Japan has the world's highest life expectancy; a Japanese child born in 1997 could expect to live 89.4 years. Poor countries have the lowest life expectancy. In most African countries, life expectancy for children born in 1997 was less than 63 years.

FINGERTIP FACTS

- Life expectancy in the U.S. is higher among whites than blacks. A white male born in 1996 could expect to live 7.8 years longer than a black born the same year.

- Females live longer than males. A white female born in 1996 had a life expectancy of 79.7 years. A white male's life expectancy in the U.S. was 73.9 years.

- More education means longer life. Death rates are lower among college graduates than among people who did not complete high school.

- Life expectancy for older people is up. In 1970, a 65-year-old American could expect to live another 15.2 years. In 1996, that same person had a life expectancy of 17.3 years.

- U.S. death rates are higher in cities than in rural areas.

- U.S. infant deaths for 1988-1990 ranged from 6.7 per 1,000 births in Maine to 22.2 per 1,000 in the District of Columbia.

- The number of births to unmarried mothers has increased. In 1996, a total of 19.9% of white mothers and 60% of black mothers were unmarried.

- In the U.S., there is one birth every 8 seconds and one death every 14 seconds, for a net gain of 4,400 people per day.

- In 1998, approximately 142.3 million babies were born in the world.

- Every 4 seconds around the world, 17 babies are born and 7 people die. This results in a net increase of 3 people every 2 seconds, or 9,000 people per hour.

- In 1997, the U.S. ranked #14 in average life expectancy. Canada ranked #4. China ranked #1.

YEARS OF LIFE EXPECTED AT BIRTH IN U.S., 1920–1997

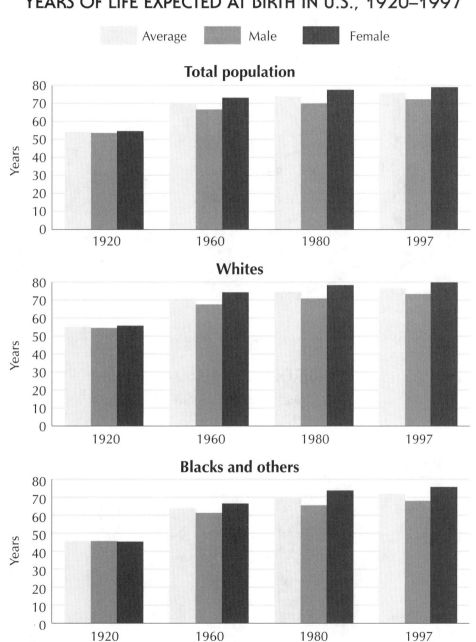

Average   Male   Female

Total population

Whites

Blacks and others

Source: National Center for Health Statistics

U.S. INFANT MORTALITY RATE, 1940–1997

(Per 1,000 live births)

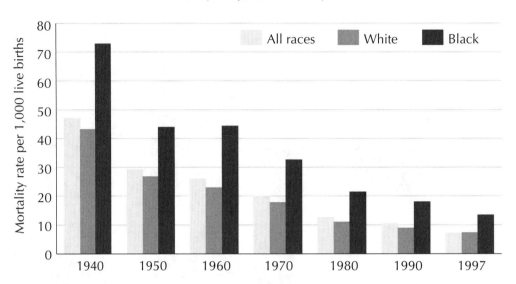

Sources: U.S. Department of Health and Human Services; National Center for Health Statistics; U.S. Centers for Disease Control

U.S. BIRTH RATE, 1960–1997

(Per 1,000 population)

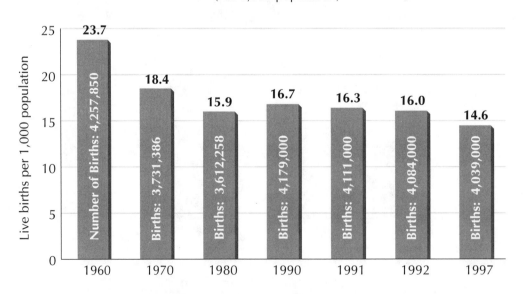

Source: National Center for Health Statistics, U.S. Department of Health and Human Services

PROFILE: LEADING CAUSES OF CHILDHOOD DEATH, BIRTH TO 4 YEARS

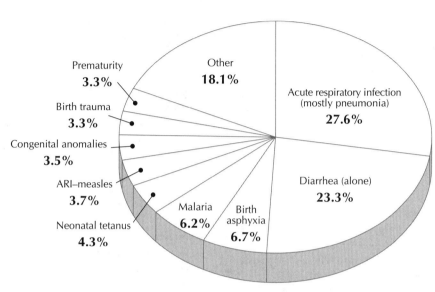

Other
18.1%

Acute respiratory infection
(mostly pneumonia)
27.6%

Prematurity
3.3%

Birth trauma
3.3%

Congenital anomalies
3.5%

ARI–measles
3.7%

Neonatal tetanus
4.3%

Malaria
6.2%

Birth
asphyxia
6.7%

Diarrhea (alone)
23.3%

Source: World Health Organization

U.S. BIRTHS AND BIRTH RATES, BY REGION, 1997

(Rates per 1,000 population)

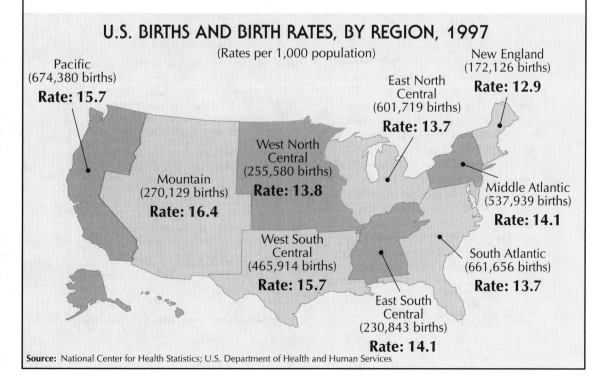

Pacific
(674,380 births)
Rate: 15.7

New England
(172,126 births)
Rate: 12.9

East North
Central
(601,719 births)
Rate: 13.7

West North
Central
(255,580 births)
Rate: 13.8

Mountain
(270,129 births)
Rate: 16.4

Middle Atlantic
(537,939 births)
Rate: 14.1

West South
Central
(465,914 births)
Rate: 15.7

South Atlantic
(661,656 births)
Rate: 13.7

East South
Central
(230,843 births)
Rate: 14.1

Source: National Center for Health Statistics; U.S. Department of Health and Human Services

H E A L T H   I N S U R A N C E

Health insurance promises to pay speci-fied health care costs—such as hospital charges, doctors' fees, and medicine bills—to a covered person. Which costs are covered depends upon the person's insurance policy. Insurance coverage in the U.S. is quite uneven. Most people are covered for most hos-pital care, and many are covered for at least some doctors' bills. But only a minority of people are covered for such costs as dental services, medicine, home care, and other, more common but expensive medical needs.

In 1996, about 24% of personal health care costs were paid for by insurance companies. The remaining 76% of costs were paid for either by the patients themselves or by the U.S. government. The two main government health insurance plans are Medicare and Medicaid. Medicare covers severely disabled people and people ages 65 and older. Medicaid covers poor people.

Most Americans' health insurance is paid for by their employers. As the cost of insurance has risen, however, companies are limiting the insurance coverage they provide for their workers. People who lose their jobs typically lose their health insurance, too.

Many Americans cannot afford to pay for health insurance on their own. According to a 1998 Census Bureau report, 43.4 million Americans are without health insurance. Of those who were not covered, 16% worked full time, 24% worked part time, and 26% did not work at all.

FINGERTIP FACTS

- The percentage of Americans without health insurance has been steadily increasing. From 1994 to 1998, the percentage of uninsured Americans rose 9% to 43.4 million.

- Whites are more likely to be insured than blacks. Hispanics have the lowest percentage of insured individuals.

- Women are more likely to have health insurance than men.

- The percentage of insured people rises as education levels rise.

- In 1997, there were 10.7 million children—16.3% of all U.S. chil-dren—who were uninsured.

- Coverage varies among regions. The Northeast has the lowest percent-age of uninsured people. The South has the highest percentage.

- The percentage of workers who are covered by employer-sponsored health care plans varies with the industry. Most high-technology workers are covered by such plans; most retail workers are not.

- In 1998, the state with the most uninsured people was Texas at 24.3%. Wisconsin had the lowest percent-age with 8.4%.

- The number of people covered by Medicare increased from 19.5 mil-lion in 1967 to 38.4 million in 1997.

- Medicaid recipients increased from 10.0 million in 1967 to 36.7 million in 1998.

PROFILE: PERCENTAGE OF U.S. POPULATION WITHOUT HEALTH COVERAGE, BY SELECTED CHARACTERISTICS

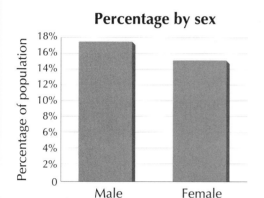

Percentage by sex

Total not covered
1998: 43.45 million

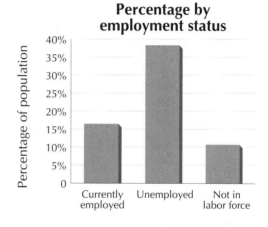

Percentage by employment status

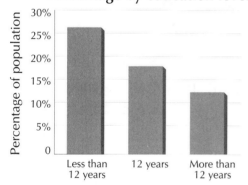

Percentage by education level

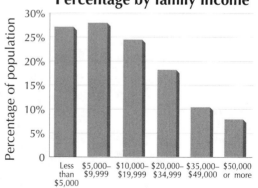

Percentage by family income

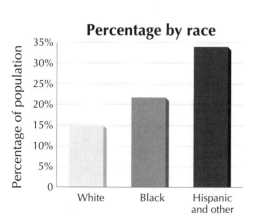

Percentage by race

Source: Bureau of the Census, U.S. Dept. of Commerce

PROFILE: AGE AND EMPLOYMENT STATUS OF THOSE WITHOUT INSURANCE

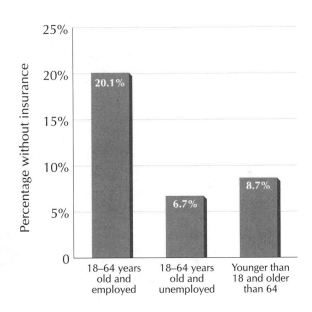

AMOUNT OF MONEY EARNED DURING ONE YEAR BY THOSE WITHOUT INSURANCE, BY INCOME LEVEL

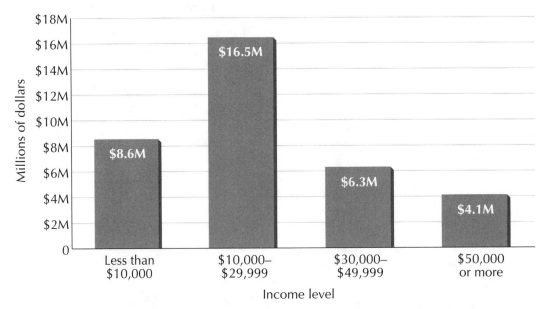

Source: U.S. Census Bureau

HEALTH COVERAGE FROM U.S. EMPLOYERS, 1991

About 74% of U.S. employees are covered by employer-sponsored health care plans in companies with 200 or more employees. The percentage of coverage, however, by industry varies:

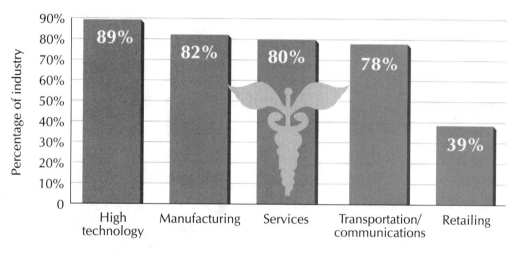

Source: Based on statistics from KPMG

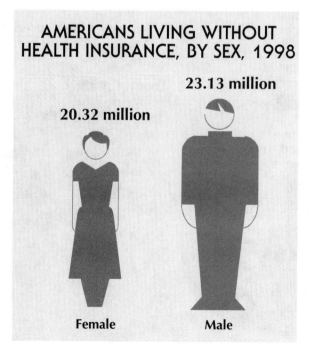

Source: U.S. Census Bureau, U.S. Dept. of Commerce

PROFILE: PERSONS WITHOUT HEALTH INSURANCE COVERAGE, BY SELECTED CHARACTERISTICS

Uninsured, by sex

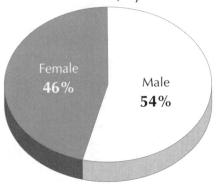

Female 46%

Male 54%

Uninsured, by employment

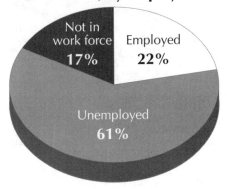

Not in work force 17%

Employed 22%

Unemployed 61%

Uninsured, by education level

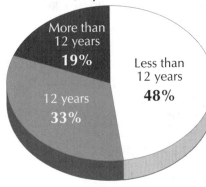

More than 12 years 19%

Less than 12 years 48%

12 years 33%

Uninsured, by family income

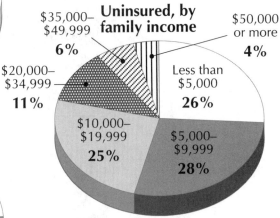

$35,000–$49,999 6%

$50,000 or more 4%

$20,000–$34,999 11%

Less than $5,000 26%

$10,000–$19,999 25%

$5,000–$9,999 28%

Uninsured, by race

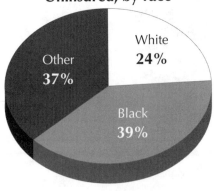

Other 37%

White 24%

Black 39%

Source: U.S. Census Bureau

PROFILE: TOP 10 STATES* WITH LOWEST PERCENTAGE OF UNINSURED POPULATION

(With rankings)

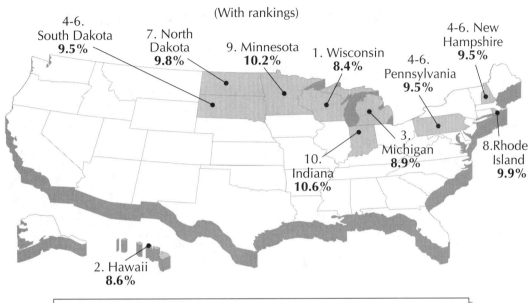

4-6. South Dakota **9.5%**

7. North Dakota **9.8%**

9. Minnesota **10.2%**

1. Wisconsin **8.4%**

4-6. Pennsylvania **9.5%**

4-6. New Hampshire **9.5%**

3. Michigan **8.9%**

8. Rhode Island **9.9%**

10. Indiana **10.6%**

2. Hawaii **8.6%**

Total uninsured in U.S.: **43.45 million (16% of population)**

PROFILE: TOP 10 STATES* WITH HIGHEST PERCENTAGE OF UNINSURED POPULATION

(With rankings)

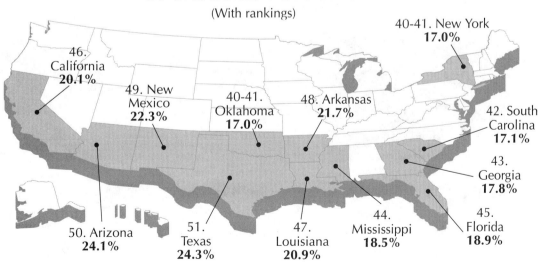

40-41. New York **17.0%**

46. California **20.1%**

49. New Mexico **22.3%**

40-41. Oklahoma **17.0%**

48. Arkansas **21.7%**

42. South Carolina **17.1%**

43. Georgia **17.8%**

50. Arizona **24.1%**

51. Texas **24.3%**

47. Louisiana **20.9%**

44. Mississippi **18.5%**

45. Florida **18.9%**

* Includes Washington, D.C.
Source: Based on statistics from the Center for National Health Program Studies, Harvard Medical School/The Cambridge Hospital

U.S. RESIDENTS WITHOUT HEALTH INSURANCE, 1980–1998

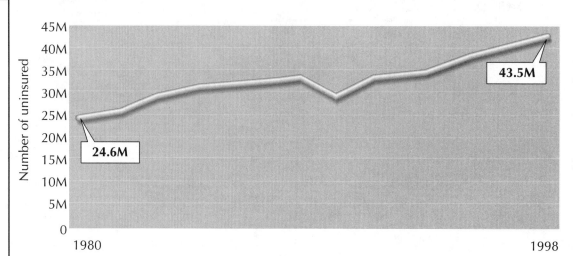

Number of uninsured

45M
40M
35M
30M
25M
20M
15M
10M
5M
0

24.6M

43.5M

1980

1998

PROFILE: NUMBER OF UNINSURED PEOPLE IN THE U.S., BY REGION

(Average, by percentage of total uninsured)

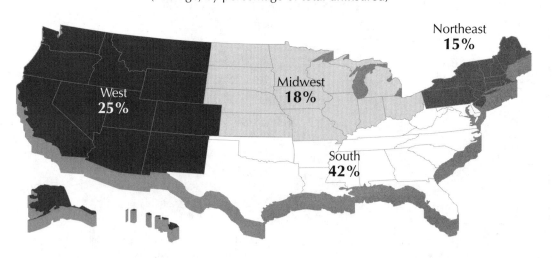

Northeast
15%

Midwest
18%

West
25%

South
42%

Source: U.S. Census Bureau

HEALTH MAINTENANCE ORGANIZATIONS (HMOs) IN THE U.S., 1980–1997

National managed care firms ranked by total HMO enrollment, July 1, 1997

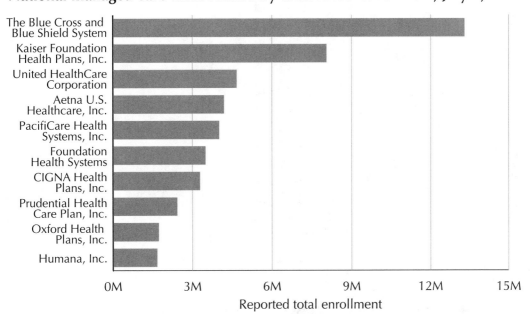

Number of people enrolled in HMOs

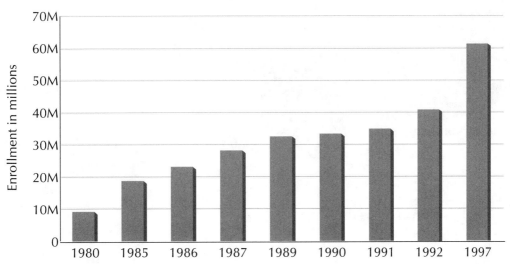

Source: American Association of Health Plans; Inter Study Statistics

MEDICARE: PERSONS 65 YEARS OLD AND OVER, 1980 vs. 1997

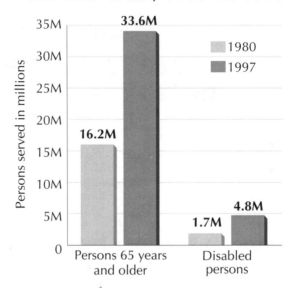

Persons served in millions

- 1980
- 1997

33.6M

16.2M

4.8M

1.7M

Persons 65 years and older

Disabled persons

Source: U.S. Health Care Financing Administration

PERSONS COVERED BY MEDICAID, 1998

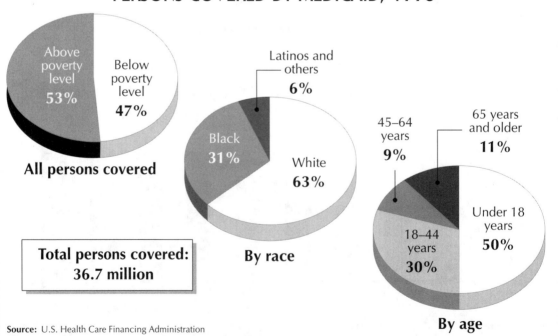

Above poverty level 53%

Below poverty level 47%

All persons covered

Latinos and others 6%

Black 31%

White 63%

By race

45–64 years 9%

65 years and older 11%

18–44 years 30%

Under 18 years 50%

By age

Total persons covered: 36.7 million

Source: U.S. Health Care Financing Administration

MEDICARE ENROLLMENT AND PAYMENTS IN THE U.S., 1970–1997

Total enrollment

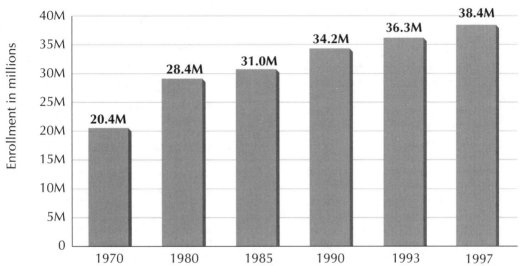

Enrollment in millions

40M
35M
30M
25M
20M
15M
10M
5M
0

20.4M — 1970
28.4M — 1980
31.0M — 1985
34.2M — 1990
36.3M — 1993
38.4M — 1997

Benefit payments

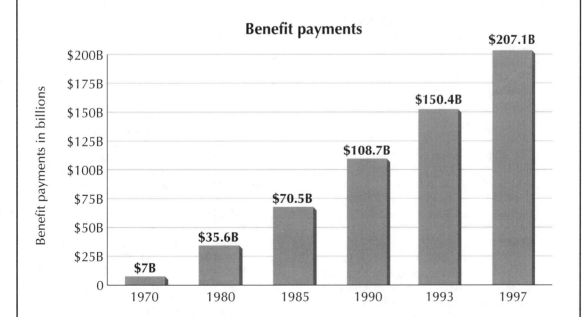

Benefit payments in billions

$200B
$175B
$150B
$125B
$100B
$75B
$50B
$25B
0

$7B — 1970
$35.6B — 1980
$70.5B — 1985
$108.7B — 1990
$150.4B — 1993
$207.1B — 1997

Source: U.S. Health Care Financing Administration

HEALTH CARE COSTS AND REFORM

The United States spends more money on health care than any other country in the world. In 1996, health care cost the U.S. an estimated $1.03 trillion. This industry accounted for 13.6% of the U.S. economy, or gross domestic product. In contrast—in 1967—the U.S. only spent a total of $51 billion, or 6.3% of the gross domestic product, on health care.

Various factors have fueled the dramatic increase in health care costs. New technologies and procedures, such as CAT scans and organ transplants, are expensive. People demand more health care than in the past. There are more elderly people today, and these people generally require more medical care than younger people. Salaries of health care professionals have also risen, and the cost of malpractice insurance has skyrocketed in recent years. In addition, it costs many millions of dollars to develop and test new medicines.

In 1996, the nations health expenditures averaged $3,759 per person, up 29% from 1990. Approximately 88% of the money was used for personal health care.

There is widespread feeling that the U.S. health care system needs to be reformed, both to control costs and to provide better coverage to all citizens. However, exactly what reforms are needed is a matter of considerable debate.

Meanwhile, the health care industry is making significant changes in an effort to control costs. For example, hospitals are shortening patient stays and performing more "standard" procedures on an outpatient basis. There is also increasing consolidation within the industry of hospitals, pharmaceutical companies, and other key health care providers.

FINGERTIP FACTS

- In 1996, U.S. health care costs totaled more than $1 trillion. This was the first time health care costs had exceeded the trillion dollar mark.
- U.S. health expenditures are projected to reach $1.74 trillion in the year 2000.
- In 1991, there were 9.8 million workers in the health care industry. About half were employed in hospitals.
- In 1996, there were 27.8 patient-care physicians for every 10,000 people in the U.S. (excluding military personnel). The ratio was lowest in Idaho (12.9) and highest in Massachusetts (42.6).
- Between 1980 and 1994, hospital inpatient admissions fell 18%, but outpatient visits jumped 50%.
- Although the average hospital stay in 1996 was 1½ days shorter than it was in 1980, it cost more than $4,000 more.
- Americans spent $1.5 billion on nursing home care in 1960. In 1996, they spent $78.5 billion.
- It costs an average of $60,000 to $110,000 to make a "test tube" baby. In comparison, the average cost of a normal delivery is $10,000.
- A 1993 study indicated that administrative expenses account for almost 25% of U.S. hospital costs.
- Drug companies often charge more for prescription drugs in the U.S. than elsewhere. A U.S. government study found that 77 commonly prescribed drugs cost an average 60% more in the U.S. than in Britain.
- Health care expenditures vary tremendously among nations. Most sub-Saharan African countries, where annual incomes are $100 to $600, spend less than $40 per person.

GOVERNMENT HEALTH CARE SPENDING, 1996

Where it is spent

Total Spending: $1.03 trillion

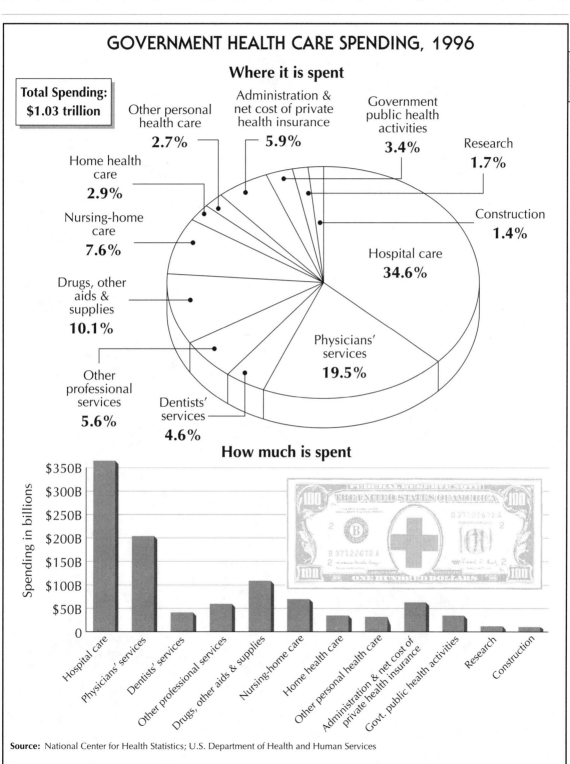

Other personal health care
2.7%

Administration & net cost of private health insurance
5.9%

Government public health activities
3.4%

Research
1.7%

Home health care
2.9%

Nursing-home care
7.6%

Drugs, other aids & supplies
10.1%

Construction
1.4%

Hospital care
34.6%

Physicians' services
19.5%

Other professional services
5.6%

Dentists' services
4.6%

How much is spent

Spending in billions

$350B
$300B
$250B
$200B
$150B
$100B
$50B
0

Hospital care
Physicians' services
Dentists' services
Other professional services
Drugs, other aids & supplies
Nursing-home care
Home health care
Other personal health care
Administration & net cost of private health insurance
Govt. public health activities
Research
Construction

Source: National Center for Health Statistics; U.S. Department of Health and Human Services

PHYSICIANS OFFICE VISITS, 1996
(Kinds of specialists visited, percentage of all visits)

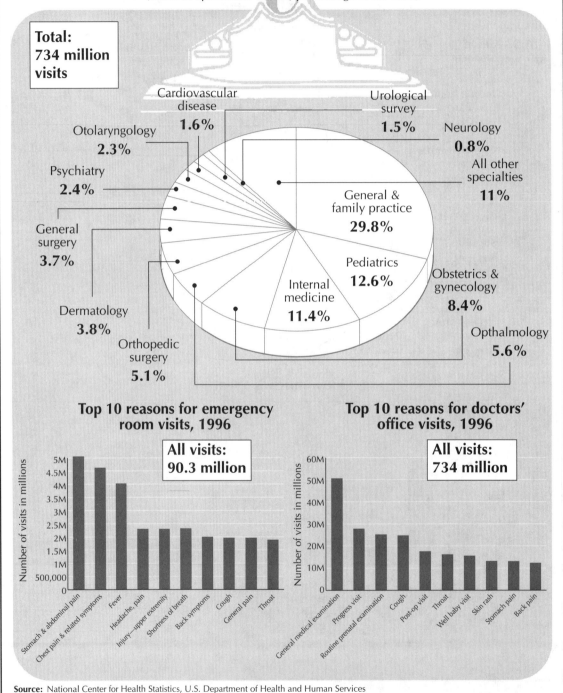

Total: 734 million visits

Cardiovascular disease **1.6%**

Urological survey **1.5%**

Neurology **0.8%**

Otolaryngology **2.3%**

All other specialties **11%**

Psychiatry **2.4%**

General & family practice **29.8%**

General surgery **3.7%**

Pediatrics **12.6%**

Dermatology **3.8%**

Internal medicine **11.4%**

Obstetrics & gynecology **8.4%**

Orthopedic surgery **5.1%**

Opthalmology **5.6%**

Top 10 reasons for emergency room visits, 1996

All visits: 90.3 million

Number of visits in millions

5M, 4.5M, 4M, 3.5M, 3M, 2.5M, 2M, 1.5M, 1M, 500,000, 0

Stomach & abdominal pain, Chest pain & related symptoms, Fever, Headache, pain, Injury—upper extremity, Shortness of breath, Back symptoms, Cough, General pain, Throat

Top 10 reasons for doctors' office visits, 1996

All visits: 734 million

Number of visits in millions

60M, 50M, 40M, 30M, 20M, 10M, 0

General medical examination, Progress visit, Routine prenatal examination, Cough, Post-op visit, Throat, Well baby visit, Skin rash, Stomach pain, Back pain

Source: National Center for Health Statistics, U.S. Department of Health and Human Services

GOVERNMENT EXPENDITURES FOR U.S. HEALTH CARE, 1975–2005*

Total amount

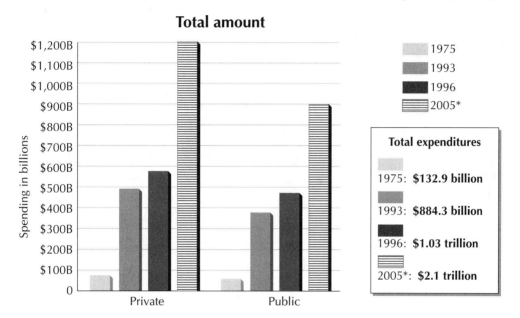

Legend:
- 1975
- 1993
- 1996
- 2005*

Total expenditures

1975: **$132.9 billion**

1993: **$884.3 billion**

1996: **$1.03 trillion**

2005*: **$2.1 trillion**

Per capita amount

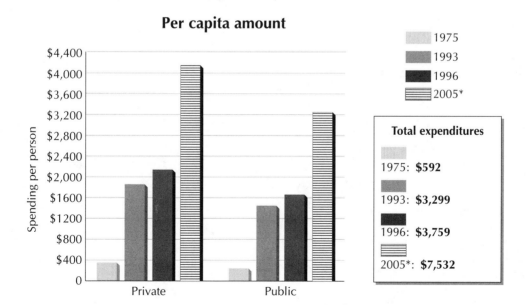

Legend:
- 1975
- 1993
- 1996
- 2005*

Total expenditures

1975: **$592**

1993: **$3,299**

1996: **$3,759**

2005*: **$7,532**

* Projected
Source: U.S. Department of Health and Human Services, Health Care Financing Administration

PERCENTAGE DISTRIBUTION OF HEALTH CARE SPENDING, 1975–1996

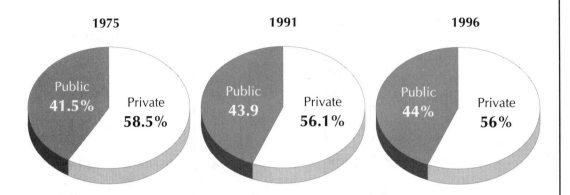

1975

Public 41.5%

Private **58.5%**

1991

Public 43.9

Private **56.1%**

1996

Public 44%

Private **56%**

Source: U.S. Department of Health and Human Services, Health Care Financing

TOP 10 COUNTRIES IN HEALTH SPENDING, 1996
(As percentage of GNP)

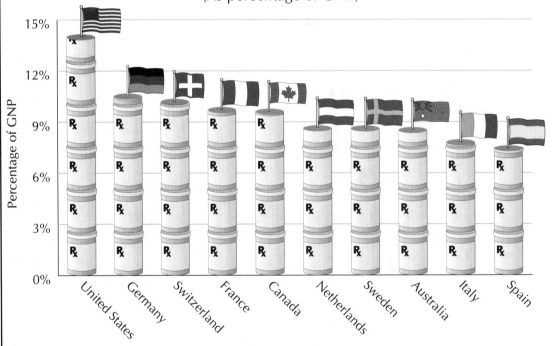

Source: U.S. Dept. of Health and Human Services, National Center for Health Statistics, *Health United States, 1995* (1996) and *OECD Health Data 98* (1998)

TOP 10 STATES IN HEALTH CARE QUALITY, 1997

(As rated by Health Risk Management, Inc.)

4. North Dakota
2. Minnesota
5. Wisconsin
3. New Hampshire
7. Maine
10. South Dakota
6. Massachusetts
8. Connecticut
9. Nebraska
1. Hawaii

TOP 10 STATES WITH POOREST QUALITY HEALTH CARE, 1997

(As rated by Health Risk Management, Inc.)

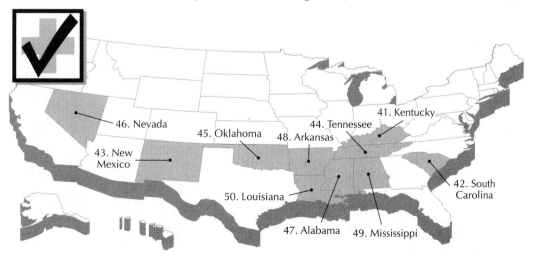

46. Nevada
45. Oklahoma
44. Tennessee
41. Kentucky
48. Arkansas
43. New Mexico
42. South Carolina
50. Louisiana
47. Alabama
49. Mississippi

Source: Health Risk Management Inc., *QualityFIRST Index*, 1998.

HOSPITAL EXPENDITURES 1972–1994
(In billions)

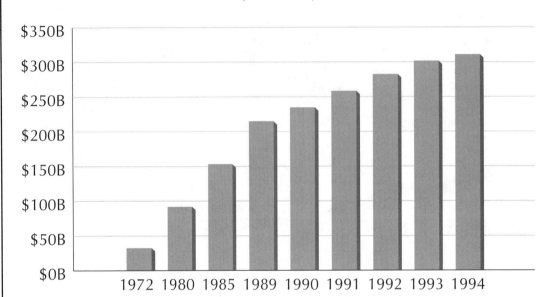

| | 1972 | 1980 | 1985 | 1989 | 1990 | 1991 | 1992 | 1993 | 1994 |

COST OF U.S. HOSPITAL CARE, 1980–1994

Average cost per day

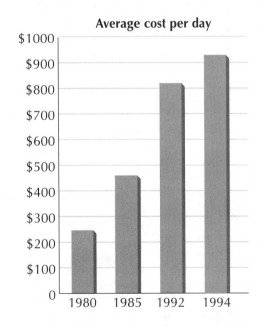

Average cost per stay

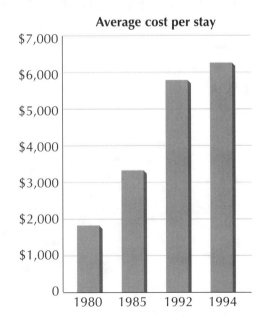

Source: Health Insurance Association of America

MOST COMMON SURGICAL PROCEDURES, 1996

(By number performed)

Men

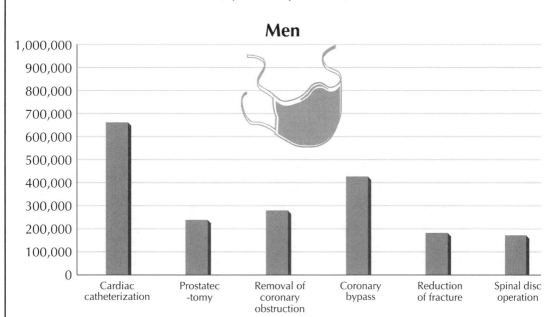

| | Cardiac catheterization | Prostatec-tomy | Removal of coronary obstruction | Coronary bypass | Reduction of fracture | Spinal disc operation |

Women

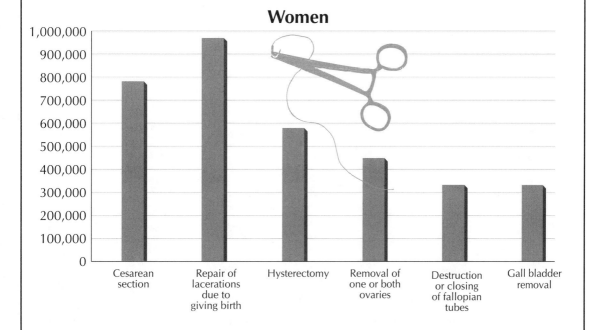

| | Cesarean section | Repair of lacerations due to giving birth | Hysterectomy | Removal of one or both ovaries | Destruction or closing of fallopian tubes | Gall bladder removal |

Source: U.S. Department of Health and Human Services, National Center for Health Statistics

VISITS TO ALTERNATIVE PRACTITIONERS, 1993

In 1993, people made 425 million visits to unconventional practitioners, such as herbalists, massage therapists, acupuncturists, and chiropractic physicians. Percentage of people with the following ailments who visited one or more of these care providers:

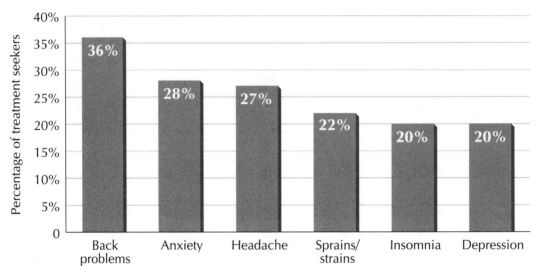

Source: *New England Journal of Medicine* survey of 1,539 adults

PROFILE: SPENDING ON PRESCRIPTION DRUGS
(Annual spending on pharmaceuticals per person, by country)

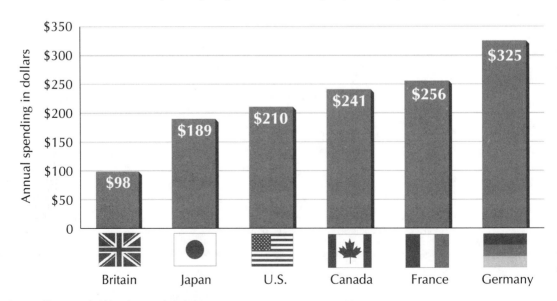

Source: Pharmaceutical Manufacturers Association

EMPLOYERS OFFERING RETIREMENT HEALTH COVERAGE, 1993–1997
(By types of employees offered coverage)

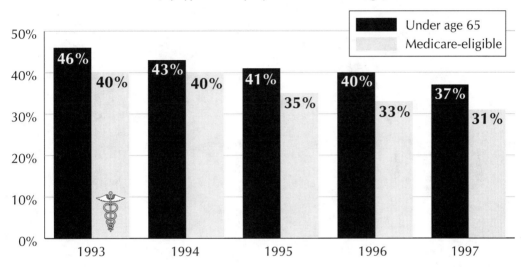

Legend: Under age 65 / Medicare-eligible

- 1993: 46% (Under age 65), 40% (Medicare-eligible)
- 1994: 43% (Under age 65), 40% (Medicare-eligible)
- 1995: 41% (Under age 65), 35% (Medicare-eligible)
- 1996: 40% (Under age 65), 33% (Medicare-eligible)
- 1997: 37% (Under age 65), 31% (Medicare-eligible)

Source: Foster Higgins

THE STEEP RISE IN U.S. HEALTH CARE COSTS, 1975–1996

From 1975 through 1996, U.S. health care costs increased from $132 billion to $1.03 trillion:

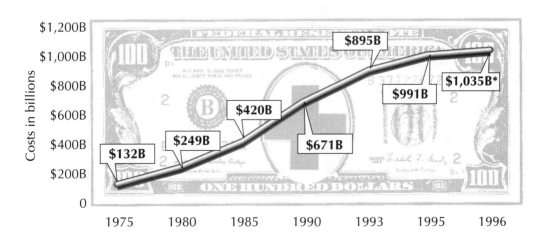

Costs in billions

- 1975: $132B
- 1980: $249B
- 1985: $420B
- 1990: $671B
- 1993: $895B
- 1995: $991B
- 1996: $1,035B*

Source: National Center for Health Statistics

*1,035 billion = 1.035 trillion

RISING PRICE INDEXES OF U.S. MEDICAL CARE, 1970–1995

(Indexes reflect cost increases per industry)

Physicians' care

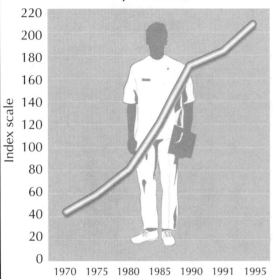

Index scale: 0, 20, 40, 60, 80, 100, 120, 140, 160, 180, 200, 220

1970 1975 1980 1985 1990 1991 1995

Dental care

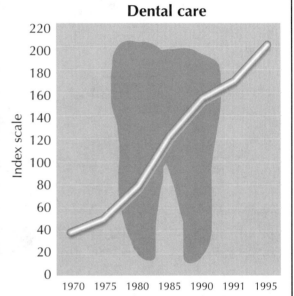

Index scale: 0, 20, 40, 60, 80, 100, 120, 140, 160, 180, 200, 220

1970 1975 1980 1985 1990 1991 1995

Hospital room charges

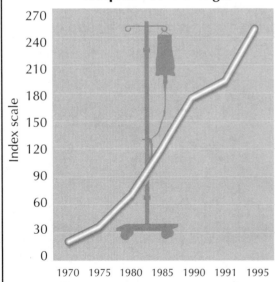

Index scale: 0, 30, 60, 90, 120, 150, 180, 210, 240, 270

1970 1975 1980 1985 1990 1991 1995

Medical care commodities

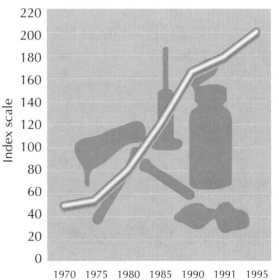

Index scale: 0, 20, 40, 60, 80, 100, 120, 140, 160, 180, 200, 220

1970 1975 1980 1985 1990 1991 1995

Source: U.S. Bureau of Labor Statistics

MOST-HEALTHY AND LEAST-HEALTHY STATES*, 1992

(Based on number of medical problems and insurance claims per capita, with rankings)

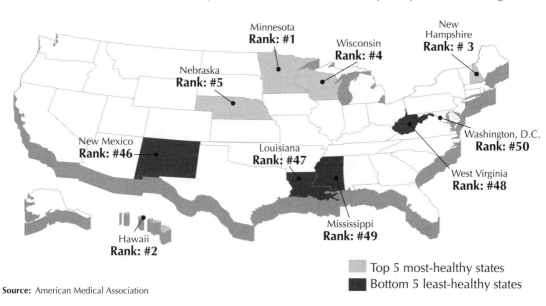

Minnesota
Rank: #1

Wisconsin
Rank: #4

New
Hampshire
Rank: # 3

Nebraska
Rank: #5

New Mexico
Rank: #46

Louisiana
Rank: #47

Washington, D.C.
Rank: #50

West Virginia
Rank: #48

Hawaii
Rank: #2

Mississippi
Rank: #49

Top 5 most-healthy states
Bottom 5 least-healthy states

Source: American Medical Association

MONEY U.S. RESIDENTS SPENT ON HEALTH CARE, BY ITEM, 1992

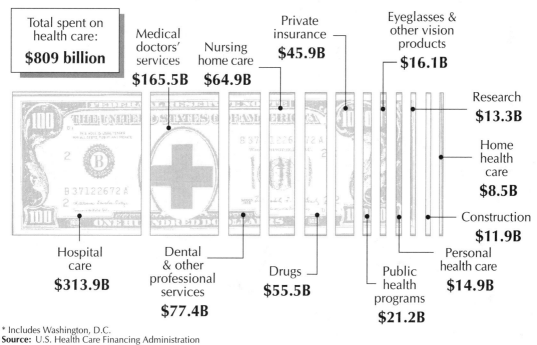

Total spent on
health care:

$809 billion

Medical
doctors'
services
$165.5B

Nursing
home care
$64.9B

Private
insurance
$45.9B

Eyeglasses &
other vision
products
$16.1B

Research
$13.3B

Home
health
care
$8.5B

Construction
$11.9B

Hospital
care
$313.9B

Dental
& other
professional
services
$77.4B

Drugs
$55.5B

Public
health
programs
$21.2B

Personal
health care
$14.9B

* Includes Washington, D.C.
Source: U.S. Health Care Financing Administration

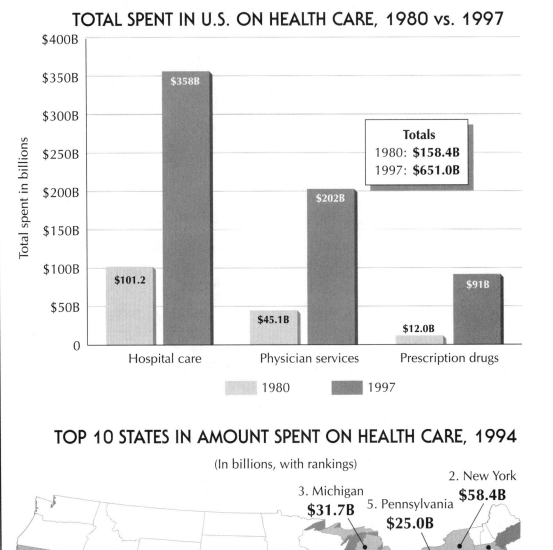

TOTAL SPENT IN U.S. ON HEALTH CARE, 1980 vs. 1997

Total spent in billions

- $400B
- $350B
- $300B
- $250B
- $200B
- $150B
- $100B
- $50B
- 0

$358B

$101.2

$45.1B

$202B

$12.0B

$91B

Totals
1980: **$158.4B**
1997: **$651.0B**

Hospital care   Physician services   Prescription drugs

☐ 1980   ■ 1997

TOP 10 STATES IN AMOUNT SPENT ON HEALTH CARE, 1994

(In billions, with rankings)

2. New York
$58.4B

3. Michigan
$31.7B

5. Pennsylvania
$25.0B

1. California
$76.0B

9. Illinois
$18.4B

8. Massachusetts
$18.7B

7. Ohio
$22.1B

4. Texas
$29.1

10. Virginia
$15.4B

6. Florida
$23.3B

Source: U.S. Health Care Financing Administration

TOP 10 DRUGS MOST FREQUENTLY PRESCRIBED IN DOCTORS' OFFICES, 1996
(By sales in millions)

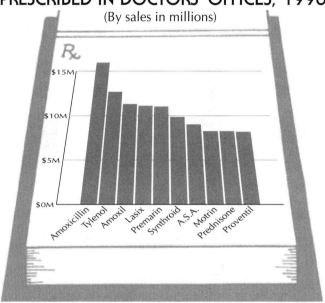

Source: National Center for Health Statistics

PROFILE: U.S. SPENDING ON PRESCRIPTION DRUGS

Where the money comes from:

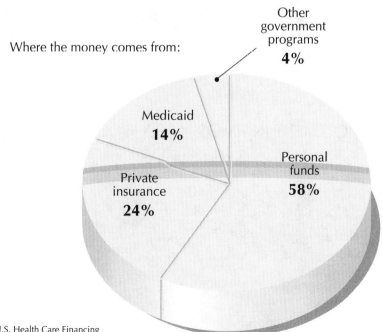

Other government programs **4%**

Medicaid **14%**

Private insurance **24%**

Personal funds **58%**

Source: U.S. Health Care Financing

AVERAGE DOCTORS' FEES, 1985 vs. 1996

(Office visits, new patient per visit)

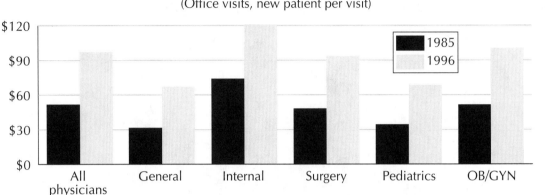

Legend: ■ 1985 □ 1996

Y-axis: $120, $90, $60, $30, $0

X-axis: All physicians, General, Internal, Surgery, Pediatrics, OB/GYN

Source: American Medical Association

U.S. BUDGET RECEIPTS, 1995 vs. 1998

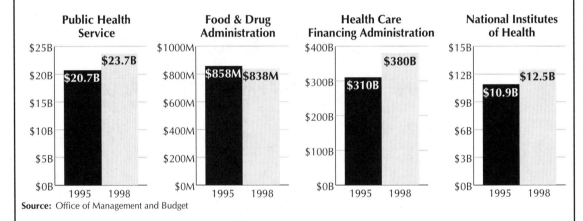

Public Health Service
$25B, $20B, $15B, $10B, $5B, $0B
$20.7B
$23.7B
1995 1998

Food & Drug Administration
$1000M, $800M, $600M, $400M, $200M, $0M
$858M $838M
1995 1998

Health Care Financing Administration
$400B, $300B, $200B, $100B, $0B
$310B
$380B
1995 1998

National Institutes of Health
$15B, $12B, $9B, $6B, $3B, $0B
$10.9B
$12.5B
1995 1998

Source: Office of Management and Budget

ENROLLMENT IN HMOS, 1980 vs. 1997

(By percentage of total regional population)

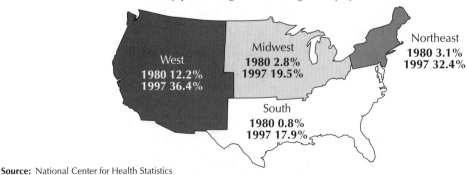

West
1980 12.2%
1997 36.4%

Midwest
1980 2.8%
1997 19.5%

Northeast
1980 3.1%
1997 32.4%

South
1980 0.8%
1997 17.9%

Source: National Center for Health Statistics

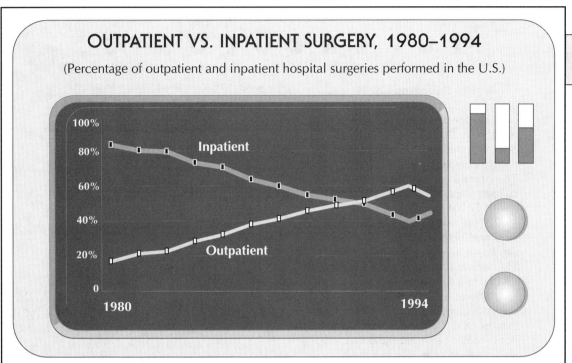

OUTPATIENT VS. INPATIENT SURGERY, 1980–1994

(Percentage of outpatient and inpatient hospital surgeries performed in the U.S.)

Source: American Hospital Association

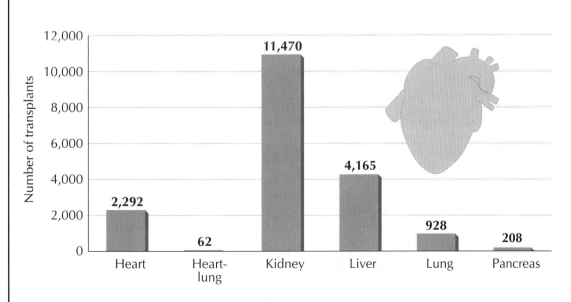

NUMBER OF TRANSPLANT OPERATIONS IN U.S., 1997

Number of transplants

Heart	Heart-lung	Kidney	Liver	Lung	Pancreas
2,292	62	11,470	4,165	928	208

Source: United Network for Organ Sharing

T U B E R C U L O S I S

In 1880, tuberculosis, or TB, was one of the most common—and most deadly—diseases in the U.S. By 1980, it had almost disappeared. Public health officials hoped they could eliminate the disease completely in the U.S., but then TB returned with a vengeance. The number of new cases jumped from a low of 22,201 in 1985 to 26,673 in 1992. There was a slight decline in 1993 and 1994, due mainly to more aggressive surveillance and treatment. The decline continued, and in 1997, TB reached a new low of 19,851 cases.

Tuberculosis is caused by rod-shaped bacteria called tubercle bacilli. In most cases, TB germs invade the lungs. But they also can infect the bones, kidneys, skin, and other parts of the body.

People can be infected with TB germs without having an active case of the disease. The bacilli may remain hidden in their bodies for their entire lives. More than 10 million Americans carry TB germs, but only about 10% of carriers will actually develop active cases. Usually, the bacilli become active when a person's immune system is weakened by illness or malnutrition.

The most obvious symptom of active pulmonary (lung) tuberculosis is a persistent cough. Other symptoms include loss of energy, fatigue, night sweats, and loss of weight. Active tuberculosis is extremely contagious. The germs are easily spread by coughing and sneezing.

Tuberculosis can almost always be cured. Treatment usually involves taking medicines for a period of 6 to 9 months. Without adequate treatment, however, a person may develop drug-resistant tuberculosis, which is very difficult to treat.

FINGERTIP FACTS

☛ Overcrowding increases the spread of TB. TB is more common in cities than in rural areas.

☛ Outdoors, ultraviolet radiation from the sun quickly kills TB germs.

☛ In 1900, the tuberculosis death rate was 194.4 per 100,000. In 1947, it was 33.5. In 1996, it was 0.5.

☛ In 1996, there were 1,194 TB deaths reported in the U.S.

☛ People infected with tuberculosis who have AIDS are up to 40 times more likely to develop active cases of TB than people without AIDS. AIDS weakens people's defenses against TB germs.

☛ Worldwide, the World Health Organization estimates that 1.7 billion people—almost one-third of the world's population—are carriers of TB germs. TB causes 2-3 million deaths each year—more than all other infectious diseases combined.

☛ Tuberculosis is one of the world's oldest diseases. Some ancient mummies found in Egypt and Peru had tuberculosis.

☛ People can acquire tuberculosis by drinking unpasteurized milk from infected animals. During pasteurization, milk is heated, which effectively kills tuberculosis bacilli and other harmful microorganisms in the milk.

☛ A tuberculosis vaccine has been injected in an estimated 3 billion people worldwide, but is not widely used in the U.S.

TUBERCULOSIS DECREASES IN U.S., 1960–1997

(Number of people with tuberculosis)

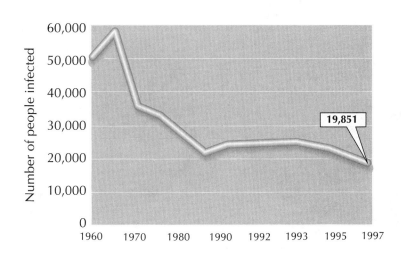

TOP 10 U.S. CITIES IN NUMBER OF CASES OF TUBERCULOSIS, 1997

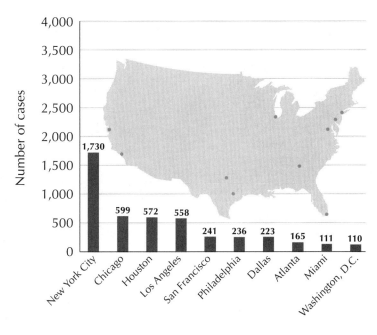

Source: U.S. Centers for Disease Control

PROFILE: TUBERCULOSIS IN THE U.S., BY AGE, RACE, AND SEX

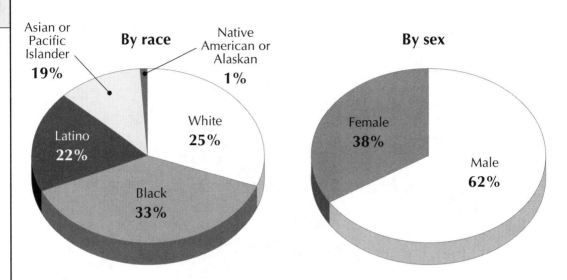

By race

Asian or Pacific Islander
19%

Native American or Alaskan
1%

White
25%

Latino
22%

Black
33%

By sex

Female
38%

Male
62%

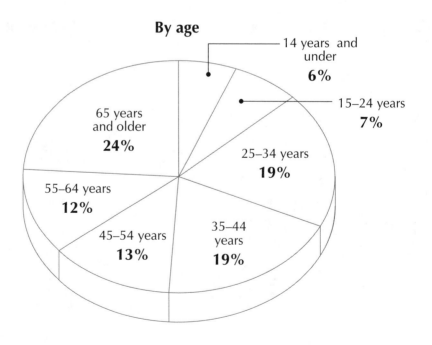

By age

14 years and under
6%

15–24 years
7%

25–34 years
19%

35–44 years
19%

45–54 years
13%

55–64 years
12%

65 years and older
24%

Source: U.S. Centers for Disease Control; American Lung Association

STATES WITH HIGHEST RATES OF TUBERCULOSIS, 1997

(Number of cases per 100,000 people)

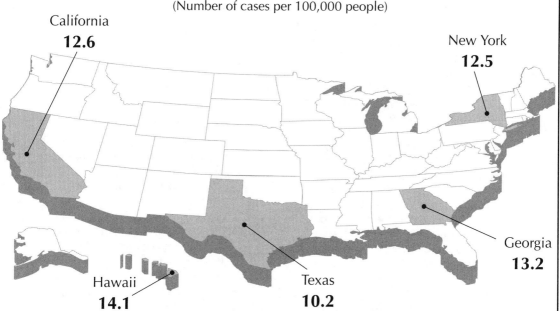

California
12.6

New York
12.5

Georgia
13.2

Hawaii
14.1

Texas
10.2

U.S. CITIES WITH HIGHEST RATES OF TUBERCULOSIS, 1997

(Number of cases per 100,000 people in cities with populations over 250,000)

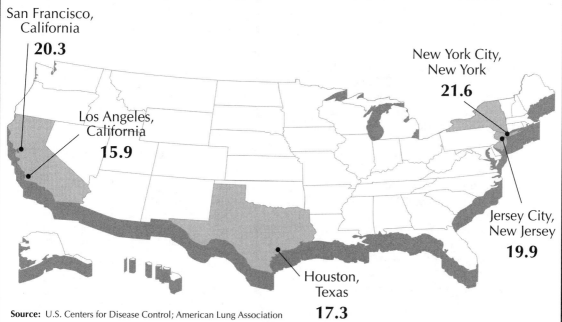

San Francisco,
California
20.3

New York City,
New York
21.6

Los Angeles,
California
15.9

Jersey City,
New Jersey
19.9

Houston,
Texas
17.3

Source: U.S. Centers for Disease Control; American Lung Association

HEART DISEASE, CANCER, AND OTHER DISEASES

Heart disease and cancer are the main causes of death in the U.S. Annually, they account for 57% of all deaths. Strokes are the third main cause, accounting for 6.6% of all deaths.

Often, heart disease and cancer develop slowly, over many years. This is why they are more common among older people than among the young. A variety of factors increases the risk of developing these diseases. For example, some people have inherited genes that cause or increase the risk of heart disease or cancer. But many risk factors can be avoided or changed. Cigarette smoking is the biggest preventable cause of heart disease and cancer.

In the early 1900s, few people with heart disease or cancer lived very long. Today, with better detection and treatment, many lives are prolonged. About 40% of people who get cancer today will be alive 5 years after diagnosis.

Some kinds of cancer are deadlier than others. For example, 79% of women who get breast cancer and 77% of men who get prostate cancer have 5-year survival rates. But the 5-year survival rate for lung cancer is 13%, and for pancreatic cancer it is only 3%.

A number of other less threatening but serious diseases plague hundreds of thousands of Americans each year. Sexually transmitted diseases (STDs), the most common of which are gonorrhea and syphilis, afflicted more than 378,000 Americans in 1996. While annual cases of other diseases, such as typhus, typhoid fever, toxic shock syndrome, and leprosy, number only in the hundreds, some serious illnesses—such as encephalitis and malaria—threaten more than 1,000 lives each year.

FINGERTIP FACTS

- Cardiovascular diseases—diseases of the heart and blood vessels—are the #1 cause of death in the U.S. Each day, they claim the lives of more than 2,000 Americans.

- Death rates from cancer and heart disease increase with age. Death rates are higher among blacks than among whites.

- Death rates from heart disease are falling. In 1960, the U.S. death rate from heart disease was 286.2 per 100,000. By 1995, it had dropped to 138.3 per 100,000.

- Up to 50 million Americans ages 6 and older have high blood pressure (hypertension). Many people die from heart attacks and strokes caused by high blood pressure.

- Smokers are twice as likely as nonsmokers to have heart attacks.

- Death rates from cancer are increasing. In 1960, the U.S. death rate from cancer was 125.8 per 100,000. By 1996, it had increased to 203.2 per 100,000.

- In 1998, about 564,800 Americans died of cancer—more than 1,500 per day.

- Cancer causes more deaths among U.S. children ages 1 to 14 than any other disease.

- Lung cancer is the leading cause of U.S. cancer deaths. Smoking is responsible for 87% of the lung cancer deaths.

- About 1,053,100 skin cancers were diagnosed in the U.S. in 1998. About 90% of these could have been prevented by avoiding exposure to the sun's rays.

HEART DISEASE AND CANCER DEATH RATES, BY REGION, 1998

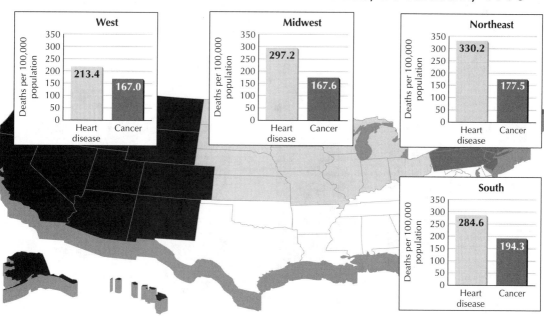

Source: U.S. National Center for Health Statistics, *Monthly Vital Statistics Report;* and unpublished data.

ESTIMATED PERCENTAGE OF U.S. POPULATION WITH HYPERTENSION, BY RACE AND SEX, AGES 18–74

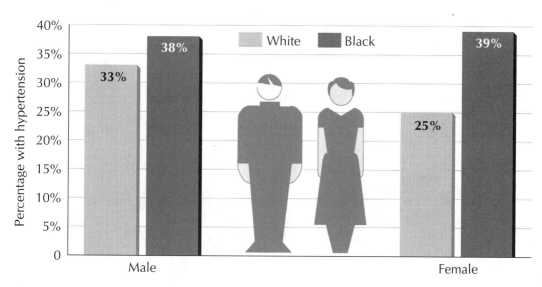

Source: National Health and Nutrition Examination Survey II

HEART DISEASE DEATH RATES, 1960–1991

(Deaths per 100,000 population)

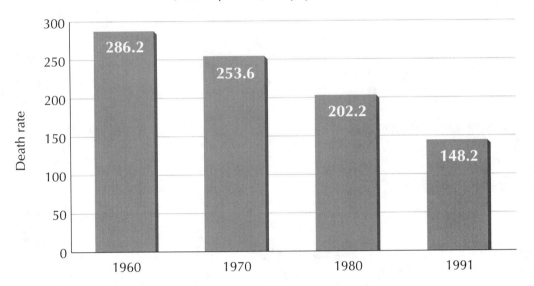

Source: U.S. Department of Health and Human Services, National Center for Health Statistics

CANCER DEATH RATES, BY SEX, 1970–1998

(Deaths per 100,000 population)

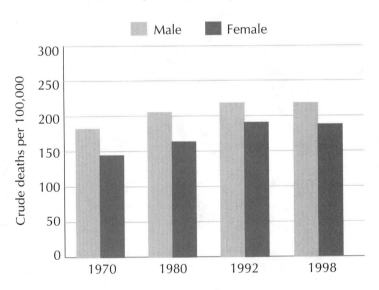

Source: National Center for Health Statistics, *Vital Statistics of the United States*, annual

ESTIMATED NEW CANCER CASES AND CANCER DEATHS, BY SITE, 1998 (est.)

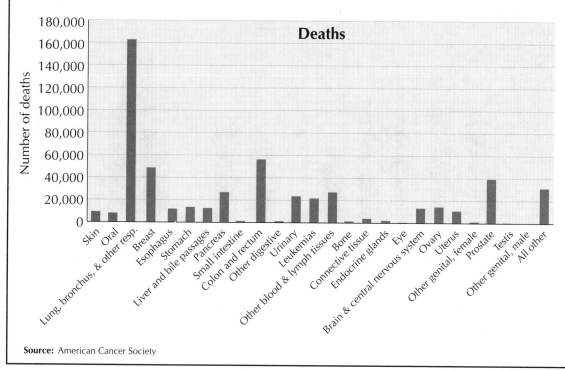

Source: American Cancer Society

5-YEAR SURVIVAL RATES FOR CANCER, BY RACE AND SITE

By race

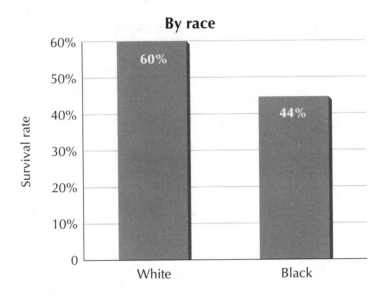

By site

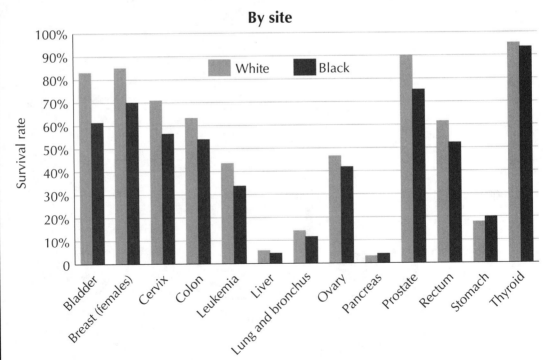

Source: American Cancer Society

FACTS AT A GLANCE

Cancer's 7 warning signals

1. A change in bowel or bladder habits
2. A sore that does not heal
3. Unusual bleeding or discharge
4. Thickening or lump in breast or elsewhere
5. Indigestion or difficulty in swallowing
6. Obvious change in wart or mole
7. Nagging cough or hoarseness

Source: American Cancer Society

HOSPICE CARE GROWS, 1974–1992

(Hospice organizations in the U.S. that serve terminally ill patients and their families)

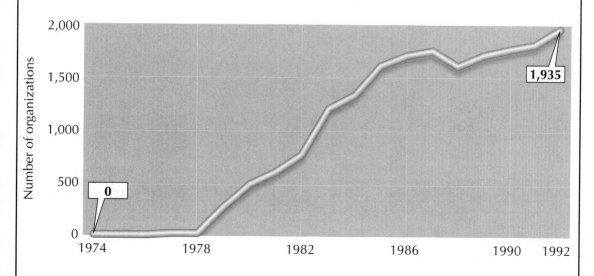

Source: National Hospice Organization

REPORTED CASES OF VENEREAL DISEASES IN U.S., 1970–1996

(Cases of selected diseases)

Syphilis

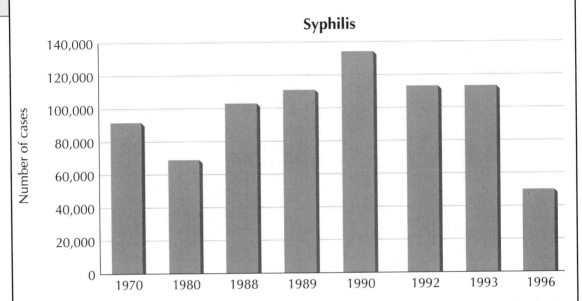

Gonorrhea

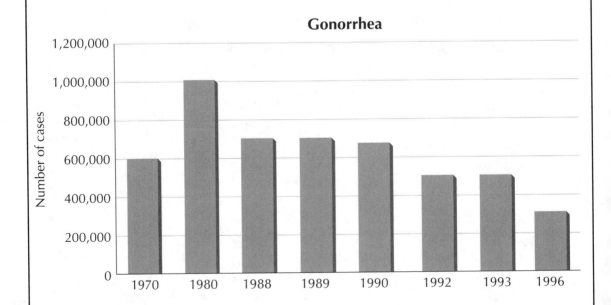

Source: U.S. Department of Health and Human Services, U.S. Centers for Disease Control

RABIES IN U.S. ANIMALS ON THE RISE

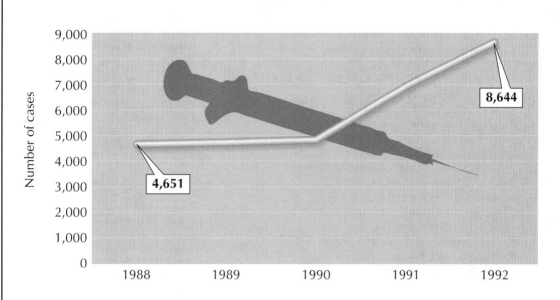

Number of cases

8,644

4,651

1988   1989   1990   1991   1992

Source: U.S. Centers for Disease Control

TOP 10 STATES IN NUMBER OF ANIMAL RABIES CASES, 1992
(With rankings)

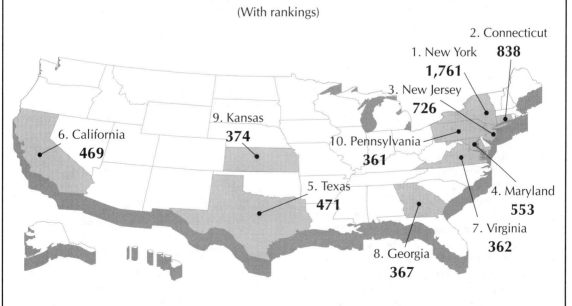

2. Connecticut **838**

1. New York **1,761**

3. New Jersey **726**

9. Kansas **374**

6. California **469**

10. Pennsylvania **361**

5. Texas **471**

4. Maryland **553**

7. Virginia **362**

8. Georgia **367**

Source: U.S. Centers for Disease Control

A I D S

Acquired immune deficiency syndrome (AIDS) was first publicly recognized in 1981. Since then, it has claimed the lives of more than 390,242 Americans. An additional 1 million Americans are estimated to be infected with human immunodeficiency virus (HIV), which causes the disease.

HIV is spread from one person to another through the exchange of body fluids, such as semen and blood. Most people become infected during sexual intercourse. The sharing of drug needles and syringes with infected people is the second most common route of transmission. Infected women can also transmit the virus to their babies during pregnancy or at birth.

HIV-infected people may feel fine and look fine. The virus may reside in their bodies for 10 years or more before AIDS symptoms actually develop. The illness weakens the body's immune system and, therefore, its ability to fight disease. People who have AIDS are vulnerable to "opportunistic diseases." These kinds of diseases are caused by microbes that usually are harmless in people with healthy immune systems. Opportunistic diseases include certain cancers as well as infections of the lungs and brain.

Scientists have not found a cure for AIDS. At present, the disease is fatal. Some drugs, however, fight the opportunistic diseases and help AIDS patients live longer. The drug AZT dramatically reduces HIV transmission from infected women to their babies. Scientists are hard at work trying to develop vaccines that would protect people from getting the disease. This is a difficult challenge, because HIV changes, or mutates, rapidly. In this way, it escapes the killing power of most drugs.

FINGERTIP FACTS

- More than 860,000 people in the U.S. have been diagnosed with AIDS since the disease was first identified.

- More than 390,000 people in the U.S. have died as a result of AIDS.

- AIDS is among the top 10 causes of death in the U.S. It is the leading cause of death of 25- to 44-year-old African-American and Latino men.

- The great majority of people with AIDS live in large cities. In the U.S., New York City has the largest number of AIDS patients.

- Although blacks make up only 13% of the U.S. population, they accounted for 57% of new HIV cases for 1998.

- In the U.S., homosexuals and bisexuals who don't use drugs make up 49% of all adult and adolescent AIDS patients. Drug abusers—both men and women—make up 32% of the total.

- The World Health Organization estimates that 30.6 million people worldwide have been infected with HIV. Approximately 1.1 million infected people are children under 15 years of age.

- The majority of people infected with HIV are in Africa.

- Worldwide, women are becoming infected as often as men. Most become infected through sexual intercourse with infected men.

- About 25% of HIV-infected women transmit the virus to their babies during pregnancy or at birth.

PROFILE: AGES OF PEOPLE LIVING WITH AIDS

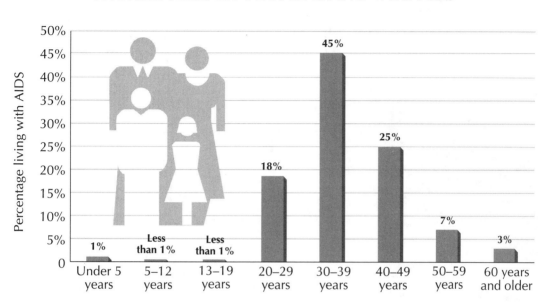

Source: U.S. Centers for Disease Control

PROFILE: MOST COMMON MODES OF AIDS TRANSMISSION

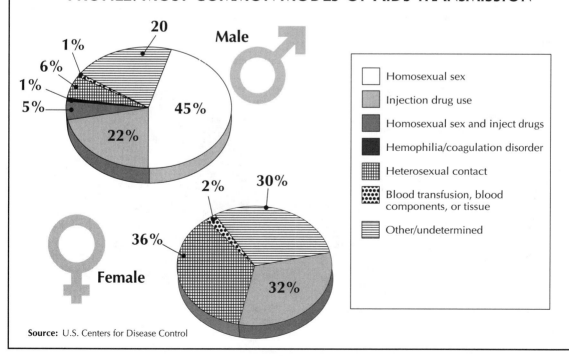

Source: U.S. Centers for Disease Control

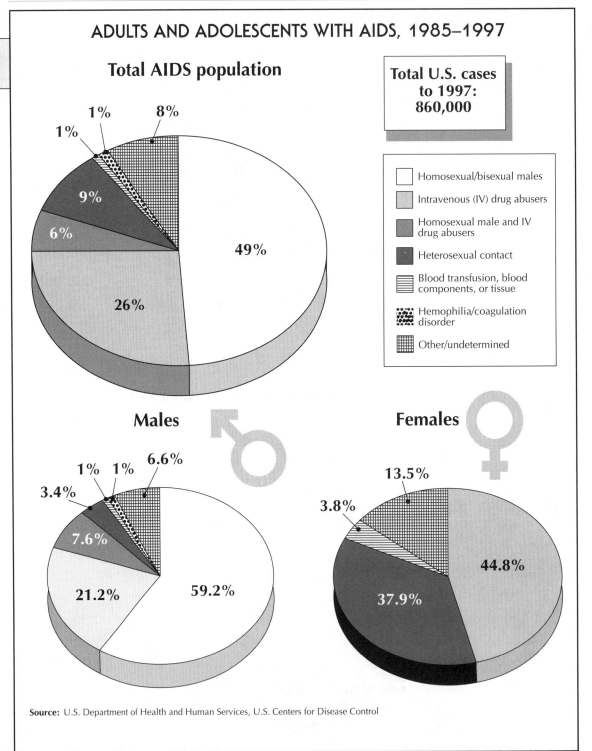

ADULTS AND ADOLESCENTS WITH AIDS, 1985–1997

Total AIDS population

Total U.S. cases to 1997: 860,000

1%
1%
8%
9%
6%
49%
26%

- Homosexual/bisexual males
- Intravenous (IV) drug abusers
- Homosexual male and IV drug abusers
- Heterosexual contact
- Blood transfusion, blood components, or tissue
- Hemophilia/coagulation disorder
- Other/undetermined

Males

3.4%
1%
1%
6.6%
7.6%
21.2%
59.2%

Females

3.8%
13.5%
37.9%
44.8%

Source: U.S. Department of Health and Human Services, U.S. Centers for Disease Control

AIDS CASES AMONG 13- TO 29-YEAR OLDS, 1989 vs. 1995

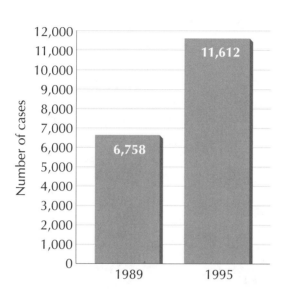

HIV INFECTION AND AIDS IN PEOPLE AGES 13–29, BY SEX AND RACE, 1995

(Percentage of AIDS population by age group)

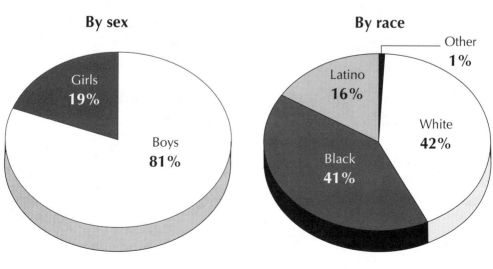

By sex

By race

Source: U.S. Centers for Disease Control & Prevention

AIDS DEATHS, BY SELECTED CHARACTERISTICS, 1997

By age

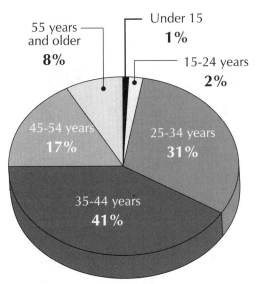

55 years and older **8%**

Under 15 **1%**

15-24 years **2%**

45-54 years **17%**

25-34 years **31%**

35-44 years **41%**

By sex

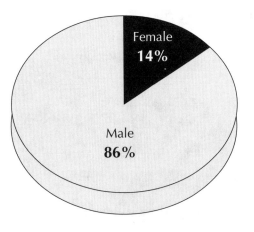

Female **14%**

Male **86%**

By race

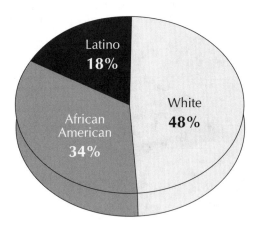

Latino **18%**

White **48%**

African American **34%**

Source: U.S. Census Bureau; U.S. Centers for Disease

HOW U.S. CHILDREN CONTRACTED AIDS, 1993

(AIDS patients under age 13, by mode of infection)

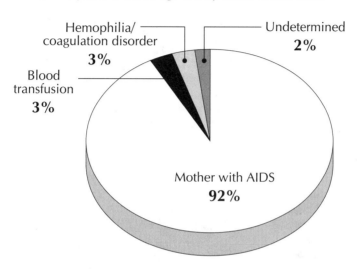

Hemophilia/
coagulation disorder
3%

Undetermined
2%

Blood
transfusion
3%

Mother with AIDS
92%

AIDS SPENDING INCREASES, 1990–1994

Where federal AIDS money is spent:

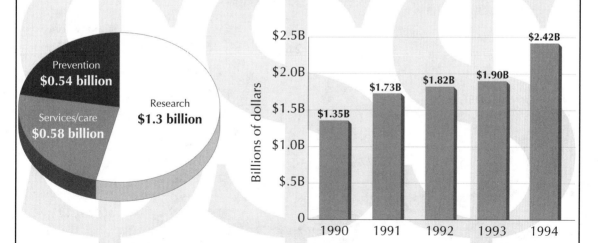

Prevention
$0.54 billion

Research
$1.3 billion

Services/care
$0.58 billion

$2.5B

$2.0B

$1.5B

$1.0B

$.5B

0

$1.35B

$1.73B

$1.82B

$1.90B

$2.42B

Billions of dollars

1990   1991   1992   1993   1994

Source: U.S. Department of Health and Human Services

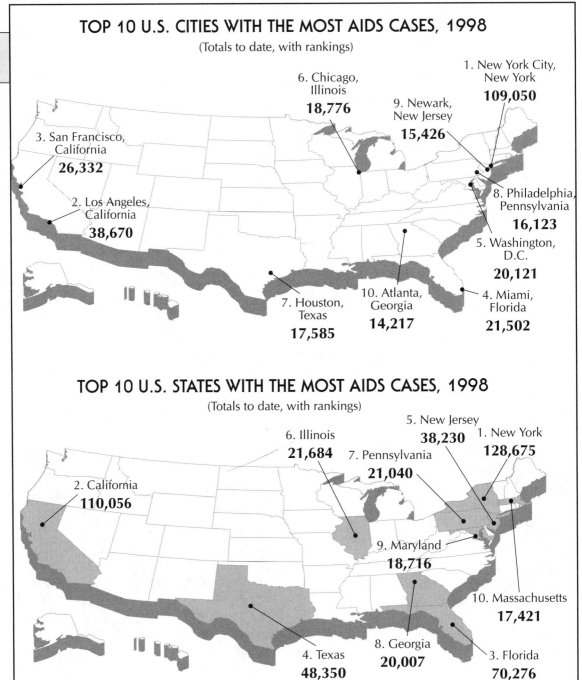

TOP 10 U.S. CITIES WITH THE MOST AIDS CASES, 1998
(Totals to date, with rankings)

6. Chicago, Illinois
18,776

9. Newark, New Jersey
15,426

1. New York City, New York
109,050

3. San Francisco, California
26,332

2. Los Angeles, California
38,670

8. Philadelphia, Pennsylvania
16,123

5. Washington, D.C.
20,121

7. Houston, Texas
17,585

10. Atlanta, Georgia
14,217

4. Miami, Florida
21,502

TOP 10 U.S. STATES WITH THE MOST AIDS CASES, 1998
(Totals to date, with rankings)

6. Illinois
21,684

7. Pennsylvania
21,040

5. New Jersey
38,230

1. New York
128,675

2. California
110,056

9. Maryland
18,716

10. Massachusetts
17,421

4. Texas
48,350

8. Georgia
20,007

3. Florida
70,276

Source: U.S. Department of Health and Human Services, U.S. Centers for Disease Control

AIDS CASES AND DEATHS IN THE U.S., 1981–1996

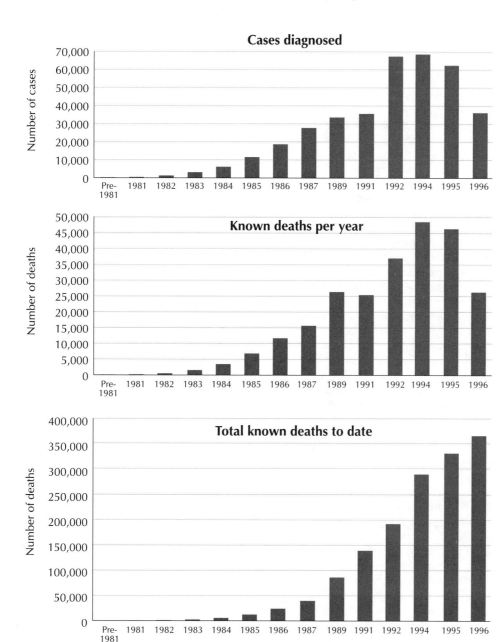

Source: U.S. Department of Health and Human Services, U.S. Centers for Disease Control

ABORTION

Abortion is one of the most controversial issues in the U.S. The purpose of an abortion is to end an unwanted pregnancy. There are many different reasons why women have abortions. Sometimes the pregnant woman's life is in danger. Sometimes a woman does not want to bear a child that is the result of incest or rape. At other times, a woman feels she is unable to accept the tremendous responsibility of having a child.

Abortion is opposed by most major religions, and many countries have laws prohibiting it. In the U.S., however, a 1973 Supreme Court ruling called *Roe v. Wade* formally guaranteed a woman's right to end an unwanted pregnancy through abortion. The Supreme Court reaffirmed this right in 1992.

A normal pregnancy lasts about 9 months. Almost 90% of all abortions are performed within the first 3 months of pregnancy. In 1972, before abortion was legal in the U.S., there were about 587,000 illegal abortions. Today there are about 1.4 million legal abortions a year. The majority of women who have abortions are white, unmarried, and under 25 years of age.

Abortion is a surgical procedure. In the 1980s, however, scientists in France developed a drug, RU-486, that induces abortion if used in the early stages of pregnancy. RU-486 is administered in combination with another drug called prostaglandin. Opponents of abortion pressured the government to keep RU-486 out of the U.S. In 1994, however, the first nationwide study of RU-486—also called mifepristone—began at U.S. clinics under the direction of the Population Council.

FINGERTIP FACTS

- In 1996, women under age 20 accounted for 20% of U.S. patients having abortions.

- The Alan Guttmacher Institute estimates that about 25% of U.S. women under age 45 have had at least one abortion.

- There were 311 abortions for every 1,000 live births in the U.S. in 1995.

- Most abortions in the U.S. are performed in clinics that are separate from hospitals, on an outpatient basis.

- Approximately 65% of all women who have abortions intend to have children later in life.

- Of all the women that had an abortion in 1996, 88.5% lived in metropolitan areas.

- In 1994, only 17% of U.S. counties had a clinic, hospital, or doctor who performed abortions. As a result, many women who wanted abortions had to travel to other parts of the country.

- A study reported in 1994 suggested that women who have abortions may increase their risk of breast cancer.

- In the 1960s, illegal abortions caused about 20% of all U.S. deaths related to pregnancy and childbirth.

- Some abortions are spontaneous; they are called miscarriages or stillbirths. As many as 75% of all conceptions may be spontaneously aborted.

PROFILE: WHO HAS ABORTIONS?

(Reported abortions in U.S., by marital status, race, and age)

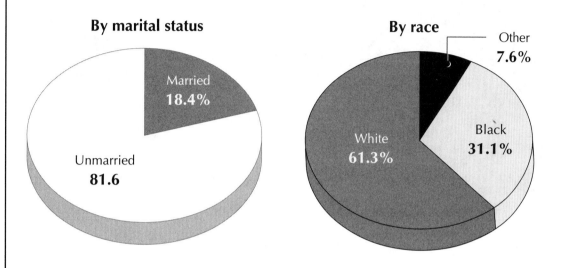

By marital status

Married
18.4%

Unmarried
81.6

By race

Other
7.6%

White
61.3%

Black
31.1%

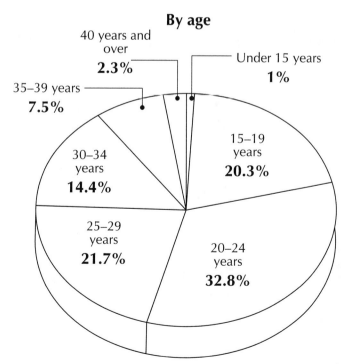

By age

40 years and
over
2.3%

Under 15 years
1%

35–39 years
7.5%

30–34
years
14.4%

15–19
years
20.3%

25–29
years
21.7%

20–24
years
32.8%

Source: Statistics based on U.S. Centers for Disease Control and Alan Guttmacher Institute

NUMBER OF ABORTIONS BY REGION, 1992

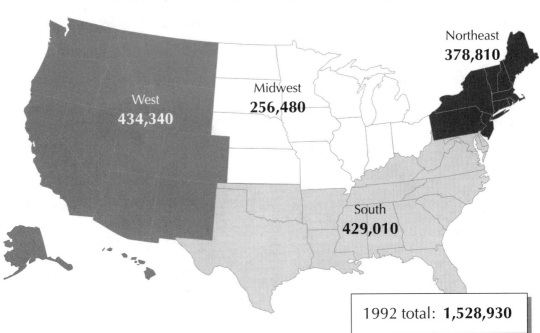

Northeast
378,810

West
434,340

Midwest
256,480

South
429,010

1992 total: **1,528,930**

REPORTED ABORTIONS IN THE U.S., 1972–1995

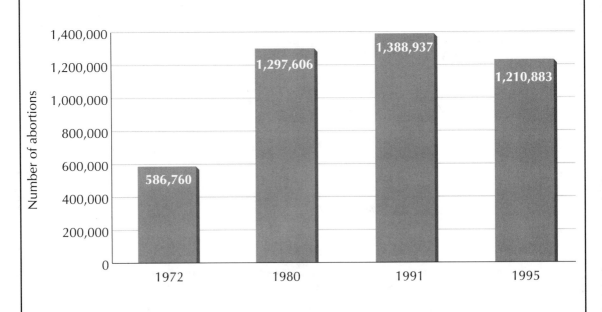

Number of abortions

1,400,000
1,200,000
1,000,000
800,000
600,000
400,000
200,000
0

586,760

1,297,606

1,388,937

1,210,883

1972   1980   1991   1995

Source: U.S. Department of Health and Human Services

PERCENTAGE OF REPORTED ABORTIONS, AVERAGE, BY WEEKS OF GESTATION

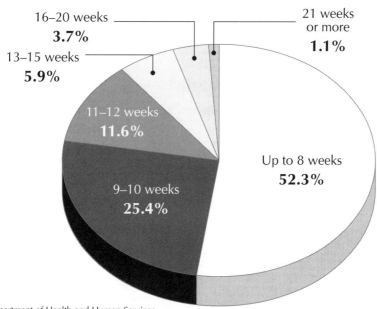

16–20 weeks
3.7%

21 weeks or more
1.1%

13–15 weeks
5.9%

11–12 weeks
11.6%

Up to 8 weeks
52.3%

9–10 weeks
25.4%

Source: U.S. Department of Health and Human Services

TOP 10 STATES* WITH HIGHEST ABORTION RATES, 1992

(Rates per 1,000 women with rankings)

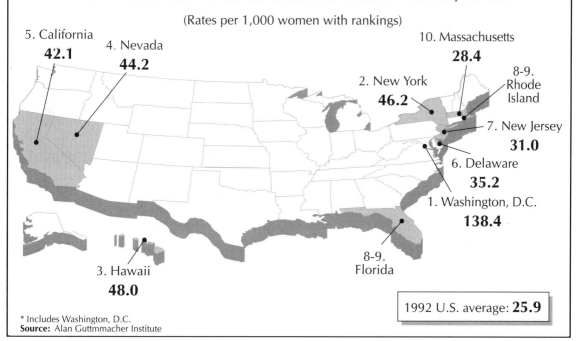

5. California
42.1

4. Nevada
44.2

10. Massachusetts
28.4

2. New York
46.2

8-9.
Rhode
Island

7. New Jersey
31.0

6. Delaware
35.2

1. Washington, D.C.
138.4

8-9.
Florida

3. Hawaii
48.0

1992 U.S. average: **25.9**

* Includes Washington, D.C.
Source: Alan Guttmmacher Institute

2

LIFESTYLES
AND
PASTIMES

SEX AND LOVE

Although they are highly personal parts of our lives, the sexual and romantic habits of America's citizens seem to be a source of never-ending interest. Scientific research—plus anecdotal evidence displayed in tabloids and on TV talk shows—indicates that a number of dramatic sexual behavioral changes have occurred over the past few decades. For example, people are having sexual relations at an earlier age but are marrying later than ever before. Divorce, contraceptive use, unwed motherhood, and homosexuality are no longer taboo subjects; nor, in the minds of many, are they taboo behaviors. Other previously "hidden" issues, including child pornography, rape, spousal violence, and sexual abuse, have come to the forefront of the news and of political debate.

Many myths about the sexual lives of Americans were contradicted in 1994 when a team of researchers based at the University of Chicago released the results of a survey of nearly 3,500 people between the ages of 18 and 59. Among many surprising things, the survey found that married couples actually reported the highest rates of sexual satisfaction—and the most frequent sex. They also found that most married people were faithful to their spouses.

Better understanding of sexual behavior and its consequences affects the lives of individuals as well as the formation of public policy. The growing threat of AIDS, for example, has led to increased monogamy and condom use. Peer pressure among teens to have sex (and even to become pregnant) has also decreased as more teens have become more educated about the realities of sexual relations and its potential consequences.

FINGERTIP FACTS

- The majority of teens ages 12 to 17 say they believe in abstinence. However, before age 18, at least 75% of American boys and 52% of American girls have had intercourse. Fewer than 20% remain virgins throughout their teenage years.

- The number of teenagers who say they have had sex before age 15 is going down. In 1990, some 34% of teens said they had sex by age 15. By 1997, that percentage had fallen to 14%.

- People are getting married at a later age. In 1970, the median age at which women first married was 20.8 years; by 1996, it had risen to 24.8 years. The median age for men rose from 23.2 to 27.1 years.

- More children are being born out of wedlock. In 1960, more than 94% were born to married women. By 1996, that percentage had shrunk to 73%.

- Americans are generally monogamous. Almost 75% of married men and 85% of married women report that they are faithful to their spouses.

- The majority of Americans (83%) have one or no sexual partners during a year. Over a lifetime, men average 6 partners, while women average 2.

- The rate of unmarried cohabitation has grown tremendously in the past 2 decades. In 1970, unmarried heterosexual couples made up about 0.5 million households; by 1997, they accounted for 4.1 million households.

PROFILE: HAPPY IN LOVE

(Percentages of married and single people in the U.S. who say their current "significant other" will be their one and only partner for the future)

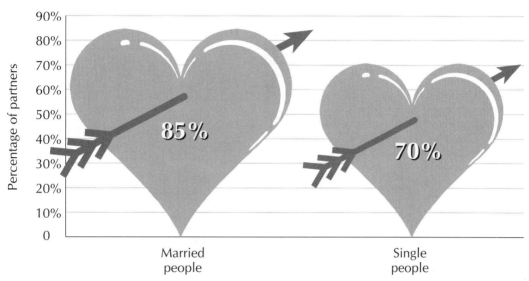

Percentage of partners

Married people

Single people

Source: Based on *USA Today* statistics

SEX THROUGH THE YEARS, BY AGE

(As self-reported, the average number of times U.S. adults have sex per year)

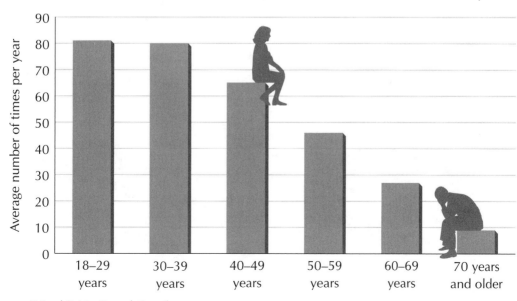

Source: National Opinion Research Council

TEEN SEX BEFORE MARRIAGE?

U.S. teens who favor abstaining
from sex before marriage, by age:

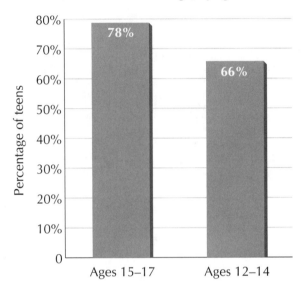

Source: MRCI

U.S. TEENS AND MARRIAGE

Percentage of U.S. teens who expect to stay single or get married, by sex:

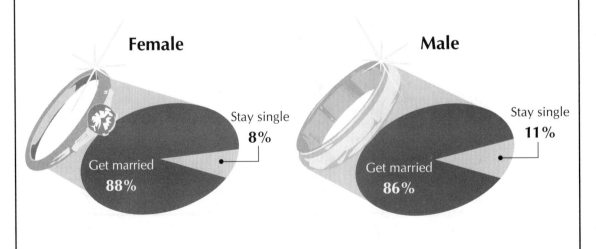

Source: Market Research Co.

U.S. MARRIAGE AND DIVORCE RATES, 1920–1997
(The rates of marriages and divorces per 1,000 population)

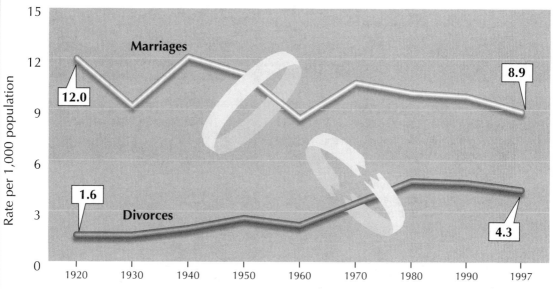

Rate per 1,000 population

Marriages

12.0

8.9

Divorces

1.6

4.3

1920 1930 1940 1950 1960 1970 1980 1990 1997

Source: U.S. Census Bureau

DIVORCED AMERICANS BY AGE, 1997
(Percentage of all divorced people)

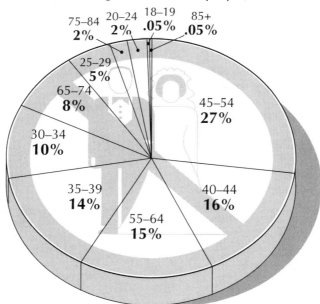

75–84 **2%** 20–24 **2%** 18–19 **.05%** 85+ **.05%**

25–29 **5%**

65–74 **8%**

45–54 **27%**

30–34 **10%**

35–39 **14%**

40–44 **16%**

55–64 **15%**

Source: National Center for Health Statistics

E A T I N G

Food is a major topic of interest for Americans. Through the centuries, eating has evolved from an activity undertaken for biological necessity into one of the nation's most popular—and most social—pastimes. While some people limit food intake to the traditional 3 meals a day, others "graze" their way through life, nibbling, snacking, and dining on everything from abalone steaks to zucchini bread.

Researchers at Rockefeller University estimate that approximately 500 foodstuffs were available to Americans 100 years ago. Today, there are more than 50,000. Advances in agriculture and food processing give us an ever-growing array of fresh, packaged, and prepared items; improved transportation has put fresher strawberries and more exotic mushrooms on menus everywhere year-round.

Eating habits have also changed for economic reasons. Women who in previous generations would have stayed at home now leave for work and thus lack the time to prepare elaborate meals. Although some 60% of all U.S. food sales—more than $320 billion per year—originate in grocery stores, including supermarkets, the remaining 40% is purchased in restaurants and other food-service establishments.

Overconsumption of fats and sugars in American diets has led to obesity, heart disease, and other health problems. But while many Americans gobble down weighty, artery-clogging foods, others have adopted healthier eating habits. Each day, more people are cutting back on red meats, avoiding fatty foods, and turning to vegetarianism and other macrobiotic, or plant-based, diets.

FINGERTIP FACTS

- A typical grocery store in 1928 stocked about 870 items. Supersize supermarkets in 1998 carried up to 30,000 items.

- A typical trip to the supermarket lasts about 44 minutes; shoppers spend an average of $45.54 per trip.

- Of all dinner orders made at U.S. restaurants, 25% include soda, 24% include french fries, 24% include pizza, and 17% included either a hamburger or cheeseburger.

- People are eating more cheese—consumption has risen from 11.4 pounds per capita in 1970 to 27.7 pounds in 1996. American cheese is the most popular type.

- In 1997, a total of 299 new soft drink products went on the market, a 56% increase from the previous year.

- On average, a person consumes about 5 gallons of frozen desserts each year; 63% of this is ice cream.

- Guacamole is America's most popular snack; on Super Bowl Sunday alone, people consume an estimated 12 million pounds of this avocado dip.

- Each year, the typical American child sees about 10,000 food ads on television.

- The U.S. government allots $50,000 to each state annually to teach children about healthy diets and nutrition.

U.S. SNACK STARS

(Most popular snacks in America, by consumption on Super Bowl Sunday)

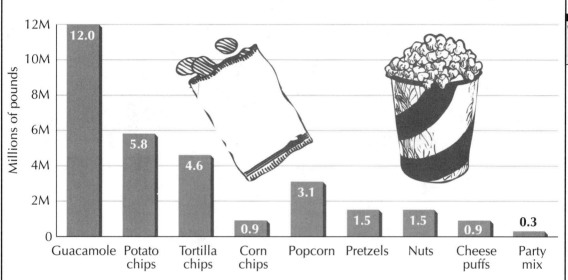

Millions of pounds

Guacamole	12.0
Potato chips	5.8
Tortilla chips	4.6
Corn chips	0.9
Popcorn	3.1
Pretzels	1.5
Nuts	1.5
Cheese puffs	0.9
Party mix	0.3

Source: Association of American Snackfoods

FOODS THAT TEENS BUY MOST

(Products that youths ages 12 to 17 spend grocery money on)

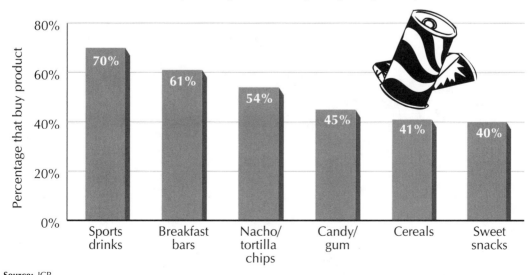

Percentage that buy product

Sports drinks	70%
Breakfast bars	61%
Nacho/ tortilla chips	54%
Candy/ gum	45%
Cereals	41%
Sweet snacks	40%

Source: ICR

WHERE IS TAKEOUT FOOD TAKEN?

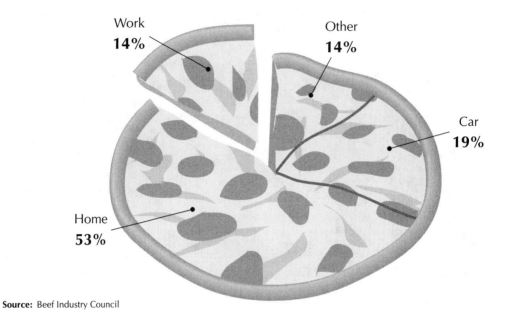

Work
14%

Other
14%

Car
19%

Home
53%

Source: Beef Industry Council

AMERICANS BUY MORE VEGETABLES, 1994

(Percentage of Americans buying more,
the same, or fewer vegetables than in years previous)

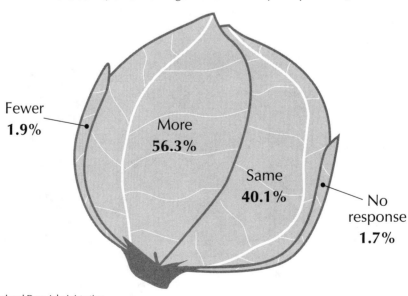

Fewer
1.9%

More
56.3%

Same
40.1%

No
response
1.7%

Source: U.S. Food and Drug Administration

SELECTED FOODS: PER CAPITA CONSUMPTION, 1970 vs. 1996

(In pounds, per person, per year)

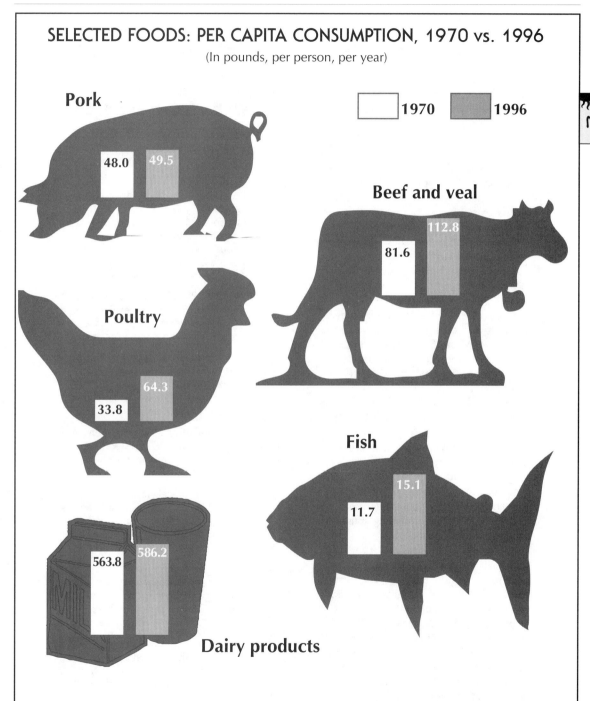

Pork

1970   1996

48.0   49.5

Beef and veal

81.6   112.8

Poultry

33.8   64.3

Fish

11.7   15.1

563.8   586.2

Dairy products

Source: U.S. Department of Agriculture

R E L I G I O N

Religion has always been an important part of American life. Today, the most widely practiced religions in America are Judaism, Christianity, and Islam. Additional thousands of Americans are adherents of Far Eastern religions, such as Buddhism, Shintoism, and Taoism.

The percentage of Americans who belong to religious groups has remained relatively stable in recent decades. In 1960, a total of 114.4 million people—64% of the population—belonged to churches and other religious groups; in 1998, a total of 64% of the population—169.1 million—were members. The apparent depth of people's commitment to their religion, however, is less than devout. For instance, fewer than half of Americans attend services 4 or more times a month. Despite their somewhat lax attendance record, Americans are generous when it comes to donations, giving their congregations some $75 billion a year.

In addition to serving as centers of worship and religious education, religious organizations perform a broad range of other functions. Many provide marriage and family counseling, meal services, and alcohol and drug abuse prevention programs.

Rapid social change and other factors have led to numerous changes in traditional religious services, and even to new religious movements. "Mainline" churches, for example, saw their congregations shrink during the 1970s and 1980s as television evangelists drew the faithful to "electronic church" ministries. A small percentage of Americans, many of them young and well educated, have increasingly embraced cults, which have a diverse variety of ideologies and practices.

FINGERTIP FACTS

☛ In 1980, there were 797 non-profit religious organizations in the U.S.; by 1993, the number had jumped to 1,230.

☛ Islam is the most rapidly growing religion in the U.S. It currently has about 4 million adherents. About 12% of U.S. Muslims are people of Arab ethnicity; 25% are people of South Asian origin; and 42% are African Americans.

☛ Some 40.7% of Americans say they attend religious services 4 or more times a month; 46.5% attend less than once a month.

☛ In a 1994 poll, 20% of Americans said they had had a revelation from God during the previous 12 months; 13% saw or sensed the presence of an angel.

☛ Revenues of U.S. religious congregations in 1997 totaled an estimated $75 billion, up 35% from 1991.

☛ Of the major religious groups in the U.S., Mormonism has the highest percentage of married members—73.1%; Islam has the most single members—39.0%.

☛ The highest percentage of Americans who say they are not religious live in the western states; Oregon residents lead, with 17.2% saying they have no religion.

☛ Roman Catholics make up more than a third of all people in the U.S. who are religiously affiliated.

PROFILE: RELIGION IN AMERICA, 1997

(Religious preferences, ages, and regions of residence of those who attend religious services in the U.S.)

Religious preference

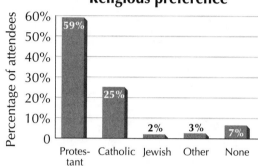

Age

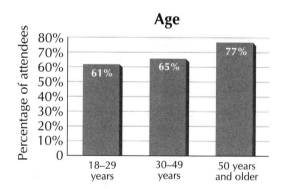

Region of residence

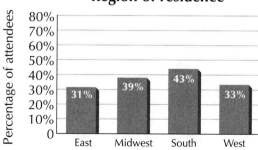

Source: Princeton Religious Research Center

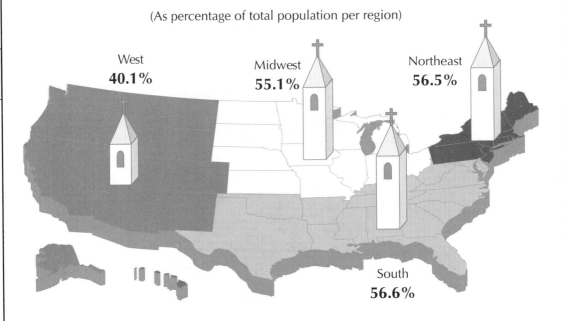

PERCENTAGE OF CHRISTIANS IN U.S., BY REGION, 1994

(As percentage of total population per region)

West
40.1%

Midwest
55.1%

Northeast
56.5%

South
56.6%

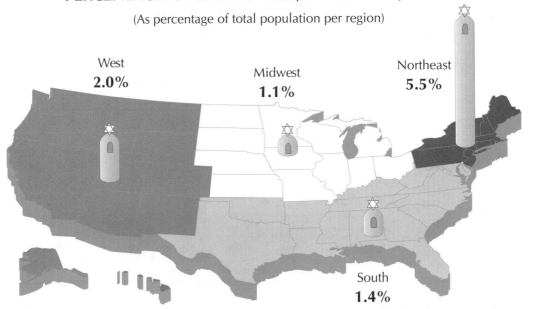

PERCENTAGE OF JEWS IN U.S., BY REGION, 1994

(As percentage of total population per region)

West
2.0%

Midwest
1.1%

Northeast
5.5%

South
1.4%

Source: U.S. Census Bureau

MAJOR RELIGIOUS AFFILIATIONS IN THE U.S.

(By percentage of total religiously affiliated population)

Roman Catholic
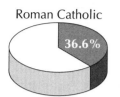
36.6%

Baptist
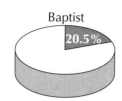
20.5%

Methodist
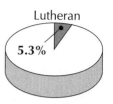
8.3%

Lutheran
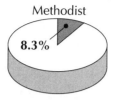
5.3%

Pentecostal
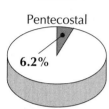
6.2%

Othodox (Eastern)
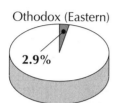
2.9%

Latter-Day Saints

2.8%

Churches of Christ

2.5%

Presbyterian
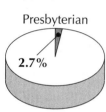
2.7%

Episcopal
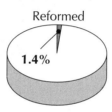
1.5%

Reformed

1.4%

Holiness

0.8%

Jehovah's Witnesses

0.5%

Adventist
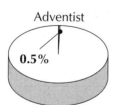
0.5%

Church of Christ, Scientist
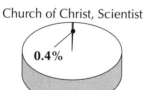
0.4%

Salvation Army

0.3%

Roman Rite
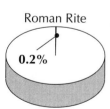
0.2%

Mennonite
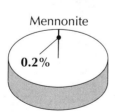
0.2%

Intl. Council of
Community Churches

0.2%

Brethren
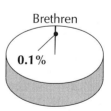
0.1%

Christian &
Missionary Alliance
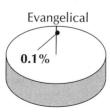
0.2%

Evangelical
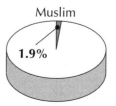
0.1%

Muslim
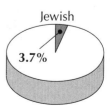
1.9%

Jewish
3.7%

Note: Religions not listed represent less than 0.1%
Source: *Yearbook of American and Canadian Churches*

FREQUENCY OF RELIGIOUS SERVICE ATTENDANCE

(By percentage of all religious attendees)

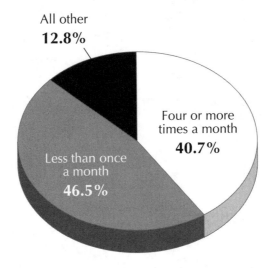

All other
12.8%

Four or more
times a month
40.7%

Less than once
a month
46.5%

Source: NFO Research, Inc.

U.S. CHURCH MEMBERSHIP, 1997

(By selected religions and religious groupings)

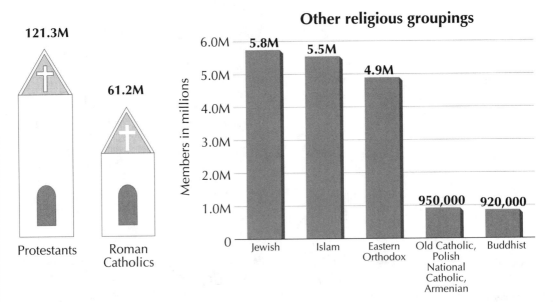

121.3M

61.2M

Protestants

Roman
Catholics

Other religious groupings

Members in millions

6.0M — **5.8M**

5.5M

4.9M

5.0M

4.0M

3.0M

2.0M

1.0M

950,000 **920,000**

0

Jewish Islam Eastern
Orthodox Old Catholic,
Polish
National
Catholic,
Armenian Buddhist

Source: Based on *Yearbook of American and Canadian Churches*

NEW PRIESTS ON THE WANE

(Average number of Roman Catholic ordinations per year in the U.S.)

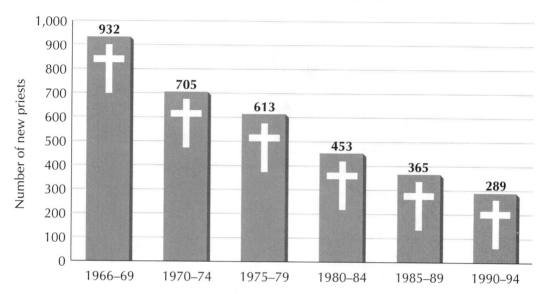

Number of new priests

- 932 — 1966–69
- 705 — 1970–74
- 613 — 1975–79
- 453 — 1980–84
- 365 — 1985–89
- 289 — 1990–94

Source: NFO Research

AMERICAN NUNS, BY AGE GROUP

The median age of the 94,022 Roman Catholic nuns in the U.S. is 65 years:

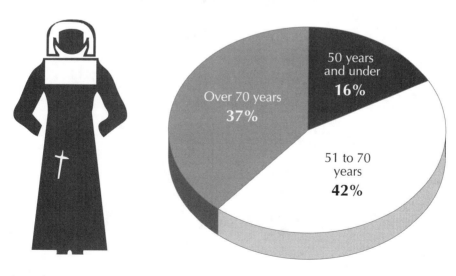

- 50 years and under **16%**
- 51 to 70 years **42%**
- Over 70 years **37%**

Note: Ages unknown for 5% of population
Source: *The Los Angeles Times*

AMERICANS SAY YES TO SCHOOL PRAYER

Most people in the U.S. favor a constitutional amendment
that would make prayer legal in public schools:

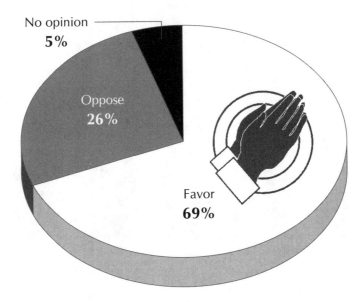

No opinion
5%

Oppose
26%

Favor
69%

Source: MRCI

GROWTH OF MUSLIM MOSQUES
IN THE U.S., 1960–1993

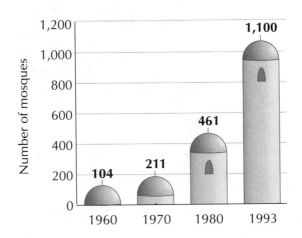

Source: The American Muslim Council; Islamic Resource Institute

TOP 10 U.S. STATES WITH HIGHEST MUSLIM POPULATION
(With rankings)

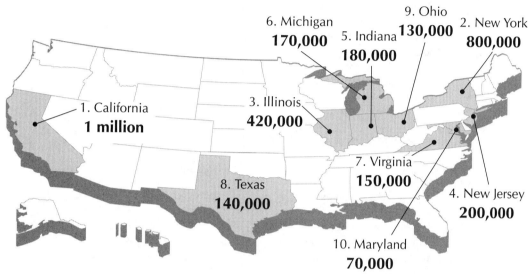

6. Michigan
170,000

9. Ohio
130,000

2. New York
800,000

5. Indiana
180,000

1. California
1 million

3. Illinois
420,000

7. Virginia
150,000

8. Texas
140,000

4. New Jersey
200,000

10. Maryland
70,000

Source: U.S. Census Bureau

ETHNIC OR RACIAL MAKEUP
OF U.S. MUSLIMS

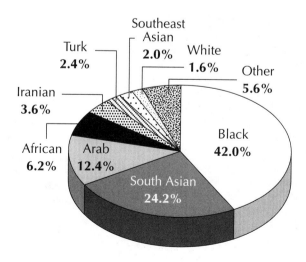

Turk
2.4%

Southeast
Asian
2.0%

White
1.6%

Other
5.6%

Iranian
3.6%

Black
42.0%

African
6.2%

Arab
12.4%

South Asian
24.2%

Source: The American Muslim Council; Islamic Resource Institute

DAILY LIFE

Not too long ago, nuclear families were the norm in America; mom spent the day at home cooking and cleaning, shopping was done in small neighborhood stores, and everyone gathered around the dinner table at night. Today, many families are headed by single parents; mothers often work outside the home, shopping is done in malls and megastores, or via phone, computer, or mail; and only 22% of American families say they eat together every night.

Fathers are now taking a more active role in caring for their children, but the majority of young American children are cared for outside their own homes during at least part of the day, either in another home, at a day care center, or at a parent's workplace. Only 35% of children today are cared for primarily in their own home. School-age children, however, still find their parents peeking over their shoulders; 44% of parents say they spend 5 hours or more each week helping children with schoolwork.

Economic status affects people's daily lives enormously. Insufficient income limits the choices people can make about where they live and how they live. Poverty was defined in 1997 as an income of $16,400 for a family of 4. By this standard, poverty afflicted some 35.6 million Americans in that year. Blacks had the highest poverty rate, and poverty was higher in rural areas than urban areas. Many of the nation's poor are children. In 1996, the number of U.S. children under age 6 who were living in poverty reached a declined to 4.9 million, or 22.7% of that age group.

FINGERTIP FACTS

- Only 31% of Americans get an average of 8 or more hours of sleep each night; 38% get 6 hours or less.

- The percentage of fathers who look after their children, ages 5 and under, increased from 14.4% in 1977 to 26.7% in 1998.

- People are getting more mail. In 1983, the U.S. Postal Service handled 119.4 billion pieces of mail; by 1997, the figure had risen to 190.4 billion.

- On average, adults have 48.6 hours of freetime per week. Americans spend the most free time watching television (20%), and the least listening to music (.04%).

- Saturday is America's favorite shopping day; Friday ranks a close second.

- Development and improvement of technology now makes it possible to go through an entire day without interacting with another person face to face. Because of this, 43% of Americans feel that life is passing by without them.

- American women outrank men more than two to one as the primary buyers of men's clothes.

- In 1987, there were 1.2 million subscribers to cellular telephone systems; by 1993, there were 16.0 million.

SLEEPY WEEKENDS

(Percentage of people who get more than
7 hours of sleep, by type of night)

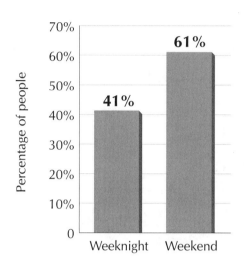

Source: Better Sleep Council

AVERAGE NUMBER OF HOURS AMERICANS SLEEP EACH NIGHT

More than 8
3%

Less than 6
12%

8
28%

6
26%

7
30%

Source: MRCI

MOST IMPORTANT FACTORS FOR GOOD SLEEP

(As percentage ranked by sleepers, based on opinion poll)

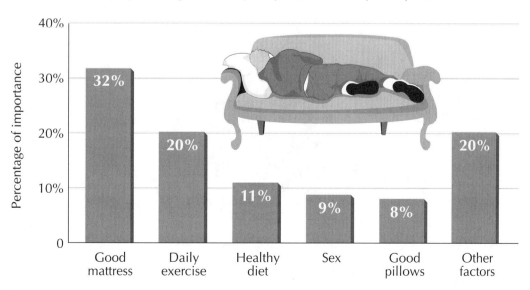

Good mattress	32%
Daily exercise	20%
Healthy diet	11%
Sex	9%
Good pillows	8%
Other factors	20%

Source: Better Sleep Council

U.S. MEN TAKE INCREASED ROLE IN CHILD CARE

Percentage of U.S. fathers who look after their children at home, 1977–1998

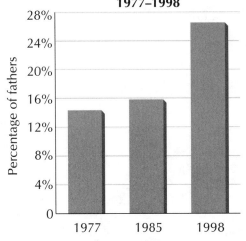

Source: U.S. Census Bureau

Where child care is given

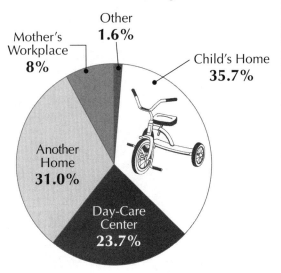

- Other **1.6%**
- Mother's Workplace **8%**
- Child's Home **35.7%**
- Another Home **31.0%**
- Day-Care Center **23.7%**

FREQUENCY OF FAMILY DINING IN U.S.

(Nights per week that families have dinner together)

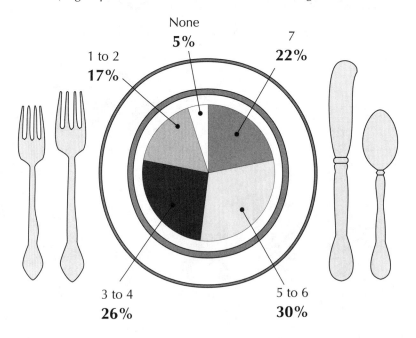

- None **5%**
- 7 **22%**
- 1 to 2 **17%**
- 3 to 4 **26%**
- 5 to 6 **30%**

Source: MRCI

WHO TAKES CARE OF U.S. CHILDREN?

(Living arrangements, by primary caregiver, of the 66 million children in the U.S.)

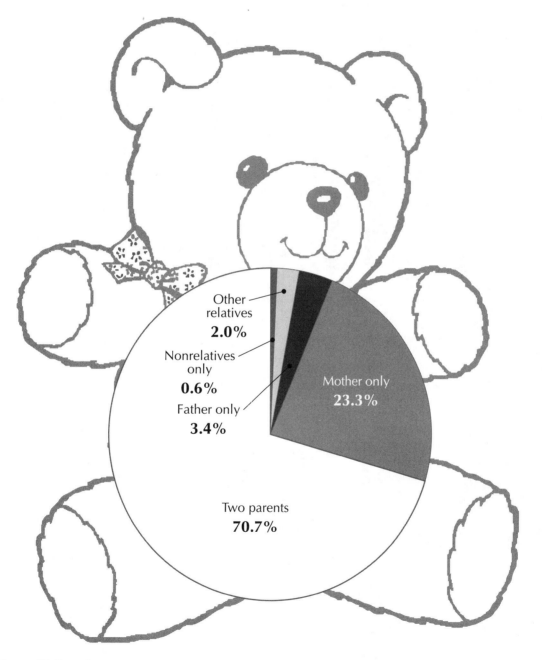

Other relatives
2.0%

Nonrelatives only
0.6%

Father only
3.4%

Mother only
23.3%

Two parents
70.7%

Source: U.S. Census Bureau

AMERICANS WANT TO KEEP IT PRIVATE

(Percentage of people in the U.S. who say they are "very concerned"
about their privacy, 1977–1993)

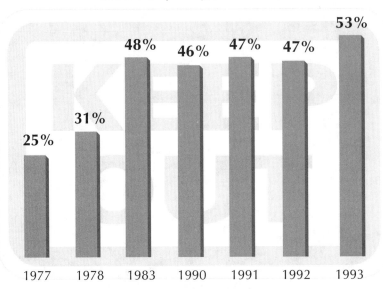

1977	1978	1983	1990	1991	1992	1993
25%	31%	48%	46%	47%	47%	53%

Source: Market Research, Inc.

BUYERS OF MEN'S CLOTHING IN THE U.S.

Men
31.4%

Women
68.6%

Source: Market Research, Inc.

U.S. MAIL STORM

Mailings in the U.S. have increased by more than 60% since 1983.
Pieces of mail, in billions:

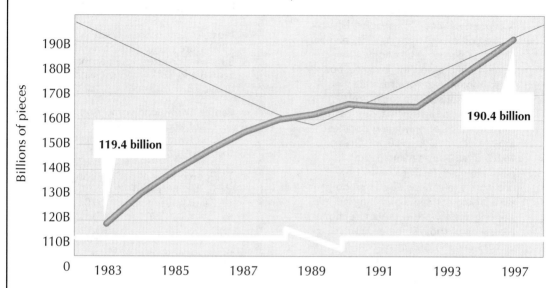

190B
180B
170B
160B
150B
140B
130B
120B
110B

Billions of pieces

119.4 billion

190.4 billion

0   1983   1985   1987   1989   1991   1993   1997

TOP 10 MOST POPULAR COMMEMORATIVE STAMPS

(In sales, by millions)

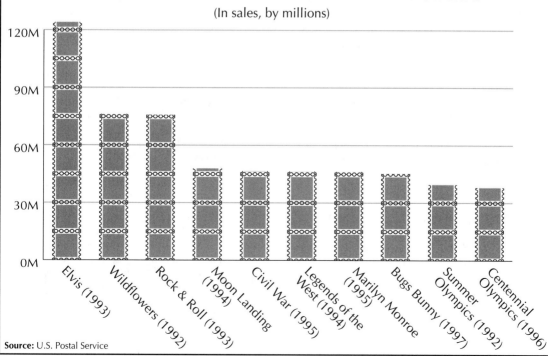

120M
90M
60M
30M
0M

Elvis (1993)
Wildflowers (1992)
Rock & Roll (1993)
Moon Landing (1994)
Civil War (1995)
Legends of the West (1994)
Marilyn Monroe (1995)
Bugs Bunny (1997)
Summer Olympics (1992)
Centennial Olympics (1996)

Source: U.S. Postal Service

H O M E   L I F E

There were some 102.5 million households in the U.S. in 1998. The typical occupants of those households, however, are constantly changing. The number of homes occupied by people living alone has increased, for instance, but most home-buyers are married.

Most households today are equipped with high-tech appliances that were unheard of only a few decades ago. As recently as 1960, for example, 16.8% of all housing units lacked complete plumbing facilities, and 21.5% did not have a telephone. By 1997, only 1.0% lacked complete plumbing facilities, and only 6.1% were without telephones. Nearly all of today's homes have refrigerators (97.2%), and most have clothes washers (76.3%), dishwashers (45.4%), microwave ovens (78.8%), freezers (32.4%), and many other conveniences.

Types of homes vary with income levels. People with limited incomes can apply to live in low-income public housing; 1,199,400 such units were occupied in 1992, an increase from 893,500 in 1970. Sadly, there also is a significant and growing homeless population in America; families with young children make up the fastest-growing component of that troubling problem.

In 1997, there were 70.2 million families in the U.S.; 32.6 million had children under age 18. The percentage of married-couple families has declined over the years, from 86.9% of all family households in 1970 to 74% in 1997. Meanwhile, the family households headed by women has increased, from 10.7% of all family households in 1970 to 14%—a total of 13.6 million—in 1996. Among black families, 33% were headed by women.

FINGERTIP FACTS

- Most American households in 1996 were occupied by couples: 33% with children younger than age 18 and 28% without children under 18.

- People living alone comprised 25.1% of households; single mothers with children younger than 18 made up 7.4%.

- The percentage of people living alone has increased—from 17.1% of households in 1970 to 25.1% in 1996.

- Renters move more frequently than homeowners; 34.3% of renters change residence during a year, as contrasted with 8.9% of homeowners.

- Most of America's 64 million children—some 64%—live with both parents; 27% live only with their mother and 4% live only with their father.

- Family homelessness has sharply increased. A 1993 survey of 26 cities indicated that 43% of the urban homeless were families, up from 32% in 1988. Despite the growing number of homeless, government cut spending for homeless assistance programs in 1997 to $1.1 billion, a 25% decrease from 1995.

- In 1970, the median sales price of a new single-family house was $23,400. In 1993, it was more than 5 times higher, at $126,500. In both years, prices were highest in the Northeast and lowest in the South.

PROFILE: U.S. HOUSEHOLDS

Composition of U.S. households, 1970 vs. 1996

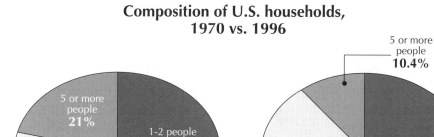

1970

5 or more people
21%

3-4 people
33%

1-2 people
46%

1996

5 or more people
10.4%

3-4 people
32%

1-2 people
57.6%

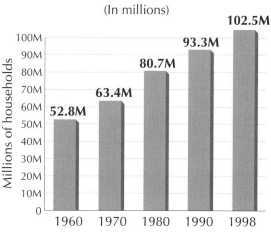

Average size of U.S. household, 1960–1998

(By number of members of household)

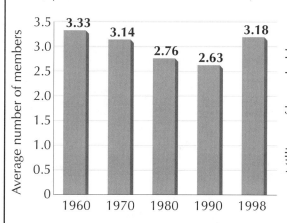

Average number of members

3.5 — **3.33**
3.0 — **3.14**
2.5 —
2.0 —
1.5 —
1.0 —
0.5 —
0 —

2.76   **2.63**   **3.18**

1960   1970   1980   1990   1998

Growth in number of U.S. households, 1960–1998

(In millions)

Millions of households

100M
90M
80M
70M
60M
50M
40M
30M
20M
10M
0

52.8M   **63.4M**   **80.7M**   **93.3M**   **102.5M**

1960   1970   1980   1990   1998

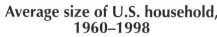

Source: U.S. Census

LIVING ARRANGEMENTS IN THE U.S., 1993

(Living arrangements of people over age 15 years, by selected characteristics)

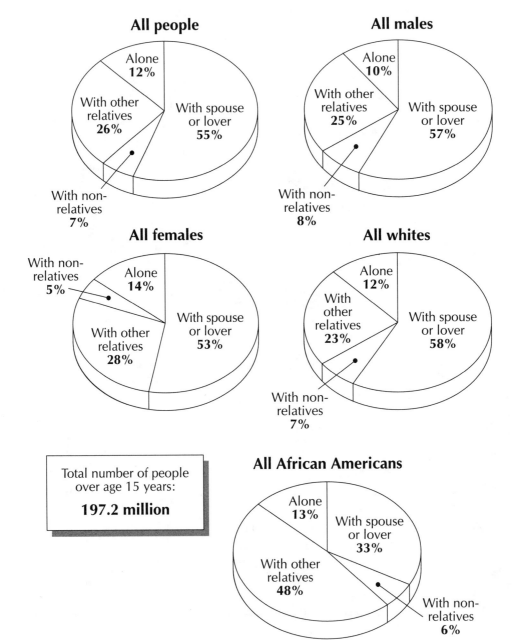

All people

Alone 12%

With other relatives 26%

With spouse or lover 55%

With non-relatives 7%

All males

Alone 10%

With other relatives 25%

With spouse or lover 57%

With non-relatives 8%

All females

With non-relatives 5%

Alone 14%

With other relatives 28%

With spouse or lover 53%

All whites

Alone 12%

With other relatives 23%

With spouse or lover 58%

With non-relatives 7%

Total number of people over age 15 years:

197.2 million

All African Americans

Alone 13%

With spouse or lover 33%

With other relatives 48%

With non-relatives 6%

Source: U.S. Census Bureau

U.S. FAMILY SIZE
(As percentage of all families)

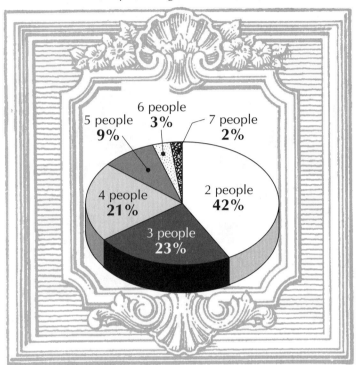

5 people
9%

6 people
3%

7 people
2%

4 people
21%

2 people
42%

3 people
23%

MARRIED-COUPLE FAMILY HOUSEHOLDS WITH CHILDREN
(By type of family, in percentage)

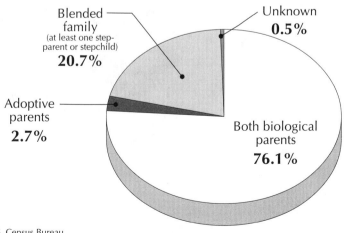

Blended
family
(at least one step-
parent or stepchild)
20.7%

Unknown
0.5%

Adoptive
parents
2.7%

Both biological
parents
76.1%

Source: U.S. Census Bureau

LIVING ARRANGEMENTS OF YOUNG ADULTS, AGES 18–24 YEARS, 1970 vs. 1995

Total number of young adults, ages 18–24

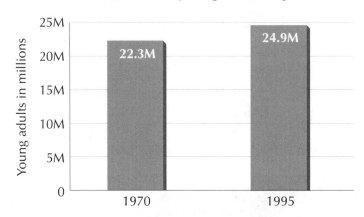

Living arrangements

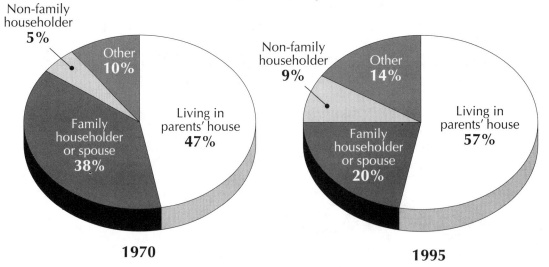

Source: U.S. Census Bureau

CHILDREN IN U.S. FAMILIES

(Percentage of families with children under
age 18 or no children)

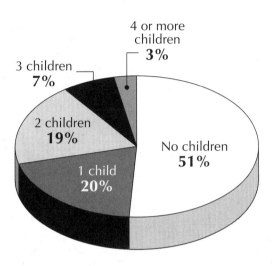

4 or more
children
3%

3 children
7%

2 children
19%

1 child
20%

No children
51%

ADULT CHILDREN IN THE FAMILY HOME, 1960–1995

(Percentage of people ages 25–30 living with parents)

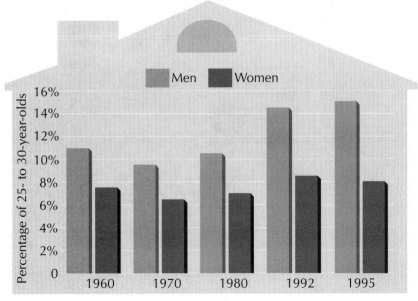

Men   Women

Percentage of 25- to 30-year-olds

16%
14%
12%
10%
8%
6%
4%
2%
0

1960   1970   1980   1992   1995

Source: U.S. Census Bureau

U.S. FAMILIES WITH CHILDREN AND MARITAL STATUS OF PARENTS, 1997

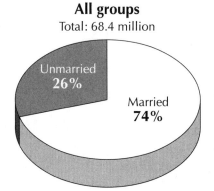

All groups
Total: 68.4 million

Unmarried **26%**
Married **74%**

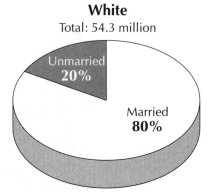

White
Total: 54.3 million

Unmarried **20%**
Married **80%**

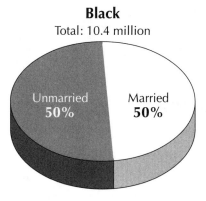

Black
Total: 10.4 million

Unmarried **50%**
Married **50%**

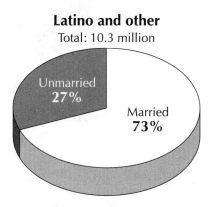

Latino and other
Total: 10.3 million

Unmarried **27%**
Married **73%**

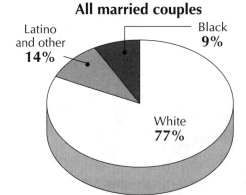

All married couples

Latino and other **14%**
Black **9%**
White **77%**

Source: U.S. Census Bureau

U.S. CHILDREN IN BLENDED FAMILIES

(In millions)

Children living with a parent and:

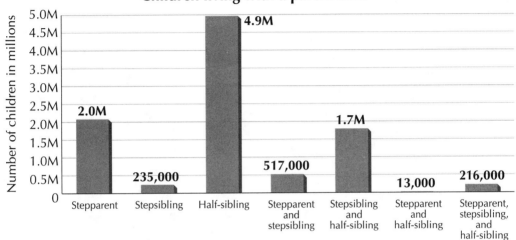

Percentage of all blended families that include a natural parent and:

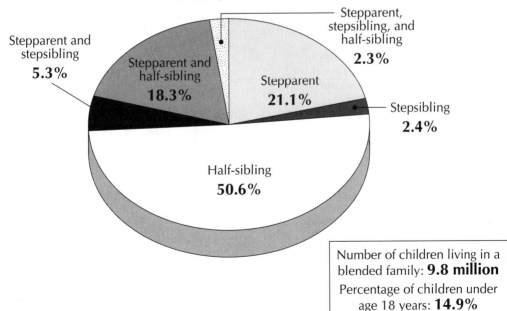

Stepparent, stepsibling, and half-sibling
2.3%

Stepparent
21.1%

Stepsibling
2.4%

Stepparent and half-sibling
18.3%

Stepparent and stepsibling
5.3%

Half-sibling
50.6%

Number of children living in a blended family: **9.8 million**

Percentage of children under age 18 years: **14.9%**

Source: U.S. Census Bureau; U.S. Department of Commerce

TWO OR MORE PEOPLE LIVING TOGETHER

Families—two or more people related by birth, marriage, or adoption—account for a smaller share of U.S. households today than they did in 1970. In 1998, more than 25% of households were people living alone.

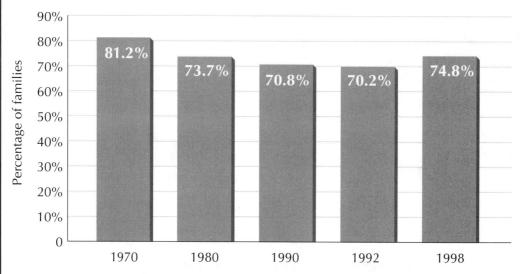

Percentage of families

1970	81.2%
1980	73.7%
1990	70.8%
1992	70.2%
1998	74.8%

WHO'S IN A HOUSEHOLD?

In 1996, people in the U.S. occupied 99.6 million households.
Number of each type of household:

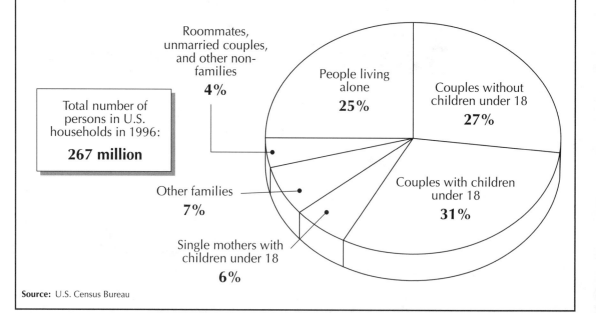

Total number of persons in U.S. households in 1996:

267 million

Roommates, unmarried couples, and other non-families
4%

People living alone
25%

Couples without children under 18
27%

Other families
7%

Couples with children under 18
31%

Single mothers with children under 18
6%

Source: U.S. Census Bureau

INCREASING HOME PURCHASES BY SINGLES

(Percentage of married or single home buyers in major metropolitan areas)

PERSONS LIVING ALONE, BY SEX, 1995

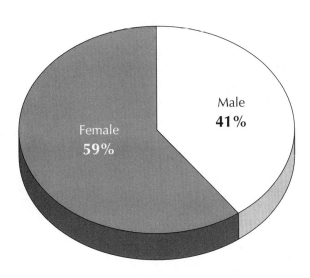

Source: U.S. Census Bureau

SINGLE-PARENT FAMILIES MAINTAINED BY WOMEN, 1960 vs. 1995

(Thousands of families, by age of mother)

Under 35

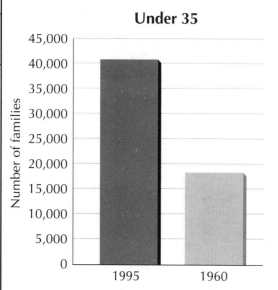

35–44 years

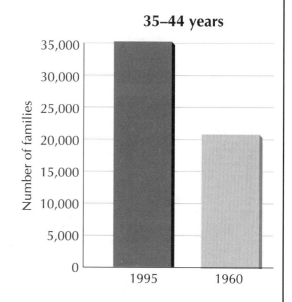

45–64 years

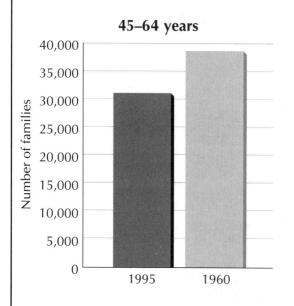

65 years and older

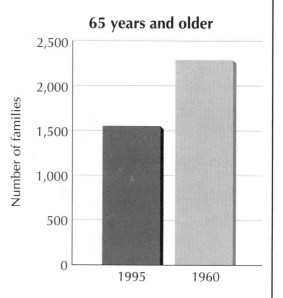

Source: U.S. Census Bureau

SINGLE-PARENT HOUSEHOLDS GROW: 1960 vs. 1993

(As percentage of all family households)

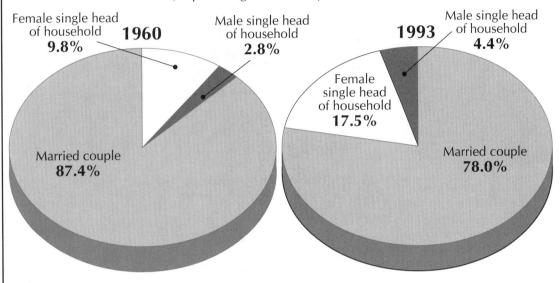

1960

Female single head of household
9.8%

Male single head of household
2.8%

Married couple
87.4%

1993

Male single head of household
4.4%

Female single head of household
17.5%

Married couple
78.0%

Source: U.S. Census Bureau

MARRIED vs. UNMARRIED MOMS, 1960–1997

(Percentage of all U.S. children born, by woman's marital status)

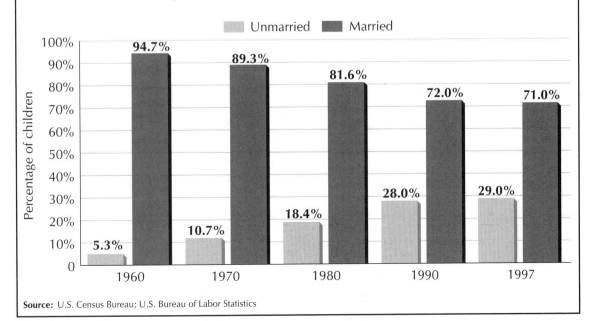

Unmarried ▪ Married

Percentage of children

	1960	1970	1980	1990	1997
Unmarried	5.3%	10.7%	18.4%	28.0%	29.0%
Married	94.7%	89.3%	81.6%	72.0%	71.0%

Source: U.S. Census Bureau; U.S. Bureau of Labor Statistics

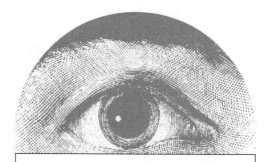

AT A GLANCE

Violence at home

More than **18%** of American women say they've been physically abused by a husband or boyfriend

For every 100 instances of violent victimization reported by men, the number reported by women: **132**

Days of hospitalization every year in the United States due to domestic violence: **100,000**

Visits to emergency rooms: **30,000**

Visits to a physician: **40,000**

Percentage of Americans who think women sometimes deserve to be hit by their husbands or boyfriends: **12%**

Percentage of Americans who believe men sometimes deserve to be hit by their wives or girlfriends: **39%**

An estimated **1.15 million** American women have been victims of one or more rapes by their husbands.

Male-on-female assaults with weapons: **25%** of all such assaults

Female-on-male assaults: **86%**

Source: Based on statistics from *U.S. News & World Report*

CHILD NEGLECT AND ABUSE CASES REPORTED IN U.S., 1980–1997

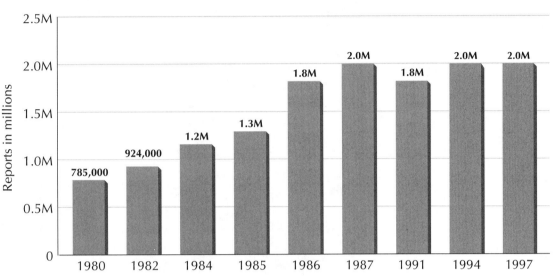

Reports in millions

- 2.5M
- 2.0M
- 1.5M
- 1.0M
- 0.5M
- 0

1980	1982	1984	1985	1986	1987	1991	1994	1997
785,000	924,000	1.2M	1.3M	1.8M	2.0M	1.8M	2.0M	2.0M

Source: American Humane Association; U.S. Department of Health and Human Services

TOP 10 STATES IN REPORTED CASES OF CHILD ABUSE AND NEGLECT, 1994
(With rankings)

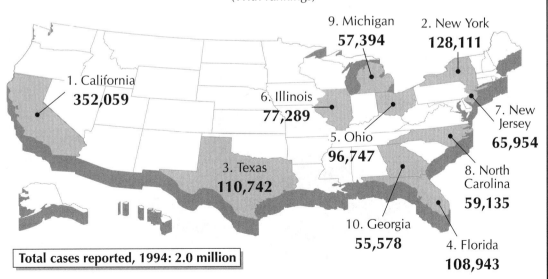

9. Michigan
57,394

2. New York
128,111

1. California
352,059

6. Illinois
77,289

7. New Jersey
65,954

5. Ohio
96,747

8. North Carolina
59,135

3. Texas
110,742

10. Georgia
55,578

4. Florida
108,943

Total cases reported, 1994: 2.0 million

Source: U.S. Department of Health and Human Services, National Center on Child Abuse and Neglect, National Child Abuse and Neglect Data System

U.S. RENTERS ON THE MOVE

(Percentage of renters and homeowners
changing residence during the year)

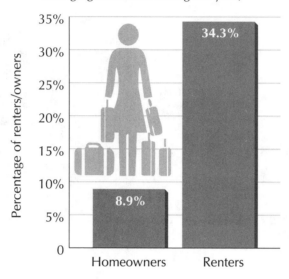

Source: U.S. Census Bureau

U.S. HOUSES: CURRENT CLEANING HABITS

How often people in the U.S. say their
current house is cleaned, compared to
the house they grew up in:

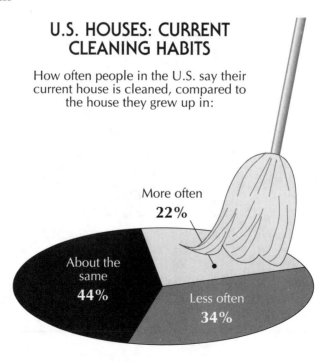

Source: Market Research, Inc.

APPLIANCES FILL THE AMERICAN HOME, 1997

Percentage of American households:

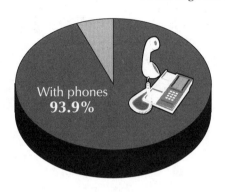

With phones
93.9%

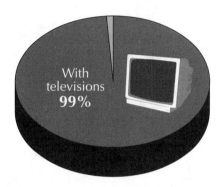

With televisions
99%

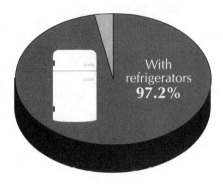

With refrigerators
97.2%

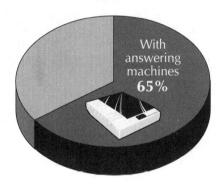

With answering machines
65%

With washing machines
76.3%

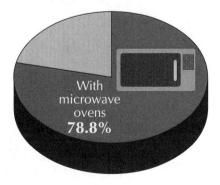

With microwave ovens
78.8%

Source: U.S. Census Bureau; U.S. Energy Information Administration

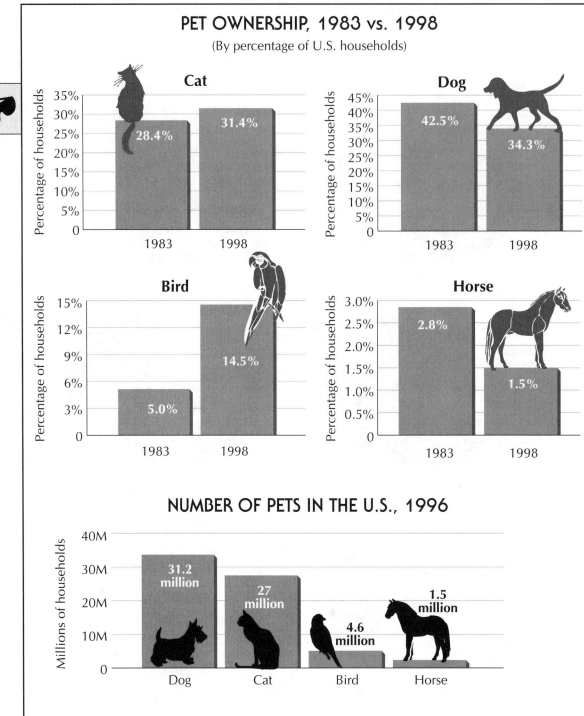

PET OWNERSHIP, 1983 vs. 1998
(By percentage of U.S. households)

Cat
Percentage of households

- 1983: 28.4%
- 1998: 31.4%

Dog
Percentage of households

- 1983: 42.5%
- 1998: 34.3%

Bird
Percentage of households

- 1983: 5.0%
- 1998: 14.5%

Horse
Percentage of households

- 1983: 2.8%
- 1998: 1.5%

NUMBER OF PETS IN THE U.S., 1996
Millions of households

- Dog: 31.2 million
- Cat: 27 million
- Bird: 4.6 million
- Horse: 1.5 million

Source: American Veterinary Medical Association

AMERICAN PET OWNERSHIP, 1996
(Millions of U.S. pets)

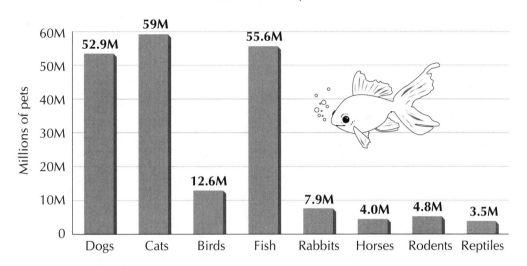

Dogs	52.9M
Cats	59M
Birds	12.6M
Fish	55.6M
Rabbits	7.9M
Horses	4.0M
Rodents	4.8M
Reptiles	3.5M

Millions of pets (y-axis: 0, 10M, 20M, 30M, 40M, 50M, 60M)

WHO OWNS DOGS?
(Percentage of all dog owners)

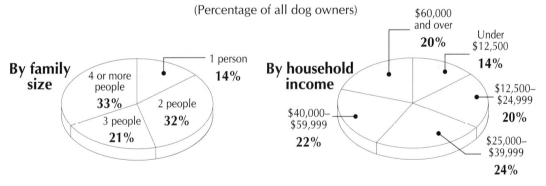

By family size
- 1 person 14%
- 2 people 32%
- 3 people 21%
- 4 or more people 33%

By household income
- Under $12,500 — 14%
- $12,500–$24,999 — 20%
- $25,000–$39,999 — 24%
- $40,000–$59,999 — 22%
- $60,000 and over — 20%

WHO OWNS CATS?
(Percentage of all cat owners)

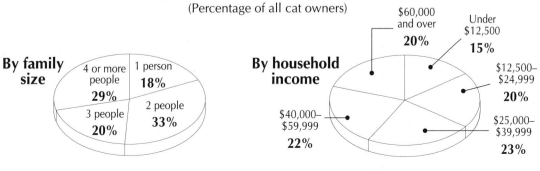

By family size
- 1 person 18%
- 2 people 33%
- 3 people 20%
- 4 or more people 29%

By household income
- Under $12,500 — 15%
- $12,500–$24,999 — 20%
- $25,000–$39,999 — 23%
- $40,000–$59,999 — 22%
- $60,000 and over — 20%

Source: American Veterinary Medical Association

LEISURE AND RECREATION

Over the past few decades, time for leisure activities has increased for most Americans. The work week has gradually decreased; people have retired at earlier ages and in better health; and growing affluence has created more disposable income and made it easier to escape from work and other responsibilities. At the same time, the range of leisure-time activities has expanded greatly. Today, people can choose from an almost infinite variety of ways to relax, amuse themselves, or participate in active forms of recreation.

Watching television and other passive activities fill much leisure time for many people. Most U.S. households have 2 or more TVs, and every day, more than 75 million Americans tune in to watch prime-time programs. Videos and movies also are enormously popular diversions; in 1997, consumers spent $13.2 billion on videos and $6.6 billion on movies. Some $25.2 billion was spent on books, with popular fiction books making up 51% of the year's top-selling titles. As more and more people buy computers, playing computer games continues to grow in popularity; sales of entertainment software totaled $1.8 billion in 1997.

More active pursuits and diversions include sports and hobbies such as gardening and photography. Tourism, camping, and exploring the great outdoors are also increasingly popular. Many of America's majestic national parks are overrun with vacationers, but the nation's most popular tourist attractions by far are Walt Disney World and Disneyland. A rapidly growing recreational activity in America is gambling. Americans wagered $47.6 billion in 1997, a sum likely to increase dramatically as the number of casinos in America continues to rise.

FINGERTIP FACTS

- Each day, more than 75 million Americans tune in to prime-time TV; Thursday is the biggest draw, averaging 94 million viewers.

- Americans have fallen in love with CDs. In 1987, CD sales made up only 11.5% of all recorded music sales. In 1997, CD sales had skyrocketed to 70%.

- In 1997, more than 54 million people owned cell phones. up 85% from 2 million in 1988.

- Hawaii is the most expensive U.S. state to visit; in 1998, the cost of 3 meals and a night in a hotel for a family of four averaged $409. New York was second at $330.

- More Americans are traveling to foreign countries—up from 34.7 million in 1985 to 52.7 million in 1996. Canada was the most popular destination in 1985, Mexico in 1996.

- National parks are growing increasingly crowded. More than 5 million people visited the Grand Canyon in 1998—twice as many as in 1983.

- The most popular national park in 1998 was the Great Smokey Mountains, with 21.8 million visitors.

- Legal gaming generated gross revenues of $43.2 billion in 1997—on a staggering total amount wagered of $47.6 billion. Revenues of various segments of the industry included casinos, $20.5 billion; Native-American-run gaming, $6.7 billion; and lotteries, $16.5 billion.

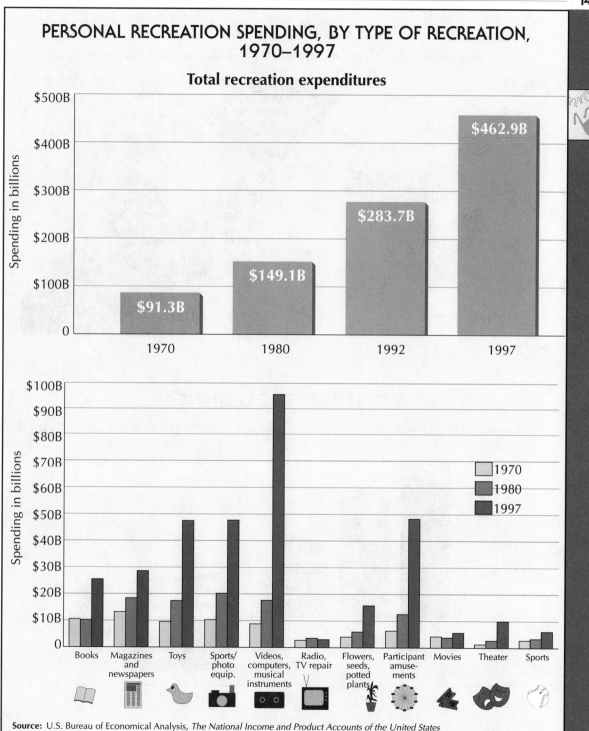

PERSONAL RECREATION SPENDING, BY TYPE OF RECREATION, 1970–1997

Total recreation expenditures

Source: U.S. Bureau of Economical Analysis, *The National Income and Product Accounts of the United States*

MORE OR LESS FREE TIME?

(How much leisure time Americans feel they have today compared to 1990, by sex)

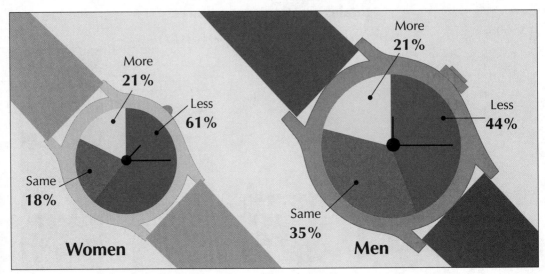

Source: Based on statistics from Market Directions

USE OF LEISURE TIME IS CHANGING

(Biggest changes in time spent on popular leisure activities, by percentages, 1991–1994)

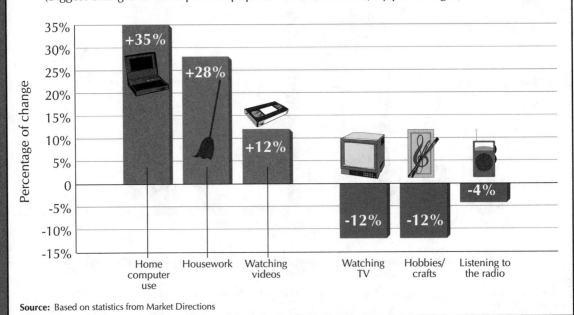

Source: Based on statistics from Market Directions

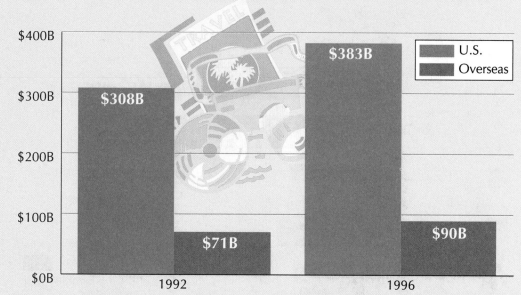

U.S. TOURIST SPENDING, 1992 vs. 1996
(In billions of dollars)

Source: Travel Industry Association of America

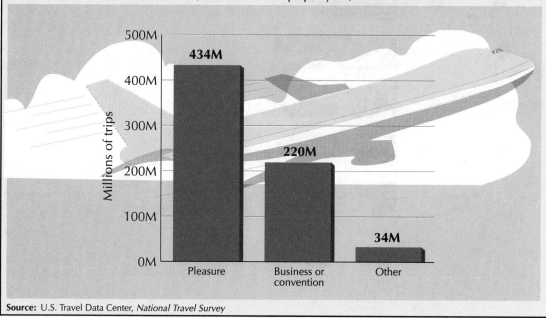

PURPOSE FOR TRAVEL BY U.S. RESIDENTS, 1994
(Millions of of trips per year)

Source: U.S. Travel Data Center, *National Travel Survey*

THE 10 MOST POPULAR SPORTS ACTIVITIES, BY SEX, 1994

(By percentage of U.S. population ages 7 years and older)

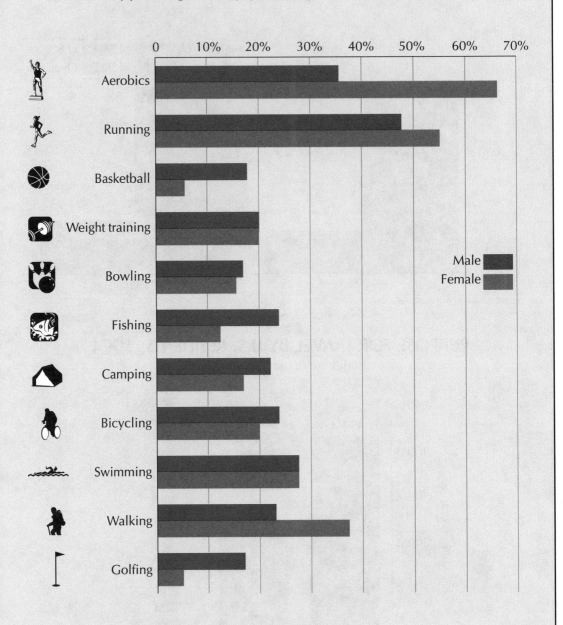

Source: U.S. Census Bureau

ANNUAL AVERAGE ATTENDANCE AT SPECTATOR SPORTS, 1995

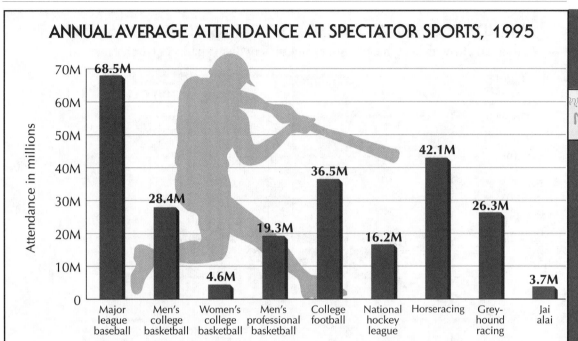

Sources: Based on statistics from National League of Professional Baseball Clubs; National Footbal League; National Hockey League; National Basketball Association; *The New York Times*

ATTENDANCE BY U.S. ADULTS FOR SELECTED LEISURE ACTIVITIES, 1997

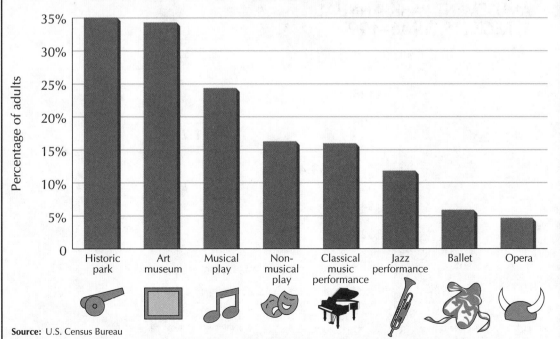

Source: U.S. Census Bureau

ATTENDANCE AT U.S. AMUSEMENT PARKS RISES, 1986–1997
(Annual attendance at the 40 busiest amusement/theme parks in North America)

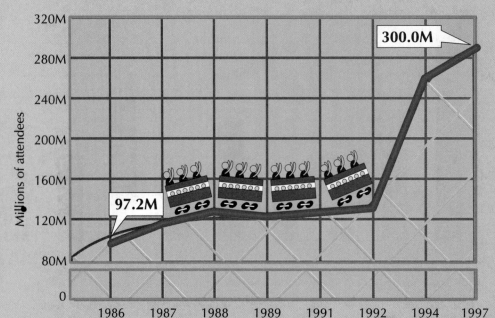

Source: Based on statistics from *Amusement Business* magazine

AMUSEMENT PARK ANNUAL RECEIPTS, 1986–1997

(In billions)

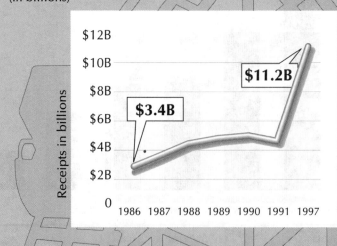

Source: U.S. Census Bureau

MOST POPULAR TOURIST ATTRACTIONS, BY NUMBER OF VISITORS, 1997

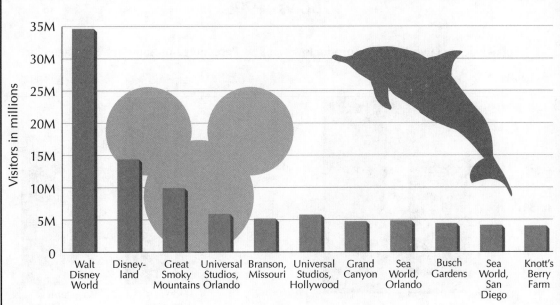

Source: U.S. Tourism Board

U.S. THEME PARK ATTENDANCE, 1997

Attendance at North American theme parks reached an estimated 300 million in 1997. Walt Disney operates the top four most popular parks in America. Annual attendance, in millions:

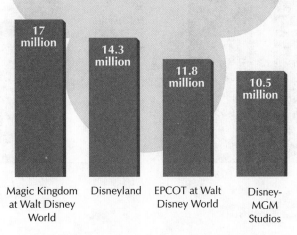

Magic Kingdom at Walt Disney World	Disneyland	EPCOT at Walt Disney World	Disney-MGM Studios
17 million	14.3 million	11.8 million	10.5 million

Source: Based on statistics from *Amusement Business* magazine

DECREASING PARTICIPATION IN LAWN AND GARDEN ACTIVITIES, 1988 vs. 1992

Retail sales of lawn & garden products
(In billions of dollars)

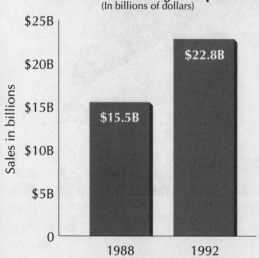

- $25B
- $20B
- $15B
- $10B
- $5B
- 0

Sales in billions

$15.5B — 1988

$22.8B — 1992

Percentage of households engaged in:

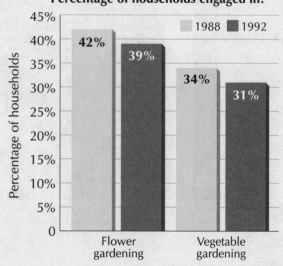

1988   1992

- 45%
- 40%
- 35%
- 30%
- 25%
- 20%
- 15%
- 10%
- 5%
- 0

Percentage of households

Flower gardening: 42% / 39%

Vegetable gardening: 34% / 31%

Percentage of households growing indoor houseplants

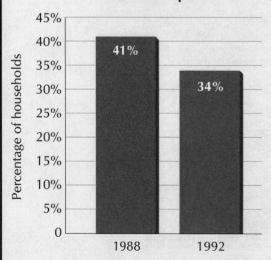

- 45%
- 40%
- 35%
- 30%
- 25%
- 20%
- 15%
- 10%
- 5%
- 0

Percentage of households

41% — 1988

34% — 1992

Percentage of households engaged in lawn care

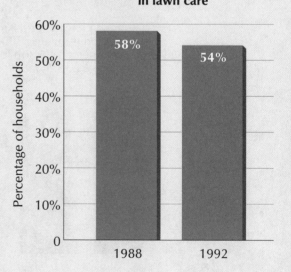

- 60%
- 50%
- 40%
- 30%
- 20%
- 10%
- 0

Percentage of households

58% — 1988

54% — 1992

Source: The National Gardening Association

AIR SHOW ATTENDANCE SOARS IN U.S.

(Annual attendance, in millions)

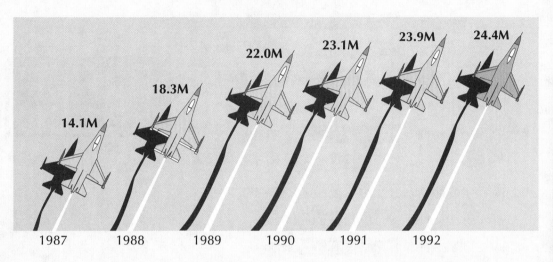

| 14.1M | 18.3M | 22.0M | 23.1M | 23.9M | 24.4M |
| 1987 | 1988 | 1989 | 1990 | 1991 | 1992 |

Source: International Council of Air Shows

STATE FAIRS DRAW BIG ATTENDANCE

(U.S. fairs that boast the greatest attendance, in millions)

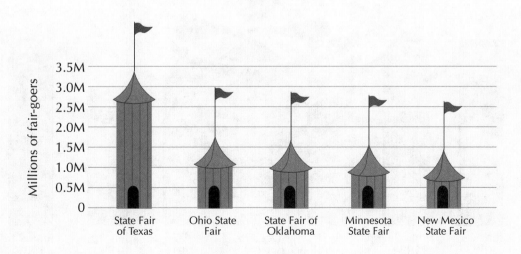

Source: Based on statistics from International Association of Fairs and Expositions

THE TOP 10 HIGHEST-GROSSING U.S. FILMS, 1990–1998

(In millions of dollars)

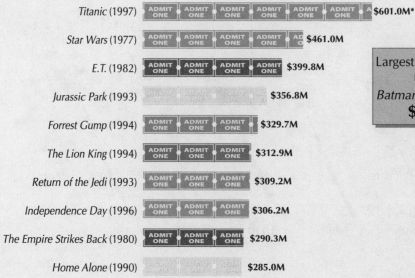

Titanic (1997) $601.0M*

Star Wars (1977) $461.0M

E.T. (1982) $399.8M

Jurassic Park (1993) $356.8M

Forrest Gump (1994) $329.7M

The Lion King (1994) $312.9M

Return of the Jedi (1993) $309.2M

Independence Day (1996) $306.2M

The Empire Strikes Back (1980) $290.3M

Home Alone (1990) $285.0M

Largest opening weekend in movie history:
Batman Forever, June 1995:
$52.8 million

Source: movieweb.com

*As of November 1998.

MEGA-HIT MOVIE WEEKENDS

(Weekends with the highest gross at the box office for each year)

$98.6M	$97.3M	$99.2M	$86.3M	$90.8M	$80.8M	$96.7M
June 24, 1995	June 24, 1994	July 9, 1993	Dec. 25, 1992	Dec. 27, 1991	July 13, 1990	June 23, 1989

Source: Based on statistics from *Variety; Entertainment Weekly*

AVERAGE BOOK PRICE
U.S. READERS WILL PAY

Most book readers will not spend
more than $15.00 on a book:

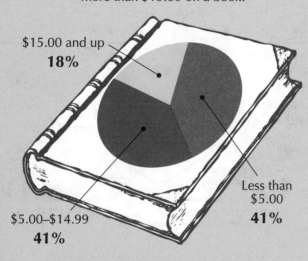

$15.00 and up
18%

Less than
$5.00
41%

$5.00–$14.99
41%

Source: Statistics based on NPD Group

SELF-IMPROVEMENT BOOKS TAKE HOLD

Of the top-selling books of 1993, a total of 19% were related to self-help.

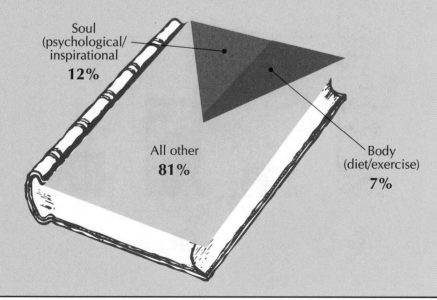

Soul
(psychological/
inspirational
12%

All other
81%

Body
(diet/exercise)
7%

Source: ABPA

U.S. GAMBLING HITS THE JACKPOT, 1987–1996

(Total amount that the U.S. gambling industry earned annually)

Source: *The Wall Street Journal; The New York Times; The Washington Post*

GAMBLING WINS BIG, 1997

(Amount that Americans spent on each form of entertainment)

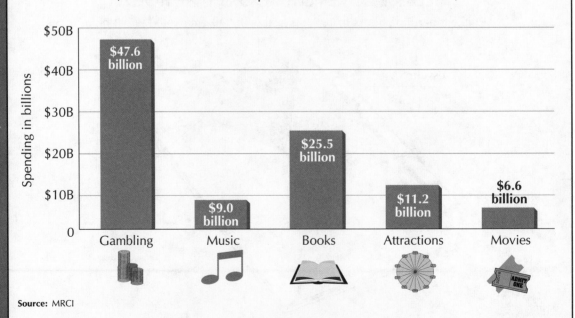

Source: MRCI

BIG SPENDERS FOR GAMBLING, 1987–1992

(Average annual amount spent in the U.S.
on gambling, per capita)

GROSS GAMBLING REVENUE, 1997

(In millions and billions of dollars)

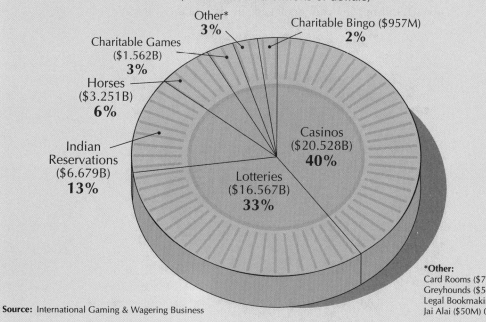

Other*
3%

Charitable Bingo ($957M)
2%

Charitable Games
($1.562B)
3%

Horses
($3.251B)
6%

Indian
Reservations
($6.679B)
13%

Casinos
($20.528B)
40%

Lotteries
($16.567B)
33%

*Other:
Card Rooms ($700M) 1%
Greyhounds ($509M) 1%
Legal Bookmaking ($96M) 0.5%
Jai Alai ($50M) 0.5%

Source: International Gaming & Wagering Business

CITY SLICKERS LIKE LOTTERIES

(Percentage of population who bought lottery tickets in 1994, by area of residence)

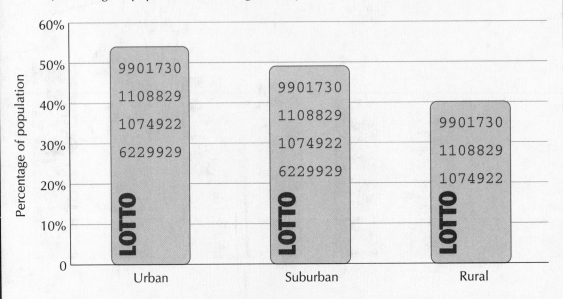

Percentage of population

Urban
- 9901730
- 1108829
- 1074922
- 6229929
- LOTTO

Suburban
- 9901730
- 1108829
- 1074922
- 6229929
- LOTTO

Rural
- 9901730
- 1108829
- 1074922
- LOTTO

Source: Statistics based on *USA Today*

SHOPPING DAYS

(Percentage of U.S. shoppers who prefer specific days of the week for shopping)

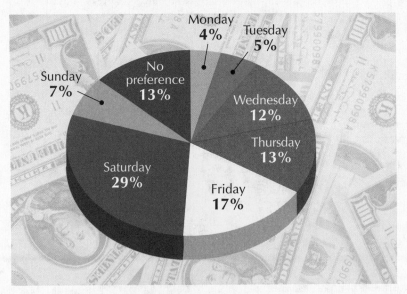

- Monday 4%
- Tuesday 5%
- No preference 13%
- Sunday 7%
- Wednesday 12%
- Thursday 13%
- Saturday 29%
- Friday 17%

Source: Statistics based on International Mass Retail Association

TEEN LIFESTYLES: U.S. vs. JAPAN

In two different cities thousands of miles apart, here's how teenagers' daily lives compare:

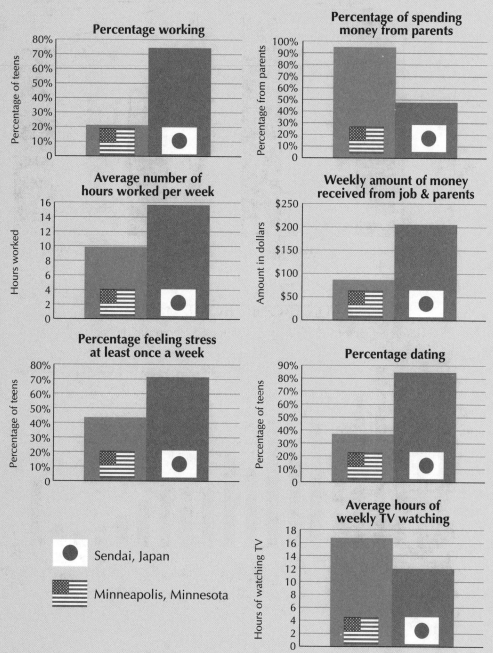

Percentage working

Percentage of spending money from parents

Average number of hours worked per week

Weekly amount of money received from job & parents

Percentage feeling stress at least once a week

Percentage dating

Average hours of weekly TV watching

● Sendai, Japan

▦ Minneapolis, Minnesota

Source: Based on statistics from the University of Michigan

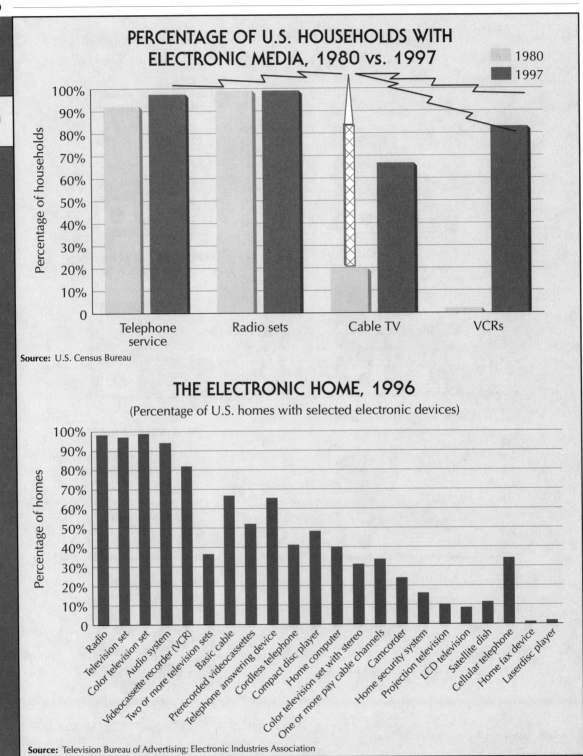

PERCENTAGE OF U.S. HOUSEHOLDS WITH ELECTRONIC MEDIA, 1980 vs. 1997

■ 1980
■ 1997

Percentage of households

100%
90%
80%
70%
60%
50%
40%
30%
20%
10%
0

Telephone service   Radio sets   Cable TV   VCRs

Source: U.S. Census Bureau

THE ELECTRONIC HOME, 1996
(Percentage of U.S. homes with selected electronic devices)

Percentage of homes

100%
90%
80%
70%
60%
50%
40%
30%
20%
10%
0

Radio
Television set
Color television set
Audio system
Videocassette recorder (VCR)
Two or more television sets
Basic cable
Prerecorded videocassettes
Telephone answering device
Cordless telephone
Compact disc player
Home computer
Color television set with stereo
One or more pay cable channels
Camcorder
Home security system
Projection television
LCD television
Satellite dish
Cellular telephone
Home fax device
Laserdisc player

Source: Television Bureau of Advertising; Electronic Industries Association

SALES OF CELLULAR TELEPHONES BOOM, 1984–1997
(Millions of people with cellular telephone service)

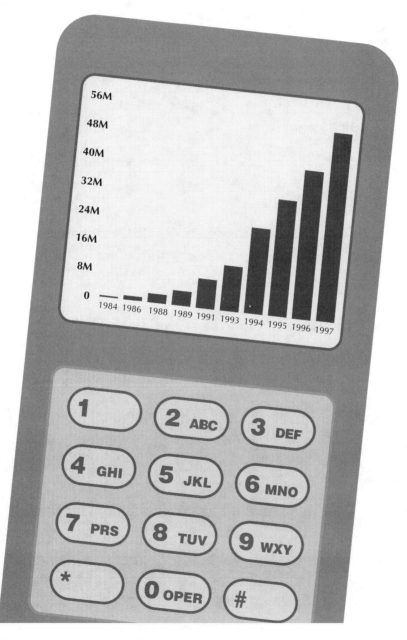

Source: Cellular Telecommunications Industry Association

SALES OF CELLULAR TELEPHONES, ANSWERING MACHINES, AND FAX MACHINES, 1983–1998

(Unit sales to dealer, in millions)

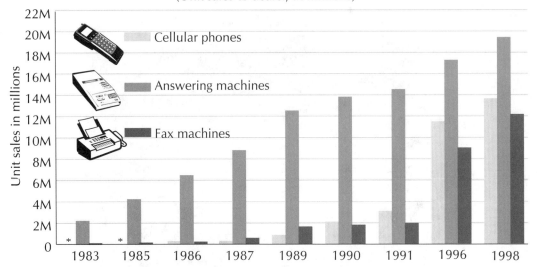

* **Note:** Data not available
Source: Electronic Industries Association; Computer and Business Equipment

THE BIGGEST NIGHTS FOR PRIME-TIME TV

(U.S. viewers per night, in millions)

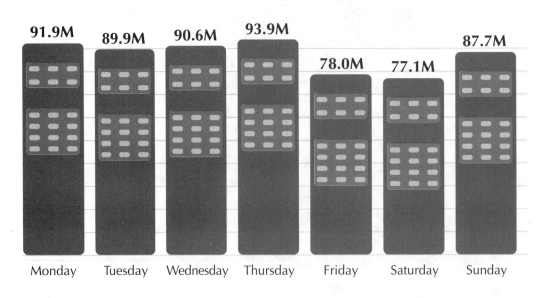

Source: NMR

MOST HOUSEHOLDS HAVE A VCR AND MULTIPLE TVs

Percentage of U.S. television households with:

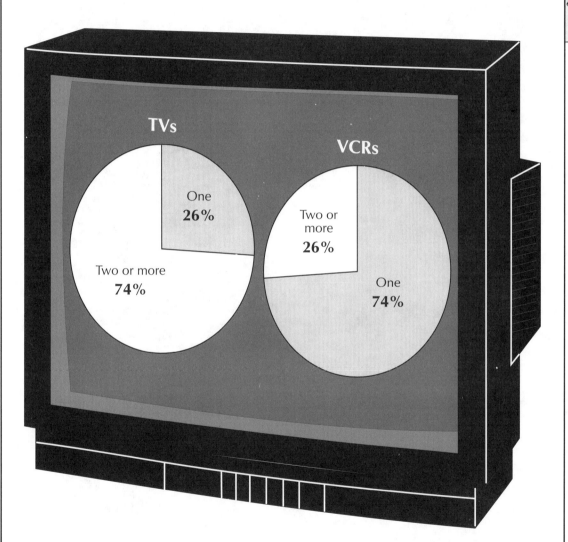

TVs

One
26%

Two or more
74%

VCRs

Two or
more
26%

One
74%

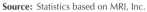

Source: Statistics based on MRI, Inc.

CHANNEL CAPACITY OF THE AVERAGE U.S. TELEVISION, 1993

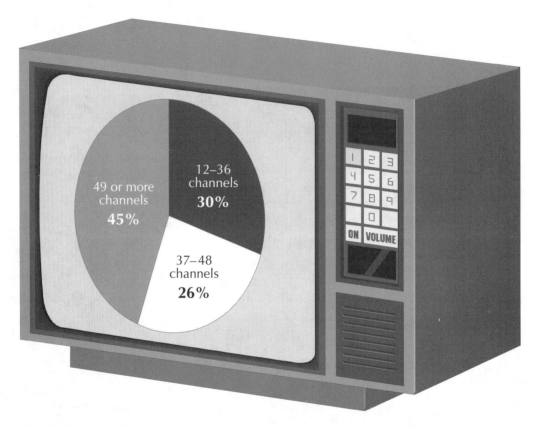

49 or more channels
45%

12–36 channels
30%

37–48 channels
26%

Source: Based on statistics from NMR; TBI

PERCENTAGE OF U.S. HOUSEHOLDS WITH TV, 1950–1998

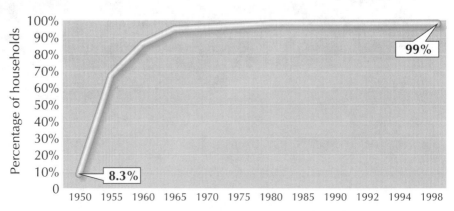

99%

8.3%

Percentage of households

1950 1955 1960 1965 1970 1975 1980 1985 1990 1992 1994 1998

Source: NMR; TBA

THE MOST POPULAR U.S. CABLE NETWORKS, 1997

(By number of subscribers, in millions)

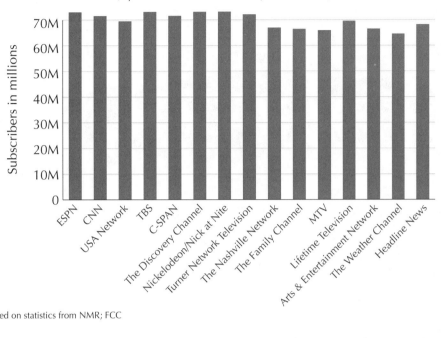

Subscribers in millions

ESPN, CNN, USA Network, TBS, C-SPAN, The Discovery Channel, Nickelodeon/Nick at Nite, Turner Network Television, The Nashville Network, The Family Channel, MTV, Lifetime Television, Arts & Entertainment Network, The Weather Channel, Headline News

Source: Based on statistics from NMR; FCC

THE MOST TRUSTED U.S. NEWS ANCHORS

(Percentage of viewers who trust one anchor over others, based on opinion polls)

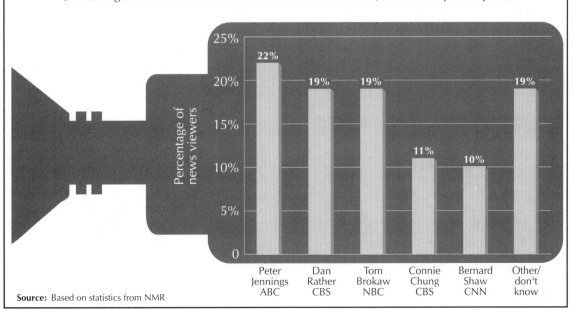

Percentage of news viewers

Peter Jennings ABC	Dan Rather CBS	Tom Brokaw NBC	Connie Chung CBS	Bernard Shaw CNN	Other/ don't know
22%	19%	19%	11%	10%	19%

Source: Based on statistics from NMR

TOP 6 BEST-SELLING ALBUMS OF ALL TIME

(By copies sold)

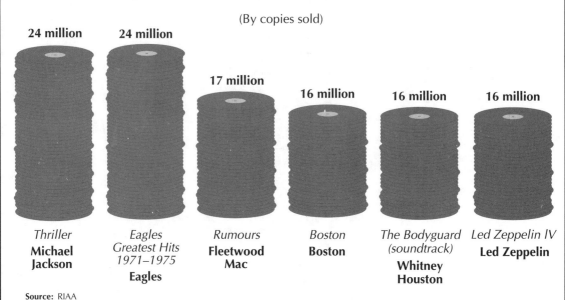

24 million	24 million	17 million	16 million	16 million	16 million
Thriller **Michael Jackson**	*Eagles Greatest Hits 1971–1975* **Eagles**	*Rumours* **Fleetwood Mac**	*Boston* **Boston**	*The Bodyguard (soundtrack)* **Whitney Houston**	*Led Zeppelin IV* **Led Zeppelin**

Source: RIAA

FALLING ROCK SALES, 1989–1998

(By percent of music purchased)

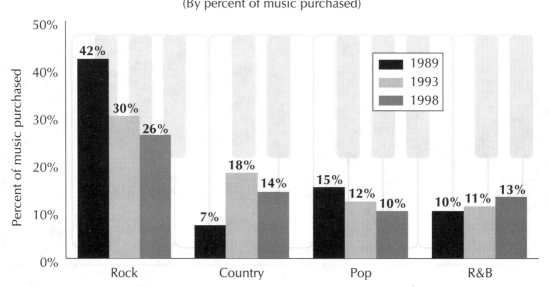

Legend:
- 1989
- 1993
- 1998

Rock: 42%, 30%, 26%
Country: 7%, 18%, 14%
Pop: 15%, 12%, 10%
R&B: 10%, 11%, 13%

Y-axis: Percent of music purchased (0% to 50%)

Source: Recording Industry Association of America

CD SALES vs. CASSETTE SALES, 1987 vs. 1997

(By percentage of people who purchased each)

62.5%

70%

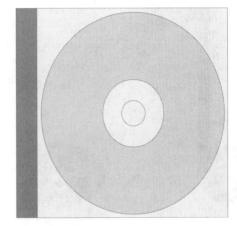

11.5%

18.2%

1987

1997

Source: Based on statistics from *SoundScan*

WHERE CDs ARE PLAYED

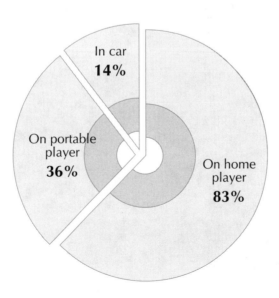

In car
14%

On portable
player
36%

On home
player
83%

Note: Some people use more than one player
Source: Based on statistics from NFO research

THE BEST-SELLING SONGS OF ALL TIME
(Songs that spent the longest time at the top of *Billboard's* music charts)

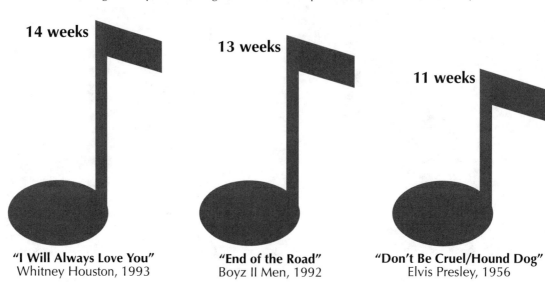

14 weeks

13 weeks

11 weeks

"I Will Always Love You"
Whitney Houston, 1993

"End of the Road"
Boyz II Men, 1992

"Don't Be Cruel/Hound Dog"
Elvis Presley, 1956

Source: Statistics from *Billboard*

GRAMMY CATEGORIES CLIMB

(Total number of Grammy categories
since the awards began)

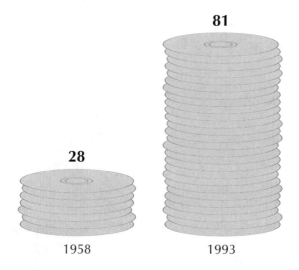

81

28

1958

1993

Source: National Academy of Recording Arts & Sciences

THE TOP-GROSSING U.S. CONCERT TOURS, 1996

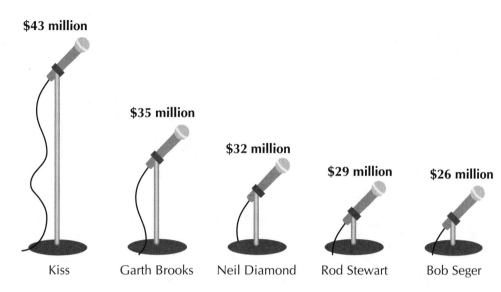

$43 million — Kiss
$35 million — Garth Brooks
$32 million — Neil Diamond
$29 million — Rod Stewart
$26 million — Bob Seger

Source: Based on statistics from *Amusement Business*

RHYTHM & BLUES PERFORMERS WITH THE MOST NO. 1 SINGLES

(Recording artists with the most number-one singles on the
Billboard Rhythm & Blues chart, since 1965)

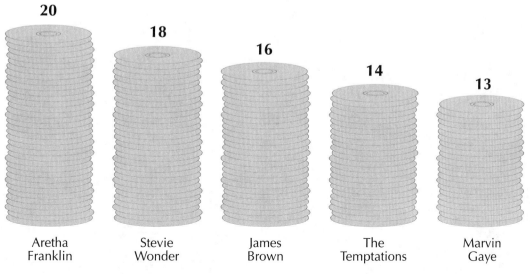

20 — Aretha Franklin
18 — Stevie Wonder
16 — James Brown
14 — The Temptations
13 — Marvin Gaye

Source: Based on statistics from *Billboard* magazine

3

POLITICS
AND
GOVERNMENT

THE GROWTH OF GOVERNMENT

Wherever they look, Americans see—or think they see—the growth of government. While it is true that local government employment has increased during the 1990s, the number of civilian federal employees has actually declined. Payrolls, however, have soared at all levels of government.

The public has demanded lower taxes and more fiscal prudence, forcing government officials to make major staff reductions. To further cut costs, obsolete programs, agencies, and departments have been consolidated or eliminated.

There has also been pressure to limit legislatures from mandating programs that provide funding without sufficient budgets. Mandated programs—covering education, Medicaid, welfare, and other areas—account for more than half of states' expenditures and for a large portion of local budgets. Since the 1970s, some 17 states have amended their constitutions or enacted statutes to limit their legislatures' ability to impose unfunded mandates on local governments. By the mid-1990s, many federal legislators were rallying to the cause, promising to limit Congress's ability to impose mandates on the states.

The "downsizing" of government promises to be a difficult and often explosive process. Decreasing government spending and size means not only a reduction in waste but also cutbacks in needed services and programs. It also means different groups in society will have to compete harder for fewer resources.

FINGERTIP FACTS

☛ In 1980, government employees—federal civilian plus state and local—totaled 16.2 million; state and local employees made up 82% of the total. In 1997, the number was 21.2 million, with state and local employees accounting for 80%.

☛ Total government revenues in 1999 were $ 1.742 trillion.

☛ Of the more than $1.56 trillion in revenues in 1998, a total of 48% came from personal/individual income taxes. Other revenue from taxes included social insurance taxes ($571 billion), and corporate income taxes ($198 billion).

☛ Between 1981-1989, the average annual deficit was about $167 billion. In 1997, it was just $22 billion.

☛ In 1980, state and local debt totaled about $336 billion, or $1,482 per capita. By 1996, this debt had grown to $447 billion, or $11,690 per capita.

☛ In 1980, the federal debt was $908 billion. By 1998, it had quadrupled, to $5.5 trillion.

☛ The Internal Revenue Service processed approximately 118 million individual income tax forms in 1998.

GOVERNMENT GROWTH, 1960–1997

(by total number of federal employees)

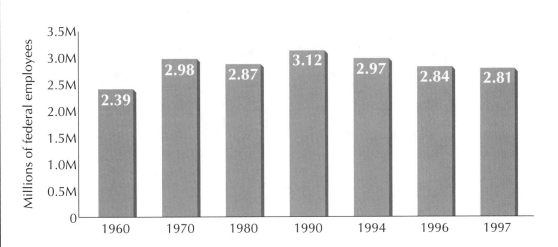

Source: Office of Management and Budget

GOVERNMENT BY THE PEOPLE, 1966–1997

While the number of federal employees has gone up modestly, per capita federal employment has also begun to rise again:

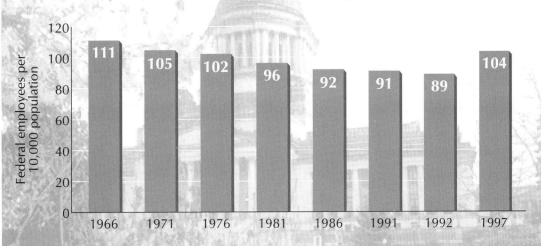

Note: Excludes post office and military
Source: U.S. Census Bureau

ANNUAL SALARIES OF FEDERAL OFFICIALS, 1998

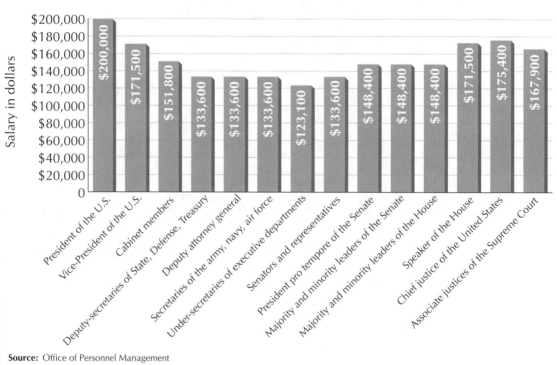

Salary in dollars

President of the U.S.	$200,000
Vice-President of the U.S.	$171,500
Cabinet members	$151,800
Deputy-secretaries of State, Defense, Treasury	$133,600
Deputy attorney general	$133,600
Secretaries of the army, navy, air force	$133,600
Under-secretaries of executive departments	$123,100
Senators and representatives	$133,600
President pro tempore of the Senate	$148,400
Majority and minority leaders of the Senate	$148,400
Majority and minority leaders of the House	$148,400
Speaker of the House	$171,500
Chief Justice of the United States	$175,400
Associate justices of the Supreme Court	$167,900

Source: Office of Personnel Management

U.S. WELFARE DECREASES, 1975 vs. 1997

After rising steadily since 1975, the average number of families receiving benefits began to decrease in 1997. Total state and federal spending on the U.S.'s primary welfare program, however, has risen by 31%. But when adjusted for inflation, the average family receives about $200 a month less.

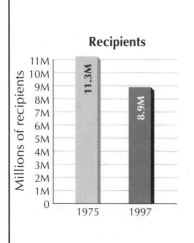

Recipients

Millions of recipients

- 1975: 11.3M
- 1997: 8.9M

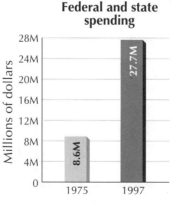

Federal and state spending

Millions of dollars

- 1975: 8.6M
- 1997: 27.7M

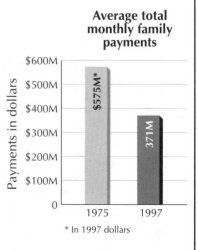

Average total monthly family payments

Payments in dollars

- 1975: $575M*
- 1997: 371M

* In 1997 dollars

Source: Office of Financial Management

WHERE THE FEDERAL GOVERNMENT GETS ITS MONEY, 1980 vs. 1998

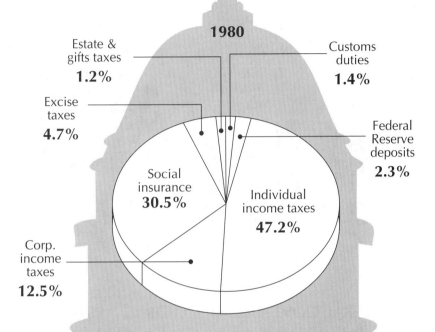

1980

Estate &
gifts taxes
1.2%

Customs
duties
1.4%

Excise
taxes
4.7%

Federal
Reserve
deposits
2.3%

Social
insurance
30.5%

Individual
income taxes
47.2%

Corp.
income
taxes
12.5%

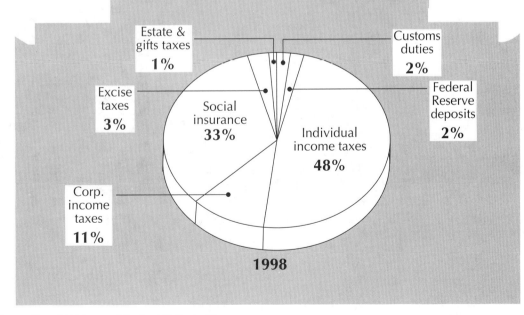

Estate &
gifts taxes
1%

Customs
duties
2%

Excise
taxes
3%

Federal
Reserve
deposits
2%

Social
insurance
33%

Individual
income taxes
48%

Corp.
income
taxes
11%

1998

Source: Financial Management Service, U.S. Dept. of Treasury

INTERNAL REVENUE GROSS COLLECTIONS, BY SOURCE, 1980 vs. 1996

(In billions; note: 1,000 billion = 1 trillion)

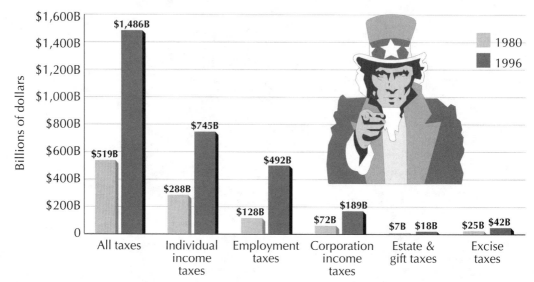

Legend:
- 1980
- 1996

Billions of dollars

	All taxes	Individual income taxes	Employment taxes	Corporation income taxes	Estate & gift taxes	Excise taxes
1980	$519B	$288B	$128B	$72B	$7B	$25B
1996	$1,486B	$745B	$492B	$189B	$18B	$42B

Source: Internal Revenue Service

FEDERAL GOVERNMENT SPENDING, 1998

(Total outlays: $1.65 trillion; note: 1,000 billion = 1 trillion)

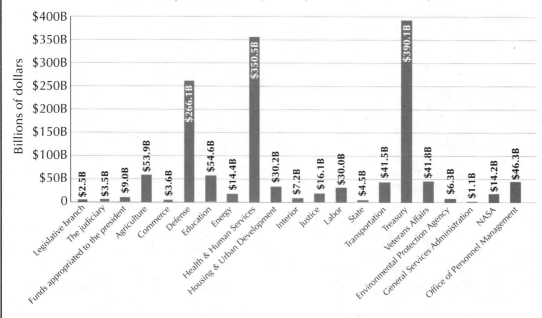

Billions of dollars

Legislative branch	$2.5B
The judiciary	$3.5B
Funds appropriated to the president	$9.0B
Agriculture	$53.9B
Commerce	$3.6B
Defense	$266.1B
Education	$54.6B
Energy	$14.4B
Health & Human Services	$350.5B
Housing & Urban Development	$30.2B
Interior	$7.2B
Justice	$16.1B
Labor	$30.0B
State	$4.5B
Transportation	$41.5B
Treasury	$390.1B
Veterans Affairs	$41.8B
Environmental Protection Agency	$6.3B
General Services Administration	$1.1B
NASA	$14.2B
Office of Personnel Management	$46.3B

Source: U.S. Office of Management and Budget, *Budget of the United States Government*

PROFILE: THE U.S. FEDERAL GOVERNMENT DOLLAR, 1999

(Note: 1,000 billion = 1 trillion)

Revenues: $1,742 billion

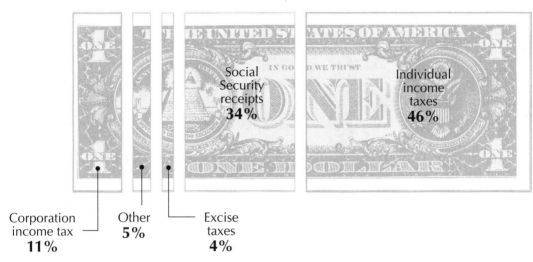

Social Security receipts **34%**

Individual income taxes **46%**

Corporation income tax **11%**

Other **5%**

Excise taxes **4%**

Outlays: $1,733 billion

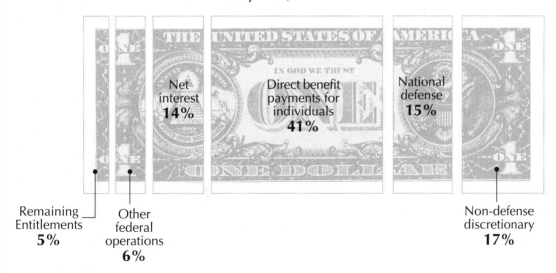

Net interest **14%**

Direct benefit payments for individuals **41%**

National defense **15%**

Remaining Entitlements **5%**

Other federal operations **6%**

Non-defense discretionary **17%**

Source: Office of Management and Budget

THE 1998 CLINTON BUDGET

(Billions of dollars projected for spending on each program or purpose)

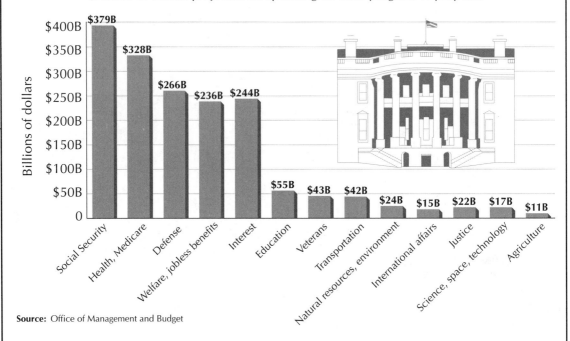

Billions of dollars

Social Security	$379B
Health, Medicare	$328B
Defense	$266B
Welfare, jobless benefits	$236B
Interest	$244B
Education	$55B
Veterans	$43B
Transportation	$42B
Natural resources, environment	$24B
International affairs	$15B
Justice	$22B
Science, space, technology	$17B
Agriculture	$11B

Source: Office of Management and Budget

U.S. FEDERAL BUDGET DEFICIT AND SURPLUS, 1975–2002

Billions of dollars

*Projected
Source: U.S. Treasury Dept. and Office of Management and Budget

STATE GOVERNMENT TAX COLLECTIONS, BY TYPE, 1970 vs. 1998

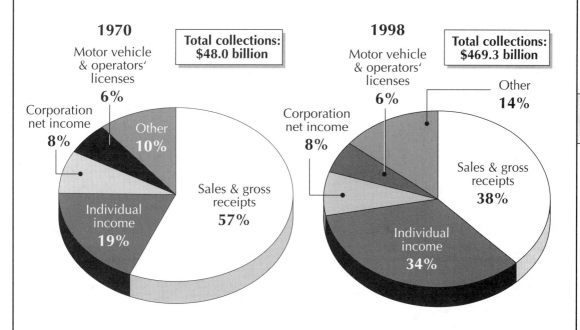

1970

Total collections:
$48.0 billion

Motor vehicle & operators' licenses
6%

Corporation net income
8%

Other
10%

Sales & gross receipts
57%

Individual income
19%

1998

Total collections:
$469.3 billion

Motor vehicle & operators' licenses
6%

Other
14%

Corporation net income
8%

Sales & gross receipts
38%

Individual income
34%

SALES TAX COLLECTIONS, BY TYPE, 1970 vs. 1998

(As percentage of total receipts)

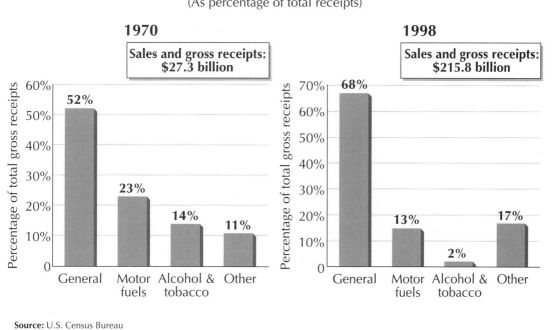

1970

Sales and gross receipts:
$27.3 billion

Percentage of total gross receipts

60%
52%
50%
40%
30%
23%
20%
14%
11%
10%
0

General   Motor fuels   Alcohol & tobacco   Other

1998

Sales and gross receipts:
$215.8 billion

Percentage of total gross receipts

70%
68%
60%
50%
40%
30%
20%
13%
17%
10%
2%
0

General   Motor fuels   Alcohol & tobacco   Other

Source: U.S. Census Bureau

STATE TAX COLLECTIONS PER CAPITA, 1998
(With rankings)

Top 10 states with highest tax collections

8. Washington
$1,997

7. Michigan
$2,080

6. Massachusetts
$2,175

4. Minnesota
$2,395

10. New York
$1,922

9. Wisconsin
$1,970

5. Delaware
$2,381

3. Connecticut
$2,491

1. Alaska
$2,659

2. Hawaii
$2,601

Top 10 states with lowest tax collections

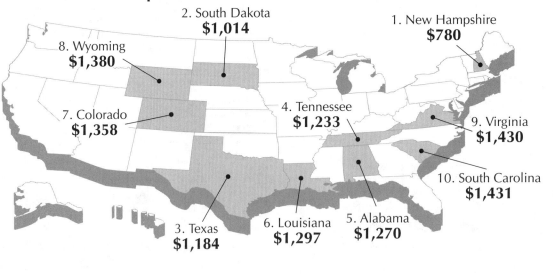

2. South Dakota
$1,014

1. New Hampshire
$780

8. Wyoming
$1,380

4. Tennessee
$1,233

7. Colorado
$1,358

9. Virginia
$1,430

10. South Carolina
$1,431

3. Texas
$1,184

6. Louisiana
$1,297

5. Alabama
$1,270

Source: U.S. Census Bureau

TOP 10 MOST EXPENSIVE CITIES, BY INCOME LEVEL, 1996

(As percentage of state and local taxes paid by a family of 4)

Family income: $25,000 per year

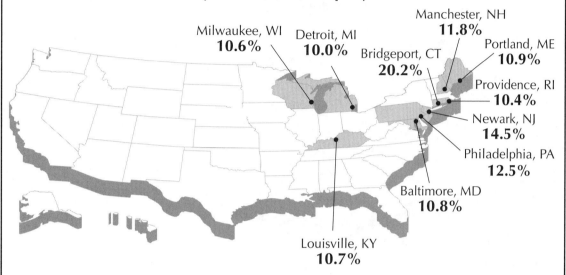

Manchester, NH
11.8%

Milwaukee, WI
10.6%

Detroit, MI
10.0%

Bridgeport, CT
20.2%

Portland, ME
10.9%

Providence, RI
10.4%

Newark, NJ
14.5%

Philadelphia, PA
12.5%

Baltimore, MD
10.8%

Louisville, KY
10.7%

Family income: $50,000 per year

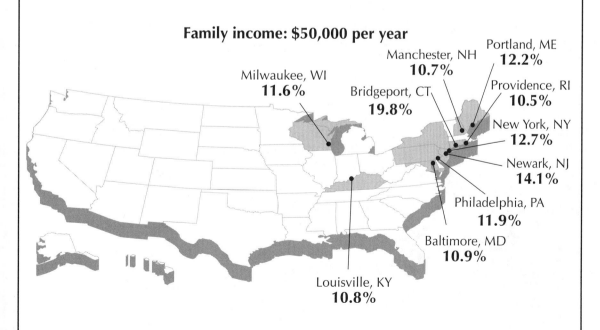

Portland, ME
12.2%

Manchester, NH
10.7%

Milwaukee, WI
11.6%

Bridgeport, CT
19.8%

Providence, RI
10.5%

New York, NY
12.7%

Newark, NJ
14.1%

Philadelphia, PA
11.9%

Baltimore, MD
10.9%

Louisville, KY
10.8%

TOP 10 MOST EXPENSIVE CITIES, BY INCOME LEVEL, 1996

(As percentage of state and local taxes paid by a family of 4)

Family income: $75,000 per year

Portland, ME
13.5%

Milwaukee, WI
12.1%

Detroit, MI
11.0%

Bridgeport, CT **22.2%**

Boston, MA
11.2%

Providence, RI
11.4%

New York, NY
14.5%

Newark, NJ
14.7%

Philadelphia, PA
11.8%

Louisville, KY
11.3%

Family income: $100,000 per year

Portland, ME
13.8%

Milwaukee, WI
12.1%

Bridgeport, CT
21.8%

Boston, MA
11.2%

Providence, RI
11.7%

New York, NY
15.0%

Newark, NJ
14.8%

Philadelphia, PA
11.5%

Baltimore, MD
11.3%

Louisville,KY
11.4%

Source: Government of the District of Columbia

GROWTH OF AFRICAN-AMERICAN ELECTED OFFICIALS
(Number of African-American officials elected since the passage of the Voting Rights Act in 1965)

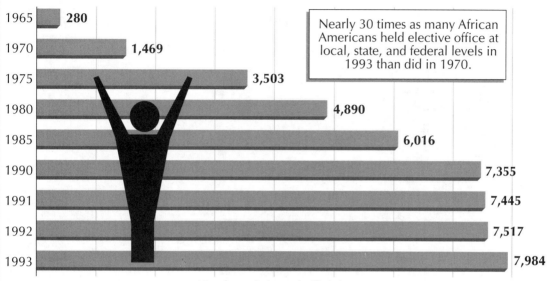

Year	Number
1965	280
1970	1,469
1975	3,503
1980	4,890
1985	6,016
1990	7,355
1991	7,445
1992	7,517
1993	7,984

> Nearly 30 times as many African Americans held elective office at local, state, and federal levels in 1993 than did in 1970.

Number of elected officials

Source: Joint Center for Political and Economic Studies

THE RISE OF WOMEN IN CONGRESS, 1979–1999

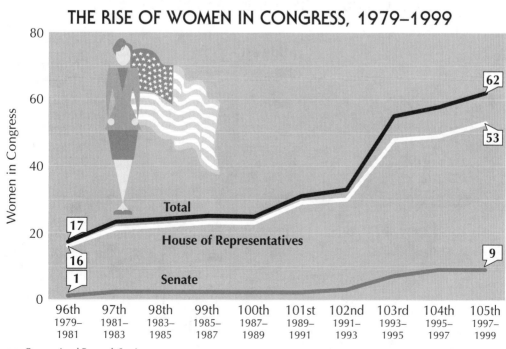

Women in Congress

Total — 62
House of Representatives — 53
Senate — 9

17, 16, 1

| 96th 1979–1981 | 97th 1981–1983 | 98th 1983–1985 | 99th 1985–1987 | 100th 1987–1989 | 101st 1989–1991 | 102nd 1991–1993 | 103rd 1993–1995 | 104th 1995–1997 | 105th 1997–1999 |

Source: Congressional Research Service

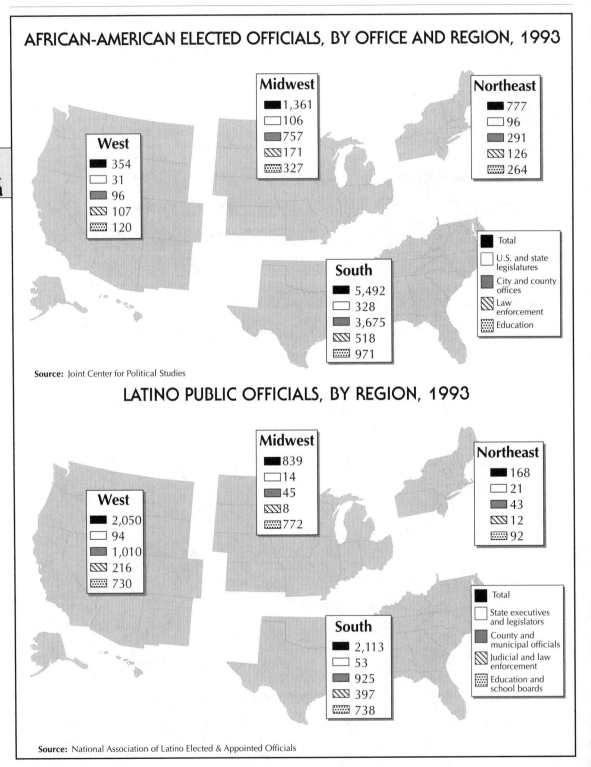

AFRICAN-AMERICAN ELECTED OFFICIALS, BY OFFICE AND REGION, 1993

Midwest
- 1,361
- 106
- 757
- 171
- 327

Northeast
- 777
- 96
- 291
- 126
- 264

West
- 354
- 31
- 96
- 107
- 120

South
- 5,492
- 328
- 3,675
- 518
- 971

- Total
- U.S. and state legislatures
- City and county offices
- Law enforcement
- Education

Source: Joint Center for Political Studies

LATINO PUBLIC OFFICIALS, BY REGION, 1993

Midwest
- 839
- 14
- 45
- 8
- 772

Northeast
- 168
- 21
- 43
- 12
- 92

West
- 2,050
- 94
- 1,010
- 216
- 730

South
- 2,113
- 53
- 925
- 397
- 738

- Total
- State executives and legislators
- County and municipal officials
- Judicial and law enforcement
- Education and school boards

Source: National Association of Latino Elected & Appointed Officials

WOMEN HOLDING PUBLIC OFFICES, BY OFFICE & STATE, 1999

(Top 10 states with highest percentage of women in legislature)

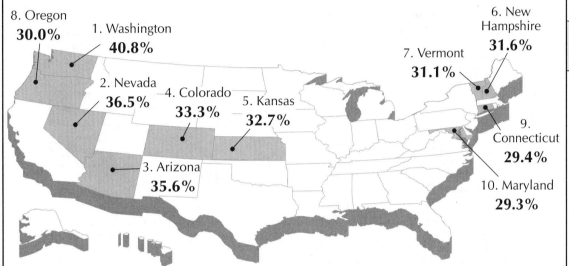

8. Oregon
30.0%

1. Washington
40.8%

2. Nevada
36.5%

4. Colorado
33.3%

5. Kansas
32.7%

3. Arizona
35.6%

6. New Hampshire
31.6%

7. Vermont
31.1%

9. Connecticut
29.4%

10. Maryland
29.3%

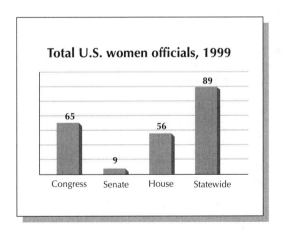

Total U.S. women officials, 1999

65	9	56	89
Congress	Senate	House	Statewide

Source: Center for the American Woman and Politics, Eagleton Institute of Politics, Rutgers University

VOTING AND ELECTIONS

In 1996, Bill Clinton became one of only three presidents to win a presidential election with less than 50% of the popular vote. Though he failed to receive a strong and clear "mandate" from the nation's voters, he did improve his popular vote percentage from 48% in 1992 to 49.2% in 1996. Republican candidate Bob Dole finished the race with 40.8% of the popular vote, and Independent third-party candidate H. Ross Perot came away with less than half of his 1992 total: only 8.5%. (Perot received 19% of the popular vote in 1992.)

Two years before the election, in 1994, President Clinton had been on shaky ground. Low approval ratings plagued him, as did Republican Speaker of the House Newt Gingrich, who successfully led the GOP's fight to gain control of Congress in 1994. But the years leading up to the '96 election turned things around. The economy continued to improve, strides were made in areas of health care and jobs, and the United States maintained its position as world leader and peacekeeper through appropriate displays of firepower and diplomacy.

The two pivotal issues of the 1996 election turned out to be the economy and Medicare/Social Security. Because the job market was expanding, the incumbent reaped the benefits. Senior citizens—whose major concern was for Medicare and Social Security—were scared by Dole's perceived plans to cut such programs.

The greatest disappointment of the 1996 election was probably the dismal voter turnout. Only 48.8% of all eligible voters showed up at the polls, marking a new low that had previously held for 72 years.

FINGERTIP FACTS

- More women (52% of voters) than men voted in the election of 1996. The percentage of male voters, however, increased from 46% in 1992 to 48% in 1996.

- Overall, the percentage of white voters was down 4% in 1996 from 87% in 1992. The percentage of black voters, however, increased from 9% in 1992 to 10% in 1996. The category classified as "other" rose notably from 4% to 7% in 1996.

- Electoral votes in 1996 broke down almost identically to the breakdown of 1992, with Clinton receiving only 9 additional votes. In 1996, Clinton lost South Carolina, Colorado, and Montana, but gained Florida and Arizona.

- By age group, 18–29 year olds had the lowest voter turnout in 1996, with only 33% of that eligible population showing up at the polls. By race, blacks had the worst attendance record, with only 35% of the eligible reporting. Of all income levels, the lowest turnout came from voters in the lowest income bracket, making less than $20,000 per year.

- California and neighboring Nevada were the worst states in voter turnout, with less than 40% of voters casting ballots. Among the best, with turnout of 60% or better, were Maine, Montana, Wyoming, South Dakota, and Minnesota.

- 1996 marked the first time since 1928 that a GOP majority was maintained in Congress for two consecutive elections.

ISSUE BREAKDOWNS OF THE VOTE, 1996

Vote of those who listed each of these top 6 issues as most important:

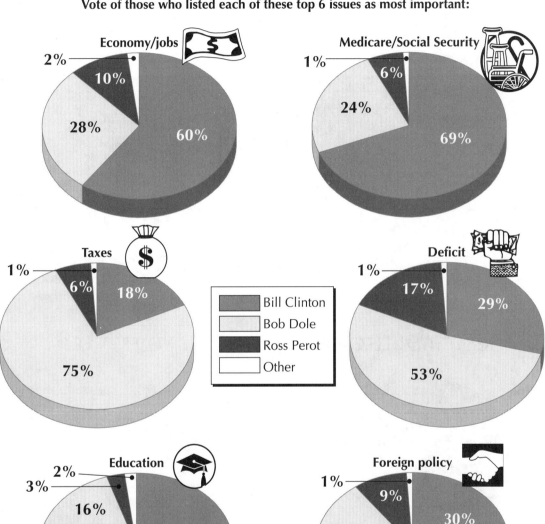

Economy/jobs
2%
10%
28%
60%

Medicare/Social Security
1%
6%
24%
69%

Taxes
1%
6%
18%
75%

Legend:
- Bill Clinton
- Bob Dole
- Ross Perot
- Other

Deficit
1%
17%
29%
53%

Education
2%
3%
16%
79%

Foreign policy
1%
9%
30%
60%

Source: Election Day exit polls.

ISSUES VOTERS CARED ABOUT, 1996

(As percentage of voters surveyed and their most important issues)

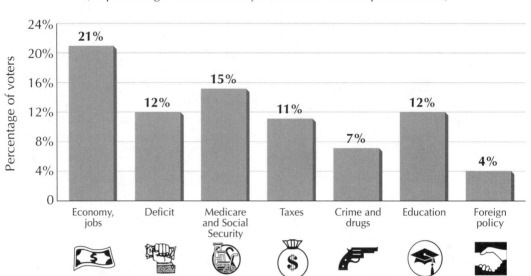

Source: Election Day exit poll; data from *Newsweek*, Nov. 18, 1996.

PRESIDENTIAL ELECTION 1996: WHO THE VOTERS WERE

(Percentages of people who voted)

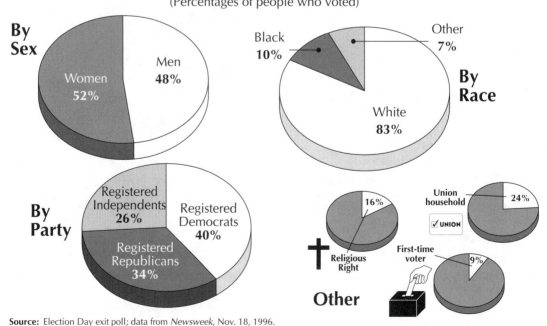

Source: Election Day exit poll; data from *Newsweek*, Nov. 18, 1996.

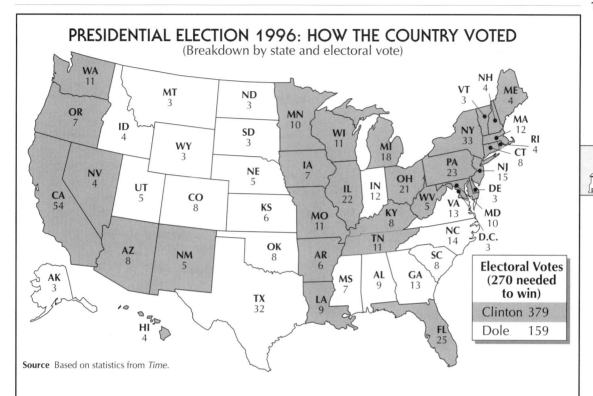

PRESIDENTIAL ELECTION 1996: HOW THE COUNTRY VOTED
(Breakdown by state and electoral vote)

WA 11	
MT 3	ND 3
OR 7	
ID 4	MN 10
WY 3	SD 3
	WI 11
	NE 5
NV 4	IA 7
UT 5	MI 18
CA 54	IL 22
CO 8	IN 12
	OH 21
KS 6	PA 23
	KY 8
AZ 8	MO 11
NM 5	WV 5
	VA 13
	NC 14
OK 8	
	AR 6
	TN 11
AK 3	MS 7
TX 32	AL 9
	GA 13
HI 4	LA 9
	SC 8
	FL 25

NH 4
VT 3
ME 4
NY 33
MA 12
RI 4
CT 8
NJ 15
DE 3
MD 10
D.C. 3

**Electoral Votes
(270 needed
to win)**

Clinton	379
Dole	159

Source Based on statistics from *Time*.

VOTER TURNOUT, 1960–1996

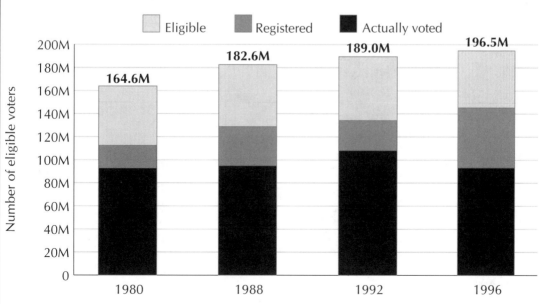

Legend: ☐ Eligible ▨ Registered ■ Actually voted

- 1980: 164.6M
- 1988: 182.6M
- 1992: 189.0M
- 1996: 196.5M

Y-axis: Number of eligible voters (0 to 200M)

Source: Based on data from *Time* and Election Day

1996 PRESIDENTIAL ELECTION ANALYSIS
(Percentage of voters who supported each candidate, by selected characteristics)

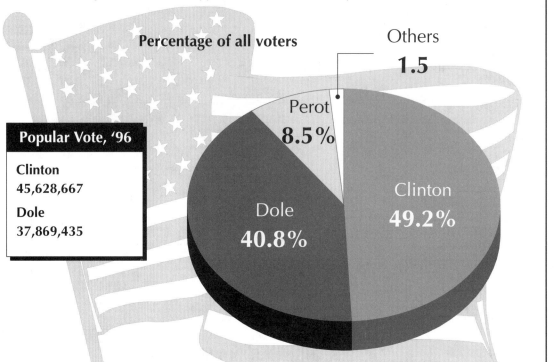

Percentage of all voters

Others
1.5

Perot
8.5%

Dole
40.8%

Clinton
49.2%

Popular Vote, '96

Clinton
45,628,667

Dole
37,869,435

Percentage of voters by age group

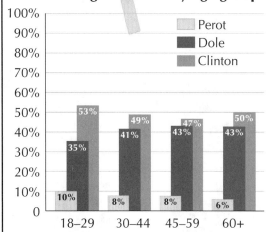

Legend: Perot, Dole, Clinton

- 18–29: 10%, 35%, 53%
- 30–44: 8%, 41%, 49%
- 45–59: 8%, 43%, 47%
- 60+: 6%, 43%, 50%

Percentage of voters by sex

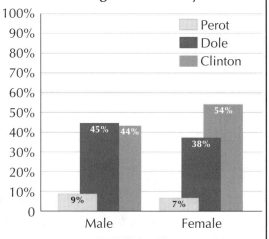

Legend: Perot, Dole, Clinton

- Male: 9%, 45%, 44%
- Female: 7%, 38%, 54%

Source: Based on data from *USA Today*; *Time*.

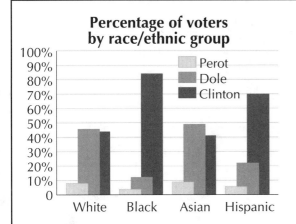

Percentage of voters by race/ethnic group

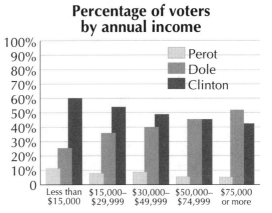

Percentage of voters by annual income

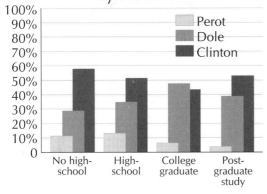

Percentage of voters by education

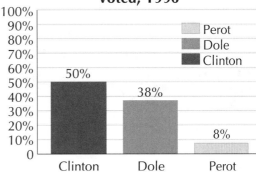

How the elderly voted, 1996

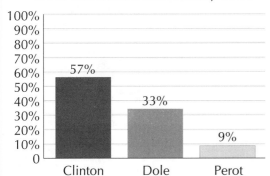

How the Moderates voted, 1996

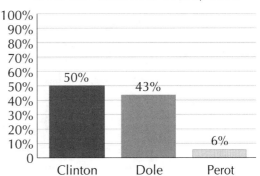

How the Catholics voted, 1996

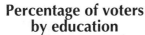

Source: Based on statistics from *Time*; USA Today; Associated Press; voter research and surveys.

LOW TURNOUT VOTER PROFILE, BY SELECTED CHARACTERISTICS

The percentage of eligible population that voted in 1996:

By sex

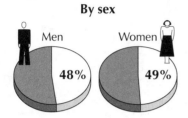

Men 48%

Women 49%

By age

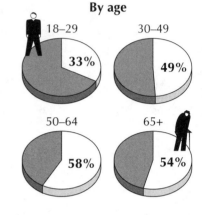

18–29 33%

30–49 49%

50–64 58%

65+ 54%

By race

White 51%

Black 35%

Other 38%

By annual income

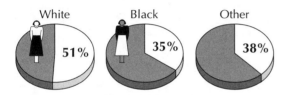

$75,000 or more 62%

$50,000–$74,999 57%

$30,000–$49,999 51%

$20,000–$29,999 45%

Less than $20,000 39%

By politics

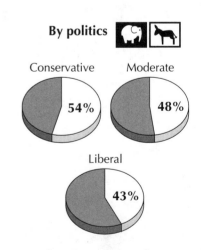

Conservative 54%

Moderate 48%

Liberal 43%

Source: Based on data from *Vital Statistics on American Politics*.

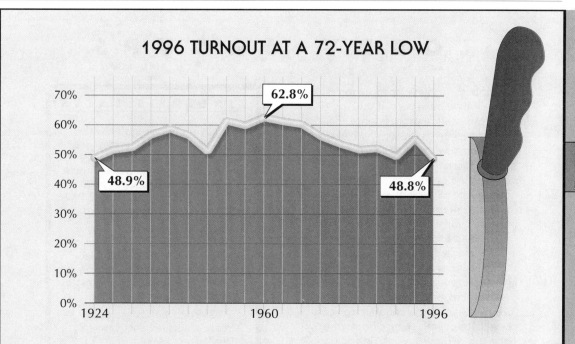

1996 TURNOUT AT A 72-YEAR LOW

62.8%

48.9%

48.8%

Source: Committee for the Study of the American Electorate

NATIONAL PROFILE OF VOTER TURNOUT
Every state had a lower turnout in 1996 than in the 1992 presidential election.
Following is a state-by-state look at the percentage of voting-age population that
actually voted, and the percentage point difference from 1992:

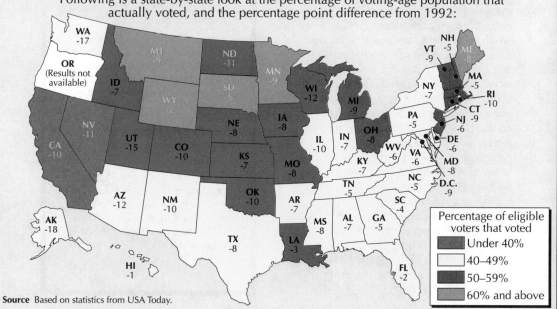

WA -17
OR (Results not available)
MT -9
ND -11
MN -9
ID -7
SD -6
WY -2
WI -12
MI -9
VT -9
NH -5
ME -8
NY -7
MA -5
RI -10
CT -9
NJ -6
PA -5
DE -6
NV -11
UT -15
CO -10
NE -8
IA -8
IL -10
IN -7
OH -8
WV -6
VA -6
MD -8
D.C. -9
CA -10
KS -7
MO -8
KY -7
NC -5
AZ -12
NM -10
OK -10
AR -7
TN -5
SC -4
AK -18
MS -8
AL -7
GA -5
TX -8
LA -3
HI -1
FL -2

Percentage of eligible voters that voted
- Under 40%
- 40–49%
- 50–59%
- 60% and above

Source Based on statistics from USA Today.

L O B B Y   G R O U P S

Even though lobbies—special-interest groups—have been part of the American political process since the nation's beginnings, citizens have always viewed them with ambivalence. While these organizations exist primarily to influence the opinions of legislators and other public officials, they can also serve the public interest, supplying valuable, practical information to busy legislators.

Today, a broad range of interests are represented by lobbies. Some of the major ones are corporations, labor, agriculture, educational and health organizations, environmental groups, foreign political and economic concerns, consumers, senior citizens, the poor, and religious groups. In addition, there are single-issue groups—such as the National Rifle Association—that lobby public officials on specific concerns, such as gun control.

The number of lobby groups in the U.S. has soared. One segment that has shown particularly strong growth is political action committees (PACs), which raise money and make contributions to candidates running for political office. PAC contributions to congressional candidates—especially incumbents—now account for a significant portion of every candidate's campaign chest. There is much evidence that money flows the fastest and most generously to candidates who share the views of well-financed PACs and influential other lobby groups. There is also much suspicion that, when it comes time to vote in Congress, these groups expect favors from elected officials in return for their contributions. During 1997-1998, PACs contributed $206.8 million to candidates, with the most going to incumbents.

FINGERTIP FACTS

☞ Lobbyists must register with Congress and file quarterly reports disclosing their clients, their objectives, and the amount of money they receive and spend. The reports are published in the Congressional Record.

☞ PACs don't always use their money to directly benefit candidates. In the 1995-1996 election, PACs spent $3.8 million in an effort to persuade voters not to elect certain candidates.

☞ PACs contribute significantly more to incumbents than to challengers. About 82% of contributions went to politicans running for re-election in 1996.

☞ PACs are a growth industry. In 1980, there were 2,551 PACs, of which 1,206 were corporate. By 1996, the number of PACs had reached 4,528, of which 1,836 were corporate.

☞ Some members of Congress have created their own PACs. Among the many fund-raising organizations created by Newt Gingrich (R-GA) is GOPAC, which raised $7.8 million from 1991 to 1994. Thirty-three of the 73 new Republicans in the 104th Congress were recruited and trained by GOPAC.

☞ Ralph Nader's group Public Citizen found that of 300 former members of the U.S. House of Representatives, 177 of them (59%) had taken lucrative lobbying-related jobs.

POLITICAL ACTION COMMITTEES, 1980–1996

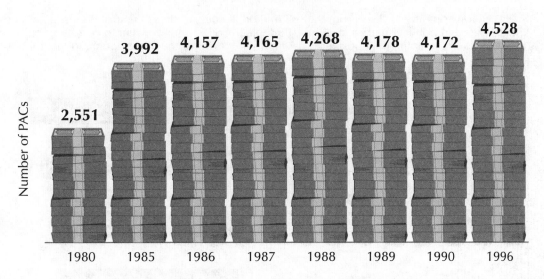

Number of PACs

Year	Number
1980	2,551
1985	3,992
1986	4,157
1987	4,165
1988	4,268
1989	4,178
1990	4,172
1996	4,528

Source: Federal Election Commission

PAC-ING BIG GUN MONEY

National Rifle Association PAC contributions to U.S. House members who favored and opposed the assault-weapon ban that narrowly passed:

To members opposing the ban:
Total: $1,161,876

**Average:
$5,429**

To members favoring the ban:
Total: $80,895

**Average:
$375**

Source: *Capital Eye: A Close Look at Money in Politics*

TOP 10 U.S. PAC SPENDERS, 1998

Political action committees dished out $206.8 million in special-interest contributions to favored legislators and political parties in 1997–1998. Nearly $158 million went to congressional candidates, up 2% over the previous period, with three-fourths of the money going to incumbents:

Association of Trial Lawyers of America	$1,730,300
American Federation of State, County, and Municipal Employees	$1,617,350
Democratic, Republican, Independent Voter Education Committee	$1,485,450
Electrical Workers Committee	$1,422,145
National Association of Realtors	$1,268,718
National Association of Home Builders	$1,258,240
American Federation of Teachers Committee on Political Education	$1,229,650
American Medical Association	$1,184,601
Dealers Election Action Committee of the National Automobile Dealers Assoc.	$1,159,675
United Auto Workers	$1,140,710

Source: Federal Election Commission

HEALTHY PAC CONTRIBUTIONS: SOURCES AND RECIPIENTS

Political action committees (PACs) that represent health and insurance industries upped their contributions to congressional members in 1993—just as debate heated up over President Clinton's health care reforms.

Top givers: political action committees, 1991 vs. 1993

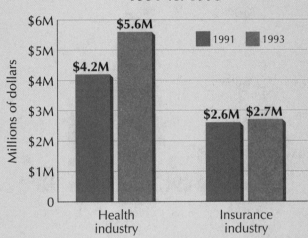

Millions of dollars

- $6M
- $5.6M (1993)
- $5M
- $4.2M (1991)
- $4M
- $3M
- $2.6M $2.7M
- $2M
- $1M
- 0

Health industry   Insurance industry

■ 1991 ■ 1993

Top PAC recipients 1997-1998

Senate

- $1,526,477 Thomas A. Daschle, D–SD
- $1,331,230 Alfonse M. D'Amato, R–NY
- $1,263,002 Christopher S. Bond, R–MO
- $1,224,053 John Breaux, D–LA
- $1,112,771 Duncan M. Faircloth, R–NC
- $1,054,793 Arlen Specter, R–PA
- $985,415 Richard Shelby, R–AL
- $956,139 Christopher Dodd, D–CT
- $930,007 Paul Coverdell, R–GA
- $875,812 Barbara Boxer, D–CA

House

- $1,033,279 Richard Gephart, D–MO
- $766,825 Martin Frost, D–TX
- $681,026 Newt Gingrich, R–GA
- $661,344 Nancy Johnson, R–CT
- $620,662 John Dingell, D–MI
- $611,178 Lois Capps, D–CA
- $600,890 Thomas Delay, R–TX
- $562,325 Charles Stenholm, D–TX
- $533,669 Thomas J. Bliley, Jr., R–VA
- $500,629 Vito J. Fossella, R–NY

Source: CAC

PAC CONTRIBUTIONS TO CONGRESSIONAL CAMPAIGNS, 1995–1996

(By political party and office-seeker experience)

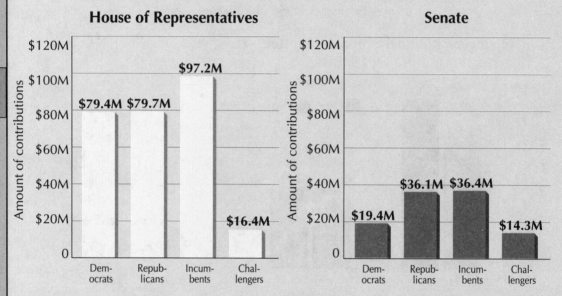

House of Representatives

Amount of contributions

- $120M
- $100M — **$97.2M**
- $80M — **$79.4M** **$79.7M**
- $60M
- $40M
- $20M — **$16.4M**
- 0

Democrats | Republicans | Incumbents | Challengers

Senate

Amount of contributions

- $120M
- $100M
- $80M
- $60M
- $40M — **$36.1M** **$36.4M**
- $20M — **$19.4M** — **$14.3M**
- 0

Democrats | Republicans | Incumbents | Challengers

Source: U.S. Federal Election Commission

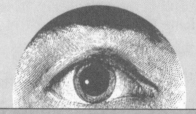

LOBBIES AND PACs: AT A GLANCE

☞ Registered lobbyists per U.S. senator: **77**; per House member: **25**

☞ State with most lobbyists per state legislator: **Arizona, 28**; fewest: **New Hampshire, 0.5**

☞ PAC that gave most money to congressional candidates in 1990: **Realtors, $3.1 million**

☞ Americans surveyed who say they are less likely to vote for a congressional candidate who accepts PAC money: **47%**

☞ Number of PACs in 1974—the year they became legal: **608**; in 1996: **4,528**

☞ Americans who rank lobbyists' ethics as excellent: **1%**

☞ Voters surveyed who think that Democrats pay more attention to lobbyists: **16%**; Republicans: **53%**

☞ Year that paid lobbyists began work on Capitol Hill: **1829**; year that federal law regulated lobbying: **1946**

Source: *U.S. News & World Report*

NAFTA VOTE, BY PARTY

The North American Free Trade Agreement
took effect on January 1, 1994.
This is how Congress voted:

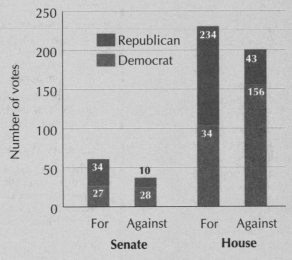

Source: Congressional Record

HOW SUPPORT FOR NAFTA WAS DIVIDED

An analysis of announced votes on NAFTA shows deep divisions within the parties, and among congressional coalitions. Even new members, expected to tilt heavily against NAFTA, were split:

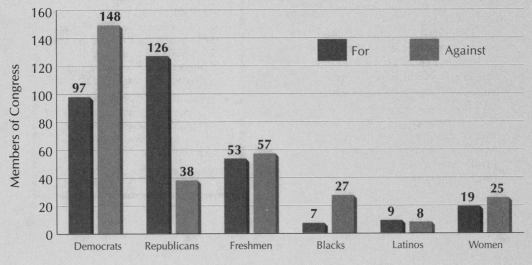

Source: Statistics based on *USA Today* research

THE FACE OF CONGRESS

As a result of the 1994 midterm elections, Congress had a dramatically new look: For the first time since 1954, Republicans were in the majority in both houses. In 1998, they controlled the Senate by 55 to 45, and the House of Representatives by 228 to 206 (204 Democrats and one Independent).

From a historical perspective, however, the most striking changes of 1998 were found in the race, gender, and class makeup of America's representatives. The 105th Congress looked more like the nation's real population than did the First Congress, which met in 1789-1790 and which contained only white males.

From an economic and social class standpoint, however, the Congress in 1998 looked quite similar to that of 1789. Most members—then as well as now—are quite wealthy. The percentage of millionaires in Congress far exceeds that in the U.S. population as a whole (and, historically, always has). Many nominees are also wealthy, perhaps reflecting the skyrocketing cost of running for office.

The 105th Congress included 86 first-term members in the House, 73 of them Republicans, and 11 new Republicans in the Senate. Nine women—a record—were seated, up from 8 in the previous Congress. Four senators belonged to minority groups: one African American, and 2 Asian Americans. In the House, there were 53 women, 39 blacks, 21 Latinos, and 4 Asian Americans.

FINGERTIP FACTS

- African Americans constitute 12.7% of the U.S. population. Black membership of the 105th Congress was 9% of the House, 1% of the Senate.

- Women, who constitute more than 50% of the U.S. population, made up 9% of the Senate and 12% of the House in the 105th Congress, 1997-1998.

- When congressional elections occur in years that do not have a presidential election, the president's party usually loses seats. In 1998, however, democrats actually gained 5 seats. This democratic gain may have helped President Clinton avoid impeachment.

- Once in office, the financial rewards are great. Most members of Congress earn $133,600 a year. The Senate's president pro tempore and the majority and minority leaders each earn $148,400, as do the majority and minority leaders of the House. The speaker of the House earns $171,500. All members of Congress are given generous allowances for expenses and staff.

- Although less than 1% of the American population are millionaires, 28% of senators and 17% of representatives have at least $1 million.

PERCENTAGE OF MILLIONAIRES IN CONGRESS

(As percentage of each group)

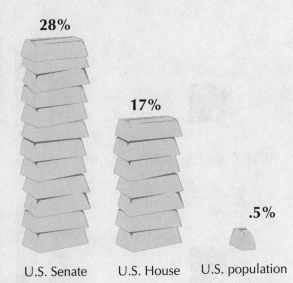

28%

17%

.5%

U.S. Senate   U.S. House   U.S. population

Source: Internal Revenue Service, Congress

MINORITY REPRESENTATION IN CONGRESS

Since the Voting Rights Act was passed in 1965, minority membership in Congress has never matched the minority population of the U.S. Here's how the makeup of Congress compared with the U.S. population in 1997:

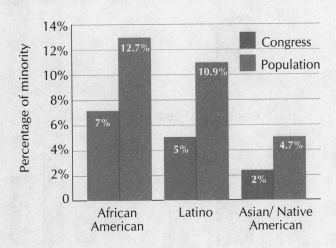

Source: Congressional Quarterly; U.S. Census Bureau

WHO MAKES UP CONGRESS? SELECTED CHARACTERISTICS, 1977–1994

95th Congress, 1977—Representatives

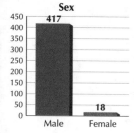

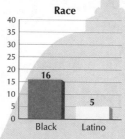

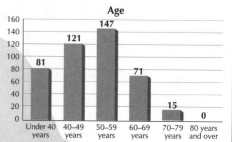

97th Congress, 1981—Representatives

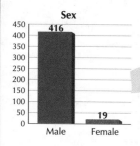

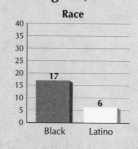

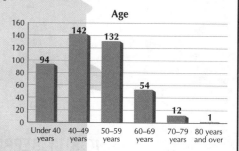

101st Congress, 1989—Representatives

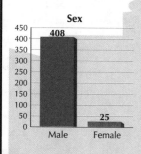

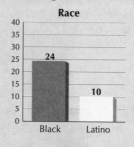

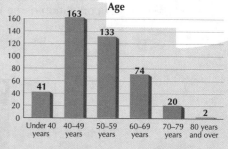

103rd Congress, 1994—Representatives

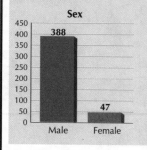

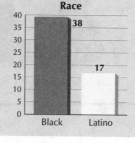

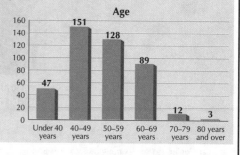

95th Congress, 1977—Senators

Sex

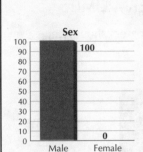

Male	Female
100	0

Race

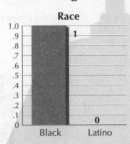

Black	Latino
1	0

Age

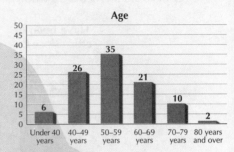

Under 40 years	40–49 years	50–59 years	60–69 years	70–79 years	80 years and over
6	26	35	21	10	2

97th Congress, 1981—Senators

Sex

Male	Female
98	2

Race

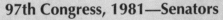

Black	Latino
0	0

Age

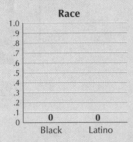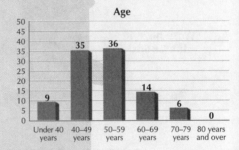

Under 40 years	40–49 years	50–59 years	60–69 years	70–79 years	80 years and over
9	35	36	14	6	0

101st Congress, 1989—Senators

Sex

Male	Female
98	2

Race

Black	Latino
0	0

Age

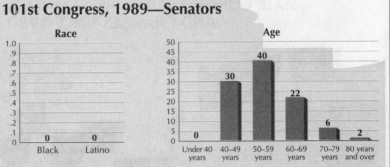

Under 40 years	40–49 years	50–59 years	60–69 years	70–79 years	80 years and over
0	30	40	22	6	2

103rd Congress, 1994—Senators

Sex

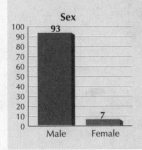

Male	Female
93	7

Race

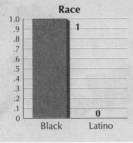

Black	Latino
1	0

Age

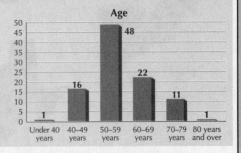

Under 40 years	40–49 years	50–59 years	60–69 years	70–79 years	80 years and over
1	16	48	22	11	1

Source: U.S. Census Bureau; *Congressional Directory*

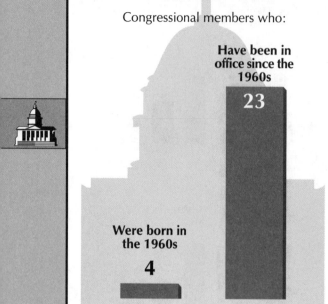

THE AGE OF CONGRESS

Congressional members who:

Have been in office since the 1960s

23

Were born in the 1960s

4

Source: *Congressional Quarterly*

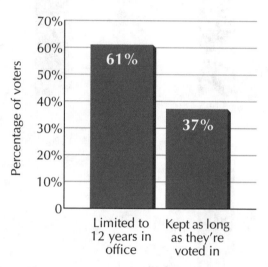

HOW AMERICANS FEEL ABOUT TERM LIMITS

Members of Congress should be:

Percentage of voters

70%
60%
50%
40%
30%
20%
10%
0

61%

37%

Limited to 12 years in office

Kept as long as they're voted in

Source: MRCI

STATE CONGRESSIONAL REPRESENTATION, 1990, AND CHANGES SINCE 1980

88
Northeast (-7)

105
Midwest (-8)

93
West (+8)

149
South (+7)

WA 9 (+1)
MT 1 (-1)
ND 1
MN 8
WI 9
VT 1
NH 2
ME 2
OR 5
ID 2
WY 1
SD 1
MI 16 (-2)
NY 31 (-3)
MA 10 (-1)
RI 2
CT 2
NE 2
NE 3
IA 5 (-1)
IL 20 (-2)
IN 10
OH 19 (-2)
PA 21 (-2)
NJ 13 (-1)
UT 3
CO 6
KS 4 (-1)
MO 9
WV 3 (+11)
KY 6 (-1)
VA 11 (+1)
MD 8
DE 1
CA 52
AZ 6 (+1)
NM 3
OK 6
AR 4
TN
NC 12
SC 6
AK 1
HI 2
TX 30
LA 7 (-1)
MS 5
AL 7
GA 11
FL 23

Change in representation (Number of changes in parentheses)

Loss (13)
No change
(29)

Source: U.S. Census Bureau

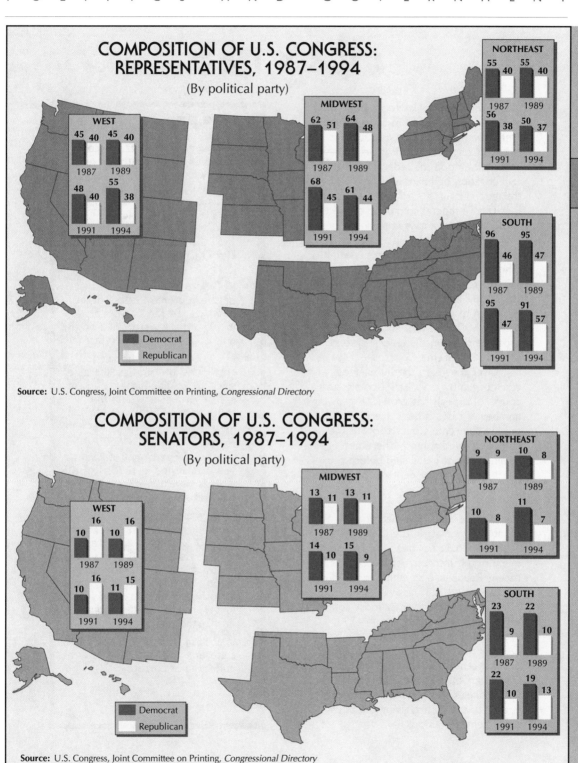

COMPOSITION OF U.S. CONGRESS: REPRESENTATIVES, 1987–1994

(By political party)

NORTHEAST

55 / 40	55 / 40
1987	1989
56 / 38	50 / 37
1991	1994

WEST

45 / 40	45 / 40
1987	1989
48 / 40	55 / 38
1991	1994

MIDWEST

62 / 51	64 / 48
1987	1989
68 / 45	61 / 44
1991	1994

SOUTH

96 / 46	95 / 47
1987	1989
95 / 47	91 / 57
1991	1994

■ Democrat
□ Republican

Source: U.S. Congress, Joint Committee on Printing, *Congressional Directory*

COMPOSITION OF U.S. CONGRESS: SENATORS, 1987–1994

(By political party)

NORTHEAST

9 / 9	10 / 8
1987	1989
10 / 8	11 / 7
1991	1994

WEST

10 / 16	10 / 16
1987	1989
10 / 16	11 / 15
1991	1994

MIDWEST

13 / 11	13 / 11
1987	1989
14 / 10	15 / 9
1991	1994

SOUTH

23 / 9	22 / 10
1987	1989
22 / 10	19 / 13
1991	1994

■ Democrat
□ Republican

Source: U.S. Congress, Joint Committee on Printing, *Congressional Directory*

J U S T I C E

Most civil and criminal litigation is begun and determined in state courts. Only when the U.S. Constitution and Acts of Congress specifically confer jurisdiction upon the federal courts may civil litigation be heard and decided by the federal courts.

The 94 federal courts that have the authority to try a case initially and pass judgment are the U.S. district courts. One or more of these courts is established in every state as well as in Washington, D.C. and the U.S. territories. Appeals from the district courts are taken to courts of appeals, of which there are 13. The final and highest appellate court in the federal system is the U.S. Supreme Court.

Over the years, the number of cases begun by U.S. district courts and courts of appeals has grown. A growing number of cases is being filed before the U.S. Supreme Court, too, but the number argued annually there has declined. Most cases filed before the Supreme Court are denied, dismissed, or withdrawn.

The composition and political leanings of the courts have become issues of intense interest in the U.S. The Supreme Court has been the focus of much of this interest. Appointments by recent Republican administrations gave the Supreme Court, as well as the other federal courts, their most conservative ideology in decades. In 1993, President Bill Clinton became the first Democratic president in more than a quarter century to appoint new Supreme Court justices. He named Ruth Bader Ginsberg and Stephen G. Breyer to the Court, giving the body a more centrist outlook.

FINGERTIP FACTS

- Almost all of the 107 members of the Supreme Courts have been white Christian males. The first Jew to sit on the court, Louis Brandeis, was appointed in 1916. The first black, Thurgood Marshall, joined the Court in 1967. The first woman, Sandra Day O'Connor, was appointed in 1981.

- In 1980, there were 5,144 cases on the Supreme Court docket, of which 154 (2.9%) were argued. In 1997, there were 7,602 on the docket and 90 (1%) were argued.

- In 1997 the prison population grew 5.1%, the smallest increase since 1990. The highest percentage of sentences was in the south with 44%, followed by the midwest with 22%, the west with 20%, and the northeast with 15%.

- The U.S. Department of Justice was established in 1870. It is the world's largest law firm, with 120,104 employees in 1998.

- In 1996, nearly 11.1 million people were arrested in the U.S. Of these, 2.1 million were arrested for serious crimes (such as murder, rape, robbery, larceny, and arson); 9.0 million were arrested for other crimes (including fraud, forgery, vandalism, drug abuse, drunkenness, and gambling).

- In 1995, a total of 438 federal, 61 state, and 191 local officials were convicted of corruption.

SEX AND RACE OF U.S. FEDERAL JUDGES

There are 837 federal judgeships, including the Supreme Court; 88 of those are vacant:

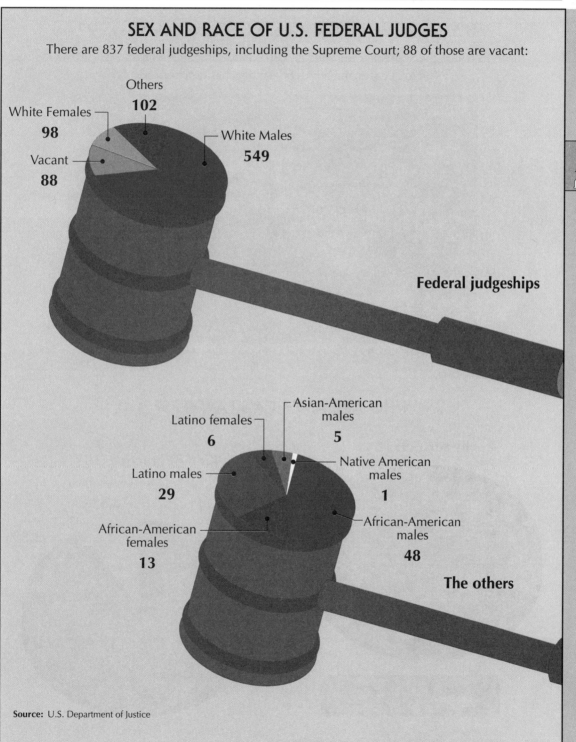

Others
102

White Females
98

Vacant
88

White Males
549

Federal judgeships

Asian-American males
5

Latino females
6

Native American males
1

Latino males
29

African-American females
13

African-American males
48

The others

Source: U.S. Department of Justice

U.S. SUPREME COURT CASES DECLINE, 1982–1997

In 1996–1997, the Supreme Court decided 80 cases, compared with 151 in 1982–1983. The total cases argued each year also has dropped sharply:

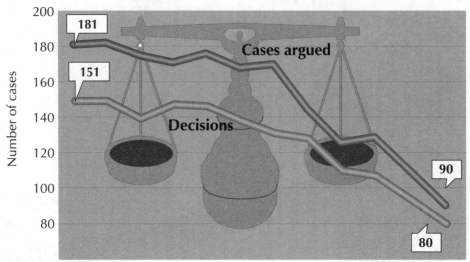

Number of cases

181

151

Cases argued

Decisions

90

80

1982–1983 1983–1984 1984–1985 1985–1986 1986–1987 1987–1988 1988–1989 1989–1990 1990–1991 1991–1992 1992–1993 1996–1997

Source: The Supreme Court

WHO ARE AMERICA'S LAWYERS?

By sex (1991)

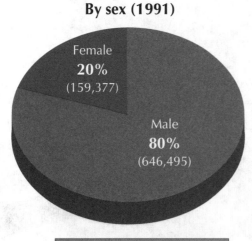

Female
20%
(159,377)

Male
80%
(646,495)

Total number of lawyers in U.S., 1991: **805,872**

Kind of practice (1991)

Salaried/staff Government
11.6% **8.3%**

Inactive/
retired
4.5%

Judicial
2.8%

Private
practice
72.8%

Source: Statistics based on data from the American Bar Association

U.S. STATE AND FEDERAL COURT SYSTEMS

How the court system works:

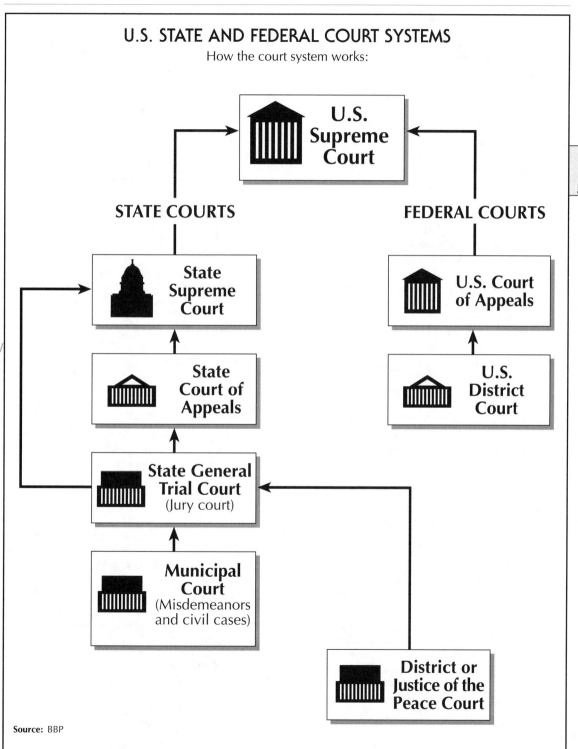

STATE COURTS

FEDERAL COURTS

U.S. Supreme Court

State Supreme Court

U.S. Court of Appeals

State Court of Appeals

U.S. District Court

State General Trial Court (Jury court)

Municipal Court (Misdemeanors and civil cases)

District or Justice of the Peace Court

Source: BBP

THE U.S. MILITARY

The U.S. ranks Number One in the world in its total amount of military expenditures, military technology, nuclear warheads and bombs, combat aircraft, naval fleet, military bases worldwide, military aid to foreign countries, and amount of military training of foreign forces.

The U.S. military budget grew rapidly during the 1980s, helping to create a massive federal budget deficit. During the 1990s, the military budget declined—from $304 billion in 1989 to an estimated $266 billion in 1998. Among the casualties of this downsizing were military bases—many of which were consolidated, closed, or subjected to cutbacks. Troop levels and budgets for new equipment were also cut. Such steps were mirrored by other developed nations, including Russia and North Atlantic Treaty Organization (NATO) members.

The end of the Cold War and the breakup of the Soviet Union in 1991 were important factors in justifying decreases in the U.S. military budget, as were growing concerns on the funding of domestic programs. However, today there is considerable pressure from conservative politicians, military leaders, and the defense industry to increase military spending once again.

Political threats to national security in the coming years are expected to be radically different from the perceived threats of the past. Two major concerns today are the epidemic of ethnic and national conflicts raging during this post-Cold War period and the possibility that nuclear materials may find their way into the hands of terrorists. Military authorities and strategists must find ways to address these and other uncertainties in a rapidly changing world.

FINGERTIP FACTS

- In 1997, global spending was more than $640 billion on military programs. The U.S. military budget accounted for 42% of the world's military expenditures.

- The U.S. ranks third on per capita military expenditures, spending about $1,097 per person. Qatar leads ($1,656); Israel is second ($1,121).

- The states with the most nuclear weapons in 1998 are New Mexico (2,450), Georgia (2,000), Washington (1,685), Nevada (1,350), and North Dakota (1,140).

- In 1999, the U.S. spent $2.7 billion on the Cooperative Threat Reduction (CTR) program. Under the program, the U.S. works with other countries to dismantle and store nuclear weapons.

- Currently, more nuclear weapons are being retired and dismantled than are being produced. By 2003, arsenals in the U.S. and Russia are expected to be at their lowest levels since the nuclear arms race began in the late 1950s.

- The U.S. states receiving the most defense dollars in 1996 were California ($30.5 billion); Virginia ($20.8 billion), and Texas (17.2 billion).

- The largest defense contractor during the fiscal year 1997 was Lockheed Martin, which was awarded contracts totaling $11.6 billion. Second was Boeing, $9.6 billion; third was Northop Grumman, $3.5 billion.

ACTIVE-DUTY PERSONNEL, 1987 vs. 1998

(Number of people on active duty in each branch of the armed forces)

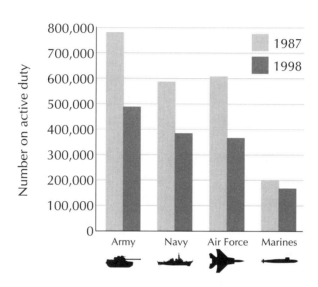

CIVILIAN STAFF IN THE MILITARY, 1985–1998

(Number of civilians who worked for the armed forces in each year)

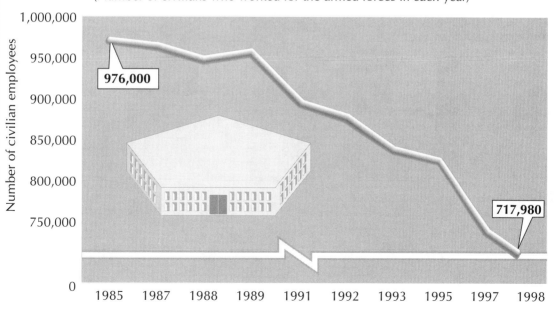

Source: U.S. Department of Defense

FEDERAL BUDGET OUTLAYS FOR NATIONAL DEFENSE FUNCTIONS, 1970–1998

Total defense budget

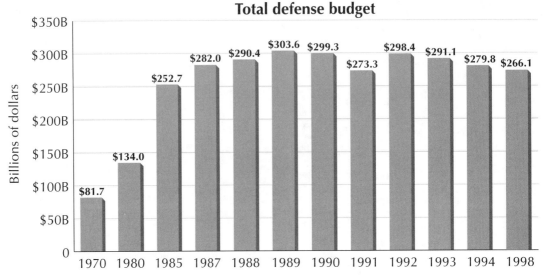

Billions of dollars

1970	$81.7
1980	$134.0
1985	$252.7
1987	$282.0
1988	$290.4
1989	$303.6
1990	$299.3
1991	$273.3
1992	$298.4
1993	$291.1
1994	$279.8
1998	$266.1

Defense budget breakdown: 1970 vs. 1994

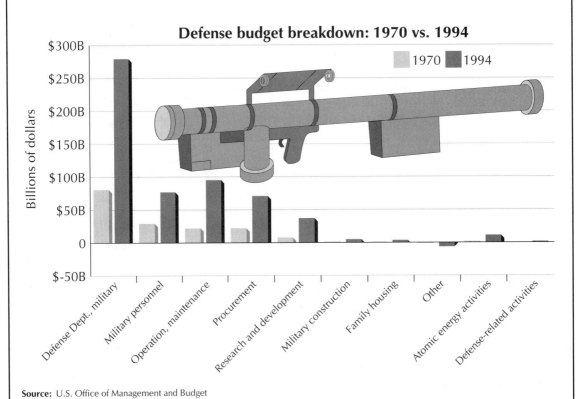

1970   1994

Billions of dollars

Categories: Defense Dept., military; Military personnel; Operation, maintenance; Procurement; Research and development; Military construction; Family housing; Other; Atomic energy activities; Defense-related activities

Source: U.S. Office of Management and Budget

MONEY FOR MILITARY EQUIPMENT, 1991–1993

(Equipment budget of each branch of the armed forces)

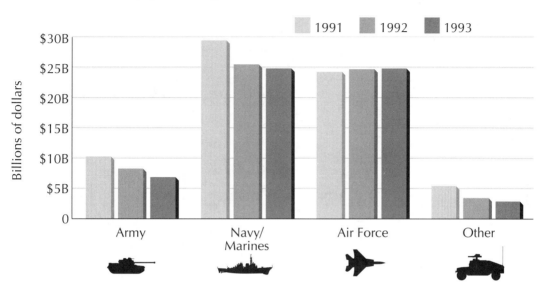

Legend: 1991 · 1992 · 1993

Billions of dollars: $30B, $25B, $20B, $15B, $10B, $5B, 0

Army · Navy/Marines · Air Force · Other

U.S. DEFENSE DEPARTMENT BUDGET, 1983–1998

(Money in the budget of the Department of Defense, in billions of dollars)

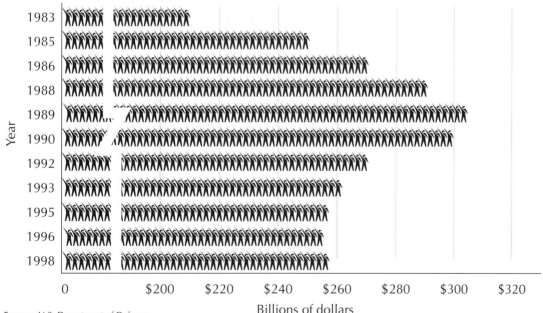

Year: 1983, 1985, 1986, 1988, 1989, 1990, 1992, 1993, 1995, 1996, 1998

Billions of dollars: 0, $200, $220, $240, $260, $280, $300, $320

Source: U.S. Department of Defense

STOCKPILES SINK

Within a decade, the strategic nuclear arsenals of the United States and Russia will be at the lowest levels since the nuclear arms race began. Warhead comparisons:

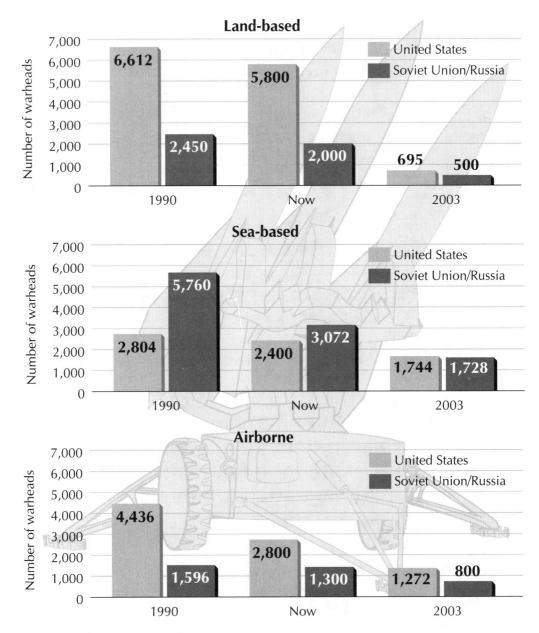

Land-based

Number of warheads

- United States
- Soviet Union/Russia

	1990	Now	2003
United States	6,612	5,800	695
Soviet Union/Russia	2,450	2,000	500

Sea-based

Number of warheads

- United States
- Soviet Union/Russia

	1990	Now	2003
United States	2,804	2,400	1,744
Soviet Union/Russia	5,760	3,072	1,728

Airborne

Number of warheads

- United States
- Soviet Union/Russia

	1990	Now	2003
United States	4,436	2,800	1,272
Soviet Union/Russia	1,596	1,300	800

Source: Arms Control Association; Bulletin of Atomic Scientists

NUMBER OF INTERCONTINENTAL BALLISTIC MISSILES (ICBMs), 1980–1997

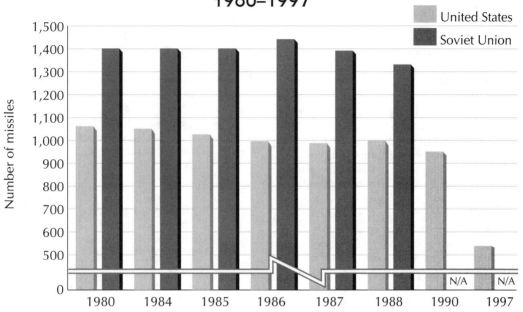

Source: Library of Congress

THE COSTS OF MAJOR AMERICAN WARS
(Estimates of total dollar costs, in descending order)

	Original costs in current dollars	Current cost to 1990
World War II	$360.0B	$466.0B
Vietnam Conflict	$140.6B	$179.0B
Korean Conflict	$50.0B	$72.0B
Persian Gulf War	$36.4B	$47.3B
World War I	$32.7B	$62.5B
Civil War: Union	$2.3B	$6.8B
Civil War: Confederacy	$1.0B	N/A
Spanish-American War	$270.0M	$2.5B
American Revolution	$100.0–$140.0M	$170.0M
War of 1812	$89.0M	$120.0M
Mexican War	$82.0M	$120.0M

Source: Congress, Joint Economic Committee

THE FACE OF THE MILITARY

In 1997, some 1.4 million Americans were on active military duty. These individuals, however, represented a somewhat skewed cross-section of the American population; males far outnumbered females; African Americans made up a disproportionate percentage of enlisted personnel; and whites were disproportionately represented among officers.

Over the years, as American society has changed, so has the U.S. military. Although African Americans have fought for their country since the Revolutionary War, they long had to serve in their own units. It wasn't until 1948 that President Harry S. Truman issued an order to desegregate the armed forces. U.S. history is also filled with women willing to risk their lives for their country, but it wasn't until the all-volunteer military was launched in 1973 that large numbers of brave women began to be integrated into the services.

Many homosexual men and women have also served with great distinction in all of America's wars, but these soldiers have historically been required to conceal their sexual orientation. During his 1992 presidential campaign, Bill Clinton indicated that he wanted to lift the longstanding ban against homosexuals in the military, although he said he would first consider the views of military leaders.

Stiff opposition resulted in a compromise policy termed "Don't ask, don't tell." Gays may now serve if they do not engage in homosexual acts, and commanders may not investigate individuals for homosexual behavior solely on the basis of suspicion or hearsay. This policy is controversial and has been challenged by people on both sides of the issue.

FINGERTIP FACTS

- The U.S. has the world's second-largest armed forces. China leads; Russia is #3.

- In 1970, there were 3.1 million military personnel on active duty; in 1997, that number was 1.4 million.

- Most U.S. military personnel are based in the U.S. In 1998, some 1.2 million were based in the U.S. and its territories; .2 million were based in foreign countries, most in Western Europe.

- In 1997, a total of 86% of the officers were males, 14% were females; 85% were white, 8% black, and 7% other races.

- African Americans make up 12.7% of the U.S. population. In 1998, they accounted for 22% of enlisted personnel and 8% of officers. The army had the largest number and percentage of blacks.

- In 1994, there were 1,137,048 people in the reserves; 68% were white, 14% black, 1% Asian, and 0.4% Native American.

- In 1998, there were 25.2 million veterans living in the U.S. and Puerto Rico, including 19.3 million wartime veterans and 5.9 million peacetime veterans.

- From 1970 to 1996, veterans benefits more than tripled, going from $10.2 billion to $34.8 billion. The fastest growing component was medical costs, which rose from $1.8 billion to $16.5 billion.

MILITARY RECRUITS, BY BRANCH

(Estimated number of recruits in each branch of the armed forces)

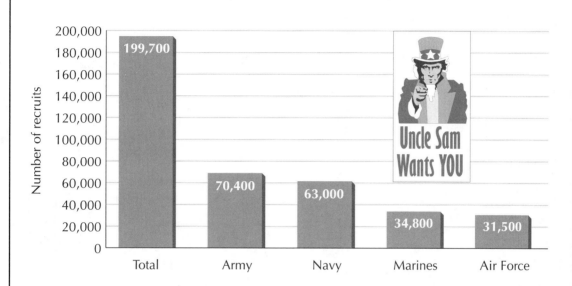

THE FACE OF THE U.S. MILITARY, BY SEX AND RACE, 1993

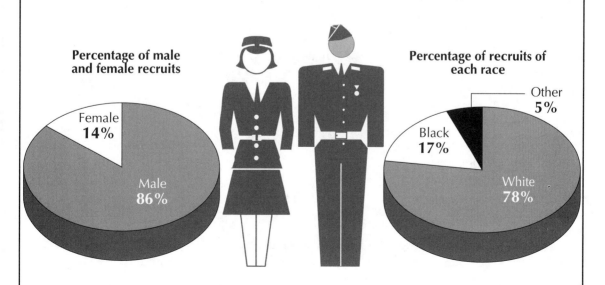

Percentage of male and female recruits

Female 14%

Male 86%

Percentage of recruits of each race

Other 5%

Black 17%

White 78%

Source: U.S Department of Defense

RECRUITS, BY RACE AND BRANCH

(Estimated number of recruits of each race in each branch)

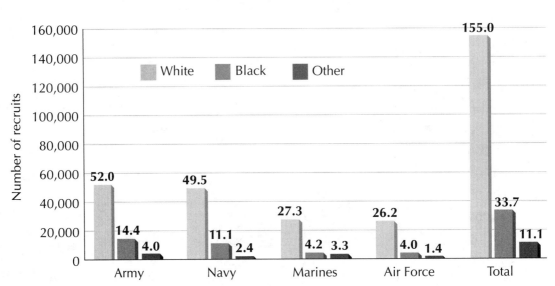

MALES AND FEMALES IN THE MILITARY, BY BRANCH

(Estimated number of male and female recruits in each branch)

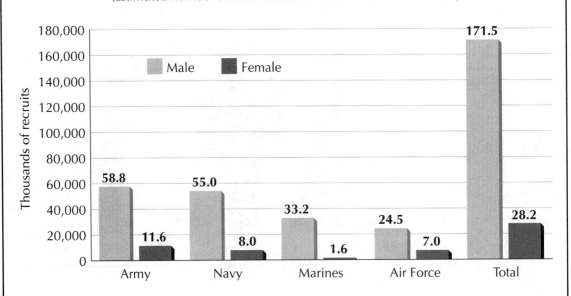

Source: U.S Department of Defense

HONORABLE DISCHARGES FOR GAY SOLDIERS, 1982–1994

(Acknowledged homosexuals honorably discharged since
the military policy barring gays started in 1982)

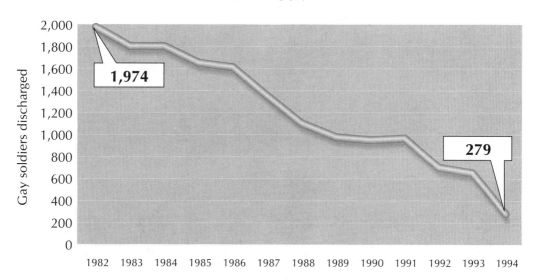

1,974

279

READY MILITARY RESERVE PERSONNEL, BY RACE AND SEX, 1994

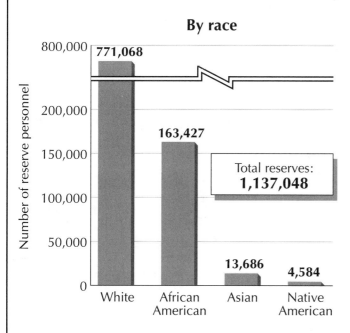

By race

Number of reserve personnel

771,068

163,427

Total reserves:
1,137,048

13,686   4,584

White   African American   Asian   Native American

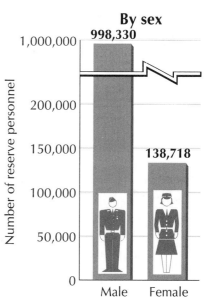

By sex

Number of reserve personnel

998,330

138,718

Male   Female

Source: U.S. Department of Defense

MINORITIES IN THE U.S. MILITARY, 1997

(As percentage of each branch)

Officers

Number of African Americans—officers

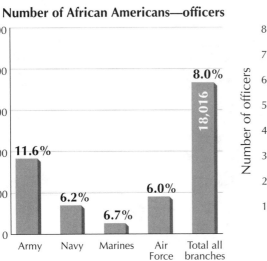

- Army: 11.6%
- Navy: 6.2%
- Marines: 6.7%
- Air Force: 6.0%
- Total all branches: 8.0% (18,016)

Number of Latinos—officers

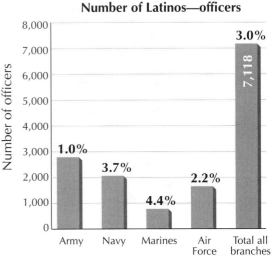

- Army: 1.0%
- Navy: 3.7%
- Marines: 4.4%
- Air Force: 2.2%
- Total all branches: 3.0% (7,118)

Number of others*— officers

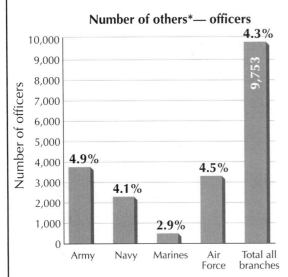

- Army: 4.9%
- Navy: 4.1%
- Marines: 2.9%
- Air Force: 4.5%
- Total all branches: 4.3% (9,753)

Total number of minorities—officers

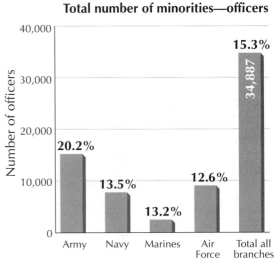

- Army: 20.2%
- Navy: 13.5%
- Marines: 13.2%
- Air Force: 12.6%
- Total all branches: 15.3% (34,887)

* Includes Native Americans, Alaskan Natives, and Pacific Islanders
Source: U.S. Department of Defense, *Defense '97*

MINORITIES IN THE U.S. MILITARY, 1997

(As percentage of each branch)

Enlisted

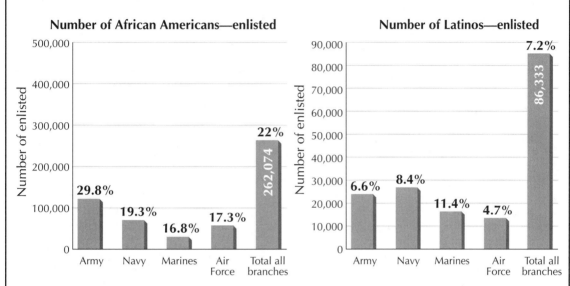

Number of African Americans—enlisted

- Army: 29.8%
- Navy: 19.3%
- Marines: 16.8%
- Air Force: 17.3%
- Total all branches: 22% (262,074)

Number of Latinos—enlisted

- Army: 6.6%
- Navy: 8.4%
- Marines: 11.4%
- Air Force: 4.7%
- Total all branches: 7.2% (86,333)

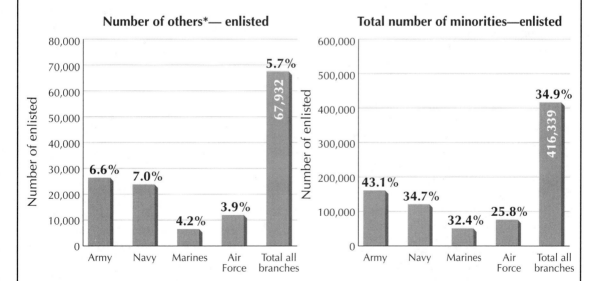

Number of others*—enlisted

- Army: 6.6%
- Navy: 7.0%
- Marines: 4.2%
- Air Force: 3.9%
- Total all branches: 5.7% (67,932)

Total number of minorities—enlisted

- Army: 43.1%
- Navy: 34.7%
- Marines: 32.4%
- Air Force: 25.8%
- Total all branches: 34.9% (416,339)

* Includes Native Americans, Alaskan Natives, and Pacific Islanders
Source: U.S. Department of Defense

WOMEN IN THE MILITARY

Officially, women have been allowed to join the U.S. armed forces since 1901. It was not until 1973, however, when the all-volunteer military was launched (while under pressure from the women's movement), that the services actively began to recruit women. In 1976, the U.S. military academies were opened to women. Today, 14% of the 1.4 million active duty personnel are female. The Air Force is the branch of the armed forces with the largest percentage of women, while the Marine Corps has the lowest.

One of the most serious problems faced by military women has been sexual harassment. The issue received widespread attention following the 1991 annual convention of the Tail Hook Association, an organization for Navy and Marine Corps pilots. During that convention, more than 2 dozen women, half of them officers, accused male aviators of mauling them and other acts of sexual misconduct. Coupled with disclosures of other incidents, including assaults of female soldiers by army men during the Persian Gulf War, this scandal finally led to serious efforts by the armed forces to enforce stricter policies designed to prevent abuse.

Another substantial obstacle faced by military women has been exclusion from combat situations. Without combat experience, a person's chances of being promoted into the military's top ranks are slim. Following the Persian Gulf War, in which more than 40,000 women participated (5% of deployed U.S. forces; 15 were killed), a movement began to repeal laws that bar women from participating equally with men in combat roles. In 1993, women were allowed to serve aboard warships and to fly combat aircraft, though they still may not serve in ground combat units.

FINGERTIP FACTS

☛ The Air Force has the highest percentage of women in any branch of the armed forces (16.3% of all officers and enlisted personnel); the Marine Corps has the lowest (4.6%).

☛ Women are underrepresented in higher military ranks. In 1997, out of a total of 192,404 women in the military, only 16% were officers.

☛ African-American women are disproportionately represented in the military. Some 31.0% of military women are black, versus approximately 12.5% of all U.S. women.

☛ According to the Pentagon, 9% of military women and 2% of military men were unable to ship out during the Persian Gulf War, a difference due mainly to pregnancy. However, studies have shown that military men lose more time because of drug and alcohol abuse than women do for drug and alcohol abuse and pregnancy combined.

☛ In 1993, President Bill Clinton appointed Sheila Widnall as secretary of the Air Force—the first woman to head a branch of the U.S. armed forces.

☛ The first major study of sexual harassment in the military, completed in 1990, found that nearly two-thirds of the 20,000 women surveyed experienced some type of sexual harassment while on the job. The most common category of unwanted behavior—experienced by a total of 52% of women surveyed—was teasing and jokes.

WOMEN IN THE MILITARY, 1997

(Active duty personnel)

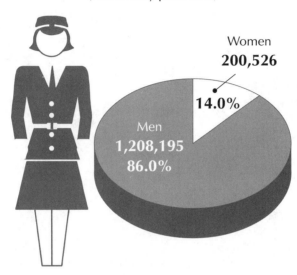

Women
200,526

14.0%

Men
1,208,195
86.0%

PERCENTAGE OF WOMEN IN THE U.S. MILITARY, 1997

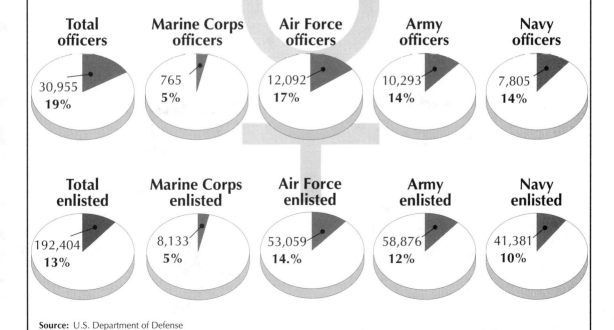

Total officers	Marine Corps officers	Air Force officers	Army officers	Navy officers
30,955 **19%**	765 **5%**	12,092 **17%**	10,293 **14%**	7,805 **14%**

Total enlisted	Marine Corps enlisted	Air Force enlisted	Army enlisted	Navy enlisted
192,404 **13%**	8,133 **5%**	53,059 **14.%**	58,876 **12%**	41,381 **10%**

Source: U.S. Department of Defense

MILITARY WOMEN ON ACTIVE DUTY, 1981–1997

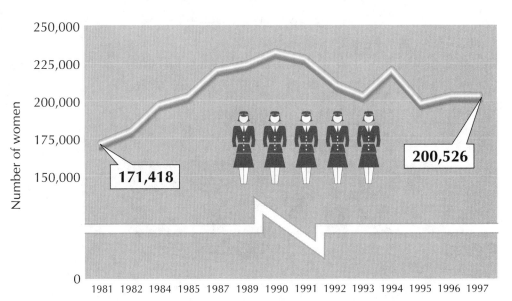

Source: U.S. Department of Defense

MILITARY WOMEN BY BRANCH, 1997

(Percentage of each service branch who are women)

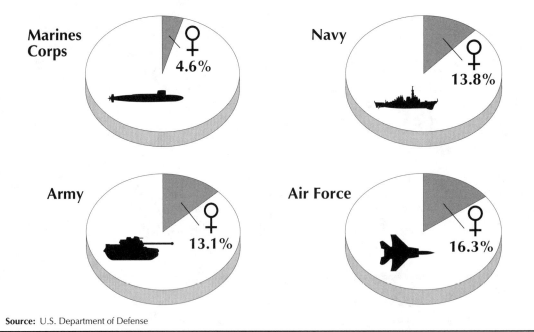

Source: U.S. Department of Defense

PROFILE: RACE OR ETHNICITY OF WOMEN IN THE MILITARY

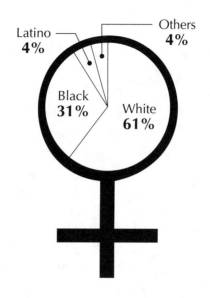

Latino
4%

Others
4%

Black
31%

White
61%

Source: U.S. Department of Defense

PROFILE: U.S. ENLISTED WOMEN vs. WOMEN OFFICERS

Women account for 19% of the military's officers and 13% of the enlisted personnel. How the 223,359 women split by rank:

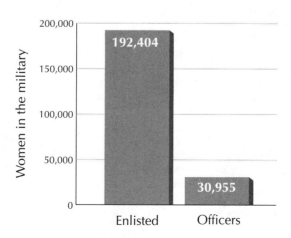

Source: U.S. Department of

PUERTO RICO

Puerto Rico, today a bustling island of 3.8 million people, has been a U.S. commonwealth since July 25, 1952. It is governed under the Constitution of the Commonwealth of Puerto Rico and the Federal Relations Statutes; the latter defines the relationship between Puerto Rico and the federal U.S. government. Residents of Puerto Rico have no voting representation in the U.S. Congress, do not vote in U.S. presidential elections, and do not pay federal taxes. The economy, however, is geared to that of the U.S., with a common currency and unrestricted free trade.

Puerto Rico's political status has been a matter of continuing debate among the island's residents. Some support independence, while others desire statehood, and still others favor continued commonwealth status but with greater autonomy. The most recent referendum occurred on November 14, 1993, when 48.9% of the voters opted to maintain commonwealth status; 46.7% favored statehood, and only 4.4% voted for independence.

The everyday problems that plague residents of Puerto Rico mirror those on the U.S. mainland. People are concerned about such issues as the economy, crime, drugs, health care, and education. In 1993, in response to a record-breaking homicide rate, a program to use the U.S. National Guard in the occupation of public housing projects known to be drug distribution spots marked the first time in the island's history that police and National Guard troops had together taken over public housing units. It also signaled a growing sense of cooperation between the two governments.

FINGERTIP FACTS

☛ The majority of Puerto Ricans are racially defined as white. Most are Christian, primarily Roman Catholic.

☛ Puerto Rican residents' median age has increased dramatically, from 18.5 years in 1960 to 23.1 years in 1998. During that period, the population of the island increased by nearly 30%.

☛ In 1960, Puerto Rico had a birth rate of 32.5 per 1,000 population. By 1998, the rate was only 17.

☛ Before 1955, Puerto Rico's economy was dominated by agriculture, with sugar the dominant agricultural product. Today, public administration and services (including tourism) prevail.

☛ In 1950, agriculture employed 246,000 people—36% of the labor force—and dominated the economy. Sugar was the primary agricultural product. In 1996, the industry employed only 114,810, or 3%.

☛ In 1980, Puerto Rico's net income was $9 billion. By 1998, net income had grown to $48.2 billion.

☛ In 1970, Puerto Rico had 1.2 million visitors and a net income of $89.8 million from tourism. By 1997, the number of visitors had grown to 23.7 million, with net income of $336 million.

PUERTO RICO AT A GLANCE

Status
U.S. commonwealth since 1952

Citizenship
- U.S.
- No travel restrictions in the U.S.
- No vote in presidential elections
- No federal taxes
- Assisted, protected by the U.S.
- Self-government in local matters, similar to U.S. states

1997 population: 3,819,023
Urban   71.2%
Rural   28.8%

Population density
(people per square mile)
Puerto Rico   1,025
Hawaii   172

Ethnicity
99.9% Hispanic

Language
Spanish, English second language

Religion
Roman Catholic   85%
Protestant and other   15%

Leading political parties
- **Popular Democratic Party:**
  Favors continued Commonwealth status

- **New Progressive Party:**
  Favors statehood

- **Independence Party:**
  Favors complete independence

Source: Puerto Rico Federal Affairs Administration

PUERTO RICO: HEALTH AND EDUCATION PROFILE

Life expectancy

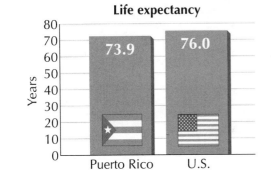

Infant mortality

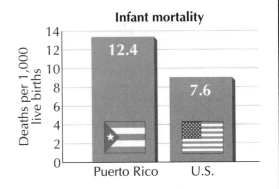

Literacy rate

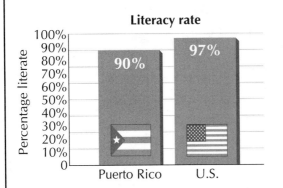

Student-teacher ratio

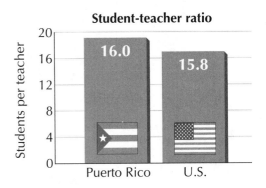

High school graduate or higher

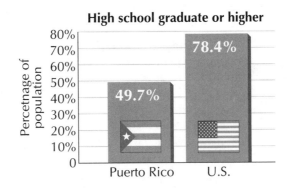

Source: Puerto Rico Federal Affairs Administration

PROFILE: THE ECONOMY OF PUERTO RICO

(Currency: U.S. dollar)

Unemployment

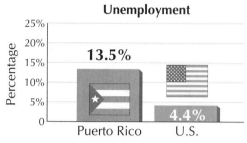

13.5%

4.4%

Puerto Rico   U.S.

Per capita income

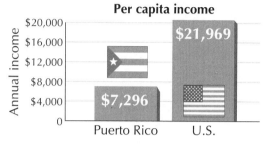

$21,969

$7,296

Puerto Rico   U.S.

Poverty rate

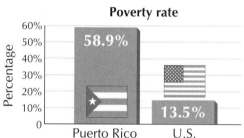

58.9%

13.5%

Puerto Rico   U.S.

Average hourly wage

$10.02

$6.66

Puerto Rico   U.S.

MAJOR INDUSTRIES IN PUERTO RICO

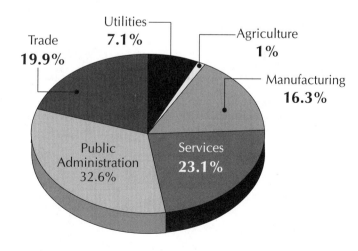

Utilities **7.1%**

Agriculture **1%**

Trade **19.9%**

Manufacturing **16.3%**

Public Administration 32.6%

Services **23.1%**

Source: Puerto Rico Federal Affairs Administration

4

POPULATION AND VITAL STATISTICS

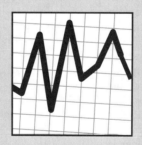

MARRIAGE AND DIVORCE

Each year in the United States, wedding bells ring for well over 2 million happy couples. Marriage is a popular convention in America. Almost 60% of Americans over age 18 are married. Yet, since the early 1980s, the number of marriages and the marriage rate have declined. There were 2,270,959 marriages in 1997, a 4% decline from 1982. One explanation is that many baby-boomers are past the ages (15 to 44) at which marriage is most likely to occur. Also, studies suggest that fewer Americans will marry during their lifetimes today than in the past.

Many marriages are successful—but many others are not. Divorce and separation are now commonplace events. Each year, more than a million marriages are legally dissolved in a court of law. Indeed, statistics suggest that the United States has the highest divorce rate in the world. Its divorce rate soared during the mid-1960s and through most of the 1970s, but has declined somewhat in more recent years. The divorce rate per 1,000 people ages 15 and older in 1997 was 4.3.

Approximately half the couples who divorce have children under age 18. In most cases, custody of the children is given to the mother, but fathers have pressed for more rights and more access to their children. Men are now increasingly being awarded custody or granted shared custody of the children. A study of divorce in 19 states released in 1995 indicated that custody went to mothers in 71.0% of the cases, to fathers in 8.5%, and was shared in 15.5%. Friends or relatives were awarded custody in the remaining cases.

FINGERTIP FACTS

- Research presented in 1995 indicates that marriage provides health, emotional, and financial benefits. For example, divorced men have higher rates of depression and drug and alcohol abuse than do married men.

- In 1996, just 10% of women ages 15 to 44 got married, compared with 14% in 1973.

- More marriages take place in California than in any other state.

- More than half of all marriages occur after a couple has lived together. In 1996, unmarried couples headed 3.7 million households, including 1.3 million with children under age 15.

- Approximately 1 in 5 Americans over age 18 has never married, compared with 1 in 6 in 1970. Only 4.2% of Americans age 65 and older have never married.

- In the U.S., 870,606 divorces were granted in 1997; the divorce rate of 4.3 per 1,000 population was the lowest since 1974.

- Divorce is most common among the young. Approximately half the people who divorce are under age 25.

- Most divorced people remarry; men are more likely to remarry than women.

- Divorce rates are highest among blacks. In 1997 the rate was 331 per 1,000 married people.

Note: Before comparing statistics, consider that different rates apply to different population ratios—for example some rates are figured per 1,000 people, other rates are figured per 100,000 people.

MARRIAGE AND DIVORCE RATES IN THE U.S., 1960–1996

(Rates per 1,000 population)

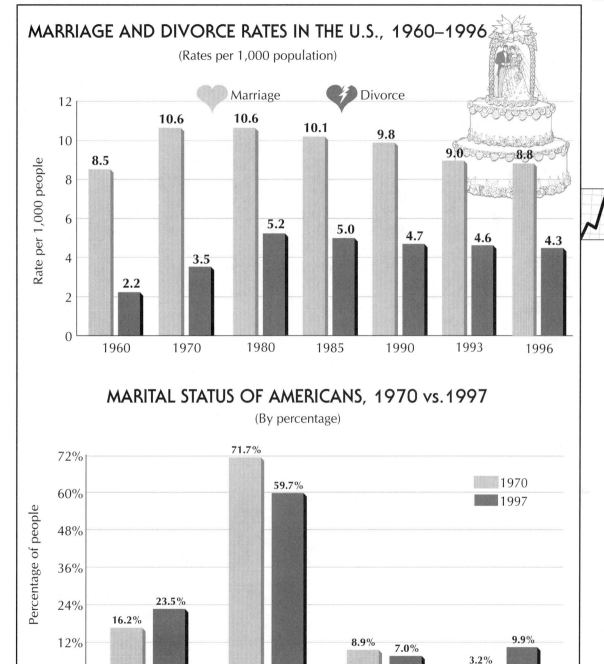

MARITAL STATUS OF AMERICANS, 1970 vs. 1997

(By percentage)

Source: U.S. Census Bureau

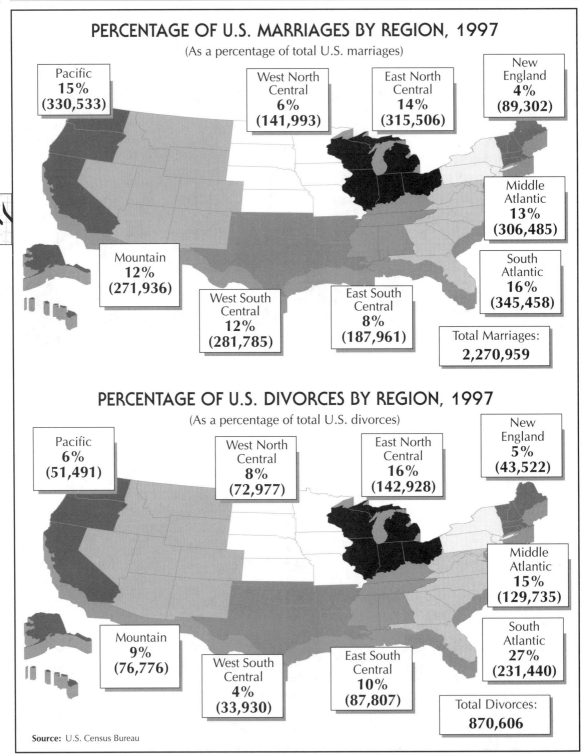

PERCENTAGE OF U.S. MARRIAGES BY REGION, 1997

(As a percentage of total U.S. marriages)

Pacific
15%
(330,533)

West North
Central
6%
(141,993)

East North
Central
14%
(315,506)

New
England
4%
(89,302)

Middle
Atlantic
13%
(306,485)

Mountain
12%
(271,936)

South
Atlantic
16%
(345,458)

West South
Central
12%
(281,785)

East South
Central
8%
(187,961)

Total Marriages:
2,270,959

PERCENTAGE OF U.S. DIVORCES BY REGION, 1997

(As a percentage of total U.S. divorces)

Pacific
6%
(51,491)

West North
Central
8%
(72,977)

East North
Central
16%
(142,928)

New
England
5%
(43,522)

Middle
Atlantic
15%
(129,735)

Mountain
9%
(76,776)

South
Atlantic
27%
(231,440)

West South
Central
4%
(33,930)

East South
Central
10%
(87,807)

Total Divorces:
870,606

Source: U.S. Census Bureau

U.S. STATES WITH THE MOST AND LEAST MARRIAGES, 1997

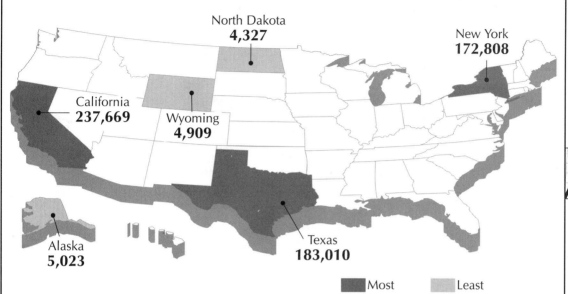

North Dakota
4,327

New York
172,808

California
237,669

Wyoming
4,909

Alaska
5,023

Texas
183,010

■ Most   ▢ Least

U.S. STATES WITH THE MOST AND LEAST DIVORCES, 1997

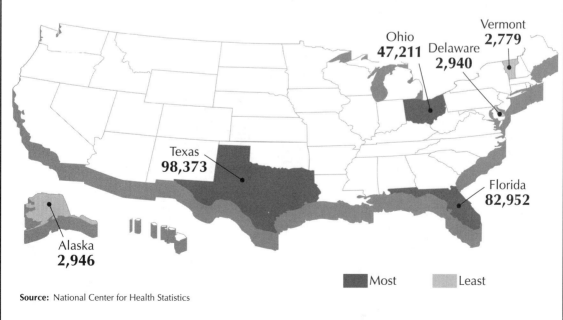

Ohio
47,211

Vermont
2,779

Delaware
2,940

Texas
98,373

Florida
82,952

Alaska
2,946

■ Most   ▢ Least

Source: National Center for Health Statistics

RACE OR ETHNICITY OF SINGLE PEOPLE OVER AGE 18, 1997

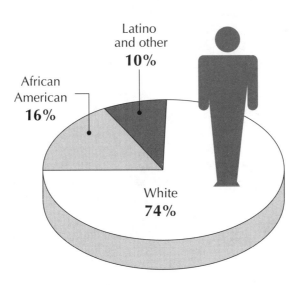

Latino
and other
10%

African
American
16%

White
74%

RACE OR ETHNICITY OF MARRIED PEOPLE OVER AGE 18, 1997

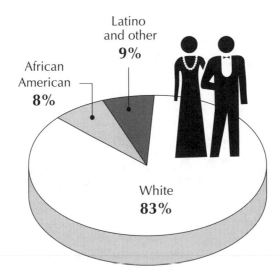

Latino
and other
9%

African
American
8%

White
83%

Source: U.S. Census Bureau

RACE OR ETHNICITY OF DIVORCED PEOPLE OVER AGE 18, 1997

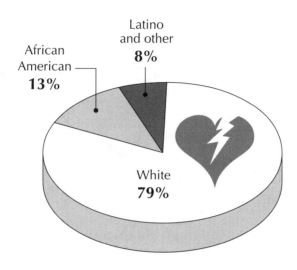

Latino and other
8%

African American
13%

White
79%

RACE OR ETHNICITY OF WIDOWED PEOPLE OVER AGE 18, 1997

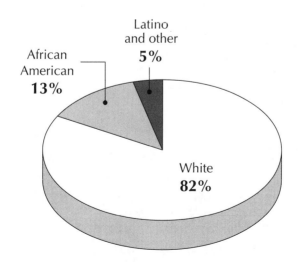

Latino and other
5%

African American
13%

White
82%

Source: U.S. Census Bureau

GROWTH IN UNMARRIED COUPLE HOUSEHOLDS, 1960–1997

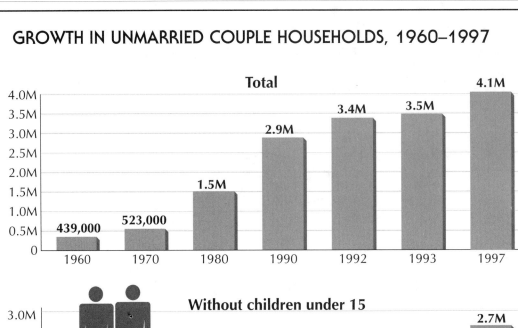

Total

439,000 — 1960
523,000 — 1970
1.5M — 1980
2.9M — 1990
3.4M — 1992
3.5M — 1993
4.1M — 1997

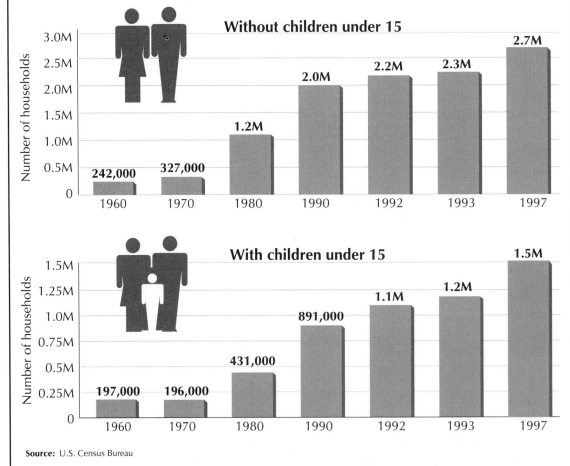

Without children under 15

242,000 — 1960
327,000 — 1970
1.2M — 1980
2.0M — 1990
2.2M — 1992
2.3M — 1993
2.7M — 1997

With children under 15

197,000 — 1960
196,000 — 1970
431,000 — 1980
891,000 — 1990
1.1M — 1992
1.2M — 1993
1.5M — 1997

Source: U.S. Census Bureau

MEDIAN AGE IN U.S. AT FIRST MARRIAGE, BY SEX, 1900–1996

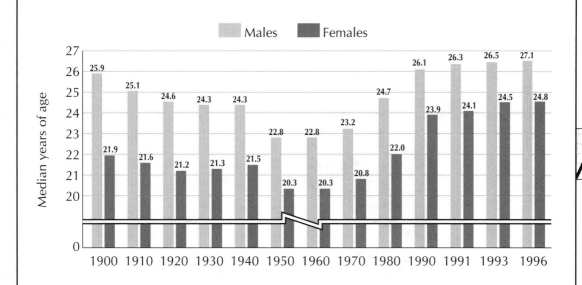

Males   Females

Source: U.S. Census Bureau

MARITAL STATUS OF AMERICANS OVER AGE 18, 1997

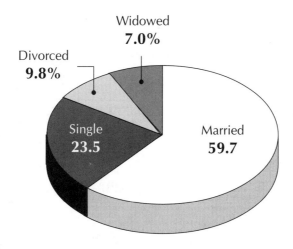

Widowed
7.0%

Divorced
9.8%

Single
23.5

Married
59.7

Source: U.S. Census

MARITAL STATUS OF WHITE AMERICANS OVER AGE 18, 1997

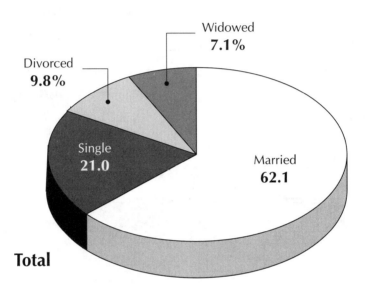

Widowed
7.1%

Divorced
9.8%

Single
21.0

Married
62.1

Total

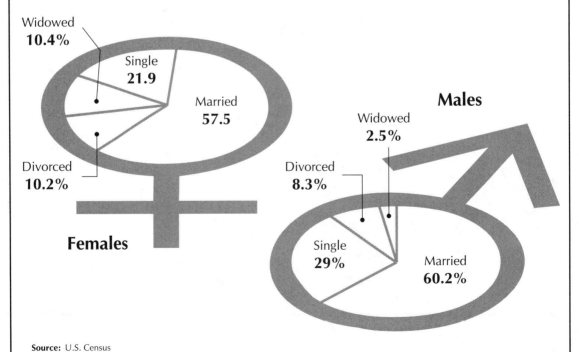

Widowed
10.4%

Single
21.9

Married
57.5

Divorced
10.2%

Females

Males

Widowed
2.5%

Divorced
8.3%

Single
29%

Married
60.2%

Source: U.S. Census

MARITAL STATUS OF AFRICAN AMERICANS OVER AGE 18, 1997

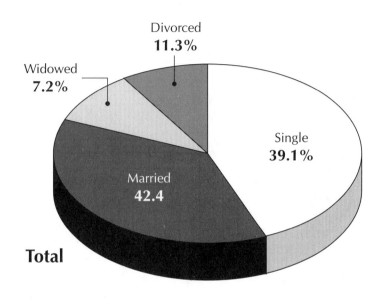

Divorced
11.3%

Widowed
7.2%

Single
39.1%

Married
42.4

Total

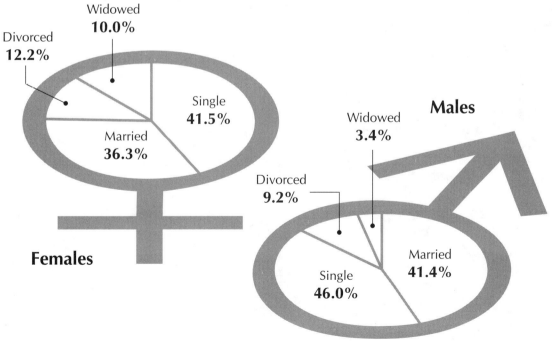

Widowed
10.0%

Divorced
12.2%

Single
41.5%

Married
36.3%

Females

Males

Widowed
3.4%

Divorced
9.2%

Married
41.4%

Single
46.0%

Source: U.S. Census

MARITAL STATUS OF LATINOS IN THE U.S. OVER AGE 18, 1997

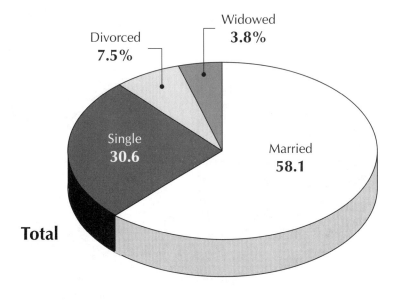

Divorced
7.5%

Widowed
3.8%

Single
30.6

Married
58.1

Total

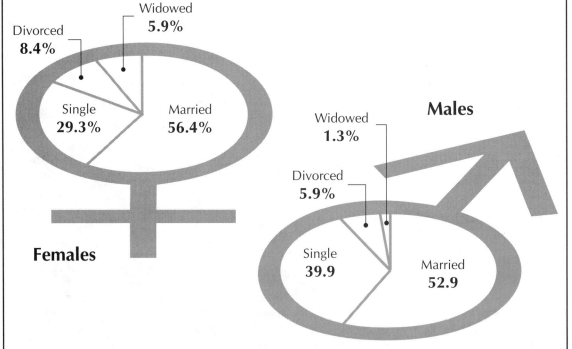

Widowed
5.9%

Divorced
8.4%

Single
29.3%

Married
56.4%

Females

Males

Widowed
1.3%

Divorced
5.9%

Single
39.9

Married
52.9

Source: U.S. Census Bureau

NUMBER OF SEXUAL PARTNERS OF ADULTS, 1991-1996

(By percentage of adults reporting number of partners)

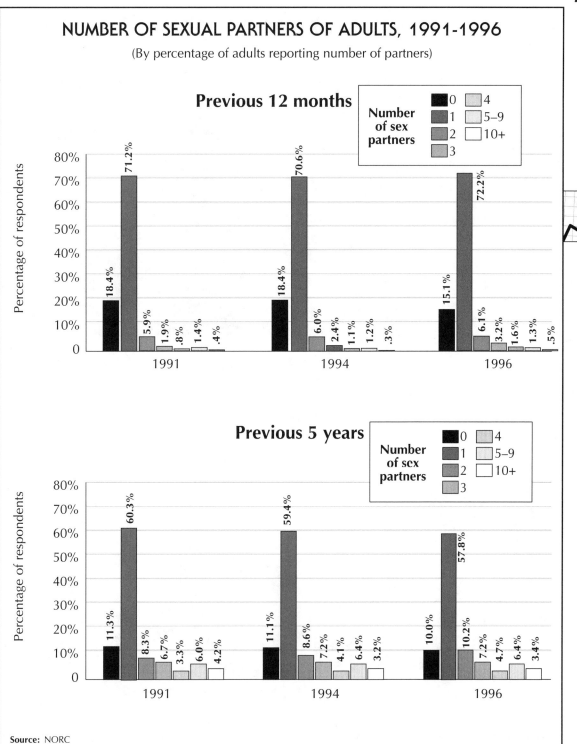

Source: NORC

MARITAL STATUS OF AMERICANS BY AGE, 1998

Marriages

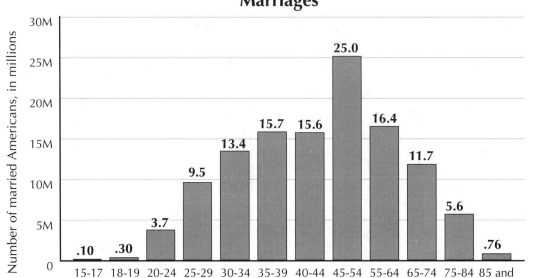

Divorces

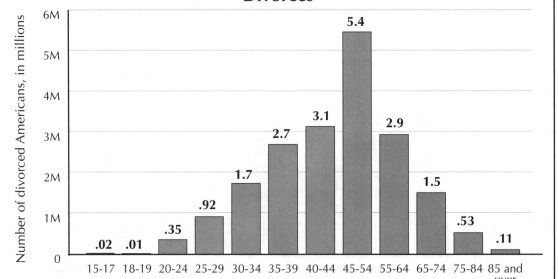

Source: National Center for Health Statistics

TOP WEDDING MONTHS, 1996
(By number of marriages each month)

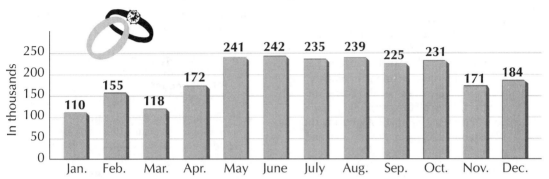

In thousands

Jan.	Feb.	Mar.	Apr.	May	June	July	Aug.	Sep.	Oct.	Nov.	Dec.
110	155	118	172	241	242	235	239	225	231	171	184

Source: U.S. Census Bureau

INTERRACIAL MARRIAGES, 1960-1997

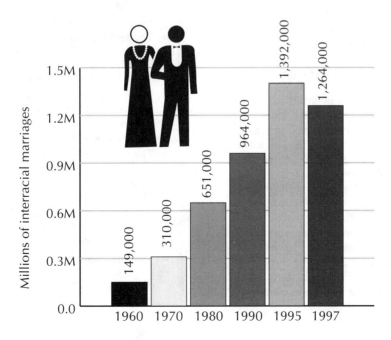

Millions of interracial marriages

1960	1970	1980	1990	1995	1997
149,000	310,000	651,000	964,000	1,392,000	1,264,000

Source: U.S. Census Bureau

BIRTHS AND DEATHS

The numbers of births and deaths in the United States are among the basic statistics tracked by the National Center for Health Statistics (NCHS), a division of the Department of Health and Human Services. Birth rates—the number of live births per 1,000 population—increased dramatically during the 1940s and 1950s, then rapidly declined in the 1960s and early 1970s. Since then, the number of live births per 1,000 women ages 15 to 44 has followed a generally downward pattern. The NCHS estimates that 3,914,900 babies were born in the U.S. in 1996, a 1% increase from 1995. This may be the beginning of a consistently upward trend for the future. Some experts expect another baby boom to take place early in the 21st century, with annual births reaching or exceeding an estimated 4.3 million.

An estimated 2,294,000 deaths occurred in the United States during 1997. This statistic was quite significant: it was the first time in U.S. history that the number of deaths actually decreased from the previous year.

The NCHS reports two kinds of death rates: the crude death rate and the age-adjusted death rate. The latter is considered a more accurate indicator of risk of death over time and of differences among racial and sexual groups. The age-adjusted death rate reached a record low of 491.6 per 100,000 population in 1996. Death rates were lower for females than males, and lower for whites than blacks ages one through 54. The estimated 1997 infant death rate of 7.0 per 1,000 live births was the lowest ever recorded for the U.S.

FINGERTIP FACTS

- In 1996, the birth rate was highest in Utah (21.0) and Texas (17.3) and lowest in Maine (11.1) and West Virginia (11.4).

- Birth rates are highest for Latinos (especially Mexican) and black women, followed by Native American, Asian American, and white women.

- In 1997, September saw the most births (353,000), January the fewest (305,000).

- More males are born each year than females. In 1996, about 1,047 male babies were born for every 1,000 female babies. However, infant death rates are higher for males.

- The fertility rate declined from 106.2 in 1950 to 65.3 in 1996.

- The fertility rate is significantly higher for black women (70.6 in 1996) than Hispanic (79.6) and white (59.0) women.

- The 15 leading causes of death—headed by heart disease and cancer —accounted for 86% of all U.S. deaths in 1997.

- The U.S. death rate in 1997 was highest in January (9.6 per 1,000), lowest in August (7.6 per 1,000).

- Death rates for infants under a year old are higher than those for people ages 1 through 54.

- The U.S. infant mortality rate is much higher for blacks (14.2) than it is for whites (6.0).

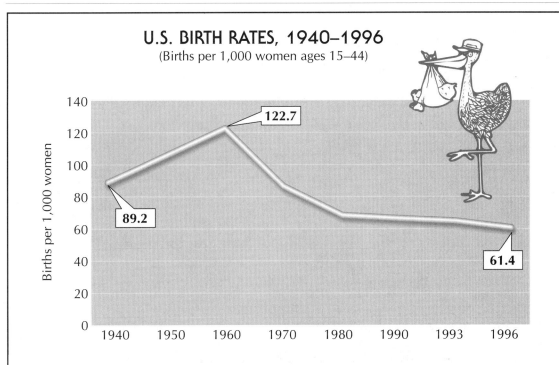

U.S. BIRTH RATES, 1940–1996
(Births per 1,000 women ages 15–44)

122.7

89.2

61.4

FERTILITY RATES OF U.S. WOMEN, 1930–1996

(Rate per 1,000 women)

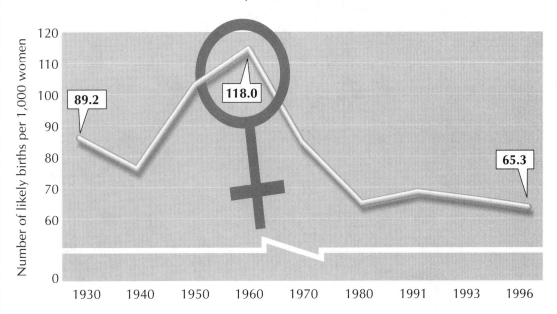

89.2

118.0

65.3

Source: U.S. Census Bureau

U.S. WOMEN AND CHILDBEARING, 1920–1998

(The average number of children born to each U.S. woman, from 1920 to 1998)

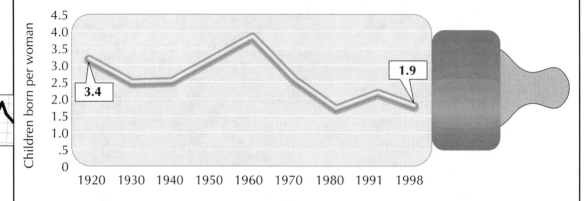

Source: U.S. Census Bureau

BABY BOOMERS' BOOM DIPS, 1970–1996

(Births per 1,000 women)

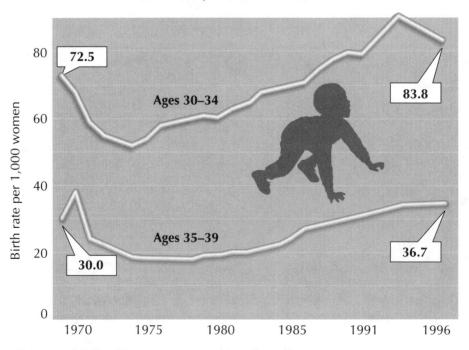

Source: U.S. Department of Health and Human Services; National Center for Health Statistics

RATE OF LIVE BIRTHS AND DEATHS
BY MONTH IN U.S., 1997

(Rate per 1,000 population)

Births

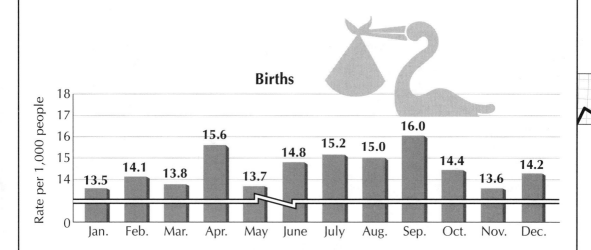

Deaths

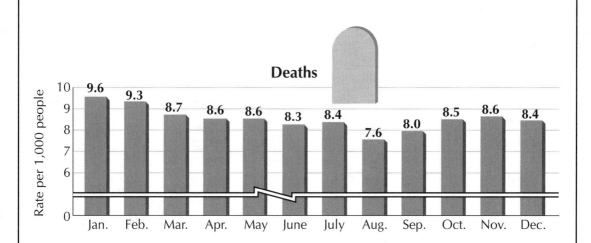

Source: U.S. Census Bureau

TOTAL DEATHS AND DEATH RATES, BY AGE AND SEX, 1996

Total deaths

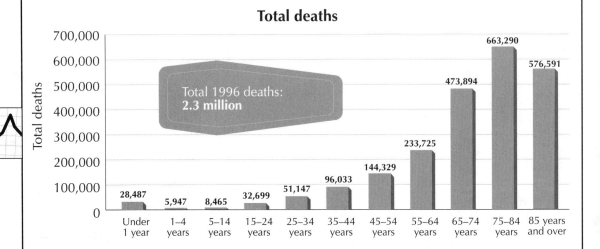

Death rates—male and female

(Rates per 100,000 people)

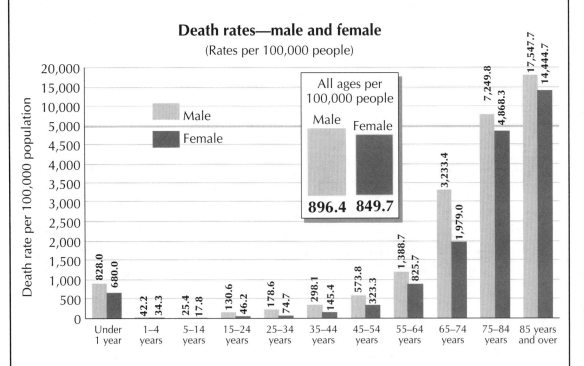

Source: U.S. Department of Health and Human Services; National Center for Health Statistics

CHANGES IN THE LEADING CAUSES OF DEATH, 1900–1997

(Rates per 100,000 population)

1900—Death rate: 1,719.1

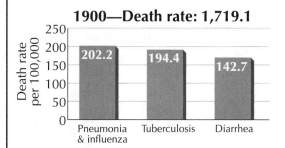

Pneumonia & influenza	202.2
Tuberculosis	194.4
Diarrhea	142.7

1920—Death rate: 1,298.9

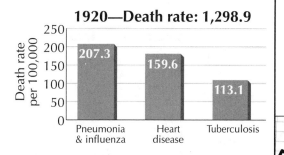

Pneumonia & influenza	207.3
Heart disease	159.6
Tuberculosis	113.1

1940—Death rate: 1,074.1

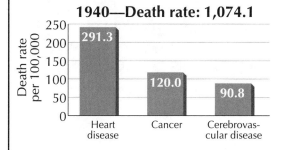

Heart disease	291.3
Cancer	120.0
Cerebrovascular disease	90.8

1960—Death rate: 954.7

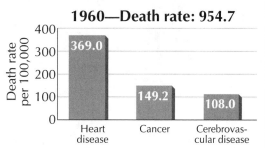

Heart disease	369.0
Cancer	149.2
Cerebrovascular disease	108.0

1980—Death rate: 878.3

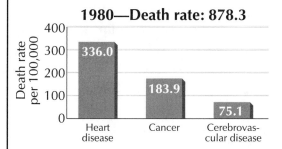

Heart disease	336.0
Cancer	183.9
Cerebrovascular disease	75.1

1990—Death rate: 863.8

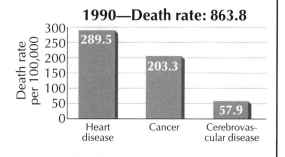

Heart disease	289.5
Cancer	203.3
Cerebrovascular disease	57.9

1992—Death rate: 853.3

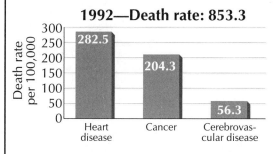

Heart disease	282.5
Cancer	204.3
Cerebrovascular disease	56.3

1997—Death rate: 872.0

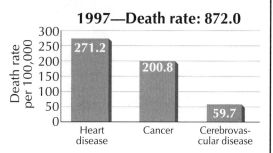

Heart disease	271.2
Cancer	200.8
Cerebrovascular disease	59.7

Source: U.S. Department of Health and Human Services; National Center for Health Statistics

CHANGES IN THE LEADING CAUSES OF DEATH, 1900–1997

(Rates per 100,000 population)

Pneumonia & influenza

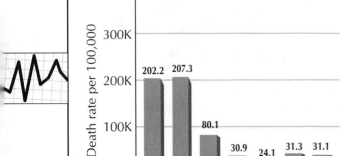

Heart disease

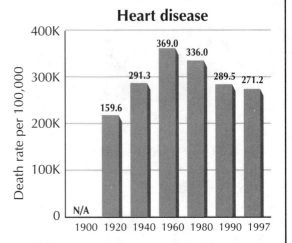

Cancer

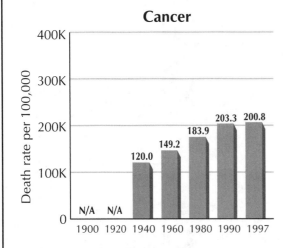

Cerebrovascular disease

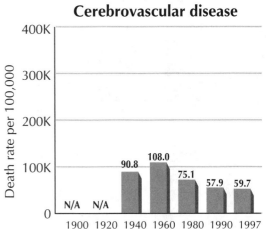

Note: N/A = Not Available
Source: U.S. Department of Health and Human Services; National Center for Health Statistics

TOP 10 STATES IN DEATH RATES, 1996

(Rates per 1,000 population, with rankings)

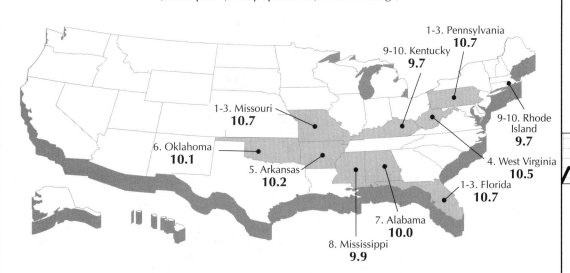

1-3. Pennsylvania
10.7

9-10. Kentucky
9.7

1-3. Missouri
10.7

9-10. Rhode
Island
9.7

6. Oklahoma
10.1

4. West Virginia
10.5

5. Arkansas
10.2

1-3. Florida
10.7

7. Alabama
10.0

8. Mississippi
9.9

Source: Department of Health and Human Services; U.S. National Center for Health Statistics

THE LEADING CAUSES OF DEATH IN THE U.S., 1997

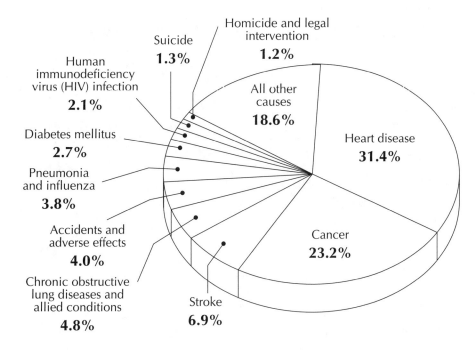

Suicide
1.3%

Homicide and legal
intervention
1.2%

Human
immunodeficiency
virus (HIV) infection
2.1%

All other
causes
18.6%

Heart disease
31.4%

Diabetes mellitus
2.7%

Pneumonia
and influenza
3.8%

Accidents and
adverse effects
4.0%

Cancer
23.2%

Chronic obstructive
lung diseases and
allied conditions
4.8%

Stroke
6.9%

Source: U.S. Department of Health and Human Services; National Center for Health

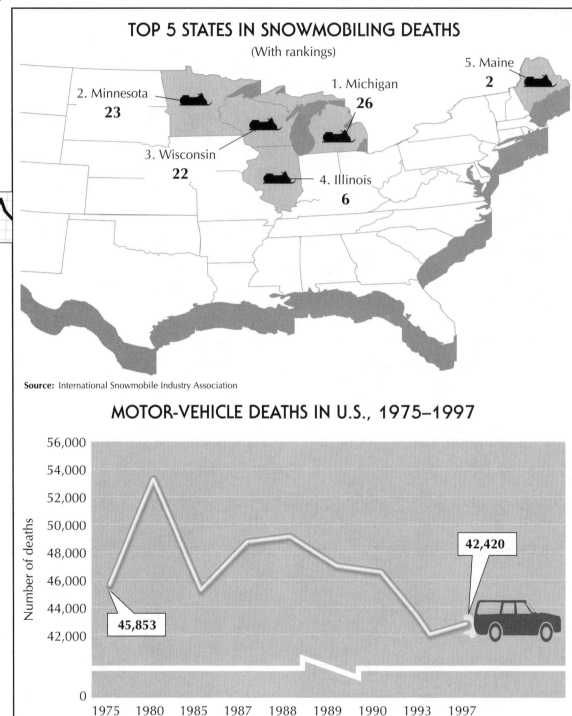

TOP 5 STATES IN SNOWMOBILING DEATHS
(With rankings)

5. Maine
2

1. Michigan
26

2. Minnesota
23

3. Wisconsin
22

4. Illinois
6

Source: International Snowmobile Industry Association

MOTOR-VEHICLE DEATHS IN U.S., 1975–1997

Number of deaths

45,853

42,420

1975 1980 1985 1987 1988 1989 1990 1993 1997

Source: National Safety Council

U.S. DEATH RATES BY RACE, 1970–1996

(Deaths per 100,000 population)

Whites

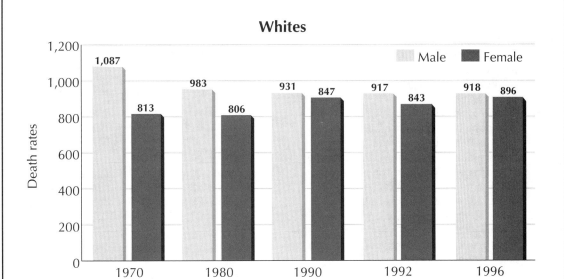

African Americans

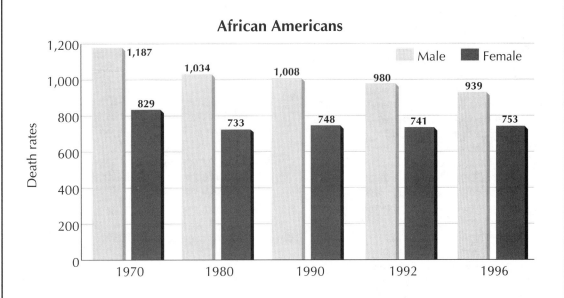

Source: U.S. Department of Health and Human Services; National Center for Health Statistics

POPULATION

The population of the United States is currently increasing at a rate of about 1% a year. In 1790, when the first federal census was conducted, about 4 million people lived in the new nation. By 1995, the population had grown by 67 times, to 269 million.

Two factors have caused the country's population growth: natural increase (the difference between the number of births and deaths), and migration increase (the difference between the number of immigrants and emigrants). Approximately two-thirds of current U.S. growth is due to natural increase, and one-third to immigration. In 1997, for example, there was a natural increase of 1.6 million and a migration increase of 1.1 million. If current fertility and immigration trends continue, the U.S. population will double by about the year 2050.

Various factors influence the actual distribution of population. For example, since the beginning of the Industrial Age in the late 18th century, people have migrated from rural areas to cities for jobs. Today, the vast majority of Americans live in urban environments. In recent years, mild climates coupled with booming economies have attracted many people to the South.

Population growth affects communities and the nation in many ways. It dramatically alters both the quality of life for each citizen and it directly affects the environment. For example, a 1994 report commissioned by the non-profit Carrying Capacity Network indicated that if current U.S. population growth and related trends continue, some 15 million acres of farmland will be lost to urbanization, highways, erosion, and pollution by the year 2000.

FINGERTIP FACTS

- The United States had a population in 1998 of approximately 269 million—the third most populous nation, after China and India.

- Nevada has been the fastest-growing state. Its population increased 50.1% during the 1980s and 39.5% from 1990 to 1997.

- California is the most populous state, with 32.6 million people in 1997. Wyoming has the fewest people—about 470,000 in 1997.

- In 1993, state population per square mile of land area ranged from one person in Alaska to 1,062 in New Jersey.

- Of the U.S. population in 1960, 69.6% lived in urban areas; by 1997, the figure had grown to 80%.

- New York City is the largest U.S. city, with a population of 7.4 million in 1996. Los Angeles, California is second (3.6 million).

- Five cities had populations of 1 million or more in 1960; by 1996, there were 10 cities in this category, accounting for 8.4% of the nation's population.

- Since 1960, most urban growth has occurred in cities of under 250,000 people.

- In 1997, a total of 9.7% of the population was foreign-born, the highest percentage since 1930. Mexicans account for 28% of foreign-born residents.

- Projections of the U.S. population by the year 2050 range from 392 million to 522 million.

NATIONAL CENSUSES

(Resident U.S. population reported by census)

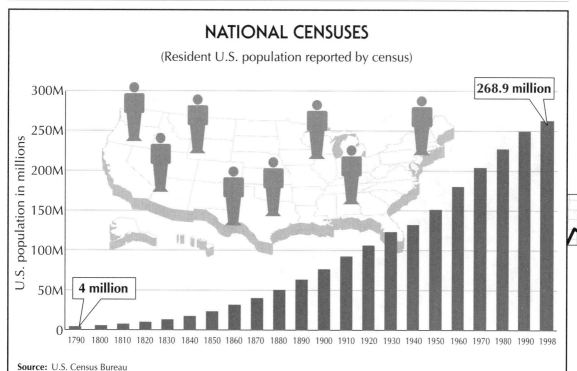

268.9 million

4 million

Source: U.S. Census Bureau

CITY POPULATION SHIFTS, 1990–1997

(U.S. cities with the greatest percentage of change in population)

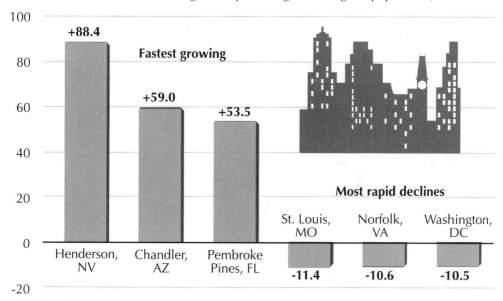

Fastest growing

+88.4

+59.0

+53.5

Most rapid declines

Henderson, NV

Chandler, AZ

Pembroke Pines, FL

St. Louis, MO

Norfolk, VA

Washington, DC

-11.4

-10.6

-10.5

Source: U.S. Census Bureau

U.S. POPULATION, BY REGION, 1970 vs. 1997

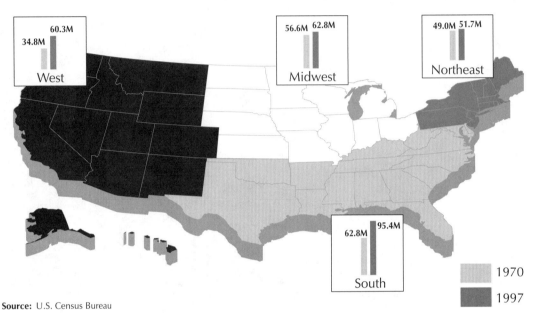

West
34.8M 60.3M

Midwest
56.6M 62.8M

Northeast
49.0M 51.7M

South
62.8M 95.4M

1970
1997

Source: U.S. Census Bureau

U.S. POPULATION GROWTH RATES, 1990–1996
(Percentage of growth for selected race and ethnic groups)

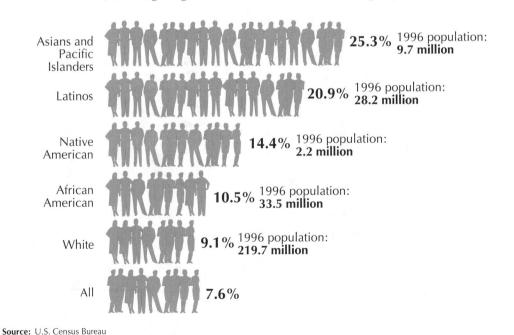

Asians and Pacific Islanders — 25.3% — 1996 population: 9.7 million

Latinos — 20.9% — 1996 population: 28.2 million

Native American — 14.4% — 1996 population: 2.2 million

African American — 10.5% — 1996 population: 33.5 million

White — 9.1% — 1996 population: 219.7 million

All — 7.6%

Source: U.S. Census Bureau

U.S. POPULATION BY STATE: THE TOP 20, 1997
(With rankings)

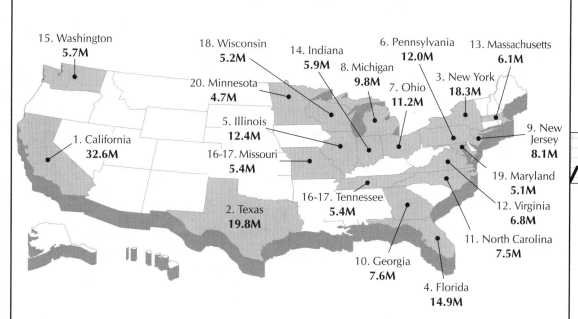

15. Washington **5.7M**

18. Wisconsin **5.2M**

14. Indiana **5.9M**

8. Michigan **9.8M**

6. Pennsylvania **12.0M**

13. Massachusetts **6.1M**

20. Minnesota **4.7M**

7. Ohio **11.2M**

3. New York **18.3M**

5. Illinois **12.4M**

9. New Jersey **8.1M**

1. California **32.6M**

16-17. Missouri **5.4M**

19. Maryland **5.1M**

12. Virginia **6.8M**

2. Texas **19.8M**

16-17. Tennessee **5.4M**

11. North Carolina **7.5M**

10. Georgia **7.6M**

4. Florida **14.9M**

OTHER STATE* POPULATIONS
(Rounded numbers)

Alabama	4.4M	Montana	880,000
Alaska	614,000	Nebraska	1.7M
Arizona	4.6M	Nevada	1.7M
Arkansas	2.5M	New Hampshire	1.2M
Colorado	4.0M	New Mexico	1.7M
Connecticut	3.3M	North Dakota	638,000
Delaware	746,000	Oklahoma	3.3M
Washington, D.C.	523,124	Oregon	3.3M
Hawaii	1.2M	Rhode Island	1.0M
Idaho	1.2M	South Carolina	3.8M
Iowa	2.9M	South Dakota	748,171
Kansas	2.6M	Utah	2.1M
Kentucky	3.9M	Vermont	590,000
Louisiana	4.3M	West Virginia	1.8M
Maine	1.3M	Wyoming	470,000
Mississippi	2.8M		

* Includes Washington, D.C.
Source: U.S. Census Bureau

TOP 20 U.S. METROPOLITAN AREAS, BY POPULATION, 1990-96

(With rankings)

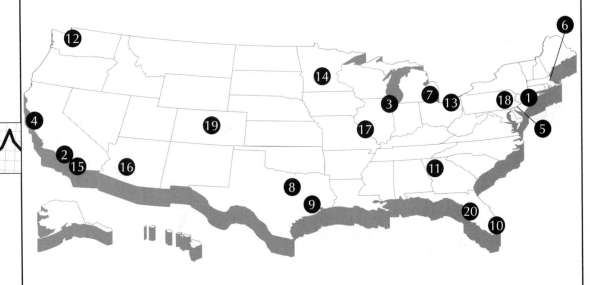

1.	NY, Northern NJ, CT	**19.9M**	11. Atlanta, GA	**3.5M**
2.	Los Angeles-Anaheim-Riverside, CA	**15.5M**	12. Seattle-Tacoma, WA	**3.3M**
3.	Chicago-Gary-Lake City, IL, IN, WI	**8.6M**	13. Cleveland-Akron-Lorain, OH	**2.9M**
4.	San Francisco-Oakland-San Jose, CA	**6.6M**	14. Minneapolis-St. Paul, MN	**2.8M**
5.	Philadelphia-Wilmington-Trenton, PA, DE, NJ	**6.0M**	15. San Diego, CA	**2.7M**
6.	Boston-Lawrence-Salem, MA, NH	**5.6M**	16. Phoenix, AZ	**2.6M**
7.	Detroit-Ann Arbor, MI	**5.3M**	17. St. Louis, MO	**2.5M**
8.	Dallas-Ft. Worth, TX	**4.6M**	18. Pittsburgh-Beaver Valley, PA	**2.4M**
9.	Houston-Galveston-Brazoria, TX	**4.3M**	19. Denver-Boulder-Greeley, CO	**2.3M**
10.	Miami-Ft. Lauderdale, FL	**3.6M**	20. Tampa-St. Petersburg, FL	**2.2M**

Source: U.S. Census Bureau

TOP 10 FASTEST-GROWING MAJOR U.S. CITIES, 1990-1996

(With rankings)

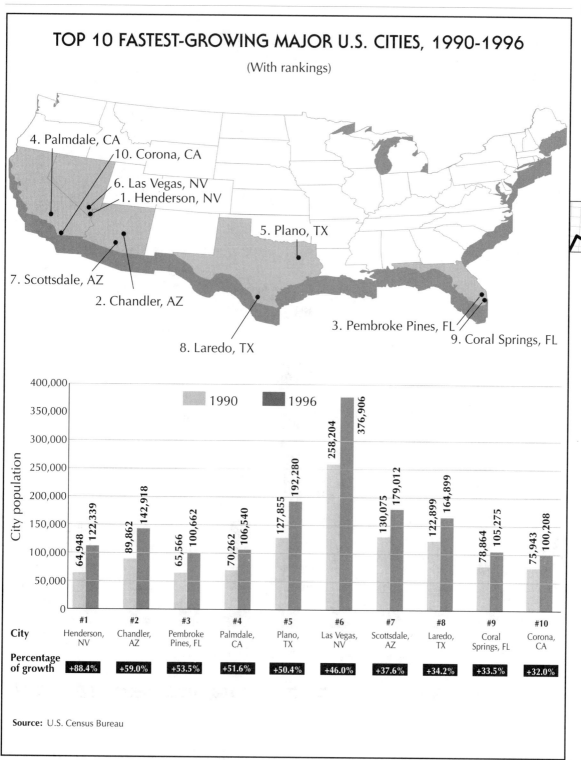

4. Palmdale, CA
10. Corona, CA
6. Las Vegas, NV
1. Henderson, NV
5. Plano, TX
7. Scottsdale, AZ
2. Chandler, AZ
3. Pembroke Pines, FL
9. Coral Springs, FL
8. Laredo, TX

City	#1 Henderson, NV	#2 Chandler, AZ	#3 Pembroke Pines, FL	#4 Palmdale, CA	#5 Plano, TX	#6 Las Vegas, NV	#7 Scottsdale, AZ	#8 Laredo, TX	#9 Coral Springs, FL	#10 Corona, CA
1990	64,948	89,862	65,566	70,262	127,855	258,204	130,075	122,899	78,864	75,943
1996	122,339	142,918	100,662	106,540	192,280	376,906	179,012	164,899	105,275	100,208
Percentage of growth	+88.4%	+59.0%	+53.5%	+51.6%	+50.4%	+46.0%	+37.6%	+34.2%	+33.5%	+32.0%

Source: U.S. Census Bureau

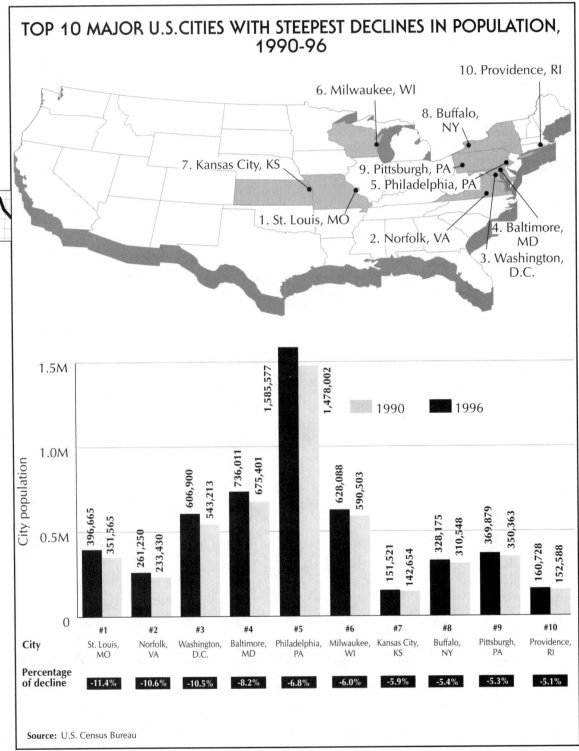

TOP 10 MAJOR U.S. CITIES WITH STEEPEST DECLINES IN POPULATION, 1990-96

10. Providence, RI

6. Milwaukee, WI

8. Buffalo, NY

7. Kansas City, KS

9. Pittsburgh, PA
5. Philadelphia, PA

1. St. Louis, MO

2. Norfolk, VA

4. Baltimore, MD

3. Washington, D.C.

1990   1996

City population

1.5M

1.0M

0.5M

0

City	#1 St. Louis, MO	#2 Norfolk, VA	#3 Washington, D.C.	#4 Baltimore, MD	#5 Philadelphia, PA	#6 Milwaukee, WI	#7 Kansas City, KS	#8 Buffalo, NY	#9 Pittsburgh, PA	#10 Providence, RI
1996	396,665	261,250	606,900	736,011	1,585,577	628,088	151,521	328,175	369,879	160,728
1990	351,565	233,430	543,213	675,401	1,478,002	590,503	142,654	310,548	350,363	152,588
Percentage of decline	-11.4%	-10.6%	-10.5%	-8.2%	-6.8%	-6.0%	-5.9%	-5.4%	-5.3%	-5.1%

Source: U.S. Census Bureau

U.S. ASIAN POPULATION, BY REGION, 1997

(By percentage of total U.S. Asian population)

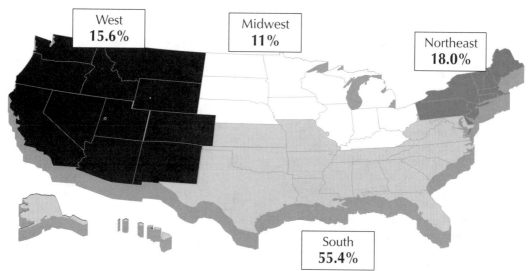

West
15.6%

Midwest
11%

Northeast
18.0%

South
55.4%

Source: U.S. Census Bureau

Total Asian or Pacific Islander population

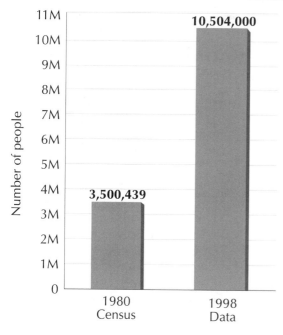

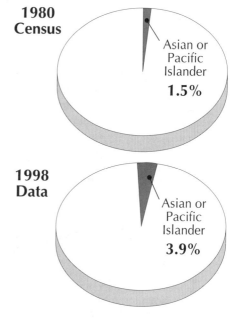

**1980
Census**

Asian or
Pacific
Islander
1.5%

**1998
Data**

Asian or
Pacific
Islander
3.9%

Source: U.S. Census Bureau

P O V E R T Y

Being poor, or living in poverty, has different meanings in different countries, in different regions of a single country, and even in different times in history. In the United States today, a primary measurement of poverty is income. The Census Bureau reported that in 1997, some 35.6 million Americans—about 13.7% of the total population—lived below the poverty line. This number has slowly been decreasing since 1993, when the number of Americans living in poverty reached an all-time high of 39.3 million.

Poverty rates vary by race, age, sex, family composition, and other factors. For example, rates are higher among blacks than whites, higher in rural areas than in metropolitan areas, higher in the South than in other regions of the U.S., and higher among immigrant families than among native-born families.

Particularly distressing is the increasing number of children who are living in poverty. In 1997, slightly less than one of every 4 American children under age 6—about 5 million youngsters—lived in families with incomes below the poverty line. The Food Research and Action Center, a nonprofit organization that works to alleviate hunger, reported that more than 5 million children under age 12 go hungry each month.

FINGERTIP FACTS

- According to the Children's Defense Fund (CDF), one U.S. infant is born into poverty every 35 seconds.

- Every 31 seconds, an infant is born to an unmarried mother, according to the CDF.

- The poverty line is adjusted periodically and varies according to family size. In 1997, for example, it was $10,468 for a family of 2; $16,404 for a family of 4; and $21,880 for a family of 6.

- In 1996, Latinos were the group with the highest poverty rate in the U.S. (29.4%), as compared to blacks (28.4%), Asians and Pacific Islanders (13.1%), and whites (11.2%).

- In 1997, the South was home to the most poor people (39% of the nation's total); the Northeast had the fewest (18%). The South also had the highest percentage of poor residents (14.6% of its total population), while the Northeast had the smallest percentage (12.6%).

- Native born Americans and naturalized citizens are more likely to live above the poverty line than unnaturalized foreign-born residents are. In 1997, about 12.5% of natives were below poverty, as opposed to 19.9% of foreign-born individuals. Similarly, 11.4% of naturalized citizens live in poverty, compared to 25% of residents who are not U.S. citizens.

- The poverty rate is higher than average in families headed by females (with no spouse present). In 1997, a total of 35.1% of these families were below the poverty level.

- Women are 32% more likely to live in poverty than men are.

- In 1997, people living inside central cities were 9.8% more likely to live in poverty than those living outside central cities.

TOP 5 RICHEST AND POOREST STATES, BY MEDIAN INCOME

Census reports show more Americans in poverty, which reflects a population increase.
The reports track state numbers on 1996 median incomes and poverty rates.
The results, with rankings:

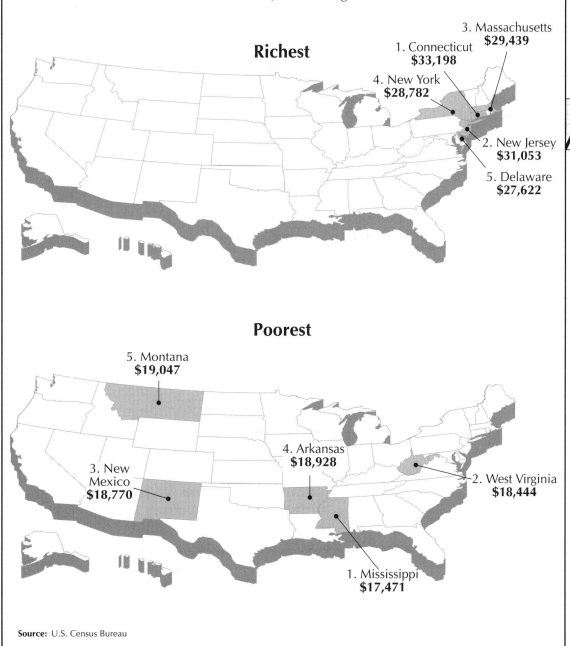

Richest

3. Massachusetts
$29,439

1. Connecticut
$33,198

4. New York
$28,782

2. New Jersey
$31,053

5. Delaware
$27,622

Poorest

5. Montana
$19,047

4. Arkansas
$18,928

2. West Virginia
$18,444

3. New
Mexico
$18,770

1. Mississippi
$17,471

Source: U.S. Census Bureau

AMERICA'S POOR AT A GLANCE, 1997

There were **35,574,000** poor people in the U.S., which was **13.3%** of the population.

27,273,000 of the poor lived in urban areas, which was **12.6%** of urban dwellers.

24,396,000 people, or **11.0%** of the poor, were whites (including Latinos).

16,491,000 people, or **8.6%** of the poor, were whites (non-Latinos).

Of the people ages 18 to 64, **11.4%,** or **18,085,000,** were poor.

13,748,000, or **14.6%** of the people in the Southern states, were poor.

39% of the poor—**13,748,000**—lived in the South.

13,422,000 people, or **19.2%** people under 18, were poor.

26.5% of African Americans, **9,116,000** people, were poor.

Outside urban areas, **8,301,000,** or **15.9%,** of the people were poor.

8,441,000 white children under 18, or **15.4%,** were poor.

In the Midwest states, **6,493,000** people—**10.4%**—were poor.

6,493,000 people, or **18%** of the poor, lived in the Midwest.

7,324,000 householders in the U.S., or 10.3%, were poor.

In the Western states, **8,858,000** of the people, or **14.6%,** were poor.

8,858,000 people, or **25.0%** of the poor, lived in the West.

8,308,000 Latinos—**27.1%**—were poor.

6,474,000, or **12.6%** of the people in the Northeast states, were poor.

18.0%, or **6,474,000,** of the poor lived in the Northeast.

9.3% of white families (including Latinos), **17,258,000** people, were poor.

4,116,000 African-American children under 18, or **36.8%,** were poor.

13,494,000 people, or **35.1%** of female-led households, were poor.

3,376,000 people over 64, or **10.5%,** were poor.

6.3% of white families (non-Latino), or **3,357,000,** were poor.

2,821,000 people—**5.2%** of all married-couple families— were poor.

Of Latino children under 18, **39.9%,** or **3,116,000,** were poor.

25.5% of African-American families, or **7,386,000** people, were poor.

39.8% of African-American female-led households, or **1,563,000** people, were poor.

24.7% of Latino families, or **1,721,000** people, were poor.

1,468,000 Asian/Pacific Islanders, or **14.0%** of their population, were poor.

8% of African-American married-couple families—**312,000** people—were poor.

244,000 people, or **10.2%** of Asian/Pacific Islander families, were poor.

Source: U.S. Census Bureau

STATES WITH HIGHEST AND LOWEST POVERTY, 1996-1997

(By percentage of resident population below poverty line)

Highest poverty percentages

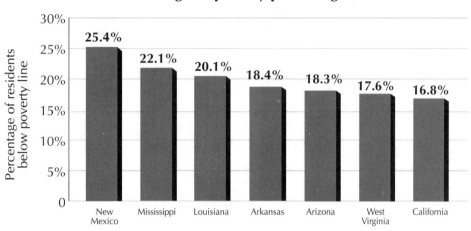

Lowest poverty percentages

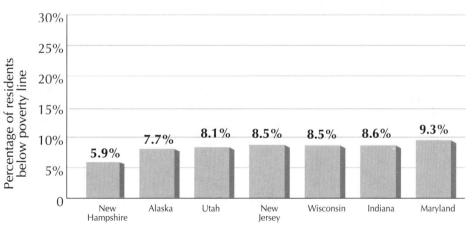

Source: U.S. Census Bureau

PROFILE: POOR IN THE U.S., BY RACE OR ETHNIC GROUP, 1996

(As percentage of all poor)

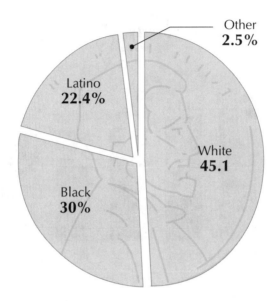

Other
2.5%

Latino
22.4%

White
45.1

Black
30%

PERCENTAGE OF ETHNIC GROUP OR RACE IN POVERTY

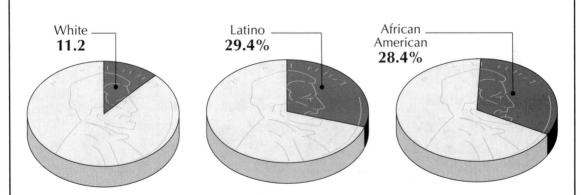

White
11.2

Latino
29.4%

African
American
28.4%

Source: U.S. Census Bureau

POVERTY HAUNTS IMMIGRANTS TO U.S.

(Percentage of immigrant families living below the poverty level)

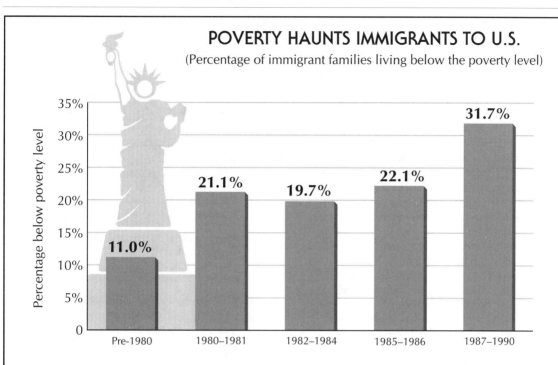

PERCENTAGE OF U.S. RACIAL / ETHNIC GROUPS UNDER POVERTY LEVEL

All racial/ethnic groups under the poverty level

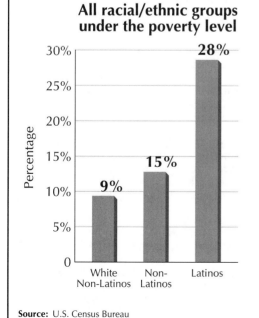

Latino groups under the poverty level

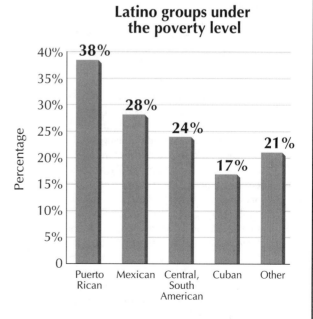

Source: U.S. Census Bureau

H O M E L E S S N E S S

One of the most troubling and tragic social problems in the U.S. is the country's large population of homeless people. Determining how many people are without permanent homes is difficult, because of the transient and often hidden nature of the population. For these reasons, estimates on the number of homeless vary widely. In 1994, U.S. Secretary of Housing and Urban Development Henry Cisneros cited "reasonable estimates" that some 600,000 Americans were homeless, and that as many as 7 million had been homeless at some point during the previous 5 years. The Interagency Council on the Homeless concluded that "the crisis of homelessness is greater than commonly known or previously acknowledged."

At one time, most U.S. homeless people were middle-age men. Today, single men account for only about 47% of the homeless population. The fastest-growing homeless group consists of substance abusers. Sadly, about 26% of the homeless are children. Many of them are in families, but a substantial number are runaways or "throwaways" —children rejected by their parents.

A primary reason for homelessness is a lack of low-cost housing. Other causes include poverty, unemployment, mental illness, substance abuse, and domestic violence. Government agencies, churches, and community groups help many homeless people, but public financing and other assistance—such as job training and drug treatment programs—are being restricted as elected officials continue to slash budgets. Many cities have cracked down on homeless people, arresting them for various public annoyances such as loitering, panhandling, public drunkenness, blocking traffic, and other disruptive behaviors.

FINGERTIP FACTS

☞ The homeless problem is most apparent in big cities. New York City has the largest homeless population in the U.S., followed by Los Angeles, Chicago, and San Francisco.

☞ About 27% of the homeless have severe mental illnesses, such as chronic schizophrenia and personality disorders.

☞ After declining 2% from 1988 to 1993, homeless single women increased 3% to an all-time high of 14% of all homeless people in 1997.

☞ About 72% of homeless families are headed by a single parent, usually a mother.

☞ In 1996, some 64% of those who sought emergency food assistance were families with children.

☞ In many cities, "food banks" and other food-assistance programs are unable to keep up with the demand. In 72% of cities surveyed in 1993, such programs had to turn people away.

☞ Approximately 25 million young Americans—about half of them under age 17—used food banks, soup kitchens, or other kinds of food-distribution programs in 1994.

☞ Federal programs to help the homeless are grouped under the Steward B. McKinney Homeless Assistance Act, which began in 1987. Most funding for homeless programs, however, comes from state and city budgets.

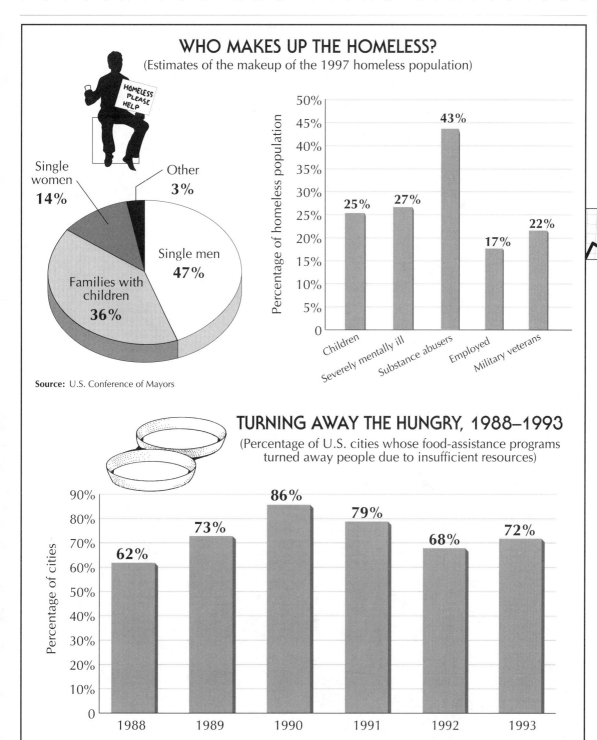

WHO MAKES UP THE HOMELESS?
(Estimates of the makeup of the 1997 homeless population)

HOMELESS
PLEASE
HELP

Single women **14%**

Other **3%**

Single men **47%**

Families with children **36%**

Source: U.S. Conference of Mayors

Percentage of homeless population

50%
45%
40%
35%
30%
25%
20%
15%
10%
5%
0

Children **25%**
Severely mentally ill **27%**
Substance abusers **43%**
Employed **17%**
Military veterans **22%**

TURNING AWAY THE HUNGRY, 1988–1993
(Percentage of U.S. cities whose food-assistance programs turned away people due to insufficient resources)

Percentage of cities

90%
80%
70%
60%
50%
40%
30%
20%
10%
0

1988 **62%**
1989 **73%**
1990 **86%**
1991 **79%**
1992 **68%**
1993 **72%**

Source: U.S. Conference of Mayors

TOP 10 U.S. CITIES IN HOMELESS POPULATION

(Estimated numbers of homeless people, with rankings)

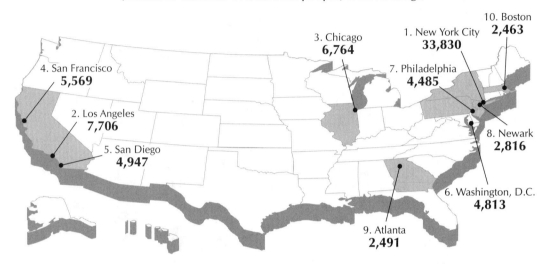

10. Boston
2,463

3. Chicago
6,764

1. New York City
33,830

7. Philadelphia
4,485

4. San Francisco
5,569

2. Los Angeles
7,706

5. San Diego
4,947

8. Newark
2,816

6. Washington, D.C.
4,813

9. Atlanta
2,491

Source: U.S. Census Bureau

HUNGRY FAMILIES IN U.S. CITIES, 1988–1996

(Percentage of people seeking emergency food
assistance who were families with children)

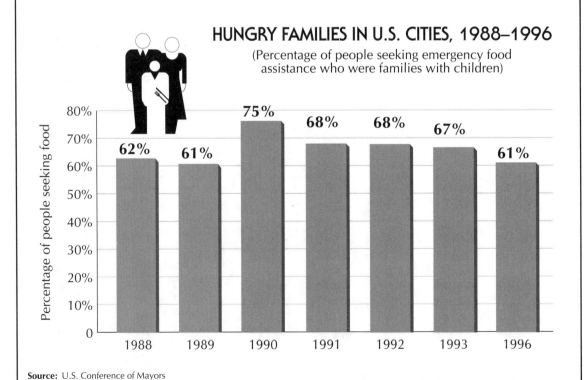

Percentage of people seeking food

Year	Percentage
1988	62%
1989	61%
1990	75%
1991	68%
1992	68%
1993	67%
1996	61%

Source: U.S. Conference of Mayors

HOMELESSNESS RISES FOR SOME, FALLS FOR OTHERS, 1988 vs. 1997

In 1997, a 26-city survey of homeless in the U.S. revealed changes in the makeup of the urban homeless since 1988. Fewer are single men; more are substance abusers or families with children:

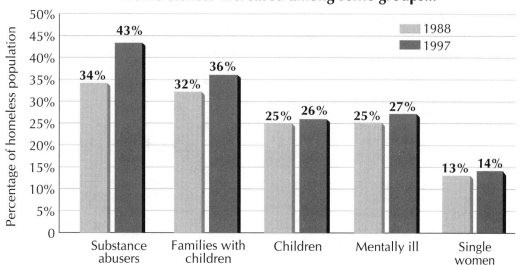

Homelessness increased among some groups...

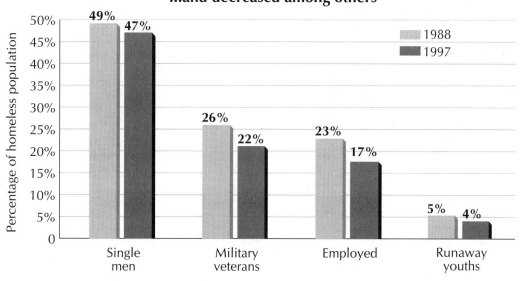

...and decreased among others

Source: U.S. Conference of Mayors

PUBLIC ASSISTANCE

During the 20th century, the U.S. government has passed a broad range of programs designed to provide financial help and social services to its citizens. The first federal U.S. program for the needy was created during the Great Depression of the 1930s. Today, programs include unemployment insurance, Social Security for retired people, health insurance plans, funds for education and training, subsidized day care for children, public housing, low-interest loans, veterans' benefits, food stamps, school lunch programs, and so on. At some time in their lives, almost all U.S. citizens will benefit from some type of government-based public assistance.

But public attention and debate have focused largely on those programs known as "welfare"—programs that provide money, food, housing, medical care, and other assistance to low-income people. In 1996, the federal government passed welfare reform legislation that restructured part of the Social Security Administration. The department of Aid to Families with Dependent Children (AFDC) was officially renamed Temporary Assistance to Needy Families (TANF) in July of 1997, and many new policies and procedures were subsequently enacted.

The process of distributing benefits changed dramatically. Instead of giving money directly to eligible people, the federal government now gives block grants to each state. This means that the money allotted for welfare benefits is proportionally distributed among the 50 states, and it is up to individual state governments to create their own welfare programs.

The qualifications and conditions of the TANF program became more strict. For example, families can only receive benefits for 60 months; unwed teenage parents must stay in school and live with

their parents; and criminals convicted of a drug-related felony cannot receive assistance.

TANF, along with a strong economy, has already helped reduce the number of people receiving benefits to 8.9 million recipients—a 27% decrease from the AFDC program. The effects on the recipients, and those no longer eligible, remain to be seen.

FINGERTIP FACTS

- ☞ Social insurance programs make up an average of 67% of federal social welfare spending. The same programs make up only 23% of such spending for states and local governments.

- ☞ Divorce or separation is the main reason why families go on welfare (45%); an unmarried woman having a child is second (30%).

- ☞ In 1997, some 22.8 million people received food stamps.

- ☞ In 1997, there were more than 750,000 pupils who participated in the national Head Start Program, at a cost of almost $3.6 billion to U.S. taxpayers.

- ☞ Between 1970 and 1994, Social Security payments to beneficiaries increased by about 850%, from $31.9 billion to $312 billion per year.

- ☞ Less than 4% of the American population was receiving welfare in 1997—the lowest percentage in more than 35 years.

- ☞ From 1996 to 1997, the number of families receiving assistance from TANF/AFDC decreased from 12.6 million to 10.9 million.

PUBLIC AID PAYMENTS IN THE U.S., 1980–1994

(In billions of dollars)

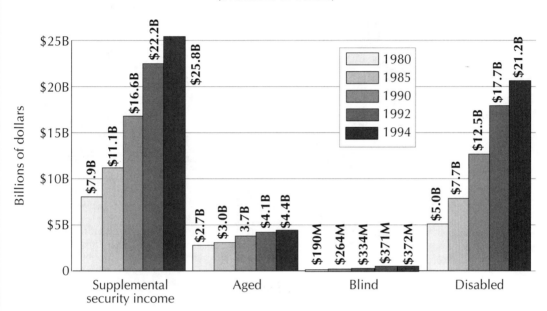

Billings of dollars

Supplemental security income: 1980: $7.9B; 1985: $11.1B; 1990: $16.6B; 1992: $22.2B; 1994: $25.8B

Aged: 1980: $2.7B; 1985: $3.0B; 1990: 3.7B; 1992: $4.1B; 1994: $4.4B

Blind: 1980: $190M; 1985: $264M; 1990: $334M; 1992: $371M; 1994: $372M

Disabled: 1980: $5.0B; 1985: $7.7B; 1990: $12.5B; 1992: $17.7B; 1994: $21.2B

Legend: 1980, 1985, 1990, 1992, 1994

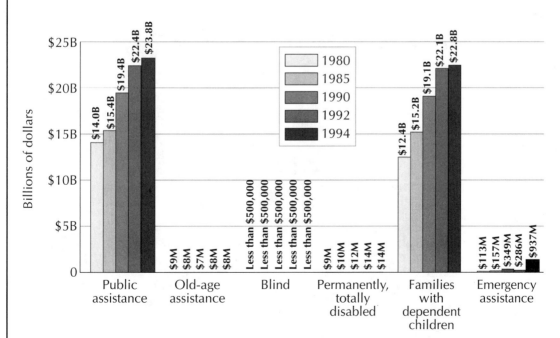

Billings of dollars

Public assistance: 1980: $14.0B; 1985: $15.4B; 1990: $19.4B; 1992: $22.4B; 1994: $23.8B

Old-age assistance: 1980: $9M; 1985: $8M; 1990: $7M; 1992: $8M; 1994: $8M

Blind: Less than $500,000 (all years)

Permanently, totally disabled: 1980: $9M; 1985: $10M; 1990: $12M; 1992: $14M; 1994: $14M

Families with dependent children: 1980: $12.4B; 1985: $15.2B; 1990: $19.1B; 1992: $22.1B; 1994: $22.8B

Emergency assistance: 1980: $113M; 1985: $157M; 1990: $349M; 1992: $286M; 1994: $937M

Legend: 1980, 1985, 1990, 1992, 1994

Source: U.S. Social Security Administration; U.S. Administration for Children and Families

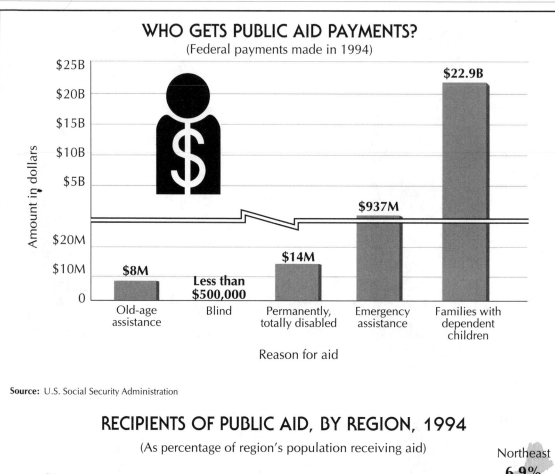

WHO GETS PUBLIC AID PAYMENTS?
(Federal payments made in 1994)

Amount in dollars

$25B
$20B
$15B
$10B
$5B

$20M
$10M
0

$8M — Old-age assistance

Less than $500,000 — Blind

$14M — Permanently, totally disabled

$937M — Emergency assistance

$22.9B — Families with dependent children

Reason for aid

Source: U.S. Social Security Administration

RECIPIENTS OF PUBLIC AID, BY REGION, 1994
(As percentage of region's population receiving aid)

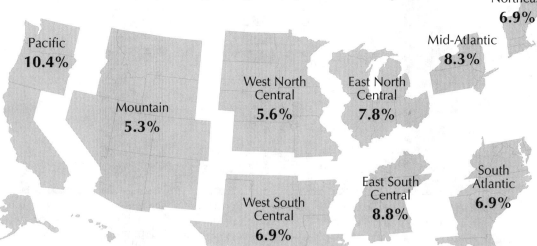

Northeast
6.9%

Mid-Atlantic
8.3%

Pacific
10.4%

West North Central
5.6%

East North Central
7.8%

Mountain
5.3%

West South Central
6.9%

East South Central
8.8%

South Atlantic
6.9%

Source: U.S. Census Bureau

GOVERNMENT SOCIAL WELFARE SPENDING, 1994

(Federal and state-and-local spending)

Federal and local

Total 1994:
$676.4 billion

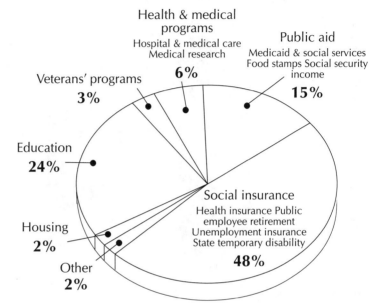

Health & medical
programs
Hospital & medical care
Medical research
6%

Public aid
Medicaid & social services
Food stamps Social security
income
15%

Veterans' programs
3%

Education
24%

Housing
2%

Other
2%

Social insurance
Health insurance Public
employee retirement
Unemployment insurance
State temporary disability
48%

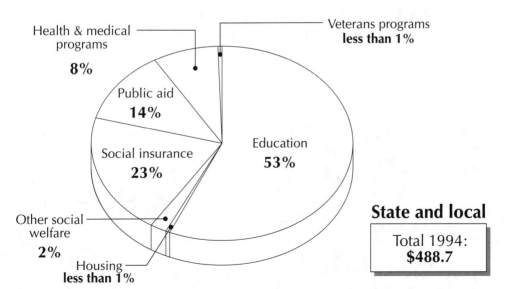

Health & medical
programs
8%

Veterans programs
less than 1%

Public aid
14%

Social insurance
23%

Education
53%

Other social
welfare
2%

Housing
less than 1%

State and local

Total 1994:
$488.7

Source: U.S. Social Security Administration

MOTHERS RECEIVING FOOD STAMPS, 1996

(By percentage of race and total recipients)

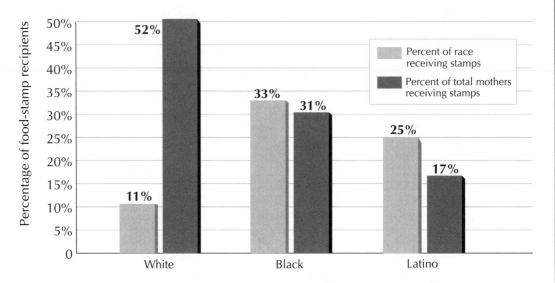

Source: U.S. Census Bureau

SOCIAL SECURITY PAYS OFF: THE NUMBER OF TOTAL PAYMENTS BY YEAR, 1970–1994

Number of beneficiaries

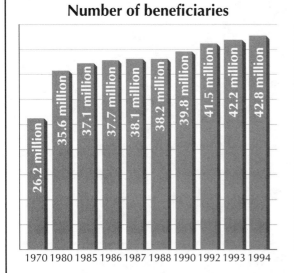

Annual payments

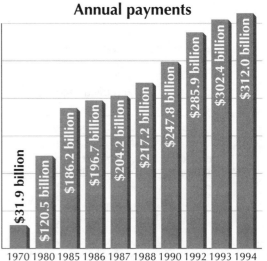

Source: U.S. Social Security Administration

TOP 10 STATES IN MEDICARE PAYMENTS, 1994

(With rankings)

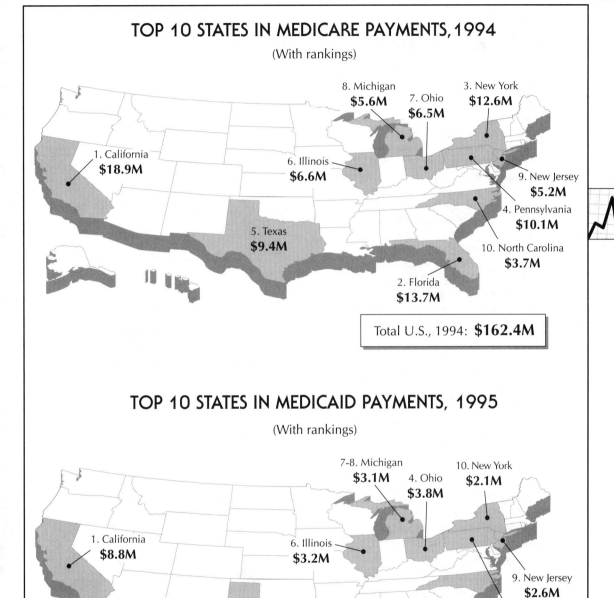

8. Michigan
$5.6M

7. Ohio
$6.5M

3. New York
$12.6M

1. California
$18.9M

6. Illinois
$6.6M

9. New Jersey
$5.2M

4. Pennsylvania
$10.1M

5. Texas
$9.4M

10. North Carolina
$3.7M

2. Florida
$13.7M

Total U.S., 1994: **$162.4M**

TOP 10 STATES IN MEDICAID PAYMENTS, 1995

(With rankings)

7-8. Michigan
$3.1M

4. Ohio
$3.8M

10. New York
$2.1M

1. California
$8.8M

6. Illinois
$3.2M

9. New Jersey
$2.6M

2. Texas
$5.7M

3. Pennsylvania
$4.3M

5. Florida
$3.5M

7-8. Louisiana
$3.1M

Total U.S., 1995: **$89.1M**

Source: U.S. Health Care Financing Administration

STANDARD OF LIVING

The term "standard of living" usually refers to the economic well-being enjoyed by a person, family, community, or nation. A standard of living is considered high when it includes not only necessities but also certain comforts and luxuries; it is considered low when food, clean water, housing, and other necessities are limited or lacking.

Economists use various methods to measure standard of living. One measurement is the percentage of income that citizens spend on certain necessities; the higher this percentage, the lower the standard of living. Another measurement is based on consumption expenditures—the amount of money spent on basic goods and services. Still another measurement calculates average disposable income—the amount left over after taxes that is available for spending or saving.

The U.S. has one of the world's highest standards of living. But income is not distributed evenly throughout the population. The nation is one of extremes. Some people enjoy great wealth, while others are trapped in extreme poverty. Major differences exist along racial, educational, and geographic lines. Household composition and family size, of course, are also factors in determining overall standards of living.

FINGERTIP FACTS

- Switzerland is the world's wealthiest nation in terms of economic output per person— $36,410 in 1993. The U.S. ranks 7th, with $24,750.

- In terms of buying power, which measures how much people get for their money, the U.S. is rated #2, behind Luxembourg.

- In 1997, personal income per capita in the U.S. was $25,660, up from $24,457 in 1996 and $9,940 in 1980.

- In 1997, disposable personal income per capita in the U.S. was $21,969. It was highest in the Northeast ($22,910), lowest in the South ($19,326).

- In 1997, about 12% of families had median incomes over $100,000. Some 10% of families lived below poverty line at $16,400.

- Connecticut ranked #1 in 1997 in personal income per capita with ($36,263); Mississippi ranked #50, with $18,272.

- According to the U.S. Census Bureau, the nation's median household income in 1997 was $44,568.

- In 1997, white men employed full-time had a median income of $36,118; for black men, it was $26,897. For white women, it was $26,470; for black women, it was $22,764.

- College graduates earn more than workers with only a high school degree. In 1996, white male college graduates ages 25 and older earned an average of $46,702; high school graduates earned $27,642.

- The median income of a single-father household ($35,658) was 40% higher than that of a single-mother household ($21,564) in 1997.

- Median household income in 1995 was higher among whites ($42,646) than among Latinos ($24,570) and blacks ($25,970).

PER CAPITA DISPOSABLE PERSONAL INCOME, BY REGION, 1997

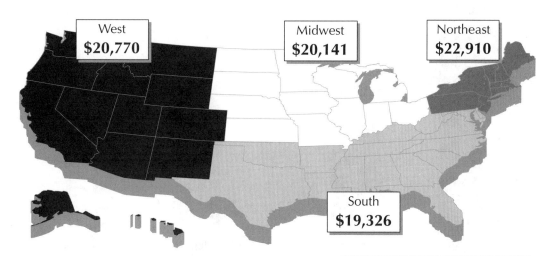

West
$20,770

Midwest
$20,141

Northeast
$22,910

South
$19,326

Average U.S. per capita income:
$21,969

Source: U.S. Bureau of Economic Analysis

PER CAPITA PERSONAL DISPOSABLE INCOME, 1929–1997
(In current dollars)

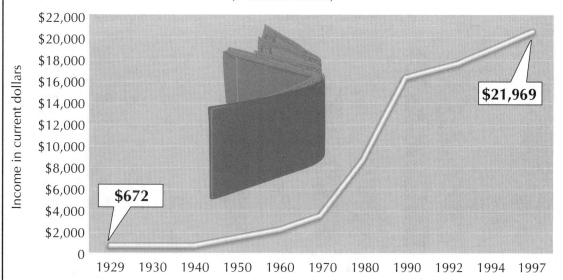

$672

$21,969

Source: U.S. Bureau of Economic Analysis

INCOME DIFFERENCES BY EDUCATION, 1997

Differences between the average incomes of full-time workers ages 25 and older:

$53,450

$31,215

$38,038

$22,067

College graduates	High school graduates		College graduates	High school graduates
Men			**Women**	

Source: U.S. Census Bureau

U.S. FAMILY MEDIAN INCOME, 1989 vs. 1995

(Figures in 1995 dollars)

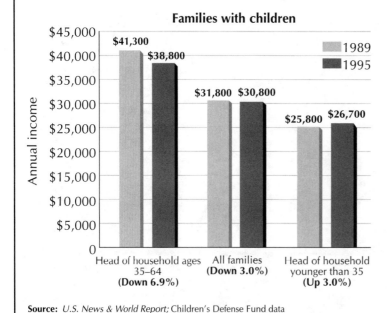

Families with children

1989
1995

$45,000
$40,000
$35,000
$30,000
$25,000
$20,000
$15,000
$10,000
$5,000
0

Annual income

$41,300 **$38,800**

$31,800 **$30,800**

$25,800 **$26,700**

Head of household ages 35–64
(Down 6.9%)

All families
(Down 3.0%)

Head of household younger than 35
(Up 3.0%)

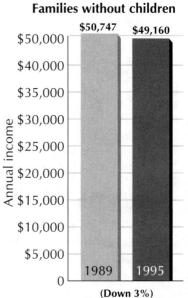

Families without children

$50,747 **$49,160**

$50,000
$40,000
$35,000
$30,000
$25,000
$20,000
$15,000
$10,000
$5,000
0

Annual income

1989   1995

(Down 3%)

Source: *U.S. News & World Report;* Children's Defense Fund data

PERSONAL CONSUMPTION EXPENDITURES, BY TYPE, 1996

(In billions of current dollars)

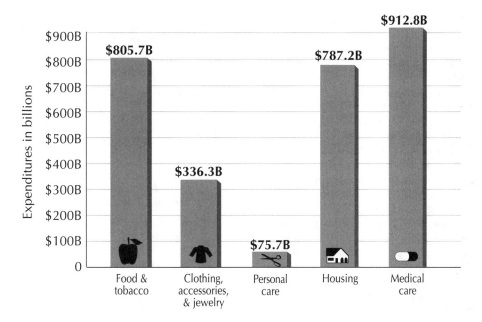

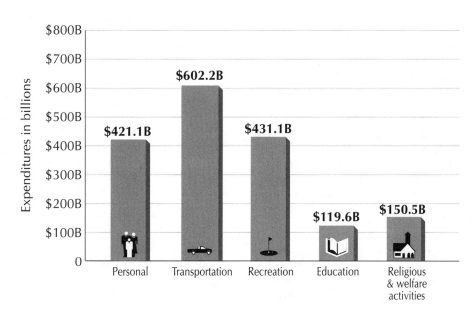

Source: U.S. Bureau of Economic Analysis

A C C I D E N T S   A N D   D E A T H

Accidents are the fourth leading cause of death in the U.S., after heart disease, cancer, and strokes. In general, accident victims are much younger than people who die from the three leading causes of death. Accidents are the #1 cause of death among Americans ages one to 38. They are the #7 cause among people ages 65 and older.

Motor-vehicle accidents are the main cause of accidental death in the U.S. Accidents in the home—mainly falls, fires, poisoning, suffocation, and drowning—are second.

The leading causes of death have changed during recent years. In 1900, a number of respiratory diseases—particularly pneumonia and influenza—were the main causes of death in the U.S. By 1996, these problems had decreased to #6. During the same period, however, cardiovascular diseases (diseases of the heart and blood vessels) and cancer grew significantly in frequency and have taken the lead.

Over the years, death rates per capita have fallen. In 1900, the U.S. death rate was 1,719 per 100,000 population. In 1950, the death rate was 963.8 per 100,000. By 1992, it had fallen to 853.3 per 100,000, but by 1997, had risen 1.2%, to 860.1 per 100,000.

Death rates vary by age, sex, race, cause, geographical location, and other factors. Death rates are rather high during the first year of life, then they drop sharply. They gradually increase again as people get older. Of course, death rates are highest among the elderly. Throughout life, however, males have higher death rates than females and black males have higher death rates than white males.

FINGERTIP FACTS

☞ Every 10 minutes, 2 people die in accidents in the U.S.

☞ Each year in the U.S., accidents cause almost half of all deaths among people ages 1 to 24. Motor-vehicle accidents are the main cause of accidental death in this age group.

☞ Among Americans ages 80 and older, falls are the main cause of accidental death.

☞ Accidental deaths caused by firearms rose 17% from 1995 to 1996.

☞ In 1993, medical expenses for accidents in the U.S. totaled about $75 billion. Damage to motor vehicles cost about $38 billion.

☞ Automobile travel is more risky than other kinds of travel. People are much more likely to be injured or killed in auto accidents than in train, bus, or airplane accidents.

☞ Deaths from motor-vehicle accidents are more common in rural areas than in cities.

☞ About 60% of Americans who die in motor-vehicle accidents are ages 15 to 44.

☞ About 30,000 people in the U.S. commit suicide each year. Males commit about 4 times as many suicides as do females.

☞ Each year, about 90 Americans are killed by lightning. More than two-thirds of all lightning deaths occur during the summer.

ACCIDENTAL DEATHS IN THE U.S., 1996

By types of accidents

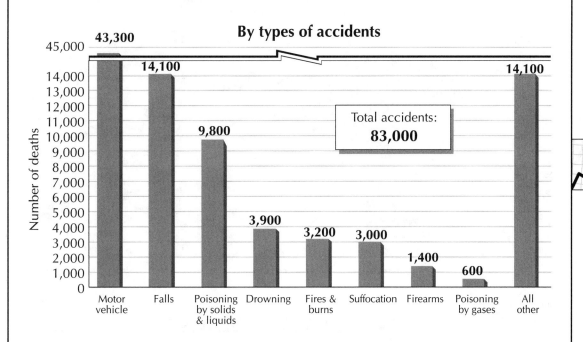

Total accidents:
83,000

Number of deaths

43,300 — Motor vehicle
14,100 — Falls
9,800 — Poisoning by solids & liquids
3,900 — Drowning
3,200 — Fires & burns
3,000 — Suffocation
1,400 — Firearms
600 — Poisoning by gases
14,100 — All other

By age group, 1997

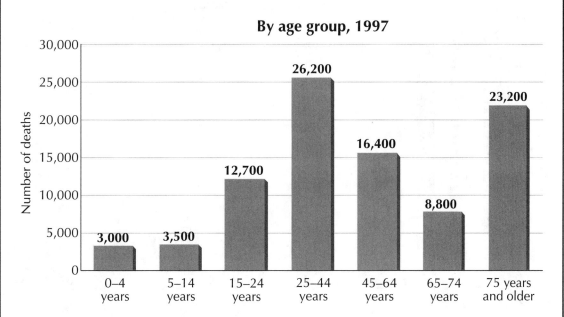

Number of deaths

3,000 — 0–4 years
3,500 — 5–14 years
12,700 — 15–24 years
26,200 — 25–44 years
16,400 — 45–64 years
8,800 — 65–74 years
23,200 — 75 years and older

Source: National Safety Council, *Accident Facts*

ACCIDENT-RELATED DEATH RATES IN THE U.S., 1930–1993

The number of deaths due to accidents has fallen steadily for 60 years,
even though the population has increased dramatically:

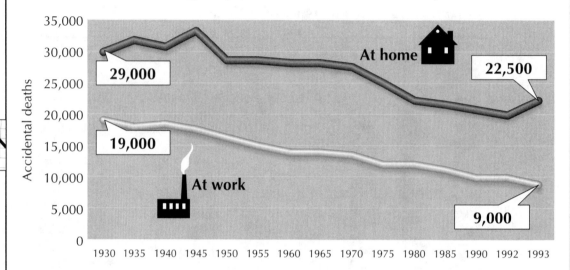

Source: National Safety Council

DEATH RATES BY CAUSE, 1997

(Rates per 100,000 population)

Death rate per 100,000

Cause	Rate
Heart diseases	271.2
Cancer	200.8
Cerebrovascular diseases	59.7
Pulmonary diseases	40.0
Accidents	34.4
Pneumonia and influenza	33.0
Diabetes mellitus	23.3
AIDS	12.3
Suicide	11.1
Kidney diseases	9.6
Liver disease and cirrhosis	9.3
Septicemia	8.1
Homicide and legal intervention	7.8
Atheriosclerosis	6.3
Perinatal-related conditions	6.2

Source: U.S. Department of Health and Human Services; National Center for Health Statistics

U.S. ACCIDENTS BY SITE, 1997

(Number of deaths and disabling injuries per site)

Accidental deaths by site

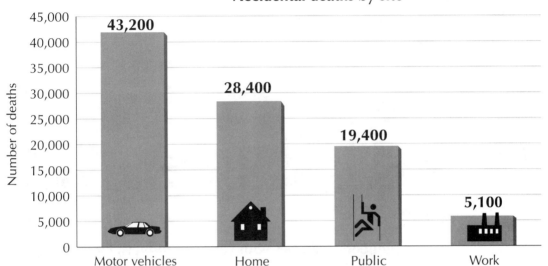

Disabling injuries

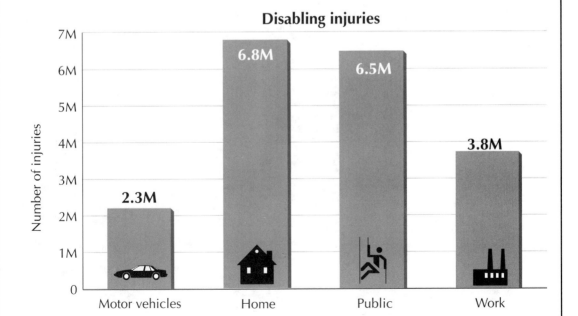

Source: National Safety Council

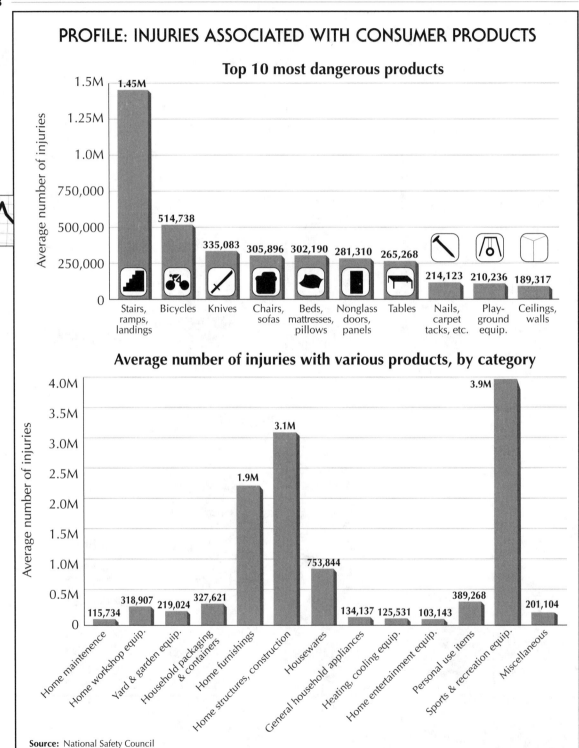

PROFILE: INJURIES ASSOCIATED WITH CONSUMER PRODUCTS

Top 10 most dangerous products

Average number of injuries

- Stairs, ramps, landings: 1.45M
- Bicycles: 514,738
- Knives: 335,083
- Chairs, sofas: 305,896
- Beds, mattresses, pillows: 302,190
- Nonglass doors, panels: 281,310
- Tables: 265,268
- Nails, carpet tacks, etc.: 214,123
- Play-ground equip.: 210,236
- Ceilings, walls: 189,317

Average number of injuries with various products, by category

Average number of injuries

- Home maintenance: 115,734
- Home workshop equip.: 318,907
- Yard & garden equip.: 219,024
- Household packaging & containers: 327,621
- Home furnishings: 1.9M
- Home structures, construction: 3.1M
- Housewares: 753,844
- General household appliances: 134,137
- Heating, cooling equip.: 125,531
- Home entertainment equip.: 103,143
- Personal use items: 389,268
- Sports & recreation equip.: 3.9M
- Miscellaneous: 201,104

Source: National Safety Council

ESTIMATED NUMBER OF INJURIES IN U.S. FROM SELECTED PRODUCTS, 1994

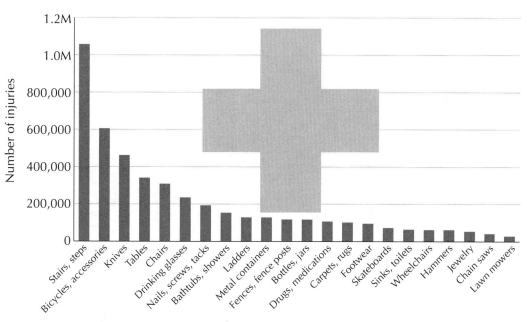

Source: Consumer Product Safety Commission, National Electronic Injury Surveillance System, *Product Summary Report* (1994)

PLANE DEATHS ON THE WANE, 1988–1993

The number of deaths and the fatal accident rate for major U.S. airlines operating scheduled flights fell drastically from 1988 to 1993:

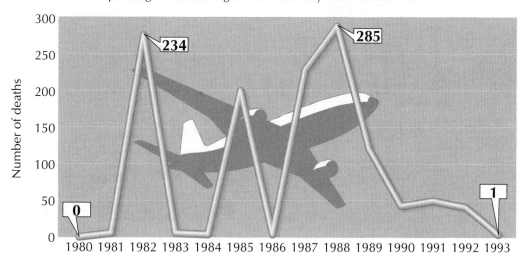

Source: National Transportation Safety Board

UP IN FLAMES: FIRE DEATHS IN THE HOME, 1983–1994

Children playing with matches or lighters caused 12% of home-fire deaths in 1994, the fourth-biggest cause after smoking, arson, and heating accidents. The number of fire fatalities caused by children:

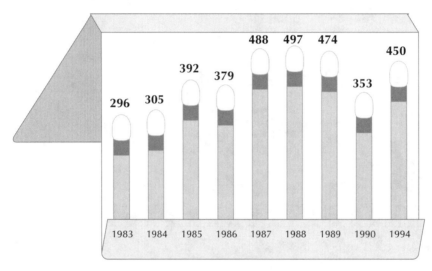

Source: U.S. Fire Administration

ACCIDENTAL DEATHS OF U.S. CHILDREN UNDER AGE 5, 1996

(Deaths by cause and number)

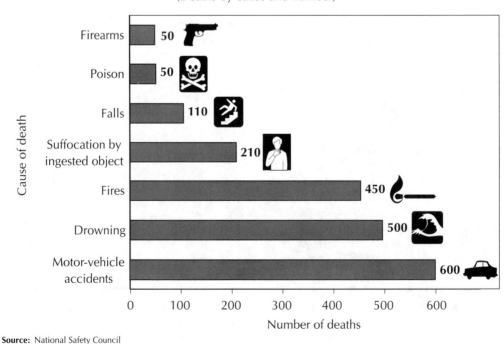

Source: National Safety Council

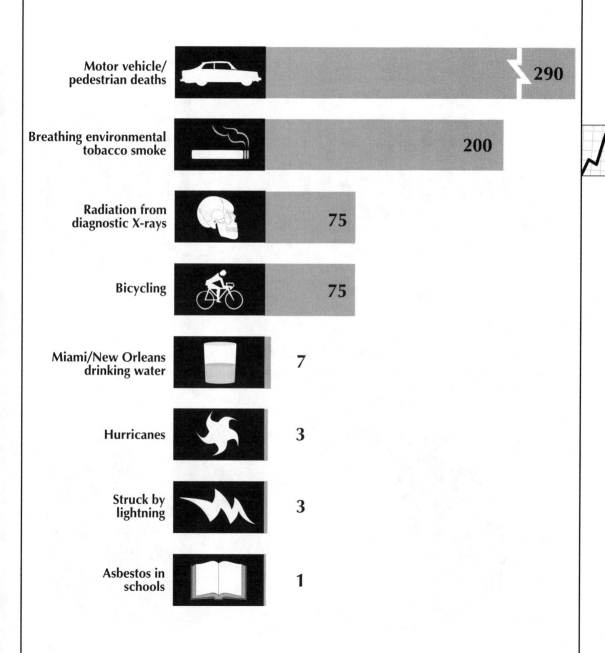

PREMATURE DEATH IN THE U.S.

(Relative probability of premature deaths by various causes; rates per 100,000 population)

Motor vehicle/ pedestrian deaths	290
Breathing environmental tobacco smoke	200
Radiation from diagnostic X-rays	75
Bicycling	75
Miami/New Orleans drinking water	7
Hurricanes	3
Struck by lightning	3
Asbestos in schools	1

Source: Energy and Environmental Policy Center

ACCIDENTAL DEATH RATES BY NATION, 1990–1991

(Rate per 100,000 population)

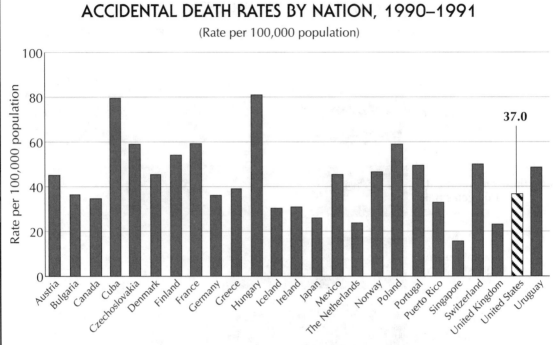

37.0

Source: World Health Organization

SEAT BELTS SAVE LIVES

Many studies by the National Highway Traffic Safety Administration show that people who wore seat belts in passenger car crashes—in which at least one person was killed— were more likely to survive and be uninjured than people who did not wear seat belts.

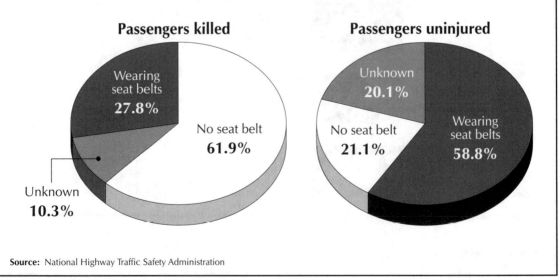

Passengers killed

Wearing seat belts **27.8%**

No seat belt **61.9%**

Unknown **10.3%**

Passengers uninjured

Unknown **20.1%**

No seat belt **21.1%**

Wearing seat belts **58.8%**

Source: National Highway Traffic Safety Administration

SEAT BELT USE IN AMERICA, 1997
(By race and gender)

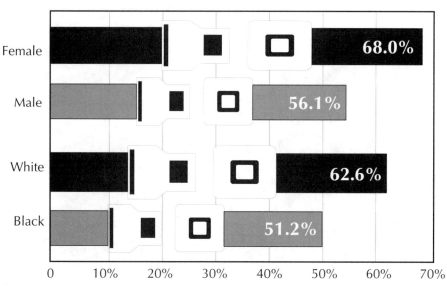

Percentage that wear seat belts

(By age)

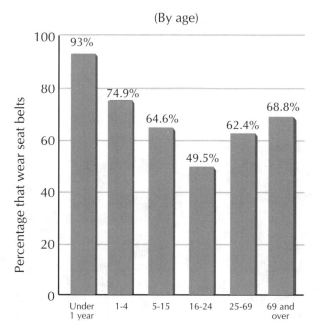

Source: National Highway Traffic Safety Administration

ALCOHOL-RELATED MOTOR-VEHICLE DEATHS DECLINE, 1982–1997

In 1982, out of 43,945 traffic deaths, 25,170 were alcohol-related. By 1997, only 17,126 of 43,200 traffic deaths were alcohol-related. How the percentage of alcohol-related deaths has declined:

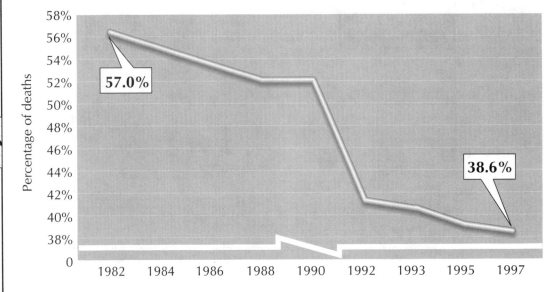

Source: National Highway Traffic Safety Administration

SAFETY ON THE ROAD, BY STATE

(Average traffic deaths per 1 million miles traveled)

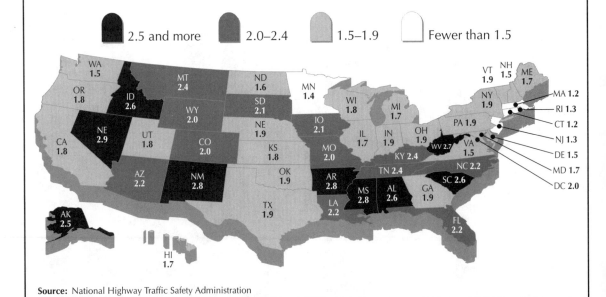

Source: National Highway Traffic Safety Administration

ROAD HAZARDS: ACCIDENTS AND DEATH, 1995

Collision deaths

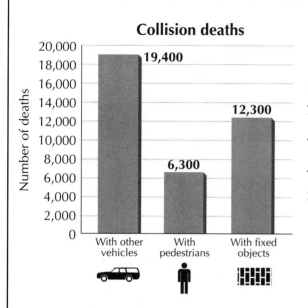

Motor-vehicle accidents

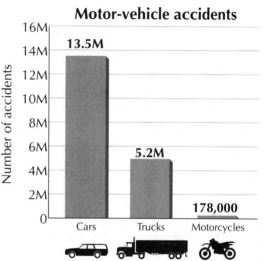

Source: National Safety Council; National Highway Traffic Safety Commission

MOST DANGEROUS JOBS, 1997

Occupations with the highest rate of fatalities per 100,000 workers:

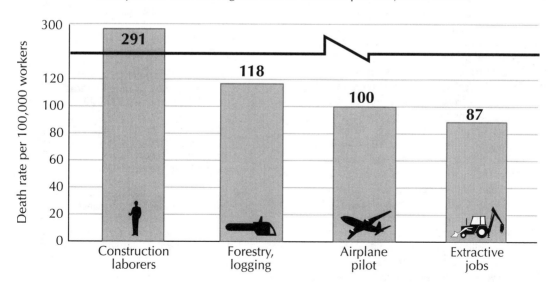

Source: Bureau of Labor Statistics

I M M I G R A T I O N

Since the first colonists settled on its shores, the United States has been a land of immigrants. More people have immigrated to this nation than to any other. Immigrants have included scientists and doctors, artists and musicians, farmers and teachers, and untold millions of hard-working laborers. They've made America their home, adopted its values, and made innumerable contributions to its economy and culture.

More than 8% of the current U.S. population were born elsewhere. In 1996, some 1.2 million people entered the country—915,900 of them legally, the rest illegally. Many of the legal immigrants were refugees escaping war, ethnic or religious persecution, or other disasters in their homelands.

Some argue that the "nation of immigrants" has a moral obligation to accept an unrestricted flow of people from other lands. Others argue for a closing of U.S. borders.

In recent years, anti-immigrant sentiment has been rising in the U.S.— as it has in other wealthy industrialized nations of the world. Many want the government to step up efforts to apprehend illegal aliens, to cut immigration quotas, and to eliminate—or at least limit—benefits and services for both legal and illegal immigrants. In 1994, in their so-called Contract With America, Republicans running for the House of Representatives included a proposal to ban welfare benefits for legal immigrants. California voters also passed the hotly debated Proposition 187, which would deny illegal aliens access to public schools, non-emergency care at public health clinics, and other social services. This result reflected the sentiments toward illegal immigrants expressed by a majority of Americans. Judicial orders at least temporarily blocked implementation of the proposition.

FINGERTIP FACTS

- Since 1970, some 20.7 million immigrants have settled in the U.S.; 915,900 people legally immigrated to the U.S. in 1996.

- Between 1820 and 1996, the largest percentage of U.S. immigrants came from Germany, followed by Great Britain, Italy, Mexico, Vietnam, the Philippines, and countries of the former Soviet Union.

- The states with the highest percentage of foreign-born residents are California (21.7%), New York (15.8%), and Hawaii (14.7%).

- Worldwide, 13.6 million people fled their homeland in 1996. Of these refugees, 491,000 were admitted to the U.S.

- The Immigration and Naturalization Service (INS) estimated in 1993 that about 300,000 people illegally enter the U.S. each year. In recent years, the greatest percentage of illegal immigrants to the U.S. have come from Mexico.

- California has the highest number of illegal immigrants. In 1997, there were an estimated 2.0 million illegal aliens living in California.

NUMBER OF IMMIGRANTS TO U.S., BY DECADE, 1820–1996

(In millions)

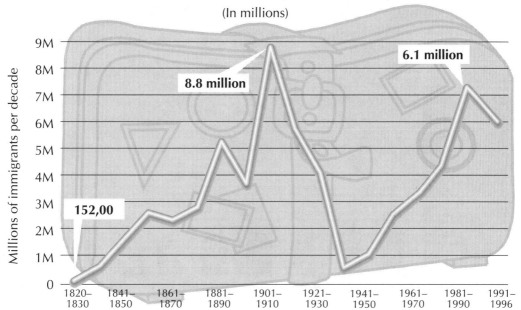

8.8 million

6.1 million

152,00

Source: U.S. Immigration and Naturalization Service

IMMIGRANTS SHORE UP U.S. POPULATION, 1901–1996

(Percentage of U.S. population growth created by immigration in the 20th century)

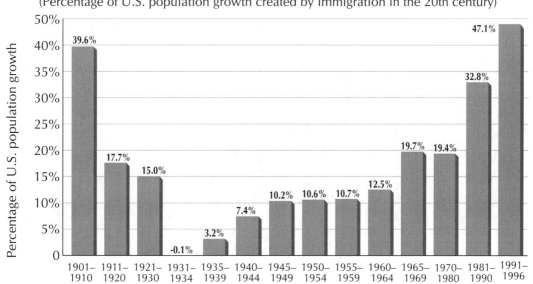

Source: U.S. Immigration and Naturalization Service; U.S. Census Bureau

U.S. IMMIGRANTS: TOP 10 COUNTRIES OF ORIGIN, 1996
(As percentage of all legal immigrants)

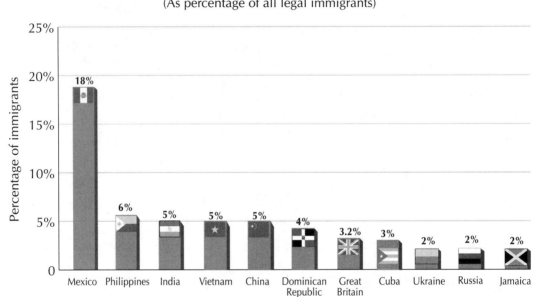

Source: U.S. Immigration and Naturalization Service

TOP 20 IMMIGRANT GROUPS IN U.S. LARGER THAN 100,000, 1994

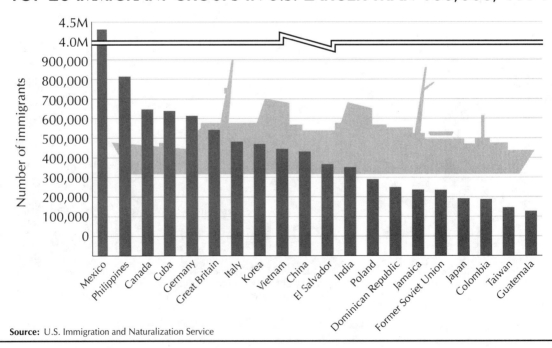

Source: U.S. Immigration and Naturalization Service

TOP 5 STATES WITH HIGHEST PERCENTAGE OF FOREIGN-BORN POPULATION, 1997
(With rankings)

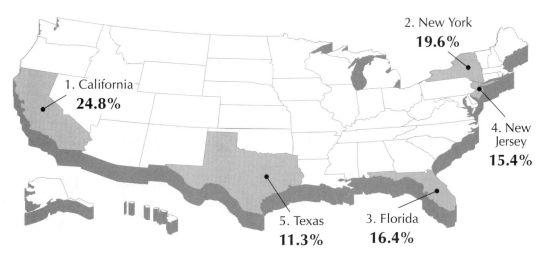

2. New York
19.6%

1. California
24.8%

4. New Jersey
15.4%

5. Texas
11.3%

3. Florida
16.4%

Source: U.S. Census Bureau

U.S. NATURALIZATION, 1990-1996

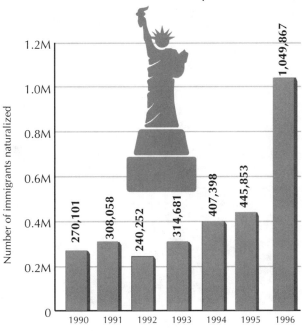

Number of immigrants naturalized

- 1.2M
- 1.0M
- 0.8M
- 0.6M
- 0.4M
- 0.2M
- 0

1990	1991	1992	1993	1994	1995	1996
270,101	308,058	240,252	314,681	407,398	445,853	1,049,867

Source: U.S. Immigration and Naturalization Service

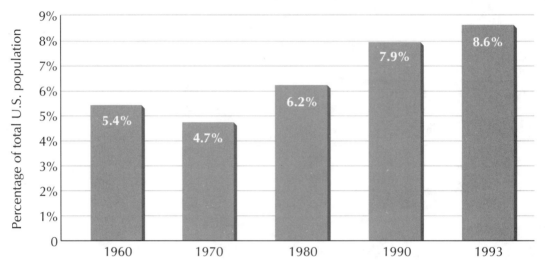

COMPARATIVE PERCENTAGES OF FOREIGN-BORN PEOPLE IN U.S., 1960–1993

Source: U.S. State Department

PROFILE: BIRTHPLACES OF FOREIGN-BORN U.S. POPULATION

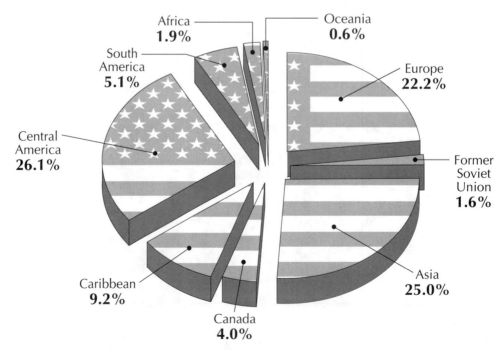

Source: U.S. Census Bureau

PROFILE: SELECTED ANCESTRY GROUPS OF U.S. POPULATION

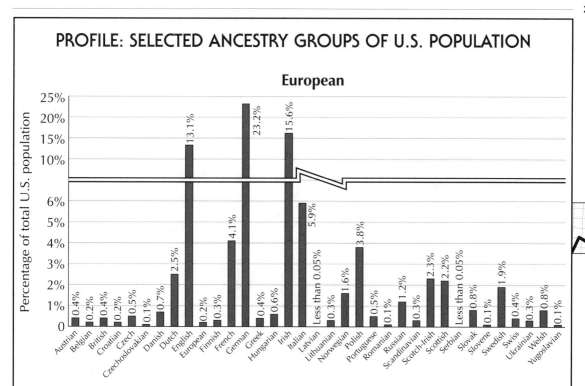

European

Percentage of total U.S. population

Group	Percentage
Austrian	0.4%
Belgian	0.2%
British	0.4%
Croatian	0.2%
Czech	0.5%
Czechoslovakian	0.1%
Danish	0.7%
Dutch	2.5%
English	13.1%
European	0.2%
Finnish	0.3%
French	4.1%
German	23.2%
Greek	0.4%
Hungarian	0.6%
Irish	15.6%
Italian	5.9%
Latvian	Less than 0.05%
Lithuanian	0.3%
Norwegian	1.6%
Polish	3.8%
Portuguese	0.5%
Romanian	0.1%
Russian	1.2%
Scandinavian	0.3%
Scotch-Irish	2.3%
Scottish	2.2%
Serbian	Less than 0.05%
Slovak	0.8%
Slovene	0.1%
Swedish	1.9%
Swiss	0.4%
Ukrainian	0.3%
Welsh	0.8%
Yugoslavian	0.1%

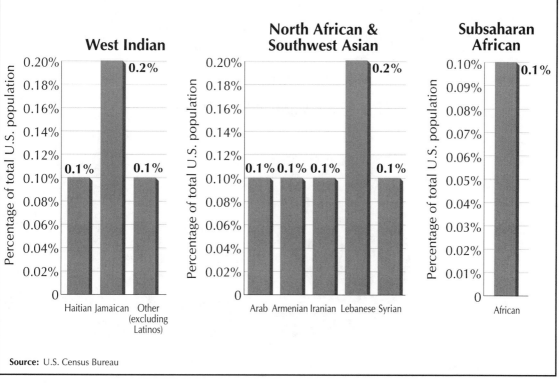

West Indian

Percentage of total U.S. population

Group	Percentage
Haitian	0.1%
Jamaican	0.2%
Other (excluding Latinos)	0.1%

North African & Southwest Asian

Percentage of total U.S. population

Group	Percentage
Arab	0.1%
Armenian	0.1%
Iranian	0.1%
Lebanese	0.2%
Syrian	0.1%

Subsaharan African

Percentage of total U.S. population

Group	Percentage
African	0.1%

Source: U.S. Census Bureau

TOP 20 COUNTRIES OF BIRTH FOR U.S. IMMIGRANTS, 1996

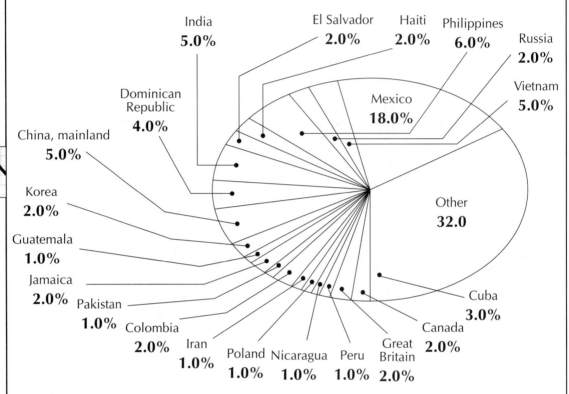

India
5.0%

El Salvador
2.0%

Haiti
2.0%

Philippines
6.0%

Russia
2.0%

Vietnam
5.0%

Dominican
Republic
4.0%

Mexico
18.0%

China, mainland
5.0%

Other
32.0

Korea
2.0%

Guatemala
1.0%

Jamaica
2.0%

Pakistan
1.0%

Colombia
2.0%

Iran
1.0%

Poland
1.0%

Nicaragua
1.0%

Peru
1.0%

Great
Britain
2.0%

Canada
2.0%

Cuba
3.0%

Source: U.S. Department of Justice; U.S. Immigration and Naturalization Service

MOST U.S. MUSLIMS ARE IMMIGRANTS

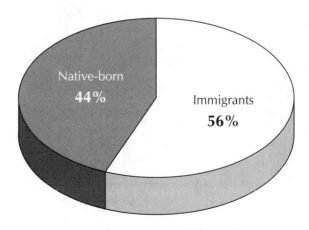

Native-born
44%

Immigrants
56%

Source: The American Muslim Council; Islamic Resource Institute

LIFESTYLES FOR IMMIGRANTS vs. AMERICAN-BORN CITIZENS

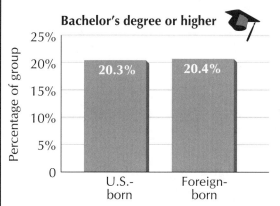

Bachelor's degree or higher

Percentage of group

- U.S.-born: 20.3%
- Foreign-born: 20.4%

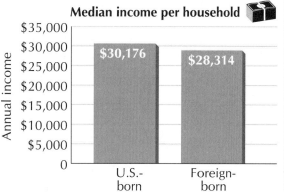

Median income per household

Annual income

- U.S.-born: $30,176
- Foreign-born: $28,314

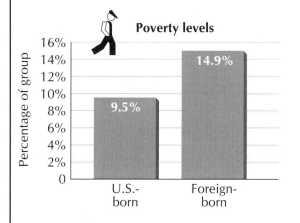

Poverty levels

Percentage of group

- U.S.-born: 9.5%
- Foreign-born: 14.9%

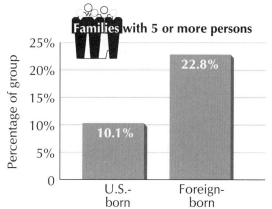

Families with 5 or more persons

Percentage of group

- U.S.-born: 10.1%
- Foreign-born: 22.8%

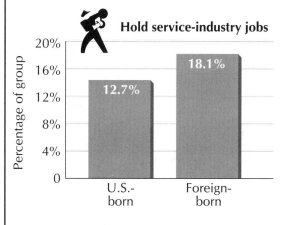

Hold service-industry jobs

Percentage of group

- U.S.-born: 12.7%
- Foreign-born: 18.1%

Self-employed

Percentage of group

- U.S.-born: 7.0%
- Foreign-born: 6.8%

Source: U.S. Census Bureau

NUMBER OF U.S. POPULATION
THAT WERE FOREIGN-BORN, 1993

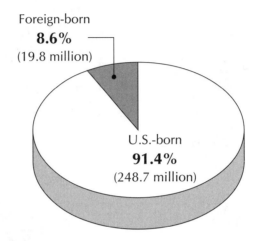

Foreign-born
8.6%
(19.8 million)

U.S.-born
91.4%
(248.7 million)

Source: U.S. Census Bureau

TOP 5 STATES IN POPULATION OF IMMIGRANTS FROM CHINA
(With rankings)

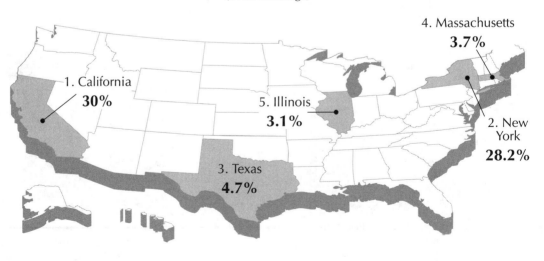

4. Massachusetts
3.7%

1. California
30%

5. Illinois
3.1%

2. New York
28.2%

3. Texas
4.7%

Source: U.S. Immigration and Naturalization Service

TOP 10 STATES WITH HIGHEST NUMBER OF ILLEGAL IMMIGRANTS

(With rankings)

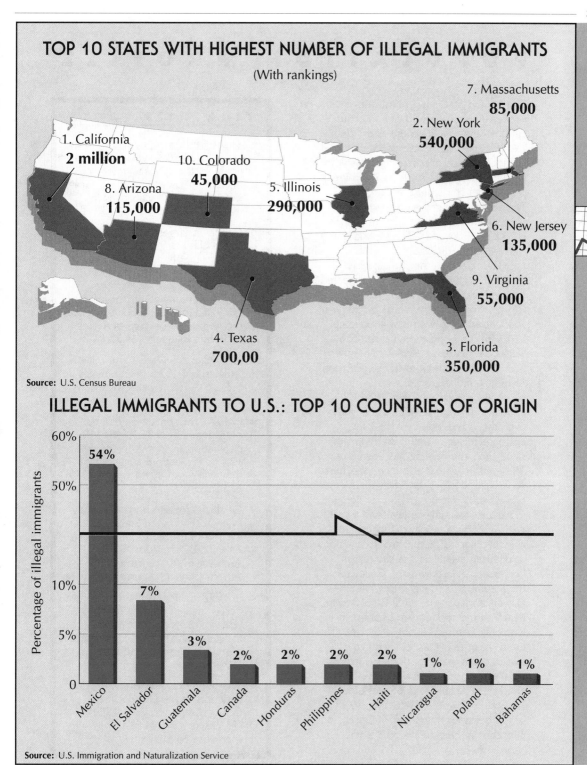

7. Massachusetts
85,000

2. New York
540,000

1. California
2 million

10. Colorado
45,000

8. Arizona
115,000

5. Illinois
290,000

6. New Jersey
135,000

9. Virginia
55,000

4. Texas
700,00

3. Florida
350,000

Source: U.S. Census Bureau

ILLEGAL IMMIGRANTS TO U.S.: TOP 10 COUNTRIES OF ORIGIN

Percentage of illegal immigrants

- 60%
- 50%
- 10%
- 5%
- 0

54% Mexico
7% El Salvador
3% Guatemala
2% Canada
2% Honduras
2% Philippines
2% Haiti
1% Nicaragua
1% Poland
1% Bahamas

Source: U.S. Immigration and Naturalization Service

POPULATION PROFILE

The United States is a pluralistic nation—it is composed of numerous cultures and ethnic groups. Less than 1% of its population are descendants of Aleuts, Eskimos, and other groups who lived on the North American continent prior to its settlement by Europeans. The other main groups are whites (72.3% of the 1998 population), blacks (12.7%), Latinos (11.2%), and Asians and Pacific Islanders (3.8%).

The nation's ethnic profile has changed over the years and is expected to continue changing in the near future. Current trends suggest that by the year 2050, non-Latino whites will make up 52.5% of the population; Latino 22.5%; blacks, 14.4%; Asians and Pacific Islanders, 9.7%; and Aleuts, Eskimos, and American Indians, 0.9%.

Many other aspects of the U.S. population profile have also changed over the years. Prior to 1950, for example, males outnumbered females; since then, the reverse has been true. The median age has also increased, more Americans are living in urban areas, more profess to having no religious preference, more are attending college, and a good deal more have interracial marriages.

Members of ethnic groups are not distributed evenly across the nation. For example, in New York, German is the leading ancestry group, while in Hawaii, it's Japanese. In El Paso, Texas, 69.6% of the residents are Latino; in Knoxville, Tennessee, only 0.5% are. The South has the highest percentage of blacks, and a majority of Asians live in the West. Florida has the highest percentage of people ages 65 and older, Alaska the lowest. In Alabama, 70.7% of residents are members of Christian churches; in Maine, only 35.8% are.

FINGERTIP FACTS

☛ The 1998 Latino population in the U.S. totaled 30.3 million. Mexicans made up the largest number (18.0 million), followed by Puerto Ricans (2.6 million) and Cubans (1.5 million).

☛ Of the 75 largest county areas in the U.S. in 1997, Baltimore County, MD, had the highest percentage of blacks (65.4%). Bexar County, Texas, had the largest percentage of Latinos (55.9%). Honolulu County, HI, had the largest percentage of Asians or Pacific Islanders (64.3%).

☛ In 1998, there were 137.6 million females and 132.5 million males in the U.S.—100 females for every 95.9 males.

☛ In 1970, residents ages 65 and older made up 9.8% of the U.S. population; in 1999, they made up 12.7%. Projections suggest that they will equal 20.4% of the 2050 population.

☛ Of all the foreign-born persons living in the United States, 22.2% are from Europe, 25.0% are from Asia, 39.4% are from North America, 5.1% are from South America, and 1.9% are from Africa.

☛ In 1997, California had the highest percentage of children under 5 years old (14% of U.S. population), as well as the highest percentage of people 65 years and older (10%).

☛ The percentage of foreign-born residents in the U.S. declined during the period from 1920 (13.2%) to 1970 (4.8%), and then rose by 1997 (9.7%).

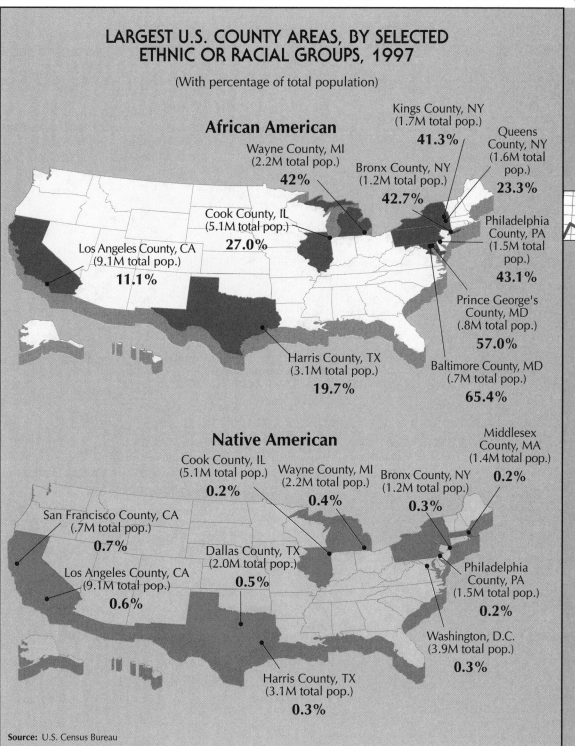

LARGEST U.S. COUNTY AREAS, BY SELECTED ETHNIC OR RACIAL GROUPS, 1997

(With percentage of total population)

African American

Kings County, NY
(1.7M total pop.)
41.3%

Queens County, NY
(1.6M total pop.)
23.3%

Wayne County, MI
(2.2M total pop.)
42%

Bronx County, NY
(1.2M total pop.)
42.7%

Cook County, IL
(5.1M total pop.)
27.0%

Philadelphia County, PA
(1.5M total pop.)
43.1%

Los Angeles County, CA
(9.1M total pop.)
11.1%

Prince George's County, MD
(.8M total pop.)
57.0%

Harris County, TX
(3.1M total pop.)
19.7%

Baltimore County, MD
(.7M total pop.)
65.4%

Native American

Middlesex County, MA
(1.4M total pop.)
0.2%

Cook County, IL
(5.1M total pop.)
0.2%

Wayne County, MI
(2.2M total pop.)
0.4%

Bronx County, NY
(1.2M total pop.)
0.3%

San Francisco County, CA
(.7M total pop.)
0.7%

Dallas County, TX
(2.0M total pop.)
0.5%

Philadelphia County, PA
(1.5M total pop.)
0.2%

Los Angeles County, CA
(9.1M total pop.)
0.6%

Washington, D.C.
(3.9M total pop.)
0.3%

Harris County, TX
(3.1M total pop.)
0.3%

Source: U.S. Census Bureau

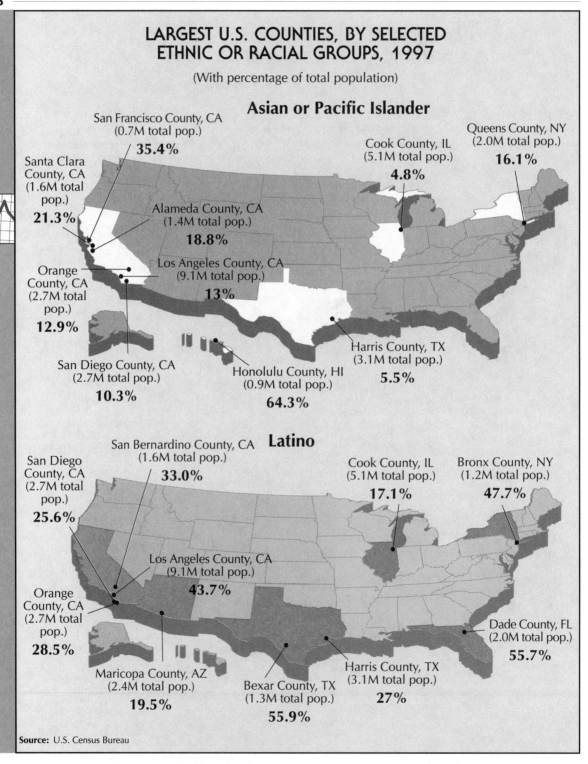

LARGEST U.S. COUNTIES, BY SELECTED ETHNIC OR RACIAL GROUPS, 1997

(With percentage of total population)

Asian or Pacific Islander

San Francisco County, CA
(0.7M total pop.)
35.4%

Santa Clara County, CA
(1.6M total pop.)
21.3%

Alameda County, CA
(1.4M total pop.)
18.8%

Orange County, CA
(2.7M total pop.)
12.9%

Los Angeles County, CA
(9.1M total pop.)
13%

San Diego County, CA
(2.7M total pop.)
10.3%

Honolulu County, HI
(0.9M total pop.)
64.3%

Cook County, IL
(5.1M total pop.)
4.8%

Queens County, NY
(2.0M total pop.)
16.1%

Harris County, TX
(3.1M total pop.)
5.5%

Latino

San Diego County, CA
(2.7M total pop.)
25.6%

San Bernardino County, CA
(1.6M total pop.)
33.0%

Los Angeles County, CA
(9.1M total pop.)
43.7%

Orange County, CA
(2.7M total pop.)
28.5%

Maricopa County, AZ
(2.4M total pop.)
19.5%

Bexar County, TX
(1.3M total pop.)
55.9%

Harris County, TX
(3.1M total pop.)
27%

Cook County, IL
(5.1M total pop.)
17.1%

Bronx County, NY
(1.2M total pop.)
47.7%

Dade County, FL
(2.0M total pop.)
55.7%

Source: U.S. Census Bureau

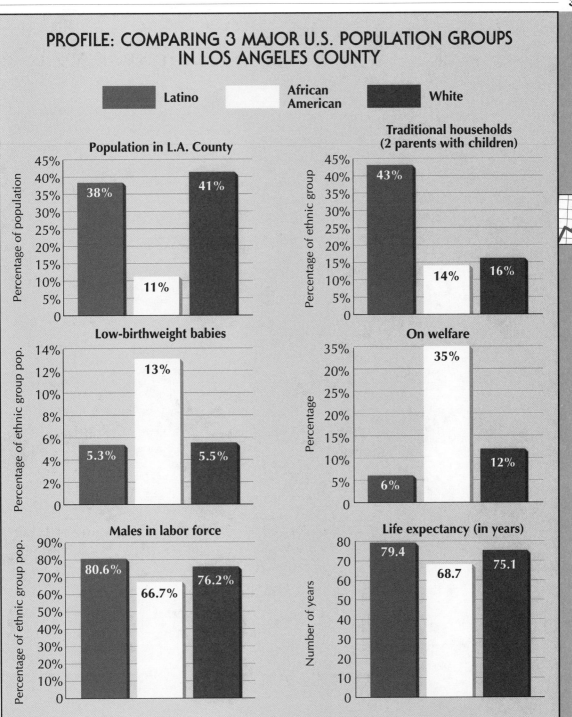

PROFILE: COMPARING 3 MAJOR U.S. POPULATION GROUPS IN LOS ANGELES COUNTY

■ Latino   □ African American   ■ White

Population in L.A. County

Percentage of population

45%
40%
35%
30%
25%
20%
15%
10%
5%
0

38%   11%   41%

Traditional households (2 parents with children)

Percentage of ethnic group

45%
40%
35%
30%
25%
20%
15%
10%
5%
0

43%   14%   16%

Low-birthweight babies

Percentage of ethnic group pop.

14%
12%
10%
8%
6%
4%
2%
0

5.3%   13%   5.5%

On welfare

Percentage

35%
20%
25%
15%
10%
5%
0

6%   35%   12%

Males in labor force

Percentage of ethnic group pop.

90%
80%
70%
60%
50%
40%
30%
20%
10%
0

80.6%   66.7%   76.2%

Life expectancy (in years)

Number of years

80
70
60
50
40
30
20
10
0

79.4   68.7   75.1

Source: U.S. Census Bureau

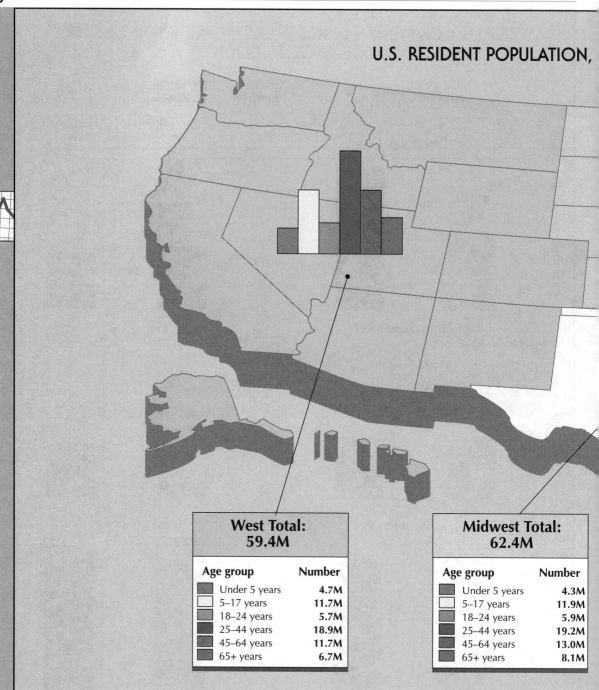

U.S. RESIDENT POPULATION,

West Total:
59.4M

Age group	Number
Under 5 years	**4.7M**
5–17 years	**11.7M**
18–24 years	**5.7M**
25–44 years	**18.9M**
45–64 years	**11.7M**
65+ years	**6.7M**

Midwest Total:
62.4M

Age group	Number
Under 5 years	**4.3M**
5–17 years	**11.9M**
18–24 years	**5.9M**
25–44 years	**19.2M**
45–64 years	**13.0M**
65+ years	**8.1M**

Source: U.S. Census

BY AGE AND REGION, 1997

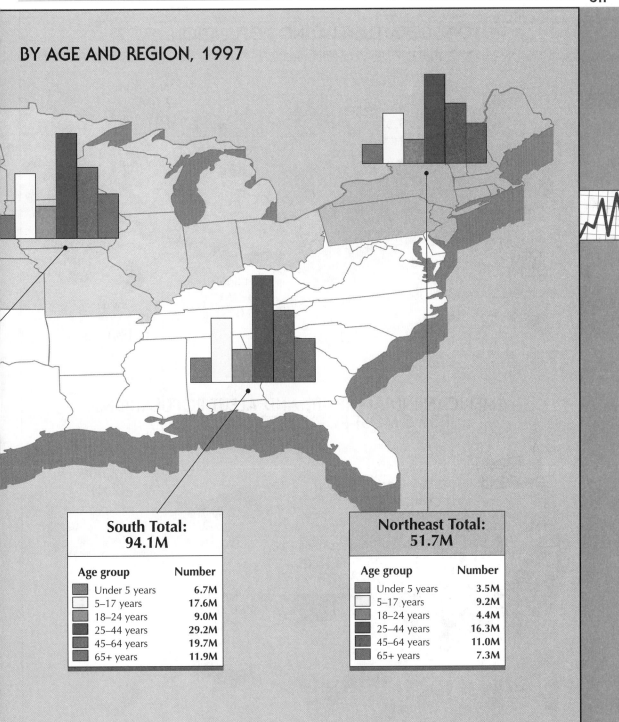

South Total:
94.1M

Age group	Number
Under 5 years	**6.7M**
5–17 years	**17.6M**
18–24 years	**9.0M**
25–44 years	**29.2M**
45–64 years	**19.7M**
65+ years	**11.9M**

Northeast Total:
51.7M

Age group	Number
Under 5 years	**3.5M**
5–17 years	**9.2M**
18–24 years	**4.4M**
25–44 years	**16.3M**
45–64 years	**11.0M**
65+ years	**7.3M**

TOP 10 STATES IN LATINO POPULATION, 1997

(Number of Latinos with percentage of state's population given in parentheses, and rankings)

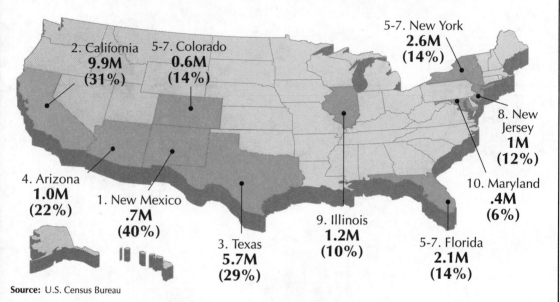

2. California
9.9M
(31%)

5-7. Colorado
0.6M
(14%)

5-7. New York
2.6M
(14%)

8. New Jersey
1M
(12%)

10. Maryland
.4M
(6%)

4. Arizona
1.0M
(22%)

1. New Mexico
.7M
(40%)

3. Texas
5.7M
(29%)

9. Illinois
1.2M
(10%)

5-7. Florida
2.1M
(14%)

Source: U.S. Census Bureau

AMERICAN INDIAN, INUIT, AND ALEUT POPULATIONS: TOP 6 MOST-POPULATED STATES, 1997

(With rankings)

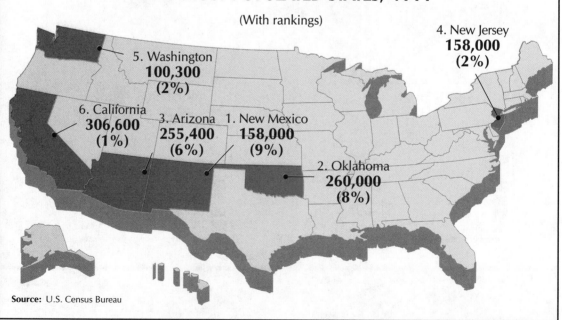

5. Washington
100,300
(2%)

4. New Jersey
158,000
(2%)

6. California
306,600
(1%)

3. Arizona
255,400
(6%)

1. New Mexico
158,000
(9%)

2. Oklahoma
260,000
(8%)

Source: U.S. Census Bureau

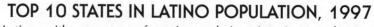

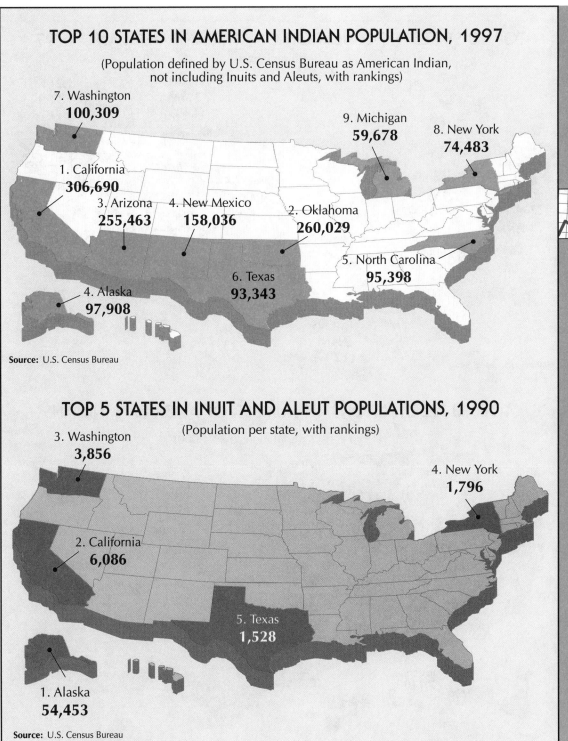

TOP 10 STATES IN AMERICAN INDIAN POPULATION, 1997

(Population defined by U.S. Census Bureau as American Indian,
not including Inuits and Aleuts, with rankings)

7. Washington
100,309

9. Michigan
59,678

8. New York
74,483

1. California
306,690

3. Arizona
255,463

4. New Mexico
158,036

2. Oklahoma
260,029

5. North Carolina
95,398

6. Texas
93,343

4. Alaska
97,908

Source: U.S. Census Bureau

TOP 5 STATES IN INUIT AND ALEUT POPULATIONS, 1990

(Population per state, with rankings)

3. Washington
3,856

4. New York
1,796

2. California
6,086

5. Texas
1,528

1. Alaska
54,453

Source: U.S. Census Bureau

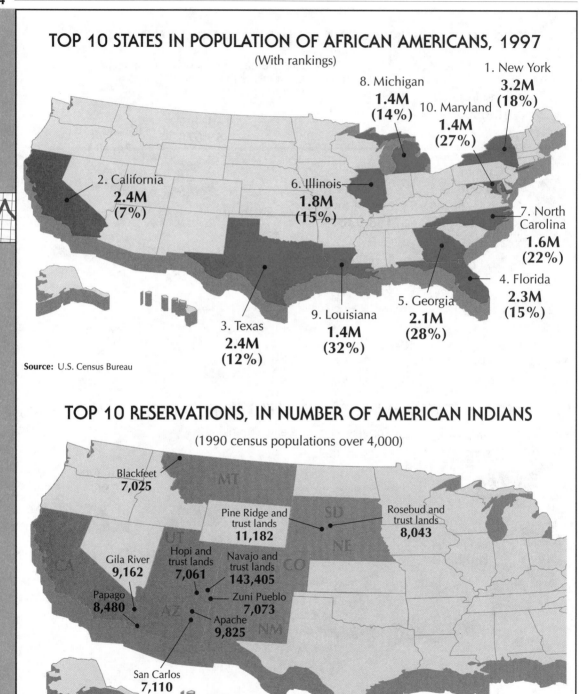

TOP 10 STATES IN POPULATION OF AFRICAN AMERICANS, 1997

(With rankings)

1. New York
3.2M
(18%)

8. Michigan
1.4M
(14%)

10. Maryland
1.4M
(27%)

2. California
2.4M
(7%)

6. Illinois
1.8M
(15%)

7. North Carolina
1.6M
(22%)

3. Texas
2.4M
(12%)

9. Louisiana
1.4M
(32%)

5. Georgia
2.1M
(28%)

4. Florida
2.3M
(15%)

Source: U.S. Census Bureau

TOP 10 RESERVATIONS, IN NUMBER OF AMERICAN INDIANS

(1990 census populations over 4,000)

Blackfeet
7,025

Pine Ridge and trust lands
11,182

Rosebud and trust lands
8,043

Gila River
9,162

Hopi and trust lands
7,061

Navajo and trust lands
143,405

Papago
8,480

Zuni Pueblo
7,073

Apache
9,825

San Carlos
7,110

Source: U.S. Census Bureau

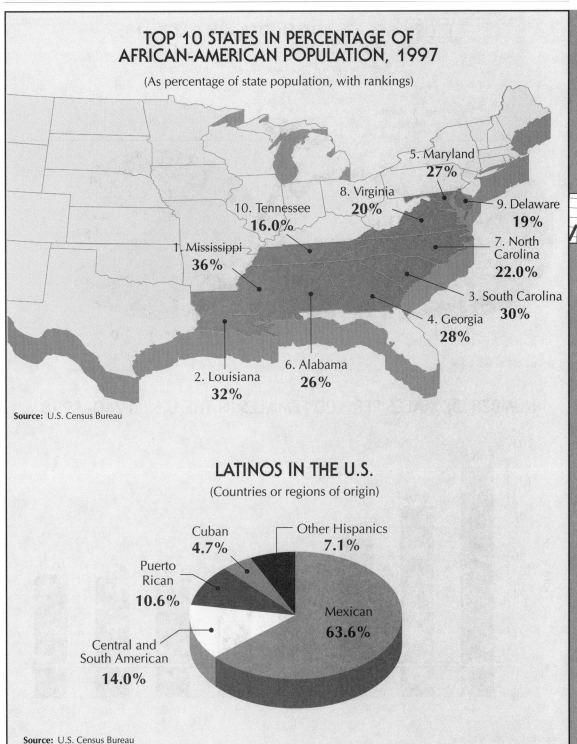

TOP 10 STATES IN PERCENTAGE OF AFRICAN-AMERICAN POPULATION, 1997

(As percentage of state population, with rankings)

5. Maryland **27%**

8. Virginia **20%**

10. Tennessee **16.0%**

9. Delaware **19%**

7. North Carolina **22.0%**

1. Mississippi **36%**

3. South Carolina **30%**

4. Georgia **28%**

6. Alabama **26%**

2. Louisiana **32%**

Source: U.S. Census Bureau

LATINOS IN THE U.S.

(Countries or regions of origin)

Cuban **4.7%**

Other Hispanics **7.1%**

Puerto Rican **10.6%**

Mexican **63.6%**

Central and South American **14.0%**

Source: U.S. Census Bureau

KIDS AGES 14 AND UNDER, BY RACE AND ETHNIC GROUP, 1994 vs. 2010

(As percentage of total age-group population)

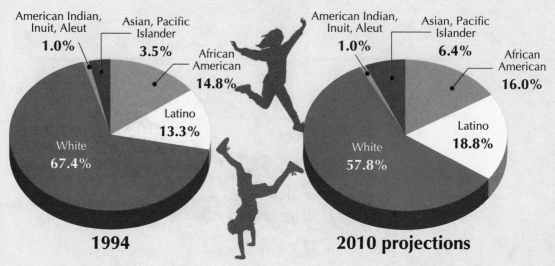

1994

American Indian, Inuit, Aleut **1.0%**

Asian, Pacific Islander **3.5%**

African American **14.8%**

Latino **13.3%**

White **67.4%**

2010 projections

American Indian, Inuit, Aleut **1.0%**

Asian, Pacific Islander **6.4%**

African American **16.0%**

Latino **18.8%**

White **57.8%**

Source: U.S. Census Bureau

NUMBER OF MALES PER 100 FEMALES IN THE U.S., 1940–1996

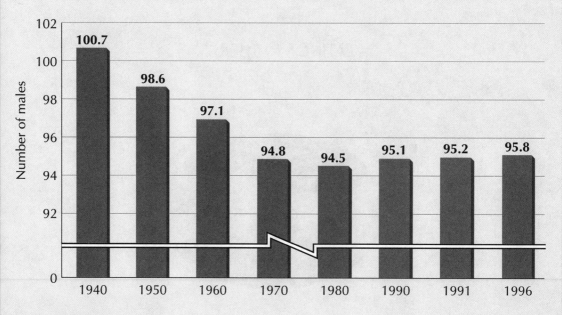

Number of males

Year	Value
1940	100.7
1950	98.6
1960	97.1
1970	94.8
1980	94.5
1990	95.1
1991	95.2
1996	95.8

Source: U.S. Census Bureau

THE AMERICAN POPULATION, 1998

(In millions, by age group)

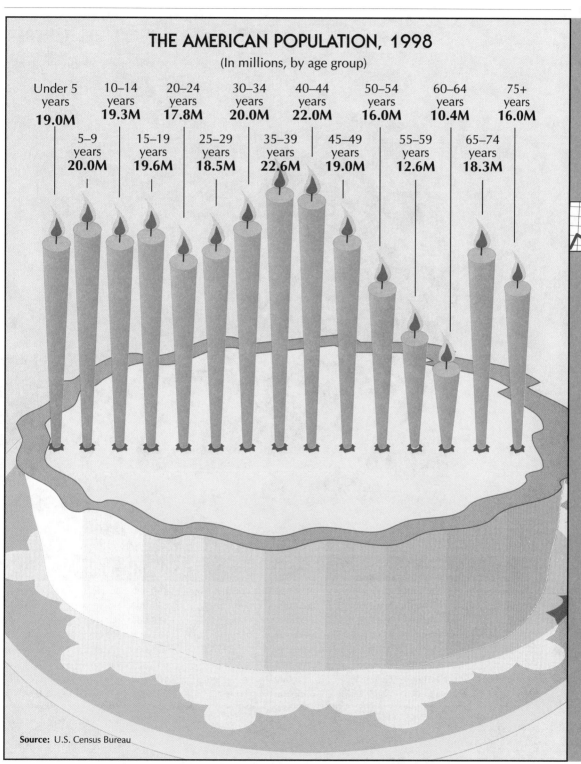

Under 5 years **19.0M**	10–14 years **19.3M**	20–24 years **17.8M**	30–34 years **20.0M**	40–44 years **22.0M**	50–54 years **16.0M**	60–64 years **10.4M**	75+ years **16.0M**
5–9 years **20.0M**	15–19 years **19.6M**	25–29 years **18.5M**	35–39 years **22.6M**	45–49 years **19.0M**	55–59 years **12.6M**	65–74 years **18.3M**	

Source: U.S. Census Bureau

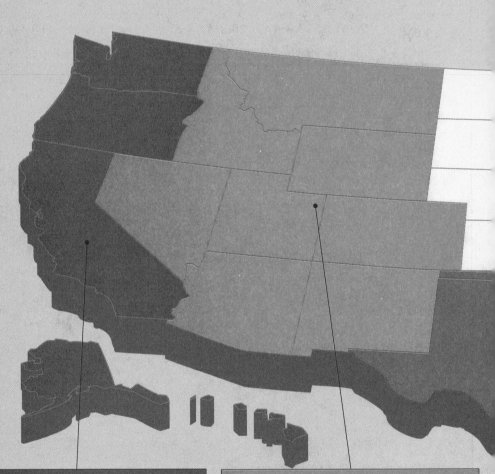

WHO LIVES WHERE?

(U.S. regions by ethnic populations)

Pacific: 12.1 million

American Indian	387,000	Vietnamese	314,000
Inuit	49,000	Hawaiian	182,000
Aleut	16,000	Samoan	52,000
Chinese	823,000	Guamanian	32,000
Filipino	960,000	Mexican	6.4 million
Japanese	609,000	Puerto Rican	166,000
Asian Indian	173,000	Cuban	76,000
Korean	327,000	Other Latino	1.5 million

West: 14.7 million

American Indian	866,000	Vietnamese	334,000
Inuit	51,000	Hawaiian	189,000
Aleut	17,000	Samoan	55,000
Chinese	863,000	Guamanian	34,000
Filipino	991,000	Mexican	7.8 million
Japanese	643,000	Puerto Rican	192,000
Asian Indian	189,000	Cuban	88,000
Korean	355,000	Other Latino	2.0 million

Source: U.S. Census Bureau

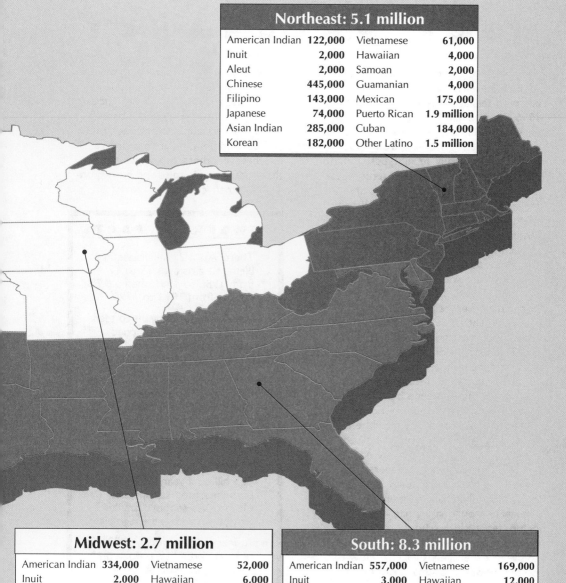

Northeast: 5.1 million

American Indian	122,000	Vietnamese	61,000
Inuit	2,000	Hawaiian	4,000
Aleut	2,000	Samoan	2,000
Chinese	445,000	Guamanian	4,000
Filipino	143,000	Mexican	175,000
Japanese	74,000	Puerto Rican	1.9 million
Asian Indian	285,000	Cuban	184,000
Korean	182,000	Other Latino	1.5 million

Midwest: 2.7 million

American Indian	334,000	Vietnamese	52,000
Inuit	2,000	Hawaiian	6,000
Aleut	2,000	Samoan	2,000
Chinese	133,000	Guamanian	3,000
Filipino	113,000	Mexican	1.2 million
Japanese	63,000	Puerto Rican	258,000
Asian Indian	146,000	Cuban	37,000
Korean	109,000	Other Latino	279,000

South: 8.3 million

American Indian	557,000	Vietnamese	169,000
Inuit	3,000	Hawaiian	12,000
Aleut	3,000	Samoan	4,000
Chinese	204,000	Guamanian	8,000
Filipino	159,000	Mexican	4.3 million
Japanese	67,000	Puerto Rican	406,000
Asian Indian	196,000	Cuban	735,000
Korean	153,000	Other Latino	1.3 million

T E E N   P R E G N A N C Y

Beginning in the mid-1980s and continuing into the early 1990s, the number of births to teenage girls increased. But in 1996, the rate had fallen to 42.5 births for every 1,000 females ages 15 to 19. This was an 8.7% decrease from 1991.

There are many stereotypes about teenage mothers. Sadly, the stereotypes are often true. Teenage mothers are more likely to drop out of school than mothers whose first child is born later. Teens with children are also more likely to live in poverty. One study showed that about 50% of all teenage mothers are on welfare within one year of their first child's birth. Teenagers also have a higher-than-average risk of giving birth to low-weight, premature babies. These babies often face serious health problems.

The majority of teenage births are to unmarried mothers. Often, the males who fathered the children abandon the mothers. It then becomes the mothers' responsibility—emotionally and financially—to raise the children.

Experts disagree about the causes of teenage pregnancy. Many point to the fact that American teenagers are sexually active at increasingly younger ages. More than half of America's teenagers report having had intercourse before leaving high school.

Experts agree that it is important to prevent teenage pregnancy. How to do this, however, is a matter of much controversy. Many communities have programs that counsel teenagers to abstain from sex until adulthood and marriage. They counsel those who do have sex to use contraceptives (birth control devices) consistently. They also encourage young people to consider—ahead of time—the responsibilities of parenthood.

Communities often offer help to teenage mothers. In some communities, day care centers accommodate infants and toddlers while their mothers are at school. Parenting classes teach mothers about infant health, diet, and development. There are programs for teenage fathers, too, which teach them how to help raise and be responsible for their children.

FINGERTIP FACTS

- There was a 27% increase in births to girls ages 15 to 17 from 1986 to 1991, then a 8.7% decline from 1994 to 1996.

- Some 71% of the births to teens in 1996 were to unmarried mothers. In 1960, only 15% were to unmarried mothers.

- Black babies have twice the risk of low birthweight as white babies. This is a reason why black babies are twice as likely as white babies to die before their first birthday.

- It costs taxpayers more than $25 billion a year in welfare payments, food stamps, and Medicaid to support families that began with a teenage birth.

- At least 56% of girls and 73% of boys in the U.S. reportedly have had intercourse before their 18th birthday.

- Fewer than 20% of U.S. school-based health clinics supply teens with contraceptives. About 28% provide teenagers with prescriptions for contraceptives.

- Most developed countries have declining birth rates among teenagers.

PROFILE: OUT-OF-WEDLOCK BIRTHS IN THE U.S.

Out-of-wedlock births have soared in recent years:

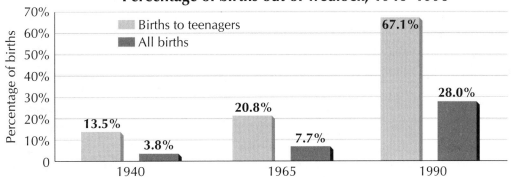

Percentage of births out of wedlock, 1940–1990

Births to teenagers
All births

- 1940: 13.5% / 3.8%
- 1965: 20.8% / 7.7%
- 1990: 67.1% / 28.0%

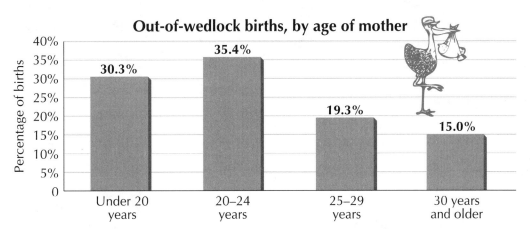

Out-of-wedlock births, by age of mother

- Under 20 years: 30.3%
- 20–24 years: 35.4%
- 25–29 years: 19.3%
- 30 years and older: 15.0%

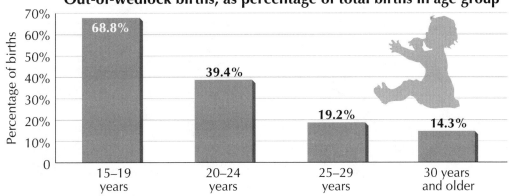

Out-of-wedlock births, as percentage of total births in age group

- 15–19 years: 68.8%
- 20–24 years: 39.4%
- 25–29 years: 19.2%
- 30 years and older: 14.3%

Source: U.S. Department of Health; National Center for Health Statistics

PROFILE: BIRTH RATES FOR UNWED MOTHERS

(Percentages of all births to unmarried women, by race or ethnic group, 1970–1996)

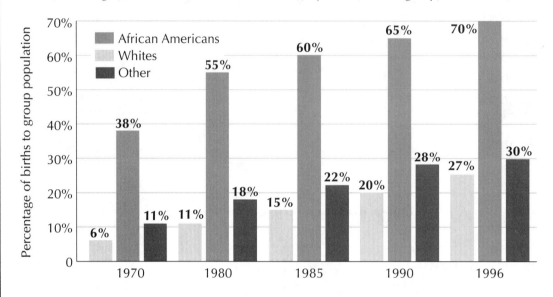

(Rates of births to unmarried women ages 15–44, per 1,000 unmarried women, 1970–1991)

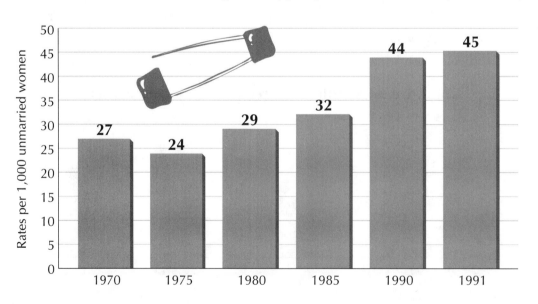

Source: U.S. Department of Health; National Center for Health Statistics

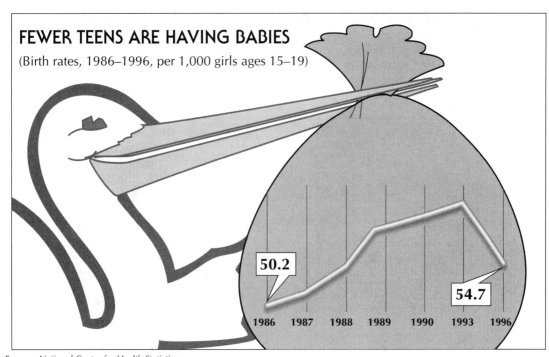

FEWER TEENS ARE HAVING BABIES

(Birth rates, 1986–1996, per 1,000 girls ages 15–19)

50.2

54.7

1986 1987 1988 1989 1990 1993 1996

Source: National Center for Health Statistics

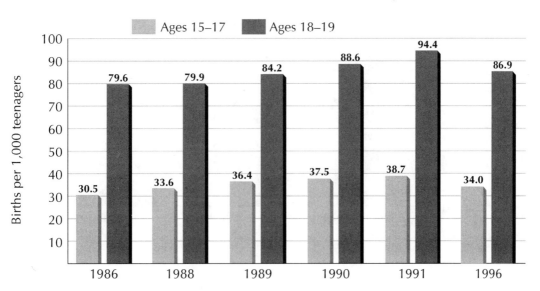

BIRTH RATES ARE HIGHER FOR OLDER TEENS, 1986–1996

Ages 15–17 Ages 18–19

Births per 1,000 teenagers

	1986	1988	1989	1990	1991	1996
Ages 15–17	30.5	33.6	36.4	37.5	38.7	34.0
Ages 18–19	79.6	79.9	84.2	88.6	94.4	86.9

Source: U.S. Census Bureau; National Center for Health Statistics

WHO ARE THE UNMARRIED MOTHERS IN THE U.S.?

Job status of unwed mothers

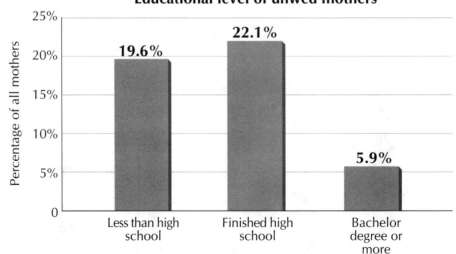

Race or ethnicity of unwed mothers

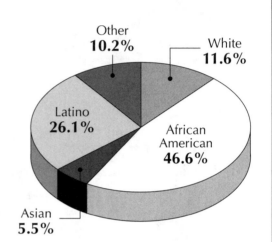

Source: U.S. Census Bureau

LOW BIRTH WEIGHT BABIES, 1997

(By age of mother)

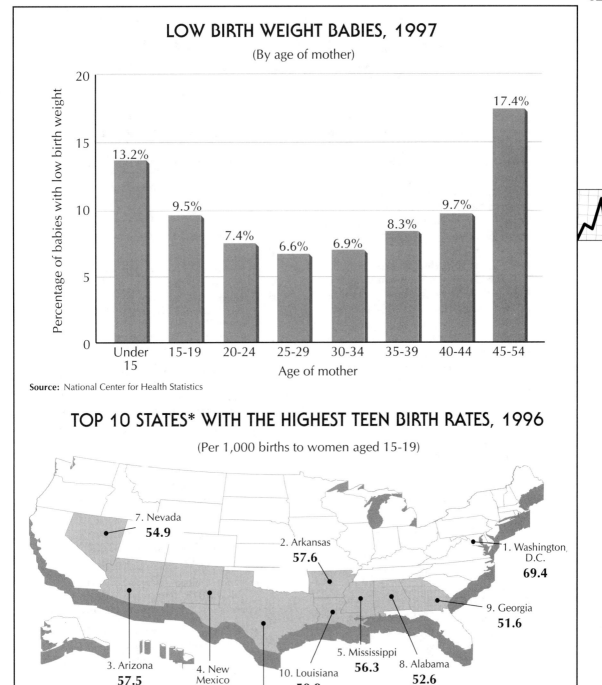

Source: National Center for Health Statistics

TOP 10 STATES* WITH THE HIGHEST TEEN BIRTH RATES, 1996

(Per 1,000 births to women aged 15-19)

7. Nevada **54.9**

2. Arkansas **57.6**

1. Washington, D.C. **69.4**

9. Georgia **51.6**

3. Arizona **57.5**

4. New Mexico **56.7**

10. Louisiana **50.9**

5. Mississippi **56.3**

8. Alabama **52.6**

6. Texas **55.5**

* Includes Washington, D.C.
Source: U.S. National Center for Health Statistics

SUICIDE AND TEEN SUICIDE

Each year, there are 30,000 Americans—more than 80 a day—who intentionally kill themselves. There are also an estimated 400,000 unsuccessful suicide attempts annually. Many mental health experts, however, believe that these figures are highly inaccurate—mostly because of the profound social stigma that is associated with suicide. They believe that many suicides are actually reported as accidental deaths.

The U.S. death rate from suicide has gradually increased, from an average of 11.4 suicide deaths per 100,000 population in 1950 to 11.9 deaths per 100,000 in 1995. Although women are more likely to attempt suicide, men more often succeed at it. Firearms, especially handguns, are the primary method used to commit suicide by both sexes. Among men, hangings are the second leading method; among women, poisonings (including overdoses of barbituates and other drugs) rank #2.

The greatest recent increase in suicide rates has occurred among America's young people; during the period between 1950 and 1995, the rate among people ages 15 to 24 tripled, from 4.5 to 13.5 deaths per 100,000. The great majority of these deaths were white males. Why so many teenagers take their lives is unclear. Possible factors include an increasing number of mental health problems, abuse of alcohol and illicit drugs, disruptive or abusive home lives, and other new or evolving pressures in school or in life with peers.

FINGERTIP FACTS

- Suicide is among the top 10 causes of death in the United States. It resulted in 31,284 deaths in 1995.

- Suicide rates are highest among those ages 35 to 44 (15.4 per 100,000).

- Suicide rates are higher among whites than blacks. In 1996, white males committed 72% of all suicides. Black males committed 6%. White females committed 17% and black females committed 2%.

- Firearms and explosives were used by 52% of the men and 41% of the women who committed suicide in 1996.

- Suicide rates vary widely from state to state. In 1995, the highest suicide rate was reported in Nevada (25.8 per 100,000), the lowest rate in New Jersey (7.3).

- Since 1980, the rate of suicide for black teens has more than doubled from 3.6 per 100,000 to 8.1 in 1995.

- In the United States, suicide is the third leading cause of death among young people ages 15-24.

- The mountain region in the U.S. had the highest suicide rate in 1997 (17.7%); the middle Atlantic region had the lowest (9.2).

TEENAGE DEATHS BY SUICIDE, 1960–1996

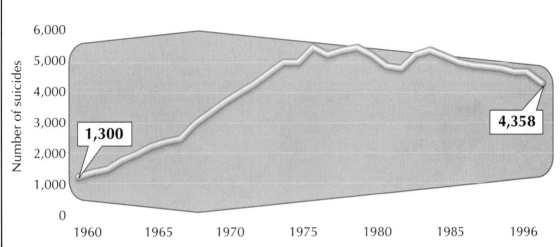

Source: Division of Vital Statistics; National Center for Health Statistics

TEENAGE SUICIDE IN 1996, COMPARED TO OTHER AGE GROUPS

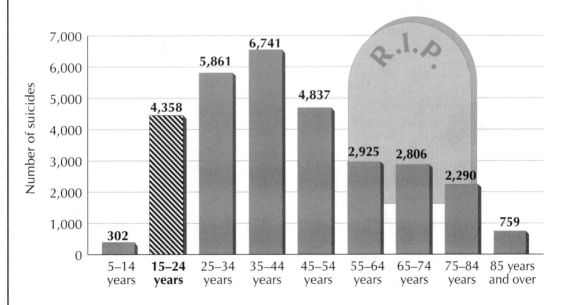

Source: Division of Vital Statistics; National Center for Health Statistics

U.S. RANKINGS OF SUICIDE RATES, BY STATE AND REGION

(Rates are number of suicides per 100,000 population)

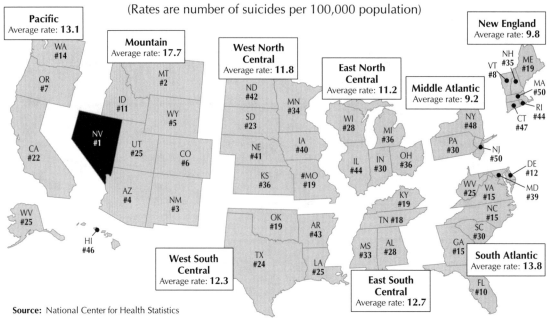

Pacific
Average rate: **13.1**

Mountain
Average rate: **17.7**

West North Central
Average rate: **11.8**

East North Central
Average rate: **11.2**

Middle Atlantic
Average rate: **9.2**

New England
Average rate: **9.8**

West South Central
Average rate: **12.3**

East South Central
Average rate: **12.7**

South Atlantic
Average rate: **13.8**

WA #14
OR #7
CA #22
NV #1
ID #11
MT #2
WY #5
UT #25
CO #6
AZ #4
NM #3
WV #25
HI #46

ND #42
SD #23
NE #41
KS #36
MN #34
IA #40
#MO #19
WI #28
MI #36
IL #44
IN #30
OH #36
KY #19
TN #18
MS #33
AL #28

OK #19
AR #43
TX #24
LA #25

NH #35
VT #8
ME #19
MA #50
RI #44
CT #47
NY #48
PA #30
NJ #50
DE #12
VA #15
MD #39
NC #15
SC #30
GA #15
FL #10

Source: National Center for Health Statistics

WHO ARE THE TEEN SUICIDES?

(As percentage of all teen suicides)

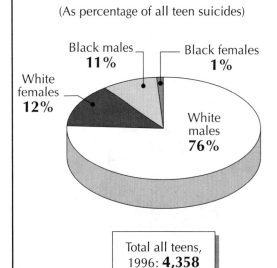

Black males **11%**

Black females **1%**

White females **12%**

White males **76%**

Total all teens, 1996: **4,358**

Source: National Center for Health Statistics

AVERAGE NUMBER OF TEEN SUICIDES, BY SEX AND RACE, 1982–1998

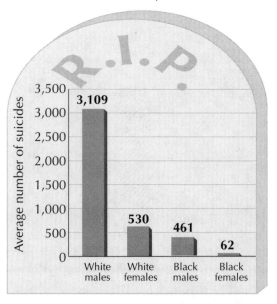

White males: 3,109
White females: 530
Black males: 461
Black females: 62

Source: Division of Vital Statistics; National Center for Health Statistics

SUICIDE IN THE U.S., BY AGE GROUP, 1996

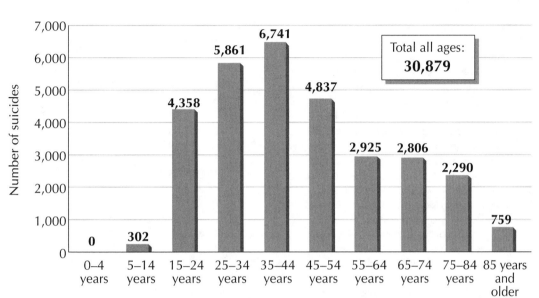

Number of suicides

Total all ages:
30,879

Age group	Number
0–4 years	0
5–14 years	302
15–24 years	4,358
25–34 years	5,861
35–44 years	6,741
45–54 years	4,837
55–64 years	2,925
65–74 years	2,806
75–84 years	2,290
85 years and older	759

Source: U.S. Department of Health and Human Services; National Center for Health Statistics

SUICIDE RATES, BY AGE GROUP, 1950 vs. 1995

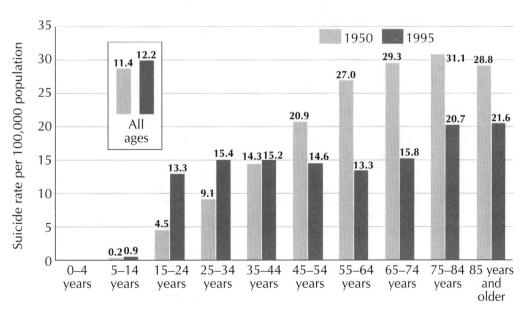

Suicide rate per 100,000 population

1950   1995

All ages: 11.4 / 12.2

Age group	1950	1995
0–4 years		
5–14 years	0.2	0.9
15–24 years	4.5	13.3
25–34 years	9.1	15.4
35–44 years	14.3	15.2
45–54 years	20.9	14.6
55–64 years	27.0	13.3
65–74 years	29.3	15.8
75–84 years	31.1	20.7
85 years and older	28.8	21.6

Source: U.S. Department of Health and Human Services

UNEMPLOYMENT

On any particular day, millions of American workers are unemployed. Some may be temporarily out of work because of the seasonal nature of their jobs. Some may be looking for new jobs because they moved, or because the firms for which they worked have downsized or gone out of business. Government statistics indicate that unemployment in America lasts an average of about 14.5 weeks, though many people remain without work for so long that they become discouraged and drop out of the labor force entirely. (The "labor force" is defined as all people, ages 16 and older, who are working or who are looking for work.)

The U.S. unemployment rate, which is tabulated monthly, indicates the percentage of the U.S. labor force that is currently unemployed. The rate does not consider non-workers who are not seeking jobs; nor does it consider people who are underemployed, such as part-time workers who want full-time jobs. In 1997, there were 136.3 million people in the U.S. labor force; the U.S. Department of Labor estimated that 6.7 million of these—5% of the total—were unemployed.

The great majority of U.S. workers are eligible for unemployment insurance if they lose their jobs. Unemployment insurance was introduced into the U.S. in 1935 as part of the Social Security Act. This insurance is designed to provide them with income for a limited period of time while they look for new jobs. The insurance is financed by a payroll tax on employers; the program is administered by the states in cooperation with the U.S. Department of Labor in Washington, D.C.

FINGERTIP FACTS

☛ In 1998, U.S. unemployment decreased by 5% from the previous year. There were 6.2 million workers without jobs.

☛ In 1998, some 49% of unemployed workers sent out their resumes, a total of 16% placed or answered ads, and 19% went to a public employment agency to find work.

☛ In 1998, unemployment lasted an average of 14.5 weeks; 14% of the unemployed were without work for 27 weeks or more.

☛ The labor force grew 95% between 1960 and 1997. This is because of population growth and an increase in working women.

☛ In 1998, there were 4.5 million unemployed whites and 1.4 unemployed blacks. Of those unemployed, 84% of whites and 92% of blacks were actively seeking jobs.

☛ Unemployment is greater among teenagers than among adults. In 1997, teenage unemployment was 16.0%, adult female 5.0%, and adult male 4.9%.

☛ Unemployment rates are lowest among whites—4.2% in late 1997, as compared to 7.7% for Latinos and 10.0% for blacks.

☛ Unemployment rates vary across the nation. In 1997, rates ranged from 2.4% in Nebraska to 7.9% in Alabama.

PERCENTAGE OF UNEMPLOYED, BY AGE AND SEX, 1998

(As percentage of group in labor force)

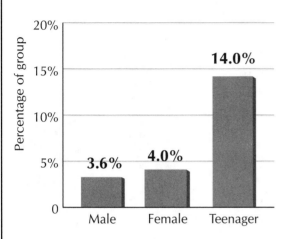

PERCENTAGE OF UNEMPLOYED, BY RACE, 1998

(As percentage of group in labor force)

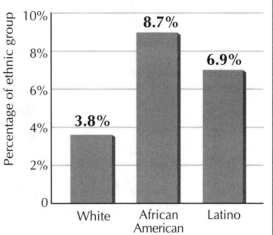

Source: Bureau of Labor Statistics

UNEMPLOYMENT RATES, 1983–1998

(For April, in each year)

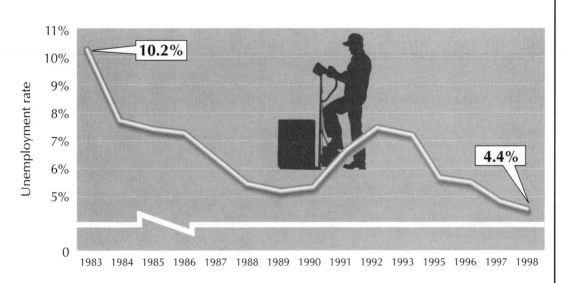

Source: U.S. Department of Labor

U.S. UNEMPLOYMENT, BY SEX AND AGE, 1992–1998

Men   Women   Teens

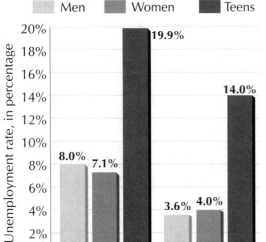

Unemployment rate, in percentage

- August 1992: Men 8.0%, Women 7.1%, Teens 19.9%
- August 1998: Men 3.6%, Women 4.0%, Teens 14.0%

Source: Bureau of Labor Statistics

U.S. UNEMPLOYMENT, BY RACE OR ETHNIC GROUP, 1992–1998

White   African American   Latino

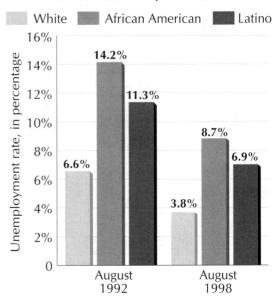

Unemployment rate, in percentage

- August 1992: White 6.6%, African American 14.2%, Latino 11.3%
- August 1998: White 3.8%, African American 8.7%, Latino 6.9%

UNEMPLOYMENT IN 10 STATES, APRIL 1999

(By number of unemployed and percentage of population)

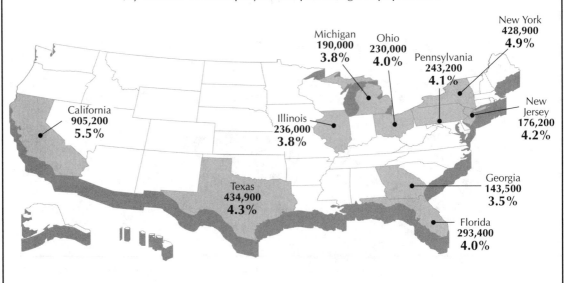

Michigan
190,000
3.8%

Ohio
230,000
4.0%

New York
428,900
4.9%

Pennsylvania
243,200
4.1%

New Jersey
176,200
4.2%

California
905,200
5.5%

Illinois
236,000
3.8%

Georgia
143,500
3.5%

Texas
434,900
4.3%

Florida
293,400
4.0%

Source: Bureau of Labor Statistics

UNEMPLOYMENT BY INDUSTRY, 1998

(By percentage of industry unemployed during
September 1998)

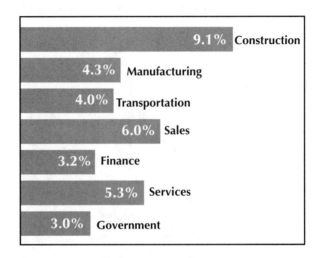

9.1% **Construction**

4.3% **Manufacturing**

4.0% **Transportation**

6.0% **Sales**

3.2% **Finance**

5.3% **Services**

3.0% **Government**

Source: U.S. Department of Labor

OUT OF WORK, 1995

About 9.4 million people in the U.S. were
unemployed in April 1995. Here is why they
were unemployed, by reasons given:

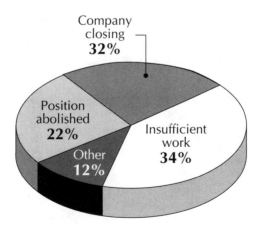

Company
closing
32%

Position
abolished
22%

Other
12%

Insufficient
work
34%

Source: U.S. Department of Labor

U.S. UNEMPLOYMENT SNAPSHOT: BY AGE AND SEX, 1998

(Percentages of men, women, and teenagers ages 16 to 19 unemployed in January 1998)

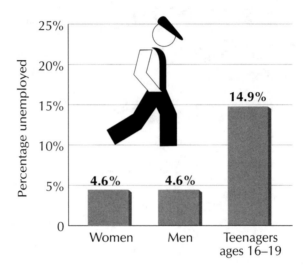

U.S. UNEMPLOYMENT SNAPSHOT: BY RACE/ETHNIC GROUP, 1998

(Percentages of people unemployed in January 1998)

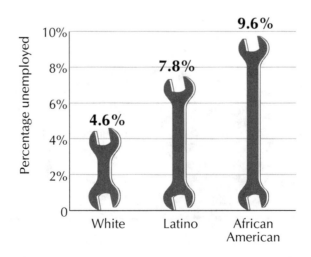

Source: U.S. Department of Labor

TOP 10 STATES IN UNEMPLOYMENT, 1997

(With rankings)

6. Oregon
5.8%

7. Minnesota
5.7%

8-10. Maine
5.4%

4. California
6.3%

5. New Mexico
6.2%

3. New York
6.4%

8-10. Texas
5.4%

2. Hawaii
6.2%

8-10. Tennessee
5.4%

1. Alabama
7.9%

Source: U.S. Department of Labor

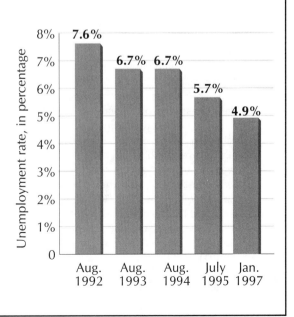

NUMBER OF JOBS IN THE U.S., 1990–1997

(In millions)

- 130M
- 125M
- 120M
- 115M
- 110M
- 105M
- 0

Millions of jobs

110.3M — July 1990
108.2M — July 1991
108.6M — July 1992
129.5M — July 1997

UNEMPLOYMENT RATES DROP, 1992–1997

- 8%
- 7%
- 6%
- 5%
- 4%
- 3%
- 2%
- 1%
- 0

Unemployment rate, in percentage

7.6% — Aug. 1992
6.7% — Aug. 1993
6.7% — Aug. 1994
5.7% — July 1995
4.9% — Jan. 1997

Source: Bureau of Labor Statistics

POPULATION GROWTH AMONG OLDER AMERICANS

Healthier lifestyles and medical advances are enabling Americans to enjoy longer, more active lives than ever before. Coupled with declining birth rates and fertility rates, this means that the percentage of people ages 65 and older is growing rapidly. This age group currently makes up about 13% of the U.S. population—up from 9.2% in 1960, and more than a 1,000% increase since 1900. The percentage is expected to increase dramatically as the baby boomers reach retirement age.

The economic quality of life has also improved for older Americans. Poverty has declined dramatically, due in large part to government programs that provide payments to retired or disabled workers, their dependents, and their survivors. Such programs also defray some of the medical expenses of retirees and their spouses. People have come to rely on Social Security and other government programs in increasing numbers. For example, in 1970, there were 26.2 million beneficiaries of Social Security; they received payments totaling $31.9 million. By 1997, there were 43.9 million beneficiaries receiving $365.6 billion.

Public debate is growing over how these massive programs are to be funded and distributed in coming years. Of particular concern is the high cost of health care for this age group. People ages 65 and over account for more than one-third of the nation's health care expenditures, fill 40% of all hospital beds, and use twice as much prescription medicine as all other age groups combined. Many Americans fear that Medicare, which pays hospital bills for older people, will run out of money within the next decade.

FINGERTIP FACTS

- In 1970, the median age of Americans was 28.0 years; by 1997, the median age was 34.9.

- Each day, about 6,000 Americans turn age 65.

- In 1996, some 33.8 million Americans were ages 65 or older. By the year 2040, the U.S. Census Bureau expects that this population will reach 76.0 million.

- In 1900, only 0.1% of Americans were age 85 or older. By 1996, the figure had grown to 1.4%—and by 2040, it is expected to reach 4.6%.

- In 1998, there were an estimated 68,000 Americans age 100 years or older—more than three-fourths of them women.

- Florida has the highest percentage of residents ages 65 and older (18.3%); Alaska has the lowest (4.1%).

- More than 47 million people—including some 18 million ages 65 and older—are grandparents of children under age 18.

- Thanks largely to Social Security, poverty among the elderly declined from 35.0% in 1959 to 10.8% in 1997.

- In 1996, some 7.4% of people ages 75 to 84 and 39.2% of those ages 90 to 94 lived in nursing homes.

- People enrolled for Medicare coverage increased from 19.5 million in 1967 to an estimated 38.3 million in 1997—a 49% increase.

U.S. POPULATION LIVES LONGER

(Number of people 85 years and older in the U.S., for each year from 1900–1990; projected increase in that age group for 1991–2050)

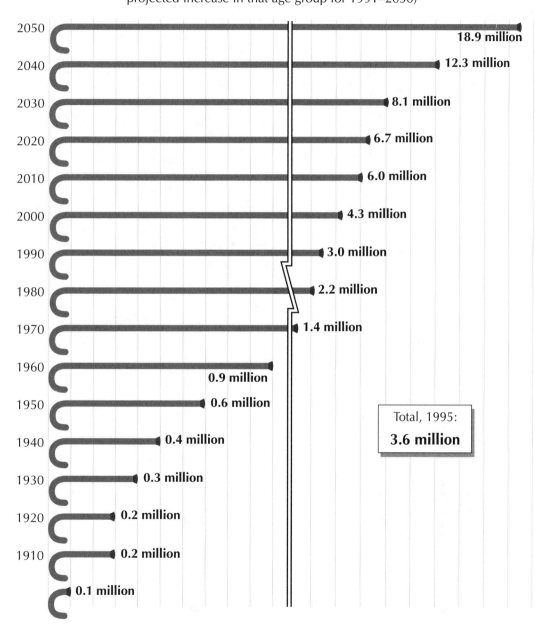

Year	Number
2050	18.9 million
2040	12.3 million
2030	8.1 million
2020	6.7 million
2010	6.0 million
2000	4.3 million
1990	3.0 million
1980	2.2 million
1970	1.4 million
1960	0.9 million
1950	0.6 million
1940	0.4 million
1930	0.3 million
1920	0.2 million
1910	0.2 million
	0.1 million

Total, 1995:
3.6 million

Source: U.S. Census Bureau

GROWTH AND PROJECTION OF POPULATION AGES 65 AND OVER, 1900–2050

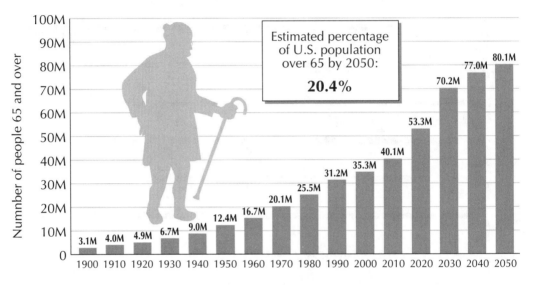

Estimated percentage of U.S. population over 65 by 2050:

20.4%

Numnber of people 65 and over

1900	3.1M
1910	4.0M
1920	4.9M
1930	6.7M
1940	9.0M
1950	12.4M
1960	16.7M
1970	20.1M
1980	25.5M
1990	31.2M
2000	35.3M
2010	40.1M
2020	53.3M
2030	70.2M
2040	77.0M
2050	80.1M

Source: U.S. Census Bureau

OVER-65 POPULATION, BY SEX, 1998

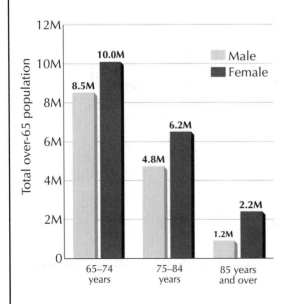

Total over-65 population

Male / Female

Age	Male	Female
65–74 years	8.5M	10.0M
75–84 years	4.8M	6.2M
85 years and over	1.2M	2.2M

OVER-65 POPULATION, BY RACE, 1998

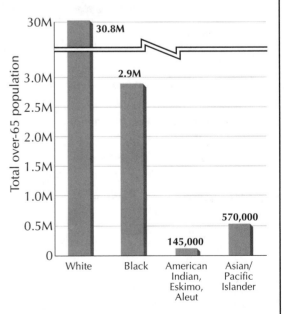

Total over-65 population

White	30.8M
Black	2.9M
American Indian, Eskimo, Aleut	145,000
Asian/ Pacific Islander	570,000

Source: U.S. Census Bureau

A NATION OF GRANDPARENTS

More than 47 million people in the U.S.
have at least one grandchild under age 18.
Here is how they add up, by age:

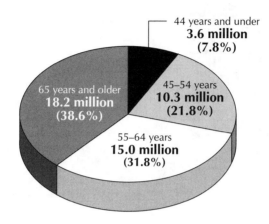

44 years and under
**3.6 million
(7.8%)**

45–54 years
**10.3 million
(21.8%)**

65 years and older
**18.2 million
(38.6%)**

55–64 years
**15.0 million
(31.8%)**

Source: U.S. Department of Health and Human Services

U.S. NURSING-HOME RESIDENTS

(By age group)

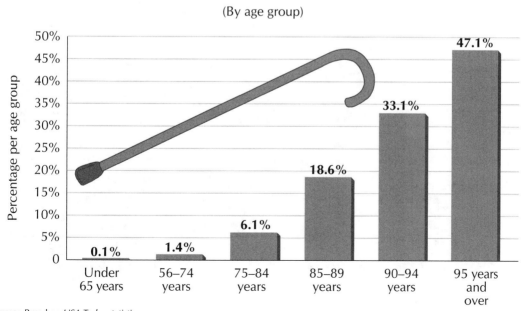

Source: Based on *USA Today* statistics

PERCENTAGE OF U.S. POPULATION AGES 65 AND OVER, BY REGION, BY 2000*

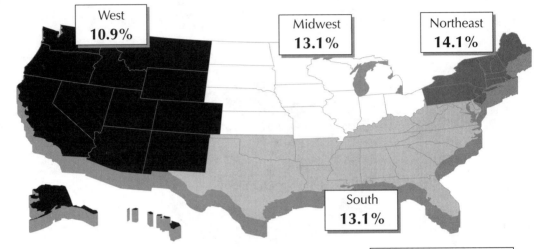

West
10.9%

Midwest
13.1%

Northeast
14.1%

South
13.1%

Total of U.S. population:
12.6%

Source: U.S. Census Bureau   *Projected

OVER-85 POPULATION ON THE INCREASE

It is projected that people in the 85-and-over age group will be the fastest-growing group in the U.S.:

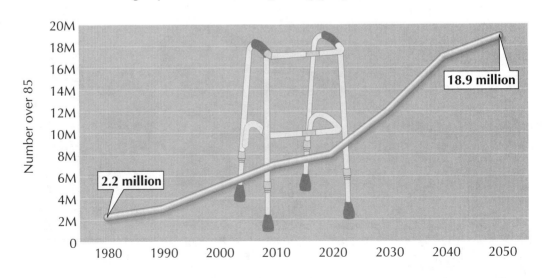

18.9 million

2.2 million

Number over 85

20M
18M
16M
14M
12M
10M
8M
6M
4M
2M
0

1980   1990   2000   2010   2020   2030   2040   2050

Source: U.S. Census Bureau

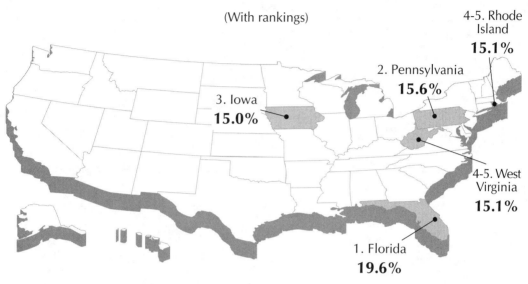

U.S. STATES WITH THE HIGHEST PERCENTAGES OF RESIDENTS OVER AGE 65, BY 2000*

(With rankings)

4-5. Rhode Island
15.1%

2. Pennsylvania
15.6%

3. Iowa
15.0%

4-5. West Virginia
15.1%

1. Florida
19.6%

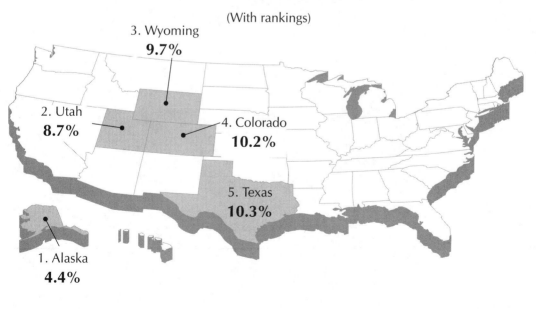

U.S. STATES WITH THE LOWEST PERCENTAGES OF RESIDENTS OVER AGE 65, BY 2000*

(With rankings)

3. Wyoming
9.7%

2. Utah
8.7%

4. Colorado
10.2%

5. Texas
10.3%

1. Alaska
4.4%

Source: U.S. Census Bureau   *Projected

5

DRUGS AND CRIME

ILLEGAL DRUGS

Much crime in the U.S. is associated with illegal drugs. Arrest rates for traffickers and users increased from 256 arrests per 100,000 population in 1980 to 410 in 1997.

There has also been a large increase in arrests of drug users for non-drug-related crimes. A Bureau of Justice Statistics study found that about 33% of convicted robbers and burglars had committed their crimes to obtain money for drugs. Urinalysis samples show that more than 50% of the people arrested in big cities for serious non-drug crimes test positive for drugs. For example, 66% of such males and 78% of such females arrested in Los Angeles, California, during the second quarter of 1993 tested positive.

The federal "war on drugs" has grown dramatically since it was begun in the early 1970s, but U.S. demand for drugs remains high, and it is difficult to determine the impact of law enforcement efforts. Surveys indicate that drug use declined in the 1990s—at least among the affluent and middle class—but drug-related crime grew. And although law enforcement agencies have confiscated unprecedented amounts of illegal drugs, there is no shortage of these substances in America.

A large portion of federal anti-drug money has been spent on fighting drugs overseas, particularly in Asia and Latin America, where most opium (heroin's main ingredient) and cocaine are produced. Nonetheless, worldwide drug production has increased significantly. Under the Clinton administration, anti-drug operations on foreign soil were scaled down, and greater emphasis was placed on drug treatment and prevention.

FINGERTIP FACTS

- More than 360,000 inmates—a third of state, and a quarter of federal prisoners—said they had participated in drug or alcohol treatment while in prison.

- Approximately 857,000 people were arrested in 1996 for violating drug laws. Of these, 86% were adults and 14% were juveniles.

- In 1970, there were 93,300 juvenile (ages 10 to 17) arrests for drug-law violations. The number dropped to 87,900 in 1987, and had increased to 220,000 by 1997.

- America's "war on drugs" was first declared in 1971. Since then, the federal government has spent about $100 billion on anti-drug efforts.

- In 1996, the most common reason stated by emergency room patients for using an illegal drug was suicide (dependency was second).

- There were an estimated 652,000 people who tried cocaine for the first time in 1996—that was about 6 potential new users every 5 minutes.

- In 1997, drug offenders accounted for more than 250,000 prisoners—21% of state and 60% of federal prisoners.

- The 1992 federal anti-drug effort had a budget of approximately $12 billion; about 68% was spent on law enforcement, including international interdiction and control programs. The 1995 budget was $12 billion, with about 59% for law enforcement.

Note: Before comparing statistics, consider that different rates apply to different population ratios—for example, some rates are figured per 1,000 people, other rates are figured per 100,000 people.

PERCENTAGE OF ILLEGAL DRUG USE, BY TYPE AND AGE GROUP, 1974 vs. 1996

(People who have ever used selected drug)

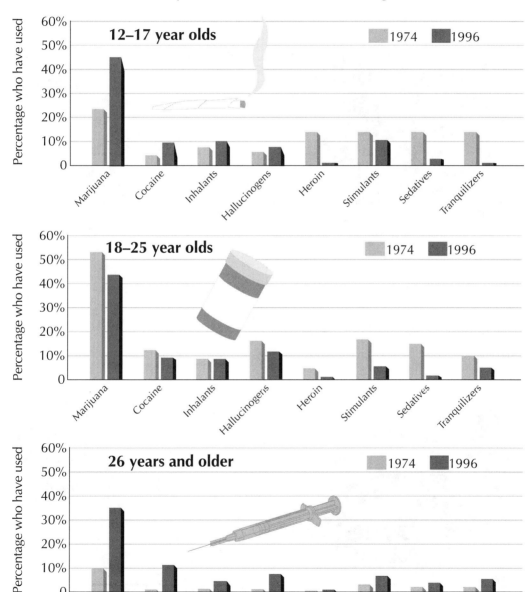

Source: National Clearinghouse for Alcohol and Drug Information

USERS OF MARIJUANA BY REGION, 1997

(Rates per 1,000 regional population)

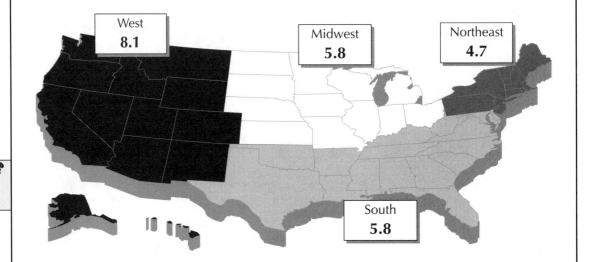

West	Midwest	Northeast
8.1	**5.8**	**4.7**

South
5.8

USERS OF COCAINE BY REGION, 1995

(As percentage of regional population)

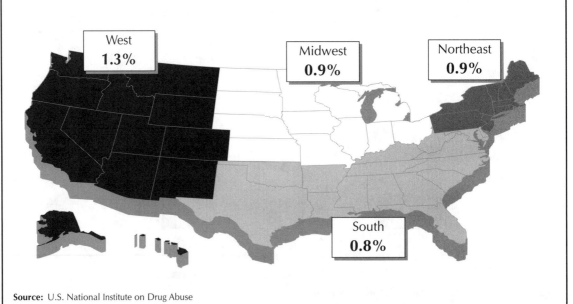

West	Midwest	Northeast
1.3%	**0.9%**	**0.9%**

South
0.8%

Source: U.S. National Institute on Drug Abuse

PROFILE: ILLEGAL DRUG USAGE AND ARRESTS

Rate of arrests by race

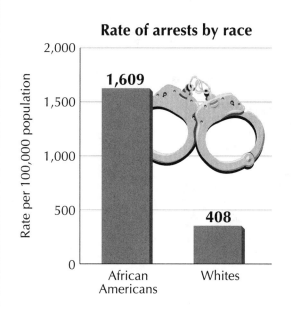

- African Americans: 1,609
- Whites: 408

(Rate per 100,000 population)

Adults who say they used illegal drugs within the past 12 months*

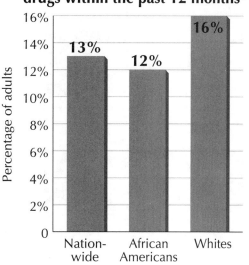

- Nation-wide: 13%
- African Americans: 12%
- Whites: 16%

(Percentage of adults)

* From time of survey

Source: Federal Bureau of Investigation

WHAT AMERICANS SPEND ON ILLEGAL DRUGS

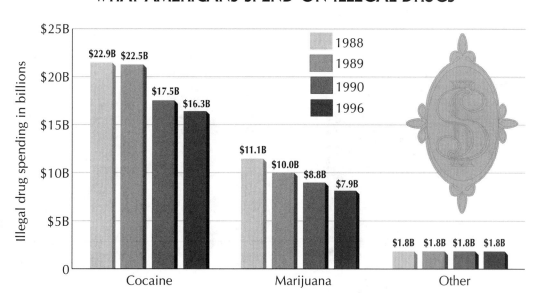

Illegal drug spending in billions

Legend: 1988, 1989, 1990, 1996

Cocaine:
- $22.9B
- $22.5B
- $17.5B
- $16.3B

Marijuana:
- $11.1B
- $10.0B
- $8.8B
- $7.9B

Other:
- $1.8B
- $1.8B
- $1.8B
- $1.8B

Source: Office of National Drug Control Policy

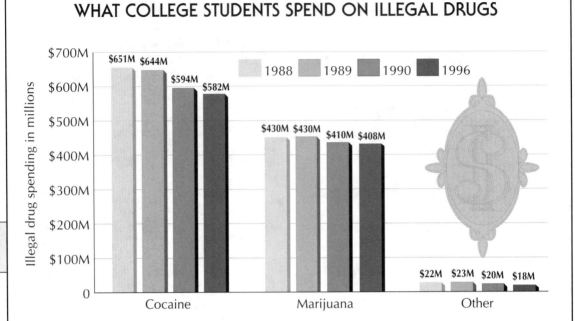

WHAT COLLEGE STUDENTS SPEND ON ILLEGAL DRUGS

Illegal drug spending in millions

Legend: 1988, 1989, 1990, 1996

Cocaine: $651M, $644M, $594M, $582M
Marijuana: $430M, $430M, $410M, $408M
Other: $22M, $23M, $20M, $18M

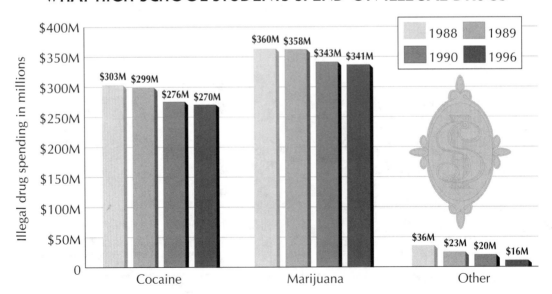

WHAT HIGH SCHOOL STUDENTS SPEND ON ILLEGAL DRUGS

Illegal drug spending in millions

Legend: 1988, 1989, 1990, 1996

Cocaine: $303M, $299M, $276M, $270M
Marijuana: $360M, $358M, $343M, $341M
Other: $36M, $23M, $20M, $16M

Source: Office of National Drug Control Policy

DRUG EMERGENCIES ON THE RISE, 1988–1996

Reports of heroin and cocaine emergencies in hospitals—an indicator of the drug problem's severity—reached an all-time record in 1996:

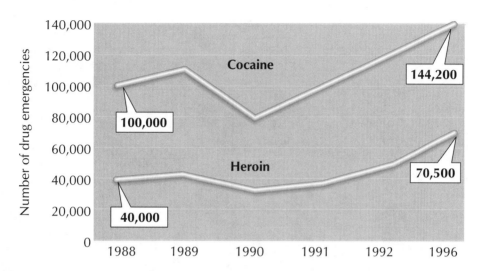

Source: Drug Abuse Warning Network

ILLEGAL DRUG USE IN HIGH SCHOOL, 1980 vs. 1997

(Percentage of seniors who have ever used selected drug)

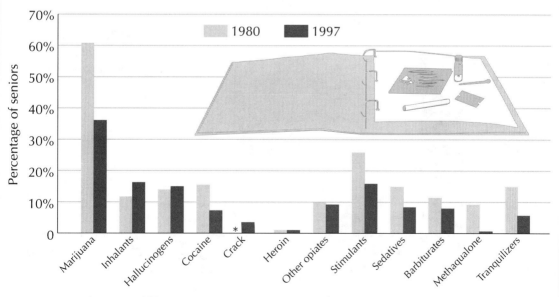

* Data on 1980 crack use not available
Source: National Institute on Drug Abuse

INCREASE IN STUDENT ILLEGAL DRUG USE, 1991 vs. 1993

After more than a decade of decline, student use of illegal drugs is on the rise again:

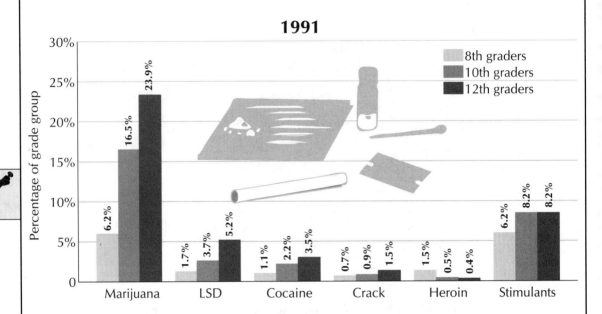

1991

Percentage of grade group

- 8th graders
- 10th graders
- 12th graders

	Marijuana	LSD	Cocaine	Crack	Heroin	Stimulants
8th graders	6.2%	1.7%	1.1%	0.7%	1.5%	6.2%
10th graders	16.5%	3.7%	2.2%	0.9%	0.5%	8.2%
12th graders	23.9%	5.2%	3.5%	1.5%	0.4%	8.2%

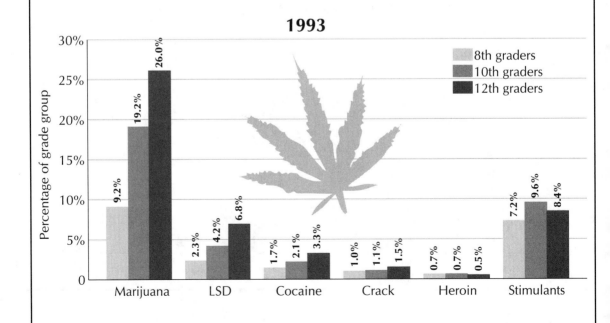

1993

Percentage of grade group

- 8th graders
- 10th graders
- 12th graders

	Marijuana	LSD	Cocaine	Crack	Heroin	Stimulants
8th graders	9.2%	2.3%	1.7%	1.0%	0.7%	7.2%
10th graders	19.2%	4.2%	2.1%	1.1%	0.7%	9.6%
12th graders	26.0%	6.8%	3.3%	1.5%	0.5%	8.4%

Source: Based on University of Michigan statistics

SPENDING ON DRUG-CONTROL SKYROCKETING, 1981–1994

(Government spending on drug interceptions and
seizures as part of the total federal drug-control budget)

Interdiction spending

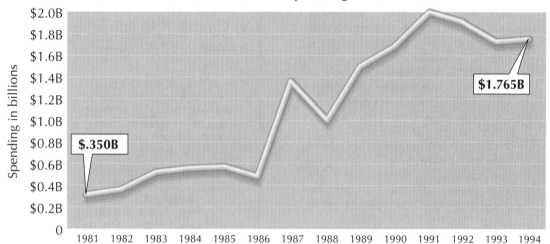

Source: Office of Management and Budget

1994 drug-control budget

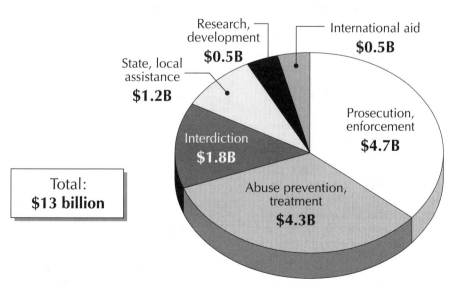

Total:
$13 billion

Source: Office of Management and Budget

CRIME

Fear of violent crime is a major concern of Americans, and for good reason: A U.S. Justice Department study found that 8 out of 10 Americans will be victims of violent crimes in their lifetimes. The U.S. has some of the highest crime rates in the world.

In 1996, there were 1.7 million violent crimes, an increase of 20% since 1980, and 11.8 million property crimes, a decrease of 2% from 1980. Violent crime rates per 100,000 inhabitants rose from 596.6 in 1980 to 634.1 in 1996, an increase of 6%. And these figures may not tell the whole story. Not all crimes are reported. National crime statistics are based on reports from police departments and other law enforcement agencies. According to federal officials, some crimes, such as rape and domestic violence, are vastly underreported as compared to other crimes.

Security at homes, schools, hospitals, shopping malls, and other buildings has increased exponentially. Police forces have grown, prison sentences have become more severe, and the number of prison inmates has soared. Attempts to fund drug-rehabilitation programs and other crime-prevention efforts have often been criticized as too expensive. Supporters, however, cite costs of more than $20,000 a year to keep a person in prison.

Another contentious issue is the glorification of violence in the media. By the time most children complete elementary school, it is estimated that each has seen some 8,000 murders and 100,000 other acts of violence on television. Many studies have found a correlation between television violence and aggressive behavior. The data, however, are not conclusive, and so the debate over cause-and-effect rages on.

FINGERTIP FACTS

- Forcible rape rates per 100,000 females increased from 30.4 in 1970 to 36.1 in 1996. There were a total of 95,770 reported forcible rapes in 1996.

- According to the U.S. Justice Department, 7,684 crimes in 1993—including 20 murders— were hate crimes motivated by prejudice based on race, ethnicity, religion, or sexual orientation.

- Juvenile crime has increased. Between 1992 and 1996, juvenile arrests increased 29%, to almost 2.1 million. Cases involving aggravated assault and other serious crimes increased 41%, to 69,000.

- The most common crime committed by juveniles is theft, followed by burglary.

- The age group with the highest violent crime victimization rate is youths aged 16-19 (102.7 per 1,000 people), followed by youths aged 12-15 (95.0). In comparison, the rate for adults aged 25-34 is 51.1.

- Blacks are more likely to be crime victims than are other racial and ethnic groups.

- In 1996, there were 11.8 million burglaries, larcenies, and motor-vehicle thefts, the lowest total in at least 20 years.

- In 1996, there were 2.4 full-time law enforcement officers for every 1,000 Americans.

- About 1 in 6 federal and state prisoners reported committing their current offense to obtain money for drugs.

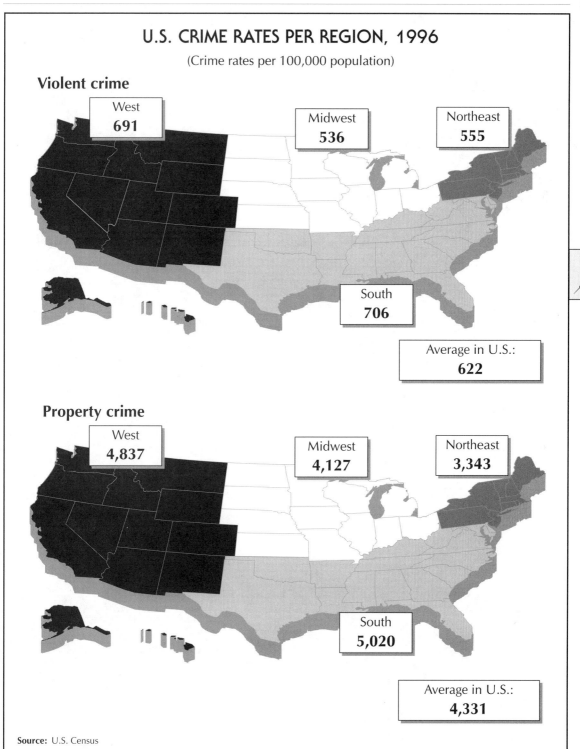

U.S. CRIME RATES PER REGION, 1996
(Crime rates per 100,000 population)

Violent crime

West
691

Midwest
536

Northeast
555

South
706

Average in U.S.:
622

Property crime

West
4,837

Midwest
4,127

Northeast
3,343

South
5,020

Average in U.S.:
4,331

Source: U.S. Census

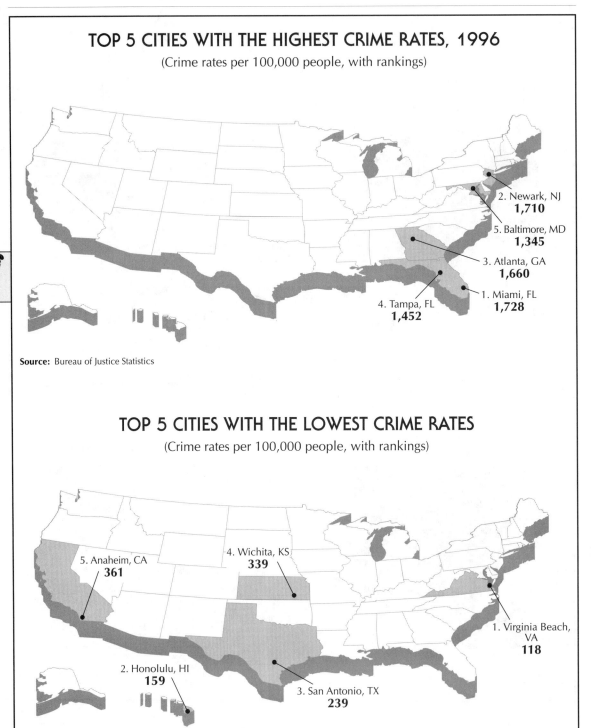

TOP 5 CITIES WITH THE HIGHEST CRIME RATES, 1996

(Crime rates per 100,000 people, with rankings)

2. Newark, NJ
1,710

5. Baltimore, MD
1,345

3. Atlanta, GA
1,660

1. Miami, FL
1,728

4. Tampa, FL
1,452

Source: Bureau of Justice Statistics

TOP 5 CITIES WITH THE LOWEST CRIME RATES

(Crime rates per 100,000 people, with rankings)

5. Anaheim, CA
361

4. Wichita, KS
339

1. Virginia Beach, VA
118

2. Honolulu, HI
159

3. San Antonio, TX
239

Source: FBI

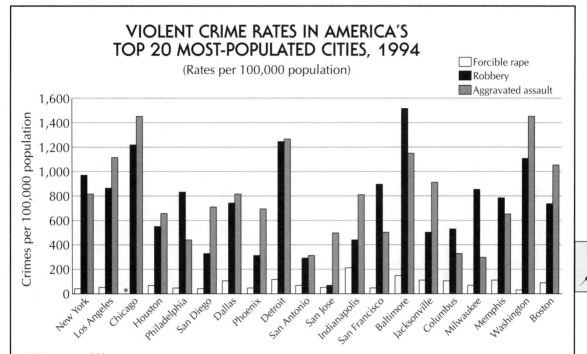

VIOLENT CRIME RATES IN AMERICA'S TOP 20 MOST-POPULATED CITIES, 1994
(Rates per 100,000 population)

Forcible rape
Robbery
Aggravated assault

* Figure not available

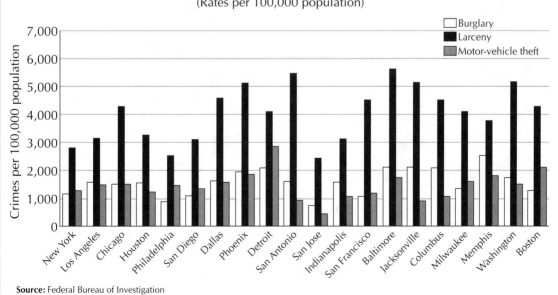

PROPERTY CRIME RATES IN AMERICA'S TOP 20 MOST-POPULATED CITIES, 1994
(Rates per 100,000 population)

Burglary
Larceny
Motor-vehicle theft

Source: Federal Bureau of Investigation

PROFILE: VICTIMS OF VIOLENCE, BY SELECTED CHARACTERISTICS

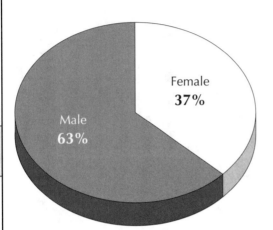

By sex

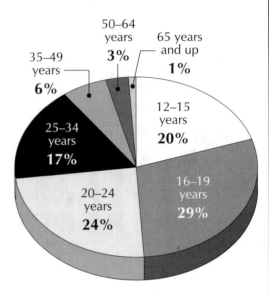

By age

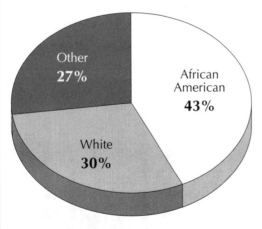

By race and ethnic group

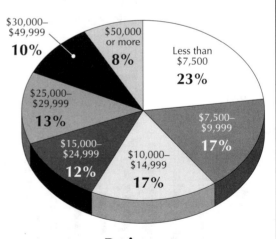

By income

Source: Federal Bureau of Investigation

VIOLENCE: WHO ATTACKS WHOM?

A new Justice Department survey shows that more than 2.5 million women are victimized each year in the U.S. Most are attacked by single offenders, usually men, and most offenders are friends or relatives. Most men, on the other hand, are attacked by acquaintances or strangers:

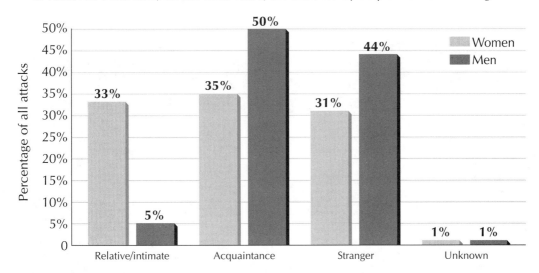

Source: Bureau of Justice Statistics

BLACK MALE TEENS ARE MOST COMMON VIOLENT CRIME TARGETS

(Violent crime victimization rates, per 1,000 persons ages 12–19)

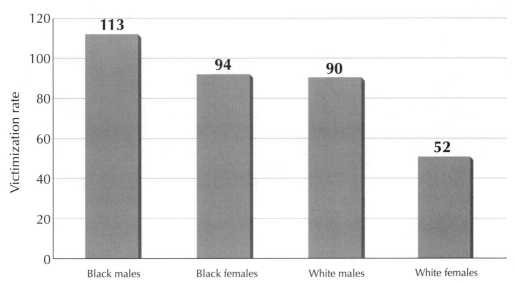

Source: Federal Bureau of Investigation

DOES VIOLENT TV REFLECT REAL LIFE?

Life on TV got safer in 1992: on average, only 2.9 violent scenes were depicted hourly. Meanwhile, real violent crime in the U.S. is increasing:

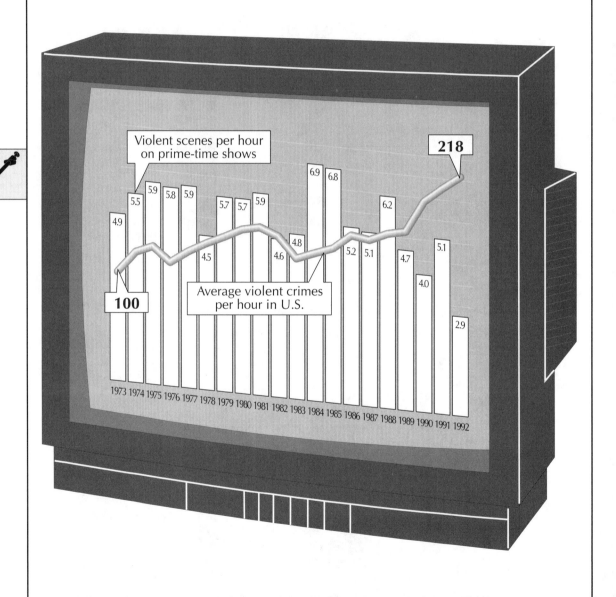

Source: University of Pennsylvania; Federal Bureau of Investigation

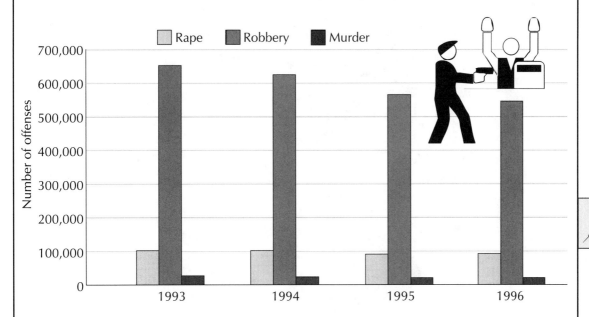

NUMBER OF VIOLENT CRIMES, BY TYPE, 1993–1996

Rape   Robbery   Murder

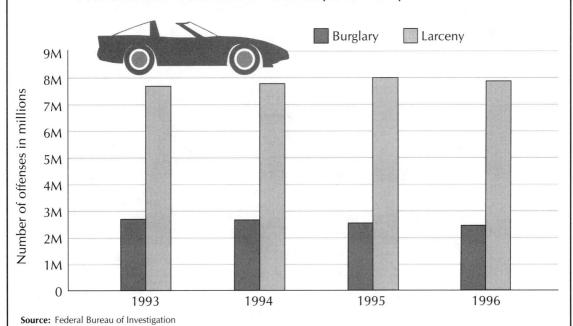

NUMBER OF PROPERTY CRIMES, BY TYPE, 1993–1996

Burglary   Larceny

Source: Federal Bureau of Investigation

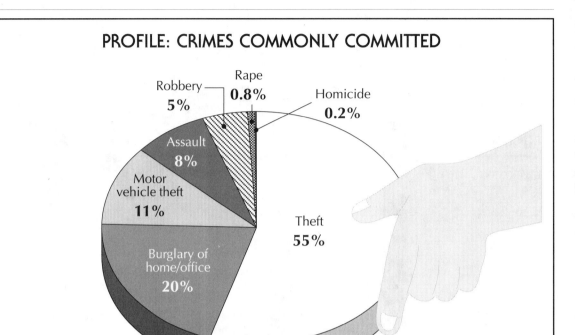

PROFILE: CRIMES COMMONLY COMMITTED

Robbery
5%

Rape
0.8%

Homicide
0.2%

Assault
8%

Motor
vehicle theft
11%

Theft
55%

Burglary of
home/office
20%

Source: Federal Bureau of Investigation

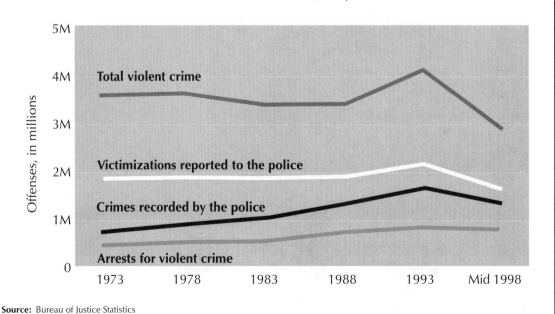

THE REALITY OF VIOLENT CRIME, 1973-1998

Offenses, in millions

5M

4M — **Total violent crime**

3M

2M — **Victimizations reported to the police**

Crimes recorded by the police

1M

Arrests for violent crime

0

1973   1978   1983   1988   1993   Mid 1998

Source: Bureau of Justice Statistics

PROFILE: CRIME VICTIMS, BY TYPES OF CRIME

(Rates per 1,000 persons or households)

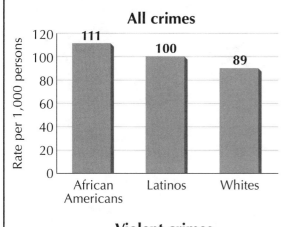

All crimes

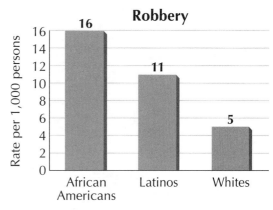

Robbery

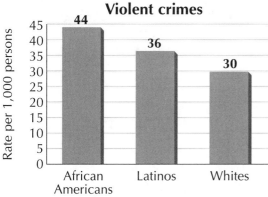

Violent crimes

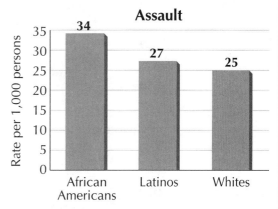

Assault

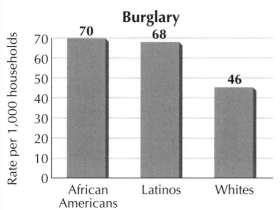

Burglary

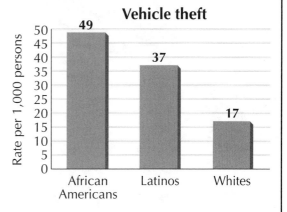

Vehicle theft

Source: Federal Bureau of Investigation

WHO DOES WHAT? TYPES OF CRIME BY RACE, 1995

(Percentage of total crime type by race of criminal)

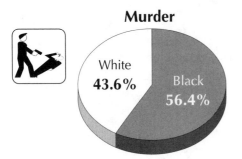

Murder

White 43.6%
Black 56.4%

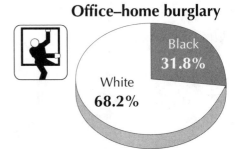

Office–home burglary

Black 31.8%
White 68.2%

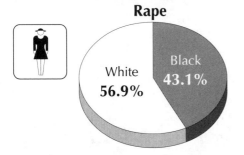

Rape

White 56.9%
Black 43.1%

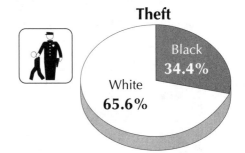

Theft

Black 34.4%
White 65.6%

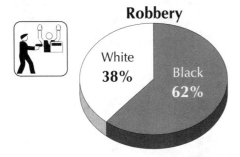

Robbery

White 38%
Black 62%

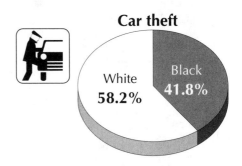

Car theft

White 58.2%
Black 41.8%

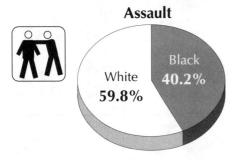

Assault

White 59.8%
Black 40.2%

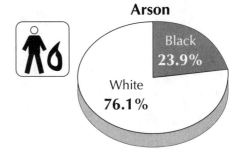

Arson

Black 23.9%
White 76.1%

Source: Federal Bureau of Investigation

JUVENILE CRIME ON THE RISE, 1983 vs. 1995

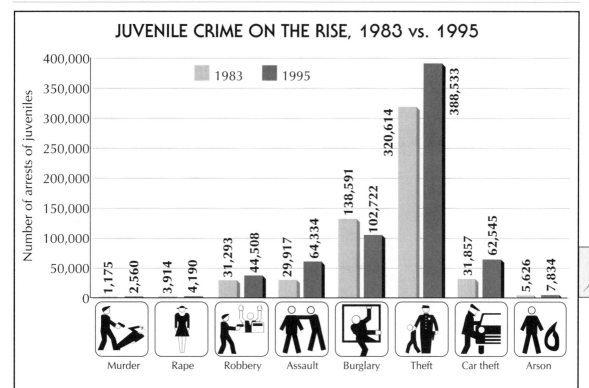

Number of arrests of juveniles

Legend: ▢ 1983 ■ 1995

Crime	1983	1995
Murder	1,175	2,560
Rape	3,914	4,190
Robbery	31,293	44,508
Assault	29,917	64,334
Burglary	138,591	102,722
Theft	320,614	388,533
Car theft	31,857	62,545
Arson	5,626	7,834

JUVENILE ARRESTS, 1965–1994

(Violent crime arrests per 100,000 juveniles, ages 10–17)

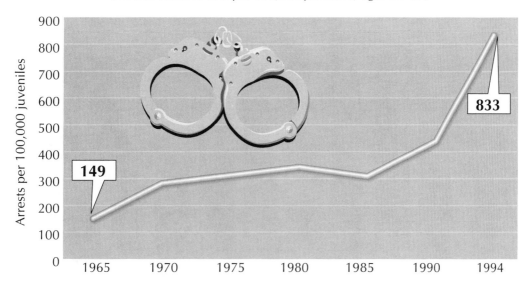

Arrests per 100,000 juveniles

149 (1965) **833** (1994)

Source: U.S. Department of Justice; Federal Bureau of Investigation

CRIMINAL ARRESTS, BY SEX, 1996

(By percentage of sex arrested for crime)

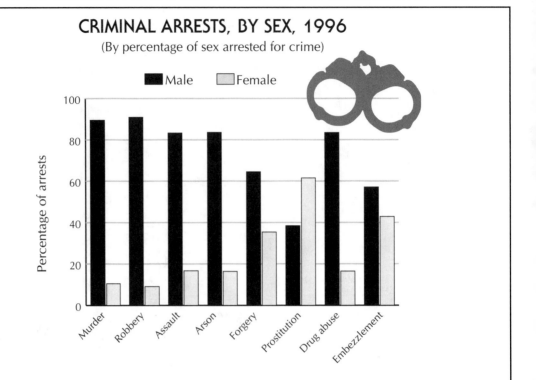

Source: FBI

TOTAL ARRESTS, BY AGE, 1994

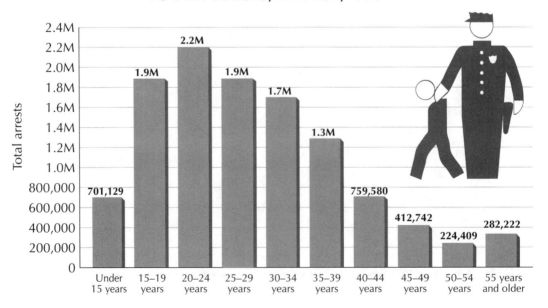

Source: U.S. Department of Justice

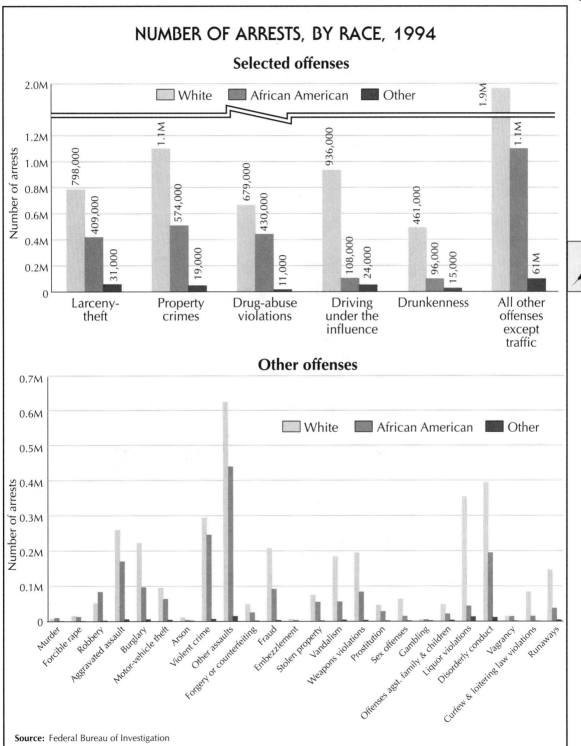

NUMBER OF ARRESTS, BY RACE, 1994

Selected offenses

Number of arrests

Legend: White, African American, Other

- Larceny-theft: 798,000 / 409,000 / 31,000
- Property crimes: 1.1M / 574,000 / 19,000
- Drug-abuse violations: 679,000 / 430,000 / 11,000
- Driving under the influence: 936,000 / 108,000 / 24,000
- Drunkenness: 461,000 / 96,000 / 15,000
- All other offenses except traffic: 1.9M / 1.1M / 61M

Other offenses

Number of arrests

Legend: White, African American, Other

Categories: Murder, Forcible rape, Robbery, Aggravated assault, Burglary, Motor-vehicle theft, Arson, Violent crime, Other assaults, Forgery or counterfeiting, Fraud, Embezzlement, Stolen property, Vandalism, Weapons violations, Prostitution, Sex offenses, Gambling, Offenses agst. family & children, Liquor violations, Disorderly conduct, Vagrancy, Curfew & loitering law violations, Runaways

Source: Federal Bureau of Investigation

DECLINE IN THE DEATHS OF POLICE OFFICERS, 1980–1994
(Total number of deaths in the line of duty and deaths by firearms)

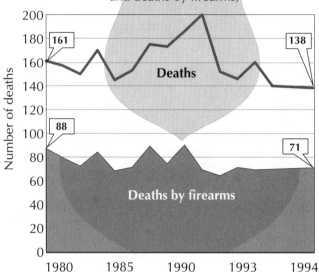

Source: American Police Hall of Fame and Museum

AMERICA'S LARGEST POLICE FORCES

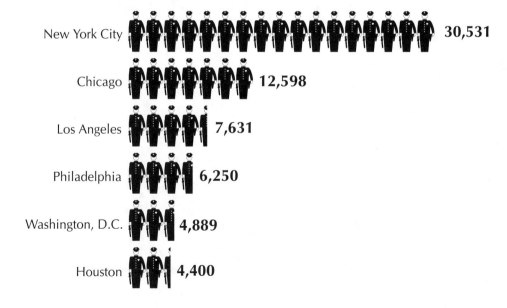

New York City — 30,531

Chicago — 12,598

Los Angeles — 7,631

Philadelphia — 6,250

Washington, D.C. — 4,889

Houston — 4,400

Source: International Association of Chiefs of Police

TEACHERS AS VICTIMS OF CRIMES

Percentage of teachers in U.S. who say they have been:

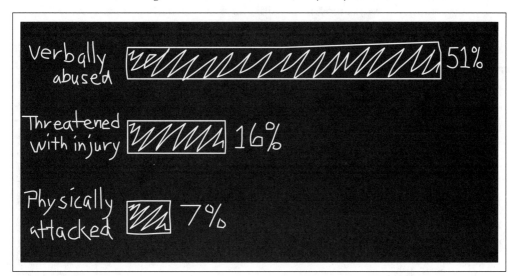

verbally abused — 51%

Threatened with injury — 16%

Physically attacked — 7%

Source: Carnegie Foundation

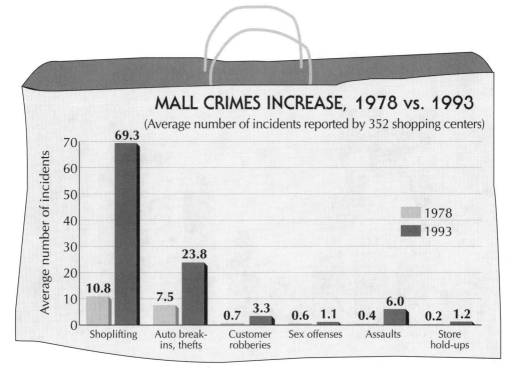

MALL CRIMES INCREASE, 1978 vs. 1993

(Average number of incidents reported by 352 shopping centers)

Average number of incidents

- 1978
- 1993

	Shoplifting	Auto break-ins, thefts	Customer robberies	Sex offenses	Assaults	Store hold-ups
1978	10.8	7.5	0.7	0.6	0.4	0.2
1993	69.3	23.8	3.3	1.1	6.0	1.2

Source: Statistics based on Burns Security Institute survey

SUBWAY CRIME ON THE WANE

New York City transit police say that their crackdown on turnstile jumpers, beginning in 1990, is most responsible for the reduction in subway crime:

Arrests of fare beaters, 1990 vs. 1993

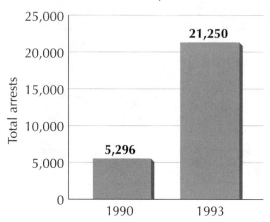

New York robberies and grand larcenies, 1983 vs. 1993

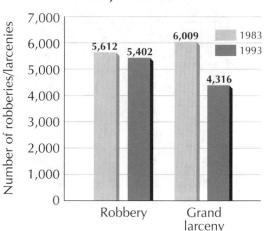

New York subway homicides, 1983–1993

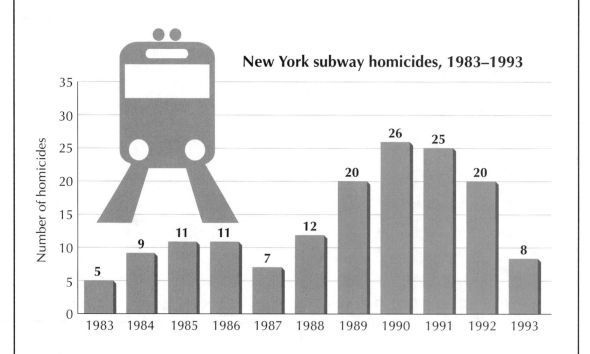

Source: New York Transit Police

STATE POLICIES ON TV CAMERAS IN COURT

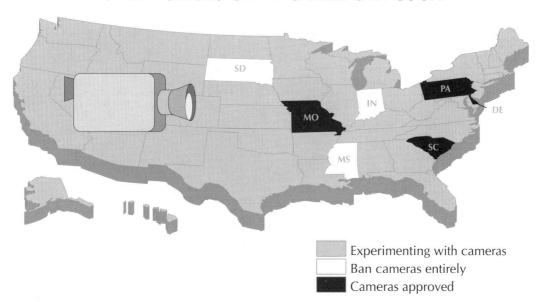

SD

PA

IN

DE

MO

SC

MS

Experimenting with cameras
Ban cameras entirely
Cameras approved

Source: National Center for State Courts; U.S. Supreme Court

PRIVATE SECURITY ON THE RISE

Private security sectors now outspend public law enforcement by 73%
and employ 2.5 times the number of people:

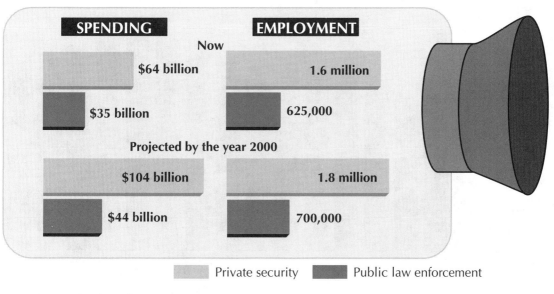

SPENDING	EMPLOYMENT
Now	
$64 billion	1.6 million
$35 billion	625,000
Projected by the year 2000	
$104 billion	1.8 million
$44 billion	700,000

Private security   Public law enforcement

Source: Statistics based on Hallcrest Systems Inc.

VIOLENCE IN ABORTION CLINICS

(Percentage of abortion clinics experiencing various
kinds of violence between January and July 1993)

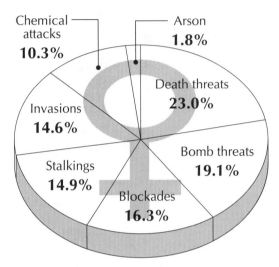

Chemical
attacks
10.3%

Arson
1.8%

Death threats
23.0%

Invasions
14.6%

Bomb threats
19.1%

Stalkings
14.9%

Blockades
16.3%

Source: The Feminist Majority Foundation

FORCIBLE RAPE AND ATTEMPTED FORCIBLE RAPE, 1970–1996

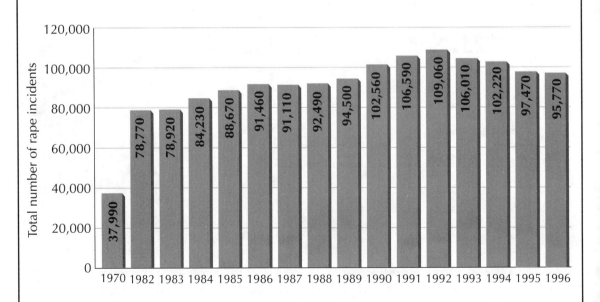

Total number of rape incidents

Year	Incidents
1970	37,990
1982	78,770
1983	78,920
1984	84,230
1985	88,670
1986	91,460
1987	91,110
1988	92,490
1989	94,500
1990	102,560
1991	106,590
1992	109,060
1993	106,010
1994	102,220
1995	97,470
1996	95,770

Source: Federal Bureau of Investigation

SEXUAL HARASSMENT COMPLAINTS BY EMPLOYEES ON THE RISE, 1989–1997

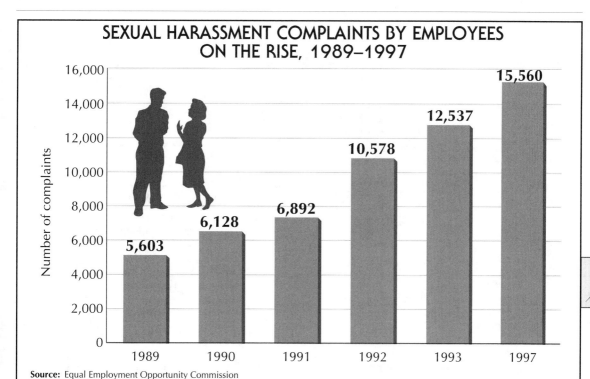

Source: Equal Employment Opportunity Commission

MALE SEXUAL HARASSMENT COMPLAINTS GROW, 1991–1993

(Number of sexual harassment cases filed by men against women)

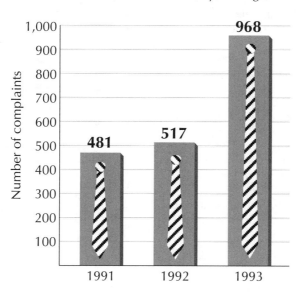

Source: Equal Employment Opportunity Commission

H O M I C I D E

Homicide—the killing of one person by another—is no longer one of the top 10 causes of death in the United States. It is, however, an event that always grabs headlines and inspires fascination on the part of the American public.

Homicide is not necessarily a crime. Killing in self-defense, to protect family members from grave bodily harm, or to prevent a felony is considered justifiable homicide. Killing someone accidentally, without gross negligence, is considered excusable homicide. There are two types of criminal homicide: murder and manslaughter. A charge of murder generally requires concrete proof of malice, or deliberate intent to kill. Manslaughter is unplanned homicide, done without malice or intent to kill.

The number of criminal homicides in the U.S. decreased from approximately 19,000 in 1985 to 18,200 in 1998. Males were the victims in more than 75% of the cases, and more blacks were killed than whites. Guns were the overwhelming weapon of choice, used in the great majority of homicide incidents.

A detailed government study of 8,063 homicides found that only 20% of the victims were killed by strangers; 64% were killed by acquaintances, and 16% were related to their killers. In family murder cases, wives were the most frequent victims. One-fifth of family murders, however, involved parents killing their children. About half the defendants in family killings had been arrested previously, as compared to three-quarters of the defendants in non-family killings.

FINGERTIP FACTS

- ☞ In 1985, there were about 19,000 criminal homicides in the U.S., or 7.9 per 100,000 population; in 1998, there were 18,200, or 7.4 per 100,000 population.

- ☞ In 1996, the states with the highest criminal homicide rates were Louisiana (17.5 per 100,000 population), Nevada (13.7), Maryland (11.6), and Mississippi (11.1). South Dakota (1.2), New Hampshire (1.7), and Iowa (1.9) had the lowest rates.

- ☞ Most homicide victims are under age 30.

- ☞ African Americans were victims in more than 50% of criminal homicides in 1994, even though they made up only 12.6% of the U.S. population.

- ☞ Black males ages 15 to 19 are more than 10 times as likely to be shot to death as are white males of that age group.

- ☞ Juvenile arrests for criminal homicide increased by almost 89% between 1986 and 1995.

- ☞ Mothers are more likely than fathers to murder their children; 64% of mothers' victims are sons, as compared to 48% of fathers' victims.

- ☞ Almost one-third of all murders committed in the U.S. are the result of an argument.

MURDER VICTIMS IN U.S., 1970–1997

Total murder victims

Number of murder victims

Year	Victims
1970	13,649
1975	18,642
1980	21,860
1985	17,545
1986	19,257
1987	17,963
1988	17,971
1989	18,954
1990	20,045
1991	21,505
1992	23,760
1993	24,530
1994	23,330
1995	21,610
1996	19,650
1997	18,209

Weapons used or cause of death, 1970–1996

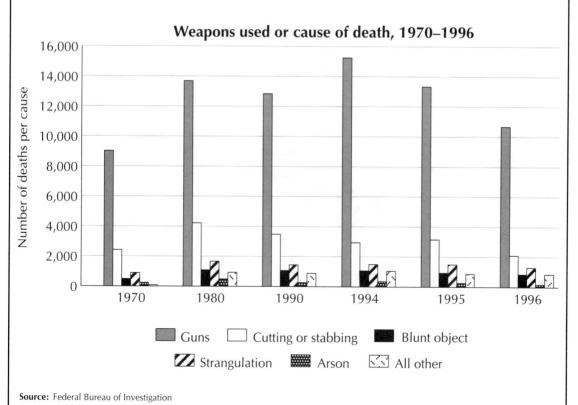

Number of deaths per cause

Guns   Cutting or stabbing   Blunt object
Strangulation   Arson   All other

Source: Federal Bureau of Investigation

MURDER RATES IN AMERICA'S TOP 20 MOST POPULATED CITIES, 1995

(Rates per 100,000 population, with rankings)

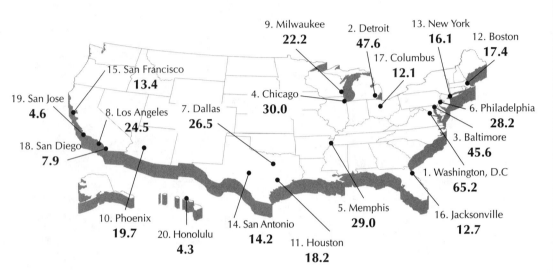

9. Milwaukee
22.2

2. Detroit
47.6

13. New York
16.1

12. Boston
17.4

17. Columbus
12.1

15. San Francisco
13.4

4. Chicago
30.0

19. San Jose
4.6

7. Dallas
26.5

6. Philadelphia
28.2

8. Los Angeles
24.5

3. Baltimore
45.6

18. San Diego
7.9

1. Washington, D.C
65.2

10. Phoenix
19.7

20. Honolulu
4.3

14. San Antonio
14.2

5. Memphis
29.0

16. Jacksonville
12.7

11. Houston
18.2

Source: Federal Bureau of Investigation

HOW U.S. HOMICIDE VICTIMS WERE KILLED, 1996

Almost three-quarters of all homicide victims in 1996 were killed by guns:

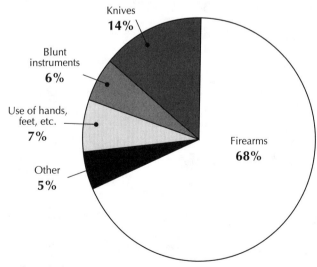

Knives
14%

Blunt instruments
6%

Use of hands, feet, etc.
7%

Firearms
68%

Other
5%

Source: Federal Bureau of Investigation

U.S. HOMICIDE INDEX TRENDS, 1995-1996

(Percentage change from 1995 to 1996, by size of city)

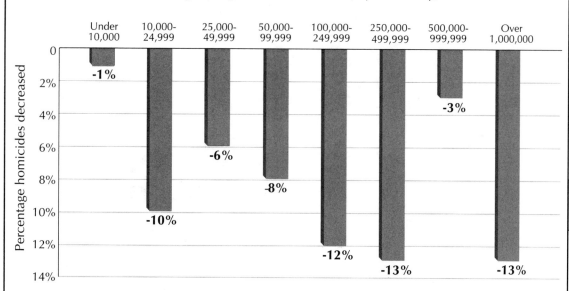

Source: FBI

MOST HOMICIDE VICTIMS ARE YOUNG

(The ages of 21,700 homicide victims
for whom ages were known in 1994)

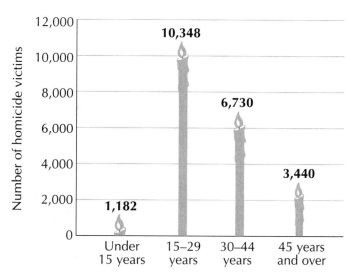

Source: Federal Bureau of Investigation

RELATED BY BLOOD:
WHO ARE THE FAMILY VICTIMS OF MURDER?

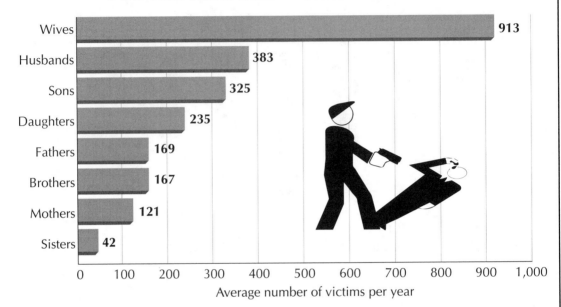

Wives	913
Husbands	383
Sons	325
Daughters	235
Fathers	169
Brothers	167
Mothers	121
Sisters	42

0   100   200   300   400   500   600   700   800   900   1,000

Average number of victims per year

VICTIM AND KILLER ARE THE SAME RACE IN MOST HOMICIDES

(A breakdown of murders in which there was a single killer and a single victim)

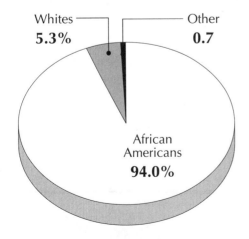

Victims of African-American murderers

Whites
5.3%

Other
0.7

African
Americans
94.0%

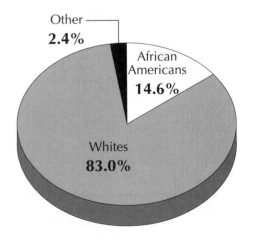

Victims of white murderers

Other
2.4%

African
Americans
14.6%

Whites
83.0%

Source: Federal Bureau of Investigation

HALF OF ALL HOMICIDE VICTIMS ARE AFRICAN AMERICAN

(Averages of statistics, 1990–1993)

Percentage of homicides

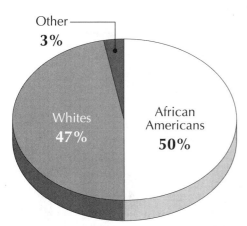

Other
3%

Whites
47%

African
Americans
50%

Percentage of population

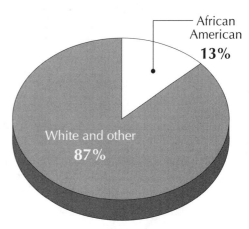

African
American
13%

White and other
87%

Source: Bureau of Justice Statistics

ANNUAL HOMICIDES, BY RACE, 1982 vs. 1993

The number of African-American homicide victims
surpassed the number of whites by 1993:

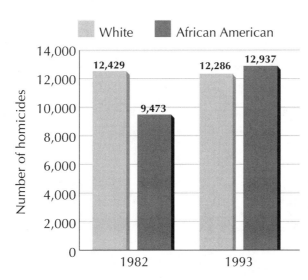

Source: Federal Bureau of Investigation

HOMICIDE VICTIMS, BY RACE AND SEX, 1970–1996

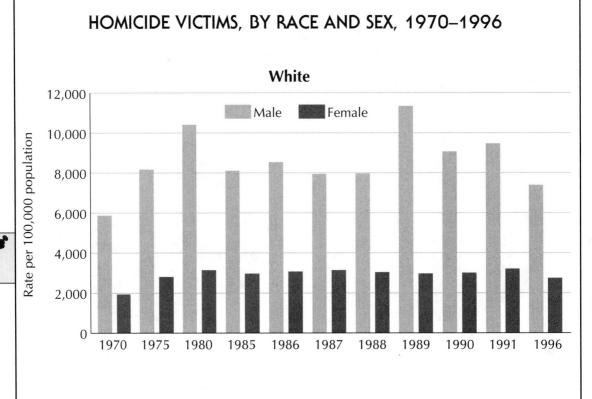

White

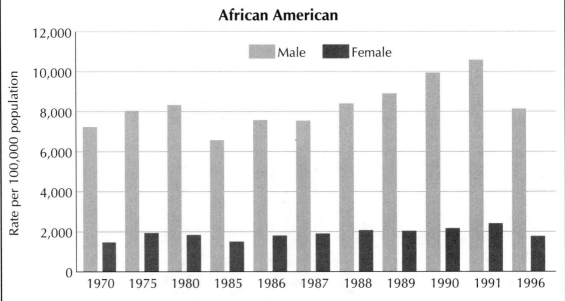

African American

Source: U.S. National Center for Health Statistics

GUNS ARE MOST USED WEAPONS IN HOMICIDE, 1976–1997

(Weapons used in homicides by juveniles under age 18)

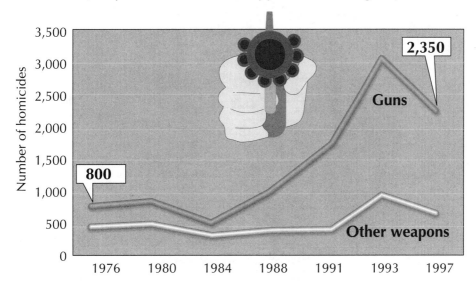

2,350

800

Guns

Other weapons

Number of homicides

3,500
3,000
2,500
2,000
1,500
1,000
500
0

1976 1980 1984 1988 1991 1993 1997

Source: U.S. Department of Justice; Federal Bureau of Investigation

HOMICIDE TRENDS OF YOUNG MALES, BY RACE, 1980-1997

(Percentage of young males who are homicide offenders or victims, in relation to their population)

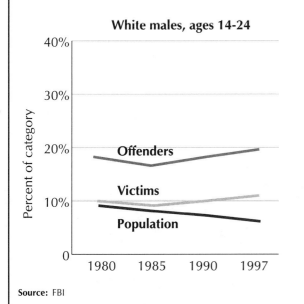

White males, ages 14-24

Percent of category

40%
30%
20%
10%
0

Offenders
Victims
Population

1980 1985 1990 1997

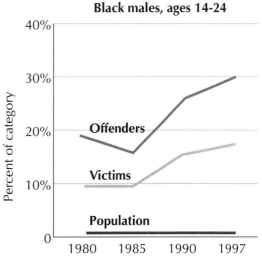

Black males, ages 14-24

Percent of category

40%
30%
20%
10%
0

Offenders
Victims
Population

1980 1985 1990 1997

Source: FBI

MURDER PROFILE: THE MOST COMMON CIRCUMSTANCES

(As percentage of all murders)

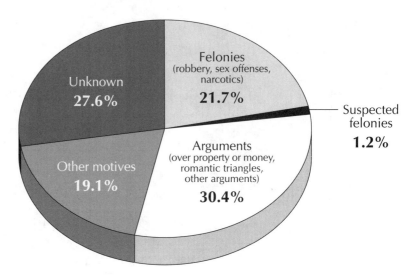

Unknown
27.6%

Felonies
(robbery, sex offenses, narcotics)
21.7%

Suspected felonies
1.2%

Other motives
19.1%

Arguments
(over property or money, romantic triangles, other arguments)
30.4%

Source: Federal Bureau of Investigation

RISKY BUSINESS, 1996

(Annual homicide rates for selected occupations per 100,000 workers)

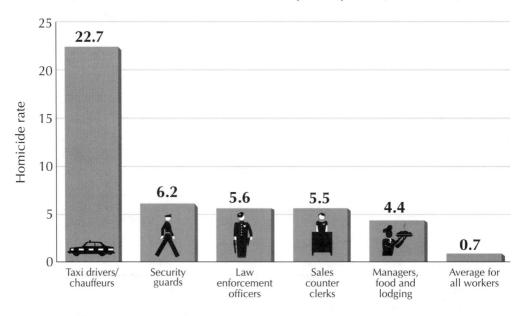

22.7	**6.2**	**5.6**	**5.5**	**4.4**	**0.7**
Taxi drivers/ chauffeurs	Security guards	Law enforcement officers	Sales counter clerks	Managers, food and lodging	Average for all workers

Homicide rate

Source: National Institute for Occupational Safety and Health

MURDER VICTIMS BY SEX, 1993

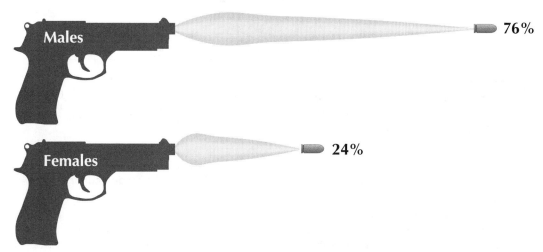

Males   76%

Females   24%

Source: Federal Bureau of Investigation

MOTIVATION OF WORKPLACE ATTACKERS
(As described by victims)

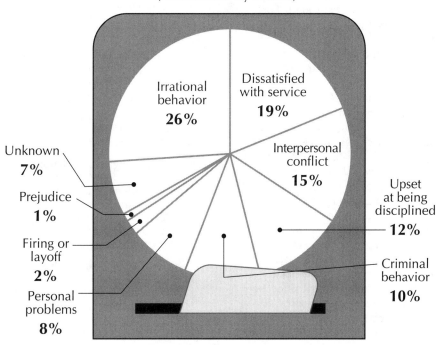

Irrational behavior 26%

Dissatisfied with service 19%

Interpersonal conflict 15%

Unknown 7%

Prejudice 1%

Firing or layoff 2%

Personal problems 8%

Upset at being disciplined 12%

Criminal behavior 10%

Source: Based on statistics from Northwestern National Life Insurance; National Institute for Occupational Safety and Health

G U N S

Guns play a central role in many of the crimes committed in the U.S. In 1996, for example, handguns were used in 47% of murders and 64% of robberies. A growing amount of this violence is committed by teenagers, for whom firearms are the weapon of choice. Between 1984 and 1994, the number of gun homicides committed by teens nearly quadrupled. Other youths frequently are the targets. Every 2 hours, a U.S. child dies of a gunshot wound.

The widespread availability of guns is one of the nation's most controversial issues. Public opinion polls have repeatedly shown that a large majority of Americans favor stricter gun controls, believing that stricter regulation will help reduce gun-related crimes. A sizable minority, however, are strongly opposed to controls of any kind. For example, the National Rifle Association (NRA)—a tremendously powerful and wealthy pro-gun organization—had 3.5 million members and revenues of $148 million in 1995.

Despite strong NRA opposition in 1993, Congress passed the Brady Bill, which requires a 5-day waiting period for handgun purchases and background checks of people who intend to buy guns. It also provided for a Crime Bill that bans 19 types of assault weapons. Both laws were applauded by police organizations nationwide. States and local communities also have enacted several types of gun-control laws. A rash of school shootings in the late 1990s—including one at Columbine High School in Colorado that killed 14 students and 1 teacher—has also caused the debate over gun-control legislation to remain a highly charged issue.

FINGERTIP FACTS

- In 1997, most firearm homicides were because of an argument (4,383), and most of the victims (4,797) knew their killers.

- In 1995, there were 35,957 firearm deaths in the U.S. Of these, suicide accounted for 18,503 deaths, homicide for 15,551.

- Handguns were used in 47% of U.S. homicides in 1996, up from 43.5% in 1982.

- Every 15 minutes during 1995, someone in the U.S. died of a gunshot wound, nearly half in homicides. In that same year, there were about 1,200 accidental firearm deaths.

- The U.S. firearms industry is booming. U.S. gun and ammunition production nearly doubled from 1987 to 1996.

- In 1995, males aged 5-24 made up 33% of all firearm deaths. Of those, 48% were suicides and 49% were homicides.

- According to the National School Safety Center, some 135,000 children carry guns into school every day. About 25% of the nation's major urban school districts have installed metal detectors.

- Of the children that have guns, 38% got them from friends, 23% from family members, and 14% bought them on the street.

HANDGUNS AND HOMICIDES, 1982 vs. 1998

Handguns were used in 47% of all homicides in 1998, up from 43.5% in 1982:

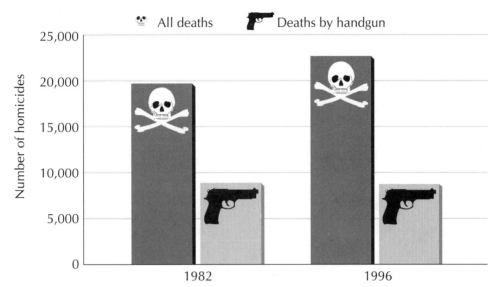

Source: Federal Bureau of Investigation

FIREARMS USED IN HOMICIDES, 1997

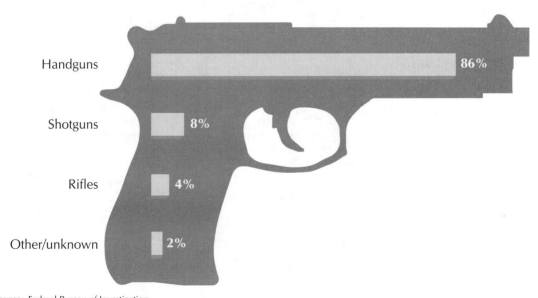

Source: Federal Bureau of Investigation

TOP 5 STATES WITH THE HIGHEST PERCENTAGE
OF HOMICIDES BY FIREARM, 1997

Authorities say there are more than 200 million firearms in circulation in the U.S. Firearms were used in most homicides in 1997, particularly in the 5 states with the highest number of slayings:

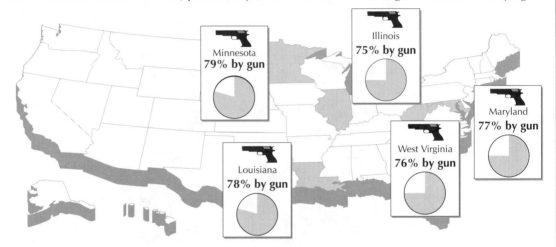

Illinois
75% by gun

Minnesota
79% by gun

Maryland
77% by gun

West Virginia
76% by gun

Louisiana
78% by gun

Source: Federal Bureau of Investigation; Florida Department of Law Enforcement

GUNS AND TYPES
OF DEATH

(Reasons for the 35,673 firearm deaths in the U.S. in 1995)

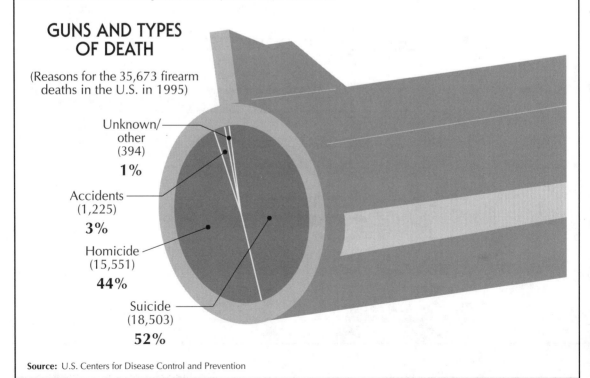

Unknown/other
(394)
1%

Accidents
(1,225)
3%

Homicide
(15,551)
44%

Suicide
(18,503)
52%

Source: U.S. Centers for Disease Control and Prevention

WHO'S KILLING WHOM?

Firearms were used in 7 of 10 U.S. homicides in 1997; usually that firearm was a handgun:

Relationship of victim to killer

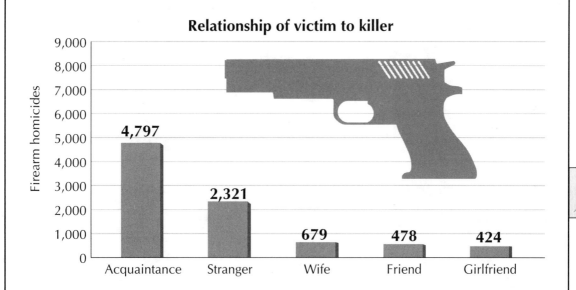

Firearm homicides

Acquaintance	4,797
Stranger	2,321
Wife	679
Friend	478
Girlfriend	424

Top reasons for 1997 homicides

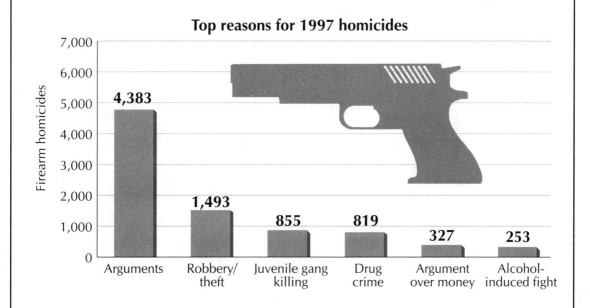

Firearm homicides

Arguments	4,383
Robbery/theft	1,493
Juvenile gang killing	855
Drug crime	819
Argument over money	327
Alcohol-induced fight	253

Source: Bureau of Justice Statistics; Federal Bureau of Investigation

MORE YOUNG AFRICAN-AMERICAN MALES SHOT TO DEATH

Young black males are 10 times more likely than white males to be firearm homicide victims. Firearm homicides per 100,000 people in the 15–19 years age group:

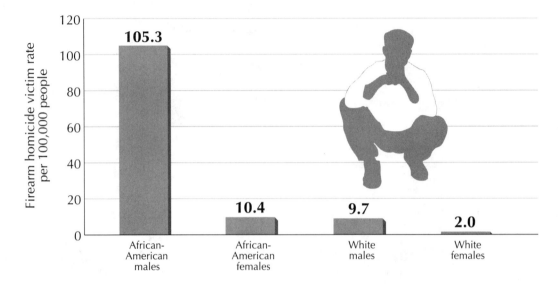

Firearm homicide victim rate per 100,000 people

- African-American males: **105.3**
- African-American females: **10.4**
- White males: **9.7**
- White females: **2.0**

Source: U.S. Centers for Disease Control and Prevention

SCHOOL SHOOTING DEATHS, 1992-1998

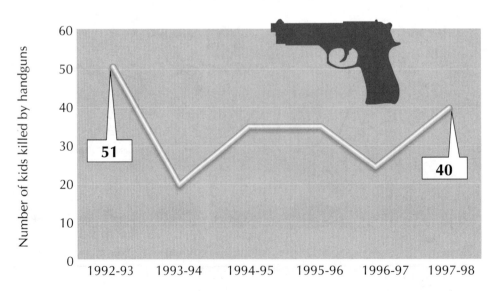

Number of kids killed by handguns

1992-93 **51** ... 1997-98 **40**

1992-93   1993-94   1994-95   1995-96   1996-97   1997-98

Source: CNN

WHICH GUNS DO KIDS HAVE?

A survey of 758 male students at 10 inner-city high schools found that 22% had possessed one or more firearms at some time. Types of guns that the 22% possessed:

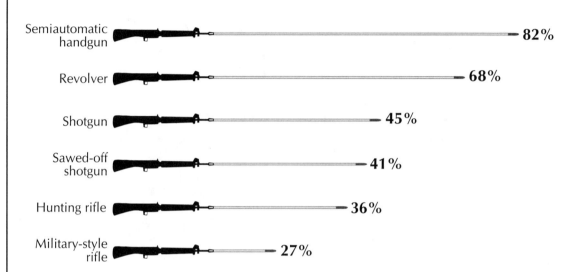

Semiautomatic handgun — **82%**

Revolver — **68%**

Shotgun — **45%**

Sawed-off shotgun — **41%**

Hunting rifle — **36%**

Military-style rifle — **27%**

Source: Federal Bureau of Investigation; National Institute of Justice

WHERE DO KIDS GET GUNS?

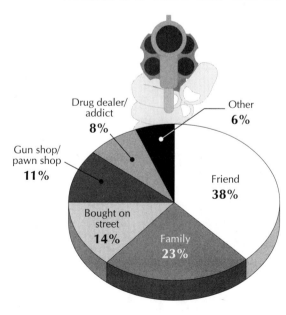

Drug dealer/addict
8%

Other
6%

Gun shop/pawn shop
11%

Friend
38%

Bought on street
14%

Family
23%

Source: Federal Bureau of Investigation; National Institute of Justice

ACCIDENTAL FIREARM DEATHS, BY AGE, 1997

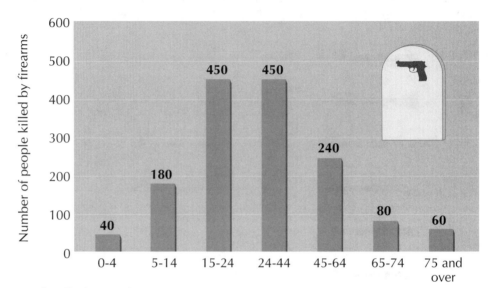

Source: National Health Safety Council

INTERNATIONAL GUN OWNERSHIP

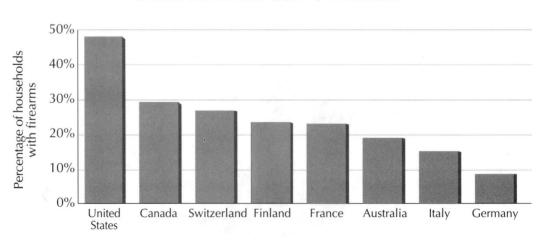

Source: Can Med Association

HOUSEHOLDS WITH FIREARMS, 1995
(By age, education, and religion of head of household)

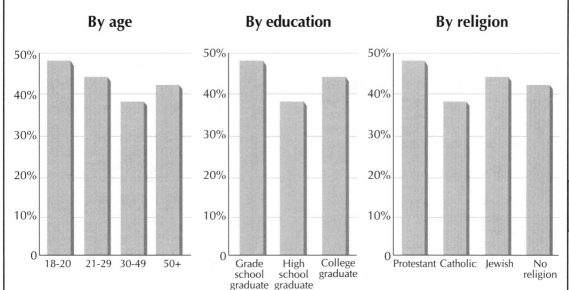

By age

By education

By religion

Source: Bureau of Justice Statistics

PROFILE: HIGH PROFIT FROM GUN SALES
(Profit margin on the sale of new handguns, according to a survey of 1,000 firearm dealers)

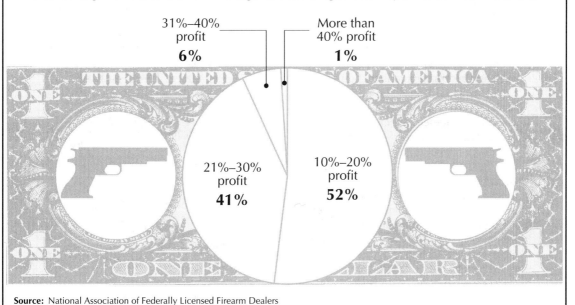

31%–40% profit
6%

More than 40% profit
1%

21%–30% profit
41%

10%–20% profit
52%

Source: National Association of Federally Licensed Firearm Dealers

JAIL

The U.S. has more people in jail and prison per capita than any other nation. In 1997, the U.S. had 1,197,590 inmates sentenced to terms of more than one year in federal and state prisons. Many U.S. jails and prisons are overcrowded, which has led to the early release of some convicts and a growing number who are placed instead under house arrest, where their movements may be electronically monitored.

Although the vast majority of people in U.S. jails and prisons are males, females make up a growing percentage of inmates. More and more juveniles are also spending time behind bars. Generally, juveniles are placed in special facilities apart from adult prisoners. There is a trend, however, to try and sentence some juveniles in adult court; for example, the 1994 federal crime bill permits juveniles ages 13 and older to be tried as adults in federal courts for such crimes as murder, rape, assault, and robbery.

Penalties for crimes vary widely from case to case and from one jurisdiction to another. Throughout the nation, it has been customary to fix minimum and maximum limitations on punishments for specific crimes; more recently, states have moved toward mandated sentences for certain crimes.

Capital punishment was suspended in the U.S. from 1967 to 1977, but was then resumed. There is strong support among Americans across the country for the death penalty, and, predictably, the number of executions has increased in recent years. Capital punishment is permitted in 38 states; in addition, some 60 crimes are subject to the federal death penalty. About 3,000 U.S. prisoners are currently on death row.

FINGERTIP FACTS

- In 1997, there were 1,197,590 prisoners in the U.S., an increase of 29% from 1992— and a whopping 72% increase from 1980.

- In the 15-year period between 1982 and 1997, the number of people in state and federal prisons more than tripled.

- In 1997, U.S. prisons held 1,197,590 inmates sentenced to more than one year, a rate of 445 per 100,000 population. This was an increase from 196,429 such prisoners in 1970, a rate of 96.7 per 100,000.

- Males in jail outnumber females by about 10 to 1.

- Drug offenders accounted for nearly 60% of the prison population in 1998. That year, the average sentence being served by prisoners was 5-10 years (30.1%), followed by 10-15 years (20.1%).

- A 1994 Gallup Poll indicated that 80% of Americans favor the death penalty for convicted murderers; their primary objective is revenge against the murderers, not any expectations that the death penalty will deter other criminals.

- Electrocution is the most frequently used method of execution in the U.S., followed closely by lethal injection. From 1977 to 1996, these methods combined were used in 96% of all executions.

PROFILE: U.S. JAILS AND PRISONS

The number of criminals in prisons in the U.S. in 1992 had increased by 168% since 1980, and the number in local jails more than doubled. The number of full-time law enforcement officers rose by 40%, yet the violent crime rate rose by 27%:

Officers vs. inmates, 1980 vs. 1990

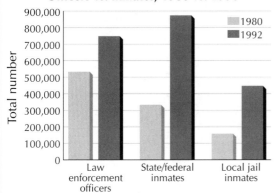

Sentences vs. time served

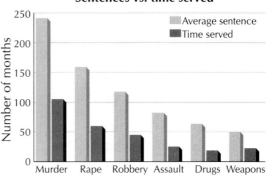

U.S. violent crime rate, 1980 vs. 1992

(Rate of violent crime per 100,000 population)

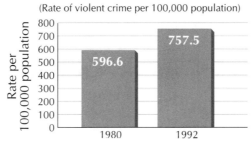

Offenders who repeat

(Percentage of violent criminals in state prisons who had served time before)

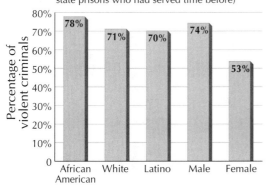

Days from arrest to sentencing

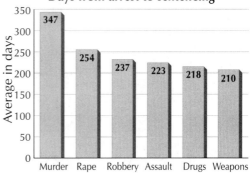

Source: Federal Bureau of Investigation

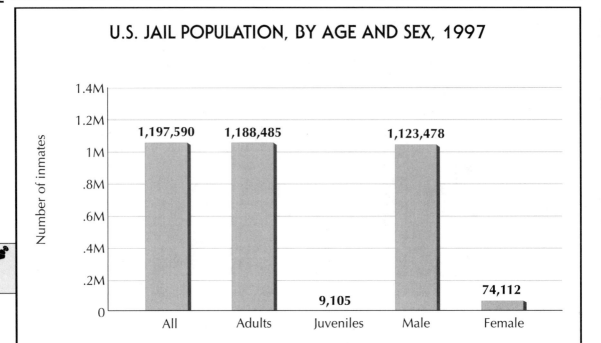

U.S. JAIL POPULATION, BY AGE AND SEX, 1997

Number of inmates

1,197,590   1,188,485   1,123,478

9,105   74,112

All   Adults   Juveniles   Male   Female

Source: Bureau of Justice Statistics

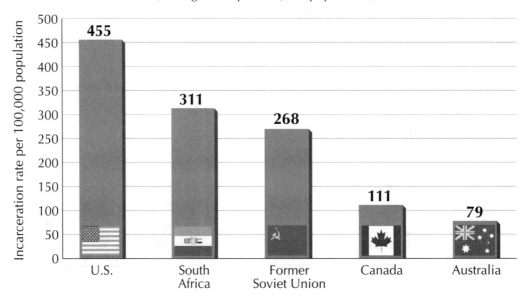

U.S. LEADS THE WORLD IN INCARCERATION RATE
(Average rates per 100,000 population)

Incarceration rate per 100,000 population

455   311   268   111   79

U.S.   South Africa   Former Soviet Union   Canada   Australia

Source: FBI Uniform Crime Report

PRISON POPULATION BOOMS AS THE CRIME RATE DROPS

State and federal prison population, 1997

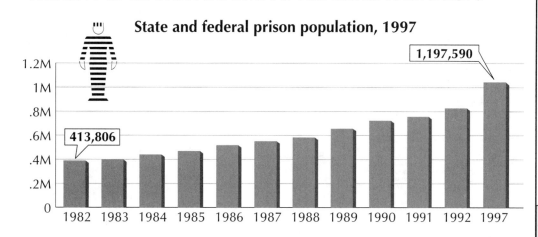

Total prison population

413,806

1,197,590

1982 1983 1984 1985 1986 1987 1988 1989 1990 1991 1992 1997

Crime rates per 100,000 people, 1997

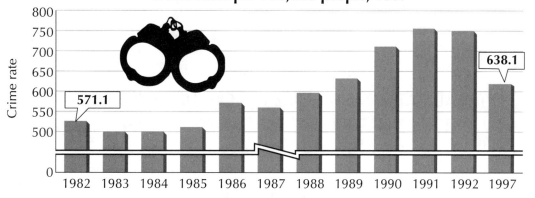

Crime rate

571.1

638.1

1982 1983 1984 1985 1986 1987 1988 1989 1990 1991 1992 1997

Percentage of prison inmates by number of prior sentences

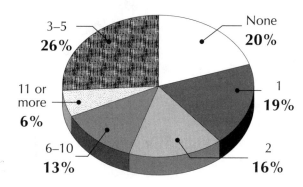

3–5
26%

None
20%

11 or
more
6%

1
19%

6–10
13%

2
16%

Source: Bureau of Justice Statistics

STATE AND FEDERAL PRISONERS IN THE U.S., 1997

Total prisoners, federal and state

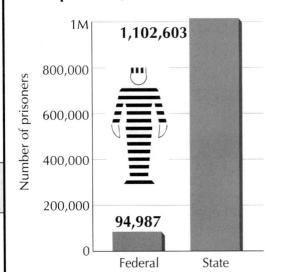

Number of prisoners

1M

1,102,603

800,000

600,000

400,000

200,000

94,987

0

Federal   State

Federal and state prisoners, by sex

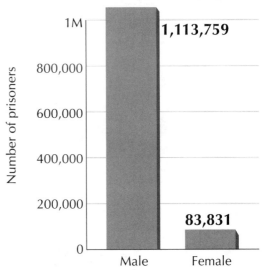

Number of prisoners

1M

1,113,759

800,000

600,000

400,000

200,000

83,831

0

Male   Female

Source: Bureau of Justice Statistics

TOTAL STATE AND FEDERAL PRISON INMATES, 1980–1997

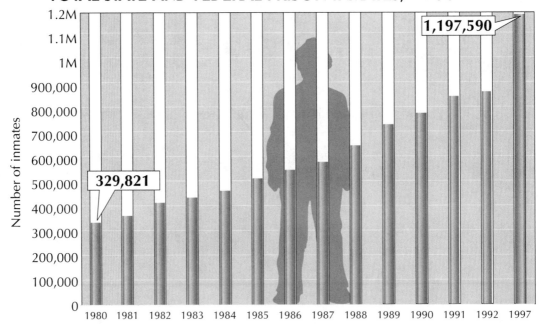

Number of inmates

1.2M
1.1M
1M
900,000
800,000
700,000
600,000
500,000
400,000
300,000
200,000
100,000
0

329,821

1,197,590

1980 1981 1982 1983 1984 1985 1986 1987 1988 1989 1990 1991 1992 1997

Source: Bureau of Justice Statistics

DOING TIME FOR CRIME

Non-violent drug offenders account for 21.1% of the federal prison population. Punishments for first-time drug offenses in months served, compared with other offenses:

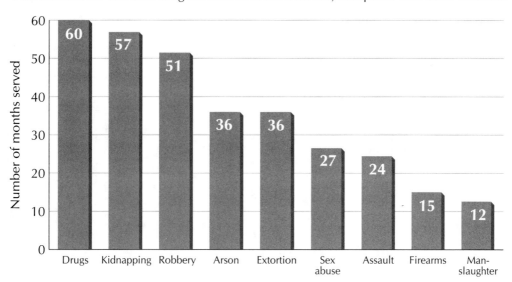

Source: U.S. Sentencing Commission; U.S. Justice Department

TOTAL ARRESTS, BY AGE, 1992

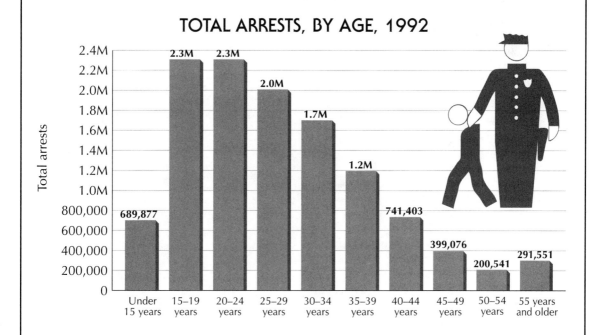

Source: U.S. Department of Justice

NUMBER OF EXECUTIONS, 1978–1996

(Death penalty was reinstated in 1977)

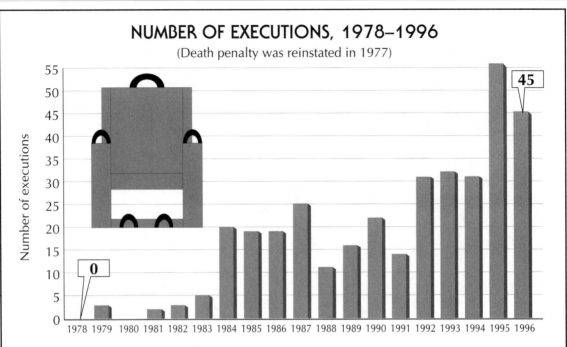

Number of executions

0

45

1978 1979 1980 1981 1982 1983 1984 1985 1986 1987 1988 1989 1990 1991 1992 1993 1994 1995 1996

Source: National Coalition to Abolish the Death Penalty

SYSTEM OF EXECUTION, BY STATE

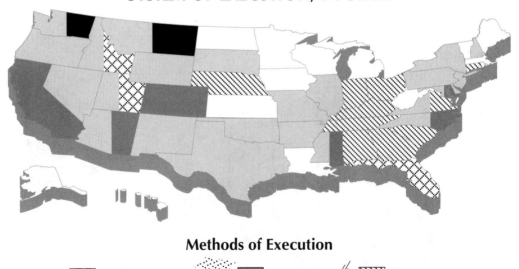

Methods of Execution

Firing squad	Gas	Electrocution
Lethal injection	Hanging	No death penalty

* Some states use more than one method of execution
Source: Bureau of Justice Statistics

COSTS OF PRISON INMATES, 1987–1992

(Average yearly price of maintaining prisoners, per capita)

Federal ☐ State ■

Source: U.S. Department of Justice

ELECTRONIC HOUSE ARRESTS GROW, 1986 vs. 1993

Because prison populations continue to climb rapidly, electronic monitoring programs are becoming more commonplace. Number of convicts under electronic house arrest:

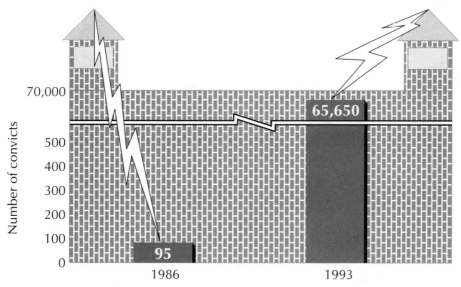

Source: U.S. Department of Justice

6

ENVIRONMENT AND GEOGRAPHY

GEOGRAPHY AND CLIMATE

The United States covers a total area of 3,732,396 square miles—3,536,338 square miles of land plus 196,058 square miles of inland and coastal waters. Of its 50 states, 49 lie on the North American continent; the 50th, Hawaii, consists of a group of islands in the Pacific Ocean. The nation's capital city, Washington, D.C., is not part of any state—it is situated on the Potomac River between Maryland and Virginia. The nation also administers several overseas territories and possessions, including the U.S. Virgin Islands, Puerto Rico, Guam, American Samoa, and the Northern Mariana Islands.

America's topography varies tremendously across the nation. In the continental U.S., there are highlands in the East and mountains in the West, with wide plains in between. Each of these three broad regions includes many smaller landforms, including vast deserts and dramatic seashores, deep-green plateaus and windswept sandhills, crystal lakes and deep canyons.

Because of the nation's great size and its varied topography, the U.S. experiences widely ranging weather. A region's climate—the average weather over a long period of time—is a factor of many elements, including latitude, prevailing winds, elevation, and distance from oceans. Earth's three major climatic zones—polar, temperate, and tropical—are all represented within the boundaries of the U.S.

FINGERTIP FACTS

☛ The major U.S. inland waterway is the Mississippi River, which is estimated at 2,340 miles long. It empties 593,000 cubic feet of water into the Gulf of Mexico every second.

☛ The U.S. Geological Survey reports that, at 2,540 miles, the Missouri River is the longest in the U.S.

☛ For all its great size, the U.S. shares borders with only two other nations: Canada to the north and Mexico to the south.

☛ Alaska is the largest state (615,230 square miles); Rhode Island is the smallest (1,231 square miles).

☛ The U.S. is the world's fourth-largest country; only Russia, Canada, and China are bigger.

☛ The largest inland bodies of water in the U.S. are the Great Lakes. Lake Michigan covers about 22,342 square miles.

☛ The highest point in the U.S. is atop Alaska's Mount McKinley, which has an elevation of 20,400 feet. The lowest point is in Death Valley, California—282 feet below sea level.

☛ The U.S. National Oceanic and Atmospheric Administration (NOAA) maintains about 11,600 weather stations.

☛ The city of Phoenix, Arizona, lies in a desert; it receives average yearly precipitation of 7.66 inches. In contrast, Mobile, Alabama, receives an average of 63.96 inches a year.

☛ The wettest spot in the U.S. is Mount Waialeale, on the Hawaiian island of Kauai; it receives about 480 inches of rainfall every year. In contrast, Death Valley, California, receives only 1.5 inches annually.

☛ Juneau, Alaska, is one of the snowiest places in the United States, averaging about 99 inches of snow every year.

5 LARGEST STATES
(In area, by square miles, with rankings)

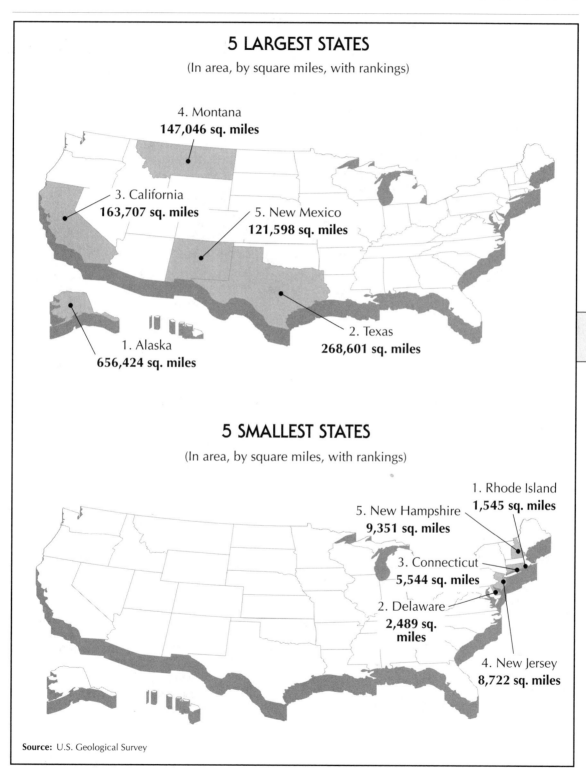

4. Montana
147,046 sq. miles

3. California
163,707 sq. miles

5. New Mexico
121,598 sq. miles

2. Texas
268,601 sq. miles

1. Alaska
656,424 sq. miles

5 SMALLEST STATES
(In area, by square miles, with rankings)

1. Rhode Island
1,545 sq. miles

5. New Hampshire
9,351 sq. miles

3. Connecticut
5,544 sq. miles

2. Delaware
2,489 sq. miles

4. New Jersey
8,722 sq. miles

Source: U.S. Geological Survey

TOP 10 LONGEST U.S. RIVERS

(In miles)

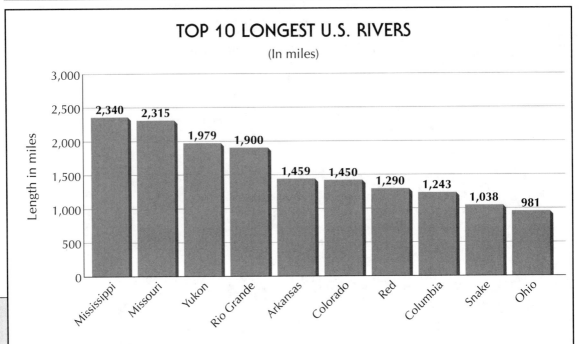

Source: U.S. Geological Survey

TOP 10 STATES WITH LARGEST STATE PARKS AND RECREATION AREAS*

(In acreage, with rankings)

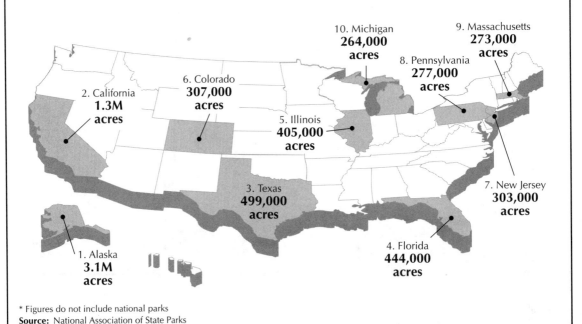

10. Michigan
264,000 acres

9. Massachusetts
273,000 acres

8. Pennsylvania
277,000 acres

6. Colorado
307,000 acres

2. California
1.3M acres

5. Illinois
405,000 acres

7. New Jersey
303,000 acres

3. Texas
499,000 acres

4. Florida
444,000 acres

1. Alaska
3.1M acres

* Figures do not include national parks
Source: National Association of State Parks

TOP 10 NATIONAL PARKS, IN ACREAGE

(With rankings)

1. Wrangell-St. Elias, Alaska
7.6M acres

7. Yellowstone, Montana/Wyoming
2.2M acres

3. Denali, Alaska
4.7M acres

10. Grand Canyon, Arizona
1.2M acres

6. Lake Clark, Alaska
2.5M acres

8. Koouk Valley, Alaska
1.7M acres

9. Everglades, Florida
1.4M acres

2. Gates of the Arctic, Alaska
7.0M acres

5. Glacier Bay, Alaska
3.2M acres

4. Katmai, Alaska
3.5M acres

TOP 10 NATIONAL PARKS, IN ANNUAL VISITS, 1998

(With rankings)

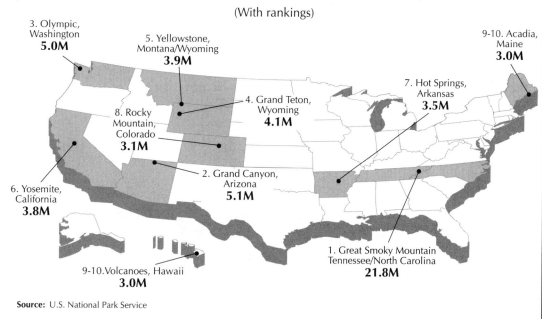

3. Olympic, Washington
5.0M

5. Yellowstone, Montana/Wyoming
3.9M

9-10. Acadia, Maine
3.0M

7. Hot Springs, Arkansas
3.5M

8. Rocky Mountain, Colorado
3.1M

4. Grand Teton, Wyoming
4.1M

6. Yosemite, California
3.8M

2. Grand Canyon, Arizona
5.1M

9-10. Volcanoes, Hawaii
3.0M

1. Great Smoky Mountain Tennessee/North Carolina
21.8M

Source: U.S. National Park Service

COLDEST U.S. TEMPERATURES ON RECORD

(In degrees Fahrenheit, with rankings and dates)

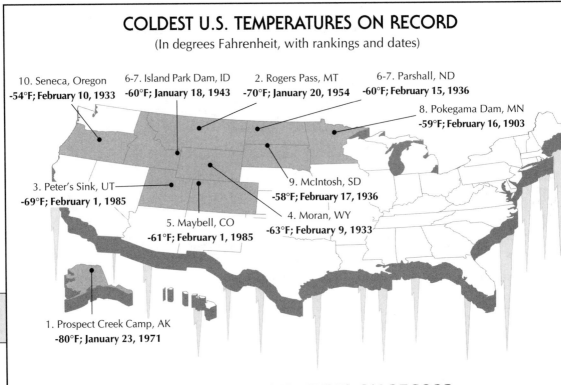

10. Seneca, Oregon
-54°F; February 10, 1933

6-7. Island Park Dam, ID
-60°F; January 18, 1943

2. Rogers Pass, MT
-70°F; January 20, 1954

6-7. Parshall, ND
-60°F; February 15, 1936

8. Pokegama Dam, MN
-59°F; February 16, 1903

3. Peter's Sink, UT
-69°F; February 1, 1985

9. McIntosh, SD
-58°F; February 17, 1936

5. Maybell, CO
-61°F; February 1, 1985

4. Moran, WY
-63°F; February 9, 1933

1. Prospect Creek Camp, AK
-80°F; January 23, 1971

HOTTEST U.S. TEMPERATURES ON RECORD

(In degrees Fahrenheit, with rankings and dates)

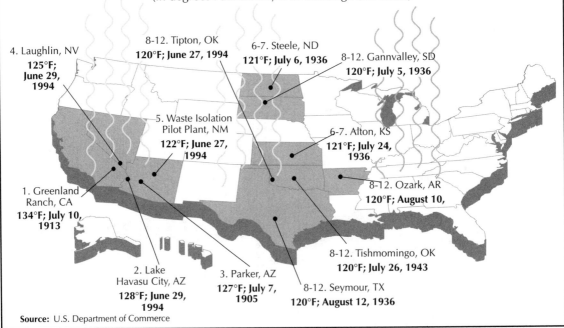

4. Laughlin, NV
**125°F;
June 29,
1994**

8-12. Tipton, OK
120°F; June 27, 1994

6-7. Steele, ND
121°F; July 6, 1936

8-12. Gannvalley, SD
120°F; July 5, 1936

5. Waste Isolation
Pilot Plant, NM
**122°F; June 27,
1994**

6-7. Alton, KS
**121°F; July 24,
1936**

1. Greenland
Ranch, CA
**134°F; July 10,
1913**

8-12. Ozark, AR
120°F; August 10,

2. Lake
Havasu City, AZ
**128°F; June 29,
1994**

3. Parker, AZ
**127°F; July 7,
1905**

8-12. Tishmomingo, OK
120°F; July 26, 1943

8-12. Seymour, TX
120°F; August 12, 1936

Source: U.S. Department of Commerce

TOP 5 STATES WITH MOST TORNADOES, 1953–1991

(Total number of tornadoes, with rankings)

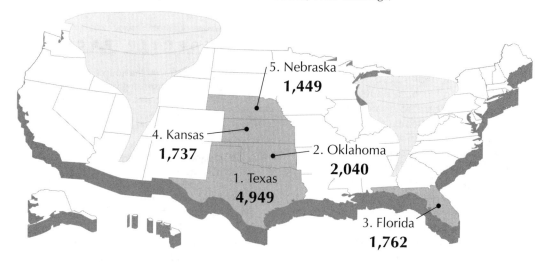

5. Nebraska
1,449

4. Kansas
1,737

2. Oklahoma
2,040

1. Texas
4,949

3. Florida
1,762

Source: U.S. Department of Commerce; National Weather Service; National Severe Storms Forecast Center

COSTLIER NATURAL DISASTERS, 1980-1998

(Clean-up and recovery costs, in billions of dollars)

■ 1980-1989   ■ 1990-1998

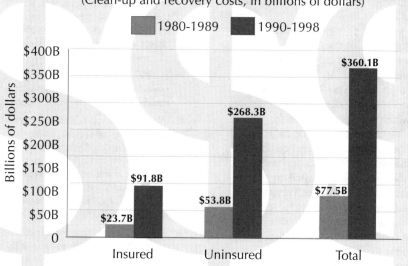

Billions of dollars

	Insured	Uninsured	Total
1980-1989	$23.7B	$53.8B	$77.5B
1990-1998	$91.8B	$268.3B	$360.1B

Source: Munich Re for Worldwatch

WATER

Water is one of the world's most precious resources. It is also one that is vastly underappreciated. People often don't value it until it becomes hard to come by. And as both population and pollution increase, so do conflicts over water rights. Communities located downstream object to water pollution created by industries upstream; cities compete with farms for scarce supplies; and taxpayers howl over increased water and sewer rates.

Water pollution that stems from emissions from factories, utilities, and municipal sewage plants is relatively easy to identify, and has been significantly controlled since passage of the Clean Water Act in 1972. Much more difficult to identify and combat is "non-point pollution," which is contamination that cannot be traced to a specific source. Dumping of used motor oil, and runoff of pesticides and fertilizer from farmland, are common examples of non-point pollution.

An important part of the water-quality equation is wetlands—swamps, marshes, estuaries, and other lands regularly saturated by water. These are essential areas for water birds. The U.S. has lost more than 50% of its wetlands, most of which has been drained for farmland. Yet, despite this serious threat to our water supply and quality, some individuals and companies have made concerted efforts to weaken the government's safeguards over wetlands, because they fear higher costs for pollution controls. Also coming under attack are the Clean Water Act and Safe Drinking Water Act, two major U.S. anti-pollution measures.

FINGERTIP FACTS

- Groundwater is the source of more than half the drinking water in the U.S. In many parts of the country, groundwater supplies are being depleted faster than they are being replaced.

- Daily water consumption in the U.S. rose steadily from 1960, reaching 100 billion gallons in 1980. It declined to 92 billion gallons in 1985, then rose again to almost 100 billion gallons in 1997.

- Everyday, the average person uses 123 gallons of water. During one year, an average household will use 110,000 gallons.

- Traditional toilets used in the U.S. use 3 to 7 gallons of water per flush. Newer water-efficient toilets use less than 2 gallons per flush.

- About 13.5% of all water consumed in New York City is used to flush toilets in people's homes. Replacing traditional toilets with water-efficient toilets would save the city about 250 million gallons every day.

- In 1997, the EPA studied the quality of water along coastlines and found that 97% of beaches were impaired.

- Wetlands are nurseries and spawning grounds for shrimp, crabs, oysters, bluefish, flounder, sea trout, striped bass, and other species of commercial importance. Since its birth, the U.S. has lost more than 50% of its wetlands. It continues to lose almost 300,000 acres each year.

- Historically, drainage for agriculture has been responsible for about 80% of all freshwater wetlands losses.

U.S. WATER CONSUMPTION, 1965–1995

(Total consumption, in billions of gallons)

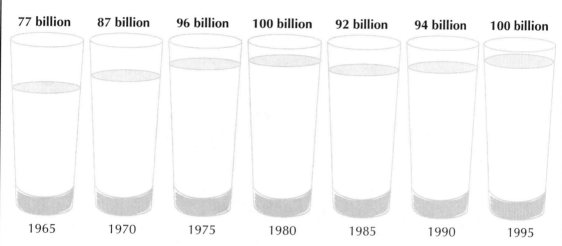

77 billion	87 billion	96 billion	100 billion	92 billion	94 billion	100 billion
1965	1970	1975	1980	1985	1990	1995

Source: U.S. Bureau of Domestic Business Development; U.S. Geological Survey

AVERAGE WATER USAGE

(Distribution of household water)

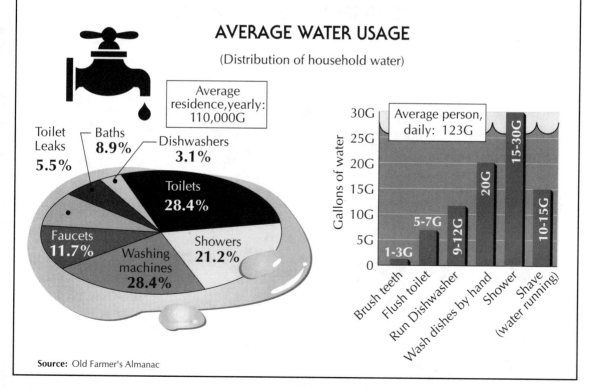

Average residence, yearly: 110,000G

Toilet Leaks 5.5%
Baths 8.9%
Dishwashers 3.1%
Toilets 28.4%
Faucets 11.7%
Washing machines 28.4%
Showers 21.2%

Average person, daily: 123G

Gallons of water

30G
25G
20G
15G
10G
5G
0

Brush teeth 1-3G
Flush toilet 5-7G
Run Dishwasher 9-12G
Wash dishes by hand 20G
Shower 15-30G
Shave (water running) 10-15G

Source: Old Farmer's Almanac

LOST WETLANDS: TOP 10 STATES

(Percentage of wetlands lost over past 200 years, with rankings)

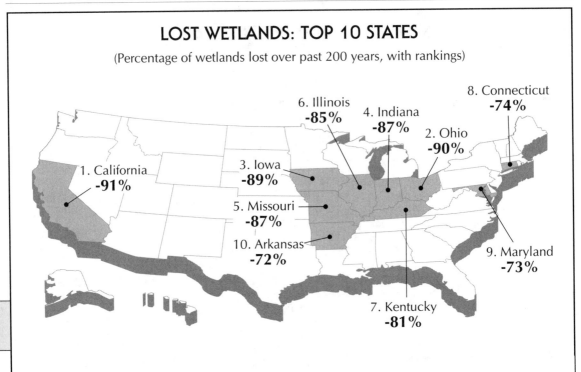

8. Connecticut
-74%

6. Illinois
-85%

4. Indiana
-87%

2. Ohio
-90%

1. California
-91%

3. Iowa
-89%

5. Missouri
-87%

10. Arkansas
-72%

9. Maryland
-73%

7. Kentucky
-81%

TOP 10 STATES WITH MOST WETLANDS

(By total wetlands acreage in state, with percentage of state covered by wetlands and rankings)

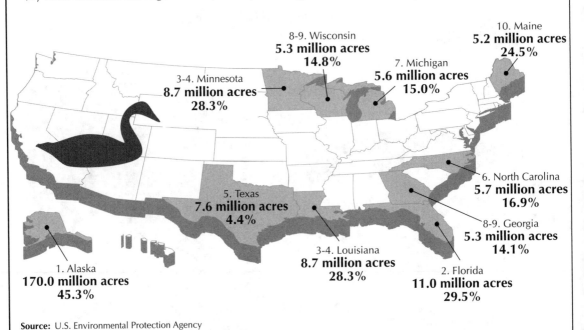

8-9. Wisconsin
5.3 million acres
14.8%

7. Michigan
5.6 million acres
15.0%

10. Maine
5.2 million acres
24.5%

3-4. Minnesota
8.7 million acres
28.3%

6. North Carolina
5.7 million acres
16.9%

5. Texas
7.6 million acres
4.4%

8-9. Georgia
5.3 million acres
14.1%

3-4. Louisiana
8.7 million acres
28.3%

2. Florida
11.0 million acres
29.5%

1. Alaska
170.0 million acres
45.3%

Source: U.S. Environmental Protection Agency

TOP 15 LARGEST LAKES OF THE WORLD

(By area, in square miles)

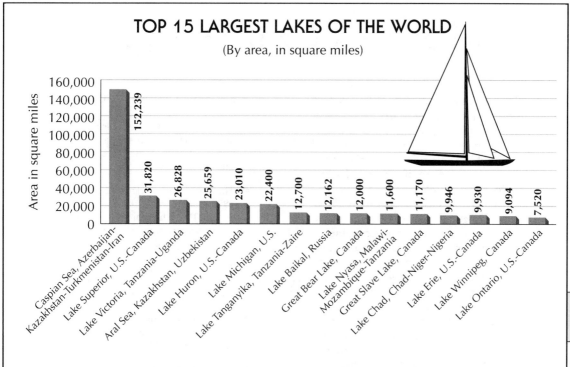

OCEANS AND SEAS: RELATIVE SIZES

(By area, in millions of square miles)

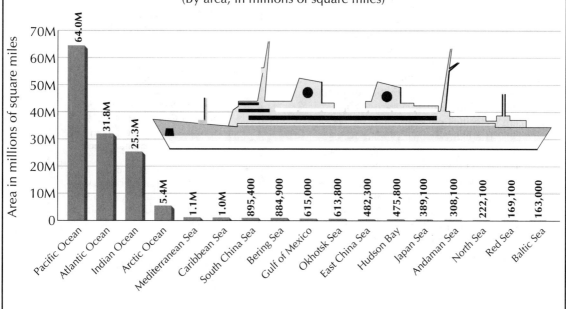

Source: U.S. Department of the Interior

E N D A N G E R E D   S P E C I E S

Thousands of the world's plant and animal species are currently in danger of becoming extinct—not from the effects of natural forces, but from the harmful actions of humans—their destruction of natural habitats, pollution, hunting, over-fishing, introduction of alien species into various environments, and so on.

In 1973, the U.S. Congress enacted the Endangered Species Act, which was intended to protect and restore endangered and threatened populations of plants and animals, whose survival was in jeopardy. The bald eagle, peregrine falcon, California sea otter, and black-footed ferret are among the species that the law has helped to save from extinction. Yet, despite strong public support for this tighter control, loggers and other businesses that are threatened by its provisions continue to try to weaken its protections.

As of March 1998, the U.S. Fish and Wildlife Service had listed 902 plant and animal species in the country as endangered and 232 other species as threatened. There were a total of 1,694 species endangered throughout the world in 1998. Many additional species, including numerous migratory birds, are in serious decline.

The U.S. National Wildlife Refuge System was established to help conserve the nation's wildlife resources. A significant portion of the current U.S. habitat of 94 species listed as endangered is located on 66 wildlife refuges. Many other listed species use refuge lands temporarily, for breeding or during migration.

FINGERTIP FACTS

☞ Scientists estimate that at least 500 plant and animal species have become extinct in the U.S. since the 1500s.

☞ The Wilderness Society reported in 1995 that if current trends continue, up to 20% of the world's plant and animal species could become extinct by the year 2000.

☞ Thirteen species have been removed from the endangered list—7 of them because they are now extinct.

☞ The states with the greatest number of endangered species are California, Hawaii, and Florida.

☞ Of all the known endangered species of plants, 97% can be found somewhere in the U.S.

☞ The U.S. National Wildlife Refuge System, which in 1994 included 499 refuges covering more than 91 million acres, comprises the only federal lands managed primarily for the benefit of wildlife.

☞ In 1996, the World Conservation Monitoring Centre listed 1,096 mammals—almost one–fourth of all mammals—as threatened species.

☞ The U.S. is home to all of the known endangered species of crustaceans and arachnids and almost all endangered species of snails and clams.

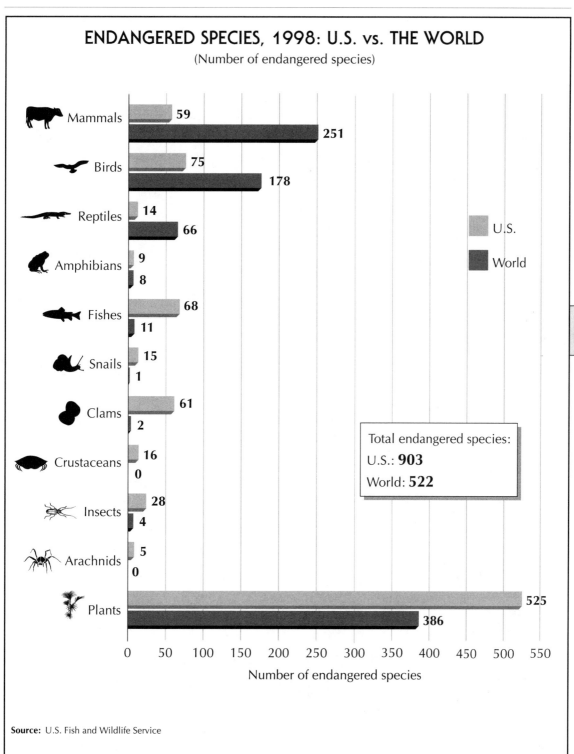

ENDANGERED SPECIES, 1998: U.S. vs. THE WORLD
(Number of endangered species)

Category	U.S.	World
Mammals	59	251
Birds	75	178
Reptiles	14	66
Amphibians	9	8
Fishes	68	11
Snails	15	1
Clams	61	2
Crustaceans	16	0
Insects	28	4
Arachnids	5	0
Plants	525	386

Total endangered species:
U.S.: **903**
World: **522**

Number of endangered species

Source: U.S. Fish and Wildlife Service

TOP 5 STATES IN ENDANGERED SPECIES, 1994

(Total number of all plant and animal species)

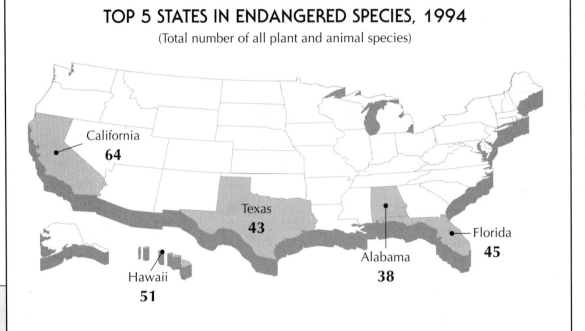

California
64

Texas
43

Hawaii
51

Florida
45

Alabama
38

TOP 4 STATES IN ENDANGERED SPECIES OF AMPHIBIANS

(Number of species)

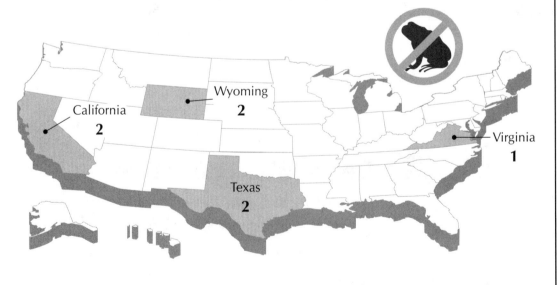

Wyoming
2

California
2

Virginia
1

Texas
2

Source: U.S. Fish and Wildlife Service

TOP 5 STATES IN ENDANGERED SPECIES OF REPTILES

(Number of species)

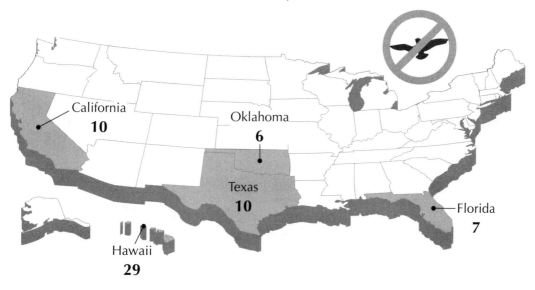

California
3

Georgia
3

Louisiana
3

Alabama
4

Florida
5

TOP 5 STATES IN ENDANGERED SPECIES OF BIRDS

(Number of species)

California
10

Oklahoma
6

Texas
10

Florida
7

Hawaii
29

Source: U.S. Fish and Wildlife Service

TOP 5 STATES IN ENDANGERED SPECIES OF MAMMALS

(Number of species)

California
8

Arizona
6

Virginia
5

North
Carolina
5

Florida
11

TOP 5 STATES IN ENDANGERED SPECIES OF PLANTS

(Number of species)

California
29

Texas
16

North
Carolina
13

Hawaii
19

Florida
31

Source: U.S. Fish and Wildlife Service

TOP 5 STATES IN ENDANGERED SPECIES OF INVERTEBRATES

(Number of species)

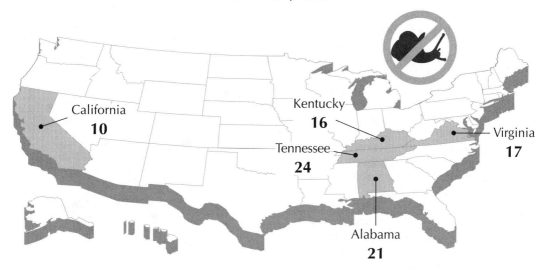

California **10**

Kentucky **16**

Tennessee **24**

Virginia **17**

Alabama **21**

TOP 5 STATES IN ENDANGERED SPECIES OF FISHES

(Number of species)

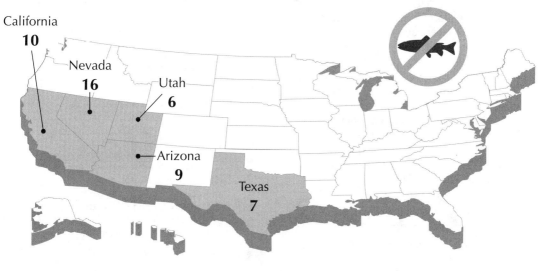

California **10**

Nevada **16**

Utah **6**

Arizona **9**

Texas **7**

Source: U.S. Fish and Wildlife Service

P O L L U T I O N

Pollution is contamination caused by the release of wastes into the environment. Today, there are multitudes of pollutants; they include everything that can harm natural surroundings; sulfur gases from smokestacks, poisonous pesticides that run off land into nearby waters, used bandages from hospitals, radioactive materials from nuclear power plants, construction debris from building sites, manure from farms, human food-and-household wastes, and so on.

Pollution occurs indoors as well as outdoors. Sick-building syndrome—characterized by occupants having burning eyes, skin irritations, and various respiratory symptoms—has been on the increase in the U.S. Inefficient ventilation systems, chemicals from office equipment and carpeting, and tobacco smoke contribute to this problem.

The effects of pollution are many. Pollution may cause or worsen a variety of illnesses among humans and animals, including cancers and respiratory ailments. It can also poison wildlife, destroy the habitats of wild creatures, and raise atmospheric temperatures (the "greenhouse effect") and destroy high altitude ozone (causing ozone "holes").

The federal government has enacted a variety of legislation directed at preventing pollution in the U.S. These measures include the Clean Water Act and the Clean Air Act.

FINGERTIP FACTS

☛ The U.S. is home to only 5% of the world's population, but it releases 20% of the world's greenhouse gases—more than any other nation.

☛ The U.S. spent $15.8 billion in 1972 for pollution abatement; the figure had grown to billion.

☛ The U.S. generates more garbage than any other nation—even China, which has 4 times as many people.

☛ Americans generated an average of 4.3 pounds of wastes per person per day in 1996—up from 2.7 pounds in 1960 and 3.3 pounds in 1970.

☛ The U.S. generated nearly 208 million tons of municipal solid wastes in 1996—up from about 88 million tons in 1960, 151 million tons in 1980, and 196 million tons in 1990.

☛ Paper and paperboard products are the heaviest component of U.S. municipal solid wastes.

☛ Americans throw away more than 242 million automotive tires each year; 77.7% are dumped illegally or in a landfill.

☛ Paper is the most recycled material in the U.S. More than 40% of all paper products generated were recycled in 1996. Metals are the second-most-recycled material.

☛ The U.S. recycled 53.8 million tons of municipal solid wastes in 1996 and composted an additional million tons.

☛ In the U.S., an estimated 200 million gallons of used motor oil are improperly disposed of each year. One gallon of used oil has the potential to contaminate up to a million gallons of drinking water.

☛ About 68% of all aluminum beverage cans and 46% of all steel cans used in the U.S. are recycled.

U.S. MUNICIPAL SOLID WASTE, 1960 vs. 1996
(In millions of tons)

Total waste generated

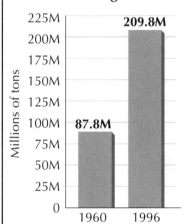

Waste generated, by type

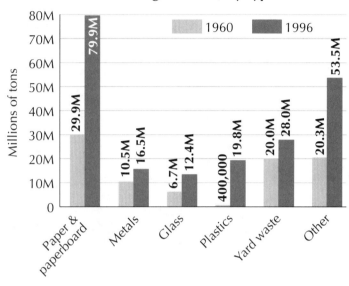

Total materials recovered

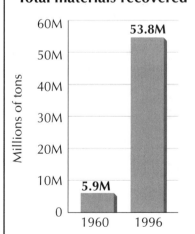

Materials recovered, by type

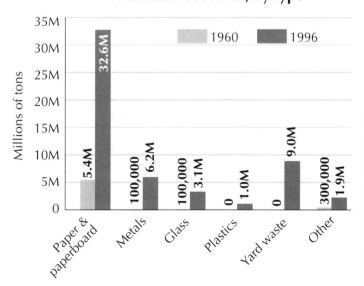

Source: U.S. Environmental Protection Agency

WHERE OLD TIRES GO

What happens to the 242 million scrap tires that are disposed of each year:

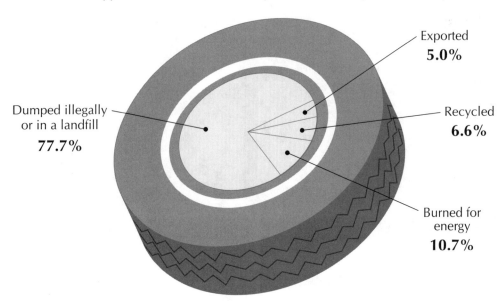

Exported
5.0%

Recycled
6.6%

Dumped illegally
or in a landfill
77.7%

Burned for
energy
10.7%

Source: National Solid Wastes Management Associates

RECYCLING OF GARBAGE IN THE U.S.

(Percentage that is recycled, by type)

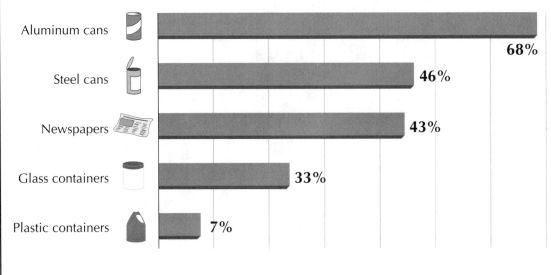

Aluminum cans — **68%**

Steel cans — **46%**

Newspapers — **43%**

Glass containers — **33%**

Plastic containers — **7%**

Source: Associated Press

WHAT CREATES SOLID WASTES?

(Percentage of solid waste)

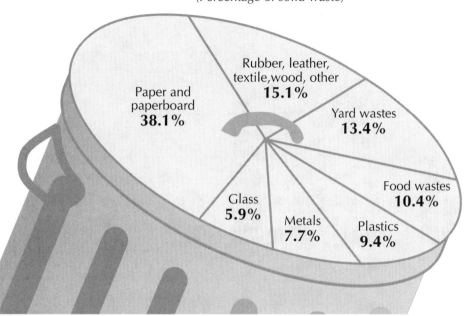

Paper and paperboard **38.1%**

Rubber, leather, textile, wood, other **15.1%**

Yard wastes **13.4%**

Food wastes **10.4%**

Glass **5.9%**

Metals **7.7%**

Plastics **9.4%**

Source: U.S. Environmental Protection Agency

MAJOR POLLUTANTS SHOW A DROP

From 1992 to 1993, overall levels of 5 major pollutants dropped in U.S. cities. Here, the percentage of change of 6 indicators during that period:

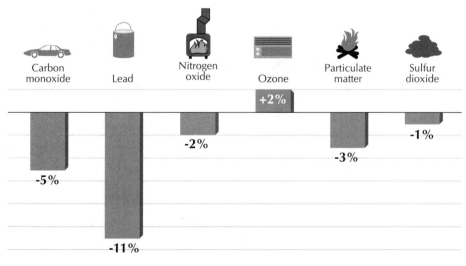

Carbon monoxide **-5%**

Lead **-11%**

Nitrogen oxide **-2%**

Ozone **+2%**

Particulate matter **-3%**

Sulfur dioxide **-1%**

Source: U.S. Environmental Protection Agency

EMISSIONS OF AIR POLLUTANTS, 1970–1996

(Emission by pollutant and source, in millions of metric tons)

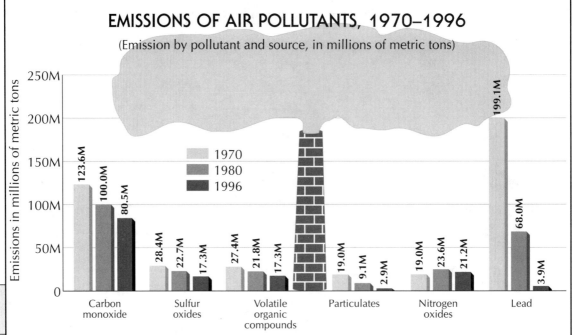

Source: U.S. Environmental Protection Agency

CFC PRODUCTION, 1971–1992

Chlorofluorocarbons (CFCs), which are used in air conditioners, refrigerators, and other products, are known to damage Earth's protective ozone layer. In the U.S., CFC production is mandated to end in 1996. Here, decline in CFC production from 1971 to 1992:

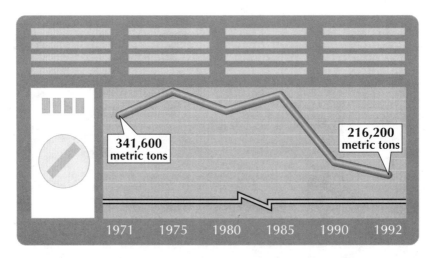

341,600 metric tons

216,200 metric tons

1971   1975   1980   1985   1990   1992

Source: U.S. Environmental Protection Agency

TOP 10 SMOGGIEST AREAS IN U.S.
(With rankings)

8.
Sacramento, CA

2.
Ventura County, CA

1.
Los Angeles, CA

7.
San Diego, CA

4.
Phoenix, AZ

3.
Houston, TX

10.
Baton Rouge, LA

9.
Providence, RI

6.
New York, NY

5.
Philadelphia, PA

Source: U.S. Environmental Protection Agency

WORLDWIDE CARBON DIOXIDE EMISSIONS, 1996
(By percentage of total gas released by country)

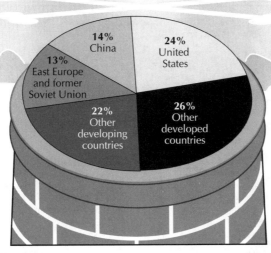

14%
China

13%
East Europe
and former
Soviet Union

22%
Other
developing
countries

24%
United
States

26%
Other
developed
countries

Source: Energy Information Administration

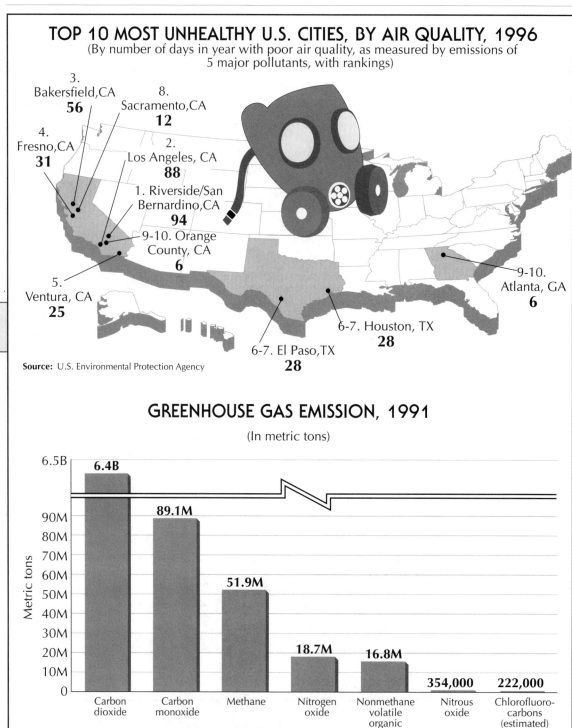

TOP 10 MOST UNHEALTHY U.S. CITIES, BY AIR QUALITY, 1996
(By number of days in year with poor air quality, as measured by emissions of 5 major pollutants, with rankings)

3.
Bakersfield,CA
56

8.
Sacramento,CA
12

4.
Fresno,CA
31

2.
Los Angeles, CA
88

1. Riverside/San
Bernardino,CA
94

9-10. Orange
County, CA
6

5.
Ventura, CA
25

9-10.
Atlanta, GA
6

6-7. Houston, TX
28

6-7. El Paso,TX
28

Source: U.S. Environmental Protection Agency

GREENHOUSE GAS EMISSION, 1991

(In metric tons)

Gas	Metric tons
Carbon dioxide	6.4B
Carbon monoxide	89.1M
Methane	51.9M
Nitrogen oxide	18.7M
Nonmethane volatile organic compounds	16.8M
Nitrous oxide	354,000
Chlorofluorocarbons (estimated)	222,000

Source: U.S. Energy Information Administration

TOP 10 U.S. CITIES WITH LEAD PROBLEMS IN WATER SUPPLY

In 1992, the EPA found that 130 of the 660 major public water systems in the U.S. exceed safe levels of lead in drinking water. Safe levels are 15 parts per billion (ppb). Here, with rankings, the cities with the highest lead content:

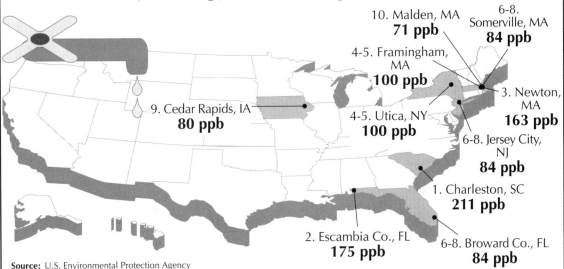

10. Malden, MA
71 ppb

6-8. Somerville, MA
84 ppb

4-5. Framingham, MA
100 ppb

3. Newton, MA
163 ppb

9. Cedar Rapids, IA
80 ppb

4-5. Utica, NY
100 ppb

6-8. Jersey City, NJ
84 ppb

1. Charleston, SC
211 ppb

2. Escambia Co., FL
175 ppb

6-8. Broward Co., FL
84 ppb

Source: U.S. Environmental Protection Agency

TOXIC DISCHARGE IN U.S. WATERS, 1990-1994

(By amount of discharge, in pounds)

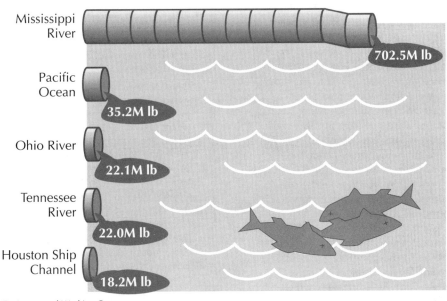

Mississippi River — 702.5M lb

Pacific Ocean — 35.2M lb

Ohio River — 22.1M lb

Tennessee River — 22.0M lb

Houston Ship Channel — 18.2M lb

Source: Environmental Working Group

H A Z A R D O U S   W A S T E

Substances known as hazardous wastes pose serious threats to all life. To avoid such threats, it is necessary to eliminate or reduce the production of hazardous wastes or to properly store, transport, and dispose of them.

The U.S. Emergency Planning and Community Right-to-Know Act of 1986 requires certain public and private facilities to prepare annual reports on their releases of toxic chemicals into the environment. The reports are to be made available to local communities. In 1993, President Bill Clinton signed an Executive Order requiring federal agencies to comply with this law. There are now 654 chemicals in the Toxic Release Inventory, a database maintained by the Environmental Protection Agency (EPA) under the act.

Since the first reports were made under the 1986 law, the amount of toxic chemicals released into the nation's environment by manufacturing facilities (not including power plants and mining facilities) has decreased. The 2.4 billion pounds released in 1996 appear to represent an encouraging downward trend with a decline of some 25% since 1992.

Since many producers of hazardous wastes were not required to prepare reports, however, and since many toxic substances were not part of the inventory, these figures are deceptive. A 1994 report from the General Accounting Office noted that an estimated 275 million tons (550 billion pounds) of hazardous waste are treated, stored, and disposed of annually in the U.S. — and the volume is growing.

Hazardous waste cleanup is both a costly and time-consuming process. The major federal cleanup effort is called the Superfund program, which by 1994 had constructed toxic waste cleanup systems in 278 communities. As of mid-1994, a total of 1,286 hazardous waste sites were targeted for cleanup. By early 1995, the federal government had spent more than $13 billion on the Superfund program. Through Superfund, polluters had, by late 1994, committed nearly $10 billion to clean up the most seriously contaminated sites.

FINGERTIP FACTS

- The Environmental Protection Agency estimates that it costs an average of $25 million to $30 million to clean up a single Superfund hazardous waste site.

- In 1996, the most hazardous waste sites on the National Priorities List were located in New Jersey (110), Pennsylvania (100), and California (96).

- In 1994, according to the EPA, 1 out of 4 Americans lived within 4 miles of a toxic dumpsite.

- Over the last ten years, the United States has seen a dramatic increase in the environmental service industry. The revenue of hazardous waste management was $6 billion in 1996.

- Nuclear power plants lack places for waste disposal. Some 86,000 tons of high-level radioactive wastes and spent fuel from nuclear power plants are in temporary storage while the government determines what to do with them. The wastes will be dangerous for more than 10,000 years.

- In 1994, the U.S. and 63 other nations signed the Basel Convention, banning the export of hazardous wastes from industrialized to developing countries.

TOP 10 INDUSTRIES IN TOXIC WASTE CREATION

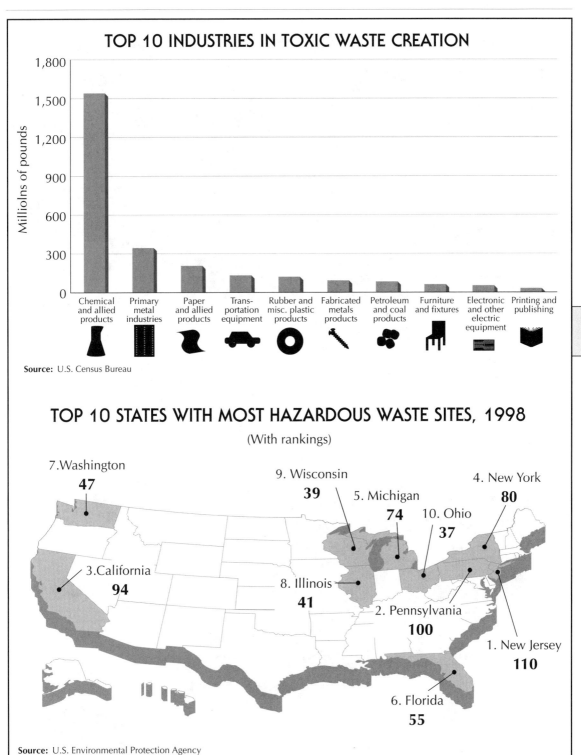

Millioins of pounds

1,800

1,500

1,200

900

600

300

0

Chemical and allied products | Primary metal industries | Paper and allied products | Trans-portation equipment | Rubber and misc. plastic products | Fabricated metals products | Petroleum and coal products | Furniture and fixtures | Electronic and other electric equipment | Printing and publishing

Source: U.S. Census Bureau

TOP 10 STATES WITH MOST HAZARDOUS WASTE SITES, 1998

(With rankings)

7. Washington
47

9. Wisconsin
39

5. Michigan
74

10. Ohio
37

4. New York
80

3. California
94

8. Illinois
41

2. Pennsylvania
100

1. New Jersey
110

6. Florida
55

Source: U.S. Environmental Protection Agency

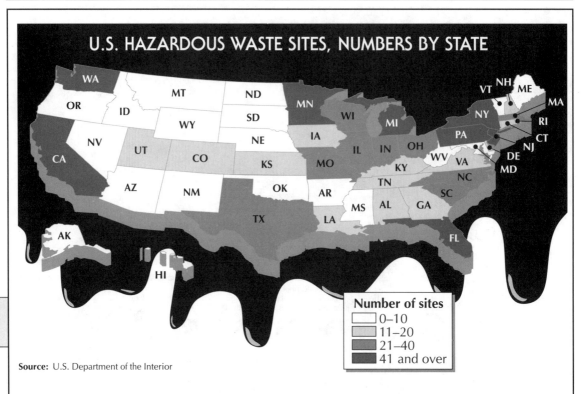

U.S. HAZARDOUS WASTE SITES, NUMBERS BY STATE

Number of sites
- 0–10
- 11–20
- 21–40
- 41 and over

Source: U.S. Department of the Interior

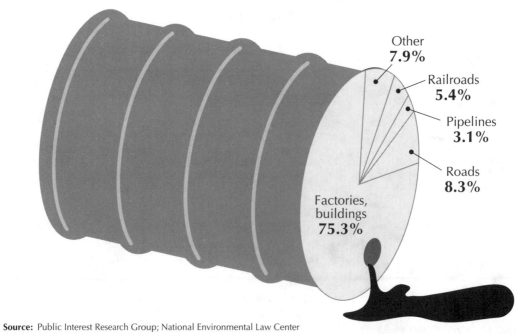

COMMON OIL-SPILL LOCATIONS

Other
7.9%

Railroads
5.4%

Pipelines
3.1%

Roads
8.3%

Factories, buildings
75.3%

Source: Public Interest Research Group; National Environmental Law Center

TOP 10 STATES FOR RELEASING TOXIC CHEMICALS, 1996

(By total pounds released, on- and off-site)

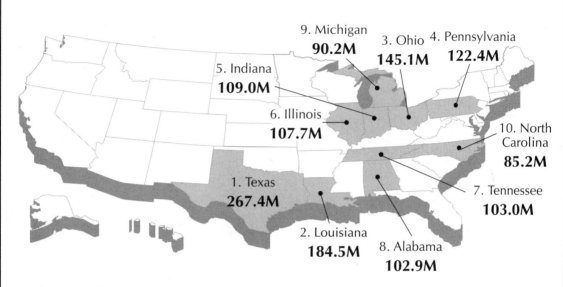

9. Michigan
90.2M

3. Ohio
145.1M

4. Pennsylvania
122.4M

5. Indiana
109.0M

6. Illinois
107.7M

10. North
Carolina
85.2M

1. Texas
267.4M

7. Tennessee
103.0M

2. Louisiana
184.5M

8. Alabama
102.9M

Source: Environmental Protection Agency

TOP 10 STATES FOR TOXIC CHEMICAL SPILLS, 1988–1992

(By number of accidents, with rankings)

9. Michigan
869

5. Ohio
1,269

4. Pennsylvania
1,395

1. California
4,820

7. Illinois
1,085

10. New
Jersey
857

6. Kentucky
1,166

2. Texas
4,532

8. Florida
905

3. Louisiana
2,505

Source: Public Interest Research Group, National Environmental Law Center

7

AGRICULTURE AND NATURAL RESOURCES

FARMS AND FARMING

Thanks to the efficiency of U.S. farms, most Americans enjoy an abundance of inexpensive food. But as the nation's population has soared, the land devoted to growing food has declined. Millions of acres of productive cropland have been lost due to such factors as erosion and housing developments. Currently, there are about 1.8 acres of cropland to grow food for each American. But if the current trends in population growth and farmland loss continue, there will be only 0.6 acre per American in the year 2050. (That is the rate that currently exists worldwide.)

The number of farms has steadily declined in recent decades—from about 6.0 million covering more than 1 billion acres in 1975, to 2.0 million farms with a total acreage of 963 million acres in 1997. Today's farms are significantly larger than farms of the past. In 1940, the average farm had 174 acres. By 1997, the average size was 471 acres.

A broad range of programs and services is designed to support the nation's agricultural sector. The U.S. Department of Agriculture, one of the largest departments of the federal government, provides aid in the way of farm price supports, crop insurance, loans to farmers, and funds for soil conservation and wetlands protection. Some of these programs have come under attack, partly from various special interest groups, partly because of their cost to consumers, and partly because they tend to enrich wealthy farmers more than help small farmers.

FINGERTIP FACTS

☛ Americans spend about 15% of their incomes on food. In most developing countries, food costs eat up 50% to 60% of people's incomes.

☛ The number of U.S. farms fell from 6.4 million in 1940 to 2.0 million in 1997.

☛ In 1997, the three states with the most acreage devoted to farming were Texas (130 million acres), Montana (60 million acres), and Kansas (48 million acres).

☛ Nebraska has the highest percentage of land used as farmland (96.1%); Alaska has the least (0.3%).

☛ Between 1980 and 1997, North Carolina lost the largest percentage of farms (39%); Texas had the largest increase (4%).

☛ Total farm income in 1998 was $216.4 billion, up from $143.2 billion in 1980. Crops accounted for $106.7 billion, livestock and products for $91.3 billion.

☛ The state with the highest 1997 farm income was California ($24.8 billion), followed by Texas ($13.4 billion), Iowa ($12.8 billion), and Nebraska ($10.1 billion).

☛ Government payments to farmers totaled $7.5 billion in 1997. Iowa farmers received the biggest chunk ($712 million), followed by Texas ($648 million), Illinois ($552 million), Nebraska ($452 million), and Minnesota ($417 million).

PROFILE OF U.S. FARMS, 1940–1997

Number of farms (in millions)

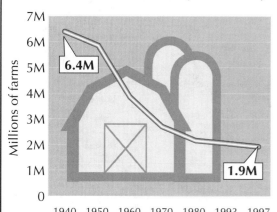

Average size of farms (in acres)

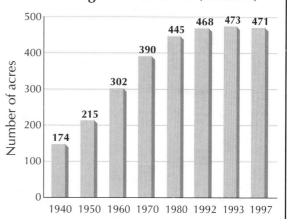

Source: U.S. Department of Agriculture

NUMBER OF U.S. FARMS, 1850–1997

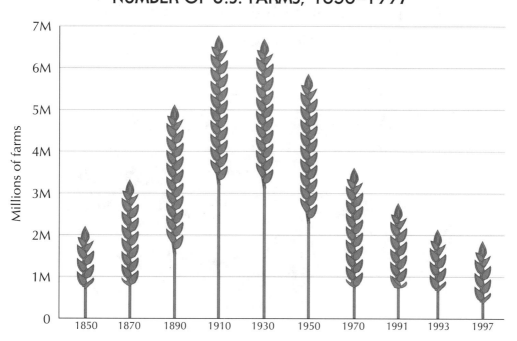

Source: U.S. Census Bureau

STATES WITH MOST AND LEAST AMOUNT OF LAND USED AS FARMLAND

(As percentage of total land)

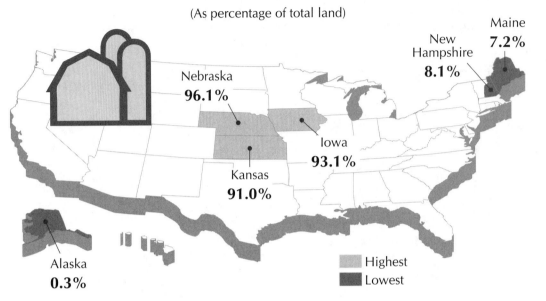

Maine
7.2%

New
Hampshire
8.1%

Nebraska
96.1%

Iowa
93.1%

Kansas
91.0%

Alaska
0.3%

Highest
Lowest

Source: U.S. Department of Agriculture

TOP 10 STATES WITH HIGHEST FARM ACREAGE

(Millions of acres, with rankings)

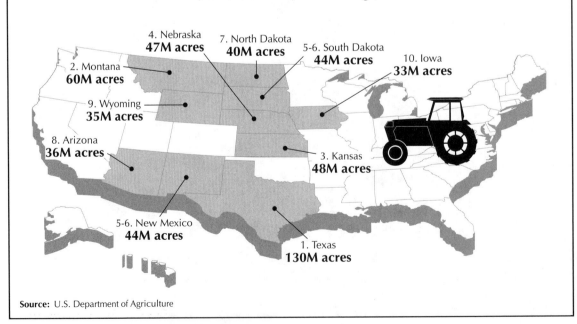

4. Nebraska
47M acres

7. North Dakota
40M acres

5-6. South Dakota
44M acres

10. Iowa
33M acres

2. Montana
60M acres

9. Wyoming
35M acres

8. Arizona
36M acres

3. Kansas
48M acres

5-6. New Mexico
44M acres

1. Texas
130M acres

Source: U.S. Department of Agriculture

U.S. FARMLAND IN DECLINE, 1959–1997

(In billions of acres)

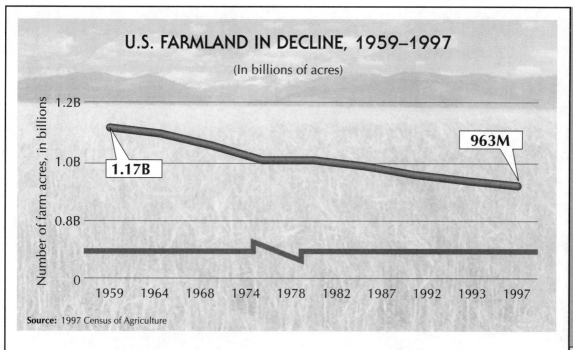

Number of farm acres, in billions

1.2B

1.0B

0.8B

0

1.17B

963M

1959   1964   1968   1974   1978   1982   1987   1992   1993   1997

Source: 1997 Census of Agriculture

TOP 10 STATES WITH LEAST FARM ACREAGE

(Millions of acres, with rankings)

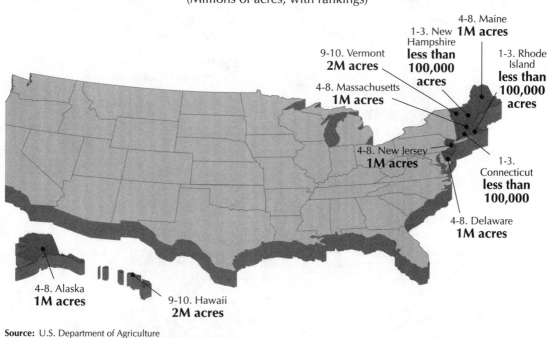

4-8. Maine
1M acres

1-3. New **1M acres**
Hampshire
**less than
100,000
acres**

1-3. Rhode
Island
**less than
100,000
acres**

9-10. Vermont
2M acres

4-8. Massachusetts
1M acres

1-3.
Connecticut
**less than
100,000**

4-8. New Jersey
1M acres

4-8. Delaware
1M acres

4-8. Alaska
1M acres

9-10. Hawaii
2M acres

Source: U.S. Department of Agriculture

U.S. HAS MOST EFFICIENT FARMS

With just 0.3% of the world's farm labor force, the U.S. produces the majority of the world's agricultural output:

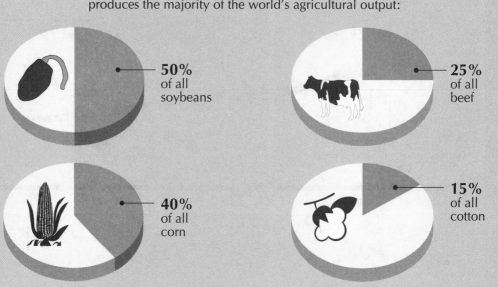

50% of all soybeans

25% of all beef

40% of all corn

15% of all cotton

Source: U.S. Department of Agriculture

FARM SUBSIDIES GROW, 1980–1993

Government aid to compensate farmers for declining crop values has increased significantly since 1980 even though farm commodity prices have remained fairly stable:

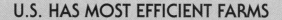

Direct government payments to farmers

Market price of corn per bushel

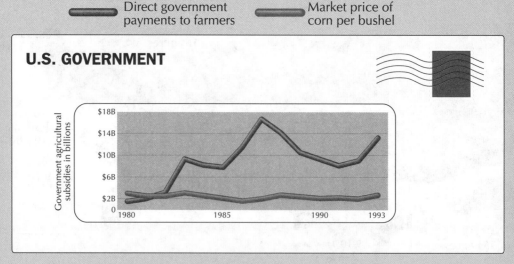

U.S. GOVERNMENT

Government agricultural subsidies in billions

$18B
$14B
$10B
$6B
$2B
0

1980   1985   1990   1993

Source: U.S. Department of Agriculture

BIGGEST FARMS, BIGGEST AID

The biggest U.S. farms receive much more government aid than do smaller and less-profitable farms:

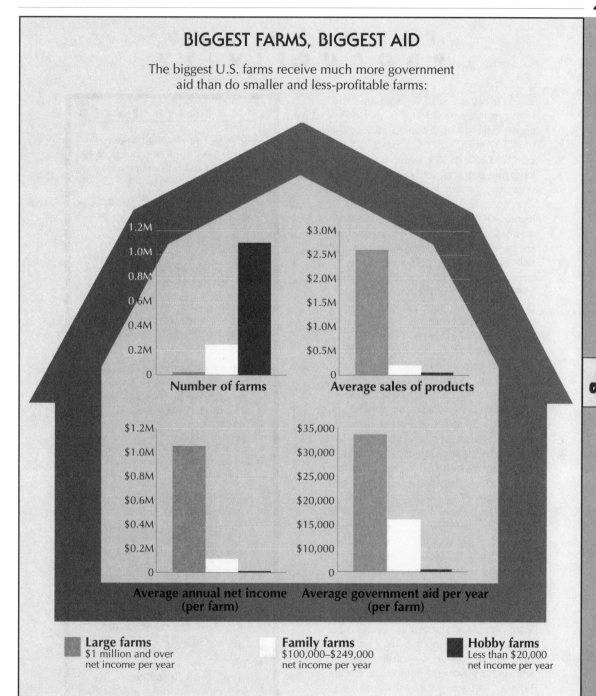

Number of farms

Average sales of products

Average annual net income (per farm)

Average government aid per year (per farm)

Large farms
$1 million and over
net income per year

Family farms
$100,000–$249,000
net income per year

Hobby farms
Less than $20,000
net income per year

Source: U.S Department of Agriculture

F A R M E R S   A N D   P R O D U C T I V I T Y

The U.S. has the world's most efficient farms. It has only 0.3% of the world's farm workers, but produces about 50% of all soybeans, 40% of all corn, 25% of all beef, and 15% of all cotton. Large-scale irrigation projects, artificial fertilizers and pesticides, genetic technology, and mechanization have been major factors in increasing the amount of food that can be produced per acre. The largest farms are highly specialized and account for the bulk of farm production; small family farms have declined. For example, in 1940, some 12% of the nation's farms produced 50% of farms sales; in 1995, only 3% of the farms produced 50% of sales.

Today's farmers are much better educated than farmers of the past. They have access to specially trained agricultural agents and up-to-the-minute weather forecasts. Many also use computers to track crop yields and other data. But the average age of farmers has increased, and a growing number of farm households rely on non-farming activities for a large part of their income. Interestingly, the number of female farmers—though small— has grown from 129,189 in 1987 to 165,102 in 1997—but the total number of farmworkers has steadily declined. This is primarily because the use of grain harvesters and other sophisticated machines has reduced the need for labor.

Farms are the main employers of migrant laborers—people who move from one place to another to take advantage of seasonal employment opportunities. These laborers are often denied safe and sanitary working conditions, decent housing, and adequate health care. Unions and government agencies, however, have had some success in improving these conditions.

FINGERTIP FACTS

☛ The U.S. had 961,560 farmers in 1997. They had a median age of 48 years and had been farmers for an average of 26.1 years.

☛ In 1880, nearly 44% of U.S. residents lived on farms. In 1997, about 2% did.

☛ In 1982, a total of 84.1% of farmers were age 35 or older; by 1997, the percentage had risen to 90.7%.

☛ Black farmers are older than white farmers. The percentage age 35 or older rose from 90.2% in 1982 to 92.9% in 1997.

☛ In 1997, about 5% of farms were owned by corporations, 9% were owned by partnerships, and 86% were owned by individuals or families.

☛ In 1993, about 801,000 people were employed as farmworkers— down from 1.1 million in 1983.

☛ In 1993, some 28.5% of the nation's farmworkers were Latinos, up from 15.9% in 1983. The percentage of black farmworkers declined to 7.0% in 1993, from 11.6% in 1983.

☛ In 1995 in the U.S., one farmworker supplied agricultural products for an average of 106 people.

☛ In 1997, women ran about 10% of farms, up from 8% in 1992.

☛ The U.S. Department of Agriculture had about 98,500 employees working in more than 14,000 offices in 1997. Its annual budget was about $52 billion.

FARM EMPLOYMENT AND WORKER PRODUCTIVITY, 1950–1995

By 1995, U.S. farms had become so productive that each worker supplied agricultural products for an average of 106 people. Farm employment, however, is down more than two-thirds from 1950:

People supplied per farmworker

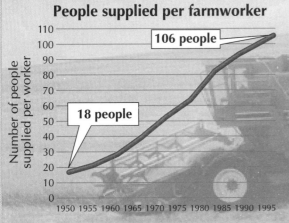

106 people

18 people

Number of people supplied per worker

110 100 90 80 70 60 50 40 30 20 10 0

1950 1955 1960 1965 1970 1975 1980 1985 1990 1995

Farm jobs

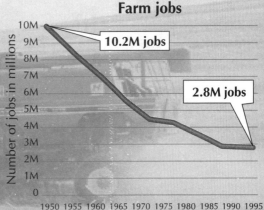

10.2M jobs

2.8M jobs

Number of jobs in millions

10M 9M 8M 7M 6M 5M 4M 3M 2M 1M 0

1950 1955 1960 1965 1970 1975 1980 1985 1990 1995

Source: U.S. Dept. of Agriculture

AMERICANS WORKING ON FARMS, 1950–1995

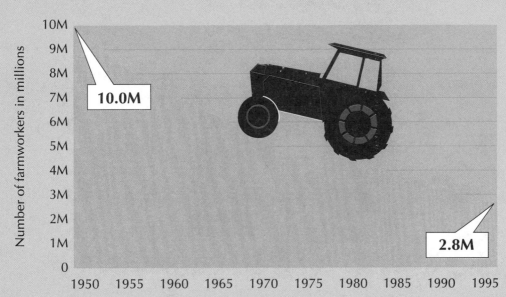

10.0M

2.8M

Number of farmworkers in millions

10M 9M 8M 7M 6M 5M 4M 3M 2M 1M 0

1950   1955   1960   1965   1970   1975   1980   1985   1990   1995

Source: U.S. Census Bureau

DECLINING FARM POPULATION, 1880–1997

The percentage of farmers in the U.S. population
has dropped dramatically since 1880:

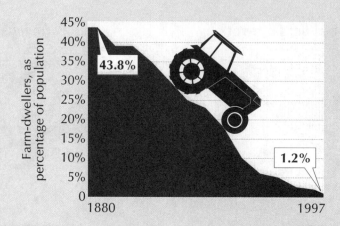

Farm-dwellers, as percentage of population

45%
40%
35%
30%
25%
20%
15%
10%
5%
0

43.8%

1.2%

1880   1997

Source: Bureau of Labor Statistics

FEMALE FARMERS, 1987 vs. 1997

The number of farmers overall in the U.S. is decreasing,
but the number of women farmers has climbed:

165,102

129,189

1987   1997

Source: U.S. Census Bureau

THE GRAYING OF U.S. FARMERS, 1982–1997

Taken as a whole, American farmers have become an older group;
Their average age is now 54.9 years. Some details about the nation's farmers:

All farmers, by age

Age groupings of all U.S. farmers

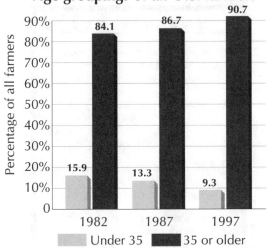

Average age of all U.S. farmers

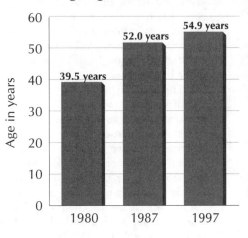

Minority-group farmers

Age of minority-group farmers

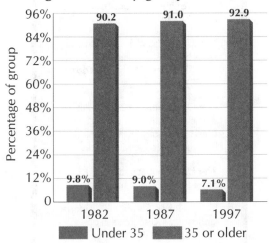

Average age of all minority-group farmers

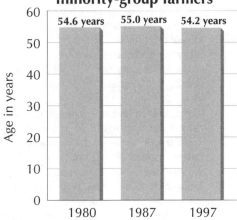

Source: U.S. Dept. of Agriculture

CROP PRODUCTION

Grains such as corn, wheat, rice, and pulses—the seed parts of legumes such as beans, soybeans, and peanuts—are the major crops in the U.S. Over the years, production of these and other crops has risen steadily, as have yields per acre. In individual years, however, dramatic production declines have resulted from drought, flooding, and other bad weather.

There are farms in every state. California is the nation's top agricultural producer, thanks to its climate and widespread irrigation. More than 200 different crops are grown in the state. It is a major source of "truck crops" (tomatoes, lettuce, celery, etc.). With Florida, California produces the bulk of the nation's citrus. Together with Texas, it accounts for more than half of all U.S. cotton production.

Midwestern states produce most of the nation's corn and soybeans; North Dakota leads in barley production; and North Carolina and Kentucky lead in tobacco production.

Farmers often switch to new crop varieties that promise higher yields and increased income. In recent years, many such varieties have been created in the laboratory using genetic-engineering techniques. "Improved crops" include potatoes that are resistant to blight disease and tomatoes that yield thicker ketchup with less processing.

Farmers also experiment with new, untried crops. For example, many farmers have added oil-seed rape to their crop-rotation schemes, hoping to meet market demands for low-saturated canola fat and to combat disease cycles in the other crops they grow. Quinoa (an Andean grain), cherimoya (an Andean fruit), and kiwi (a fruit native to China) are other crops that have enjoyed increased production in the U.S. in recent years.

FINGERTIP FACTS

- Corn is the nation's biggest cash crop, with $18.8 billion worth of production in 1997.

- Soybeans, introduced into the U.S. from China in 1765, are the nation's second most valuable crop, at $15.6 billion worth of production in 1997.

- Average yield per acre for cotton rose from 614 pounds in 1989 to 629 pounds in 1997.

- Iowa and Illinois are the leading corn-growing states, producing 1.656 billion and 1.425 billion bushels respectively in 1997.

- Tobacco is the nation's sixth-largest cash crop. It is grown in 51 of the 435 congressional districts. Two-thirds of annual production comes from North Carolina and Kentucky.

- Tobacco is the most lucrative U.S. crop, bringing growers $3,862 an acre. Peanuts ($691) and cotton ($380) are next.

- The U.S. produced 2,526 million bushels of wheat in 1997. Kansas, North Dakota, and Montana are the leading wheat-growing states.

- The U.S. produces nearly 11 billion pounds of apples each year.

- In the United States, 46% of farmland was used to raise crops in 1997. Of this land, 72% was harvested, 15% was pastured, 5% was idle, and 8% was made up of failed crops.

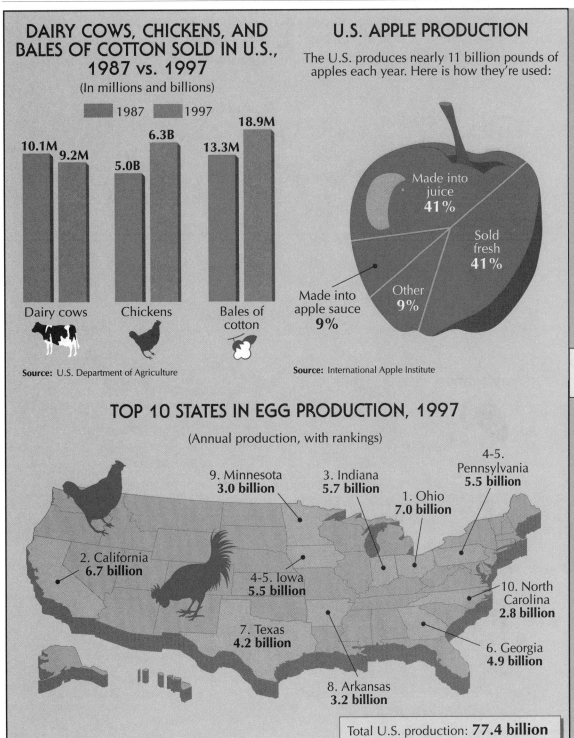

DAIRY COWS, CHICKENS, AND BALES OF COTTON SOLD IN U.S., 1987 vs. 1997

(In millions and billions)

■ 1987 ■ 1997

10.1M 9.2M — Dairy cows

5.0B 6.3B — Chickens

13.3M 18.9M — Bales of cotton

Source: U.S. Department of Agriculture

U.S. APPLE PRODUCTION

The U.S. produces nearly 11 billion pounds of apples each year. Here is how they're used:

Made into juice **41%**

Sold fresh **41%**

Made into apple sauce **9%**

Other **9%**

Source: International Apple Institute

TOP 10 STATES IN EGG PRODUCTION, 1997

(Annual production, with rankings)

9. Minnesota **3.0 billion**

3. Indiana **5.7 billion**

4-5. Pennsylvania **5.5 billion**

1. Ohio **7.0 billion**

2. California **6.7 billion**

4-5. Iowa **5.5 billion**

10. North Carolina **2.8 billion**

7. Texas **4.2 billion**

6. Georgia **4.9 billion**

8. Arkansas **3.2 billion**

Source: U.S. Department of Agriculture

Total U.S. production: **77.4 billion**

CORN, SOYBEAN, AND COTTON HARVESTS

U.S. soybean, corn, and cotton crops have reached record levels:

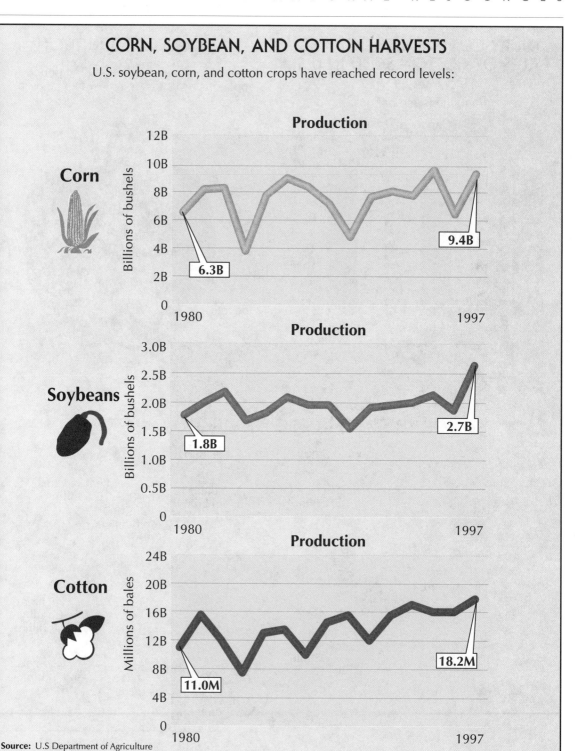

Corn

Production

Billions of bushels

6.3B

9.4B

1980   1997

Soybeans

Production

Billions of bushels

1.8B

2.7B

1980   1997

Cotton

Production

Millions of bales

11.0M

18.2M

1980   1997

Source: U.S Department of Agriculture

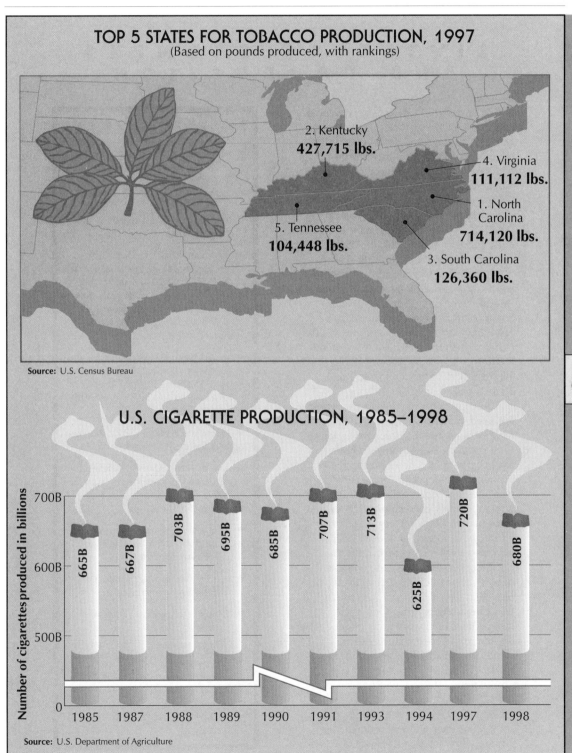

TOP 5 STATES FOR TOBACCO PRODUCTION, 1997
(Based on pounds produced, with rankings)

2. Kentucky
427,715 lbs.

4. Virginia
111,112 lbs.

1. North
Carolina
714,120 lbs.

5. Tennessee
104,448 lbs.

3. South Carolina
126,360 lbs.

Source: U.S. Census Bureau

U.S. CIGARETTE PRODUCTION, 1985–1998

Number of cigarettes produced in billions

700B

600B

500B

0

| 1985 | 1987 | 1988 | 1989 | 1990 | 1991 | 1993 | 1994 | 1997 | 1998 |

665B | 667B | 703B | 695B | 685B | 707B | 713B | 625B | 720B | 680B

Source: U.S. Department of Agriculture

L I V E S T O C K   F A R M I N G
A N D   P R O D U C T I O N

Approximately 50% of U.S. farm income is derived from livestock—cattle, hogs, chickens, turkeys, and other domesticated animals. Cattle and calves bred for beef are the primary source of farm income, earning $20.3 billion in 1997 (20.6% of total farm income). Dairy products are second, at $18.9 billion (19.2%). The leading 1997 plant crop, corn, brought in $18.8 billion (9.6%).

Most livestock in the U.S. is now raised by large, specialized operations, which has resulted in greater productivity and lower prices for consumers. Some farms, for example, specifically raise and market broiler chickens (about 5.8 billion annually). One study found that the retail price of broilers fell from $1.62 a pound in 1960 to $0.37 a pound in 1997.

Automation and other technologies are used in livestock farming to keep down labor costs and improve agricultural productivity. Automated feeders are programmed to give livestock a proper mix of food and water. Milking machines milk cows and keep track of how much milk each cow produces. Automatic sorters sort eggs according to weight and color and electrically powered cleaners sweep out barns.

Selective breeding and genetic engineering create new breeds of livestock as well as new drugs to boost production of existing breeds. One of the most controversial products of genetic engineering is recombinant bovine somatotropin (rBST), a growth hormone that significantly boosts milk production in dairy cows. Approved by the U.S. Food and Drug Administration (FDA) in 1993, it has been opposed by some consumer and environmental groups, who question its safety.

FINGERTIP FACTS

☞ In 1997, some 50.2% of U.S. farm income came from livestock, including cattle and calves (20.6%), dairy products (11.3%), hogs (7.0%), poultry (11.3%), sheep and lambs (0.3%), and other commodities.

☞ The number of U.S. farms with milk cows declined from 334,000 in 1980 to 116,874 in 1997. But over the same periods, total milk production increased, from 128 billion pounds to 156 billion pounds.

☞ In 1997, farmers received $13.36 for every 100 pounds of milk they sold, $52.90 for every 100 pounds of hogs, and $78.90 for every 100 pounds of veal.

☞ U.S. farmers spent $32.8 billion on feed for their livestock in 1997.

☞ There were 99.5 million head of cattle on U.S. farms at the start of 1997. Texas led the states, with 14.3 million head.

☞ At the start of 1998, there were more than 60.9 million hogs and pigs on America's farms.

☞ In 1997, U.S. farmers produced 25.5 billion pounds of beef.

☞ Ohio is the leading egg-producing state, with 6.97 billion eggs in 1997.

☞ Poultry production has been steadily rising in the U.S. In 1994, farmers produced 29.1 billion pounds; In 1997, they produced 33.0 billion pounds—a 12% increase.

U.S. HOG FARMS INCREASE IN SIZE, 1983–1993

Small hog farms are declining in number in the U.S.,
but the number of larger operations is growing dramatically:

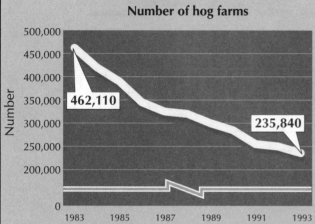

Number of hog farms

462,110

235,840

Number

500,000
450,000
400,000
350,000
300,000
250,000
200,000
0

1983   1985   1987   1989   1991   1993

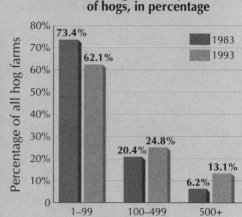

**Size of hog farms, by number
of hogs, in percentage**

Percentage of all hog farms

80%
70%
60%
50%
40%
30%
20%
10%
0

73.4%
62.1%

20.4%   24.8%

6.2%   13.1%

1983
1993

1–99   100–499   500+

THE TOP 5 STATES IN HOG PRODUCTION

(Number of hogs in inventory, in millions, with rankings)

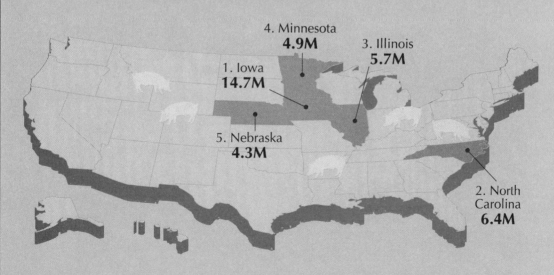

4. Minnesota
4.9M

3. Illinois
5.7M

1. Iowa
14.7M

5. Nebraska
4.3M

2. North
Carolina
6.4M

Source: U.S. Department of Agriculture

U.S. PORK PRODUCTION, 1980–1997

(In billions of pounds)

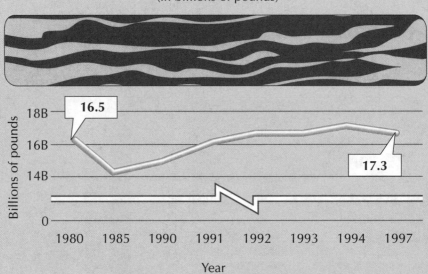

Source: U.S. Department of Agriculture

WHOLESALE HOG PRICES RISE, 1982–1997

It costs U.S. farmers as much as $0.40 a pound to raise hogs.
The average price that farmers receive compared to the average retail price, per pound:

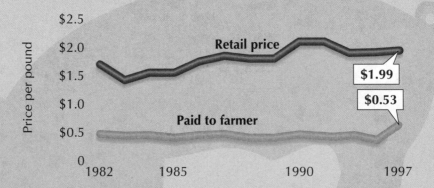

Source: U.S. Department of Agriculture

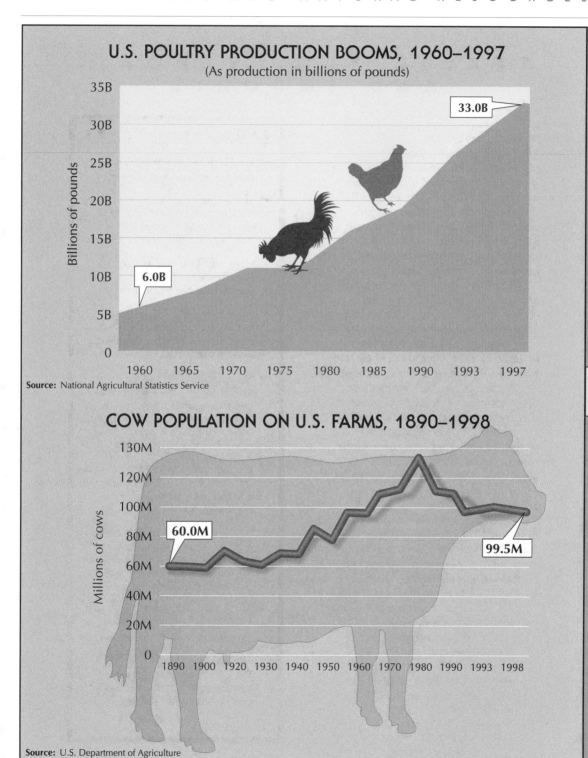

U.S. POULTRY PRODUCTION BOOMS, 1960–1997
(As production in billions of pounds)

33.0B

6.0B

Billions of pounds

35B
30B
25B
20B
15B
10B
5B
0

1960 1965 1970 1975 1980 1985 1990 1993 1997

Source: National Agricultural Statistics Service

COW POPULATION ON U.S. FARMS, 1890–1998

60.0M

99.5M

Millions of cows

130M
120M
100M
80M
60M
40M
20M
0

1890 1900 1920 1930 1940 1950 1960 1970 1980 1990 1993 1998

Source: U.S. Department of Agriculture

AGRICULTURE EXPORTS AND IMPORTS

U.S. farmers produce crops in excess of the country's domestic needs. While some of the excess is stockpiled, most of it is sold in foreign markets. America is the world's top food exporter, with exports in 1998 valued at $44.0 billion. Grains and feeds are the major U.S. exports, followed by oilseeds, animals and animal products, cotton, fruits, and vegetables. Asian countries, led by Japan, are the top U.S. food importers.

Government policies and trade agreements affect exports and imports in various ways. For example, if U.S. government subsidies for sugar growers were dropped, the percentage of imported sugar consumed in the U.S. —currently about 13%—would probably increase.

Political unrest, bad weather, and other calamities in foreign countries also create markets for U.S. farmers. For example, a severe drought in Australia in 1994 reduced that nation's wheat crop by more than 50%; wheat buyers who usually purchase Australian wheat had to turn to U.S., Canadian, and European sources.

Of course, the reverse can also occur. In 1994, the U.S. imported millions of tons of grain—mainly wheat, oats, and barley—in part because U.S. production was severely reduced by the 1993 floods in the Midwest. Food imports to the U.S. totaled $27.4 billion in 1998. Canada, Mexico, and Brazil were the leading countries of origin. Fruits, vegetables, beef and veal, coffee, and grains and feed were the leading imports. Yet from 1980 to 1998, the percentage of imports to the U.S. made up of agricultural products declined from 7% to 4%.

FINGERTIP FACTS

- The U.S. is the world's leading exporter and importer of tobacco.

- The U.S. exported 6.3 million tons of fruits, nuts, and vegetables in 1998, and imported 9.1 million tons—including 4.2 million tons of bananas.

- More than 41% of all agricultural exports are bought by Asia, with Japan taking the largest share.

- Exports revenue is rising in the U.S. In 1980, the U.S. earned $41.5 billion in exports. In 1996 that number had increased 28% to $57.2 billion.

- The approval in 1993 of the North American Free Trade Agreement, NAFTA, plus strong growth in the Mexican economy led to a substantial increase in U.S. corn and soybean exports to Mexico during 1994.

- The U.S. imported $4.0 billion worth of fruits in 1998. Chile, Mexico, and Brazil were the leading countries of origin.

- U.S. farmers produced 45% of the world's soybeans, 40% of its corn, and 10% of its wheat. The majority of these crops were sold to Asia and Latin America.

- The U.S. imported $4.2 billion worth of vegetables in 1998, with Mexico, Canada, and Spain the main countries of origin.

- The U.S. exported 16% of its corn production, 41% of its wheat, 34% of its soybeans, and 37% of its cotton crop in 1997.

EXPORT AND IMPORT VALUE OF SELECTED COMMODITIES, 1980 vs. 1998

(Exports and imports from and to the U.S.)

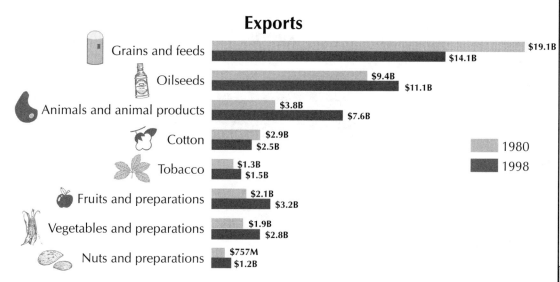

Exports

Commodity	1980	1998
Grains and feeds	$19.1B	$14.1B
Oilseeds	$9.4B	$11.1B
Animals and animal products	$3.8B	$7.6B
Cotton	$2.9B	$2.5B
Tobacco	$1.3B	$1.5B
Fruits and preparations	$2.1B	$3.2B
Vegetables and preparations	$1.9B	$2.8B
Nuts and preparations	$757M	$1.2B

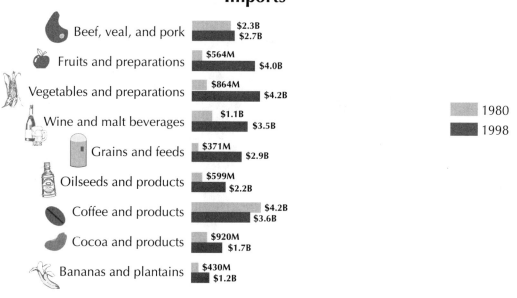

Imports

Commodity	1980	1998
Beef, veal, and pork	$2.3B	$2.7B
Fruits and preparations	$564M	$4.0B
Vegetables and preparations	$864M	$4.2B
Wine and malt beverages	$1.1B	$3.5B
Grains and feeds	$371M	$2.9B
Oilseeds and products	$599M	$2.2B
Coffee and products	$4.2B	$3.6B
Cocoa and products	$920M	$1.7B
Bananas and plantains	$430M	$1.2B

Source: U.S. Department of Agriculture

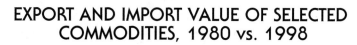

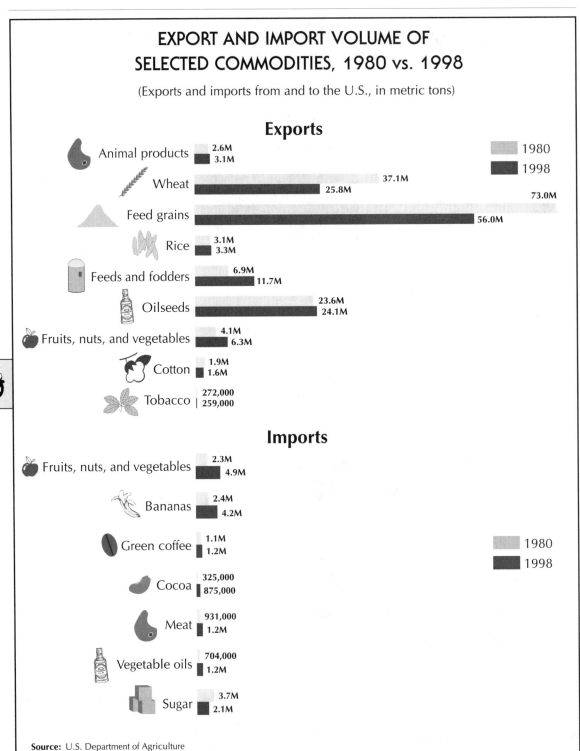

EXPORT AND IMPORT VOLUME OF SELECTED COMMODITIES, 1980 vs. 1998

(Exports and imports from and to the U.S., in metric tons)

Exports

Commodity	1980	1998
Animal products	2.6M	3.1M
Wheat	37.1M	25.8M
Feed grains	73.0M	56.0M
Rice	3.1M	3.3M
Feeds and fodders	6.9M	11.7M
Oilseeds	23.6M	24.1M
Fruits, nuts, and vegetables	4.1M	6.3M
Cotton	1.9M	1.6M
Tobacco	272,000	259,000

Imports

Commodity	1980	1998
Fruits, nuts, and vegetables	2.3M	4.9M
Bananas	2.4M	4.2M
Green coffee	1.1M	1.2M
Cocoa	325,000	875,000
Meat	931,000	1.2M
Vegetable oils	704,000	1.2M
Sugar	3.7M	2.1M

Source: U.S. Department of Agriculture

WHO EXPORTS THE MOST WHEAT, RICE, CORN?

(By millions of metric tons, 1997)

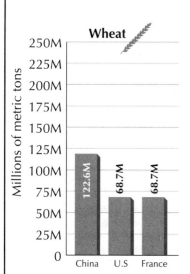

Wheat

Millions of metric tons

122.6M	68.7M	68.7M
China	U.S	France

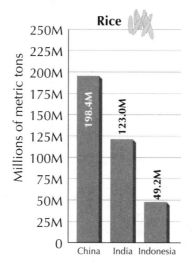

Rice

Millions of metric tons

198.4M	123.0M	49.2M
China	India	Indonesia

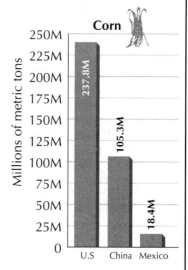

Corn

Millions of metric tons

237.8M	105.3M	18.4M
U.S	China	Mexico

Source: U.S. Department of Agriculture

WHO IMPORTS THE MOST WHEAT, RICE, CORN?

(By millions of metric tons, 1996)

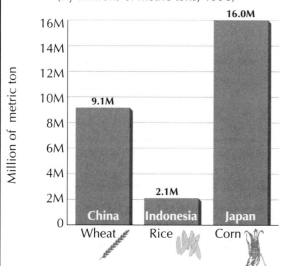

Million of metric ton

Wheat	Rice	Corn
9.1M	2.1M	16.0M
China	Indonesia	Japan

Source: U.S. Department of Agriculture

WHO BUYS THE MOST FOOD FROM THE U.S.?

Asia	$19.7 billion
Western Europe	$18.4 billion
Latin America	$11.2 billion
Canada	$7.0 billion
Africa	$2.2 billion
Former Soviet Union	$1.1 billion
Eastern Europe	$320 million

Source: U.S. Department of Agriculture

AGRICULTURE AND THE ENVIRONMENT

While technological advancements have substantially increased agricultural productivity and the competitiveness of U.S. farmers, some of these practices have had undesirable effects. For example, large expanses of single crops (called monocultures) and the removal of "belts" of sheltering trees and shrubs between fields have contributed to soil erosion. The U.S. loses an estimated 4 billion tons of topsoil annually, making farmland less fertile and causing ecological damage. Overgrazing of rangelands also causes extensive erosion.

Damming rivers for irrigation destroys natural habitats. For example, California's Central Valley Project—which includes 5 major dams and thousands of miles of aqueducts—has contributed to the destruction of 92% of the valley's waterfowl wetlands habitat. Fertilizer- and pesticide-laden runoff from farms also causes terrible damage to wildlife habitats. In addition, pesticides create health risks to farmworkers and to the general public, as people ingest pesticide residues in food and water.

Agriculture, especially rice growing and cattle raising, is also a major source of atmospheric methane, a gas that is a prime contributor to "greenhouse warming."

During the past decade, however, progress has been made in combating the harmful environmental effects of agriculture. Scientists have been able to engineer crops to be resistant to diseases that once had to be controlled with pesticides. Farmers are cutting their per-acre use of chemicals, partly by switching to biological pest controls; manure is being used instead of fossil-based fertilizers to improve soil; and federal programs such as the Conservation Reserve Program and the Swampbuster Initiative protect wildlife and natural habitats.

FINGERTIP FACTS

- Each year, the U.S. loses more than 2 million acres of prime cropland to erosion, salinization, and waterlogging. Another 1 million acres are lost to urbanization, industry, road construction, and other development.

- U.S. topsoil is being lost 17 times faster than it is being replaced. It takes nature more than 200 years to form one inch of topsoil.

- In 1776, when the U.S. declared its independence, the average topsoil was 9 inches deep. Today, it's 5.9 inches deep.

- More than 500 million tons of livestock wastes—manure, feathers, and so on—are produced in the U.S. each year.

- More than 20,000 different pesticide products, containing more than 600 different active ingredients, are sold in the U.S.

- Although the number of forest fires in the U.S. decreased to 52,390 in 1994, more than 2.2 million acres were damaged.

PESTICIDE USE BY SECTOR, 1997
(By people using pesticides, in millions)

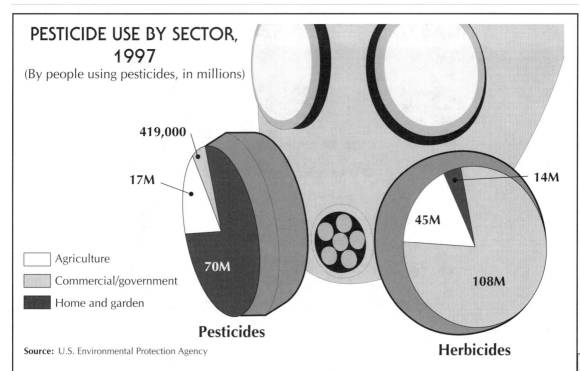

419,000

17M

14M

45M

70M

108M

- ☐ Agriculture
- ▨ Commercial/government
- ■ Home and garden

Pesticides

Herbicides

Source: U.S. Environmental Protection Agency

NATURAL GASES IN THE ATMOSPHERE

Major sources of methane released into the atmosphere, in millions of tons a year:

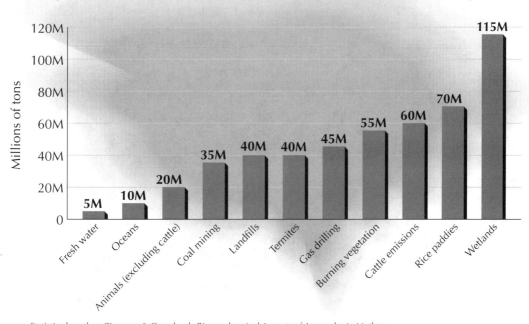

Millions of tons

120M	
100M	
80M	
60M	
40M	
20M	
0	

5M — Fresh water
10M — Oceans
20M — Animals (excluding cattle)
35M — Coal mining
40M — Landfills
40M — Termites
45M — Gas drilling
55M — Burning vegetation
60M — Cattle emissions
70M — Rice paddies
115M — Wetlands

Source: Statistics based on Cicerone & Oremland, *Biogeochemical Aspects of Atmospheric Methane*

TOP 5 FISH CATCHES IN THE WORLD, 1996
(In thousands of metric tons)

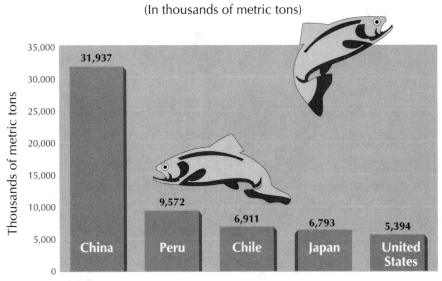

China 31,937
Peru 9,572
Chile 6,911
Japan 6,793
United States 5,394

Thousands of metric tons

U.S. COMMERCIAL FISH CATCHES, 1991-1996
(In thousands of metric tons)

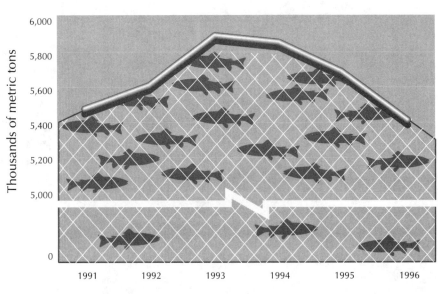

Thousands of metric tons

1991   1992   1993   1994   1995   1996

Source: U.S. Dept. of Commerce

FIRE FREQUENCY AND DAMAGE IN THE U.S., 1985–1994

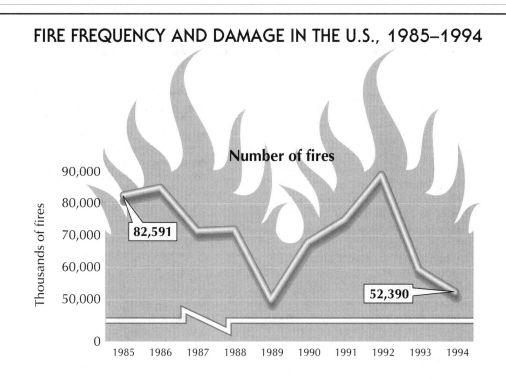

Number of fires

82,591

52,390

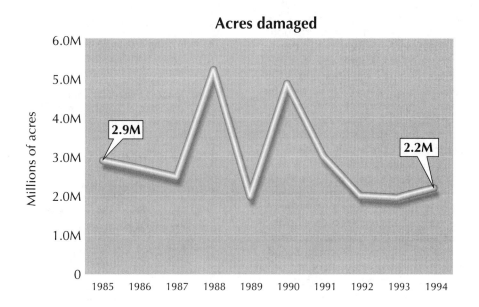

Acres damaged

2.9M

2.2M

Source: National Interagency Fire Center, National Oceanic and Atmospheric Administration

USING NATURAL RESOURCES

Today's farmers depend on 3 major groups of natural resources: fertile soil rich in nitrogen, phosphorus, and other nutrients; water from rivers and other surface supplies plus water pumped from groundwater supplies; and energy, derived primarily from oil and other non-renewable fossil fuels. About 400 gallons of oil equivalents are used annually to produce the food used by each American—to operate tractors and other equipment, and to produce fertilizers and pesticides.

Raising livestock uses far more resources than does growing fruits and vegetables. An estimated 20,000 pounds of potatoes can be grown on one acre—only 165 pounds of beef can be grown on the same land.

Farming methods also are a factor in the efficiency of resource use. No-till farming—where new seeds are planted directly into the previous crop's stubble—reduces soil erosion. Surge irrigation regulates water delivery rather than let water flow into all furrows at once, saving water, energy, and labor costs. Crop rotation cuts the need for nitrogen fertilizer. Organic farming uses cover crops instead of fertilizers to enrich the soil, and beneficial insects instead of pesticides to fight harmful pests.

Like other natural resources on which modern society depends, supplies of many of the natural resources needed by farmers are dwindling. Major efforts are being made to develop alternate sources. For example, scientists are developing environmentally sound processes to convert manure and other animal wastes into methane gas for fuel, liquid nutrients for aquaculture, and high-nutrient feed additives for livestock.

FINGERTIP FACTS

- ☞ About 14% of U.S. farms are irrigated. Although this percentage has remained the same for 10 years, the average number of acres irrigated per farm has grown 19%. In 1987, about 15 acres per farm were irrigated. In 1997, about 197 acres were.

- ☞ Irrigation is wasteful. Worldwide, 70% of the water used for irrigation never reaches the crops.

- ☞ More than 2,000 gallons of water are used to produce one pound of butter or beef; fewer than 250 gallons of water are needed to produce one pound of grain crops such as oats and corn.

- ☞ About 9 pounds of feed are needed to produce one pound of beef; about 2 pounds of feed are needed to produce one pound of chicken.

- ☞ In commercial pork-farming operations, about one pound of meat can be produced from 3 pounds of feed.

- ☞ Timber harvested in national forests jumped from 3.5 billion board feet in 1950 to more than 24.5 billion board feet in 1997.

- ☞ Alaska's rainforests are dwindling rapidly. From 1930 to 1939, only 27.2 million board feet of timber were harvested in southeastern Alaska. From 1994 to 1996, there were 1.802 billion board feet cut.

- ☞ Fertile soil contains up to 1,000 pounds of earthworms per square acre.

- ☞ Certain techniques, such as no-till farming, can reduce erosion.

FEED REQUIREMENTS: POUND FOR POUND

Pounds of feed required per pound of product produced:

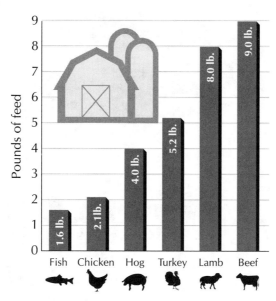

Pounds of feed

1.6 lb.	2.1lb.	4.0 lb.	5.2 lb.	8.0 lb.	9.0 lb.
Fish	Chicken	Hog	Turkey	Lamb	Beef

Source: Statistics based on M.E. Ensminger, *Animal Science*

TOBACCO EXPENSES

Tobacco is one of the most profitable but also most labor-intensive crops grown in the U.S.:

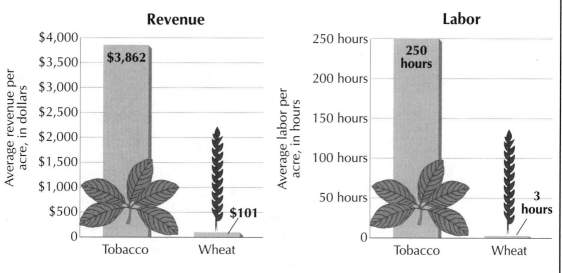

Revenue

Average revenue per acre, in dollars

Tobacco: $3,862
Wheat: $101

Labor

Average labor per acre, in hours

Tobacco: 250 hours
Wheat: 3 hours

Source: Tobacco Institute

WATER REQUIREMENTS: OUNCE FOR OUNCE
(Gallons of water used per pound of food produced)

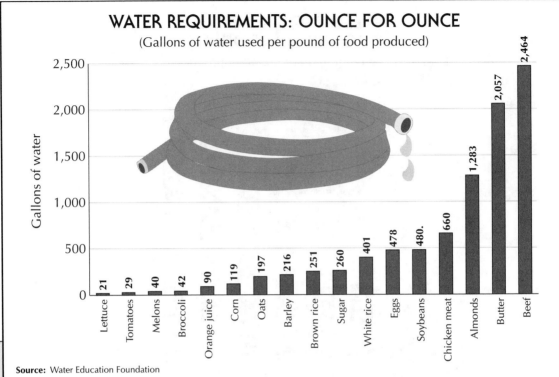

Source: Water Education Foundation

TOP 10 STATES IN NUMBER OF IRRIGATED FARMS

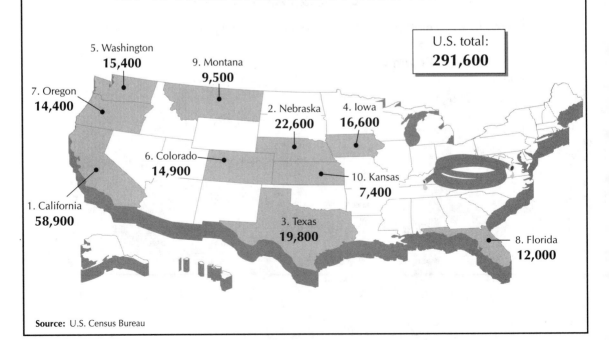

U.S. total: **291,600**

5. Washington **15,400**
9. Montana **9,500**
7. Oregon **14,400**
2. Nebraska **22,600**
4. Iowa **16,600**
6. Colorado **14,900**
10. Kansas **7,400**
1. California **58,900**
3. Texas **19,800**
8. Florida **12,000**

Source: U.S. Census Bureau

TAKING TIMBER FROM ALASKA, 1930–1996

The rainforests of Alaska's 17-million acre Tongass National Forest are dwindling rapidly, as more and more timber is cut. Mean average timber harvest each decade in southeastern Alaska, in millions and billions of board feet:

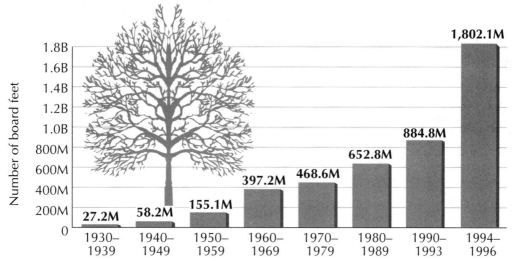

Source: Alaska Department of Fish and Game

TIMBER HARVESTED IN NATIONAL FORESTS, 1950 vs. 1997

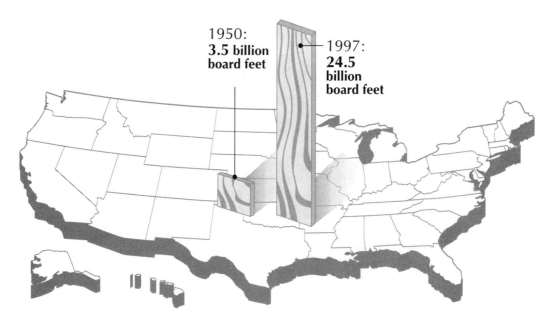

1950:
3.5 billion board feet

1997:
24.5 billion board feet

Source: U.S. Forest Service

8

TRANSPORTATION AND ENERGY

GETTING AROUND

Whether it is for business or pleasure, most Americans depend on their cars to get around—or, at least, to try to get around. Growth in traffic has led to increasing congestion, especially during "rush hours," when people travel to and from work. Despite these problems, the U.S. transportation program remains focused on highway travel, with a much greater percentage of federal transportation funds going to highway programs than to mass transit.

Airplanes, railroads, and buses are the primary alternatives to automobiles for long-distance travel. For short distances, there are various mass transit options. Buses are the primary mass transit vehicles for "commuter services" between cities and the suburbs. About 950 U.S. cities have mass transit systems; almost all of these consist solely of bus service. Most of the largest cities, however, are also equipped with subway or surface rail systems or combinations of the two. New York City has the longest and most developed rail system in the country, with 492.9 miles of route in its famed subway system.

FINGERTIP FACTS

☞ In 1997, private automobiles carried 78.9% of all intercity passenger traffic, followed by airlines (19.4%), buses (1.0%), and railroads (0.7%).

☞ Between 1980 and 1997, the percentage of intercity passenger traffic carried by cars declined from 86.9% to 78.9%. Meanwhile, the airlines'

share of this traffic rose from 10.1% to 19.4%—in part because airfares have risen much more slowly than fares for other transportation.

☞ In 1996, the U.S. had 3.9 million miles of public roads—785,000 in urban areas and more than 3.1 million in rural areas.

☞ As of 1997, there were 46,319 miles of road in the U.S. interstate system. The longest interstate was I-90, with 3,081 miles; the shortest was I-878 in New York City—only 0.7 mile.

☞ On average, males drove 32 miles a day while females drove 26 miles a day in 1998.

☞ Most American workers—86.5%—commute via car, truck, or van.

☞ Driving is by far the most common method of commuting in 9 of the nation's 10 largest cities; only in New York City is public transportation the favored mode.

☞ According to 1996 data, Los Angeles, California, is the nation's most traffic-congested metropolitan area.

☞ In Michigan, 81.5% of commuters drive alone, compared to 54.3% in New York.

☞ "Carpooling" is practiced by 20.5% of Hawaiian commuters, but only 10.1% of South Dakotans.

☞ New Yorkers spend an average of 27.8 minutes traveling to work; North Dakotans spend an average of only 11.9 minutes.

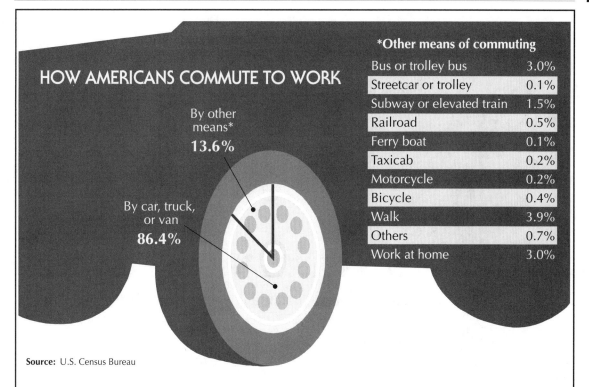

HOW AMERICANS COMMUTE TO WORK

By other means*
13.6%

By car, truck, or van
86.4%

*Other means of commuting

Bus or trolley bus	3.0%
Streetcar or trolley	0.1%
Subway or elevated train	1.5%
Railroad	0.5%
Ferry boat	0.1%
Taxicab	0.2%
Motorcycle	0.2%
Bicycle	0.4%
Walk	3.9%
Others	0.7%
Work at home	3.0%

Source: U.S. Census Bureau

HOW AMERICANS GET TO WORK IN THE 10 LARGEST CITIES

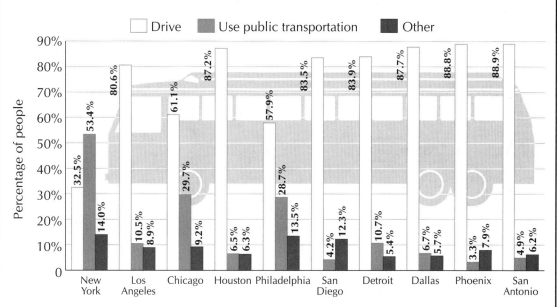

□ Drive   ■ Use public transportation   ■ Other

Percentage of people

City	Drive	Use public transportation	Other
New York	32.5%	53.4%	14.0%
Los Angeles	80.6%	10.5%	8.9%
Chicago	61.1%	29.7%	9.2%
Houston	87.2%	6.5%	6.3%
Philadelphia	57.9%	28.7%	13.5%
San Diego	83.5%	4.2%	12.3%
Detroit	83.9%	10.7%	5.4%
Dallas	87.7%	6.7%	5.7%
Phoenix	88.8%	3.3%	7.9%
San Antonio	88.9%	4.9%	6.2%

Source: U.S. Census Bureau

U.S. COMMUTER FACTS

When going to work, states where the most and least number of people:

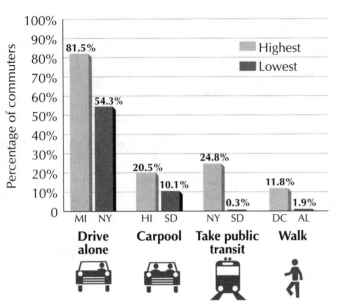

Percentage of commuters

- Highest
- Lowest

	Drive alone	Carpool	Take public transit	Walk
MI NY	81.5% 54.3%			
HI SD		20.5% 10.1%		
NY SD			24.8% 0.3%	
DC AL				11.8% 1.9%

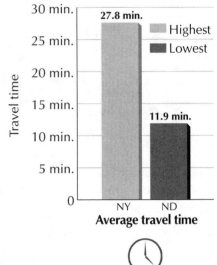

Travel time

- Highest
- Lowest

27.8 min. 11.9 min.

NY   ND

Average travel time

Source: Federal Highway Administration

TOP 11 U.S. METRO AREAS IN TRAFFIC CONGESTION, 1993

(With rankings)

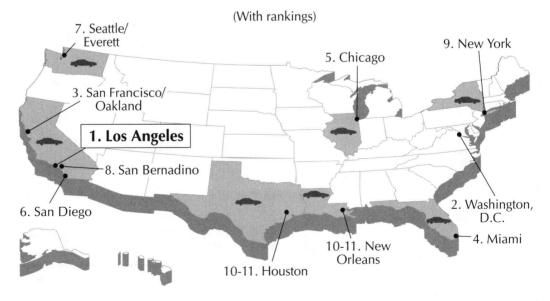

7. Seattle/Everett

3. San Francisco/Oakland

5. Chicago

9. New York

1. Los Angeles

8. San Bernadino

6. San Diego

2. Washington, D.C.

4. Miami

10-11. New Orleans

10-11. Houston

Source: National Research Council

HOW AMERICANS TRAVEL

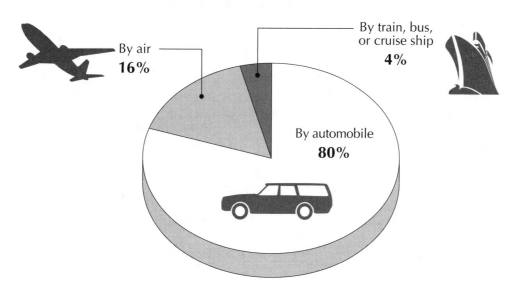

By train, bus,
or cruise ship
4%

By air
16%

By automobile
80%

Source: Travel Industry Association of America

BEST-SELLING BRANDS OF MOTORCYCLES IN U.S., 1993

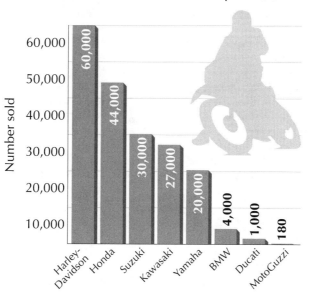

Number sold

Harley-Davidson	60,000
Honda	44,000
Suzuki	30,000
Kawasaki	27,000
Yamaha	20,000
BMW	4,000
Ducati	1,000
MotoGuzzi	180

Source: Based on statistics from DJB

AMERICA'S LOVE AFFAIR WITH AUTOMOBILES

Americans drove their cars 1.5 trillion miles in 1996—more than 11,000 miles per vehicle—as they traveled to malls and mountains, farms and factories, homes and hospitals—indeed, to every conceivable destination.

All this freedom of movement, however, has a price. It cost 48.31 cents per mile to own and operate an automobile in 1997, up from 27.95 cents in 1980. Some costs are fixed. For example, car insurance averaged $690 in 1996, while depreciation averaged $2,780. Other costs—gasoline and oil, tires, and maintenance—are variable, depending on mileage. Society pays, too, especially as it deals with the air pollutants emitted by cars. But there is good news on this front. Engine modifications, such as the addition of catalytic converters, have helped reduce harmful emissions like carbon monoxide and nitrogen oxides.

Accidents are another problem. There were some 11.8 million motor-vehicle accidents and 41,967 deaths in 1997. These cost the nation an estimated $167.3 billion in damages, medical expenses, wage losses, and so on.

People over age 65 drive less than younger drivers do—but they are at greater risk when they get behind the wheel. For example, drivers ages 70 to 74 have more than twice as many fatal crashes—based on number of miles traveled—than do drivers ages 40 to 49.

FINGERTIP FACTS

- Motor-vehicle registrations in the U.S. reached 129 million in 1996.

- Males made up just over half (51%) of the 179.5 million licensed drivers in 1996, but they drove about 65% of the miles driven that year.

- Americans drove their cars a total of 1.5 trillion miles in 1996, up from 1.1 trillion in 1980.

- People in the Los Angeles, California, area drive 266 million miles a day.

- In 1996, U.S. passenger cars consumed 68.9 billion gallons of fuel. The average passenger car used 531 gallons.

- New Hampshire had the highest number of automobiles per capita (.63) in 1996; Arkansas had the lowest (.34). The U.S. average number of automobiles per capita per state was .48.

- A car must be driven 800 miles to cause as much pollution as an outboard motor does in one hour.

- In 1997, males were involved in 14.4 million motor-vehicle accidents; females were involved in 9.6 million. Safety belts were effective in preventing about 50% of fatalities and severe injuries.

- In 1997, there were 41,967 motor-vehicle fatalities; 65.2% occurred in rural areas; 51.9% occurred at night.

- In 1997, the use of safety belts saved an estimated 5,226 lives. An estimated 268 toddlers and infants were saved by child-restraint systems.

- From 1975 to 1995, the number of U.S. drivers ages 65 and older more than doubled, reaching 13 million. By the year 2020, there will be 30 million drivers in this age group.

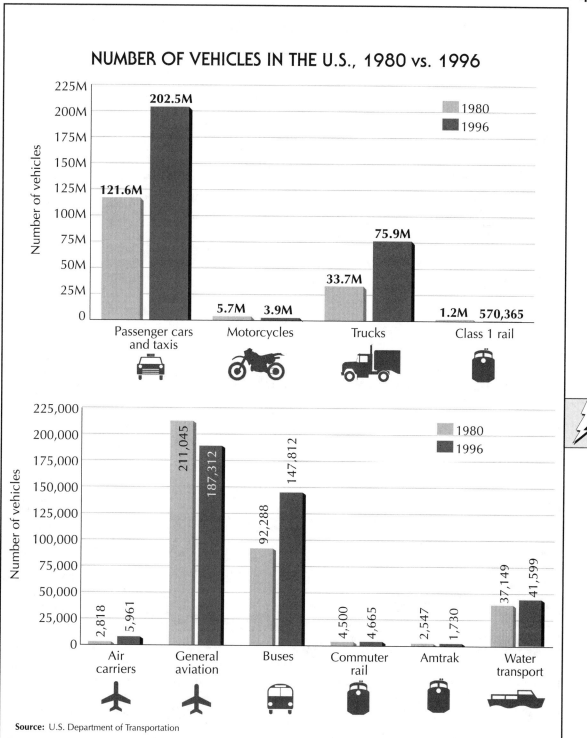

NUMBER OF VEHICLES IN THE U.S., 1980 vs. 1996

Source: U.S. Department of Transportation

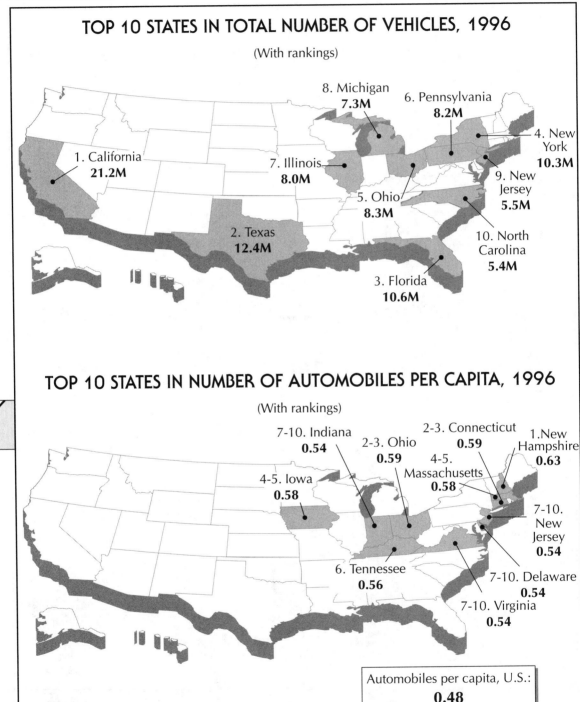

TOP 10 STATES IN TOTAL NUMBER OF VEHICLES, 1996

(With rankings)

8. Michigan
7.3M

6. Pennsylvania
8.2M

4. New York
10.3M

1. California
21.2M

7. Illinois
8.0M

9. New Jersey
5.5M

5. Ohio
8.3M

2. Texas
12.4M

10. North Carolina
5.4M

3. Florida
10.6M

TOP 10 STATES IN NUMBER OF AUTOMOBILES PER CAPITA, 1996

(With rankings)

7-10. Indiana
0.54

2-3. Ohio
0.59

2-3. Connecticut
0.59

1.New Hampshire
0.63

4-5. Iowa
0.58

4-5. Massachusetts
0.58

7-10. New Jersey
0.54

6. Tennessee
0.56

7-10. Delaware
0.54

7-10. Virginia
0.54

Automobiles per capita, U.S.:
0.48

Source: U.S. Department of Transportation

AVERAGE ANNUAL MILES DRIVEN PER VEHICLE IN U.S.

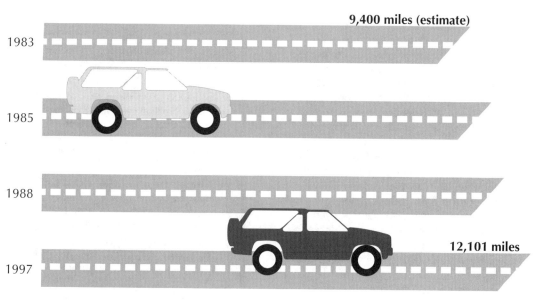

1983

9,400 miles (estimate)

1985

1988

1997

12,101 miles

Source: U.S. Energy Information Administration

TOP 10 STATES FOR MILES DRIVEN PER VEHICLE

(Number of miles driven annually per vehicle, with rankings)

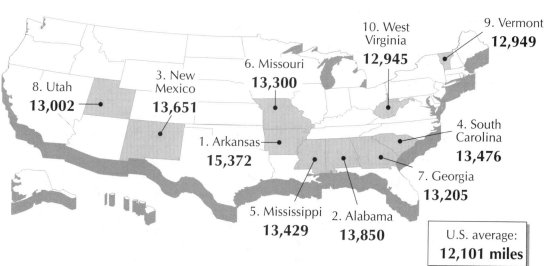

8. Utah
13,002

3. New Mexico
13,651

6. Missouri
13,300

10. West Virginia
12,945

9. Vermont
12,949

1. Arkansas
15,372

4. South Carolina
13,476

7. Georgia
13,205

5. Mississippi
13,429

2. Alabama
13,850

U.S. average:
12,101 miles

Source: Federal Highway Administration; U.S. Department of Transportation

THE U.S. AUTO INDUSTRY

U.S. automakers produced 5.9 million passenger cars in 1997. But the nation's auto industry is much broader, including importers (4.4 million cars in 1997); dealers; gasoline service stations; manufacturers and sellers of tires, batteries, and other parts; parking garages; and rental services.

Consumer demands have resulted in cars that are sleeker, faster, and more comfortable than ever before. They have better fuel efficiency, too. And today, the "family car" may not even be what has previously been considered a "car." Sales of light trucks and sport-utility vehicles (SUVs) for personal use have zoomed. Recreational-vehicle sales also are on the rise, after hitting a low in 1991.

People are holding onto vehicles longer than they did in the past. One reason may be "sticker shock." During the past 20 years, new car prices have risen at faster rates than most people's incomes have. By the end of 1994, the average cost of a new car exceeded $20,000, including taxes and other charges, as compared to $4,400 in 1974 (the equivalent of $12,800 after adjusting for inflation). As a result, used cars were outselling new cars 2 to 1 in 1994, accounting for one-third of all the dollars spent on vehicles.

FINGERTIP FACTS

- In 1997, General Motors produced the most cars (2.6 million); 29% of them were Chevys. Ford Motor Corp. produced 1.28 million cars; 71% were Fords.

- Business-related car sales increased significantly from 1983 to 1997, going from 33% of all sales to 51%.

- U.S. auto plants produced 5.9 million passenger cars in 1997, second only to Japan's 8.5 million.

- Production has declined since 1985, when 8.2 million cars were manufactured in the U.S. Importation of new cars, which has remained fairly steady for the last 10 years, totaled 4.4 million in 1997.

- Canada is the major source of imported cars in the U.S. (1.7 million in 1997), followed by Japan (1.4 million) and Mexico (0.5 million).

- The U.S. exported 536,000 new passenger cars to other countries in 1997, up from 489,000 in 1993.

- At General Motors, labor costs an average of $2,388 per vehicle; at Honda's U.S. plants, labor costs an average of $920 per vehicle.

- The fuel efficiency of new cars has improved over the years, from an average of 16.1 miles per gallon in 1955 to an average of 27.9 miles per gallon in 1997.

- The Toyota Camry was the best-selling car of 1997; Ford F-Pickups headed light-truck sales.

- Luxury cars and large cars accounted for only one-quarter of U.S. car sales in 1997; most Americans buy small and mid-size cars.

- Leasing is growing quickly in popularity—it has more than doubled in the past decade and is expected to continue as a major force in car sales.

- More car buyers are choosing American-made vehicles. In 1996, about 85% of cars sold were American, up 3% from 1983. A total of 8.5% of cars sold were from Japan, down 12% from 1983.

U.S. AUTOMOBILE SALES, BY SIZE AND TYPE, 1997

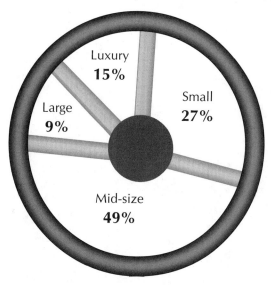

Luxury
15%

Small
27%

Large
9%

Mid-size
49%

TOTAL U.S. PERSONAL SPENDING ON MOTOR VEHICLES, 1993

How total spending breaks down for personal transportation in the U.S.:

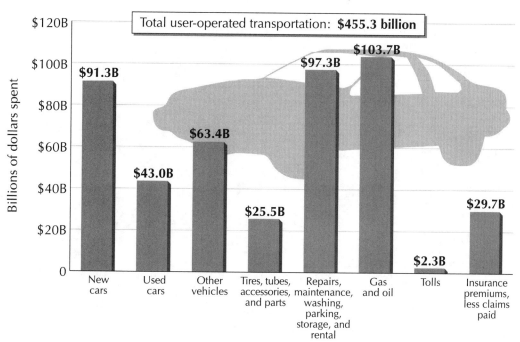

Total user-operated transportation: **$455.3 billion**

Billions of dollars spent

$120B

$100B

$80B

$60B

$40B

$20B

0

$91.3B New cars

$43.0B Used cars

$63.4B Other vehicles

$25.5B Tires, tubes, accessories, and parts

$97.3B Repairs, maintenance, washing, parking, storage, and rental

$103.7B Gas and oil

$2.3B Tolls

$29.7B Insurance premiums, less claims paid

Source: American Automobile Manufacturers Association; Bureau of Economic Analysis; U.S. Commerce Department

TOP 10 BEST-SELLING CARS AND LIGHT TRUCKS IN THE U.S., 1996

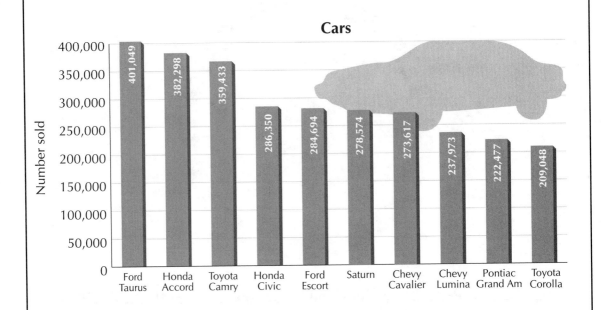

Cars

Number sold (y-axis: 0 to 400,000)

Model	Number sold
Ford Taurus	401,049
Honda Accord	382,298
Toyota Camry	359,433
Honda Civic	286,350
Ford Escort	284,694
Saturn	278,574
Chevy Cavalier	273,617
Chevy Lumina	237,973
Pontiac Grand Am	222,477
Toyota Corolla	209,048

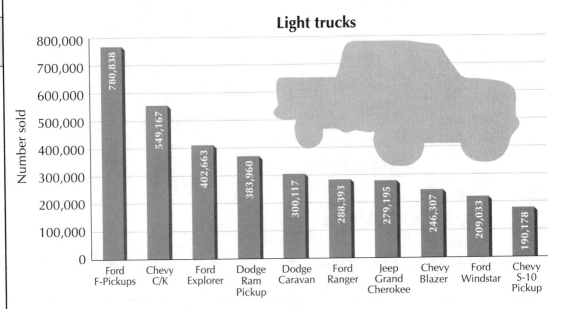

Light trucks

Number sold (y-axis: 0 to 800,000)

Model	Number sold
Ford F-Pickups	780,838
Chevy C/K	549,167
Ford Explorer	402,663
Dodge Ram Pickup	383,960
Dodge Caravan	300,117
Ford Ranger	288,393
Jeep Grand Cherokee	279,195
Chevy Blazer	246,307
Ford Windstar	209,033
Chevy S-10 Pickup	190,178

Source: Based on statistics from Ward's Automotive Reports

LEASING IS INCREASING

Consumers are leasing more new cars, not buying them. This trend has continued through the 1990s:

Percentage of new cars leased

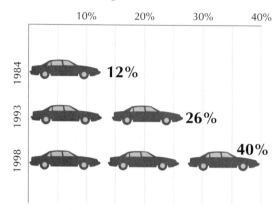

10%   20%   30%   40%

1984 — 12%

1993 — 26%

1998 — 40%

Source: Based on statistics from CNW

TOTAL LABOR COST FOR SELECTED VEHICLES

General Motors — $2,388

Chrysler — $1,872

Ford — $1,629

Honda — $920

Source: Based on statistics from Economic Strategy Institute; Harbour and Associates; The WEFA Group

AIRBAG SALES EXPLODE, 1987–1994

(Percentage of new cars and vans with driver-side airbags)

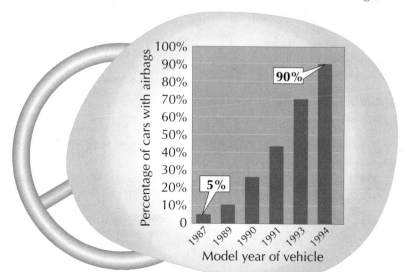

Source: Insurance Institute for Highway Safety; Highway Loss Data Institute

AIR TRAVEL

More people are taking to the skies than ever before, a trend that shows no signs of slowing. Indeed, U.S. air traffic is expected to double by the year 2010, with an estimated 1.0 billion passengers a year. Most passengers in the U.S. fly on major airlines, such as Delta, American, United, USAir, and Northwest. But the nation also has 125 scheduled commuter carriers, which fly short hauls and cover smaller cities no longer serviced by the major airlines. Commuter air traffic—about 58 million boardings annually—is growing steadily at the rate of 6% to 10% a year. Business travelers make up about 65% of these customers.

Safety concerns are always a big issue among air travelers, even though during the years 1990 to 1994, a person's chances of being killed on a flight with a major U.S. airline was 1 in 6.5 million. On international carriers, the risk was even less; 1 in 7.0 million.

The risk of death is higher on prop/turboprop planes, which are more likely to be used by commuter services. From 1985 to 1994, the risk was 1 in 2.0 million. In 1994, the Department of Transportation announced plans to improve commuter-airline safety standards to those of the major carriers, particularly in such areas as aircraft maintenance and pilot training.

FINGERTIP FACTS

☛ In 1997, passenger revenue on air travel in the U.S. totaled more than $79 billion, up from $70 billion in 1995.

☛ Delta carried the most passengers in 1997, followed closely by American; United was third but had the most revenue, followed by American and Delta.

☛ There were 8.2 million scheduled departures from U.S. airports in 1997. Chicago's O'Hare was the busiest airport, with 69.1 million passengers.

☛ The busiest domestic route in 1997 was between New York City and Los Angeles (3.7 million passengers).

☛ From 1985–1994, a U.S. traveler's chance of being killed on a domestic flight was 0 on American, Southwest, and TWA; it was 1 in 10 million on Continental; 1 in 8 million on Delta; and 1 in 2 million on USAir.

☛ Thunderstorm wind shear leads to more passenger deaths in U.S. domestic jet crashes (419 deaths from 1975 to 1994) than any other cause, including collisions (159 deaths) and ice buildup (122 deaths).

☛ The U.S. has 125 scheduled commuter carriers, which serve about 58 million travelers a year. The largest is American Eagle, which had 280 planes in mid-1995.

☛ The average length of a passenger trip was 1,011 miles in 1997. The revenue per passenger mile totaled 13.1¢.

☛ Compared to inflation, airplane ticket prices have increased at a much slower rate. Using constant dollars, tickets were actually 18% cheaper in 1996 than were in 1986.

TOP 10 U.S. AIRLINES, 1997

By number of passengers in 1997

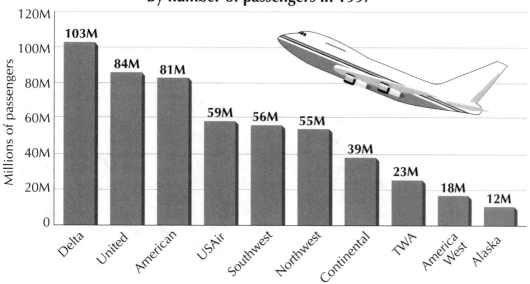

Airline	Passengers
Delta	103M
United	84M
American	81M
USAir	59M
Southwest	56M
Northwest	55M
Continental	39M
TWA	23M
America West	18M
Alaska	12M

Millions of passengers

By revenue miles flown in 1997

(Revenue miles are miles for which passengers paid to fly)

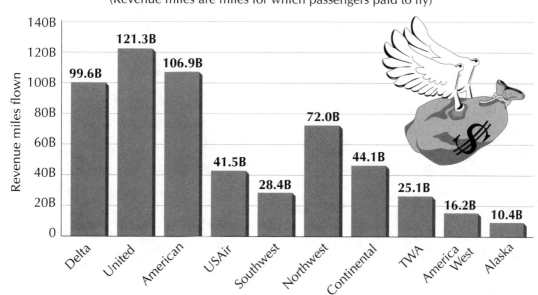

Airline	Revenue miles flown
Delta	99.6B
United	121.3B
American	106.9B
USAir	41.5B
Southwest	28.4B
Northwest	72.0B
Continental	44.1B
TWA	25.1B
America West	16.2B
Alaska	10.4B

Revenue miles flown

Source: Air Transport Association of America

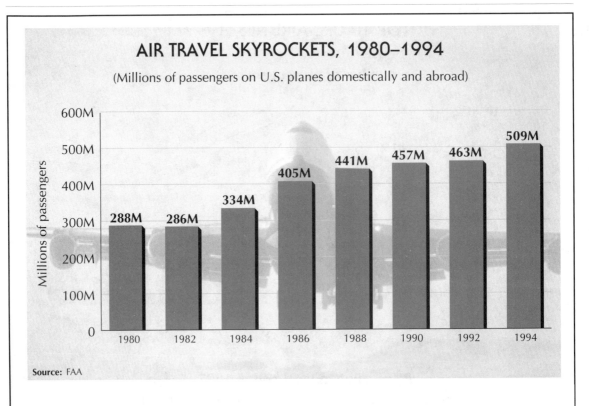

AIR TRAVEL SKYROCKETS, 1980–1994

(Millions of passengers on U.S. planes domestically and abroad)

Source: FAA

WORLD'S 10 BUSIEST AIRPORTS, 1997

The U.S. had 5 of the world's 10 busiest airports in 1997. The total number of passengers:

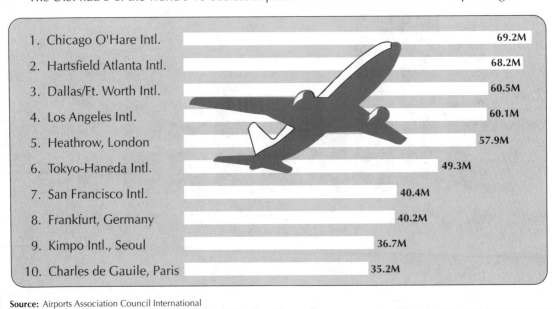

1. Chicago O'Hare Intl. — 69.2M
2. Hartsfield Atlanta Intl. — 68.2M
3. Dallas/Ft. Worth Intl. — 60.5M
4. Los Angeles Intl. — 60.1M
5. Heathrow, London — 57.9M
6. Tokyo-Haneda Intl. — 49.3M
7. San Francisco Intl. — 40.4M
8. Frankfurt, Germany — 40.2M
9. Kimpo Intl., Seoul — 36.7M
10. Charles de Gauile, Paris — 35.2M

Source: Airports Association Council International

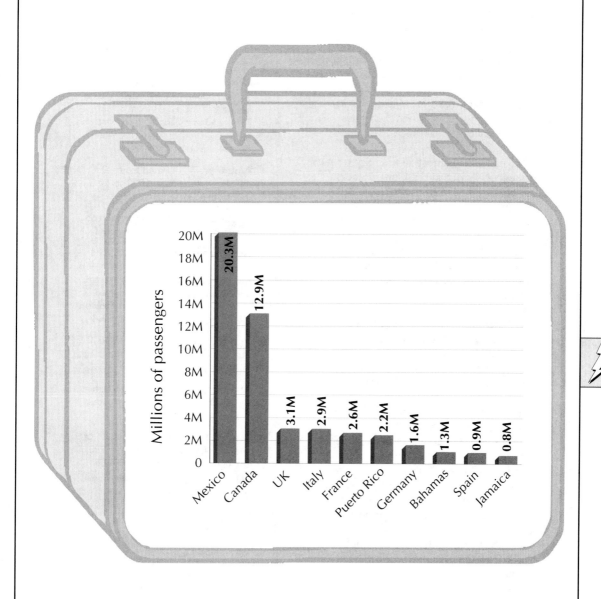

TOP 10 U.S.–OVERSEAS AIR TRAVEL DESTINATIONS, 1996

Source: U.S. Department of Transportation

R A I L R O A D S

Railroads play a significant role in the transportation of both people and freight in America, even though competing modes of transport—particularly the various kinds of motor vehicles, but also airplanes—have been favored with more generous government subsidies and less strict regulation over the past 50 years.

Since 1971, almost all intercity train passenger service in the United States has been provided by the federally subsidized National Railroad Passenger Corporation, better known as Amtrak. Each year, more than 20 million passengers ride Amtrak trains, and the system takes in more than $1 billion in revenues. However, reduced federal funding has forced deep cuts in Amtrak maintenance and service.

Amtrak and other railroads are classified by the Interstate Commerce Commission according to annual gross operating revenues. Currently, the revenue levels are: Class 1: $250 million or more; Class 2: more than $20 million but less than $250 million; and Class 3: $20 million or less.

Mergers and consolidations helped lead to a decline in the number of Class 1 freight lines. But freight traffic on railroads has increased in recent years, despite that downward trend. This is due in part to a shift to intermodal transport—the movement of freight by more than one method (for example, truck trailers transferred to freightcars for part of their journey, then transferred back to trucks for transport to the final destination).

FINGERTIP FACTS

- Even though Amtrak's revenue increased from $1.3 billion in 1990 to $1.6 billion in 1997, their net losses also increased from $183 million to $318 million. This is partly because expenses increased while federal subsidies decreased.

- Amtrak traffic declined from 22.4 million passengers in 1990 to 20.2 million in 1997.

- The average U.S. passenger rail trip covered 285.1 miles in 1992.

- According to 1994 timetables, the fastest scheduled passenger trains in the U.S. take 42 minutes, at average speeds of 97.7 miles per hour, to travel the 68.4 miles from Wilmington, Delaware, to Baltimore, Maryland.

- In 1980, U.S. railroads had 458,000 employees; by 1992, the number had fallen to 197,000.

- The cheapest way to move freight is by water. Using trains costs about 3 times as much.

- In 1940, railroads handled 61.3% of the nation's freight traffic; by 1980, the figure had dropped to 37.2%. Since then, there has been an increase, to an estimated total of 40.2% in 1996.

- In 1997, the freight railroad company with the highest operating revenue was Union Pacific with $9.8 billion.

- Class 1 freight trains covered 584 million miles in 1995, up from lows of 347 million in 1985 and 1986.

- In 1995, there were 3.71 accidents per 1 million train miles for Class 1 railroads.

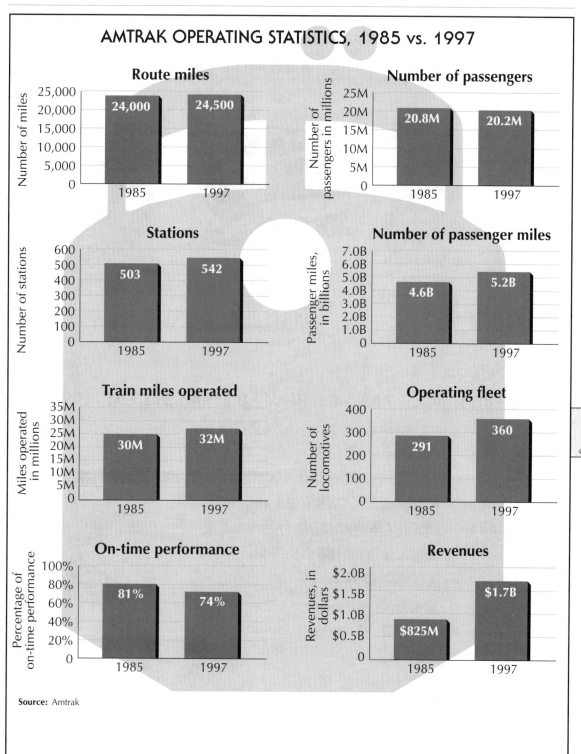

AMTRAK OPERATING STATISTICS, 1985 vs. 1997

Route miles

Number of miles

24,000 — 1985
24,500 — 1997

Number of passengers

Number of passengers in millions

20.8M — 1985
20.2M — 1997

Stations

Number of stations

503 — 1985
542 — 1997

Number of passenger miles

Passenger miles, in billions

4.6B — 1985
5.2B — 1997

Train miles operated

Miles operated in millions

30M — 1985
32M — 1997

Operating fleet

Number of locomotives

291 — 1985
360 — 1997

On-time performance

Percentage of on-time performance

81% — 1985
74% — 1997

Revenues

Revenues, in dollars

$825M — 1985
$1.7B — 1997

Source: Amtrak

U.S. RAILROAD TRAFFIC RISES

Railroad traffic dropped in 1991 and recovered in 1992.
Container shipping, air freight, and trucking have also been rising:

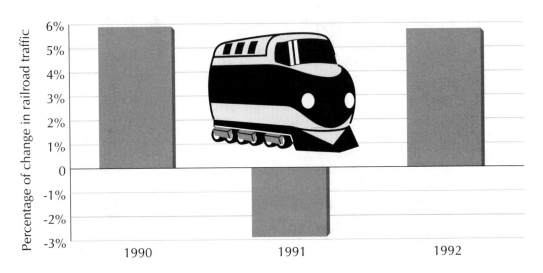

Source: American Association of Railroads

TOP 10 LARGEST RAPID OR HEAVY U.S. RAIL SYSTEMS, 1996

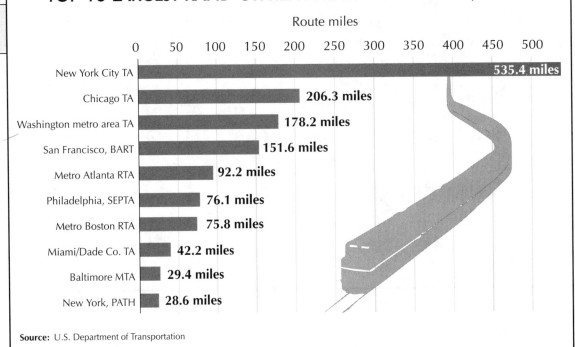

Route miles

	Route miles
New York City TA	535.4 miles
Chicago TA	206.3 miles
Washington metro area TA	178.2 miles
San Francisco, BART	151.6 miles
Metro Atlanta RTA	92.2 miles
Philadelphia, SEPTA	76.1 miles
Metro Boston RTA	75.8 miles
Miami/Dade Co. TA	42.2 miles
Baltimore MTA	29.4 miles
New York, PATH	28.6 miles

Source: U.S. Department of Transportation

NUMBER OF RAILROAD VEHICLES DECLINE, 1970-1996

Class 1 freight cars

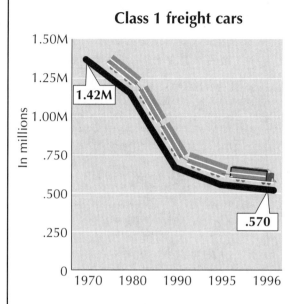

In millions

1.50M
1.25M
1.00M
.750
.500
.250
0

1.42M

.570

1970   1980   1990   1995   1996

Class 1 locomatives

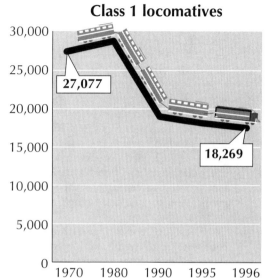

30,000
25,000
20,000
15,000
10,000
5,000
0

27,077

18,269

1970   1980   1990   1995   1996

Source: U.S. Department of Transportation

HOW FREIGHT AND PASSENGERS ARE MOVED, 1996

Freight traffic

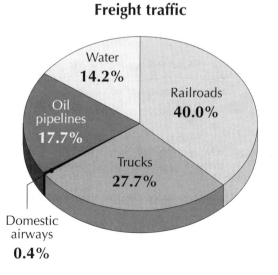

Water
14.2%

Railroads
40.0%

Oil pipelines
17.7%

Trucks
27.7%

Domestic airways
0.4%

Passenger traffic

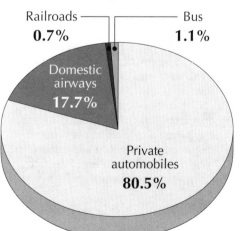

Railroads
0.7%

Bus
1.1%

Domestic airways
17.7%

Private automobiles
80.5%

Source: U.S. Department of Transportation

ENERGY GENERATION AND PRODUCTION

Fossil fuels—which include coal, petroleum, and natural gas—provide almost 80% of the total energy used in the U.S. Other sources, primarily hydropower and nuclear power, supply the remaining 20%. Energy production from 1960 to 1997 increased more than 43%, from 41.5 quadrillion British thermal units (Btu's) to 72.3 quadrillion Btu's. Over that period, coal and nuclear power met growing percentages of the nation's energy needs, while petroleum's role declined significantly.

Fossil fuels are nonrenewable resources, so these fuels are limited in supply. They also are associated with environmental problems, including oil spills and air pollution. Many people oppose nuclear power generation because of the dangerous radioactive spent fuel that it creates. This relatively new form of extremely hazardous material is piling up quickly, but scientists still are not sure how—or if— such waste can be safely transported, disposed of, or stored.

A number of economic and technological problems have limited the development of safer and cleaner alternative energy sources, such as wind power and solar energy. Researchers continue to improve our access to these sources, but they are also searching for additional ones that are more practical on a large scale. For instance, hydrogen may become the fuel of the future if researchers can find an inexpensive and relatively speedy method of extracting it from water or natural gas.

FINGERTIP FACTS

☛ In 1997, the U.S. produced more than 72 quadrillion Btu's of energy—almost twice that produced by China and the former Soviet Union, the second and third-largest energy producers.

☛ In 1997, daily U.S. petroleum production was 8.2 million barrels.

☛ In 1994, for the first time, more new wells were drilled in the U.S. for natural gas than for petroleum.

☛ Today, almost 80% of all energy production is from fossil fuels, down from 95.3% in 1973. To make up the difference, Americans have turned to nuclear energy (9.9%) and solar and wind power (9.7%).

☛ Most electricity generated in the U.S. comes from coal (56.9%). Nuclear energy (21.2%), hydroelectric power (9.3%), and gas (9.0%) are the other leading sources.

☛ In 1996, some 110 commercial nuclear power reactors were operating in the U.S., more than in any other nation.

☛ In 1997, the U.S. imported 24.96 quadrillion Btu's of petroleum, and exported 4.57 quadrillion Btu's.

☛ Producing electricity from natural gas costs about 3.0 cents per kilowatt-hour, less than from wind (5.0 cents), geothermal energy (5.5 cents), or solar energy (14.0 cents).

ELECTRICITY GENERATION BY U.S., 1950–1992

(Net generation by energy source, in billions of kilowatt-hours)

Coal

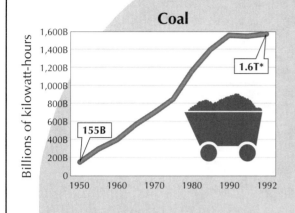

155B
1.6T*

Nuclear power

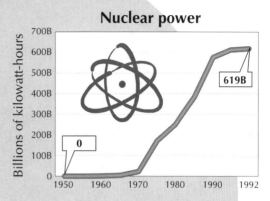

0
619B

Natural gas

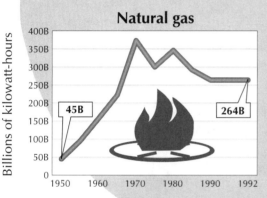

45B
264B

Hydroelectric power

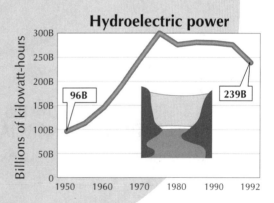

96B
239B

Petroleum

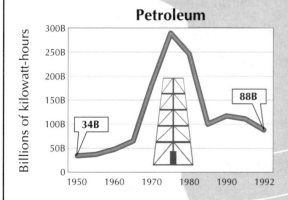

34B
88B

Geothermal and other

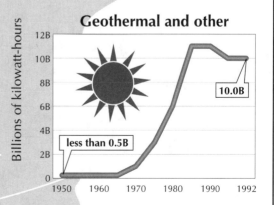

less than 0.5B
10.0B

Source: U.S. Department of Energy

*T=Trillion (1,000 Billion)

U.S. ELECTRICITY GENERATION, 1997
(Sources of electricity, in percentage)

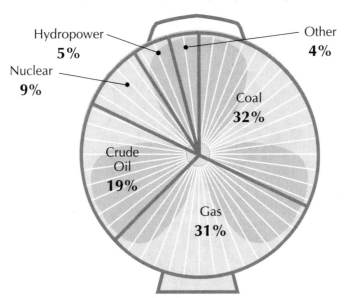

Hydropower
5%

Nuclear
9%

Other
4%

Coal
32%

Crude
Oil
19%

Gas
31%

Source: Energy Information Administration

TOP 12 STATES IN NUMBER OF
OPERATING COMMERCIAL NUCLEAR PLANTS, 1997

(With rankings)

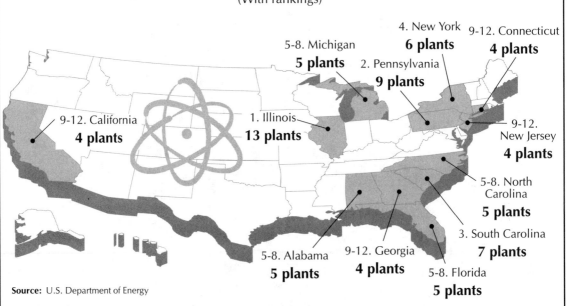

4. New York
6 plants

9-12. Connecticut
4 plants

5-8. Michigan
5 plants

2. Pennsylvania
9 plants

9-12. California
4 plants

1. Illinois
13 plants

9-12.
New Jersey
4 plants

5-8. North
Carolina
5 plants

3. South Carolina
7 plants

5-8. Alabama
5 plants

9-12. Georgia
4 plants

5-8. Florida
5 plants

Source: U.S. Department of Energy

U.S. ELECTRICITY GENERATION BY NUCLEAR POWER, 1965–1997

Net generation of electricity

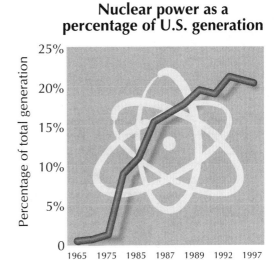

Billions of kilowatt hours

700B
600B
500B
400B
300B
200B
100B
0

1965 1975 1985 1987 1989 1992 1997

Nuclear power as a percentage of U.S. generation

Percentage of total generation

25%
20%
15%
10%
5%
0

1965 1975 1985 1987 1989 1992 1997

Source: U.S. Department of Energy

RESERVES OF NATURAL GAS BEGIN TO RISE AGAIN, 1980–1997

(In trillions* of cubic feet)

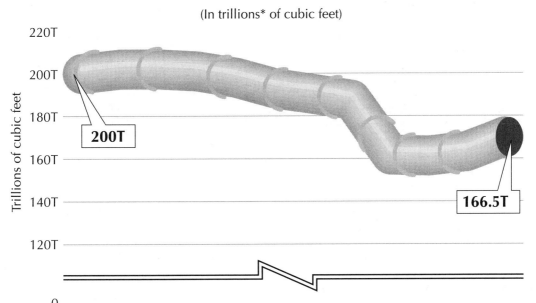

Trillions of cubic feet

220T
200T
180T
160T
140T
120T
0

200T

166.5T

1980 1981 1982 1983 1984 1985 1986 1987 1988 1990 1991 1997

Source: U.S. Department of Energy

*Trillion=1,000 billion

ENERGY CONSUMPTION

As the U.S. population has increased, so has its thirst for energy. The most dramatic increase has been in demand for electricity. The nation used 380 times more electricity in 1980 than it did in 1900. Furthermore, the U.S. uses more energy than any other nation in the world.

Growth in energy consumption has continued steadily in recent years. At the same time, however, people have become more energy-conscious, thanks to public education campaigns about environmental concerns and the growing realization that fossil fuel reserves are dwindling. This has led to energy-saving measures in industry, residences, and commercial establishments. Cars today travel farther on a gallon of gas, and new home appliances consume significantly less energy than their counterparts of 10 or 20 years ago. Economics also has spurred conservation efforts. The average price of electricity rose from 1.7 cents per kilowatt-hour in 1970 to 7.9 cents in 1996.

From 1980 to 1995, the average annual energy consumption per U.S. household dropped from 126 million Btu's to 93 million Btu's. Nonetheless, Americans continue to consume more energy per capita than residents of any other country.

FINGERTIP FACTS

☛ The U.S. produces less energy than it consumes. In 1997, it produced 72.3 quadrillion Btu's and consumed a record 94.2 quadrillion.

☛ In per capita terms, the leading U.S. energy consumer is Alaska (1.1 billion Btu's per person in 1995).

☛ In 1993, more than half of the oil used in the U.S. was imported.

☛ Although the United States had about one-fourth the population China did in 1996, the U.S. used 60% more energy than China. In fact, the U.S. used 25% of the total energy consumed in the entire world.

☛ U.S. consumption increased only 1% from 1996 to 1997. This slow growth was due mainly to the cool summer and warm winter, which cut down on energy use.

☛ The state with the highest overall energy consumption in 1995 was Texas with 10,511 trillion Btu. The state with the lowest total consumption was Vermont with 149 trillion Btu.

☛ Of the 94.2 quadrillion Btu's consumed in the U.S. in 1997, electricity generation consumed the largest portion (36.3%).

☛ Between 1980 and 1997, U.S. energy consumption increased 19%. During this time, 20 million new households were formed, using 14 million new microwaves, 17 million new televisions, and 15 million new air conditioners.

☛ Almost all (96%) U.S. commercial buildings use electricity; 55.5% use natural gas.

☛ Most U.S. homes are heated with natural gas (51.7%). Electricity heats 21.5% of U.S. homes.

☛ Households use energy mainly for heating (52% of energy consumed), followed by water heating (18%), cooking and refrigeration (11%), air conditioning (8%), and combined other uses (11%).

U.S. CONSUMPTION OF ENERGY, 1950–1995

(Total and per capita consumption of energy, in quadrillions* of British thermal units, or Btu's)

Total energy consumption

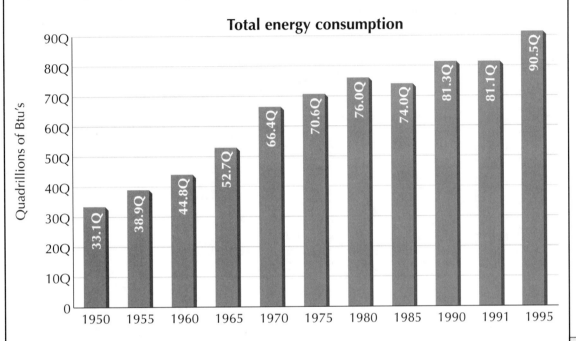

Quadrillions of Btu's

1950	1955	1960	1965	1970	1975	1980	1985	1990	1991	1995
33.1Q	38.9Q	44.8Q	52.7Q	66.4Q	70.6Q	76.0Q	74.0Q	81.3Q	81.1Q	90.5Q

Per capita consumption

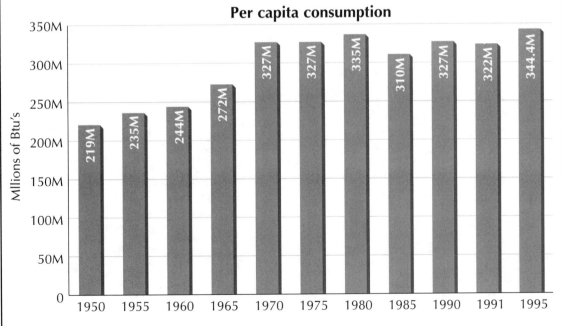

Millions of Btu's

1950	1955	1960	1965	1970	1975	1980	1985	1990	1991	1995
219M	235M	244M	272M	327M	327M	335M	310M	327M	322M	344.4M

Source: U.S. Department of Energy

*Quadrillion=1,000 trillion

WORLD'S MAJOR ENERGY CONSUMERS, 1996

The following countries rank highest in global consumption of primary energy, which includes petroleum, coal, nuclear energy, hydroelectricity, and natural gas, consumption in quadrillions* of British thermal units, or Btu's:

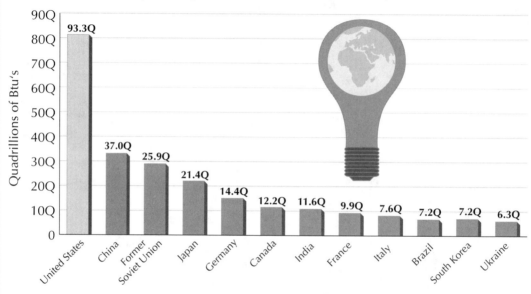

Source: Energy Information Administration

*Quadrillion=1,000 trillion

TOP 10 ENERGY-CONSUMING STATES, PER CAPITA, 1995

(In British thermal units, or Btu's, with rankings)

10. Montana
435.4M

5. North Dakota
545.8M

9. Indiana
447.2M

3. Wyoming
845.6M

8. West Virginia
448.7M

7. Alabama
455.3M

1. Alaska
1.1B

4. Texas
559.1M

2. Louisiana
879.1M

6. Kentucky
459.0M

Source: Energy Information Administration

U.S. ENERGY OVERVIEW, 1960 vs. 1997
(In quadrillions* of British thermal units, or Btu's)

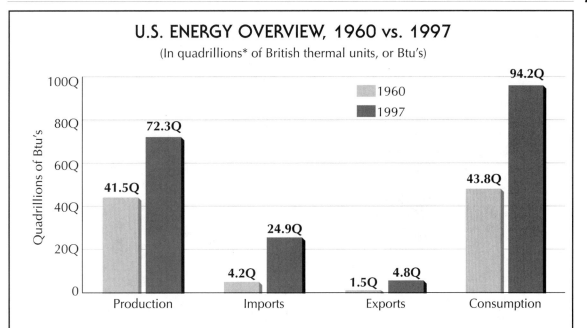

Production	1960	1997
Crude Oil	14.9Q	13.6Q
Natural gas and plant liquids	1.5Q	2.5Q
Natural gas	12.7Q	19.5Q
Coal	10.8Q	23.2Q
Nuclear electric power	0.01Q	6.7Q
Hydroelectric power	1.6Q	3.7Q
Others	Less than 0.005Q	0.2Q

Imports	1960	1997
Crude Oil	2.2Q	18.2Q
Petroleum products	1.8Q	3.4Q
Natural gas	0.2Q	3.0Q
Others	0.1Q	0.5Q

Exports	1960	1997
Coal	1.1Q	2.2Q
Crude oil and petroleum products	0.4Q	2.1Q
Others	0.1Q	0.3Q

Consumption	1960	1997
Petroleum products	19.9Q	36.3Q
Natural gas	12.4Q	22.6Q
Coal	9.8Q	22.6Q
Nuclear power	0.0Q	6.7Q
Hydroelectric power	1.7Q	3.9Q
Others	Less than 0.005Q	0.8Q

Source: U.S. Department of Energy

*Quadrillion=1,000 trillion

HOW AMERICAN HOMES ARE HEATED

(By source of heat, in percentage of homes)

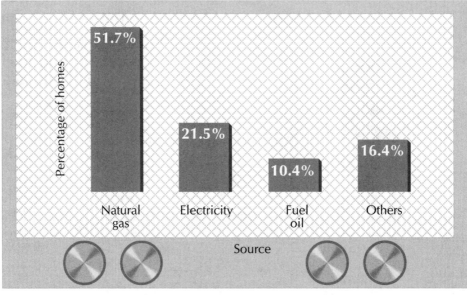

Percentage of homes

51.7%

21.5%

10.4%

16.4%

Natural gas | Electricity | Fuel oil | Others

Source

Source: Energy Information Administration

HOUSEHOLD ENERGY USE

(How energy is used in U.S. households, in percentage)

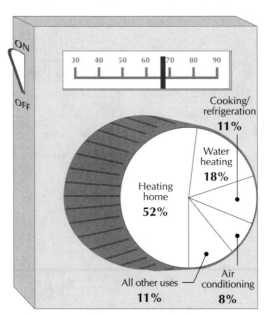

ON

OFF

30 40 50 60 70 80 90

Cooking/
refrigeration
11%

Water
heating
18%

Heating
home
52%

Air
conditioning
8%

All other uses
11%

Source: U.S. Energy Information Administration

U.S. PRODUCTION AND CONSUMPTION OF PETROLEUM PRODUCTS, 1970–1997

(In quadrillions* of British thermal units, or Btu's)

■ Production
■ Consumption

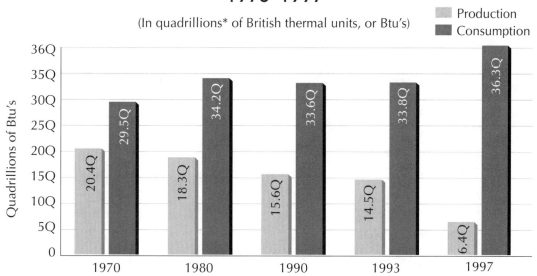

Quadrillions of Btu's

20.4Q 29.5Q 18.3Q 34.2Q 15.6Q 33.6Q 14.5Q 33.8Q 6.4Q 36.3Q

1970   1980   1990   1993   1997

Source: U.S. Energy Information Administration

*Quadrillion=1,000 trillion

PERCENTAGE OF IMPORTED OIL IN U.S., 1973 vs. 1997

In 1973, immediately after the Arab oil embargo, a much smaller percentage of foreign oil was used in the U.S. than in 1997:

36.1%

1973

61%

1997

Source: Statistics based on American Petroleum Institute

9

MONEY
AND
BUSINESS

B I G   B U S I N E S S

The generally good health of big business during 1997 and the first half of 1998 was reflected in record profits and soaring stock market prices. General Motors, the largest corporation in the U.S., had 1997 sales of $178 billion and profits of $5.7 billion.

Even large corporations face stiff competition, both domestically and internationally. One response has been to "downsize" to make the company's operations "leaner and meaner." Another has been a movement toward mergers, alliances, and other agreements. This latter course has been particularly widespread in the health care and communications industries. In 1995, for example, United Healthcare, an operator of health maintenance organizations (HMOs), paid $1.65 billion to buy Metrahealth, a more traditional health insurance company. Two California HMOs merged to form a company with a stock market value exceeding $4 billion.

Even whole industries are merging. This is best seen among the communications, information, and entertainment industries, which have been dramatically changed by technological advances. Several record-setting mergers occurred in 1998, each involving purchases of more than $70 billion. The first was Citicorp's acquisition of Travelers Group, Inc., followed by Ameritech Corporation's purchase of SBC Communications. And back in 1995, the already massive Disney bought the television network ABC, while Westinghouse acquired ABC's rival, CBS. The impact of this move was felt throughout the entertainment industry and many other fields.

FINGERTIP FACTS

- In 1997, the U.S. companies with the highest sales were General Motors ($178 billion), Ford ($154 billion), and Exxon ($122 billion). The top-ranking companies in terms of profits were Exxon ($8.4 billion), General Electric ($8.2 billion), and Intel ($6.9 billion).

- The top U.S. companies, based on stock values on December 31, 1997, were General Electric ($272 billion), Coca-Cola ($229 billion), Exxon ($182 billion), Merek & Co. ($78.6 billion), and Philip Morris ($127 billion).

- Wal-Mart is the world's largest retailer, with a market value of $90 billion in 1997 and sales of $119 billion. In second place is Sears—valued at $38.7 billion, with 1997 sales of $41.3 billion.

- IBM is the top-ranked corporation in the computer industry, with assets totaling $86.1 billion, 1997 sales of $78.5 billion, and profits of $6.1 billion.

- In 1997, the companies with the most franchises were McDonald's (13,748), 7-Eleven (12,857), Subway (12,233), Burger King (7,278), and Century 21 Real Estate (6,176).

- The average number of shares traded daily on the New York Stock Exchange reached a record 521 million in 1997.

- Major deals of 1998 included Citicorp's $73 billion acquisition of Travelers Group Inc., Ameritech Corporation's $72 billion purchase of SBC Communications, and the $70 billion merger of Bell Atlantic and GTE Corporation.

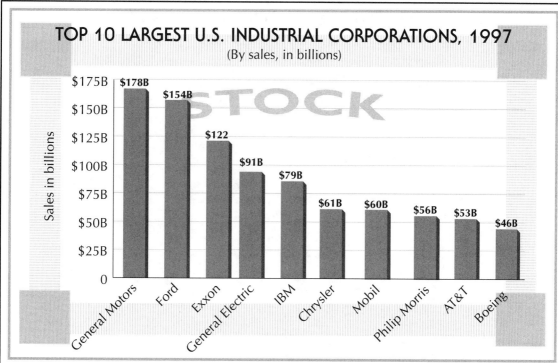

TOP 10 LARGEST U.S. INDUSTRIAL CORPORATIONS, 1997
(By sales, in billions)

- General Motors: $178B
- Ford: $154B
- Exxon: $122
- General Electric: $91B
- IBM: $79B
- Chrysler: $61B
- Mobil: $60B
- Philip Morris: $56B
- AT&T: $53B
- Boeing: $46B

Source: Statistics from *Fortune* magazine

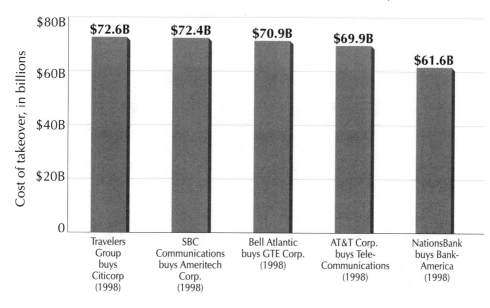

TOP 5 U.S. BUSINESS BUYOUTS
Most expensive takeovers in U.S. history:

- Travelers Group buys Citicorp (1998): $72.6B
- SBC Communications buys Ameritech Corp. (1998): $72.4B
- Bell Atlantic buys GTE Corp. (1998): $70.9B
- AT&T Corp. buys Tele-Communications (1998): $69.9B
- NationsBank buys Bank-America (1998): $61.6B

Source: Based on statistics from *USA Today; U.S. News & World Report*

TOP 10 U.S RETAIL COMPANIES, 1997
(By sales in billions of dollars)

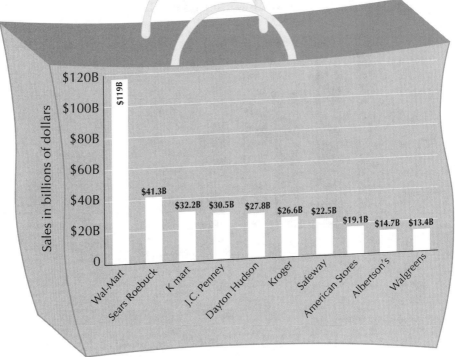

Sales in billions of dollars

Wal-Mart	$119B
Sears Roebuck	$41.3B
K mart	$32.2B
J.C. Penney	$30.5B
Dayton Hudson	$27.8B
Kroger	$26.6B
Safeway	$22.5B
American Stores	$19.1B
Albertson's	$14.7B
Walgreens	$13.4B

Source: Statistics from *Fortune* magazine

DAILY TRADING ON NEW YORK STOCK EXCHANGE, 1900–1997
(Average number of shares traded daily)

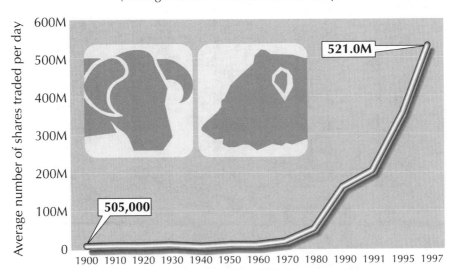

Average number of shares traded per day

521.0M

505,000

1900 1910 1920 1930 1940 1950 1960 1970 1980 1990 1991 1995 1997

Source: New York Stock Exchange

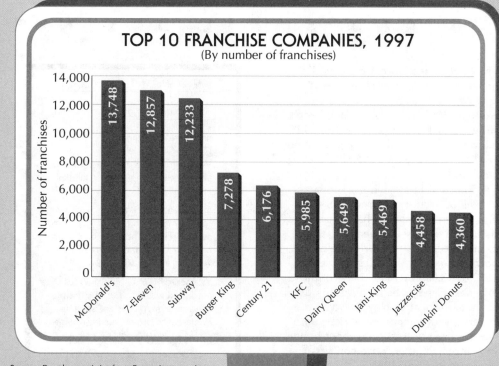

TOP 10 FRANCHISE COMPANIES, 1997
(By number of franchises)

Number of franchises

Company	Number
McDonald's	13,748
7-Eleven	12,857
Subway	12,233
Burger King	7,278
Century 21	6,176
KFC	5,985
Dairy Queen	5,649
Jani-King	5,469
Jazzercise	4,458
Dunkin' Donuts	4,360

Source: Based on statistics from *Enterprise* magazine

LARGEST AFRICAN-AMERICAN-OWNED BUSINESSES, 1997

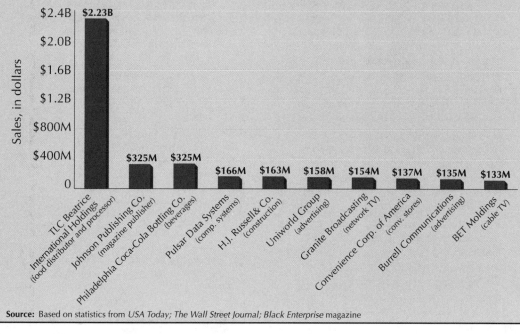

Sales, in dollars

Company	Sales
TLC Beatrice International Holdings (food distributor and processor)	$2.23B
Johnson Publishing Co. (magazine publisher)	$325M
Philadelphia Coca-Cola Bottling Co. (beverages)	$325M
Pulsar Data Systems (comp. systems)	$166M
H.J. Russell & Co. (construction)	$163M
Uniworld Group (advertising)	$158M
Granite Broadcasting (network TV)	$154M
Convenience Corp. of America (conv. stores)	$137M
Burrell Communications (advertising)	$135M
BET Holdings (cable TV)	$133M

Source: Based on statistics from *USA Today; The Wall Street Journal; Black Enterprise* magazine

J O B S   A N D   S M A L L   B U S I N E S S

The "civilian labor force" consists of all non-institutionalized civilians ages 16 and older who work or who are seeking work. In 1997, some 129 million people were working in the U.S.—up from 126 million in 1996. Of the 1997 population aged 16 years and older, 63.8% were employed.

The 1990s has been marked by the loss of job security for many U.S. workers. Large corporations have slashed thousands of jobs; Lockheed Martin, for example, cut its huge workforce by nearly 60%—from 32,000 employees in 1990 to 13,000 by 1995. Many of those lost jobs will never be replaced. In other cases, permanent employees have been replaced with temporary workers who work at lower wages and without health insurance and other fringe benefits. Between 1985 and 1995, the number of temporary workers in the American workforce tripled, to 2.1 million.

The corporate "downsizing" trend has contributed to the sharp decline in job stability. In the 1970s, employees had an average of only one or no job changes during that decade; in the 1980s, only 52% enjoyed such stability. The likelihood for the 1990s is that job instability will continue to worsen throughout the decade. Such instability hurts workers squarely in their wallets. In general, people who change jobs frequently, whether voluntarily or not, are more likely to experience wage declines; they will also have more difficulty accumulating pension benefits.

The good news is that there has been robust growth in new jobs. By 2006, more than 18 million new jobs are projected. Small and start-up businesses will be responsible for a significant portion of these jobs.

FINGERTIP FACTS

☞ The urban areas projected to gain the most new jobs in the U.S. between 1993 and 2015 are Atlanta, Georgia (1.46 million new jobs), Washington, D.C. (1.4 million), and Los Angeles-Long Beach, California (1.39 million).

☞ In 1997, about 16 million workers spent time on some entrepreneurial activity. These entrepreneurs represented 13% of all non-agricultural workers in the U.S.

☞ Women own 66% of businesses that are based in the home, but the percentage of men who are starting home-based businesses is growing.

☞ In 1997, the U.S. had 6.9 million incorporated businesses, 798,917 new incorporations, and 71,811 business failures.

☞ In 1996, there were 7.95 million women-owned businesses in the U.S. These businesses employed more than 18.5 million workers and generated $2.3 trillion in sales.

☞ The restaurant/food service industry is the largest small business employer ($4.7 million employees). The health care industry is second (4.4 million employees).

☞ In 1997, the Small Business Administration made a total of 47,198 loans to small, independently owned and operated businesses in the U.S; 15% of the loans, were to minority-owned businesses.

☞ The fastest-growing occupation in the U.S. is expected to be home health aides, rising from 347,000 in 1992 to between 794,000 and 835,000 by 2005—an increase of up to 140.6%

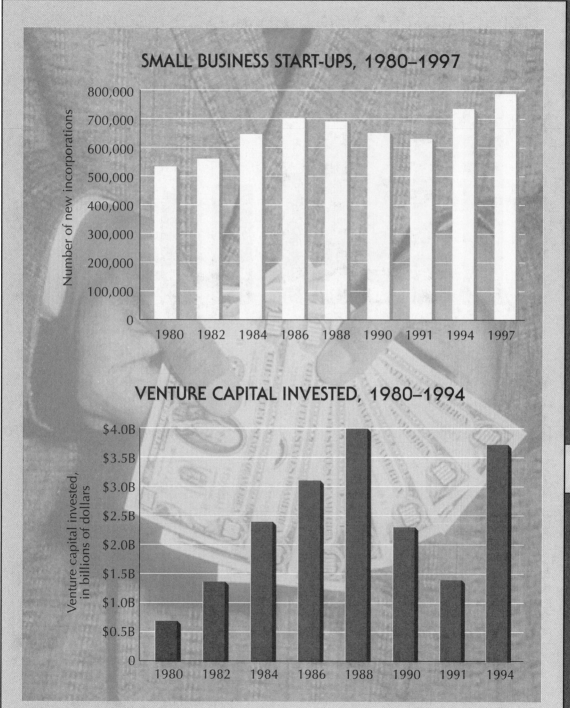

SMALL BUSINESS START-UPS, 1980–1997

Number of new incorporations

| | 1980 | 1982 | 1984 | 1986 | 1988 | 1990 | 1991 | 1994 | 1997 |

VENTURE CAPITAL INVESTED, 1980–1994

Venture capital invested, in billions of dollars

| | 1980 | 1982 | 1984 | 1986 | 1988 | 1990 | 1991 | 1994 |

Source: U.S. Small Business Administration

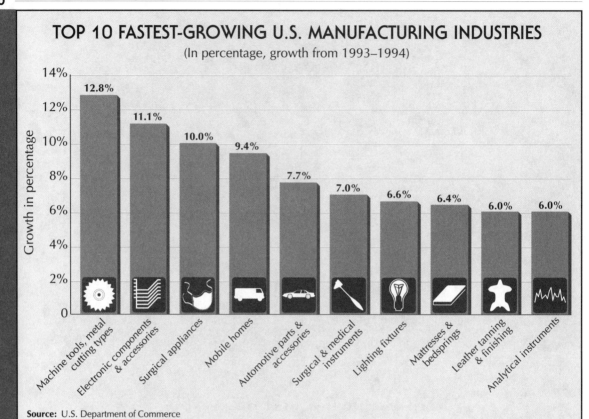

TOP 10 FASTEST-GROWING U.S. MANUFACTURING INDUSTRIES
(In percentage, growth from 1993–1994)

Growth in percentage

- Machine tools, metal cutting types — 12.8%
- Electronic components & accessories — 11.1%
- Surgical appliances — 10.0%
- Mobile homes — 9.4%
- Automotive parts & accessories — 7.7%
- Surgical & medical instruments — 7.0%
- Lighting fixtures — 6.6%
- Mattresses & bedsprings — 6.4%
- Leather tanning & finishing — 6.0%
- Analytical instruments — 6.0%

Source: U.S. Department of Commerce

TOP 10 FASTEST-GROWING OCCUPATIONS IN AMERICA, 1990–2005
(Growth in percentage)

Growth in percentage

- Home health aides
- Systems analysts & computer scientists
- Personal & home care aides
- Medical assistants
- Human services workers
- Radiologic technologists & technicians
- Medical secretaries
- Psychologists
- Travel agents
- Corrections officers

Source: U.S. Bureau of Labor Statistics

JOB CATEGORIES OF EMPLOYED PERSONS BY RACE, 1993

(Persons age 16 or older)

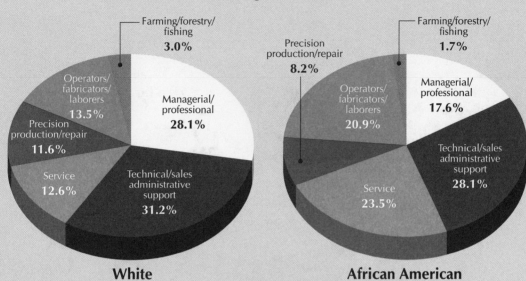

White

African American

Source: U.S. Department of Labor

U.S. BUSINESS SECTORS, BY NUMBER OF EMPLOYEES

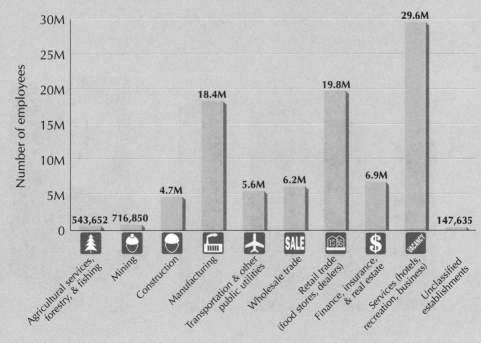

Source: U.S. Census Bureau

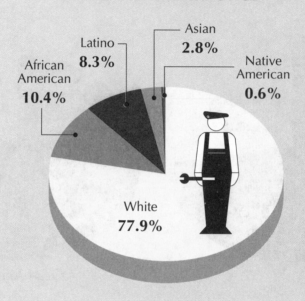

RACE OR ETHNICITY OF PEOPLE IN THE U.S. WORKFORCE

Asian **2.8%**

Latino **8.3%**

Native American **0.6%**

African American **10.4%**

White **77.9%**

Source: U.S. Census Bureau

PART-TIME WORKERS ON THE RISE, 1990–1993

More Americans are working part-time because they cannot get full-time jobs:

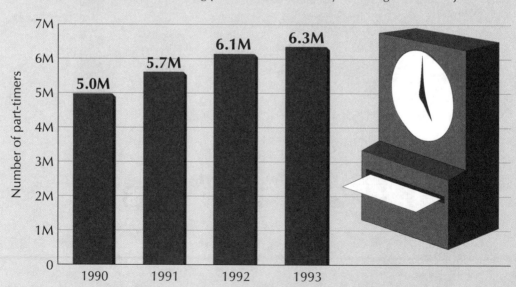

Source: U.S. Bureau of Labor Statistics

TOP 5 U.S. CITIES FOR BUSINESS

(In quality of labor pool, colleges, business resources; with rankings)

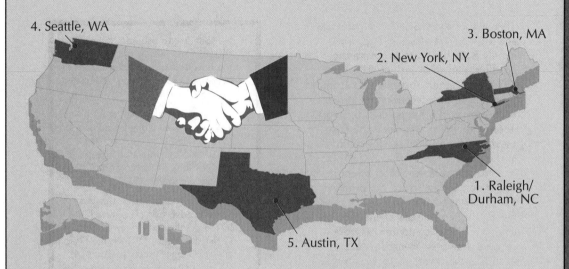

4. Seattle, WA

3. Boston, MA

2. New York, NY

1. Raleigh/
Durham, NC

5. Austin, TX

Source: Based on statistics from *Fortune*

GROWTH IN HISPANIC FIRMS CONTINUES

Hispanic-owned businesses are a bright spot in the sluggish U.S. economy:

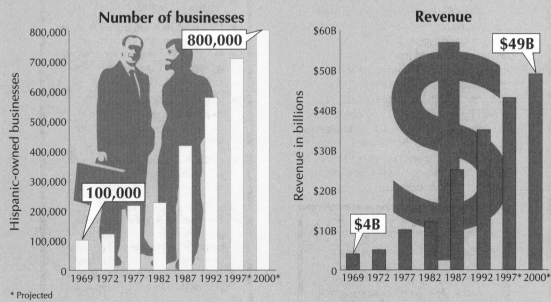

Number of businesses

Hispanic-owned businesses

800,000

100,000

1969 1972 1977 1982 1987 1992 1997* 2000*

Revenue

Revenue in billions

$60B

$50B

$40B

$30B

$20B

$10B

0

$49B

$4B

1969 1972 1977 1982 1987 1992 1997* 2000*

* Projected
Source: U.S. Census Bureau; *Hispanic Business*

ADVERTISING

Throughout the U.S. in 1997, national and local advertisers spent approximately $188 billion to promote their products and services—up 21% from 1994. Altogether, American companies spend more on advertising than their counterparts in other parts of the world. These expenditures include the costs of creating ads and then placing them in the media.

Newspapers, television, direct mail, magazines, and radio are the primary advertising media in the U.S. As greater numbers of consumers spend time "on-line" on various computer network services, however, advertisers are exploring that medium, too; in 1994, McDonald's aired what it called the first "on-line TV commercial."

The leading advertiser in 1997 was General Motors, which spent $2.2 billion for that year. General Motors was followed by Procter & Gamble ($1.7 billion), Philip Morris ($1.3 billion), and Chrysler ($1.1 billion). Much of their advertising money was spent on national network and "spot" television (spot ads, which target local markets, appear on selected network stations). When viewed by product category, the automotive industry was the biggest spender, followed by retail; business and consumer services; entertainment and amusements; foods; toiletries and cosmetics; drugs and remedies; travel, hotels, and resorts; direct response companies; and candy, snacks, and soft drinks.

FINGERTIP FACTS

☛ The largest industries involved in direct marketing are non-store retailers ($92 billion in sales), real estate ($46.5), and general merchandise stores ($39 billion).

☛ Ad spending to promote cigarettes totaled $569 million in 1997, with the bulk of it going to consumer magazines ($307 million) and television ($91 million).

☛ The largest catalog marketers in 1997 were Dell Computer Corp. ($11.9 billion in sales), Gateway 2000 ($6.3 billion), J.C. Penney Co. ($3.8 billion), and International Business Machines ($3.0 billion).

☛ Television gets the largest market share of advertising revenues (24% in 1997), followed by newspapers (22%), direct mail (20%), radio (7%) and telephone "yellow pages" (6%).

☛ Among magazine publishers, Time Warner receives the most advertising revenue, followed by Hearst, Condé Nast, and *The New York Times*.

☛ The automobile industry spent the most money on advertising in 1997 (12.8 billion), followed by retail (10.8 billion), and business ($9.0 billion).

☛ Magazines received the most advertising dollars from the automobile industry ($1.7 billion), the cosmetics industry ($1.1 billion), and the computer industry ($1.0 billion).

☛ In 1995, it cost about $325,000 to place a single 30-second ad on the television sitcom "Home Improvement."

☛ McCann-Erikson Worldwide topped U.S.-based ad agencies in 1997, with an income of approximately $1.8 billion.

☛ Many advertisers use celebrities to promote their products. In the early 1990s, Michael Jordan earned an estimated $30 million annually from endorsing products for Nike, McDonald's, and other companies.

TOP 10 U.S. AD AGENCIES, 1997

(By gross income, in millions and billions)

	0	$200M	$400M	$600M	$800M	$1.0B	$1.2B	$1.4B	$1.6B	$1.8B
McCann-Erickson Worldwide										$1.8B
DDB Needham Worldwide									$1.6B	
BBDO Worldwide								$1.5B		
J. Walter Thompson						$1.2B				
Ogilvy & Mather						$1.13B				
Young & Rubicam					$1.0B					
Ammirati Puris Lintas Worldwide					$973M					
Grey Advertising					$955M					
MVBMS/ EURO RSCG Worldwide					$952M					
Leo Burnett Co.				$878M						

Source: Statistics based on *Advertising Age* magazine

TOP 10 U.S. ADVERTISERS, 1997

(By annual spending)

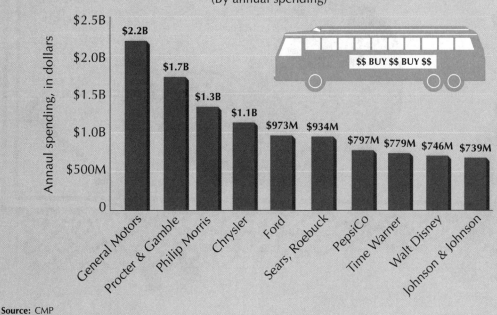

$$ BUY $$ BUY $$

	$2.2B	$1.7B	$1.3B	$1.1B	$973M	$934M	$797M	$779M	$746M	$739M
Annaul spending, in dollars	General Motors	Procter & Gamble	Philip Morris	Chrysler	Ford	Sears, Roebuck	PepsiCo	Time Warner	Walt Disney	Johnson & Johnson

Source: CMP

U.S. ADVERTISING SPENDING, 1776–1997

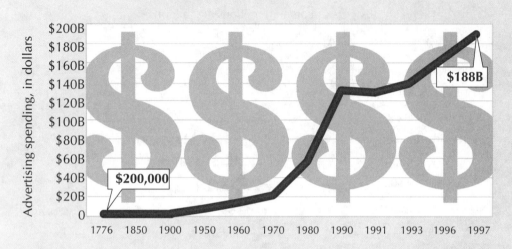

Source: Based on statistics from McCann-Erickson Worldwide

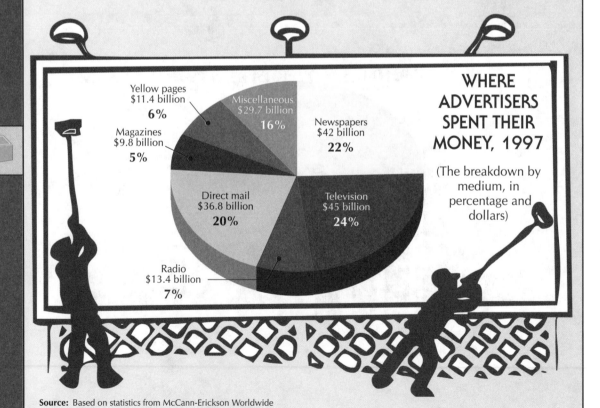

Yellow pages
$11.4 billion
6%

Magazines
$9.8 billion
5%

Miscellaneous
$29.7 billion
16%

Newspapers
$42 billion
22%

Direct mail
$36.8 billion
20%

Television
$45 billion
24%

Radio
$13.4 billion
7%

WHERE ADVERTISERS SPENT THEIR MONEY, 1997

(The breakdown by medium, in percentage and dollars)

Source: Based on statistics from McCann-Erickson Worldwide

TOP 10 ADVERTISING CAMPAIGNS, 1997

(Companies rated by television audiences)

1. Nissan
2. Budweiser
3. Pepsi
4. Milk
5. McDonalds

6. Coke
7. Little Caesars
8. M&M's
9. Ford
10. Levi's

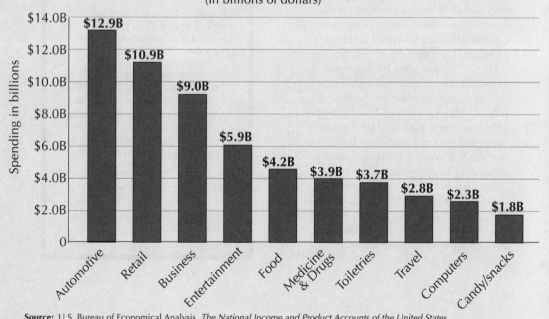

TOP 10 HIGHEST-SPENDING AD CATEGORIES, 1997

(In billions of dollars)

Spending in billions

Category	Spending
Automotive	$12.9B
Retail	$10.9B
Business	$9.0B
Entertainment	$5.9B
Food	$4.2B
Medicine & Drugs	$3.9B
Toiletries	$3.7B
Travel	$2.8B
Computers	$2.3B
Candy/snacks	$1.8B

Source: U.S. Bureau of Economical Analysis, *The National Income and Product Accounts of the United States*

THE COST OF LIVING

American consumers spent $4.4 trillion in 1993, up from $3.8 trillion in 1990, and $1.7 trillion in 1980. Increasingly, much of this money is not "cold cash," but, rather, hard plastic—outstanding balances on credit cards are growing much faster than the growth in consumer spending. At the end of 1994, balances outstanding on Visa and MasterCard credit cards were a record $256 billion, up 24% from 1993's $206 billion. And the number of credit cards has soared. At the end of 1993, there were 266.5 million Visa and MasterCard credit cards in circulation, up more than 25% from 208.3 million in 1990.

Everyone feels the pressure to "keep up"—whether it's a teenager who wants the latest footwear and CDs, parents who want their children to receive the best education and health care, or a company that needs high-tech equipment in order to meet customer demands. And few of us escape the costs of the unexpected—flood damage from a hurricane; hospital stays after an accident; losses from burglary, fraud, and other crimes. All these costs of living have continued to increase year by year.

The costs of some products and services have risen much faster than the consumer price index (which tracks the average change in prices over time); medical bills and the costs of attending college are examples of quick risers. Other products and services, however, have become bargains. Today, for example, personal computers far more powerful than the multi-million-dollar goliaths used to send men to the moon are affordable for millions of Americans.

FINGERTIP FACTS

☛ In 1996, residents of every state except North Dakota and Hawaii were able to stay ahead of inflation. The states with the highest 1-year gains were Rhode Island (7.3%), and New Hampshire (6.2%).

☛ The average cost of a house in the U.S. in 1997 was $159,700.

☛ By the time American babies born in 1997 reach age 18, their parents will have spent an average of $153,660 on them. Housing accounts for 33%, followed by food (18%), transportation (15%), and childcare (9%).

☛ Outstanding consumer credit totaled $1.23 trillion in 1997. Of this debt, 43% was for credit cards (528 billion), 34% was for automobiles ($414 billion), and 23% was for noninstallment credit (292 billion).

☛ Tuition and fees at 4-year public colleges averaged $3,111 in 1997–1998; at private colleges, they averaged $12,994.

☛ The number of young people living with their parents has increased— 61% of 18- to 24-year-olds lived at home or in college dorms in 1996, up from 47% in 1970. Among persons 25 to 34, the percentage rose from 8% in 1970 to 14% in 1996.

☛ Between 1993 and 1998, the cost of a concert ticket rose by more than 43%, amusement park admission increased 23%, and monthly cable television rates rose 41%.

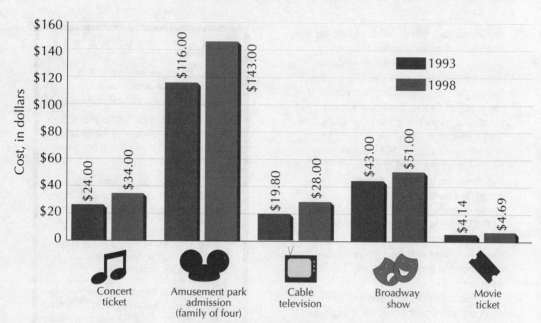

U.S. INFLATION IMPACT, 1993 vs. 1998
How costs have changed over the years for selected items, as a result of inflation:

Legend: 1993, 1998

Cost, in dollars

Concert ticket: $24.00 / $34.00
Amusement park admission (family of four): $116.00 / $143.00
Cable television: $19.80 / $28.00
Broadway show: $43.00 / $51.00
Movie ticket: $4.14 / $4.69

Source: U.S. Department of Commerce; U.S. Department of Labor; *USA Today*

PRICES AND INFLATION EASE, 1982–1993

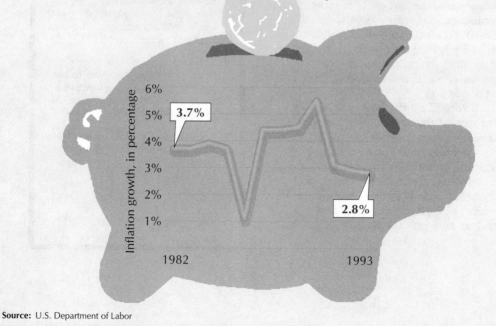

Inflation growth, in percentage

3.7% (1982) ... 2.8% (1993)

Source: U.S. Department of Labor

BANKING

American taxpayers—who picked up the multi-billion-dollar tab for the savings and loan crisis of the 1980s—may be surprised to learn that the U.S. banking industry is no longer quite so rocky. It has enjoyed robust profits in recent years, thanks to the growth of loans, low loan losses, and healthy interest income. Indeed, more than 97% of banks were profitable in the third quarter of 1997. But the industry is not out of the woods. There are more than 10,000 banks in America, with a total of some 54,000 branches. Various changes in the banking industry are expected to cut these numbers and lead to significant lay-offs among the nation's nearly 1.5 million bank employees.

The trend of recent years toward mergers and consolidations is expected to continue. The use of automated teller machines (ATMs) and personal-computer-based home banking is expected to rise. Brokerage houses and other financial institutions will become increasingly powerful competitors to banks—but banks are fighting back by adding the sale of annuities, mutual funds, and other financial products and services to their list of offerings.

Before June 1997, interstate banking was allowed, though bank "holding companies"—companies with controlling stock holdings in one or more subsidiaries—to maintain separate banks in each state. Once this requirement was lifted, "interstate branching" brought the industry's big players into many small markets once only served by local banks.

FINGERTIP FACTS

- The U.S. has more than 10,000 commercial banks, with an average of 5.8 bank employees per 1,000 citizens.

- Of the nation's top 100 banks, 39% offered fully-functioning Internet banking in 1998. This number has increased more than 50% from 1997.

- Of the world's 50 largest banks in 1998, the greatest percentage (28%) were Japanese; Germany came in second with 18%.

- Chase Manhattan Corp. is the largest U.S. commercial bank, with more than $365 billion in assets.

- About 1,200 banks and credit unions offered online banking in 1998 (6% of the market). By 2003, this number is expected to grow to 15,845 banks (75% of the market).

- Banks process about 64 billion checks per year. Automated banking would reduce the number of checks handled to 40 billion by 2003.

- The total net income of insured commercial banks continues to rise. In 1989, the net income was $15.5 billion dollars. By 1998, it had risen to $61.5 billion—a 75% increase.

- About 55% of all retail banking transactions take place at ATMs or via the telephone; only 43% occur at bank branches.

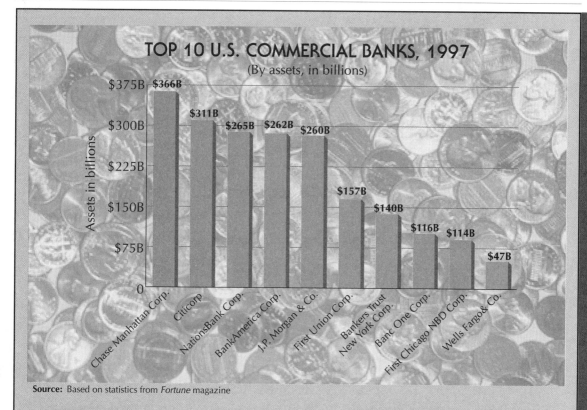

TOP 10 U.S. COMMERCIAL BANKS, 1997
(By assets, in billions)

Assets in billions

- Chase Manhattan Corp.: $366B
- Citicorp: $311B
- NationsBank Corp.: $265B
- BankAmerica Corp.: $262B
- J.P. Morgan & Co.: $260B
- First Union Corp.: $157B
- Bankers Trust New York Corp.: $140B
- Banc One Corp.: $116B
- First Chicago NBD Corp.: $114B
- Wells Fargo& Co.: $47B

Source: Based on statistics from *Fortune* magazine

TOP 10 BANKING COMPANIES IN AMOUNT OF MUTUAL FUND ASSETS
(In billions)

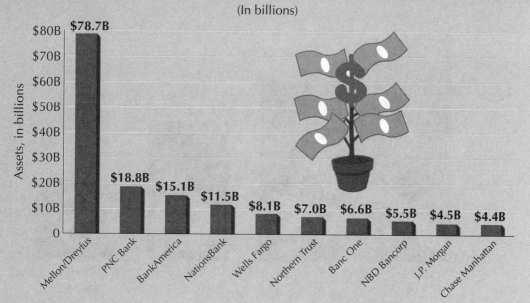

Assets, in billions

- Mellon/Dreyfus: $78.7B
- PNC Bank: $18.8B
- BankAmerica: $15.1B
- NationsBank: $11.5B
- Wells Fargo: $8.1B
- Northern Trust: $7.0B
- Banc One: $6.6B
- NBD Bancorp: $5.5B
- J.P. Morgan: $4.5B
- Chase Manhattan: $4.4B

Source: Based on statistics from Lipper Analytical Services

OFF-SITE BANKING

Less than half of all banking transactions are done at bank branch offices.
Automated teller machines (ATMs) are the most popular off-site option:

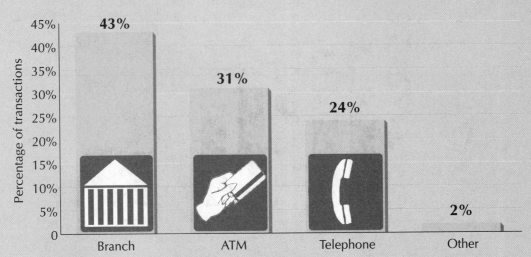

43% Branch
31% ATM
24% Telephone
2% Other

Percentage of transactions

Source: Bank Administration Institute

BANKING FEES RISE

Average bank service fees soared from 1990 to 1993. Here, some representative fee increases,
compared to the consumer price index increase during the same period:

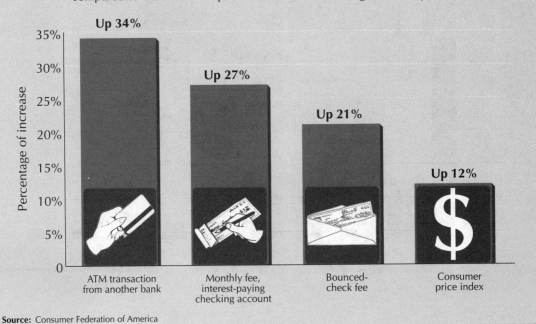

Up 34% ATM transaction from another bank
Up 27% Monthly fee, interest-paying checking account
Up 21% Bounced-check fee
Up 12% Consumer price index

Percentage of increase

Source: Consumer Federation of America

MUTUAL FUNDS FLOURISH, 1983–1997
(Assets of all U.S. mutual funds, in billions and trillions* of dollars)

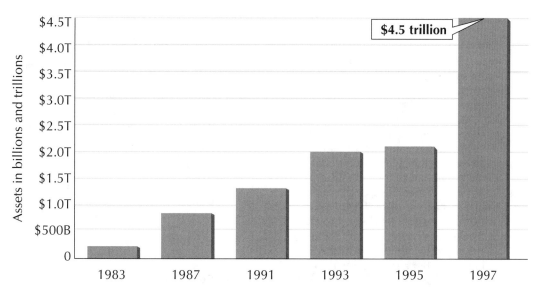

*1 trillion = 1,000 billion
Source: Based on statistics from Investment Company Inst.

THE AMERICAN CREDIT CRUNCH, 1980–1992
(Household debt as a percentage of personal income)

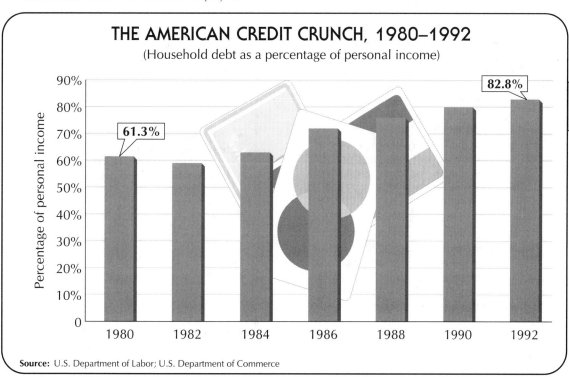

Source: U.S. Department of Labor; U.S. Department of Commerce

E X P O R T S   A N D   I M P O R T S

International trade has a major impact on the U.S. economy and Americans' lives. Workers at exporting firms have wages that average 15% higher than workers at non-exporting firms; their benefits are 33% higher.

Because the U.S. has been spending more for its imports than it has been receiving for its exports, it has had a trade deficit. In May 1995, for example, the nation had an $11.43 billion deficit, as exports reached $64.81 billion but imports climbed to $76.24 billion.

Governments have always imposed tariffs and other trade barriers, generally to protect local industries from foreign competition. But a move away from such protectionism and toward the free flow of goods and services has become a strong trend in recent years. For example, the North American Free Trade Agreement (NAFTA), concluded in 1992, eliminated most trade barriers among Canada, Mexico, and the U.S. And this trade organization might grow in coming years—several Latin American countries have expressed interest in becoming part of an expanded NAFTA.

Exporting is not just for the large corporations. Twenty–three percent of U.S. companies with fewer than 500 employees exported products and services in 1996—up from 16% in 1993 and 11%in 1992.

The U.S. government would like to see more American companies prosper in international trade. It funds several trade-promotion programs that provide firms with business counseling, training, market research information, export subsidies, and export finance assistance.

FINGERTIP FACTS

☞ In 1997, U.S. exports totaled $689.2 billion, excluding goods and services under U.S. military grant programs. Manufactured goods accounted for the largest portion ($550.6 billion), followed by agricultural commodities (55.3 billion) and mineral fuels ($12.6 billion).

☞ Imports to the U.S. totaled $870.6 billion in 1997. Manufactured goods, accounted for the largest share ($728.9 billion), followed by mineral fuels ($78.2 billion) and agricultural commodities ($35.1 billion).

☞ Coca-Cola sells 69% of its soft drinks outside the U.S. Latin America is its biggest customer, taking 2.4 billion cases a year.

☞ In 1997, the United States earned the most export trade dollars from Canada ($151.7 billion), Mexico (71.4 billion), and Japan ($65.5 billion). The U.S. paid the most export dollars to Canada ($168.2), Japan ($121.6 billion), and Mexico ($85.9 billon).

☞ The United States exported $17.4 billion in clothing and textiles in 1997. That same year the U.S. imported $60.5 billion worth, a 70% difference.

☞ The U.S. imported $14.0 billion worth of footwear in 1997; South Korea ($2.3 billion) was the major source.

☞ In 1997, the U.S. exported $3.9 billion in furniture, with Canada importing nearly half of the total.

WORLD EXPORTS: THE U.S. SHARE, 1997

(By selected commodities)

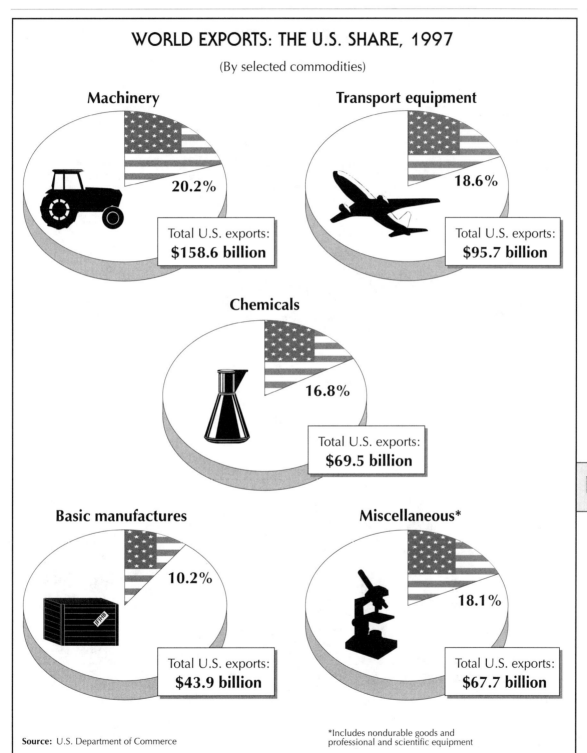

Machinery

20.2%

Total U.S. exports:
$158.6 billion

Transport equipment

18.6%

Total U.S. exports:
$95.7 billion

Chemicals

16.8%

Total U.S. exports:
$69.5 billion

Basic manufactures

10.2%

Total U.S. exports:
$43.9 billion

Miscellaneous*

18.1%

Total U.S. exports:
$67.7 billion

Source: U.S. Department of Commerce

*Includes nondurable goods and
professional and scientific equipment

TOP 5 STATES IN EXPORTS

(States whose economies rely most on exports, with rankings)

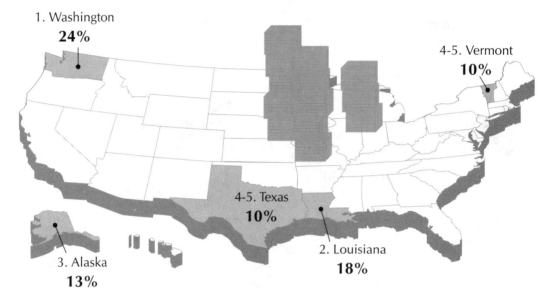

1. Washington
24%

4-5. Vermont
10%

4-5. Texas
10%

3. Alaska
13%

2. Louisiana
18%

Source: U.S. Department of Commerce; Regional Financial Associates

TOP 10 U.S. EXPORTS TO JAPAN
(In billions)

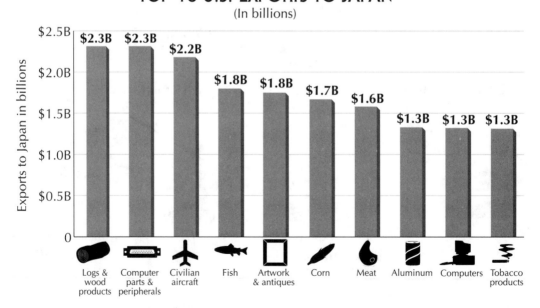

Source: U.S. Department of Commerce

AMERICAN FOOD IS BIG BUSINESS OVERSEAS

Some U.S. food and beverages businesses earn a large portion of their profits through exports. Here, the foreign earnings of some top American companies, in percentages of sales:

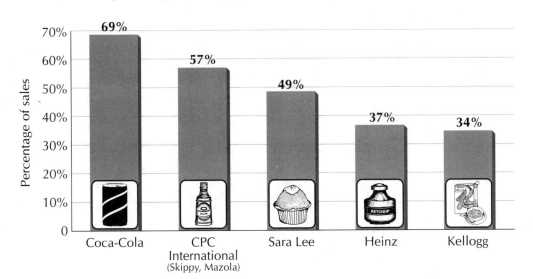

Percentage of sales

- Coca-Cola: **69%**
- CPC International (Skippy, Mazola): **57%**
- Sara Lee: **49%**
- Heinz: **37%**
- Kellogg: **34%**

Source: Prudential Securities; *Food Business* magazine

NUMBER OF U.S. JOBS SUPPORTED BY EXPORTS TO MEXICO, 1986–1992

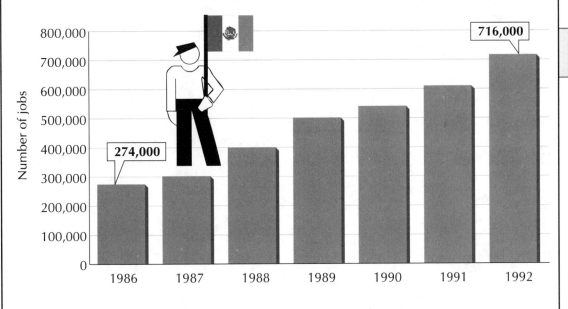

Number of jobs

- 1986: **274,000**
- 1992: **716,000**

Source: U.S. Government Accounting Office; Embassy of Mexico

10

SCIENCE
AND
TECHNOLOGY

TECHNOLOGY

Throughout history, people have vastly underestimated the impact of new technologies. Never has this been more true than for semiconductors, which are used to form miniaturized electronic components and integrated circuits. The microprocessors of personal computers (PCs) are made up of semiconductors, as are the electronic components of many other pieces of equipment critical to today's world.

Indeed, semiconductors and related technologies—especially the integration of computers and telephones—have so dramatically changed the American home and workplace environments that they have made hundreds of other technologies and machines obsolete. Among many things, computers have made the process of creating and communicating information infinitely faster and easier.

Electronic mail (e-mail) and fax machines deliver messages and information around the world in seconds, while airplane telephones allow people to call air-to-ground and ground-to-air. Cable services now enable people to shop, bank, and order movies from home. Desktop videoconferencing allows face-to-face meetings via PCs, saving time and money for busy executives.

An important result of these technological developments has been the growth of telecommuting—employees working at home or on the road, and communicating with their offices via computer and modem. Similarly, doctors in rural communities can consult instantly with medical experts and specialists at large urban hospitals, astronauts in space can beam photographs to Earth stations, and students in remote areas can review lessons with teachers at distant schools and universities.

FINGERTIP FACTS

☛ The number of in-vitro fertilized babies is growing. In 1984, only 180 babies were fertilized this way. By 1995, more than 11,600 were.

☛ There are about 200 satellites orbiting Earth solely for the purpose of private communications services, including pagers, telephones, and computers.

☛ In 1997, Americans placed 498 billion local calls, generating $52.9 billion in revenues.

☛ In the 10 years between 1987 and 1997, the number of people using pagers in the U.S. increased 88%.

☛ In 1984, there were 91,600 cellular telephone subscribers in the U.S. By 1997, the number had jumped to 54.0 million.

☛ The telephone was invented in 1876, and 70 years passed before it was found in 50% of U.S. households. Television, introduced in 1946, took only 8 years to get into 50% of the nation's homes.

☛ In 1980, the U.S. Patent and Trademark Office received 104,300 patent applications for inventions, from both U.S. citizens and residents of other countries. In 1998, it received 189,300. It issued 61,800 patents for inventions in 1980 and 151,020 in 1998. The company that received the most patents was IBM with 2,682.

☛ Despite the great boom in the use and sale of fax machines, they are still utilized by less than 10% of Americans.

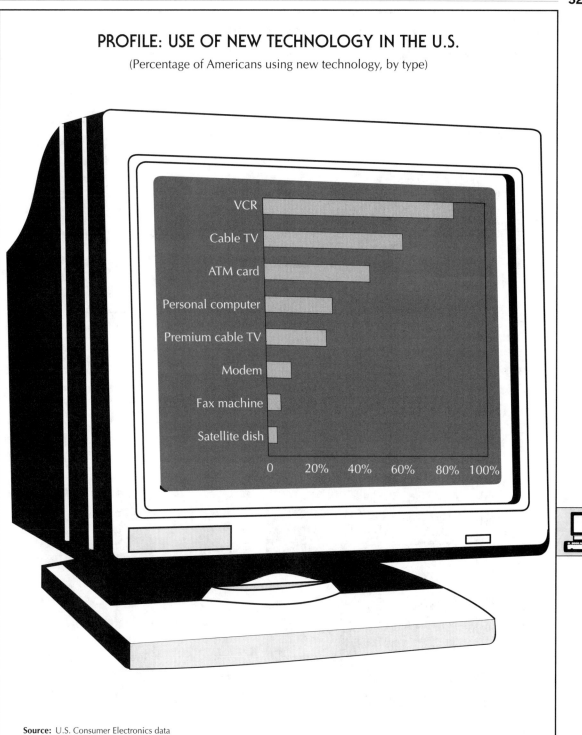

PROFILE: USE OF NEW TECHNOLOGY IN THE U.S.

(Percentage of Americans using new technology, by type)

VCR	
Cable TV	
ATM card	
Personal computer	
Premium cable TV	
Modem	
Fax machine	
Satellite dish	

0   20%   40%   60%   80%   100%

Source: U.S. Consumer Electronics data

THE ROAD TO ACCEPTING NEW TECHNOLOGY

(Number of years it took these inventions to be found in at least 50% of U.S. households)

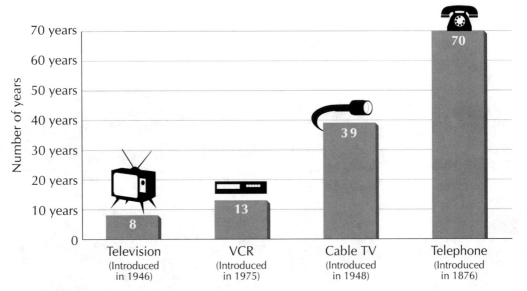

Number of years

- 70 years — 70 (Telephone)
- 60 years
- 50 years
- 40 years — 39 (Cable TV)
- 30 years
- 20 years
- 13 (VCR)
- 10 years — 8 (Television)
- 0

Television (Introduced in 1946)
VCR (Introduced in 1975)
Cable TV (Introduced in 1948)
Telephone (Introduced in 1876)

Source: Technologic Partners

SALES OF TELEPHONE ANSWERING DEVICES, 1989–1998

(Sales to dealers, in millions of devices)

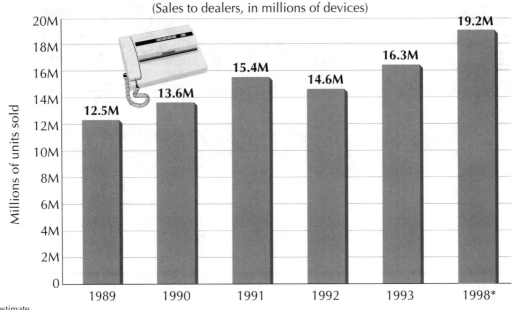

Millions of units sold

- 20M
- 19.2M (1998*)
- 18M
- 16.3M (1993)
- 16M — 15.4M (1991)
- 14.6M (1992)
- 14M — 13.6M (1990)
- 12.5M (1989)
- 12M
- 10M
- 8M
- 6M
- 4M
- 2M
- 0

1989   1990   1991   1992   1993   1998*

*estimate
Source: U.S. Consumer Electronics Industry

VIDEOCONFERENCING BOOMS, 1989–1995

(By number of teleconferencing systems sold)

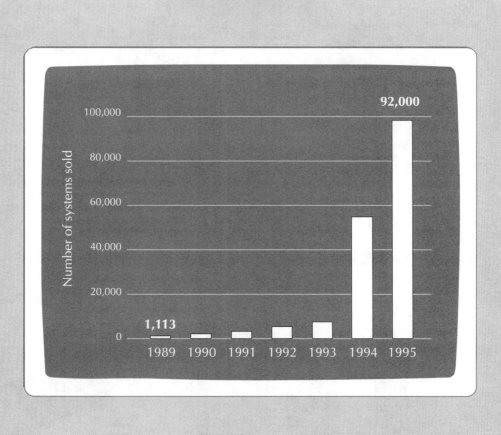

Number of systems sold

100,000
80,000
60,000
40,000
20,000
0

92,000

1,113

1989 1990 1991 1992 1993 1994 1995

Source: The Yankee Group

CELLULAR PHONE USE SKYROCKETS, 1984–1997

An estimated 17,000 people per day are joining the ranks
of cellular phone subscribers. The number of subscribers
increased from fewer than 100,000 in 1984 to
more than 54 million in 1997:

91,600

54.0M

December 1984

June 1997

Source: Cellular Telecommunications Industry Association; New York City Department of Consumer Affairs

PROFILE: MOST COMMON USES OF CELLULAR PHONES

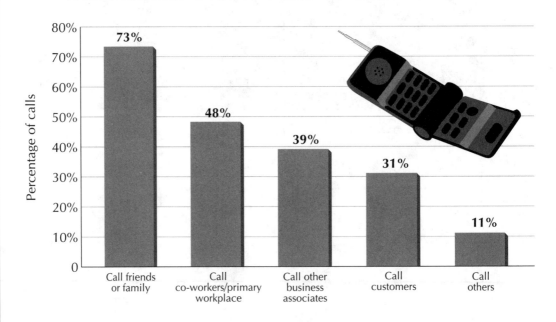

Percentage of calls

- 73% — Call friends or family
- 48% — Call co-workers/primary workplace
- 39% — Call other business associates
- 31% — Call customers
- 11% — Call others

Source: The Yankee Group

TOP CELLULAR PHONE CITIES, 1998

(Cities with the highest percentage of cellular phone owners)

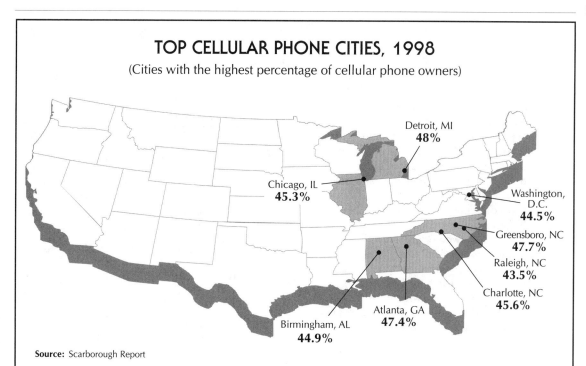

Detroit, MI
48%

Chicago, IL
45.3%

Washington, D.C.
44.5%

Greensboro, NC
47.7%

Raleigh, NC
43.5%

Charlotte, NC
45.6%

Atlanta, GA
47.4%

Birmingham, AL
44.9%

Source: Scarborough Report

IN-VITRO FERTILIZATIONS MULTIPLY

(Number of in-vitro fertilized babies
reported in the U.S., 1984 vs. 1995)

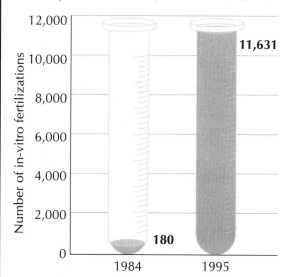

Number of in-vitro fertilizations

11,631

180

1984   1995

Source: American Fertility Society

USE OF SEMICONDUCTORS, AVERAGE BY INDUSTRY

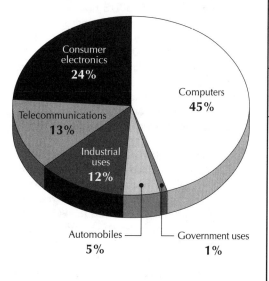

Consumer electronics
24%

Computers
45%

Telecommunications
13%

Industrial uses
12%

Automobiles
5%

Government uses
1%

Source: Semiconductor Industry Association

C O M P U T E R S

In the beginning, only some 50 years ago, there were mainframes—bulky computers so large they filled cavernous rooms. Today, personal computers (PCs) that sit on desktops or are carried in briefcases are commonplace, and their capabilities far outshine those of the first computers. There has also been an evolution in how computers are used. Originally viewed primarily as high-speed calculators and dedicated single-purpose data processing devices, they now are multipurpose tools that can be plugged into local and worldwide networks.

The PC market is more developed in the U.S. than anywhere else on the planet. Worldwide, 97.3 million PCs were shipped in 1998, while by 1998, some 118 million PCs were being used in the U.S. A survey of adults indicated that 83% used their computers for game-playing and other personal pursuits, 67% used them for work, and 46% for school. A 1998 survey of consumers found that 47.8% of U.S. households had one or more PCs, as compared to 28% in Germany, 23% in Great Britain, 15% in France, and 10% in Japan.

Technological development has been phenomenally rapid in the computer industry, providing users with ever faster and more powerful options. PCs have become smaller, lighter, more mobile, and more energy-efficient. CD-ROM and fax/modem hardware and software sales have soared. Going "on-line" and "surfing" the Internet attracts thousands of new participants daily. Even greater capabilities are predicted for PCs in the coming decade, including simple command and control voice recognition, miniature read-write CDs, and the ability to send and receive both voice and data simultaneously over wireless links.

FINGERTIP FACTS

☛ A typical 1995 desktop computer weighed about 25 pounds and had a processor about the size of a fingernail; it had 8 megabytes of internal memory plus a 1 gigabyte hard drive and 1.44 megabyte floppies for storage.

☛ Worldwide, the top computer vendors in 1997 were Compaq (16% market share), Dell (9.3%), Packard Bell (8.8%), IBM (8.7%), and Gateway 2000 (7.1%).

☛ American consumers spent an estimated $69.6 billion in 1998 to buy 35.5 million PCs.

☛ The federal government buys some 20% of all PCs sold in the U.S.

☛ By the year 2000, PC penetration in U.S. homes is predicted to reach 62.8%, as compared to 52.4% in Germany, France, and Great Britain.

☛ Approximately 24% of U.S. households had more than 1 computer in 1998.

☛ People living in households with PCs report that the machines are used about 30 hours per week. The most time is spent using entertainment software (32%), followed by word processing (22%), Internet games (16%), and business (19%).

☛ In 1997, Microsoft was the top software publisher with $944 million in sales—20% of the market share.

☛ An estimated 30 million people worldwide have access to the Internet and World Wide Web.

COMPUTER USE IN U.S. HOUSEHOLDS, 1998

(By characteristic, in percentage of households)

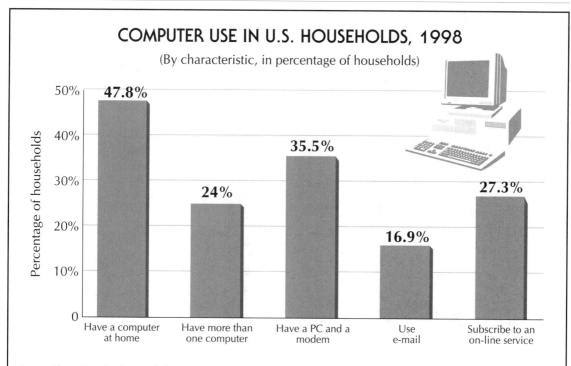

Source: Electronic Industries Association

HOW ADULTS USE THEIR HOME COMPUTERS

(Percentage of adult computer users)

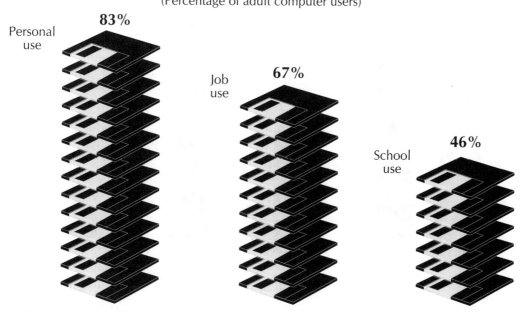

Source: Times Mirror Center for People and the Press

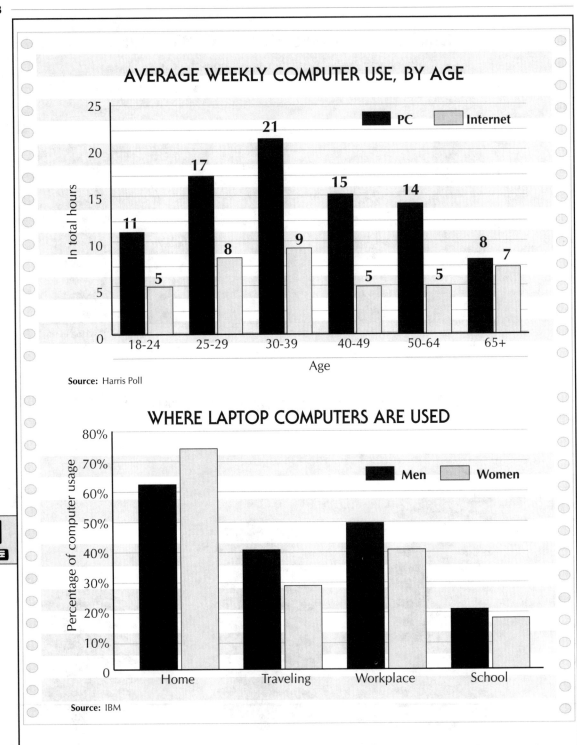

AVERAGE WEEKLY COMPUTER USE, BY AGE

PC   Internet

In total hours

Age	PC	Internet
18-24	11	5
25-29	17	8
30-39	21	9
40-49	15	5
50-64	14	5
65+	8	7

Source: Harris Poll

WHERE LAPTOP COMPUTERS ARE USED

Men   Women

Percentage of computer usage

Home   Traveling   Workplace   School

Source: IBM

TOP SELLERS OF PERSONAL COMPUTERS IN U.S., 1992–1997

(As percentage of all personal computers sold in U.S.)

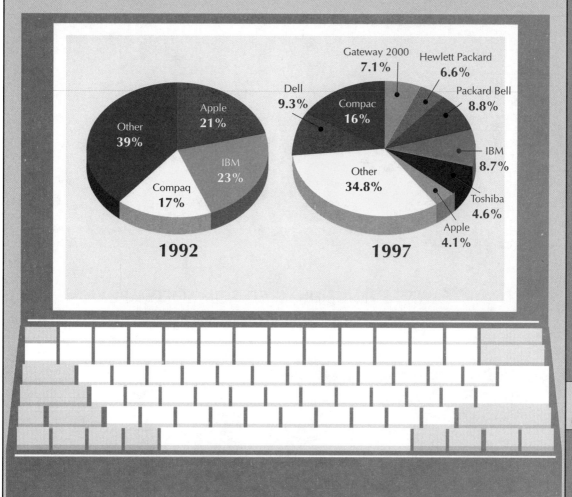

1992

Other 39%
Apple 21%
IBM 23%
Compaq 17%

1997

Dell 9.3%
Gateway 2000 7.1%
Hewlett Packard 6.6%
Packard Bell 8.8%
Compac 16%
IBM 8.7%
Toshiba 4.6%
Apple 4.1%
Other 34.8%

Source: Based on statistics from *USA Today; The New York Times; The Washington Post*

COMPUTER USERS DISC-COVER CD-ROM, 1988–1993

(Sales of CD-ROM drives and compact disc players)

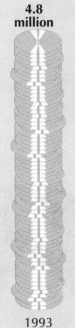

4.8 million

1.5 million

75,000

240,000

1988   1990   1992   1993

Source: Dataquest

SALES REVENUE FROM CD-ROM SOFTWARE

(Sales for first quarters of 1993 and 1994)

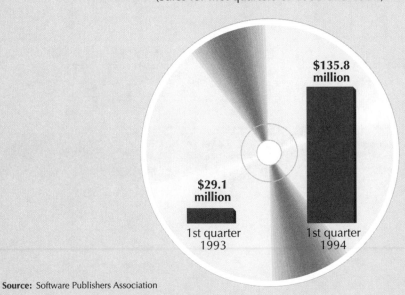

$135.8 million

$29.1 million

1st quarter 1993

1st quarter 1994

Source: Software Publishers Association

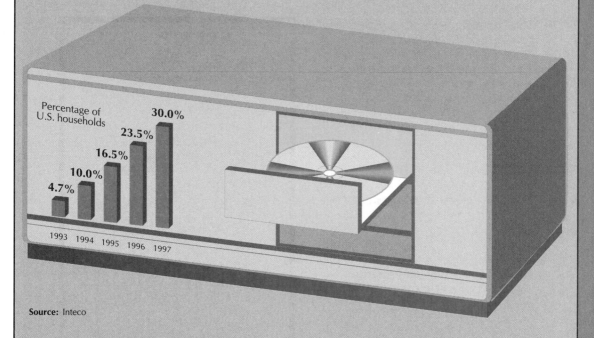

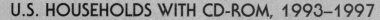

U.S. HOUSEHOLDS WITH CD-ROM, 1993–1997
(U.S. households projected to have computer-installed CD-ROM drives, in percentage)

Percentage of
U.S. households

30.0%

23.5%

16.5%

10.0%

4.7%

1993 1994 1995 1996 1997

Source: Inteco

PCs THAT BECOME OBSOLETE EACH YEAR

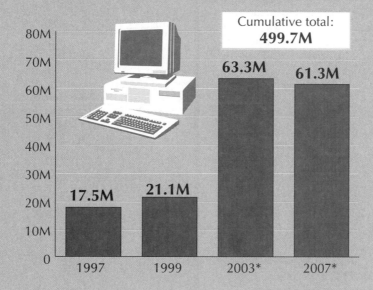

Cumulative total:
499.7M

80M

70M

63.3M

61.3M

60M

50M

40M

30M

20M

17.5M

21.1M

10M

0

1997   1999   2003*   2007*

* projected
Source: Stanford Resources, Inc.

THE INTERNET

Each day, millions of people explore a new communications frontier called "cyberspace"— the term for the electronic world that spans the globe and allows people to send letters, pay bills, post messages on computer bulletin boards, transfer computer files, converse with friends and strangers, gain access to libraries and newspapers that have gone "on-line," and much more. Today, the world of cyberspace seems infinite.

At the center of cyberspace is the Internet, a network of networks. The Net links literally millions of computers around the world. By late 1998, some 45.2 million households worldwide were using the Internet. The largest on-line services by the middle of 1998 were America Online (11.0 million subscribers), CompuServe (5.9 million), and Prodigy (3.7 million).

Accessibility to the Internet has been simplified by the World Wide Web, a system of viewing information stored on tens of thousands of computers connected to the Internet. The function known as "hypertext" allows people to move quickly from one document to another related document within the system—even if the latter document is on a computer halfway around the world. Software programs called "browsers" make it relatively easy to maneuver the Web and, in turn, to explore and use Internet resources. Many browsers are being marketed, and major on-line information services have incorporated browsers into the services they offer subscribers.

Males in their 20s and 30s are the primary users of the Internet. Females make up about 40% of the on-line community. Children under age 18 make up about 2.3% of users.

FINGERTIP FACTS

☞ Worldwide, in 1998, there were 20 million host computers on the Internet that provided interactive services of one type or another.

☞ In 1998, companies worldwide reported that they received about 6% of their business from Internet users. This percentage is expected to more than triple in 5 years.

☞ Alaska led the U.S. with the highest percentage of residents online (44%) in 1997. Mississippi had the lowest percentage (13.6%) that year.

☞ The number of domain names registered in the system reached 1.3 million in 1997—a 98% increase from 1993.

☞ By 1997, there were more than 100 million people connected to the Internet, and Internet traffic was doubling every 100 days.

☞ American consumers spent $518 million on-line in 1997, compared to more than $1.5 trillion in retail stores.

☞ The United States is the top country in world Internet usage, with 55% of the total Internet users. But, Finland is the top country in Internet usage per capita, with 244 users per 1,000 people.

☞ Of all U.S. Internet users, 83% use it for e-mail, 81% use it for access to the World Wide Web (including 67% who use search engines), and 44% visit company sites.

☞ Analysts estimate that the potential market for "information highway" goods and services will be approximately $3 trillion by the year 2000.

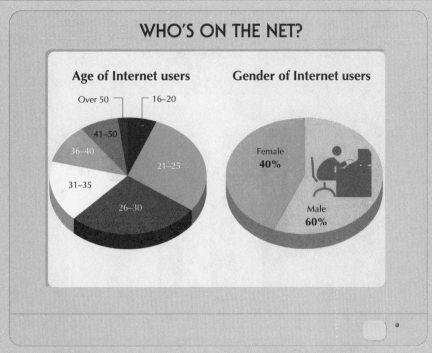

WHO'S ON THE NET?

Age of Internet users

Over 50

16–20

41–50

36–40

21–25

31–35

26–30

Gender of Internet users

Female
40%

Male
60%

Source: Based on statistics from *Time* magazine

HOW THE INTERNET IS USED BY U.S. COMPANIES

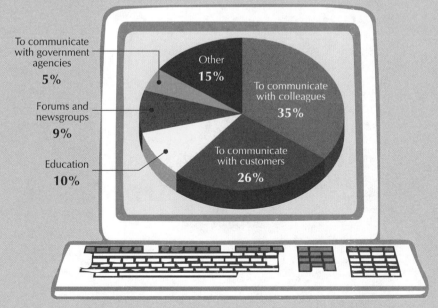

To communicate
with government
agencies
5%

Other
15%

To communicate
with colleagues
35%

Forums and
newsgroups
9%

Education
10%

To communicate
with customers
26%

Source: Based on statistics from Mark Lottor, Network Wizards; IBM; *USA Today*

HOW USERS LEARN ABOUT WEB SITES

About 75% of people who use the World Wide Web say they browse it about once a day. How they find out about Web sites:

Note: Many users get information from multiple sources
Source: Statistics based on Georgia Institute of Technology

TOP TEEN WEB SITES, AGES 12–17

(As percentage of age group that accessed site at least once)

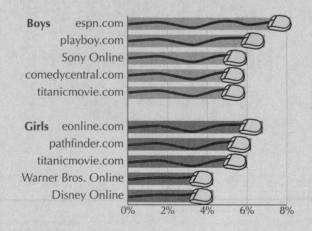

Source: Media Metrix

TOP 5 STATES WITH HIGHEST INTERNET USE

(By percentage of residents using Internet weekly)

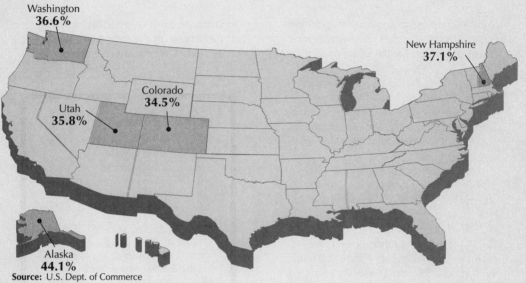

Washington
36.6%

New Hampshire
37.1%

Colorado
34.5%

Utah
35.8%

Alaska
44.1%

Source: U.S. Dept. of Commerce

TOP 5 STATES WITH LOWEST INTERNET USE

(By percentage of residents using Internet weekly)

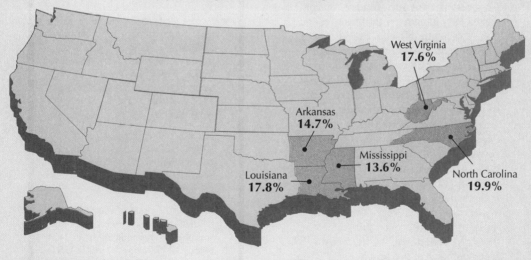

West Virginia
17.6%

Arkansas
14.7%

Mississippi
13.6%

Louisiana
17.8%

North Carolina
19.9%

Source: U.S. Dept. of Commerce

RESEARCH AND DEVELOPMENT

Scientific research and the development of technologies based on that research form the underpinnings of many modern societies. Without such work, the world would be lacking high-speed computers and telecommunications equipment, miracle medicines and diagnostic tools, efficient vehicles and appliances, and a host of other items that we take for granted today.

Each year, billions of dollars are spent worldwide on research and development (R&D). Although the percentage of Gross Domestic Product (GDP) devoted to R&D by the U.S. (2.7%) is similar to those of its main economic competitors (Japan, 2.0% and Germany, 2.8%) the U.S. devotes a large part of these funds to defense R&D, while the other two nations do not.

Federal funds traditionally have paid for a significant portion of research in the U.S.—of the $205.7 billion spent on R&D in 1997, about 30% were federal funds. In recent years, however, Congress has cut such funding sharply, particularly in areas without immediately recognizable applications. Corporations and large universities, which have made major contributions to science, have also cut back on basic research. Some scientists approve of this focused direction of funding. Others, however, point out that most modern technology arose from research undertaken without any obvious practical applications.

In 1970, about 543,800 scientists and engineers were employed in R&D at corporations, universities and colleges, other non-profit institutions, and federally funded R&D centers. By 1989, that number had grown to 949,300. In the 1990s, though, funding cutbacks have resulted in reduced employment

opportunities in some fields. In 1997, for example, an estimated 676,000 full-time R&D scientists and engineers were employed in industry—down 18,000 from 1991.

FINGERTIP FACTS

☞ In 1997, some 74.8% of R&D scientists and engineers were employed by industry; 7.2% worked for the federal government; and the remainder were employed at universities and other institutions.

☞ In 1960, the U.S. spent $13.5 billion on R&D; about 56% ($7.5 billion) of this was defense- or space-related. In 1997, R&D expenditures were $205.7 billion, of which 30% ($61.7 billion) were defense- or space-related.

☞ In 1997, two-thirds of R&D expenditures in science and engineering at universities and colleges were spent on basic research, the remainder on applied R&D.

☞ Of the funds that went to research and development in 1997, a total of 65% came from industry, 30% came from federal government, 2% came from colleges and universities, 2% came from other non-profits, and 1% came from non-federal government.

☞ In 1997, the largest portion of federal R&D funding was devoted to life sciences (51%), followed by engineering (19%) and physical sciences (11%).

☞ The largest group of the 461 Nobel Prize laureates in chemistry, physics, and physiology/medicine from 1901 through 1997 came from the U.S. (201), followed by Great Britain (72), Germany (60), and France (26).

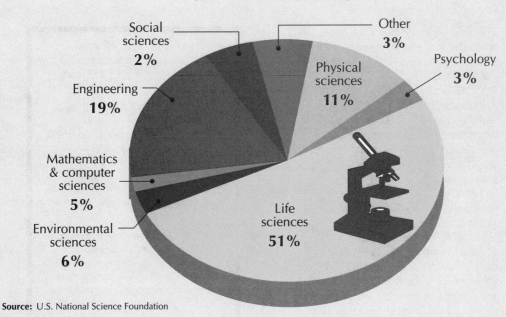

FEDERAL FUNDING FOR RESEARCH, 1997
(By science field, in percentage)

- Social sciences **2%**
- Engineering **19%**
- Mathematics & computer sciences **5%**
- Environmental sciences **6%**
- Life sciences **51%**
- Physical sciences **11%**
- Other **3%**
- Psychology **3%**

Source: U.S. National Science Foundation

FEDERAL RESEARCH & DEVELOPMENT SPENDING, 1960–1997
(In billions of dollars)

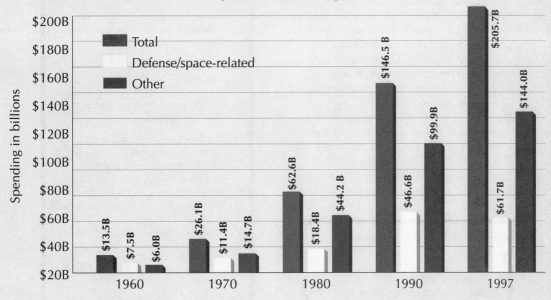

Spending in billions

- Total
- Defense/space-related
- Other

Year	Total	Defense/space-related	Other
1960	$13.5B	$7.5B	$6.0B
1970	$26.1B	$11.4B	$14.7B
1980	$62.6B	$18.4B	$44.2 B
1990	$146.5 B	$46.6B	$99.9B
1997	$205.7B	$61.7B	$144.0B

$200B
$180B
$160B
$140B
$120B
$100B
$80B
$60B
$40B
$20B

Source: U.S. National Science Foundation

N A S A

The Space Age began on October 4, 1957, when the first satellite was launched— a metal ball named *Sputnik I*, owned by the Soviet Union.

The National Aeronautics and Space Administration (NASA) is the government agency in the U.S. responsible for space technology and exploration. It was created by the National Aeronautics and Space Act of 1958—though many people may be surprised to learn that its roots go back to 1915, when the National Advisory Committee for Aeronautics was created.

NASA has had many successes since its founding. Its *Apollo* flights landed men on the moon; probes have sent back photographs from distant planets; and dozens of complex space-shuttle missions have been successfully completed, with many more planned. A major project under development is *Alpha*, a multinational space station that is scheduled to be completed in the year 2002. Weighing 443 tons and able to house a crew of 6, it will orbit Earth at an altitude of about 250 miles.

Today NASA faces growing pressure to justify its existence. It is being asked to demonstrate social relevance, practicality, and affordability at the same time that it continues to provide a bold vision of the future. Its budget for fiscal 1998 was $14.2 billion, a reduction of $152 million from its 1997 budget. Particularly hard hit was the portion earmarked for human space flight.

FINGERTIP FACTS

☛ The average cost per space shuttle flight in 1998 was $400 million, down from $590 million in 1993.

☛ In fiscal year 1998, NASA spent $2.9 billion on space-shuttle operations, up from $2.4 billion in 1995.

☛ From 1993 to 1998, NASA has concentrated on cost reduction in many areas of operation. Over this six-year period, the space shuttle budget decreased 29%, the shuttle work force decreased 23%, overtime work decreased 43%, and the cost per space flight decreased 31%.

☛ NASA spent the largest percentage of its budget, 41%, on science, aeronautics, and technology in 1995. A close second was human space flight, making up 40% of the budget.

☛ Through 1997, a total of 328 people had traveled into space, including 212 Americans. The U.S. had launched 112 manned flights.

☛ The first space-shuttle flight began on April 12, 1981. Ninety-one flights had occurred by the end of 1997.

☛ In 1994, two Russian cosmonauts flew on U.S. space shuttles. In 1995, Norman E. Thagard became the first U.S. astronaut to travel into space aboard a Russian spacecraft.

☛ The U.S. Space Command uses radar to track some 7,000 pieces of orbiting debris that are softball-size or bigger, ranging from burned-out rocket boosters to spent satellites. Millions of other, smaller pieces also orbit Earth. The debris are a hazard to space shuttles and satellites.

☛ In May 1998, NASA had 18,985 employees and spent $93.7 million on payroll.

HOW NASA SPENDS ITS MONEY

In 1995, the National Aeronautics and Space Administration had a budget of $14.3 billion. Here, a breakdown of how NASA distributed that money:

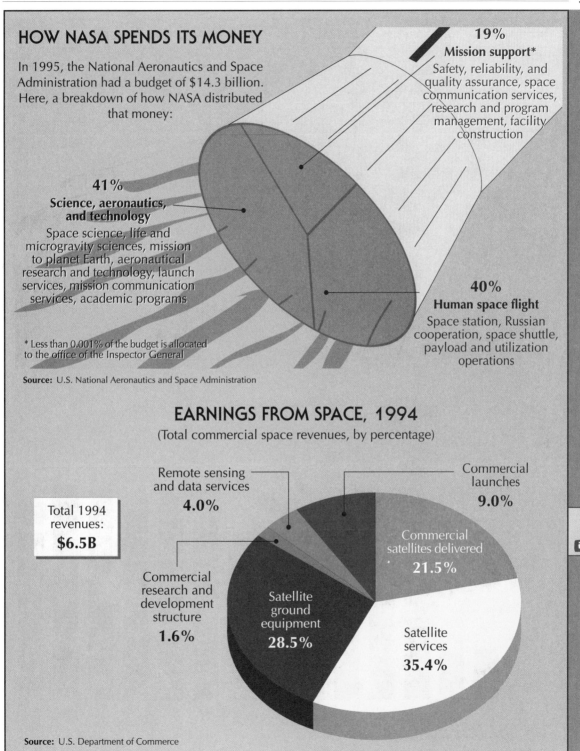

19%
Mission support*
Safety, reliability, and quality assurance, space communication services, research and program management, facility construction

41%
Science, aeronautics, and technology
Space science, life and microgravity sciences, mission to planet Earth, aeronautical research and technology, launch services, mission communication services, academic programs

40%
Human space flight
Space station, Russian cooperation, space shuttle, payload and utilization operations

* Less than 0.001% of the budget is allocated to the office of the Inspector General

Source: U.S. National Aeronautics and Space Administration

EARNINGS FROM SPACE, 1994

(Total commercial space revenues, by percentage)

Total 1994 revenues:
$6.5B

Remote sensing and data services
4.0%

Commercial launches
9.0%

Commercial satellites delivered
21.5%

Commercial research and development structure
1.6%

Satellite ground equipment
28.5%

Satellite services
35.4%

Source: U.S. Department of Commerce

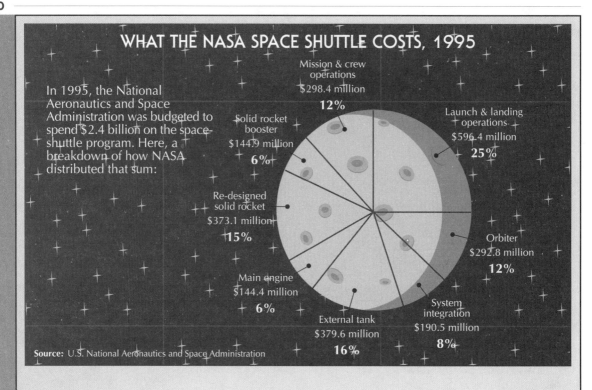

WHAT THE NASA SPACE SHUTTLE COSTS, 1995

In 1995, the National Aeronautics and Space Administration was budgeted to spend $2.4 billion on the space-shuttle program. Here, a breakdown of how NASA distributed that sum:

Mission & crew operations
$298.4 million
12%

Launch & landing operations
$596.4 million
25%

Solid rocket booster
$144.9 million
6%

Re-designed solid rocket
$373.1 million
15%

Orbiter
$292.8 million
12%

Main engine
$144.4 million
6%

System integration
$190.5 million
8%

External tank
$379.6 million
16%

Source: U.S. National Aeronautics and Space Administration

NASA's SPENDING DECLINES, 1970–1996
(In billions of dollars)

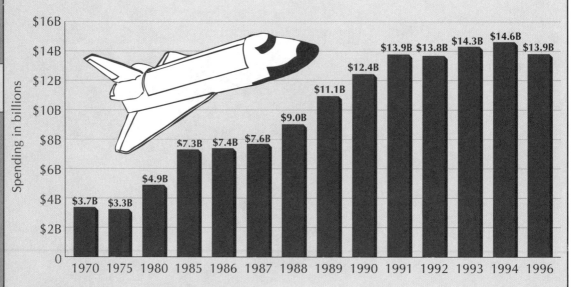

Spending in billions

Year	Spending
1970	$3.7B
1975	$3.3B
1980	$4.9B
1985	$7.3B
1986	$7.4B
1987	$7.6B
1988	$9.0B
1989	$11.1B
1990	$12.4B
1991	$13.9B
1992	$13.8B
1993	$14.3B
1994	$14.6B
1996	$13.9B

Source: U.S. National Aeronautics and Space Administration

SUCCESS IN COST REDUCTION, 1993-1998

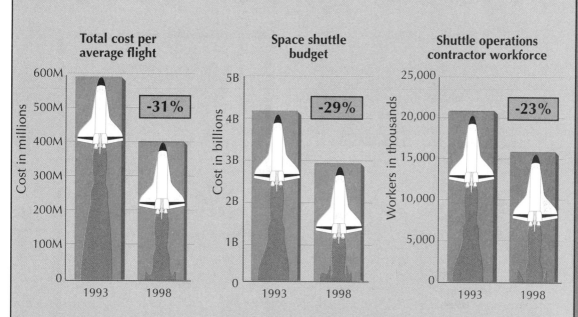

Total cost per average flight

Cost in millions

-31%

1993   1998

Space shuttle budget

Cost in billions

-29%

1993   1998

Shuttle operations contractor workforce

Workers in thousands

-23%

1993   1998

Source: U.S. National Aeronautics and Space Administration

SPACE JUNK GROWS

(Comparison of number of working satellites to pieces of "space junk")

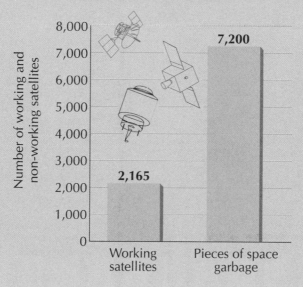

Number of working and non-working satellites

2,165   7,200

Working satellites   Pieces of space garbage

SCIENCE EDUCATION

Each year, about 350,000 students earn bachelor's degrees in science or engineering fields. An additional 75,000 master's degrees and 21,000 doctorates are awarded in these fields. Male degree recipients greatly outnumber females in agriculture, computer sciences, engineering, and physical sciences; females outnumber males in social sciences, health sciences, and psychology. In the life sciences, degrees are about evenly divided by sex.

Science education begins in kindergarten and continues through every level of primary and secondary school. Enrollment drops significantly in higher grades. About 85% of junior high school students are enrolled in science classes, compared to 75% of 10th graders taking biology and 20% of seniors enrolled in physics.

A certain degree of science literacy is important for all members of society. For most people, the foundations of this literacy are learned in primary and secondary schools. Critics have charged that science curricula at the primary and secondary levels have focused too heavily on the rote memorization of facts and figures, at the expense of teaching observation, problem solving, and the application of science to everyday life. In Benchmarks for Science Literacy, a 4-year study released in 1993, the American Association for the Advancement of Science (AAAS) advises that by teaching less material—but teaching it better—students will learn more and have greater understanding of facts and concepts.

FINGERTIP FACTS

- Foreign citizens received 31.5% of the science doctorates in 1994.

- In 1971, more than 50,000 bachelor's degrees in engineering were awarded, only 0.8% of them to females. In 1997, that number rose 17%, and 18% of the degrees were awarded to females.

- In 1971, some 2,388 bachelor's degrees were awarded in computers and information sciences, 12.6% to females. In 1997, females earned 41% of the nearly 89,000 computer science degrees awarded.

- In social sciences, females earned 68% of the master's degrees and 52% of the doctorates in 1997.

- In mathematics, females earned 28% of the master's degrees and 19.7% of the doctorates awarded in 1997.

- Social science garnered one-half of the master's degrees in science awarded in 1997, followed closely by computer science and life science.

- Almost 70% of 1997 science doctorates were awarded to men.

- In general, the job market is better for young scientists who majored in fields with practical applications than for those in more theoretical fields. For example, the American Institute of Physics reported in 1994 that 75% of scientists with degrees in optics and lasers found jobs right after receiving their doctorates, as compared to only 14% of those with degrees in astrophysics.

- In 1997, male college-bound high school students averaged science-reasoning test scores of 22.1 on the American College Testing (ACT) program (maximum score 36.0); females averaged 20.7.

BACHELOR'S DEGREES AWARDED IN SCIENCE, 1994

(By field, in percentages)

1994 total: **289,600**

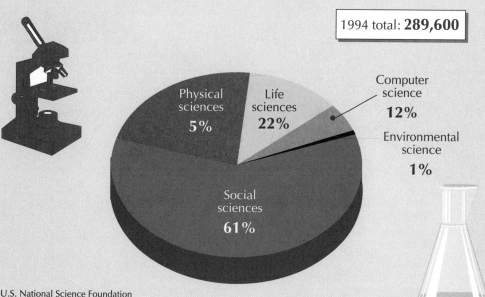

Physical sciences **5%**

Life sciences **22%**

Computer science **12%**

Environmental science **1%**

Social sciences **61%**

Source: U.S. National Science Foundation

BACHELOR'S DEGREES AWARDED IN ENGINEERING, 1994

(By engineering specialty, in percentages)

1994 total: **60,100**

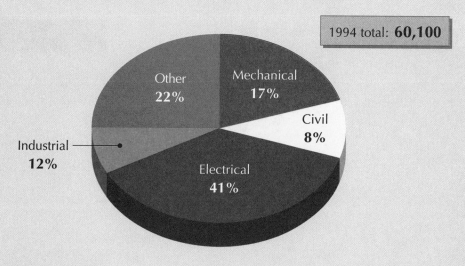

Other **22%**

Mechanical **17%**

Civil **8%**

Industrial **12%**

Electrical **41%**

Source: U.S. National Science Foundation

MASTER'S DEGREES AWARDED IN SCIENCE, 1994

(By field, in percentages)

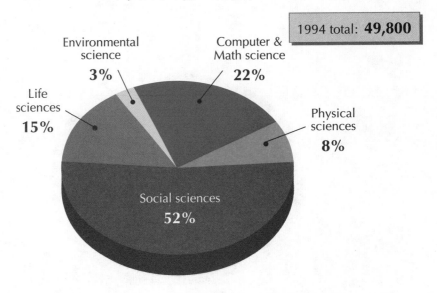

1994 total: **49,800**

Environmental science
3%

Computer & Math science
22%

Life sciences
15%

Physical sciences
8%

Social sciences
52%

Source: U.S. National Science Foundation

MASTER'S DEGREES AWARDED IN ENGINEERING, 1994

(By engineering specialty, in percentages)

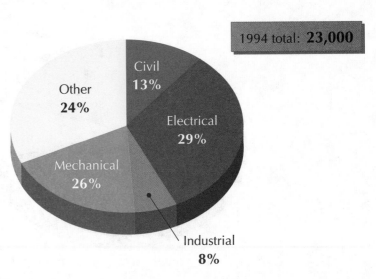

1994 total: **23,000**

Civil **13%**

Other
24%

Electrical
29%

Mechanical
26%

Industrial
8%

Source: U.S. National Science Foundation

WHO GETS THE DOCTORATES?

(Doctorates given in 1997 for engineering, physical sciences, earth sciences, mathematics, computer sciences, biological sciences, agricultural sciences, social sciences, and psychology)

By sex

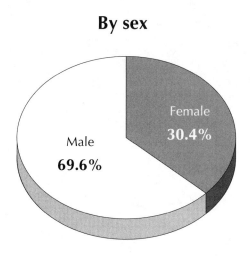

Female
30.4%

Male
69.6%

By citizenship

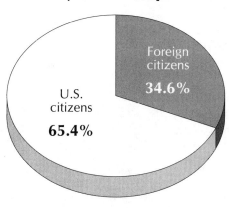

Foreign citizens
34.6%

U.S. citizens
65.4%

By race or ethnic group

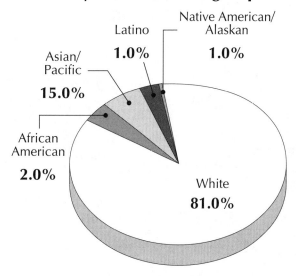

Native American/ Alaskan
1.0%

Latino
1.0%

Asian/ Pacific
15.0%

African American
2.0%

White
81.0%

Source: U.S. National Science Foundation

11

SPORTS
AND
RECORDS

SPORTS IN AMERICA

Participating in and watching sports consumes a larger percentage of Americans' time than ever before. Children start swimming and throwing balls even before they start preschool, while increasing numbers of people in their eighties and nineties are walking and lifting weights. The volume of sports teams, from youth soccer leagues to tandem bicycling clubs, keeps multiplying. There is growing openness to new and less well-known sports, plus a willingness to spend money on often-pricey equipment, memberships in gyms, and vacations in sports camps or distant scuba-diving havens.

Spectator sports—everything from local Little League games and college track meets to the Olympic Games and Monday night football—are a significant part of the nation's multi-billion-dollar entertainment industry. Professional sports keeps expanding at a rapid pace. Since 1945, major league baseball has added 12 new teams; since 1966, the National Hockey League has awarded 14 additional franchises; the National Basketball Association grew from 22 teams in 1980 to 30 teams by 1998; and so on. And the American thirst for sports seems only to intensify with each passing year.

FINGERTIP FACTS

☞ Some 16.6 million people ages 6 and older played soccer in 1998; fully 40% played 25 or more days a year.

☞ In 1975, about 308.6 million rounds of golf were played in the U.S., with 13 million golfers playing at least 1 round. By 1998, some 27.5 million golfers were on the greens, and 550 million rounds were played.

☞ The number of women participating in college sports increased about 15% from the 1984-1985 academic year (91,669 participants) to 1996-1997 (107,400).

☞ Basketball is played in the U.S. by 28.2 million males, but only by 12.2 million females.

☞ The most popular U.S. youth team sports are basketball (29.4 million participants in 1998), softball (15.6 million), volleyball (14.8 million), and soccer (13.2 million).

☞ Across the U.S., the number of bowlers decreased from 62.5 million in 1975 to 40.1 million in 1998.

☞ Wisconsin and North Dakota have the largest percentages of golf-playing residents (20.2%); Louisiana (5.3%) and Arkansas (5.6%) have the lowest percentages.

☞ Women's participation in some sports varied greatly between 1993 and 1998. The sports with the largest increases in participation were wind surfing (78.1%), muzzleloading (57.7%), and ice hockey (51.7%). The sports with the largest decreases were fresh water fishing (-20.3%), touch football (-16.6%), and alpine skiing (-16.0%).

☞ Prior to the infamous 1994 "strike" season, attendance at major league baseball games topped 55 million annually.

☞ The 1998 Winter Olympics were held in Nagano, Japan, and between 40-60 million Americans tuned in to watch each night. The U.S. won 13 medals— 6 gold, 3 silver, and 4 bronze.

☞ From 1980 to 1998, the number of pro basketball teams grew from 22 to 30, and average attendance per game rose from 11,017 to 16,103.

TOP 10 MOST POPULAR HIGH SCHOOL SPORTS, BY SEX, 1993–1994

(Numbers of students participating, by sport and sex)

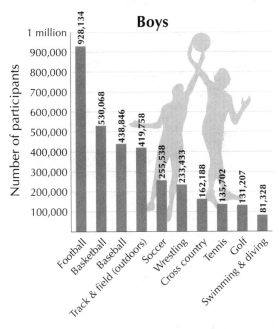

Boys

Number of participants

- Football: 928,134
- Basketball: 530,068
- Baseball: 438,846
- Track & field (outdoors): 419,758
- Soccer: 255,538
- Wrestling: 233,433
- Cross country: 162,188
- Tennis: 135,702
- Golf: 131,207
- Swimming & diving: 81,328

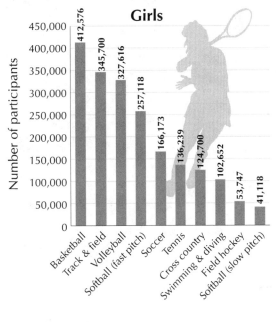

Girls

Number of participants

- Basketball: 412,576
- Track & field: 345,700
- Volleyball: 327,616
- Softball (fast pitch): 257,118
- Soccer: 166,173
- Tennis: 136,239
- Cross country: 124,700
- Swimming & diving: 102,652
- Field hockey: 53,747
- Softball (slow pitch): 41,118

Source: National Federation of State High School Associations

YOUNGSTERS' FAVORITE SPORTS

(Youth participants under age 18 in 1993, by sport)

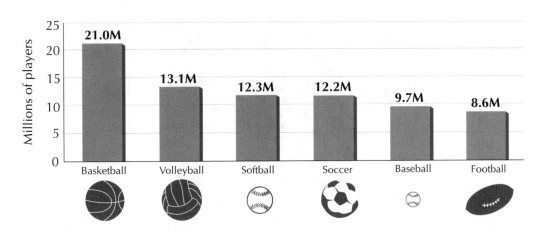

Millions of players

- Basketball: 21.0M
- Volleyball: 13.1M
- Softball: 12.3M
- Soccer: 12.2M
- Baseball: 9.7M
- Football: 8.6M

Source: Based on *USA Today* Research statistics

WHO PLAYS TENNIS?

The average U.S. tennis fan is age 32, has a college education, and has an average household income of $55,400. Further breakdowns:

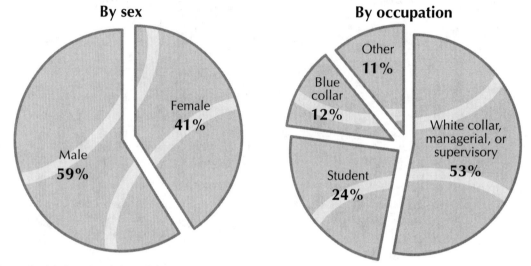

By sex

Female
41%

Male
59%

By occupation

Other
11%

Blue collar
12%

White collar, managerial, or supervisory
53%

Student
24%

Source: Tennis Industry Association statistics

WHO PLAYS BASKETBALL?

(Number of Americans participating in basketball, by age and sex)

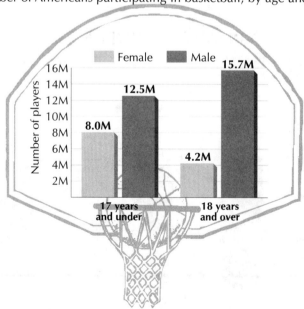

Female   Male

Number of players

16M
14M
12M
10M
8M
6M
4M
2M

8.0M

12.5M

15.7M

4.2M

17 years and under

18 years and over

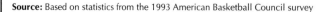

Source: Based on statistics from the 1993 American Basketball Council survey

TOP 5 STATES WHERE MOST GOLF IS PLAYED

(By percentage of people who play golf, with rankings)

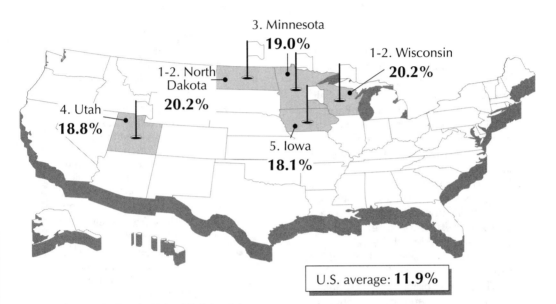

3. Minnesota
19.0%

1-2. Wisconsin
20.2%

1-2. North
Dakota
20.2%

4. Utah
18.8%

5. Iowa
18.1%

U.S. average: **11.9%**

Source: Based on statistics from the National Golf Foundation

AMERICA'S MOST AND LEAST EXPENSIVE SPORTS

(Average yearly expenditures in U.S. households buying this kind of sports gear)

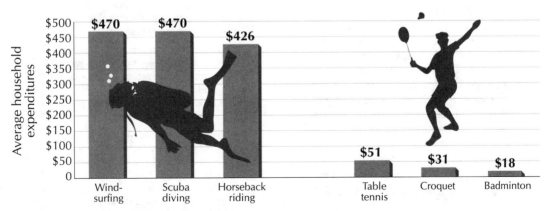

Average household expenditures

$500
$450
$400
$350
$300
$250
$200
$150
$100
$50
0

$470 Wind-surfing

$470 Scuba diving

$426 Horseback riding

$51 Table tennis

$31 Croquet

$18 Badminton

Most expensive

Least expensive

Source: National Sporting Goods Association

THE BIG BUSINESS OF SPORTS

It is not only the promise of fame that makes many high school athletes dream of playing professional sports; it is also the enticement of great wealth. They are spurred on by National Basketball Association and Major League Baseball salaries that, in the 1990s, average more than $1 million, coupled with endorsement contracts that may bring in additional millions.

Every aspect of professional sports is big business. Buying a pro team generally offers an excellent return on a person's investment. For example, the people who purchased the Baltimore Orioles for $70 million in 1989 sold the team just 4 years later for $173 million.

Fans spend billions of dollars annually not only to attend sports events but to wear team jerseys and hats, collect autographed memorabilia, and even buy cards and pogs featuring the images of their favorite players.

But fan loyalty is increasingly being soured by labor disputes, including the lengthy and bitter 1994-1995 baseball strike. Also bothersome to fans are the rising costs to attend games played by athletes who are already millionaires, playing for clubs owned by millionaires; and the all-too-frequent arrests of athletes for charges such as drug use, rape, and general mayhem. There are signs that the big business of sports will pay heavily if it continues to ignore the real interests of its fans.

FINGERTIP FACTS

☞ The top annual salary earned by baseball legend Babe Ruth was $80,000 in 1930. In 1998, Chicago White Sox right-fielder Albert Belle's salary was $10.0 million.

☞ In 1980, the average salary of a major league baseball player was $144,000. By 1998, it had jumped to $1.4 million.

☞ Following the 1994-1995 baseball strike, many free agents took pay cuts. Dave Stewart, whose 1994 salary with the Toronto Blue Jays had been $4.25 million, signed with the Oakland Athletics for $1 million.

☞ Basketball great Michael Jordan was the highest-earning athlete in 1999, with $42 million from product endorsements. Tiger Woods was #2.

☞ Tennis player Martina Hingis was the highest-earning female athlete in 1997. She earned $3.4 million in salary and winnings.

☞ The cost of a thirty-second television advertisement run during the Super Bowl increased from less than $100,000 in 1970 to about $1.2 million in 1997.

☞ The 1999 Women's World Cup drew 650,000 spectators, totaling almost $23 million. In addition, 19 companies paid more than $6 million for sponsorship rights.

☞ Despite declining ratings for sports programs on television, the National Basketball Association (NBA) made a deal worth $2.6 billion for television rights to basketball games for the next four years.

☞ Professional sports leagues average ticket prices are increasing rapidly. From 1991 to 1998, MLB ticket prices increased 37%, the price of NBA tickets went up 36%, NFL ticket prices rose 34%, and NHL ticket prices grew 18%.

☞ The 107 franchises in professional baseball, football, basketball, and hockey are worth a total of $11.4 billion.

BASEBALL SALARIES OUT OF THE PARK, 1967–1998

(Average and minimum salaries for major league baseball players)

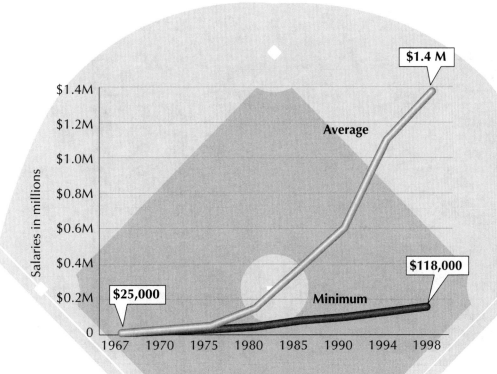

Source: Based on statistics from the Major League Baseball Players

FREE AGENCY SPIKES NFL SALARIES

In 1986, the average National Football League salary was under $200,000.
Base salaries increased at an annual rate of 16.4% until the start of free agency.
Since the first year of free agency in 1993, the average salary jumped 46%:

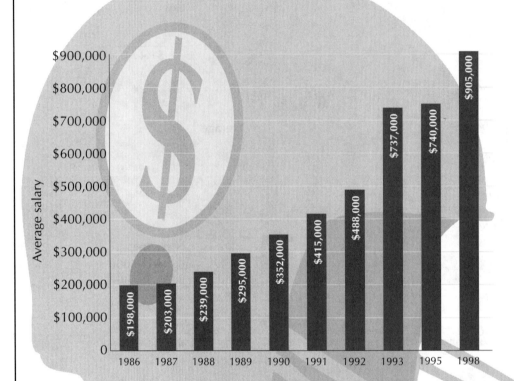

Average salary

Year	Salary
1986	$198,000
1987	$203,000
1988	$239,000
1989	$295,000
1990	$352,000
1991	$415,000
1992	$488,000
1993	$737,000
1995	$740,000
1998	$905,000

Source: Based on statistics from the National Football League Players

TOP 10 WEALTHIEST BASEBALL OWNERS, 1993

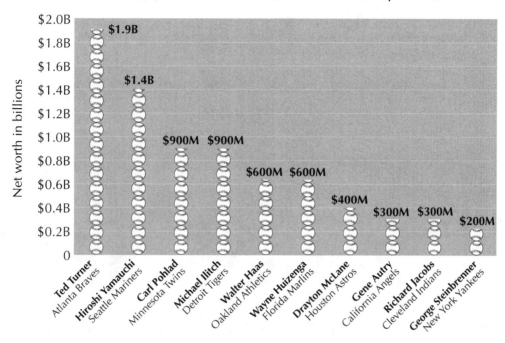

Net worth in billions

- $2.0B
- $1.8B
- $1.6B
- $1.4B
- $1.2B
- $1.0B
- $0.8B
- $0.6B
- $0.4B
- $0.2B
- 0

$1.9B — **Ted Turner** Atlanta Braves

$1.4B — **Hiroshi Yamauchi** Seattle Mariners

$900M — **Carl Pohlad** Minnesota Twins

$900M — **Michael Ilitch** Detroit Tigers

$600M — **Walter Haas** Oakland Athletics

$600M — **Wayne Huizenga** Florida Marlins

$400M — **Drayton McLane** Houston Astros

$300M — **Gene Autry** California Angels

$300M — **Richard Jacobs** Cleveland Indians

$200M — **George Steinbrenner** New York Yankees

Source: Based on statistics from *Sports Illustrated*

AVERAGE VALUE OF PRO TEAMS

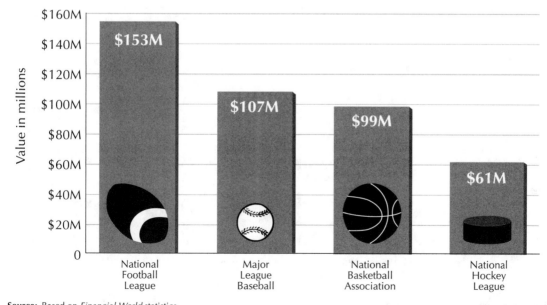

Value in millions

- $160M
- $140M
- $120M
- $100M
- $80M
- $60M
- $40M
- $20M
- 0

$153M — National Football League

$107M — Major League Baseball

$99M — National Basketball Association

$61M — National Hockey League

Source: Based on *Financial World* statistics

NCAA WOMEN'S BASKETBALL REBOUNDS

The National Collegiate Athletic Association women's basketball tournament has grown in popularity in recent years. Here, the bottom line on attendance and gross receipts from 1982–1993:

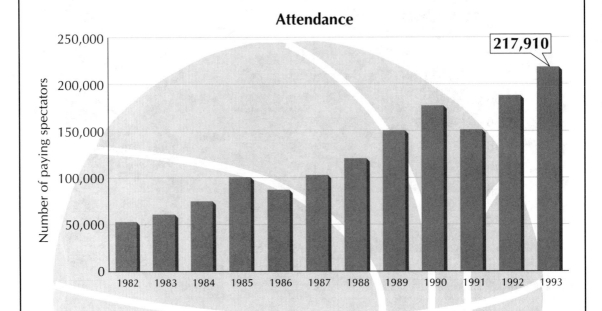

Attendance

217,910

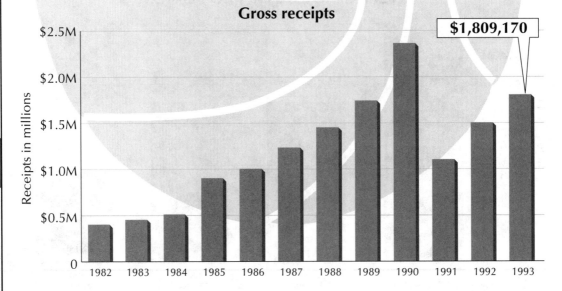

Gross receipts

$1,809,170

Source: Based on statistics from the National Collegiate Athletic Association

NCAA FUNDING SOURCES

The 1991–1992 operating budget of the National Collegiate Athletic Association was $168.7 million. The bulk of this—75%—came from a single contract with CBS Sports for televised coverage of the NCAA basketball tournament. A breakdown of the NCAA's revenues for that season:

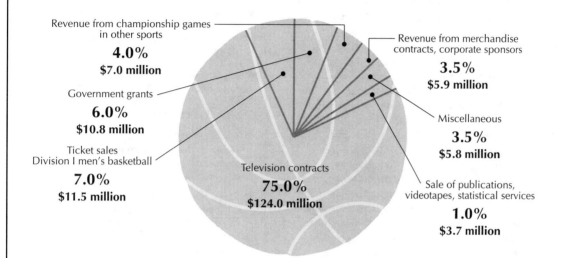

Revenue from championship games in other sports
4.0%
$7.0 million

Revenue from merchandise contracts, corporate sponsors
3.5%
$5.9 million

Government grants
6.0%
$10.8 million

Miscellaneous
3.5%
$5.8 million

Ticket sales
Division I men's basketball
7.0%
$11.5 million

Television contracts
75.0%
$124.0 million

Sale of publications, videotapes, statistical services
1.0%
$3.7 million

Source: Based on statistics from *U.S. News & World Report*

BUDGET FOR THE WINTER OLYMPIC GAMES, 1932 vs. 1994

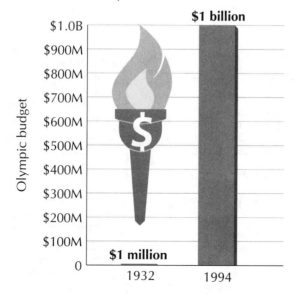

Source: IBM

SPORTS RECORDS

In 1954, when Roger Bannister became the first runner to break the 4-minute mile, the historic feat made headlines around the world. Since then, more than 700 athletes have run a mile in less than 4 minutes, and the record has been lowered by more than 15 seconds. In the 1970s, football professionals kicked field goals with 63.1% accuracy. Today, 80.1% of kicks are successful.

Clearly, athletes are getting swifter and stronger—slamming tennis serves across the net at more than 100 miles per hour, vaulting over ever-higher bars, shaving seconds off records as they streak through swimming pools. Improved nutrition, more efficient training methods, and high-tech equipment are some of the factors in the never-ending breaking of records.

Still, some records have remained on the books for decades. For example, Ty Cobb's career total of 892 stolen bases was a major league record for almost half a century before being broken by Lou Brock in 1977. And Cobb's record of 3 season batting averages over .400 stands to this day.

FINGERTIP FACTS

☛ Through 1994, Martina Navratilova had the best tennis career-record totals, with 167 singles and 162 doubles titles. Margaret Smith Court won the most grand slam titles—24.

☛ Ivan Lendl headed the men's tennis players ranking charts for a record 270 weeks, followed closely by Jimmy Connors at 268.

☛ In 1990, Pete Sampras became the youngest men's singles tennis champ in U.S. Open history. And Jennifer Capriati made her professional debut, becoming the youngest tennis player ever to play a pro title match.

☛ Brazil, Germany, and Italy have dominated World Cup Soccer since 1930, having won 3 championships each.

☛ A.J. Foyt won CART (Championship Auto Racing Teams) titles a record 67 times. Mario Andretti holds second place, with 52 wins.

☛ Ray Floyd had the longest winning career in the PGA, with his first tournament win in 1963 and his last such win in 1992.

☛ Speed skater Bonnie Blair has 5 Olympic gold medals, more than any other U.S. female. Swimmer Mark Spitz won a record 7 gold medals in a single Olympic Games (1972).

☛ Wilt Chamberlain once amassed 55 rebounds in a game and led the NBA in rebounding for 11 seasons, but his career-points total of 31,419 was surpassed by Kareem Abdul-Jabbar, who hit 38,387.

☛ In September 1998, Mark McGwire of the St. Louis Cardinals hit his 62nd home run to break Roger Maris's 37-year-old record for the most home runs hit in a season. McGwire ended the season with an amazing 70 home runs. Sammy Sosa of the Chicago Cubs finished second with an impressive 66 home runs.

☛ Hank Aaron led the National League in home runs for 4 seasons and had a career total of 755 homers.

☛ Ty Cobb, the first member of the Baseball Hall of Fame, batted over .400 in 3 amazing seasons of his career, and over .300 in 23 seasons.

☛ Cy Young won 511 games during his career, more than any other baseball pitcher. He also holds the records for most games completed (751) and most innings pitched (7,356).

TOP 10 MAJOR LEAGUE BASEBALL ALL-TIME CAREER PERFORMERS

(Figures calculated as of the end of the 1998 baseball season)

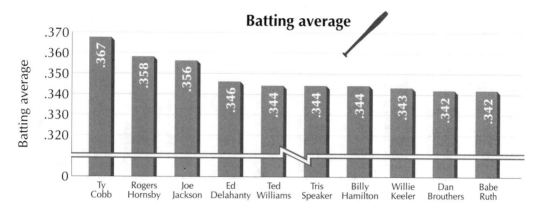

Batting average

Player	Batting average
Ty Cobb	.367
Rogers Hornsby	.358
Joe Jackson	.356
Ed Delahanty	.346
Ted Williams	.344
Tris Speaker	.344
Billy Hamilton	.344
Willie Keeler	.343
Dan Brouthers	.342
Babe Ruth	.342

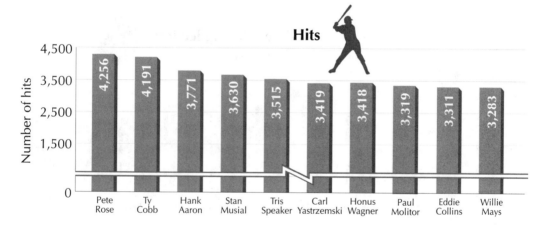

Hits

Player	Number of hits
Pete Rose	4,256
Ty Cobb	4,191
Hank Aaron	3,771
Stan Musial	3,630
Tris Speaker	3,515
Carl Yastrzemski	3,419
Honus Wagner	3,418
Paul Molitor	3,319
Eddie Collins	3,311
Willie Mays	3,283

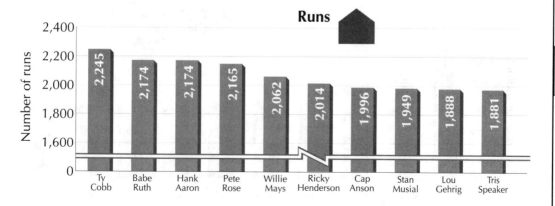

Runs

Player	Number of runs
Ty Cobb	2,245
Babe Ruth	2,174
Hank Aaron	2,174
Pete Rose	2,165
Willie Mays	2,062
Ricky Henderson	2,014
Cap Anson	1,996
Stan Musial	1,949
Lou Gehrig	1,888
Tris Speaker	1,881

Source: Based on statistics from Major League Baseball

TOP 10 MAJOR LEAGUE BASEBALL ALL-TIME CAREER PERFORMERS

(Figures calculated as of the end of the 1998 baseball season)

Strikeouts

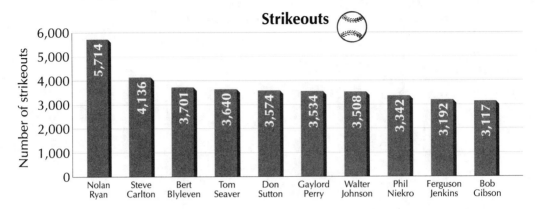

Player	Number of strikeouts
Nolan Ryan	5,714
Steve Carlton	4,136
Bert Blyleven	3,701
Tom Seaver	3,640
Don Sutton	3,574
Gaylord Perry	3,534
Walter Johnson	3,508
Phil Niekro	3,342
Ferguson Jenkins	3,192
Bob Gibson	3,117

Lifetime pitching leaders

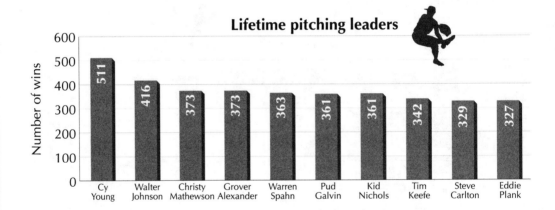

Player	Number of wins
Cy Young	511
Walter Johnson	416
Christy Mathewson	373
Grover Alexander	373
Warren Spahn	363
Pud Galvin	361
Kid Nichols	361
Tim Keefe	342
Steve Carlton	329
Eddie Plank	327

Shutouts

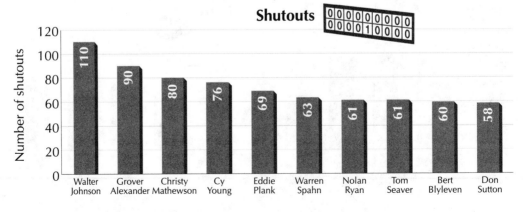

Player	Number of shutouts
Walter Johnson	110
Grover Alexander	90
Christy Mathewson	80
Cy Young	76
Eddie Plank	69
Warren Spahn	63
Nolan Ryan	61
Tom Seaver	61
Bert Blyleven	60
Don Sutton	58

Source: Based on statistics from Major League Baseball

TOP 10 NHL GOAL-SCORING LEADERS

(National Hockey League figures as of the end of the 1997–1998 season)

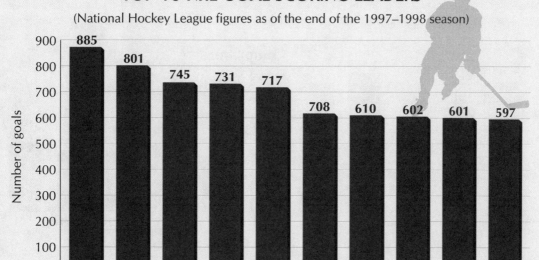

Source: Based on statistics from the National Hockey League

TOP 10 NBA CAREER PERFORMERS

(Rebounds and points statistics for National Basketball Association players; calculated at the end of the 1997–1998 season)

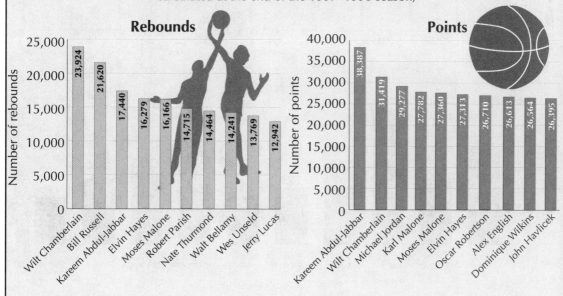

Source: Based on statistics from the National Basketball Association

TOP 10 NFL PASSING LEADERS

(National Football League figures as of the end of the 1997 season)

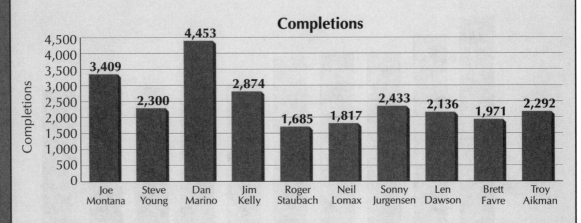

Completions

Joe Montana 3,409
Steve Young 2,300
Dan Marino 4,453
Jim Kelly 2,874
Roger Staubach 1,685
Neil Lomax 1,817
Sonny Jurgensen 2,433
Len Dawson 2,136
Brett Favre 1,971
Troy Aikman 2,292

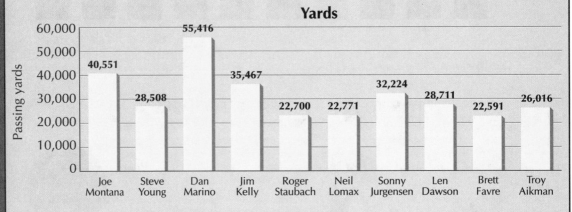

Yards

Joe Montana 40,551
Steve Young 28,508
Dan Marino 55,416
Jim Kelly 35,467
Roger Staubach 22,700
Neil Lomax 22,771
Sonny Jurgensen 32,224
Len Dawson 28,711
Brett Favre 22,591
Troy Aikman 26,016

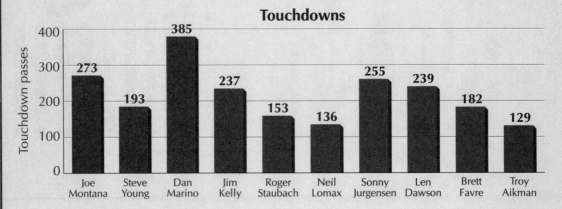

Touchdowns

Joe Montana 273
Steve Young 193
Dan Marino 385
Jim Kelly 237
Roger Staubach 153
Neil Lomax 136
Sonny Jurgensen 255
Len Dawson 239
Brett Favre 182
Troy Aikman 129

Source: Based on statistics from the National Football League

TOP 10 NFL RUSHERS

(National Football League figures as of the end of the 1997 season)

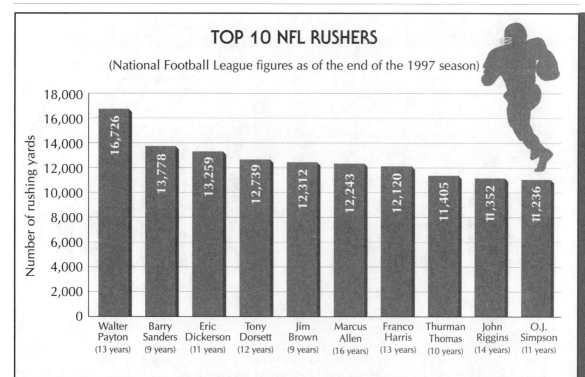

Source: Based on statistics from the National Football League

WORLD CUP CHAMPIONS

Teams from 58 countries have played in the 16 World Cup soccer championships held since 1930. Winners and number of World Cup titles:

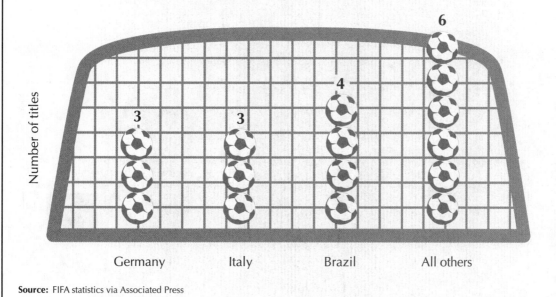

Source: FIFA statistics via Associated Press

TOP WINNERS OF GRAND SLAM TENNIS TITLES, 1968–1998

Men

Number of titles

- Bjorn Borg — 11
- Rod Laver — 11
- Pete Sampras — 11
- Jimmy Connors — 8
- Fred Perry — 8
- Ivan Lendl — 8
- Ken Rosewall — 8

Women

Number of titles

- Margaret Smith Court — 24
- Steffi Graf — 21
- Helen Wills Moody — 19
- Chris Evert — 18
- Martina Navratilova — 18
- Billie Jean King — 12
- Monica Seles — 9
- Evonne Goolagong — 7

Source: Based on statistics from the National Tennis Association

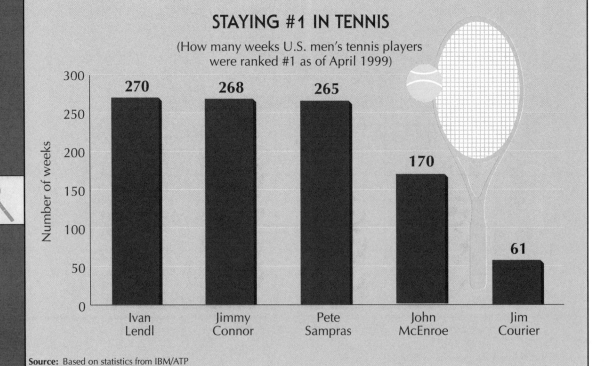

STAYING #1 IN TENNIS

(How many weeks U.S. men's tennis players
were ranked #1 as of April 1999)

Number of weeks

- Ivan Lendl — 270
- Jimmy Connor — 268
- Pete Sampras — 265
- John McEnroe — 170
- Jim Courier — 61

Source: Based on statistics from IBM/ATP

GRAND SLAM TITLES FOR U.S. PLAYERS, 1968–1998

(How many singles titles U.S. players won at grand slam tennis tournaments)

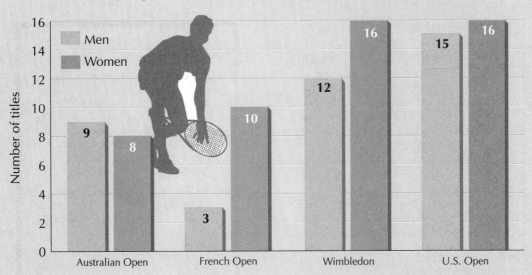

Source: Based on statistics from U.S. Tennis Association

TOP 5 ALL-TIME INDYCAR WINNERS

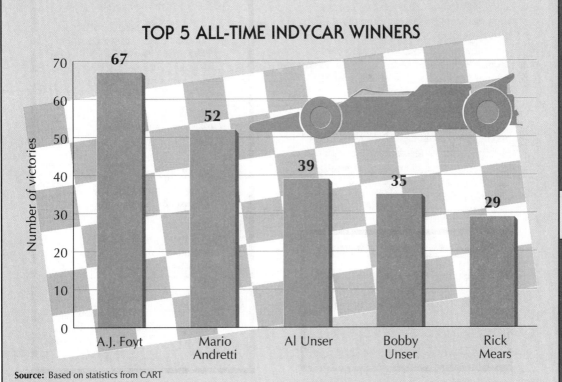

Source: Based on statistics from CART

SPORTS TRENDS

Skydiving and scuba diving, bungee jumping and shooting the rapids, rock climbing and rollerblading—these activities and sports trends are enjoying fantastic growth because adventurous athletes are seeking new challenges and thrills. The search for things new and different has affected spectator sports, too; soccer and jai-alai, for example, are pulling in ever-growing audiences. But what is trendy one year may be passé the next. For instance, the number of racquetball players has dropped steadily since 1985, and many courts have been converted to squash courts, aerobics facilities, and other uses.

Unfortunately, many amateur athletes resort to dangerous practices while pursuing their sports. They undertake activities without first getting proper training, preparation, or equipment. Too often, the result is serious injury, or even death. The majority of bicyclists do not wear helmets, for example, even though helmets reduce the risk of bicycle-related head injury by 85%.

Public and private groups are currently using various tactics to educate people about the risks of sports. In one Maryland county, legislation accompanied by an educational campaign increased bicycle helmet use from 4% to 47% within one year.

FINGERTIP FACTS

- One of the fastest-growing sports in the U.S. is rock climbing, with an estimated 500,000 enthusiasts.

- The number of in-line skaters increased from 3 million in 1989 to 27 million in 1998. Youths aged 7-17 make up 58% of participants, and women account for 52%.

- The sport with the largest participation decline between 1993 and 1998 was volleyball. It declined 17.1% to 14.8 million participants in 1998. The sport with the largest increase during the same time period was snowboarding. It increased 29.1% to 3.6 million participants.

- An estimated 20,000 Americans participate in triathlons, which include a sequence of swimming, biking, and running.

- The number of golfers aged 5-17 increased 29% in 1997. Participation on high school golf teams also went up 17%, as about 179,600 young golfers took to the courses.

- A worldwide TV audience of almost 2.9 million households watched the 1999 Women's World Cup final at the Rose Bowl in Pasadena, California, about 7 times as many people as watch the NHL Stanley Cup Finals.

- Attendance at jai-alai games rose from 3.9 million in 1980 to 6.1 million in 1996.

- In 1995, the U.S. National Park Service began charging a $150 "user fee" for climbers of Mount McKinley, to help offset costs of rescuing people.

- Each year, bicyclists in the U.S. sustain injuries that result in 550,000 emergency room visits and nearly 1,000 deaths. Of the deaths, 52% involve head injuries.

- Sales of bicycle helmets jumped from 386,000 in 1985 to 17.2 million in 1998. Still, only about 69% of child bicyclists and 38% of all bicyclists wear helmets.

INCREASE OR DECREASE IN POPULARITY OF SELECTED SPORTS, 1992–1993

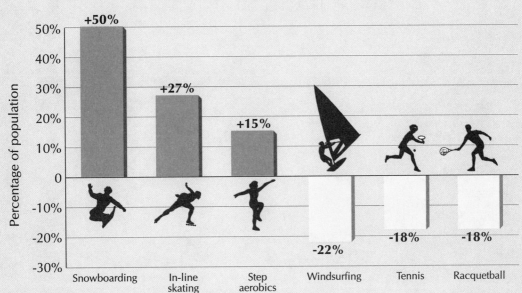

Source: National Sporting Goods Association

TEEN SPORT ATTENDANCE vs. OTHER ACTIVITIES, 1993

(Percentage of U.S. teens who attended various events)

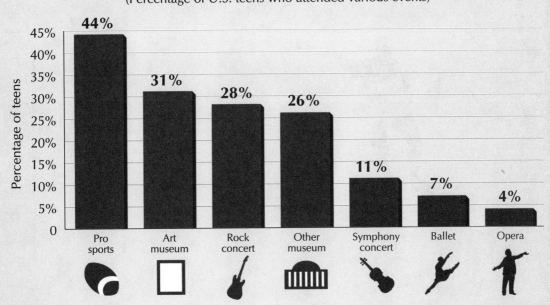

Source: GPA

MOUNTAIN BIKE SALES SHIFT INTO HIGH GEAR, 1982–1993

U.S. sales of mountain bikes have climbed steeply,
since 1982, from about $113 million to $2.3 billion in 1993:

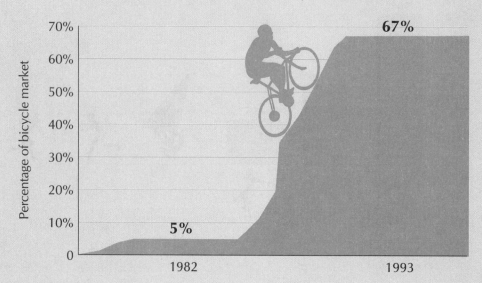

Source: Based on statistics from Interbike

IN-LINE SKATES SALES JUMP, 1989–1993

(U.S. consumer spending on rollerblade skates)

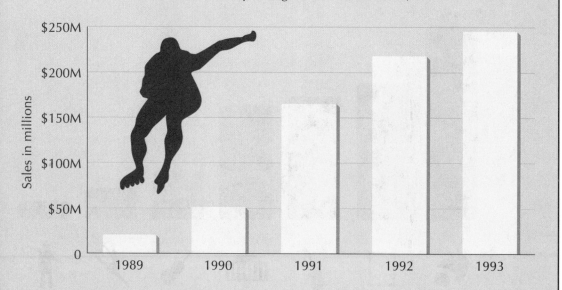

Source: Based on statistics from the National Sporting Goods Association

ROLLERBLADING ON A ROLL

Rollerblading is one of the fastest-growing sports in the U.S. Here is how the number of in-line skaters mounted from 1989–1993:

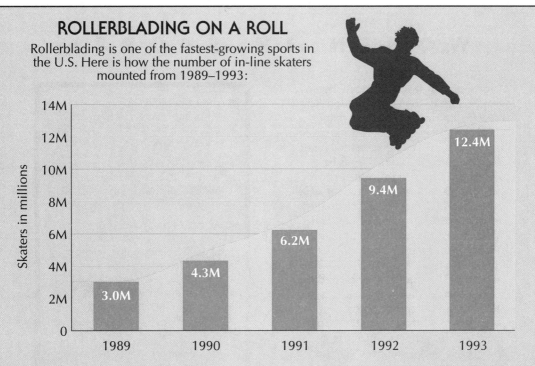

Source: Based on statistics from Rollerblade

CHESS POPULARITY RISING

Membership in U.S. Chess Federation after 1972, when Bobby Fischer beat Boris Spassky for the world championship:

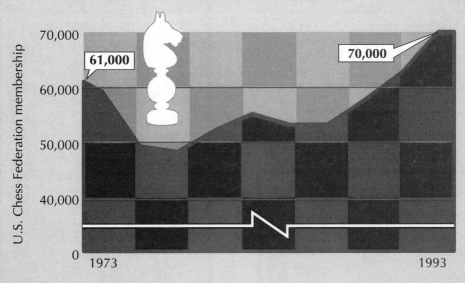

Source: U.S. Chess Federation

WOMEN IN SPORTS

A revolution in women's sports began with passage of the U.S. Education Act of 1972. Its Title IX prohibits gender discrimination in sports at all educational institutions that receive federal funds. Since then, schools and colleges have moved to provide female athletes with facilities, coaching, and scholarships equal to those received by men. This has helped increase the number of women athletes; for instance, the number of girls involved in high school sports rose from 200,000 in the late 1970s to 2 million today. The impact has trickled down to elementary schools, and trickled up into professional sports. The paying public is also increasingly enthusiastic about women's sports, which has led to larger crowds—and hence greater earning potential—higher salaries and more endorsement opportunities for athletes.

Although female athletes enjoy more opportunities than ever before, and are receiving increasing respect for their athleticism, gender inequities continue to bedevil them. For example, a 1994 survey by the National Collegiate Athletic Association (NCAA) found that colleges award twice as much money in athletic scholarships to men as to women, and that female coaches earn much lower salaries than their male counterparts do.

FINGERTIP FACTS

- By 1996, one in three high school girls played sports.
- Female athletes graduate at higher rates (69% in 1996) than the general female college population (58%).

- During the 1970-1971 school year, 8% of high school athletes were girls. By 1996-1997, the figure had grown to 41%.
- During the 1996-1997 academic year, 171,022 girls nationwide played high school soccer, up from 11,534 in 1976-1977.
- According to the National Collegiate Athletic Association, 77 of its 752 member institutions in the 1981-1982 academic year operated soccer programs for women. In 1998-1999, there were 791 such programs at 895 institutions.
- Only 20% of collegiate athletics for women are headed by female coaches. Women hold only 31% of jobs in collegiate women's programs.
- In 1994, the U.S. Department of Education received 50 complaints nationwide alleging sex discrimination in various public school athletic programs.
- Female high school athletes have a lower pregnancy rate than non-athletes. In 1997, about 11% of non-athletes became pregnant while only 5% of athletes did.
- Walking for exercise is the most popular sports activity among U.S. females (done by more than 49.3 million females in 1998), followed by swimming (31.3 million), bicycle riding (20.6 million), and aerobic exercise (20.0 million).
- Women comprise a significant portion of the professional sports audience; 35.1%, for example, say they are interested in the National Football League.

WOMEN JOIN THE ROOTING

(Percentages of U.S. women who reported that they were
interested or not interested in these leagues)

National Football League

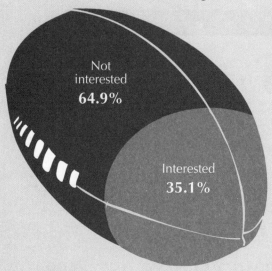

Not interested
64.9%

Interested
35.1%

Major League Baseball

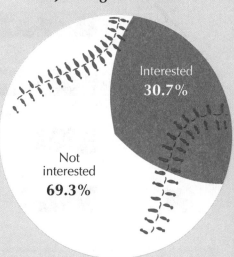

Interested
30.7%

Not interested
69.3%

National Basketball Association

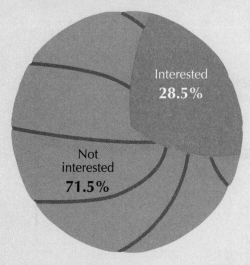

Interested
28.5%

Not interested
71.5%

National Hockey League

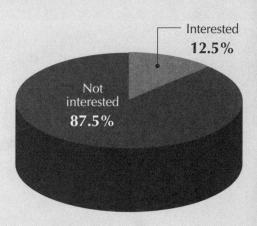

Interested
12.5%

Not interested
87.5%

Source: Based on ESPN statistics

HIGH SCHOOL GIRLS IN MALE-DOMINATED SPORTS

(Number of U.S. high school girls who participate in male-dominated sports)

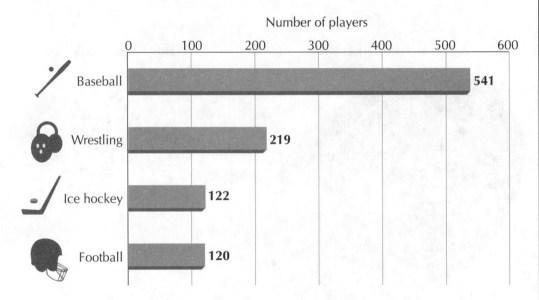

Number of players

Source: National Federation of State High School Associations

HIGH SCHOOL SPORTS PARTICIPATION TRENDS, 1971–1994

The number of boys participating in high school athletics slipped somewhat
in the period from 1971 to 1994, but girls' participation increased significantly:

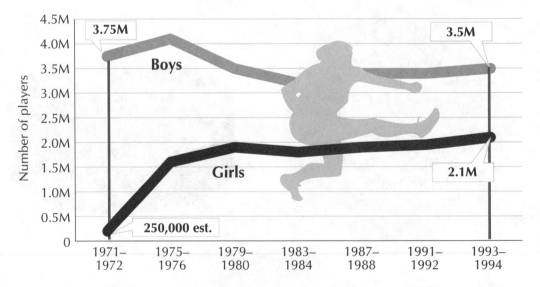

Source: Based on National Federation of State High School statistics

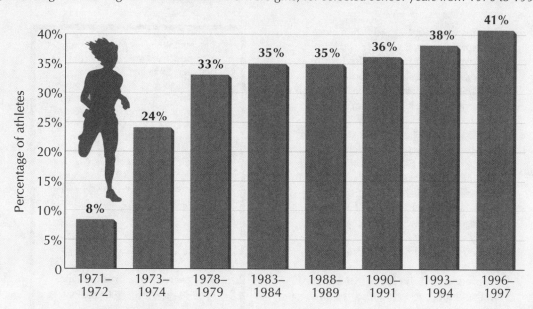

FEMALE ATHLETES MAKING STRIDES

(Percentage of U.S. high school athletes who were girls, for selected school years from 1970 to 1997)

Source: National Federation of State High School Associations

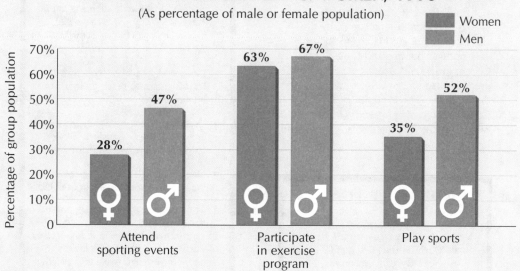

SPORTS IN AMERICA: MEN vs. WOMEN, 1996

(As percentage of male or female population)

Source: National Sporting Goods Association

HUNTING AND FISHING

Humans have hunted and fished since prehistoric times, but the purpose of these activities gradually shifted from survival to sport. Today's hunters and fishermen chase, catch, and kill more for excitement and pleasure than for the need to obtain a meal.

Some 39 million Americans (19% of the population) go fishing each year, and about 14 million (7%) go hunting. These activities are far more popular among males than females—74% of the fishing tackle bought in 1998 and 91% of the hunting equipment was purchased for use by males.

Various methods of hunting and fishing are used, depending on people's preferences and the species of animal being pursued. Most hunting is done with firearms: rifles for big game—such as deer, bear, and moose—and shotguns for small game and birds in flight. Trolling, casting, and still fishing are the basic methods of sport fishing.

Public lands, including national forests and areas administered by the U.S. Bureau of Land Management, are very popular hunting and fishing sites. Conservation and safety concerns, however, have led to growing restrictions on these sports. For example, in 1992, Colorado voters approved a measure restricting the hunting of black bears, and Iowa enacted a law protecting bats as a non-game species.

FINGERTIP FACTS

☛ If recreational fishing were considered a corporation, it would rank 13th on the Fortune 500 list of America's biggest companies.

☛ The number of women who hunt with bows and arrows is increasing. Between 1993 and 1998, the percentage rose 37.9% to about half a million. The number of women who hunt with firearms, however, has declined 1% in the same time period to 1.8 million.

☛ Of the 17.3 million people who hunted in 1998, some 12.9 million pursued big game, 9.3 million small game, and 3.6 million hoped to shoot migratory birds.

☛ There were 9.4 million saltwater anglers and 29.7 million freshwater anglers in 1998. About one-quarter of saltwater anglers and one-third of freshwater anglers were women.

☛ People in the U.S. spent an estimated $2.9 billion in 1993 on hunting equipment, including firearms—up from $1.4 billion in 1980.

☛ Recreational fishing supports about 1.2 million jobs and creates $28 billion in wages. It also contributes $3.1 billion in federal income taxes.

☛ More than 50% of hunters travel at least 25 miles to reach their favorite hunting sites.

☛ Wyoming hosts the highest percentage of out-of-state anglers (64%), followed by Delaware (58%).

☛ Deer hunting is the most popular type of big-game hunting in the U.S.

☛ The majority of anglers— approximately 58%–practice the catch and release method. This is an important practice for recreational anglers to adopt in order to maintain a healthy fish population.

PROFILE: WHAT AMERICANS HUNT MOST

Millions of hunters

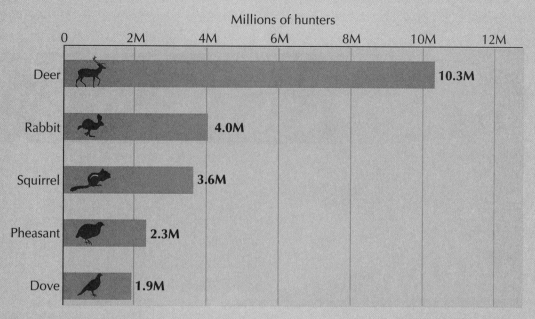

Deer	10.3M
Rabbit	4.0M
Squirrel	3.6M
Pheasant	2.3M
Dove	1.9M

Source: U.S. Department of the Interior; U.S. Department of Commerce

THE TRAVELING HUNTER

How far hunters will travel to get to their favorite hunting sites:

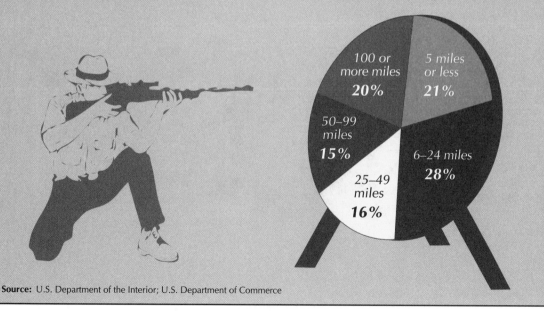

100 or more miles **20%**

5 miles or less **21%**

50–99 miles **15%**

6–24 miles **28%**

25–49 miles **16%**

Source: U.S. Department of the Interior; U.S. Department of Commerce

AVERAGE AGE OF FIRST HUNTING EXPERIENCE

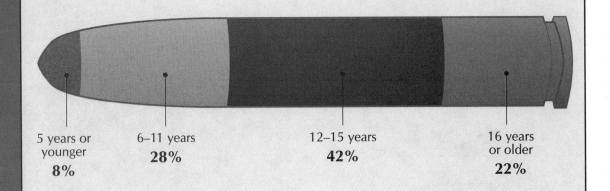

5 years or
younger
8%

6–11 years
28%

12–15 years
42%

16 years
or older
22%

Source: U.S. Department of the Interior; U.S. Department of Commerce

WHERE ANGLERS ANGLE

(Top 5 states with the highest percentage of fishermen from out of state, with rankings)

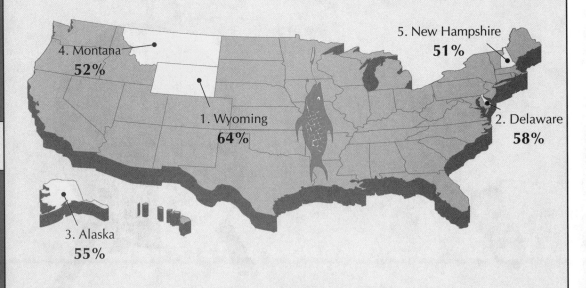

5. New Hampshire
51%

4. Montana
52%

1. Wyoming
64%

2. Delaware
58%

3. Alaska
55%

Source: U.S. Fish and Wildlife Service; U.S. Census Bureau

PROFILE: ANGLERS' FAVORITE WATERS

(Overall averages, for persons over age 16)

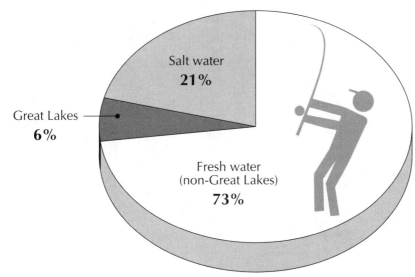

Salt water
21%

Great Lakes
6%

Fresh water
(non-Great Lakes)
73%

Source: U.S. Fish and Wildlife Service

PROFILE: HUNTERS' FAVORITE GAME

(Overall averages, for persons over age 16)

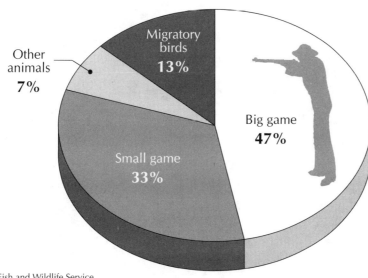

Migratory
birds
13%

Other
animals
7%

Big game
47%

Small game
33%

Source: U.S. Fish and Wildlife Service

12

EDUCATION AND LEARNING

PROFILE OF EDUCATION IN THE U.S.

Some 50 million children are enrolled in elementary and secondary schools in the U.S. An additional 15 million people are enrolled full-time in institutions of higher learning. The nation's educational system also encompasses millions of others from preschoolers to senior citizens—a majority of children ages 3 to 5 (56%) participate in preschool programs, and millions of people take courses in adult education programs, primarily to improve their job skills or for other personal and social reasons.

The majority of students attend public—that is, tax-supported—institutions. At the elementary and secondary levels, control of education is in the hands of the states, with local school districts charged with operating individual schools. Most schools, both public and private, teach a standard curriculum that focuses on language arts, mathematics, science, social studies, and health. The methods used to teach these and other subjects vary greatly, however, depending on school philosophy, student abilities, availability of teaching aids, and other factors.

Test scores are the most widely used indicator of what students have learned. On average, the more educated their parents, the higher students score on proficiency tests. Schools are increasingly developing programs to help parents and teachers work together, to ensure that children receive the education they need to succeed as adults—and that the nation's workforce needs—as the U.S. faces ever-tougher economic competition from other countries.

FINGERTIP FACTS

- More than 14.8 million U.S. youths were enrolled in high school in 1996.

- In 1998, almost 5.0 million students were enrolled in private elementary and secondary schools. The majority of these attended Catholic schools.

- The average public elementary school has 458 students; the average high school has 678 students.

- In 1893, the average number of school days for U.S. students was 193.5. Today, it's 180.

- In the U.S., 5th graders were found to spend 46 minutes a day on homework as compared to 57 minutes in Japan and 114 minutes in China.

- In the 1984-1985 school year, 77.7% of public elementary and secondary schools had computers, averaging 62.7 students per computer. By 1997-1998, some 98.8% had them, with 6.4 students per computer.

- Only 47% of parents with young children read to them daily.

- Higher family income correlates with greater parental involvement in children's schooling—74% of parents in households earning $50,000 or more belong to parent groups at school, vs. 38% of parents in low-income households.

- The number of children home-educated in the U.S. is on the rise. In 1983, only 92,500 children received their primary education at home. By 1997, that number had increased 93% to 1.34 million children.

SCHOOL ENROLLMENT, BY SEX AND LEVEL, 1960–1996

Total   Male   Female

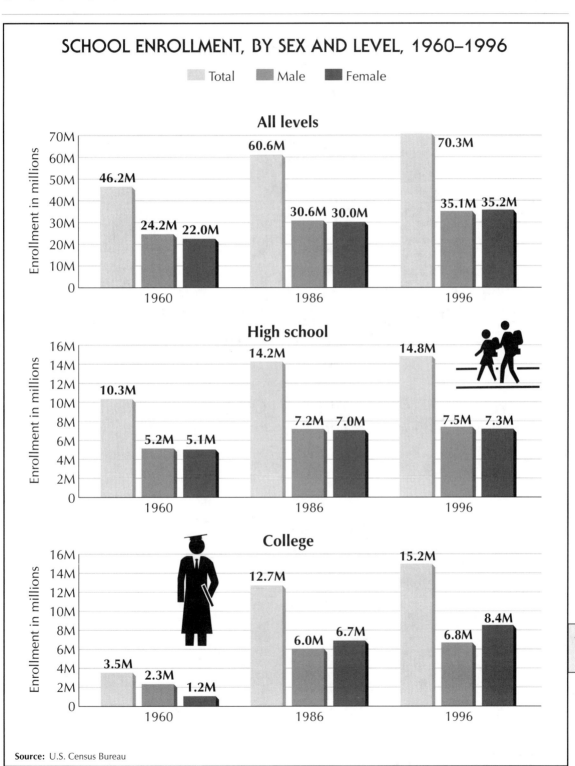

All levels

Enrollment in millions

- 1960: 46.2M (Total), 24.2M (Male), 22.0M (Female)
- 1986: 60.6M (Total), 30.6M (Male), 30.0M (Female)
- 1996: 70.3M (Total), 35.1M (Male), 35.2M (Female)

High school

Enrollment in millions

- 1960: 10.3M (Total), 5.2M (Male), 5.1M (Female)
- 1986: 14.2M (Total), 7.2M (Male), 7.0M (Female)
- 1996: 14.8M (Total), 7.5M (Male), 7.3M (Female)

College

Enrollment in millions

- 1960: 3.5M (Total), 2.3M (Male), 1.2M (Female)
- 1986: 12.7M (Total), 6.0M (Male), 6.7M (Female)
- 1996: 15.2M (Total), 6.8M (Male), 8.4M (Female)

Source: U.S. Census Bureau

U.S. SCHOOL ENROLLMENT, 1970–2000
(By grade level)

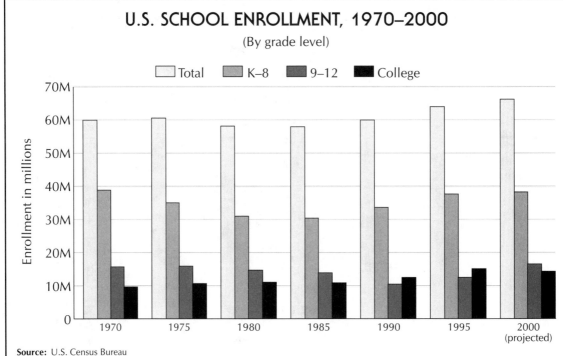

Total   K–8   9–12   College

Enrollment in millions

70M / 60M / 50M / 40M / 30M / 20M / 10M / 0

1970   1975   1980   1985   1990   1995   2000 (projected)

Source: U.S. Census Bureau

1997 STUDENT POPULATION
(By number and percentage of total student population)

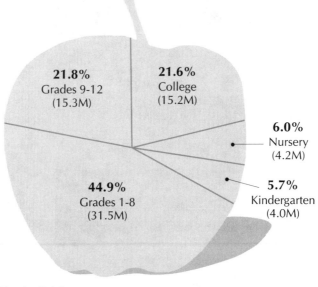

21.8% Grades 9-12 (15.3M)

21.6% College (15.2M)

6.0% Nursery (4.2M)

44.9% Grades 1-8 (31.5M)

5.7% Kindergarten (4.0M)

Source: U.S. National Center for Education Statistics

AVERAGE VERBAL SAT SCORES, 1967–1998

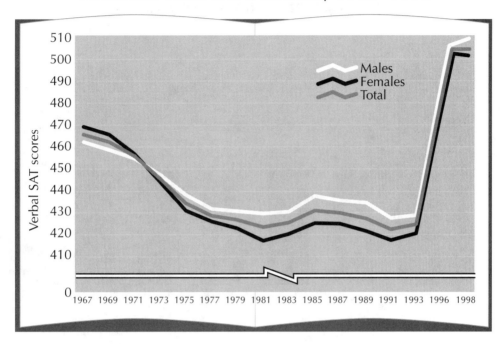

AVERAGE MATH SAT SCORES, 1967–1998

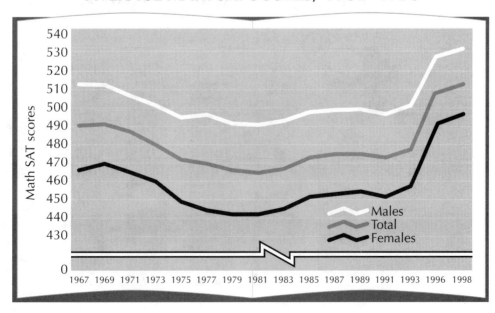

Source: The College Board

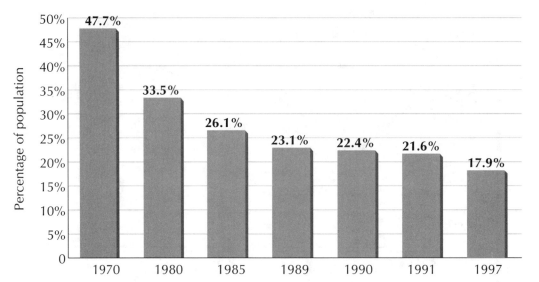

PERCENTAGE OF POPULATION WITH LESS THAN 12 YEARS OF SCHOOL, 1970–1997

Source: U.S. Census Bureau

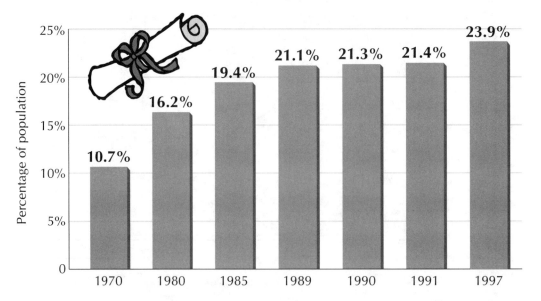

PERCENTAGE OF POPULATION WITH 4 YEARS OF COLLEGE OR MORE, 1970–1997

Source: U.S. Census Bureau

HIGHEST EDUCATIONAL DEGREE EARNED, OF PEOPLE WITH SOME EDUCATION

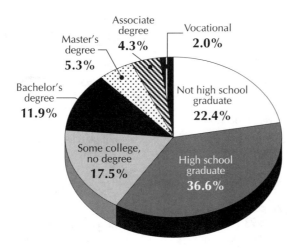

Associate degree
4.3%

Vocational
2.0%

Master's degree
5.3%

Bachelor's degree
11.9%

Not high school graduate
22.4%

Some college, no degree
17.5%

High school graduate
36.6%

Source: U.S. Census Bureau

PROFILE: AVERAGE NUMBER OF YEARS OF EDUCATION, BY RACE OR ETHNIC GROUP

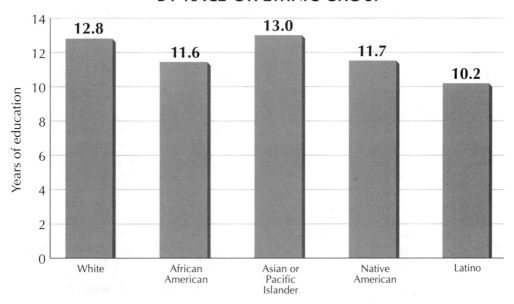

	Years of education
White	12.8
African American	11.6
Asian or Pacific Islander	13.0
Native American	11.7
Latino	10.2

Source: U.S. Department of Education

HIGH SCHOOL AND COLLEGE

Four out of 5 adult Americans have graduated from high school. The Goals 2000: Educate America Act, originally adopted in 1989, calls for a 90% completion rate by the year 2000. Educators and the public, however, agree that competency is as important as completion. There is growing debate over educational standards and society's expectations of students—with good reason. For example, the failure of many graduating students to attain even basic language and math skills has forced colleges and universities to provide remedial courses for incoming freshmen. A 1993 study of literacy found that up to 47% of adult Americans do not know how to use a bus schedule or cannot distinguish between two employee benefits.

Another concern is preparedness for the labor force. Technological advances have reduced the number of well-paying opportunities for semi-skilled and un-skilled high school graduates. High school dropouts have an even harder time being hired for decent jobs.

In 1970, college enrollment was about 7.4 million; by 1997, about 14.3 million people were enrolled in U.S. colleges and universities. More people than ever before are also completing 4 or more years of college. For example, in 1960, only 7.7% of Americans age 25 or older had college degrees; by 1997, the figure had reached 23.9%.

As more Americans have gained access to educational opportunities, the college population has grown increasingly diverse. In 1960, there were almost 2 males for every female college student, and 92.2% of public college students and 96.3% of those in private colleges were white. By 1996, female students outnumbered men, and the percentage of white students had declined to 71%.

FINGERTIP FACTS

☛ Among Americans ages 25 and older in 1997, a total of 82.1% had completed high school—82.0% of males and 82.2% of females.

☛ In 1997, about 89% of the youths enrolled in private high schools were white, and 8% were black. In private colleges and universities, 82% of students were white and 12% were black.

☛ Males are more likely than females to drop out of high school. Latinos have the highest dropout rates, followed by blacks, then whites.

☛ Scholastic Aptitude Test (SAT) scores have increased over the years. In 1970, verbal scores averaged 460; in 1998, the average was 505. In the same period, average math scores rose from 488 to 512.

☛ In 1997, fully 86% of college freshmen had A or B grade averages in high school.

☛ The South has the largest number of institutions of higher learning in the U.S. (1,148), followed by the Midwest (959).

☛ In 1996, the majority of college freshmen (56%) were female.

☛ In 1970, 4.4 million males and 3.0 million females attended college. In 1996, a total of 6.3 million males and 8.0 million females attended.

☛ In the 1997-1998 collegiate school year, 1.7 million degrees were conferred. Sixty-nine percent were bachelor's degrees, 24% were master's degrees, 3% were doctorates, and 4% were medical degrees.

TOTAL U.S. PUBLIC HIGH SCHOOL GRADUATES, 1980–1994

(In millions)

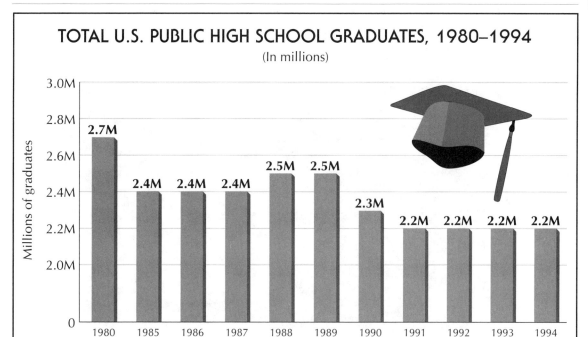

Source: U.S. National Center for Health Statistics

HIGH SCHOOL DROPOUT RATES, BY GENDER, 1967–1995

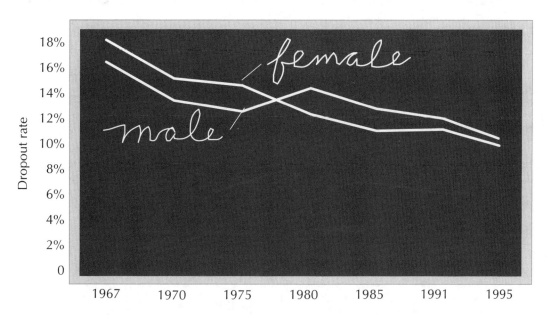

Source: U.S. Department of Education

HIGH SCHOOL DROPOUT RATES, BY RACE OR ETHNIC GROUP, 1983–1995

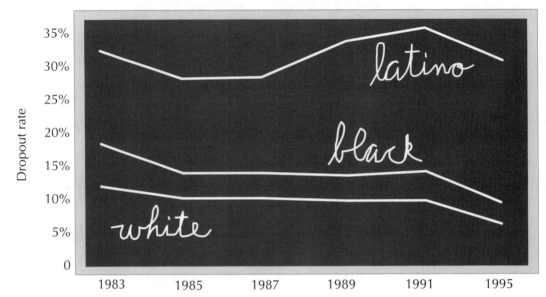

Source: American Federation of Teachers

INTENDED FIELDS OF STUDY FOR COLLEGE FRESHMEN, 1997

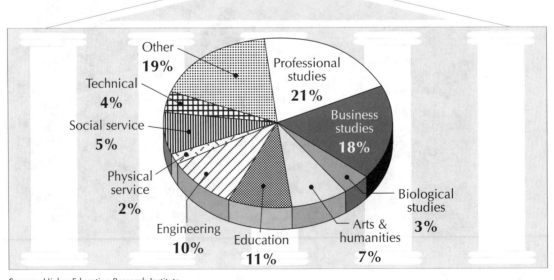

Source: Higher Education Research Institute

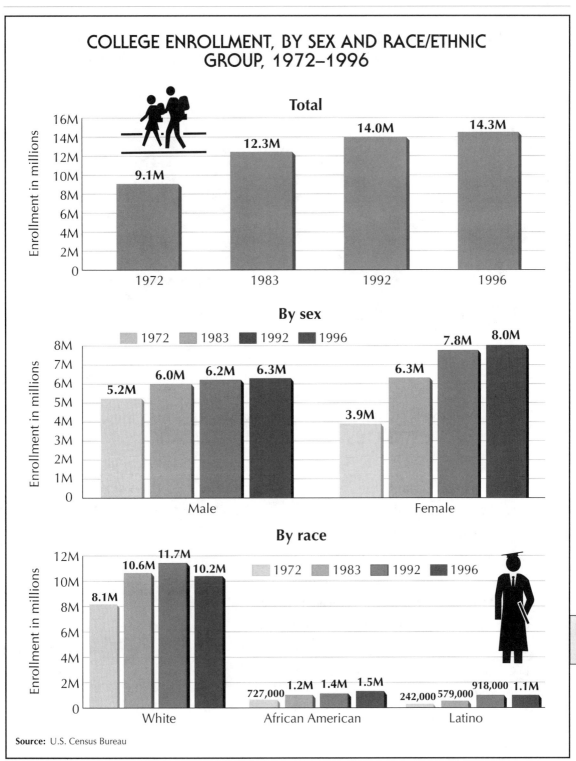

COLLEGE ENROLLMENT, BY SEX AND RACE/ETHNIC GROUP, 1972–1996

Total

(Enrollment in millions)

- 1972: 9.1M
- 1983: 12.3M
- 1992: 14.0M
- 1996: 14.3M

By sex

Legend: 1972, 1983, 1992, 1996

Male:
- 1972: 5.2M
- 1983: 6.0M
- 1992: 6.2M
- 1996: 6.3M

Female:
- 1972: 3.9M
- 1983: 6.3M
- 1992: 7.8M
- 1996: 8.0M

By race

Legend: 1972, 1983, 1992, 1996

White:
- 1972: 8.1M
- 1983: 10.6M
- 1992: 11.7M
- 1996: 10.2M

African American:
- 1972: 727,000
- 1983: 1.2M
- 1992: 1.4M
- 1996: 1.5M

Latino:
- 1972: 242,000
- 1983: 579,000
- 1992: 918,000
- 1996: 1.1M

Source: U.S. Census Bureau

TENURED PROFESSORS AT COLLEGES AND UNIVERSITIES, BY GENDER, 1991

Females

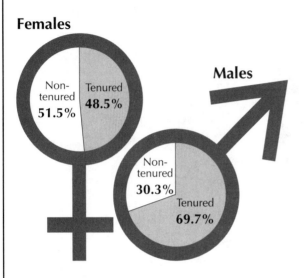

Non-tenured 51.5%
Tenured 48.5%

Males

Non-tenured 30.3%
Tenured 69.7%

Source: National Center for Education Statistics

PERCENTAGE OF COLLEGE FRESHMEN, BY GENDER, 1996

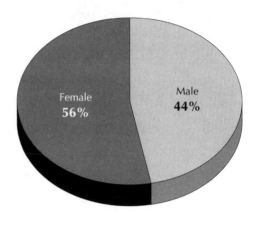

Female 56%
Male 44%

Source: Higher Education Research Institute

TOP 10 UNIVERSITIES CONSIDERED MOST PRESTIGIOUS BY PEOPLE IN EDUCATION

Rank	School	Average score on scale of 1–5
1.	**Harvard University**	4.7
2–3.	**Stanford University**	4.6
2–3.	**Northwestern University** (Kellogg)	4.6
4.	**University of Michigan at Ann Arbor**	4.5
5.	**Massachusetts Institute of Technology** (Sloan)	4.4
6–8.	**European Institute of Business Administration**	4.2
6–8.	**University of Pennsylvania** (Wharton)	4.2
6–8.	**University of Virginia** (Darden)	4.2
9.	**Columbia University**	4.1
10.	**Duke University** (Fuqua)	4.0

Source: Based on statistics from *U.S. News and World Report*

ASIANS DOMINATE FOREIGN STUDENTS IN U.S. UNIVERSITIES, 1998

Two-thirds of the foreigners studying at American universities in 1998 were from Asia:

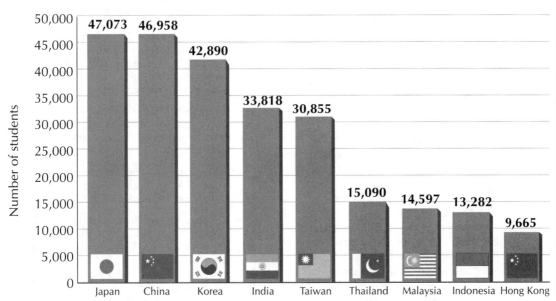

Source: Based on statistics from *Asia Week*

WHERE U.S. STUDENTS STUDY ABROAD: THE MOST POPULAR COUNTRIES, 1996-1997 SCHOOL YEAR

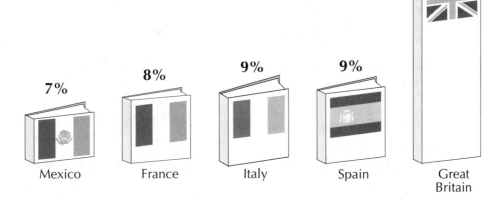

Source: Institute of International Education

TEACHERS

The United States has some 2.9 million elementary and secondary school teachers. Most of them are women, and the great majority are non-Latino whites. Increasingly, they are burdened by large classes, fearful of violence in the classroom, overwhelmed by the needs of children with social and emotional problems, discouraged by unrealistic community demands, and fed up with mediocre school bureaucracies. Frustrated and disillusioned, many quit their careers.

Although American society depends on teachers to educate its youth, it does not grant teachers a social and economic status that reflects that enormous responsibility. Average teacher salaries—from starting salaries to those of people with many years of experience—are lower than those in many other professions, though there has been significant improvement in teachers' wages during the past 2 decades. It is hoped that reforms in teacher training, including the establishment in 1987 of a National Board for Professional Teaching Standards, will improve public opinion of the teaching profession. By 1998, the board had standards and assessments in 33 certificate areas.

At the college and university level, there are some 890,000 professors and other faculty members. Typically, a beginning college instructor gradually advances through the ranks of assistant professor and associate professor to full professor. Advancement depends on a combination of teaching ability, research work, and publication of books and articles.

FINGERTIP FACTS

☛ In 1997, South Dakota teachers earned the least in the U.S., with an average of $26,764. Alaska had the best-paid teachers, averaging $50,647.

☛ In 1996, there were 2.97 million elementary and secondary school teachers. Eighty-seven percent of them worked at public schools and 13% worked at private schools.

☛ There were 470,537 professors teaching at public colleges and 198,282 professors teaching at private colleges in 1996.

☛ Each elementary school teacher was responsible for 18.9 students in 1996, down from 24.3 students in 1970.

☛ U.S. teachers spend more time in the classroom than their counterparts in other countries. U.S. elementary school teachers spend 1,093 hours teaching each year, compared to 624 hours in Sweden, 790 hours in Germany, and 944 hours in France.

☛ The two largest teachers' unions—the National Education Association and the American Federation of Teachers—have a combined membership of more than 2 million.

☛ In 1980, the average salary for classroom teachers was $15,970. By 1997, it had risen to $38,611.

☛ The average teacher salary in a private school was $23,395 in 1997, about 35% lower than the average public school teacher's salary.

☛ Most elementary and secondary teachers over age 40 have master's or other advanced degrees. White teachers are more likely than their African American or Latino counterparts to have advanced degrees.

☛ Average salaries for full-time college professors vary enormously, and they are not always highest at the most prestigious schools. For the 1994-1995 year, these salaries were $104,200 at Harvard University, $79,900 at Nassau Community College (Long Island, New York), and $69,700 at Vassar College.

EDUCATION OF EDUCATORS: DEGREES HELD BY ELEMENTARY AND SECONDARY SCHOOL TEACHERS

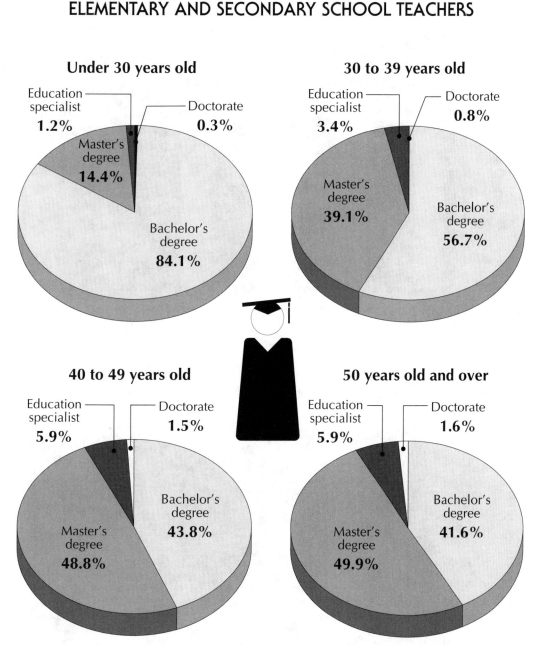

Under 30 years old

Education specialist **1.2%**

Doctorate **0.3%**

Master's degree **14.4%**

Bachelor's degree **84.1%**

30 to 39 years old

Education specialist **3.4%**

Doctorate **0.8%**

Master's degree **39.1%**

Bachelor's degree **56.7%**

40 to 49 years old

Education specialist **5.9%**

Doctorate **1.5%**

Bachelor's degree **43.8%**

Master's degree **48.8%**

50 years old and over

Education specialist **5.9%**

Doctorate **1.6%**

Bachelor's degree **41.6%**

Master's degree **49.9%**

Source: U.S. National Center for Education Statistics

PROFILE: AVERAGE PAY FOR TEACHERS COMPARED TO OTHER PROFESSIONS

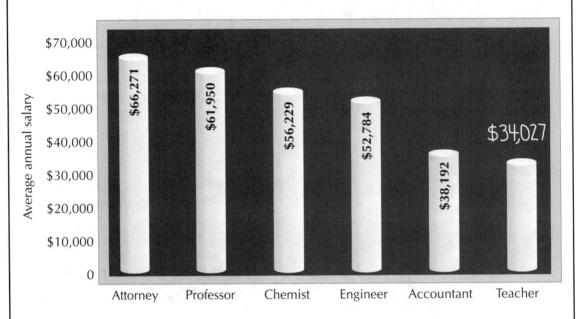

Average annual salary

Attorney	$66,271
Professor	$61,950
Chemist	$56,229
Engineer	$52,784
Accountant	$38,192
Teacher	$34,027

Source: American Federation of Teachers

WHO'S TEACHING U.S. STUDENTS?

(Number of elementary and secondary school teachers, by race or ethnic group)

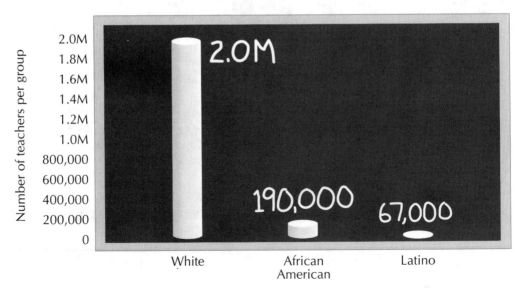

Number of teachers per group

White	2.0M
African American	190,000
Latino	67,000

Source: U.S. National Center for Education Statistics

NUMBER OF ELEMENTARY AND SECONDARY SCHOOL TEACHERS, BY GENDER

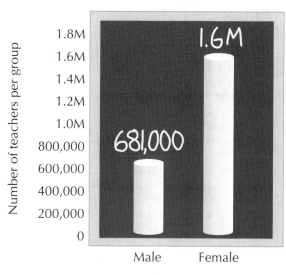

Number of teachers per group

1.8M
1.6M
1.4M
1.2M
1.0M
800,000
600,000
400,000
200,000
0

681,000

1.6M

Male   Female

Source: U.S. National Center for Education Statistics

PROFILE: WHERE PUBLIC SCHOOL FUNDING COMES FROM

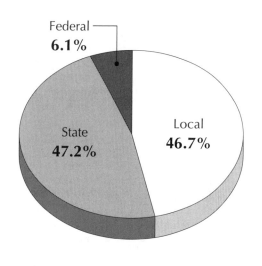

Federal
6.1%

State
47.2%

Local
46.7%

Source: U.S Department of Education

TEACHERS' MARKET: WHERE U.S. INSTITUTIONS OF HIGHER EDUCATION ARE LOCATED, BY REGION, 1992

(Number of institutions, by region)

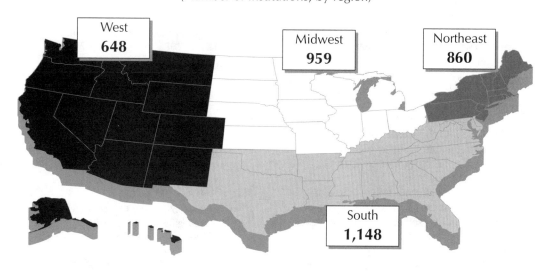

West
648

Midwest
959

Northeast
860

South
1,148

Source: U.S. National Center for Health Statistics

THE COST OF EDUCATION

School costs are going up, up, up! While the general public focuses on salaries of teachers and administrators, and parents fret over college tuition payments, these are only part of the picture. Schools need to find millions of dollars to buy computers and other equipment. Insurance premiums have skyrocketed. Maintenance and repair expenditures, which have often been deferred for years, can no longer be delayed.

Yet school districts are under growing pressure to hold the line on budgets. State and federal governments have slashed aid to schools, and taxpayers are rejecting yearly jumps in local taxes (the large majority of school funding comes from local and state taxes). This has led to deep cuts in summer remedial programs, shortened kindergarten hours, ever-larger class sizes, the elimination of extracurricular activities, and other cost-saving moves.

In many U.S. school systems, teachers who want classroom supplies must often pay for them themselves. Even corporations—recognizing their need for a skilled workforce in the future—are getting into the act, donating money for scholarships, equipment, teacher training, and other programs.

Americans agree that spending money on education is of critical value to both society and the individual. Only with a solid education will today's students be able to survive in the increasingly complex and competitive global economy.

Educational accomplishment also contributes enormously to the development of positive self-esteem and greater control over one's life path. For example, spending more time learning translates into higher salaries and higher net worth.

FINGERTIP FACTS

- The bulk of public school funding comes from state (47.2%) and local (46.6%) monies; 6.1% comes from the federal government.

- Expenditures per student vary from state to state. In 1997, New Jersey spent an average of $9,455 per pupil; Utah spent $3,837.

- A 1995 government report projected that the nation's elementary and secondary schools need about $112 billion in repairs and upgrades to restore them to good condition.

- About 14 million students attend schools that need extensive repairs or replacement.

- In 1996-1997, federal student aid totaled about $39 billion.

- At private colleges and universities, a growing portion of tuition income is used to subsidize scholarships for needy students. A study of 31 institutions found that in 1995, 19.7% of the average $19,110 tuition and fees bill went for needs-based scholarships. This contrasted with 12.8% in 1985 and 9.1% in 1975.

- Men earn more than women. In 1996, salaries of men with high school degrees averaged $27,642; their female counterparts averaged $16,161.

- The higher the level of education, the greater the salary discrepancy between the sexes. In 1996, the average salary of men with advanced degrees was $74,406; for women, it was $42,625.

- A household headed by a person with a high school degree has an average net worth of $33,254, while one headed by a college graduate has an average net worth of $72,373.

AVERAGE PUBLIC SCHOOL COSTS, PER U.S. PUPIL, 1983–1996

(In thousands of dollars)

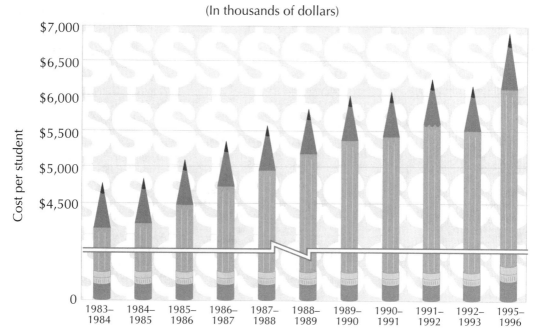

Cost per student

$7,000
$6,500
$6,000
$5,500
$5,000
$4,500
0

| 1983–1984 | 1984–1985 | 1985–1986 | 1986–1987 | 1987–1988 | 1988–1989 | 1989–1990 | 1990–1991 | 1991–1992 | 1992–1993 | 1995–1996 |

Source: U.S. Department of Education

AVERAGE COST OF COLLEGE, 1983 vs. 1997

(Including tuition, food, and housing)

$5,854

$7,792

1983–1984

1996–1997

STUDENT AID AVAILABLE, 1985 vs. 1997

(From all sources, in billions)

$55.0B

$29.1B

1985–1986

1996–1997

Source: The College Board; U.S. Department of Education

Index